I0084057

BRITISH ALIENS
IN THE UNITED STATES
DURING THE WAR OF 1812

Compiled By
KENNETH SCOTT

CLEARFIELD

Copyright © 1979
Genealogical Publishing Co., Inc.
Baltimore, Maryland
All Rights Reserved

Library of Congress Catalog Card Number 79-89271

Reprinted for Clearfield Company by
Genealogical Publishing Company
Baltimore, Maryland
1999, 2014

ISBN 978-0-8063-0865-4

CONTENTS

INTRODUCTION

HE RECORDING of ships' passenger lists was not required by law until 1819, and prior to that date only scattered lists of immigrants exist. It is, therefore, of the greatest importance that another source can supply information concerning thousands of British subjects—Canadian, English, Irish, Scottish, Welsh, and West Indian, most of them immigrants—who were residing in the United States during the War of 1812. On June 1, 1812, President Madison sent his war message to Congress, which on June 18 declared war. Subjects of Great Britain were henceforth enemy aliens and were to be dealt with in accordance with an Act of July 6, 1798, and a supplementary Act of July 6, 1812.

Accordingly, notice was promptly given that all British subjects in the United States were to report to the marshal of the state or territory of their residence "the persons composing their families, the places of their residence and their occupations or pursuits; and whether, and at what time they have made the application to the courts required by law, as preparatory to their naturalization." It was ordered that notice was to be published in the newspapers and that reports by the aliens were to be sent by the several marshals to the Department of State.

The returns, long in the custody of that department, were many years ago deposited in the National Archives and appear to be complete, with the exception of some returns of Pennsylvania and some *detailed* items of Connecticut, although there is a complete list of all British aliens in Connecticut. Extensive supplementary material from the Navy Department (now in the National Archives) deals with British aliens living in or near New York City and a few others who applied for indulgence when ordered inland from coastal towns.

Normally a return gave the name of the alien, aged fourteen or more, years of residence in the United States, number of persons in the family, place of residence and status. Happily, many returns supply further data of no little genealogical value—country of origin, for example.

Massachusetts returns are especially useful, for they usually give month and year of arrival in the United States, names and ages of wives and children, with an indication as to whether they were born in this country or abroad, names and ages of other occupants of the house—relatives, children of the wife by a former marriage, apprentices or servants. Sometimes height, complexion, and color of hair and eyes are indicated.

Naval returns for New York City and vicinity regularly include physical descriptions, while street and often street number are supplied in the case of residents of the city.

For some states additional material is found beyond what was required in the returns: aliens in New Jersey usually reported the exact date of arrival in the country (day, month and year); in Pennsylvania, likewise, the exact time of arrival is stated, while residents of Philadelphia indicated street and number; reports from Virginia, Georgia and Louisiana in numerous instances include physical descriptions; North Carolina, Ohio, East Tennessee and Missouri returns very frequently indicate country of origin; in the case of passengers and crews of two cartels allowed to proceed to the West Indies, ages, physical descriptions and places of birth are stated.

Special attention was paid to half-pay British officers (some of whom had served in the Revolution), persons who derived income from property in Great Britain, or who failed to report or desired to leave the country, and individuals of bad character.

This material is not only of value for genealogical research. It is clearly of importance for economic and social history. For example, the great number of weavers, spinners, carders and makers of cotton machines throw light on the rapid growth of the cloth industry, notably in Rhode Island, New Jersey and sections of New York. Many British subjects were engaged in the gunpowder business, in Delaware particularly. Almost all crafts and employments are represented: some of the aliens were artists, engravers, printers, silversmiths, gunsmiths, cabinetmakers, schoolmasters, ministers of the Gospel, to mention only a few occupations.

To facilitate location of the original returns, at the end of each item, where possible, the date of the return by the Federal marshal is noted. Naval records for New York City are indicated by the word "Navy" at the end.

The transcription of the records from microfilm has been extremely difficult because of the many hands involved in the returns. Sometimes the writing is miniscule; frequently a marshal or deputy wrote many different letters which look alike (failure to dot the letter i adds to the burden); spelling is often erratic (some used the British *our* and others the *or*). Where a name does not appear certain a question mark has been appended.

Warmest thanks are due for assistance given the compiler of this book: to Mr. James D. Walker of the National Archives (who brought to the attention of the compiler the existence of such records as had been microfilmed, reels R 588, 2 and 3); to Mr. Michael P. Musick of the Navy and Old Army Branch of the Military Archives Division of the National Archives (who located and arranged for the microfilming of further alien returns and pertinent Naval records); to Mr. Joel Buchwald, head of the Federal Records Branch of the National Archives in Bayonne, N.J. (who kindly made available reels R 588, 2 and 3 until copies could be secured from Washington); to Dr. Kenn Stryker-Rodda (who rendered valuable assistance in connection with the preparation of the index); to Mrs. Joanne Sanger (who helped with some of the typing of the manuscript); to Dr. Aurelia G. Scott (who proofread almost all the typescript).

MAINE

Alcorn, John, age 24, 2 days in U.S., no family, Portland, weaver (12 Aug. 1812)

Allen, Peter, age 53, 28 years in U.S., 10 in family, Penobscot, weaver (31 Aug. 1812)

Allen, Thomas, age 28, 7 years in U.S., no family, Wells, mariner (12 Aug. 1812)

Arter, Nicholas, age 25, 7 years in U.S., no family, Wiscassett, ropemaker (12 Aug. 1812)

Aymor, Daniel, age 26, 5 years in U.S., 4 in family, Eastport, blockmaker (31 Aug. 1812)

Baird, John, age 20, 2 days in U.S., no family, Portland, baker (12 Aug. 1812)

Baird, Martha, age 40, 2 days in U.S., 2 in family, Portland, spinster, weaver (12 Aug. 1812)

Balger, James, age 12, 1 year in U.S., no family, Newcastle (12 Aug. 1812)

Balger, John, age 46, 9 years in U.S., 7 in family, Newcastle, boat builder (12 Aug. 1812)

Balger, Lestshay, age 21, 1 year in U.S., no family, Newcastle (12 Aug. 1812)

Banager, Stephen, age 24, 8 years in U.S., no family, Castine, labourer; applied 1812 (31 Aug. 1812)

Bancraft, John age 55, 30 years in U.S., 3 in family, Castine, bricklayer; naturalized 1800 (31 Aug. 1812)

Banks, Rose, age 20, a few weeks in U.S., just arried from Ire-land, spinster (19 Oct. 1812)

Barnett, Thomas, age 45, 4 days in U.S., 9 in family, Portland, farmer (12 Aug. 1812)

Barr, Enos, age 36, 6 years in U.S., 5 in family, Castine, sail-maker (31 Aug. 1812)

Bennett, Obadiah, age 25, 4 days in U.S., no family, Portland, farmer (12 Aug. 1812)

Black, John, age 32, 14 years in U.S., 7 in family, Ellsworth, merchant; naturalized 1810 (31 Aug. 1812)

Boice, Joseph, age 68, 1 year in U.S., 4 in family, Eastport, housewright (31 Aug. 1812)

Bostwith, John S., age 42, 3 years in U.S., 8 in family, Eastport, mariner (31 Aug. 1812)

Bowring, George, age 37, 14 years in U.S., no family, Penobscot, labourer (31 Aug. 1812)

Boyce, William, age 37, a few weeks in U.S., just arrived from Ireland, 6 in family, farmer (19 Oct. 1812)

Braham, John, age 28, 3 years in U.S., no family, Portland, hatter; applied June, 1811 (12 Aug. 1812)

Brosup, William J., age 16, 2 years in U.S., no family, Penobscot, seaman (31 Aug. 1812)

Brown, Ann, age 56, 4 days in U.S., no family, Portland (12 Aug. 1812)

Brown, Cornelius, age 22, 4 days in U.S., no family, Portland, cooper (12 Aug. 1812)

Brown, George, age 64, 4 days in U.S., no family, Portland, farmer (12 Aug. 1812)

Brown, Jane (?) or possibly James, age 25, 4 days in U.S., no family, Portland, farmer (12 Aug. 1812)

Brown, John, age 28, 4 days in U.S., no family, Portland, farmer (12 Aug. 1812)

Brown, Joseph, age 50, 20 years in U.S., 5 in family, Deer Isles, clergyman (25 Nov. 1812)

Brown, Luke, age 61, 10 years in U.S., 3 in family, Portland, caulker (12 Aug. 1812)

Brown, Philemon, age 21, 20 years in U.S., no family, Deer Isles, farmer (25 Nov. 1812)

Brown, Samuel, age 58, 8 years in U.S., 3 in family, Eastport, labourer (31 Aug. 1812)

Buckley, James, age 72, 29 years in U.S., no family, Castine, labourer (25 Nov. 1812)

Bulger, Nelly, age 23, a few weeks in U.S., just arrived from Ireland (19 Oct. 1812)

Bunten, Samuel, age 77, 7 years in U.S., 2 in family, Portland, labourer (12 Aug. 1812)

Burgoin, John, age 50, 32 years in U.S., 2 in family, Penobscot, labourer (31 Aug. 1812)

Burns, John, age 46, 1 year in U.S., 5 in family, Penobscot, carpenter (25 Nov. 1812)

Burns, Michael, age 24, 3 years in U.S., 2 in family, Gardiner, tailor (12 Aug. 1812)

Burns, Patrick, age 30, 3 years in U.S., Eastport, labourer (31 Aug. 1812)

Byrne, John, age 28, a few weeks in U.S., just arrived from Ireland, labourer (19 Oct. 1812)

Cane, John, age 51, 28 years in U.S., 11 in family, Castine, labourer; applied in 1784; married in U.S. (12 Aug. 1812)

Caneday, James, age 30, 2 days in U.S., 4 in family, Portland, weaver (12 Aug. 1812)

Cannavan, John, age 27, 5 years in U.S., 3 in family, Hallowell, tailor (12 Aug. 1812)

Carpenter, William, age 22, 5 years in U.S., 2 in family, Bethel, farmer (31 Aug. 1812)

Carrol, James, age 45, 1 year in U.S., 5 in family, Wiscassett, mariner (12 Aug. 1812)

Carrol, Michael, age 42, 19 years in U.S., no family, Castine, mason (12 Aug. 1812)

Clark, Connor, age 56, a few weeks in U.S., just arrived from Ireland, labourer (19 Oct. 1812)

Clark, Terrence, age 40, a few weeks in U.S., 4 in family, just arrived from Ireland, farmer (19 Oct. 1812)

Coad, Edward, age 35, 6 years in U.S., 2 in family, Limington, York Co., joiner (12 Aug. 1812)

Cochran, Alexander, age 22, 4 days in U.S., no family, Portland, weaver (12 Aug. 1812)

Cockran, . . ., age 55, a few weeks in U.S., just arrived from Ireland, 11 in family, farmer (19 Oct. 1812)

Codd, Nicolas, age 50, 16 years in U.S., no family, Newcastle, merchant (12 Aug. 1812)

Codd, Thomas, age 28, 16 years in U.S., no family, Newcastle, merchant (12 Aug. 1812)

Coole, James, age 21, 2 days in U.S., no family, Portland, weaver (12 Aug. 1812)

Cope, Richard S., age 30, 8 years in U.S., Eastport, cordwainer (31 Aug. 1812)

Copp, David, age 60, 8 years in U.S., 4 in family, Eastport, trader (31 Aug. 1812)

Core, Margaret, age 21, 4 days in U.S., no family, Portland, spinster (12 Aug. 1812)

Cormie, Joseph, age 28, 8 years in U.S., Eastport, merchant (31 Aug. 1812)

Coston, Daniel, age 50, 29 years in U.S., 3 in family, Castine, labourer (31 Aug. 1812)

Cox, William H., age 23, 1 year in U.S., no family, Hallowell, weaver and spinner (12 Aug. 1812)

Crawford, Levi, age 43, 4 years in U.S., 6 in family, Eastport, labourer (31 Aug. 1812)

Crawley, Phillip, age 25, 7 years in U.S., Eastport, fisherman (31 Aug. 1812)

Creighton, Abraham, age 19, 5 in family, just arrived from Ireland, farmer (19 Oct. 1812)

Crenner, Charles, age 28, 7 years in U.S., no family, Parsons-
field, tailor (12 Aug. 1812)
Cummings, Margaret, age 50, 4 days in U.S., 4 in family, Port-
land (12 Aug. 1812)
Cummins, Edward, age 28, 10 years in U.S., 6 in family, Hallo-
well, tailor (12 Aug. 1812)
Cunningham, John, age 24, 3 years in U.S., no family, Penobscot,
sailor (25 Nov. 1812)
Curren, John, age 30, a few weeks in U.S., just arrived from
Ireland, farmer (19 Oct. 1812)
Curry, Andrew, age 48, 2 years in U.S., 6 in family, Eastport,
victualer (31 Aug. 1812)
Dampsay, Daniel, age 22, 4 mos. in U.S., no family, Wiscassett,
mariner (12 Aug. 1812)
Davis, (illegible), age 50, 19 years in U.S., 6 in family, Port-
land, tobacconist (12 Aug. 1812)
Davis, Christopher, age 23, a few weeks in U.S., just arrived
from Ireland, farmer (19 Oct. 1812)
Davis, John, age 22, 3 mos. in U.S., no family, Wiscassett, ma-
riner (12 Aug. 1812)
Deckle, George, age 23, 3 mos. in U.S., 4 in family, Eastport,
mason (31 Aug. 1812)
Dockel, William, age 67, 33 years in U.S., 7 in family, Winthrop,
yeoman (12 Aug. 1812)
Doherty, Neal, age 23, 4 days in U.S., no family, Portland, farmer (12 Aug. 1812)
Donaghly, Neal, age 20, 4 days in U.S., no family, Portland,
farmer (12 Aug. 1812)
Donell, David, age 23, 1 year in U.S., no family, Buckstown,
cooper (25 Nov. 1812)
Dorsey, Patrick, age 30, 6 years in U.S., no family, Wiscassett,
yeoman (12 Aug. 1812)
Doug(aah?), ..., age 36, 2 days in U.S., 3 in family, Portland,
farmer (12 Aug. 1812)
Dougheaty, William, age 28, 4 days in U.S., 3 in family, Port-
land, linen weaver (12 Aug. 1812)
Douglass, James, age 53, 33 years in U.S., 13 in family, Cas-
tine, labourer (31 Aug. 1812)
Downey, Patrick, age 47, 28 years in U.S., no family, Newcastle,
yeoman (12 Aug. 1812)
Doyle, Patrick, age 27, 12 years in U.S., no family, Newcastle,
merchant (12 Aug. 1812)
Dunlap, Saml., age 25, 4 days in U.S., no family, Portland, wea-
ver (12 Aug. 1812)
Durmady, Edward, age 50, a few weeks in U.S., just arrived from
Ireland, farmer (19 Oct. 1812)
Dyas, James, age 40, a few weeks in U.S., just arrived from Ire-
land, 4 in family (19 Oct. 1812)
Edgerton, Robert, age 28, 8 years in U.S., no family, Noblebo-
rough, block and pump maker (12 Aug. 1812)
Edmonds, Daniel, age 31, 9 years in U.S., no family, Edgcomb,
mariner (12 Aug. 1812)
Elder, David, age 30, 4 days in U.S., 2 in family, Portland,
farmer (12 Aug. 1812)
Elder, William, age 49, 4 days in U.S., no family, Portland,
farmer (12 Aug. 1812)
Farrell, Michael, age 48, 2 years in U.S., no family, Bristol,
blacksmith (12 Aug. 1812)
Farrow, Thomas, age 48, 6 years in U.S., 4 in family, Cape Elizabeth, mariner (12 Aug. 1812)
Feltis, Mark, age 29, 5 years in U.S., no family, Bristol, tailor
(12 Aug. 1812)
Feny, Barnard, age 24, 4 days in U.S., 3 in family, Portland,
labourer (12 Aug. 1812)

Ferguson, Easter, age 60, 4 days in U.S., 5 in family, Portland
  (12 Aug. 1812)
Ferguson, John, age 30, 4 days in U.S., no family, Portland, wea-
  ver (12 Aug. 1812)
Finch, Simon, age 55, 4 years in U.S., 8 in family, Eastport,
  labourer (31 Aug. 1812)
Fitzsimons, Ally, age 23, a few weeks in U.S., just arrived from
  Ireland, spinster (19 Oct. 1812)
Flood, Wm., age 20, a few weeks in U.S., just arrived from Ire-
  land (19 Oct. 1812)
Foye, Isaac, age 44, 10 years in U.S., no family, Wiscassett,
  rigger (12 Aug. 1812)
Francis, Robert, age 63, 18 years in U.S., 6 in family, Winthrop,
  baker (12 Aug. 1812)
Fulton, Mary, age 42, 4 days in U.S., 3 in family, Portland (12
  Aug. 1812)
Furey, Mathew, age 23, a few weeks in U.S., just arrived from
  Ireland, farmer (19 Oct. 1812)
Gallaghan, Hugh, age 20, 4 days in U.S., no family, Portland,
  labourer (12 Aug. 1812)
Gardiner, Archibald, age 17, 4 days in U.S., no family, Portland,
  blacksmith (12 Aug. 1812)
Gardiner, Elisha, age 30, 5 years in U.S., 3 in family, Hampden,
  caulker (31 Aug. 1812)
Gardiner, Hugh, age 20, 4 days in U.S., no family, Portland,
  blacksmith (12 Aug. 1812)
Gardiner, Mary, age 23, 4 days in U.S., no family, Portland,
  spinster (12 Aug. 1812)
Garmly, William, age 20, a few weeks in U.S., just arrived from
  Ireland, farmer (19 Oct. 1812)
Gay, James, age 38, 6 years in U.S., 6 in family, Cape Elizabeth,
  merchant; applied in 1811 (12 Aug. 1812)
Gay, Samuel, age 34, 8 years in U.S., 3 in family, Portland,
  tailor (12 Aug. 1812)
Gilbert, Anne, age 37, a few weeks in U.S., just arrived from
  Ireland, 5 in family (19 Oct. 1812)
Gilley, Robert, age 28, 4 days in U.S., 2 in family, Portland,
  linen weaver (12 Aug. 1812)
Goff, John, age 43, 11 years in U.S., 8 in family, Frankfort,
  farmer (31 Aug. 1812)
Gold, William G., age 20, a few weeks in U.S., just arrived from
  Ireland (19 Oct. 1812)
Gorham, Prince, age 45, 5 years in U.S., 8 in family, Hampden,
  cooper (25 Nov. 1812)
Greason, Thomas, age 24, 3 years in U.S., 2 in family, Eastport,
  labourer (31 Aug. 1812)
Grier, Adam, age 19, 4 days in U.S., no family, Portland, far-
  mer (12 Aug. 1812)
Grier, M., age 35, a few weeks in U.S., just arrived from Ire-
  land, labourer (19 Oct. 1812)
Hamilton, George, age 27, a few weeks in U.S., just arrived from
  Ireland, farmer (19 Oct. 1812)
Hanley, Patrick, age 29, 2 years in U.S., Bristol, carpenter (19
  Oct. 1812)
Hanly, Roger, age 47, 27 years in U.S. (19 Oct. 1812)
Hanson, William, age 37, 10 years in U.S., no family, Portland,
  carpenter (12 Aug. 1812)
Hardy, Charles, age 35, 4 days in U.S., no family, Portland, li-
  nen weaver (12 Aug. 1812)
Harmon, Thomas, age 30, 13 years in U.S., 4 in family, Portland,
  mariner (12 Aug. 1812)
Harris, Eli, age 26, 1 year in U.S., 4 in family, Eastport, cord-
  wainer (31 Aug. 1812)
Harris, Gilbert, age 47, 6 weeks in U.S., 7 in family, Eastport,
  preacher (31 Aug. 1812)

Haycock, Thomas, age 27, 3 years in U.S., 4 in family, Eastport,
    baker (31 Aug. 1812)
Hayden, Samuel, age 55, 23 years in U.S., 3 in family, Hallowell,
    watchmaker (12 Aug. 1812)
Hayes, George, age 45, 7 years in U.S., 9 in family, Hampden,
    caulker (31 Aug. 1812)
Hazelburn, Nils, age 28, 6 years in U.S., 2 in family, Wiscassett,
    mariner (12 Aug. 1812)
Heath, Noble, age 17, 1 year in U.S., no family, Falmouth, tan-
    ner (12 Aug. 1812)
Henderson, Joseph, age 25, 4 days in U.S., no family, Portland,
    clerk (12 Aug. 1812)
Henderson, William, age 26, 2 days in U.S., no family, Portland,
    baker (12 Aug. 1812)
Hill, John L., age 56, 16 years in U.S., no family, Edgcomb, yeo-
    man (12 Aug. 1812)
Hill, Thomas, age 30, a few weeks in U.S., just arrived from Ire-
    land, 5 in family, farmer (19 Oct. 1812)
Hockenhull, Thomas, age 45, 19 years in U.S., 3 in family, Port-
    land, cordwainer (12 Aug. 1812)
Howard, Robert, age 18, 4 days in U.S., no family, Portland,
    farmer (12 Aug. 1812)
Hughes, Hugh, age 22, a few weeks in U.S., just arrived from
    Ireland, 2 in family, clerk (19 Oct. 1812)
Hunt, Henry, age 30, 2 years in U.S., Eastport, tallow chandler
    (31 Aug. 1812)
Hunter, John, age 34, 4 years in U.S., no family, Wiscassett,
    mariner (12 Aug. 1812)
Hunter, Thomas, age 51, 6 years in U.S., 4 in family, Portland,
    watchmaker; applied in March, 1810 (12 Aug. 1812)
Hysam, John, age 33, 19 years in U.S., no family, Newcastle, yeo-
    man (19 Oct. 1812)
Jacobs, Thomas, age 47, 22 years in U.S., 8 in family, Winthrop,
    yeoman (12 Aug. 1812)
Jerard, William, age 42, 8 years in U.S., no family, Wiscassett,
    rigger (12 Aug. 1812)
Johnson, Edward, age 20, a few weeks in U.S., just arrived from
    Ireland. farmer (19 Oct. 1812)
Killey, John, age 36, 10 years in U.S., 9 in family, Gouldsbo-
    rough, labourer (31 Aug. 1812)
Kilpatrick, Mathew, age 16, 2 days in U.S., no family, Portland,
    farmer (12 Aug. 1812)
Kindol, Andrew, age 55, 9 years in U.S., 12 in family, Malta,
    yeoman (12 Aug. 1812)
Kindol, Michael, age 22, 9 years in U.S., no family, Malta, shoe-
    maker (12 Aug. 1812)
Kindol, Patrick, age 26, 9 years in U.S., no family, Malta, yeo-
    man (12 Aug. 1812)
Lanegan, John, age 38, 7 years in U.S., 5 in family, Boston,
    merchant (31 Aug. 1812)
Larey, John, age 30, 8 years in U.S., 4 in family, Malta, yeo-
    man (12 Aug. 1812)
Law, William, age 42, 2 days in U.S., 11 in family, Portland,
    farmer (12 Aug. 1812)
Lawrence, John, age 23, 1 year in U.S., Eastport, printer (31
    Aug. 1812)
Lawry, Robert, age 52, 2 days in U.S., no family, Portland, far-
    mer (12 Aug. 1812)
Leach, James, age 36, 4 days in U.S., 2 in family, Portland, wea-
    ver (12 Aug. 1812)
Leach, William, age 21, 4 days in U.S., no family, Portland, wea-
    ver (12 Aug. 1812)
Leppard, James, age 29, 11 years in U.S., no family, Wiscassett,
    mariner (12 Aug. 1812)

6 MAINE

Lewis, John, age 27, 6 years in U.S., 4 in family, Winthrop,
yeoman (12 Aug. 1812)
Logue, Catherine, age 28, 2 days in U.S., 2 in family, Portland
(12 Aug. 1812)
Longridge, John, age 22, 4 days in U.S., no family, Portland,
farmer (12 Aug. 1812)
Lumsden, Francis, age 45, 1 year in U.S., no family, Hallowell,
gentleman (12 Aug. 1812)
Lunt, Joseph, age 23, 12 years in U.S., Eastport, seaman (31 Aug.
1812)
Lynch, Hugh, age 55, a few weeks in U.S., 6 in family, no settled
place, as just arrived from Ireland, farmer (19 Oct. 1812)
Lynn, James O., age 32, 4 days in U.S., 4 in family, Portland,
farmer (12 Aug. 1812)
McCesky, Paul, age 24, 2 days in U.S., no family, Portland, wea-
ver (12 Aug. 1812)
McClug, Robert Wilson, age 29, 2 years in U.S., 3 in family,
Portland, carpenter (12 Aug. 1812)
McCluky, John, age 15, 4 days in U.S., no family, Portland, far-
mer (12 Aug. 1812)
McColley, Daniel, age 18, 4 days in U.S., no family, Portland,
farmer (12 Aug. 1812)
McColley, Patrick, age 18, 4 days in U.S., no family, Portland,
farmer (12 Aug. 1812)
McCristal, Francis, age 22, 2 days in U.S., no family, Portland,
weaver (12 Aug. 1812)
McDurmot, William, age 30, 2 days in U.S., no family, Portland,
farmer (12 Aug. 1812)
McElroy, Michael, age 22, 4 days in U.S., no family, Portland,
cordwainer (12 Aug. 1812)
McGuire, Thomas, age 46, 9 years in U.S., no family, Bristol,
merchant (12 Aug. 1812)
McIntire, William, age 30, 2 days in U.S,, no family, Portland,
weaver (12 Aug. 1812)
M'Intyre, Argus, age 53, 34 years in U.S., 2 in family, North-
port, stone layer; married at Castine (12 Aug. 1812)
McKeen, James, age 38, 8 years in U.S., 8 in family, Robinston,
labourer (31 Aug. 1812)
McKenney, Samuel, age 49, 2 days in U.S., 8 in family, Portland,
farmer (12 Aug. 1812)
McKinley, John, age 20, 8 years in U.S., no family, Eastport,
cordwainer (31 Aug. 1812)
McNaught, James, age 32, 4 days in U.S., 5 in family, Portland,
linen weaver (12 Aug. 1812)
McNechell, Dennis, age 40, 2 days in U.S., 2 in family, Portland,
farmer (12 Aug. 1812)
McNeil, Jane, age 27, 4 days in U.S., no family, Portland, Spinster (12 Aug. 1812)
McTacley, James, age 48, 4 days in U.S., 9 in family, Portland,
tailor (12 Aug. 1812)
McWilliam, Patrick, age 18, 2 days in U.S., no family, Portland,
weaver (12 Aug. 1812)
Mack, John, age 41, 11 years in U.S., no family, Wiscassett, ma-
riner (12 Aug. 1812)
Macter, Joseph, age 24, 4 days in U.S., 2 in family, Portland,
weaver (12 Aug. 1812)
Madigan, John, age 18, 8 years in U.S., no family, Nobleborough;
applied in May 1811 (12 Aug. 1812)
Madigan, Walter, age 45, 8 years in U.S., 9 in family, Wiscassett,
merchant; applied in May 1811 (12 Aug. 1812)
Marquize, William, age 22, a few weeks in U.S., just arrived from
Ireland, farmer (19 Oct. 1812)
May, William, age 30, 14 years in U.S., Union, shipwright (19
Oct. 1812)
Mercer, Robert, age 47, 27 years in U.S., 10 in family, Sullivan,
joiner (25 Nov. 1812)

Miller, William, age 26, 4 days in U.S., no family, Portland,
  spinner (12 Aug. 1812)
Mitchel, Charles, age 45, 9 years in U.S., 8 in family, Freeport,
  caulker (12 Aug. 1812)
Mitchel, David, age 46, 4 days in U.S., 6 in family, Portland,
  farmer (12 Aug. 1812)
Molloy, Daniel, age 22, 17 days in U.S., no family, París, dis-
  tiller (31 Aug. 1812)
Mooney, Martin, age 40, a few weeks in U.S., just arrived from
  Ireland, farmer (19 Oct. 1812)
Mooney, Michael, age 24, a few weeks in U.S., just arrived from
  Ireland, farmer (19 Oct. 1812)
Moore, John, age 37, 2 years in U.S., 2 in family, Portland, tra-
  der; applied in May, 1812 (12 Aug. 1812)
Moore, William, age 60, 4 days in U.S., 8 in family, Portland,
  wheelwright (12 Aug. 1812)
Moore, William, age 23, 4 days in U.S., no family, Portland, cooper
  (12 Aug. 1812)
Morgan, James R., age 24, 15 years in U.S., 4 in family, Eastport,
  fisherman (31 Aug. 1812)
Morong, Francis, age 68, 28 years in U.S., 2 in family, No. 9,
  cooper (31 Aug. 1812)
Morong, William, age 29, 28 years in U.S., 3 in family, No. 9,
  farmer (31 Aug. 1812)
Morrice, James, age 49, 37 years in U.S., 6 in family, Prospect,
  labourer (31 Aug. 1812)
Morris, Robert, age 45, 2 years in U.S., 9 in family, Eastport,
  labourer (31 Aug. 1812)
Morton, John, age 23, 4 days in U.S., no family, Portland, farmer
  (12 Aug. 1812)
Mullens, James, age 40, a few weeks in U.S., 6 in family, just
  arrived from Ireland, farmer (19 Oct. 1812)
Munn, John, age 23, 4 days in U.S., no family, Portland, weaver
  (12 Aug. 1812)
Murphey, Thomas, age 27, a few weeks in U.S., just arrived from
  Ireland, labourer (19 Oct. 1812)
Murray, John, age 25, 3 years in U.S., Eastport, labourer (31 Aug.
  1812)
Neilson, Sally, age 45, 2 days in U.S., 5 in family, Portland,
  weaver (12 Aug. 1812)
Nelly, Catherine, age 60, 4 days in U.S., no family, Portland
  (12 Aug. 1812)
Nelly, James, age 20, 4 days in U.S., no family, Portland, far-
  mer (12 Aug. 1812)
Newcomb, John, age 33, 11 years in U.S., 3 in family, Portland,
  caulker (12 Aug. 1812)
Nicolson, James, age 42, 4 days in U.S., no family, Portland, far-
  mer (12 Aug. 1812)
Nowlin, Robert, age 31, 9 years in U.S., 3 in family, Eastport,
  labourer (31 Aug. 1812)
O'Donnel, David, age 23, 4 days in U.S., no family, Portland, dis-
  tiller (12 Aug. 1812)
O'Donold, Michael, age 35, 8 mos. in U.S., 3 in family, Eastport,
  cooper (31 Aug. 1812)
O'Neal, Dennis, age 35, 4 mos. in U.S., no family, Bangor, labourer (31 Aug. 1812)
Owen, Luke, age 39, 15 years in U.S., 9 in family, Paris, farmer
  (31 Aug. 1812)
Parker, John, age 16, 4 days in U.S., no family, Portland, farmer
  (12 Aug. 1812)
Parker, Thomas, age 22, 2 years in U.S., no family, Portland, sailmaker (12 Aug. 1812)
Parker, Timothy, age 53, 2 years in U.S., 5 in family, Eastport,
  victualer (31 Aug. 1812)

Pendlebury, Thomas, age 24, 1 year in U.S., 3 in family, Eastport, labourer (31 Aug. 1812)

Phillips, George, age 34, 9 years in U.S., 4 in family, Bangor, labourer (31 Aug. 1812)

Pierpint, Richard, age 21, 1 year in U.S., 2 in family, Union, cotton manufacturer (19 Oct. 1812)

Pinkerton, John, age 48, 2 days in U.S., no family, Portland, farmer (12 Aug. 1812)

Pollock, Mary, age 38, 2 days in U.S., 5 in family, Portland (12 Aug. 1812)

Pollock, Sarah, age 37, 2 days in U.S., Portland (12 Aug. 1812)

Prey, John, age 35, 8 years in U.S., no family, Buckstown, farmer (31 Aug. 1812)

Ramsay, Saml., age 30, 4 days in U.S., no family, Portland, farmer (12 Aug. 1812)

Ramsey, John, age 42, 8 years in U.S., 3 in family, Portland, mariner (12 Aug. 1812)

Rankin, Henry, age 50, 4 days in U.S., no family, Portland, farmer (12 Aug. 1812)

Ranney, William, age 30, 2 days in U.S., no family, Portland, tailor (12 Aug. 1812)

Reading, Timothy, age 42, 8 years in U.S., 3 in family, Portland, butcher (12 Aug. 1812)

Retalick, Richard, age 28, 2 years in U.S., 2 in family, Portland, mariner (12 Aug. 1812)

Robens, Richard, age 40, 5 years in U.S., 4 in family, Frankfort, labourer (31 Aug. 1812)

Robertson, James, age 35, 11 years in U.S., 6 in family, Castine, labourer; married at Wiscassett (12 Aug. 1812)

Robinson, Richard, age 21, 4 days in U.S., no family, Portland, weaver (12 Aug. 1812)

Rowse, Edward, age 25, 9 years in U.S., Bristol, clerk (19 Oct. 1812)

Roynor, Richard, age 25, 4 years in U.S., no family, Portland, mariner (12 Aug. 1812)

Russell. James, age 26, 2 days in U.S., no family, Portland, weaver (12 Aug. 1812)

Sample, John, age 20, 4 days in U.S., no family, Portland, farmer (12 Aug. 1812)

Semple, Samuel, age 27, 2 days in U.S., 2 in family, Portland, weaver (12 Aug. 1812)

Sherlock, E., age 19, a few weeks in U.S., just arrived from Ireland (19 Oct. 1812)

Shortall, George, age 40, 2 days in U.S., 8 in family, Portland, farmer (12 Aug. 1812)

Shortell, Andrew, age 29, 8 years in U.S., no family, Wiscassett, house-carpenter (12 Aug. 1812)

Smart, John, age 37, 7 years in U.S., no family, Wiscassett, mariner (12 Aug. 1812)

Smith, Henry, age 26, 1 year in U.S., no family, Wiscassett, mariner (12 Aug. 1812)

Smith, Hugh, age 21, a few weeks in U.S., just arrived from Ireland, farmer (19 Oct. 1812)

Smyth, Joseph, age 56, 27 years in U.S., 11 in family, Castine, millwright (31 Aug. 1812)

Smyth, Peter, age 32, 4 days in U.S., no family, Portland, tailor (12 Aug. 1812)

Sposite, Michael, age 30, 7 years in U.S., 4 in family, Cape Elizabeth, mariner (12 Aug. 1812)

Steele, Andrew, age 57, 36 years in U.S., 14 in family, Castine, farmer; married at Castine (12 Aug. 1812)

Steele, Archibald, age 37, 18 years in U.S., no family, Falmouth, paper maker (12 Aug. 1812)

Steeling, Thomas, age 28, 4 days in U.S., 2 in family, Portland, farmer and weaver (12 Aug. 1812)

Stevenson, Hugh, age 29, 11 years in U.S., no family, Portland, cordwainer (12 Aug. 1812)

Steward, Henry, age 36, 2 days in U.S., no family, Portland, farmer (12 Aug. 1812)

Stewart, Charles, age 45, 26 years in U.S., 7 in family, Sedgwick, farmer (31 Aug. 1812)

Stoop, James, age 18, 2 days in U.S., no family, Portland, farmer (12 Aug. 1812)

Stringer, John, age 37, 18 years in U.S., no family, Hallowell, chairmaker (12 Aug. 1812)

Strut, George, age 23, 16 years in U.S., 'Eastport, cordwainer (31 Aug. 1812)

Stuart, George, age 28, 8 years in U.S., no family, Harlem, shipcarpenter (12 Aug. 1812)

Sweney, Lawrence, age 16, 1 year in U.S., no family, Prospect, seaman (25 Nov. 1812)

Swiney, George, age 28, 4 days in U.S., 2 in family, Portland, merchant (12 Aug. 1812)

Tate, William, age 39, 2 days in U.S., 2 in family, Portland, sadler (12 Aug. 1812)

Taylor, James, age 16, 12 years in U.S., no family, Wiscassett (12 Aug. 1812)

Taylor, John, age 54, 13 years in U.S., no family, Wiscassett, yeoman (12 Aug. 1812)

Taylor, William, age 40, 23 years in U.S., 11 in family, Eastport, fisherman (31 Aug. 1812)

Tease, James, age 28, 4 days in U.S., Portland, farmer (12 Aug. 1812)

Thompson, John, age 45, 2 days in U.S., 3 in family, Portland, farmer (12 Aug. 1812)

Turnbull, William, age 52, 27 years in U.S., 6 in family, Portland, ropemaker (12 Aug. 1812)

Van Buskirk, Abraham, age 50, 6 years in U.S., 10 in family, Eastport, cooper (31 Aug. 1812)

Walker, James, age 50, 2 years in U.S., 9 in family, Eastport, labourer (31 Aug. 1812)

West, Joseph, age 44, 19 years in U.S., no family, Wiscassett, painter (12 Aug. 1812)

Whelan, Patrick, age 26, a few weeks in U.S., just arrived from Ireland (19 Oct. 1812)

Whilpley, Joseph, age 34, 2 years in U.S., 5 in family, Eastport, blacksmith (31 Aug. 1812)

White, Archibald, age 36, 15 years in U.S., no family, Wiscassett, mariner (12 Aug. 1812)

Whitiera, John, age 21, 1 year in U.S., no family, Castine, joiner (12 Aug. 1812)

Wilkins, James, age 23, a few weeks in U.S., just arrived from Ireland, clerk (19 Oct. 1812)

Wilkinson, Richard, age 38, 15 years in U.S., 6 in family, Portland, painter (12 Aug. 1812)

Willkens, John, age 32, years in U.S., 10 in family, Penobscot, weaver (31 Aug. 1812)

Wilson, Thomas, age 20, 2 days in U.S., no family, Portland, farmer (12 Aug. 1812)

Woodwith, James, age 34, 6 years in U.S., 6 in family, Eastport, seaman (31 Aug. 1812)

Woodworth, Samuel, age 64, 6 years in U.S., 5 in family, Eastport, victualer (31 Aug. 1812)

NEW HAMPSHIRE

Clementson, Henry, age 39, 3 mos. in U.S., self, wife, 1 young
    child & a Mulatto woman, Portsmouth (7 Aug. 1812)
Forrester, George, age 30, 20 mos. in U.S., self, wife & 1 young
    child, Portsmouth, teacher of mathematics (7 Aug. 1812)
Lee-Ashington, Ralph, age 42, 3 mos. in U.S., self & a black
    man named George, Portsmouth, no occupation; intends to return
    to "Demerary" in spring or summer of next year (7 Aug. 1812)
Wade, T. (or J.?), age 40, 3 mos. in U.S., self, wife, 1 young
    child & a black woman, Portsmouth, no occupation (7 Aug. 1812)

VERMONT

Bates, James T., age 47, 25 years in U.S. (from England), wife &
    8 children, Pawlet, Rutland Co., farmer(16 Aug.-7 Sept. 1812)
Fegan, Michael, age 27, 2 years in U.S., wife & 1 child, Winsor,
    weaver (10 Sept. - 26 Oct. 1812)
Hamilton, Richard C., age 24, 3 years in U.S., wife, Poultney,
    manufacturer of woolen (10 Sept. - 26 Oct. 1812)
Head, Benjamin, age 38, 8 years in U.S., Hartford, tailor; applied
    last time (10 Sept. - 26 Oct. 1812)
Hodson, John, age 28, 3 years in U.S., wife & 1 child, Winsor,
    printer (10 Sept. - 26 Oct. 1812)
Hughes, John M., age 23, 1 year in U.S., Chester, tailor (10
    Sept. - 26 Oct. 1812)
McMeecham, Burney, age 53, 28 years in U.S. (from Ireland),
    Pownal, Bennington Co., farmer, a poor man (16 Aug.-7 Sept.
    1812)
Petree, James, age 47, 17 years in U.S., wife & 9 children, Hart-
    ford, farmer (10 Sept. - 26 Oct. 1812)
Rule, Henry, age 47, 10 years in U.S. (native of Great Britain),
    wife & 7 children (of whom 3 born in U.S.), Sunderland, Co. of
    Bennington, farmer (16 Aug.-7 Sept. 1812)
Walsh, Michael, age 24, 1 year in U.S., Winsor, hatter (10 Sept.-
    26 Oct. 1812)
Warner, William, age 22, 3 years in U.S., Danby, spinner (10 Sept.-
    26 Oct. 1812)
Wiseman, John, age 47, 19 years in U.S. (native of England), a
    wife & 9 children, Pawlet, Rutland Co., weaver (16 Aug.- 7 Sept.
    1812)

MASSACHUSETTS

*An asterisk indicates some 30 items which could not be completed
with accuracy.

Adams, Alfrd Gordon, age 28, arrived in U.S. July 1812, surveyor,
Boston (30 July 1812)

Adams, James, age 48, arrived in U.S. 1801, labourer, Boston -
wife Mary (born in U.S.), age 46; child: Fanny (born in U.S.),
age 14; inmate: Mary Jourdan, age 22 (6 Aug. 1812)

Adams, John, age 45, 5ft. 3in., light complex., brown hair, blue
eyes, cordwainer, Marblehead (30 Mar. 1813)

Adams, John, age 44, arrived U.S. 1800, applied 1809, mariner,
Salem -wife Molly (born abroad), age 42 (29 Aug. 1812)

Aigen, Thomas, age 28, arrived U.S. Aug. 1807, lemon dealer, Boston (31 July 1812)

Ainslee, George, age 27, arrived U.S. 1809, locksmith, Boston
(29 July 1812)

Ainsworth, Richard, age 29, arrived U.S. July 1801, clerk, Barns-
table - wife Betsey (born in U.S.), age 31; children: Eliza D.,
age 9, Allen C., age 7, Consider, age 5, Stephen, age 3, James,
age ½ (all born in U.S.) (30 July 1812)

Aldwell, John, age 36, arrived in U.S. July 1805, labourer, Boston (10 Mar. 1813)

Alexander, Robert, age 25, arrived U.S. June 1804, mariner, Boston (31 July 1812)

Allen, Alexander F., age 45, arrived U.S. Feb. 1812, cordwainer,
Boston (27 Feb. 1813)

Anderson, George, age 23, arrived U.S. July 1804, applied March
1810, mariner, Scituate (28 Aug. 1812)

Anderson, George, age 23, 5ft. 6in., light complex., dark hair,
blue eyes, arrived U.S. Mar. 1811, labourer, Scituate (12 June
1813)

*Andrew, Jonah, age 30, 5ft. 6in., dark complex., dark hair, dark
eyes (9 Apr. 1813)

Andrews, Thomas, age 43, arrived U.S. June 1806, gentleman, Boston - wife Jane (born in U.S.), age 25 (25 Oct. 1812)

Armstrong, James, age 18, arrived U.S. 1810, printer's apprentice,
Boston (7 Sept. 1812)

Ashby, William, Jr., age 24, arrived U.S. 1804, trader, Marblehead (3 Aug. 1812)

Ashton, Henry, age 29, arrived U.S. July 1812, merchant, Boston
(14 Aug. 1812)

Atkins, John, age 24, arrived U.S. 1794, tobacconist, Boston (26
Feb. 1813)

Atkinson, John, age 42, arrived U.S. 1803, mariner, Boston (20
Mar. 1813)

Atkinson, John, age 32, arrived U.S. Sept. 1812, cordwainer, Boston - wife Jane (born in U.S.); children: Mark (?), age 8, Margaret, age 5 (both born in U.S.)

Atkinson, William, age 35, arrived U.S. Aug. 1801, coachman, Boston - wife Pheabe (born in U.S.), age 26 (13 Mar. 1813)

Ault, Thomas, age 38, arrived U.S. June 1795, cordwainer, Claremont (?) - children: George J., age 13, Egbert, age 10, Thomas,
age 3, Elizabeth, age 1 (all born in U.S.) (3 Aug. 1812)

Ayling, Henry, age 27, arrived U.S. 1802, turner, Boston - wife
Elizabeth (born in U.S.), age 30; children: Charles, age 5,
Richar..., age 3, Elizabeth, age 4 mos. (all born in U.S.) (5
Sept. 1812)

Ayling, Thomas, age 32, arrived U.S. 1802, turner, Boston - wife
Susan (born in U.S.), age 32; children: Alfred (born abroad),
Thomas, age 5, Maria, age 4 (both born in U.S.)(1 Sept. 1812)

Bail, James, age 44, arrived U.S. 1782, truckman, Boston - wife
Sally (born abroad), age 33; children: James, age 13, George,
age 10, Gerrish, age 8, William, age 6, John, age 1 (all born
in U.S.) (19 Apr. 1813)

Baker, Charles, age 19, arrived U.S. 1809, mariner, Boston (29
    Aug. 1812)
Baker, John J., age 53, arrived U.S. July 1801, weaver, Hingham -
    wife Anna (born in U.S.), age 53 (8 Mar. 1813)
Bales, John, age 31, arrived U.S. 1808, yeoman, Concord (20 Mar.
    1813)
Bales, Robert, age 25, arrived U.S. Aug. 1801, coachman, Boston
    (9 Mar. 1813)
Balfour, Walter, age 33, arrived U.S. May 1807, applied July
    1811, minister of Congregational Society in Charlestown - wife
    Mary (born in U.S.), age 25; children: Betsey, age 2, Donald
    M., age 8 mos. (both born in U.S.) (25 July 1812)
Bally, James, age 30, arrived U.S. 1803, manufacturer, Newbury
    (29 Aug. 1812)
Bannigan, Thos., age 39, arrived U.S. 1798, labourer, Salem (29
    Aug. 1812)
Barnes, William, age 33, arrived U.S. 8 June 1800, comedian,
    Boston - wife Sarah (born in U.S.), age 25; inmate: Charles
    Bates, age 8 (4 Jan. 1813)
Barney, James, age 34, arrived U.S. 1804, merchant, New York
    (22 July 1812)
Barry, Thomas, age 28, arrived U.S. Sept. 1812, labourer, Boston
    (30 Sept. 1812)
Barry, William, age 40, 5ft. 5in., light complex., light hair,
    light eyes, arrived U.S. 1783, labourer, Dorchester - wife
    Betsey (born abroad); children: William, age 18, Peggy, age 12,
    Edward, age 10, Betsey, age 5, Joshua, age 4, Thomas, age 14
    (all born in U.S.) (10 Apr. 1813)
Bartlett, William, age 45, arrived U.S. 1793, gardener, Boston -
    wife Mary (born in U.S.); children: Emeline, age 9, Mary Ann,
    age 5, John, age 2 (all born in U.S.) (16 Mar. 1813)
*Barton, John, age 52, 5ft. 4in., dark complex., dark hair, grey
    eyes - wife Penelope (born abroad), age 40 (5 Apr. 1813)
Bates, Barnabas, age 25, arrived U.S. May 1801, minister, Barn-
    stable - wife Abigel (born in U.S.), age 25; children: Abigel
    A., age 2, Mary B., age ½ (both born in U.S.) (3 Aug. 1813)
Bathe, John, age 48, arrived U.S. Sept. 1796, painter, Boston -
    wife Mary (born abroad); child: Elizabeth, age 22 (born abroad)
    (6 Jan. 1813)
Bean, Joseph R., age 24, arrived U.S. Dec. 1811, mariner, Boston
    (27 July 1812)
Beer, Joseph, age 25, arrived U.S. Nov. 1810, mariner, Boston
    (19 Apr. 1813)
Bell, Samuel, age 27, arrived U.S. Oct. 1811, blacksmith, Boston -
    wife Margaret (born abroad); children: Jane, age 3 (born abroad),
    Margaret, age 3 mos. (born in U.S.) (14 Aug. 1812)
Benson, Thomas, age 47, arrived U.S. Oct. 1794, paper stainer,
    Worcester - wife Sarah (born abroad); children: Jane, James,
    Mary Ann, Sarah (all born abroad) (5 Aug. 1812)
Bergess, William, age 26, arrived U.S. May 1806, cotton weaver,
    Watertown (12 Sept. 1812)
Bettely, Andrew, age 32, arrived U.S. Apr. 1795, labourer, Boston -
    wife Mary (born in U.S.), age 32; children: Mary, age 5, Thomas,
    age 2, Elizabeth, age 1 (all born in U.S.) (27 Feb. 1813)
Blackburn, John, age 35, arrived U.S. 1803, cotton machine maker,
    Walpole - wife Olive (born in U.S.), age 28; children: George,
    age 13, Hannah, age 11 (both born abroad), William, age 7, Mary
    Ann, age 5 (both born in U.S.) (24 July 1812)
Blagdon, John, age 28, arrived U.S. July 1808, brewer, Charles-
    town (23 Sept. 1812)
Blanchfield, Oliver, age 28, arrived U.S. 1810, shoemaker, Salem
    (14 Aug. 1812)
Blandon, Patrick, age 26, arrived U.S. Aug. 1811, weaver, Water-
    town (7 Oct. 1812)

Blendon, Nicholas, age 57, arrived U.S. Aug. 1811, farmer, Watertown - wife Rossana (born abroad), age 50; children: James, age
16, Mary, age 19 (both born abroad) (21 Nov. 1812)
Boden, John, age 22, arrived U.S. July 1811, weaver, Watertown
(16 Sept. 1812)
Bogan, Walter, age 28, arrived U.S. 1806, manufacturer, Newbury -
wife Mary (born in U.S.), age 25; child: Margaret, age 4 (born
in U.S.) (28 Aug. 1812)
Bohan, Thomas, age 50, arrived U.S. Oct. 1806, labourer, Boston -
wife Mary (born abroad), age 30; children: John, age 8 (born
abroad), James, age 6, Margaret, age 3 (both born in U.S.) (24
Feb. 1813)
Bolton, Robert, age 28, arrived U.S. May 1808, blacksmith, Bos-
ton (26 Sept. 1812)
Boucker, Abraham, shoemaker, Boston - wife Abigal (born in U.S.);
children: Abigal, age 4, Mary, age 3 mos. (both born in U.S.)
(18 July 1812)
Bower, James, age 48, arrived U.S. 1807, gardener, Newtown (24
Mar. 1813)
Bowerbank, Thomas, age 72, arrived U.S. Sept. 1812, merchant,
Boston (28 Oct. 1812)
Bowman, James, age 53, 5 ft. 6in., dark complex., dark hair,
dark eyes, arrived U.S. Feb. 1785, chairmaker, Milton - wife
Susanna (born abroad); children: William, age 25, Harriet, age
24, Susannah, age 21, Abigail, age 18, Jefner (?), age 16,
James, age 14, Margaret, age 12, Eliza, age 10, Rebecca, age 8,
Oliver, age 6 (7 Apr. 1813)
Boyd, David, age 33, arrived U.S. 1797, ropemaker, Boston - wife
Hannah (born in U.S.), age 25; child: David, age 2 (born in U.
S.) (18 Aug. 1812)
Braatz, Michael Henry, age 62, arrived U.S. May 1777, labourer,
Worcester - wife Christiana (born abroad), age 59; children:
Eleanor, age 33, Benjamin, age 22 (both born in U.S.) (16 Sept.
1812)
Brabiner, Wm. A., age 20, arrived U.S. 1808, clock- and watch-
maker (24 July 1812)
Bracket, James, age 60, arrived U.S. Jan. 1802, domestic, Boston -
wife Mary (born in U.S.), age 40 (31 July 1812)
Brady, Francis, age 29, arrived U.S. Nov. 1807, labourer, Boston
(23 Feb. 1813)
Brady, James, age 28, arrived U.S. Aug. 1812, weaver, Watertown -
wife Judith (born abroad), age 20 (8 Mar. 1813)
Brady, Owen, age 19, arrived U.S. July 1812, weaver, Boston (31
July 1812)
Braine, Daniel, age 20, arrived U.S. Mar. 1806, accountant, Bos-
ton (22 Sept. 1812)
Brandy, Patrick, age 32, arrived U.S. Sept. 1811, labourer, Boston (31 July 1812)
Bready, Bernard, age 28, arrived U.S. July 1812, currier, Lynn
(22 Mar. 1813)
Brewer, Thomas, age 31, scrivener, Boston - wife Margaret Elizabeth (born in U.S.), age 21; children: Francis Elizabeth, age
4, Mary Ann, age 2, Catherine, age 2 mos. (all born in U.S.);
inmate: Hannah Hill Deverett, age 8 (18 July 1812)
Bricket, Obadiah, age 35, arrived U.S. July 1799, gentleman,
Boston - wife Francis (born abroad), age 35; children: Sarah
(born abroad), Ann, Hannah, Judith (last 3 born in U.S.) (3
Aug. 1812)
Brien, William, age 40, arrived U.S. 1800, labourer, Boston -
wife Elizabeth (born in U.S.), age 40; child: George, age 12
(29 July 1812)
Brimmer, John, age 22, arrived U.S. 1812, gardener, Roxbury (4
Jan. 1813)
Bristow, John, age 48, arrived U.S. July 1792, mariner, Hingham
(19 Apr. 1813)

Britt, John, age 26, arrived U.S. Aug. 1809, carpenter, Boston -
wife Elenor (born in U.S.); child: Susan, age 2 (3 Aug. 1812)

Brown, Francis, age 43, arrived U.S. 1786, labourer, Boston -
wife Abigail (born in U.S.), age 49; children: Thursey (?), age
14, John (both born in U.S.) (20 Mar. 1813)

Brown, Patrick, age 27, arrived U.S. 1807, trader, Boston (21
July 1812)

Brown, William, age 50, arrived U.S. May 1804, cordwainer, Boston - wife Abigal (born abroad), age 30; children: William, age
11, Nancy, age 13 (both born in U.S.) (30 July 1812)

Bruce, Thomas, age 27, arrived U.S. June 1803, applied Mar. 1812,
slater, Boston (30 July 1812)

Brunan, Edward, age 26, arrived U.S. June 1807, labourer, Boston
(31 July 1812)

Bryant, Martin, age 29, arrived U.S. Nov. 1811, labourer, Boston - wife Annis (born abroad), age 30; children: James, age 7,
Patrick, age 5 (both born abroad) (19 Mar. 1813)

Buckley, Peter, age 29, arrived U.S. 1812, woolen manufacturer,
Boston (30 Sept. 1812)

Buckley, William, age 37, arrived U.S. Sept. 1812, manufacturer,
Boston (23 Sept. 1812)

Bunt, Edward, age 50, arrived U.S. Apr. 1788, mariner, Boston -
children: William, age 22, Clark, age 20, Edward, age 17 (all
born in U.S.) (22 Sept. 1812)

Burbank, Elisha, age 41, arrived U.S. 1793, morocco tanner,
Charlestown - wife Nancy (born abroad), age 33; children: Eliza
(born abroad), age 15, Lydia, age 13, Nancy, age 11, Mary, age
9, William, age 6, Eloisa, age 4, Elisha, age 2 (last 6 all born
in U.S.) (21 Aug. 1812)

Burke, Martin, age 19, arrived U.S. Sept. 1810, domestic, Boston
(25 Aug. 1812)

Burke, William, age 32, arrived U.S. Mar. 1805, cotton weaver,
Canton - wife Esther (born in U.S.), age 21 (12 Sept. 1812)

Burke, William, age 20, arrived U.S. July 1812, accountant, Boston (28 Oct. 1812)

Burnatt, James, age 25, arrived U.S. June 1811, mariner, Watertown (17 Sept. 1812)

Burnett, Henry, age 31, arrived U.S. July 1812, merchant, Boston
(7 Aug. 1812)

Burnett, Sophia (?), age 30, arrived U.S. July 1813, labourer,
Salem (10 July 1813)

Burnett, Thomas, age 32, arrived U.S. July 1812, weaver, Waltham -
wife Elizabeth (born abroad), age 22; child: James, age 2 (born
abroad) (16 Sept. 1812)

Burns, John, age 43, arrived U.S. 1798, labourer, Boston - wife
Eleanor (born abroad), age 40; child: John, Jr., age 5; wife
Eleanor arrived U.S. 1796 (20 July 1812)

Burns, William, age 48, arrived U.S. 1808, born in Quebec, now
labourer in Boston (20 July 1812)

Burroughs, George, age 60, arrived U.S. Aug. 1794, labourer, Boston - wife Nancy (born abroad), age 30; children: Mabela, age
38, Abigail, age 28, Peggy, age 24, Robert, age 31 (all born
abroad) (2 Mar. 1813)

Byrne, John, umbrella maker, Boston - wife Elizabeth (born abroad),
age 27; children: Mary Ann, age 7, Franklin Sydney, age 6 (both
born abroad), Jane, age 3, William John, age 2, Edward, age 7
mos. (last 3 born in U.S.) (27 July 1812)

Byrne, Kavin, age 24, arrived U.S. 1807, trader, Boston (21 July
1812)

Byrne, Mark, age 19, arrived U.S. 1809, merchant, Boston (4 Aug.
1812)

*Byrne, Patrick, age 27, 5ft. 7in., florid complex., brown hair,
grey eyes (30 Mar. 1813)

Caddy, William, age 29, arrived U.S. 1805, labourer, Boston -
wife Flora (born abroad), age 30; children: Mary, age 4, Margaret, age 15 mos. (both born in U.S.) (3 Aug. 1812)

Caffeld, John, age 30, arrived U.S. June 1805, cordwainer, Boston (7 Jan. 1813)

Cahill, Patrick, age 28, arrived U.S. Oct. 1807, labourer, Boston - wife Alice (born in U.S.), age 22; child: Thomas, age 2
(born in U.S.) (19 Apr. 1813)

Cain, Robert, age 26, arrived U.S. Sept. 1805, tailor, Boston -
wife Phebe (born in U.S.), age 24; child: Eliza, age 15 mos.
(born in U.S.) (31 July 1812)

Cakely, Jeremiah, age 26, arrived U.S. Aug. 1812, weaver, Watertown - wife Julien (born abroad), age 25 (21 Nov. 1812)

Calton, Thomas, age 55, arrived U.S. 1789, labourer, Salem - wife
Margaret (born abroad), age 51 (18 Sept. 1812)

Cameron, George, age 28, arrived U.S. Feb. 1805, tailor, Boston
(22 Mar. 1813)

Campbell, James, age 57, arrived U.S. Dec. 1777, weaver, Worcester - wife Ann (born in U.S.), age 54; children: Anna, age 25,
Charlotte, age 23, James, Jr., age 22, Alexander, age 17, Joseph, age 11, Nelly, age 26 (all born in U.S.) (16 Sept. 1812)

Campbell, Luke, age 30, arrived U.S. Aug. 1802, labourer, Boston
(13 Aug. 1812)

Cane, Alexander, age 23, arrived U.S. June 1803, cooper, Charlestown - wife Lucinda (born in U.S.), age 20 (19 Apr. 1813)

Cann, John, age 25, arrived U.S. 1804, labourer, Boston - wife
Mary (born in U.S.), child: John, age 2 (20 Mar. 1813)

Cantwell, William, age 19, arrived U.S. 1812, scrivener, Boston
(30 July 1812)

Cardiff, Philip, age 21, arrived U.S. Nov. 1810, victualer, Boston (30 July 1812)

Cardy (or Caidy?), Henry, age 24, arrived U.S. Mar. 1805, mariner,
Dartmouth - wife Sally (born in U.S.), age 19 (2 Sept. 1812)

Carew, John, age 27, arrived U.S. Oct. 1807, labourer, Boston
(23 Feb. 1813)

Carew, Richard, age 37, arrived U.S. Oct. 1810, labourer, Boston
(24 Feb. 1813)

Carey, Dennis, age 56, arrived U.S. Nov. 1795, labourer, Boston -
wife Margaret Bell (born abroad), age 40; child: Maria, age 17
(24 Feb. 1813)

Carmichael, Peter, age 33, arrived U.S. 1803, trader, Boston (29
July 1812)

Carmoody, James, age 51, arrived U.S. Oct. 1806, labourer, Boston
(27 Feb. 1813)

Carney, John, age 42, arrived U.S. Sept. 1806, coachman, Worcester (10 Aug. 1812)

Carney, Thomas, age 34, arrived U.S. July 1801, trader, Boston -
wife Ann (born abroad), age 38; children: Rossanna, age 9, Mary,
age 7, Sarah, age 5, Margaret, age 4, Helen, age 2, Elizabeth,
age 1 (all born in U.S.) (14 Aug. 1812)

Carr, Michael, age 34, 5ft. 9in., sallow complex., dark hair,
grey eyes, arrived U.S. Oct. 1811, labourer, Boston (11 May
1813)

Carrigue, Richard, age 33, arrived U.S. May 1797, labourer, Boylston - wife Sally (born in U.S.), age 30; children: Richard, age
13, Betsey, age 11, Henry, age 9, Ann Maria, age 7, Pammila,
age 5, Edward Turner, age 2 (all born in U.S.) (28 Aug. 1812)

Carrol, Barnabas, age 37, arrived U.S. May 1807, labourer, Boston - wife Rose (born abroad), age 26; children: John, age 7,
Catharine, age 2, James, age 2 mos. (all born in U.S.) (19 Apr.
1813)

Carrol, Robert, age 16, arrived U.S. Dec. 1808, mariner, Boston
(7 Nov. 1812)

Carroll, Edward, age 31, arrived U.S. Oct. 1806, grocer, Boston
(30 July 1812)

Carroll, James, age 29, arrived U.S. Aug. 1810, weaver, Pittsfield (1 Aug. 1812)
Carry, James, age 37, arrived U.S. 1796, carpenter, Salem - wife
Deborah (born in U.S.), age 32; child: Martha, age 4 (born in
U.S. (7 Aug. 1812)
Carter, William, age 29, arrived U.S. Apr. 1808, gardener, Cam-
bridge - wife Silence (born in U.S.), age 29; child: Mary Ann,
age 3 mos. (born in U.S.) (29 Jan. 1813)
Cary, Isaac Thomas, age 35, arrived U.S. May 1804, cotton machine
maker, Watertown - wife Lucretia (born in U.S.), age 37;
children: Isaac, age 4, Betsey, age 2 (both born in U.S.) (4
Aug. 1812)
Cary, Lucius, age 30, arrived U.S. Sept. 1812, merchant, Chelsea
(30 Sept. 1812)
Caton, Richard, age 38, arrived U.S. Oct. 1806, labourer, Boston (25 Feb. 1813)
Cavacher, James, age 32, arrived U.S. Aug. 1796, labourer (31
July 1812)
*Cavill, John, age 38, 5ft. 9in., florid complex., dark hair,
grey eyes, wife Mary (born abroad), age 29, child: John, age 2
(born in U.S.) (16 Mar. 1813)
Cawles, Richard, age 28, arrived U.S. Oct. 1805, labourer, Bos-
ton - wife Ruth (born in U.S.), age 27; child: Daniel, age 5
(24 Feb. 1813)
Chapman, John, age 30, arrived U.S. May 1796, boatbuilder, Boston - wife Betsey (born in U.S.), age 25; children: John, age
7, Thomas, age 3, Hannah, age 1 (all born in U.S.) (5 Aug.
1812)
Child, William, age 45, arrived U.S. Sept. 1808, gluemaker,
Charlestown (14 Sept. 1812)
Chilton, William, age 32, arrived U.S. Mar. 1797 - wife Betsey,
age 21 (31 July 1812)
Clark, Joseph W., age 28, arrived U.S. July 1810, applied June
1812, trader, Boston (27 July 1812)
Clark, William, age 53, arrived U.S. 1784, stevedore, Boston -
wife Ann (born abroad), age 43 (23 Mar. 1813)
Clarke, George, age 20, arrived U.S. Aug. 1806, comedian, Boston - wife Elizabeth (born in U.S.), age 22; children: Eliza-
beth, age 5, George, age 4 (both born in U.S.) (4 Jan. 1813)
Clarke, Patrick, age 78, arrived U.S. June 1805, applied June
1807, labourer, Boston - wife Eleanor (born abroad), age 32;
children: Patrick, age 10, Mary, age 7 (both born abroad), John,
age 2 (born in U.S.) (10 Sept. 1812)
Cleary, Edmund, age 22, arrived U.S. July 1806, stone cutter,
Boston (9 Mar. 1813)
Cleary, William, age 25, arrived U.S. 1810, blacksmith, Boston
(22 Mar. 1813)
Clement, William, age 30, arrived U.S. Aug. 1801, labourer, Bos-
ton (25 Feb. 1813)
Clench, John, age 24, arrived U.S. July 1812, yeoman, Boston (31
July 1812)
Cock, John, age 26, arrived U.S. 1792, whitesmith, Boston - wife
Lydia (born in U.S.), age 23; children: Rebecca, age 4, Lydia,
age 2 (both born in U.S.) (20 July 1812)
Codd, James, age 38, arrived U.S. Aug. 1811, labourer, Boston -
wife Bridget (born abroad), age 37 (3 Aug. 1812)
Cogen, Hugh, age 29, arrived U.S. Mar. 1807, labourer, Boston -
wife Nancy (born in U.S.), age 28; children: John, age 6, Ja-
mes, age 2 (both born in U.S.) (1 Mar. 1813)
Collings, James, age 33, arrived U.S. May 1805, labourer, Boston
(19 Apr. 1813)
Collings, Jeremiah, age 35, arrived U.S. Oct. 1801, labourer,
Boston - wife Joanah (born in U.S.), age 30; children: John,
age 5, Mary, age 2 (both born in U.S.) (27 Feb. 1813)

Collings, Michael, age 40, arrived U.S. Oct. 1804, labourer,
Boston - children: John, age 8 (born abroad), William, age 4,
Michael (both born in U.S.) (24 Feb. 1813)
Collins, Patrick, age 40, arrived U.S. 1807, labourer, Boston -
wife Cathrine (born in U.S.), age 30; children: Cornelius, age
14, Daniel, age 10, Martha, age 7, William, age 4, John, age
20 mos. (21 July 1812)
Collins, Patrick, age 22, arrived U.S. June 1812, yeoman, Dor-
chester (24 Mar. 1813)
Collisan, John, age 45, arrived U.S. 1802, labourer, Boston (29
Aug. 1812)
Commins, Thomas, age 17, arrived U.S. June 1810, apprentice to
E.G. Huse, Boston (9 July 1812)
Condon, John, age 35, arrived U.S. May 1799, labourer, New Bedford - wife Cathrine (born abroad), age 30; children: Mary,
age 11, Cathrine, age 7, William, age 3 (all born in U.S.)
(28 July 1812)
Condon, Patrick, age 58, arrived U.S. 1788, fisherman, Boston -
wife Martha (born in U.S.), age 48; inmate: James Daniels, age
24 (18 July 1812)
Connelly, Richard, age 24, shoemaker, Boston (26 Feb. 1813)
Connor, Peter, age 30, arrived U.S. Aug. 1805, labourer, New Bedford - wife Eleanor (born abroad), age 27; children: Thomas,
age 10, Nancy, age 8 (both born abroad), Michael, age 6, Abbey,
age 3, Sarah, age 2 (last 3 born in U.S.) (28 July 1812)
Conway, Wallis Thomas, age 41, arrived U.S. Aug. 1808, chemist,
Boston - wife Susannah (born abroad), age 33 (27 July 1812)
Cooke, James, age 38, labourer, Boston - wife Margret (born
abroad), age 24; children: Mary, age 4½, John, age ¼ (30 July
1812)
Cooper, John, age 29, arrived U.S. Oct. 1808, weaver, West Boylston - wife Esther (born abroad), age 29; children: Ann, age
10, Ele, age 8, Isaac, age 6 (all 3 born abroad), Sally (born
in U.S.), age 6 mos. (22 July 1812)
Cooper, William, age 48, arrived U.S. July 1800, labourer,
Charlestown - wife Agness (born abroad), age 47; children: John,
age 24, William, age 16, James, age 12 (all born abroad) (21
Nov. 1812)
Cordwell, William, age 34, arrived U.S. 1800, mariner, Salem -
wife Abigal (born in U.S.), age 28 (3 Aug. 1812)
Cosgrave, Simon, age 35, arrived in U.S. Oct. 1812, merchant,
Salem (5 Nov. 1812)
Cotter, Edmund J., age 28, arrived U.S. Apr. 1811, glassmaker,
Boston (23 Jan. 1813)
Cottrell, William, age 60, arrived U.S. 1793, labourer, Boston -
wife Mary (born in U.S.), age 60 (22 Mar. 1813)
Couch, James, age 21, arrived U.S. Sept. 1807, mason, Boston (15
Mar. 1813)
Coughlan, Cornelius, age 40, arrived U.S. 1801, labourer, Boston
(25 July 1812)
Coulson, William, age 30, arrived U.S. May 1804, mariner, Boston
(20 Oct. 1812)
Cowan, James, age 19, arrived U.S. May 1811, woolen spinner, Bos-
ton (2 Oct. 1812)
Cowan, William, age 31, arrived U.S. Aug. 1804, labourer, Boston
(23 Feb. 1813)
Cowley, Edward, age 22, arrived U.S. Oct. 1812, servant, Boston -
wife Sarah (born abroad), age 29; child: Susanah, age 6 mos.
(born in U.S.) (26 Mar. 1813)
Cox, Edward L., age 26, arrived U.S. Sept. 1812, tinplate maker,
Boston (29 Sept. 1812)
Cox, Joseph, age 40, arrived U.S. 1778, painter, Concord - wife
Nabby (born in U.S.), age 41; children: Joseph, Jr., age 15,
Amos W., age 13, Nabby, age 12, Mary, age 10, Horatio, age 7,
Harriet, age 2 (all born in U.S.) (4 Aug. 1812)

Cromack, Joseph, age 34, arrived U.S. Sept. 1806, manufacturer, Boston - wife Judith (born in U.S.), age 25; children: Martha, age 8 (born abroad), Isack, age 2, Joseph, age 4 mos. (both born in U.S.) (5 Oct. 1812)

Crothers, Edward, age 36, arrived U.S. June 1812, maltster, Roxbury (28 Oct. 1812)

Culbert, Mathew, age 25, arrived U.S. May 1807, hatter, Watertown (31 July 1812)

Cummings, Andrew, age 48, arrived U.S. 1795, lemon trader, Boston - wife Sussan (born abroad), age 32; children: Andrew, age 4, Mary, age 3, Catherine, age 14 mos., Susan, age 7 mos. (all born in U.S.) (18 July 1812)

Currey, James, age 20, 5ft. 7in., light complex., sandy hair, blue eyes, arrived U.S. Aug. 1812, cordwainer, Charlestown (15 July 1813)

Curton, Christian, age 35, arrived U.S. June 1808, labourer, Roxbury - wife Elizabeth (born abroad), age 33 (26 Sept. 1812)

Daase, Edward, age 23, arrived U.S. 1804, labourer, Boston (19 Mar. 1813)

Daggen, Daniel, age 25, arrived U.S. June 1807, mariner, Cohassett (17 Nov. 1812)

Daley/Dayley, James, age 55, arrived U.S. June 1801, mason, Boston - wife Mary (born abroad), age 60 (22 Mar. 1813)

Dalton, Thomas, age 24, arrived U.S. Apr. 1810, mariner, Boston (1812 or 1813)

Danon, William, age 24, arrived U.S. 1809, mariner, Boston (19 Aug. 1812)

Darby, Daniel, age 45, arrived U.S. 1807, shoemaker, Boston - wife Hannah B. (born abroad), age 45; children: Sydney, age 7, Emma, age 5, Thomas P., age 9 (all born abroad) (24 July 1812)

Darrell, John, age 23, arrived U.S. May 1807, labourer, Boston (25 Feb. 1813)

Davis, Thomas, age 33, arrived U.S. July 1803, mariner, Boston (19 Apr. 1813)

Dawes, Caleb, age 58, arrived U.S. 1793, mason, Boston - wife Susan (born abroad), age 35; children: William, age 12, Mary Ann, age 10, Susannah, age 8, Hannah, age 3 (all born in U.S.) (21 Aug. 1812)

Dayle, Patrick, age 34, arrived U.S. Feb. 1812, stone cutter, Greenfield (19 Apr. 1813)

Dealy, Peter, age 23, arrived U.S. 1810, gentleman, Boston (20 July 1812)

Deamer, James, age 22, 5ft. 6in., dark complex., dark hair, dark eyes, arrived U.S. Dec. 1807, mariner, Ipswich (13 Apr. 1813)

Deblois, Basil, arrived U.S. 1811, applied 7 Jan. 1812, brushmaker, Roxbury (20 July 1812)

Delaney, John, age 35, arrived U.S. July 1801, tailor, Boston (16 Nov. 1812)

Delany, Patrick, age 32, arrived U.S. 1799, applied July 1812, trader, Boston - wife Susan (born in U.S.), age 25; children: Susan, age 7, John, age 4, James, age 3 (all born in U.S.) (1812 or 1813)

Delany, Patrick, age 24, arrived U.S. Apr. 1804, labourer, Lynn (19 Apr. 1813)

Dent, George, age 21, arrived U.S. Dec. 1811, mariner, Boston (27 July 1812)

Dewhurst, John, age 63, arrived U.S. Mar. 1801, cabinetmaker, Boston - wife Nancy (born abroad), age ?1; children: Jan, age 18, Thomas, age 16 (both born abroad) (5 Aug. 1812)

Dezell, Robert, age 33, arrived U.S. Aug. 1805- wife Mary (born abroad), age 33; children: Margaret, age 7, Nancy M., age 5, Mary Jane, age 3, Robert, age 2 mos. (all born in U.S.) (24 Feb. 1813)

Dick, John, age 36, arrived U.S. July 1803, labourer, Boston - wife Margaret (born abroad), age 36; children: William, age 14, John, age 12 (both born abroad), Catharine, age 7, Mary Ann, age 4, Andrew, age 1 (last 3 born in U.S.) (26 Feb. 1813)

Dickerson, Thomas, age 55, arrived U.S. 1812, yeoman, Boston - wife Jane (born abroad), age 45; children: Mary, age 19, James, age 17, Thomas, age 15, Charles, age 13, Ann, age 9 (all born abroad) (14 Aug. 1812)

Dickson, Thomas, age 22, arrived U.S. June 1805, stone cutter, Danvers - wife Betsey (born abroad), age 20 (16 Oct. 1812)

Dirck, James, age 22, arrived U.S. 1810, tailor, Boston (29 July 1812)

Disney, Thomas, age 28, arrived U.S. July 1812, tallow chandler, Boston - wife Ann (born abroad), age 24 (31 July 1812)

Dodd, John, age 36, arrived U.S. Oct. 1809, cabinetmaker, Boston (5 Jan. 1813)

Dodman, Thomas J, age 21, arrived U.S. Oct. 1807, joiner, West Springfield (11 Aug. 1812)

Donnaly, Michael, age 27, arrived U.S. 1808, mariner, Boston (30 July 1812)

Doran, Edward, age 71, arrived U.S. Sept. 1802, applied 1805, grocer, Boston (31 July 1812)

*Dorrison, Nicholas, age 49, 5ft. 4in., dark complex., dark hair, dark eyes (20 Apr. 1813)

Doull, John, age 29, arrived U.S. 1806, clock- and watchmaker, Boston (24 July 1812)

Dowling, Richard, age 30, 5ft. 9in., dark complex., brown hair, dark eyes, arrived U.S. Feb. 1812, printer, Roxbury - wife Elizabeth (born abroad), age 28 (13 Mar. 1813)

Dowling, Thomas, age 32, 5ft. 8in., dark complex., dark hair, dark eyes, labourer, Boston (17 Mar. 1813)

Doyle, Darby, age 41, arrived U.S. 1796, labourer, Boston (17 Aug. 1812)

Doyle, George, age 27, arrived U.S. 1806, labourer, Canton (20 Mar. 1813)

Doyle, Lawrence, age 30, arrived U.S. 1800, mariner, Boston (19 Mar. 1813)

Doyle, Michael, age 39, arrived U.S. 1811, labourer, Boston (22 Mar. 1813)

Drake, Sam. A., age 46, arrived U.S. Nov. 1810, comedian, Boston - wife Martha (born abroad), age 34; children: Samuel, Jr., age 14, Martha, age 17, Alexander, age 13, James, age 11, Julia, age 8 (all born abroad), Georgian (born in U.S.) (4 Jan. 1813)

Dunn, John, age 30, arrived U.S. Aug. 1805, gardener, Boston - wife Sarah (born in U.S.), age 31; children: Alexander, age 2, John, age 2 mos. (both born in U.S.); inmate: Samuel Beardman, age 9 (11 Jan. 1813)

*Durfee, Neil, age 40, 5ft. 6in., florid complex., dark hair, dark eyes (6 Apr. 1813)

*Durffee, Francis, age 41, 5ft. 7in., florid complex., grey hair, blue eyes (10 Apr. 1813)

Earter, Philip, age 30, arrived U.S. Nov. 1809, mariner, Boston (2 Mar. 1813)

Eaton, James B., age 34, arrived U.S. 1803, mechanic, Cambridge - wife Elizabeth J. (born in U.S.), age 25; children: Mary, age 7, Frederick, age 5, Sydney, age 3, Harriet, age 1 (all born in U.S.) (20 July 1812)

Eaton, Thomas, age 29, arrived U.S. 1803, ropemaker, Boston - wife Rebecca (born in U.S.), age 33 (18 Aug. 1812)

Eday, John Mead, age 24, arrived U.S. July 1812, merchant, Boston (31 July 1812)

Edey, Richard Thomas Atkins, age 33, arrived U.S. 1805, gentleman, Watertown - wife Julia (born abroad); children: Simmonds, age 8 (born abroad), Julia A., age 3 (born in U.S.); inmate: Susannah Stewart, age 40 (25 July 1812)

Edwards, John, age 29, arrived U.S. 1804, ropemaker, Boston -
wife Nancy (born in U.S.), age 29; children: Maria, age 8 mos.,
John, age 2 (both born in U.S.) (18 Aug. 1812)
Ellwood, James, age 27, arrived U.S. May 1801, labourer, Boston -
children: James, age 9, Lucy, age 19 (sic!), Elenor, age 7
(all born in U.S.) (30 July 1812)
Enesey (?), Martin, age 27, arrived U.S. May 1806, mariner, Bos-
ton (12 Nov. 1812)
Entwisle, James, age 27, arrived U.S. Sept. 1810, comedian, Boston (4 Jan. 1813)
Evans, George, age 25, arrived U.S. Aug. 1807, mariner, Fairhaven
(13 Aug. 1812)
Evens, Jacob, age 40, arrived U.S. Sept. 1806, maltster, Rutland -
wife Thankfull (25 Aug. 1812)
Fagan, Peter, age 32, arrived U.S. 1810, labourer, Boston (22
July 1812)
Fahy, Henry, age 30, arrived U.S. 1811, applied Oct. 1811, a do-
mestic, Boston (21 July 1812)
Fahy, Peter, age 45, arrived U.S. Oct. 1811, labourer, Boston -
wife Eleanor (born abroad), age 34; children: Mary, age 5, Mar-
gret, age 3, Thomas, age 2 (all born abroad) (27 July 1812)
Fahy, Philip, age 46, arrived U.S. Aug. 1803, labourer, Boston
(31 July 1812)
*Fair, Thomas, age 42, 5ft. 6in., florid complex., dark hair, grey
eyes - wife Betsey (born abroad), age 44; child: Eliza (born in
U.S.), age 14 (1 Apr. 1813)
Fales, John, age 23, arrived U.S. 1808, cotton manufacturer,
Walpole (15 Aug. 1812)
Fargie, Andrew, age 26, arrived U.S. June 1812, wheelwright, Bos-
ton (9 Mar. 1813)
Farley, James, age 36, minister, Taunton - inmate:Hannah Farley
(5 Aug. 1812)
Farley, Patrick, age 36, arrived U.S. 1801, labourer, Boston (20
Mar. 1813)
Farmer, Thomas, age 30, arrived U.S. Aug. 1812, weaver, Waltham -
wife Ann (born abroad), age 30 (5 Oct. 1812)
Farrar (?), Samuel, age 32, 5ft. 5½in., dark complex., dark hair,
blue eyes, merchant, Boston, on 19 Mar. 1812 was ordered to re-
move to Northampton, Hampshire Co. (Mass. passport No.2)
Farrell, Lawrence, age 49, arrived U.S. Sept. 1812, blacksmith,
Boston - wife Catherine (born abroad), age 49; children: John,
age 25, Richard, age 21, Mary, age 19, Lawrence, age 17,Cathe-
rine, age 15, Margaret, age 13, Mathias, age 11, Patrick, age 9,
Thomas, age 4 (all born abroad) (30 Sept. 1812)
Farrell, Thomas, age 25, arrived U.S. Nov. 1809, gardener, Boston (14 Jan. 1813)
Farrow (or Farron?), Samuel, age 32, arrived U.S. Oct. 1804,
merchant, Boston (given pass to North(ampton?) (24 Feb. 1813)
Fenby, Samuel, age 29, arrived U.S. 1803, tobacconist, Boston -
wife Catherine (born in U.S.), age 23; child: Mariah, age 2
(born in U.S.) (30 July 1812)
Ferris, George, age 15, arrived U.S. 1805, "a papist," an ap-
prentice, Boston (25 Aug. 1812)
Ferris, Peter, age 31, arrived U.S. Aug. 1812, mariner, Boston -
wife Catharine, age 24 (25 Feb. 1813)
Ferris, William, age 20, arrived U.S. 1805, scrivener, Boston,
"a doubtful character" (22 Aug. 1812)
Fiche, Peter, age 32, arrived U.S. 1803, gilder, Boston - wife
Hannah (born in U.S.), age 23 (25 July 1812)
Field, Samuel, arrived U.S. 1804, mariner, Salem - wife Sally
(born abroad); child: Sally (born in U.S.) (24 Mar. 1813)
Fielding, John, age 42, arrived U.S. Oct. 1807, shoemaker, Marble-
head - wife Elizabeth (born abroad), age 42 (3 Aug. 1812)

Fielding, John, age 29, arrived U.S. Dec. 1803, labourer, Boston - wife Abigail (born in U.S.); children: John, age 3, Abigail, age 2 (19 Mar. 1813)

Fielding, John, age 14, arrived U.S. Aug. 1812; he came here to proceed to his uncle, a coachmaker in Philadelphia (14 Aug. 1812)

Fincsey, Stephen, age 53, arrived U.S. June 1796, fruit dealer, Boston (25 Feb. 1813)

Fipinders, James, age 22, arrived U.S. Sept. 1810, labourer, Boston (31 July 1812)

Fisher, John, age 33, arrived U.S. 1801, manufacturer, Newbury (28 Aug. 1812)

Fisher, William, age 37, arrived U.S. 1810, salt-maker, Marblehead - wife Rachel (born abroad) (12 Aug. 1812)

Fitzgerald, Edward, age 33, arrived U.S. June 1799, mariner, Boston - wife Rachael (born in U.S.), age 29; child: Mary, age 9 (24 Feb. 1813)

Fitzgerald, Michael, age 23, arrived U.S. 1793, tailor, Boston (12 Mar. 1813)

Fitzhanis, Lawrence, age 15, arrived U.S. 1812, yeoman, Boston (14 Aug. 1812)

Fitzhanis, Nicholas, age 18, arrived U.S. 1812, yeoman, Boston (14 Aug. 1812)

Fitzpatrick, Barnard, age 40, arrived U.S. 1803, tailor, Boston - wife Eleanor (born abroad), age 30; children: Mary (born abroad), age 11, Thomas, age 8, Cathrine, age 6, Eleanor, age 2 (last 3 born in U.S.) (21 July 1812)

Fitzpatrick, Patrick, age 24, arrived U.S. Mar. 1812, labourer, Boston (9 Mar. 1813)

Fitzroy, James, age 30, 5ft. 10 in., light complex., brown hair, brown eyes, arrived U.S. 1810, gardener (9 Apr. 1813)

Fitzsimmons, Peter, age 27, arrived U.S. Aug. 1805, trader, Boston - wife Mary (born abroad), age 31; children: James, age 3, John, age 1 (both born in U.S.) (31 July 1812)

Flaman, James, age 31, arrived U.S. Aug. 1805, trader, Boston (31 July 1812)

*Flemming, Thomas, age 55, 5ft. 10in., dark complex., grey hair, grey eyes - wife Hannah (born abroad), age 52; child: William, age 6 (born in U.S.) (13 Mar. 1813)

Fletcher, Robert, age 45 (24 Feb. 1813)

Fling, David, age 29, arrived U.S. 1808, labourer, Boston (29 July 1812)

Flinn, John, age 31, arrived U.S. May 1797, labourer, Worcester - wife Hannah (born in U.S.), age 32; children: Nancy, age 6, Edmund, age 4, Hannah, age 2 (all born in U.S.); inmate: Ruth Nicholson, age 10 (7 Sept. 1812)

Flinn, Thomas, age 29, arrived U.S. 1809, labourer, Boston (25 Mar. 1813)

Foley, Maurice, age 47, arrived U.S. Aug. 1799, innkeeper & grocer, Boston - wife Elen (born abroad), age 27; children: Sarah Ann, age 9, Edward, age 5, Bridget, age 3, Mary Ann, age 18 mos. (8 Aug. 1812)

Foley, Morris, age 40, arrived U.S. 1787, mariner, Boston (19 Mar. 1813)

Foley, Thomas, age 37, arrived U.S. July 1800, labourer, Boston (23 Feb. 1813)

Ford, John, age 34, arrived U.S. May 1810, hatter, Boston - wife Hannah (born abroad), age 34; children: John, age 6, Edward, age 5 (both born abroad) (7 Aug. 1812)

Ford, Thomas, age 45, arrived U.S. May 1801, paper stainer, Boston - wife Cathrine (born in U.S.), age 25; children: Mary Ann, age 6, John, age 4, Cathrine, age 3½, Eliza, age 6 mos. (all born in U.S.) (4 Aug. 1812)

Foster, Charles, age 42, arrived U.S. Aug. 1805, yeoman, East
    Sudbury - wife Rebecca (born in U.S.), age 36; children: Nancy
    B., age 9, Samuel, age 1 (both born in U.S.) (23 Mar. 1813)
Foster, William, age 30, arrived U.S. 30 Aug. 1809, applied in
    S,C. Jan. 1811, innholder, Boston - wife Mary (born in U.S.),
    age 32, widow of James Clay (a naturalized citizen) by whom
    she had two children, Mary Ann, age 12, and Louisa, age 9, both
    born in U.S. (1812 or 1813)
Fowler, Enoch, age 22, arrived U.S. Sept. 1794, cabinetmaker,
    Salisbury (5 Sept. 1812)
Fowler, James, age 20, carpenter, Salisbury (11 Mar. 1813)
Frazier, John, age 41, arrived U.S. Dec. 1808, gardener, Water-
    town - wife Elizabeth (born abroad), age 39; children: Eliza-
    beth, age 20, Mathew, age 15, Charles, age 12 (all born abroad),
    James, age 10, John, age 8, George, age 6, Isabella, age 2½
    (all 4 born in U.S.) (11 Jan. 1813)
Freeman, Charles, age 37, arrived U.S. Jan. 1798, labourer, Bos-
    ton - wife Betsey (born in U.S.), age 27; children: Elizabeth
    & Ann (both born in U.S.) (30 Sept. 1812)
Fry, William, age 43, arrived U.S. Aug. 1811, blacksmith, Wal-
    pole (7 Aug. 1812)
Fullerton, James, Jr., age 26, arrived U.S. May 1809, scrivener,
    Boston (31 July 1812)
Fullerton, John, age 42, arrived U.S. June 1812, gentleman, Water-
    town (22 Mar. 1813)
Furlong, John, age 45, arrived U.S. Aug. 1797, labourer, Boston
    (3 Aug. 1812)
Fury, Mathew, age 28, arrived U.S. Aug. 1811, labourer, Cambridge
    (20 Mar. 1813)
Fussel, James, age 29, arrived U.S. 1807, tailor, Boston - wife
    Mary Ann (born abroad), age 25; children: John, age 19 mos.,
    Elizabeth Motley, age 4 days (both born in U.S.) (29 July 1812)
Gaiety, Timothy, age 32, arrived U.S. Aug. 1812, yeoman, Lynn
    (11 Nov. 1812)
Gains, John, age 30, tailor, Boston - wife Susannah (born in U.S.),
    age 40; children: Cathrine, age 4, Maria, age 2 (both born in
    U.S.) (3 Aug. 1812)
Galley, James, age 31, arrived U.S. Sept. 1807, barber, Haver-
    hill (7 Dec. 1812)
Galvin, Nicholas, age 19, arrived U.S. July 1812, labourer, Bos-
    ton (31 July 1812)
Gareven, Jeremiah, age 29, arrived U.S. Aug. 1805, labourer, Bos-
    ton - wife Nancy (born in U.S.), age 29 (Mar. 1813)
Garlick, Robert, age 42, arrived U.S. Oct. 1810, machine maker,
    Sharon - wife Hannah (born abroad), age 40; children: Thomas,
    age 12, Joseph, age 9 (both born abroad), John (born in U.S.)
    (19 Mar. 1813)
Garry, William, age 24, arrived U.S. May 1812, yeoman, Lynn (19
    Apr. 1813)
Gately, Malachi, age 33, arrived U.S. Aug. 1812, cordwainer,
    Lynn - wife Kitty (born abroad), age 28; children: Timothy,
    age 8, James, age 4, Bridget, age 14 mos. (16 Nov. 1812)
Gay, John, age 24, arrived U.S. July 1806, yeoman, Charlestown
    (23 Mar. 1813)
Geddes, Alexander, age 56, arrived U.S. 1804, manufacturer of
    twine, Boston - wife Maria J. (born abroad), age 45; children:
    Maria, age 15, James, age 13, Margaret, age 10 (all born in
    U.S.) (18 July 1812)
Geoghegan, William, arrived U.S. 1811, mariner, Salem (11 Mar.
    1813)
Gerry, Patrick, age 42, arrived U.S. Aug. 1807, dyer & clothier,
    West Boylston (29 Aug. 1812)
Gerry, Thomas, age 32, arrived U.S. July 1802, Boston - wife
    Sarah (born in U.S.), age 32; children: Mary Ann, age 4, Re-
    becca, age 1 (19 Mar. 1813)

Gibbin, William, age 59, arrived U.S. May 1806, gerdener, Worcester - wife Lewis (born abroad), age 57 (26 Aug. 1812)

Gibbon, Daniel, age 37, arrived U.S. Dec. 1812, carpenter, Boston (9 Mar. 1813)

Gidney, Philip, age 48 - arrived U.S. June 1802, yeoman, Tewksbury - wife Elizabeth (born abroad), age 51; inmates:.Moses Shattuck, age 25, Joseph Stevens, age 23, Asa Parker, age 20, Tryphane Woods, age 44, Mathew Kimbell, age 20, Peter (a Negro), age 16 (4 Aug. 1812)

Gilden, Dennis, age 23, arrived U.S. Oct. 1807, morocco tanner, Boston (6 Aug. 1812)

Gilligan, John, age 24, arrived U.S. 1812, labourer, Boston (19 Aug. 1812)

Gilroy, John, age 39, arrived U.S. Aug. 1812, weaver, Watertown - wife Mary (born abroad), age 36; children: John, age 13, James, age 7, Martha, age 4, Alexander, age 1½ (all born abroad) (8 Oct. 1812)

Gilson, Richard, age 35, arrived U.S. Aug. 1812, weaver, Watertown - wife Bridget, age 30 (7 Oct. 1812)

Glannon, Thomas, age 19, arrived U.S. Aug. 1812, trader, Boston (13 Aug. 1812)

Gledhill, Thomas, age 26, arrived U.S. 1809, upholsterer, Boston - wife Frances (born abroad), age 22 (29 July 1812)

Glen, Patrick, age 28, arrived U.S. Aug. 1812, yeoman, Lynn - wife Elizabeth (born abroad), age 24; child: John, age 1½ (16 Nov. 1812)

Good, James, age 23, arrived U.S. June 1812, labourer, Taunton (25 Mar. 1813)

Goods, John, age 25, arrived U.S. 1801, mariner, Boston - wife Martha (born in U.S.) (21 July 1812)

Gordon, George, age 30, arrived U.S. Nov. 1808, yeoman, Dorchester (19 Apr. 1813)

Gordon, William, age 38, arrived U.S. 1793, cordwainer, Boston - wife Sarah (born in U.S.), age 38; children: William, age 6, James, age 5, Sarah, age 1 (all born in U.S.) (10 Mar. 1813)

Gorman, Mustie, age 70, arrived U.S. 1801, brewer, Boston - wife Beddy (born abroad), age 70; children: John, age 22, Mary, age 30, Easter, age 22, Betsey, age 20 (all born abroad) (18 Aug. 1812)

Gowan, George, age 30, arrived U.S. May 1798, hatter, Boston (12 Sept. 1812)

Grace, James, age 25, arrived U.S. Aug. 1811, labourer, Cambridge (10 Aug. 1812)

Grace, Mary, age 56, merchant, Boston - children: Ann(born abroad), Elizabeth (born in U.S.) (25 July 1812)

Grace, William, age 52, arrived U.S. Oct. 1796, shipwright, Boston - wife Margaret (born abroad), age 45; children: Michael, age 22, Joseph, age 18, Mary, age 16 (all born abroad), James, age 15, Deborah, age 9, Eliza, age 4 (last 3 born in U.S.) (24 Sept. 1812)

Graham, John, age 39, arrived U.S. July 1803, cordwainer, Boston (5 Oct. 1812)

Grant, John, age 44, arrived U.S. Aug. 1804, labourer, Boston (19 Apr. 1813)

Grant, Lawrence, age 55, arrived U.S. Dec. 1791, labourer, Boston (25 Feb. 1813)

Grant, William, age 29, arrived U.S. Aug. 1803, trader, Boston - wife Elizabeth (born abroad), age 21; children: Mary Jane, age 2½, William H., age 4 mos. (both born in U.S.) (30 July 1812)

Gray, George, age 35, arrived U.S. 1805, mathematical instrument maker, Lynn (10 Sept. 1812)

Gready, Thomas, age 28, arrived U.S. 1805, labourer, Boston - wife Mary (born in U.S.), age 21; child: Mary, age 1 (born in U.S.) (7 Aug. 1812)

Green, Robert, age 39, arrived U.S. Nov. 1799, labourer, Charlestown - wife Eunis (born in U.S.), age 46; children: Elvis, age 9, Mary Ann, age 7, William Jan, age 3 (all born in U.S.) (4 Aug. 1812)

Greene, Horace, age 19, arrived U.S. 1811, mariner, Boston (29 Aug. 1812)

Greene, John, age 29, arrived U.S. Mar. 1808, baker, New Bedford (28 July 1812)

Greene, William, age 34, arrived U.S. Sept. 1812, trader, Boston (6 Nov. 1812)

Greenwod, John, age 34, arrived U.S. 1809, merchant, Boston (20 July 1812)

Greenwood, James, age 37, arrived U.S. 1811, merchant, Boston - wife Elizabeth (born abroad), age 37; children: Francis, age 4 (born abroad), Louisa, age 1½, James, age 3 days (both born in U.S.) (22 July 1812)

*Gregson, Isaac, age 22, 5ft. 3in., florid complex., sandy hair, grey eyes (14 June 1813)

Greves, John, arrived U.S. Oct. 1807, labourer, Boston - wife Priscilla (born in U.S.), age 23; child: Henry, age 3 (born in U.S.) (30 July 1812)

Grigson, James, age 21, arrived U.S. May 1812, hatter, Boston (7 Aug. 1812)

Gunn, Richard, age 30, 5ft. 3in., dark complex., dark hair, dark eyes, arrived U.S. July 1806, mariner, Charlestown - wife Isabella (born abroad), age 25 (13 Mar. 1813)

Gurnow, Michael, age 20, arrived U.S. Apr. 1810, manufacturer of woolen cloth, Stockbridge (21 Aug. 1812)

Halford, Giles, age 22, arrived U.S. Feb. 1804, labourer, Shelburn (10 Aug. 1812)

Hall, James, age 21, arrived U.S. Oct. 1809, spinner, Hingham - wife Susannah (born abroad), age 24; child: James, age 2 (born in U.S.) (8 Mar. 1813)

Hall, Joseph, age 25, arrived U.S. 1810, gardener, Brookline (17 Aug. 1812)

Hall, Patrick H., age 38, arrived U.S. Nov. 1804, labourer, Boston - wife Francis (born in U.S.), age 27; children: John, age 5, Mary, age 4, Maria E., age 1 (15 Mar. 1813)

Hall, Robert, age 25, arrived U.S. Oct. 1811, seaman, Boston (25 Feb. 1813)

Halpin, Patrick, age 29, arrived U.S. Aug. 1806, coachman, Boston (13 Feb. 1813)

Hamil, Patrick, age 32, arrived U.S. Dec. 1805, manufacturer, Canton (26 Mar. 1813)

Hamilton, John, age 25, 5ft. 10in., dark complex., dark hair, grey eyes, arrived U.S. July 1806, grocer, Boston (2 Apr. 1813)

Hanable, Hannah, age 17, arrived U.S. 1811, servant, Boston (27 Feb. 1813)

Hancock, Edward, age 27, arrived U.S. 1799, truckman, Boston - wife Susannah (born in U.S.), age 28 (19 Mar. 1813)

Hanly, Robert, age 27, arrived U.S. Aug. 1810, carpenter, Bristol (19 Apr. 1813)

Harlett, William, age 44, arrived U.S. 1801, weaver, Roxbury - wife Elizabeth (born in U.S.), age 28; children: Evis, age 9, Elizabeth, age 5, William, age 18 mos. (all born in U.S.) (8 Aug. 1812)

Harney, Thomas, age 49, arrived U.S. Oct. 1798, labourer, Boston - wife Rebecca Henry (born abroad), age 48

*Harrison, Thomas, age 50, 5ft. 8in., florid complex., grey hair, blue eyes - children: John, age 16, Elizabeth, age 14 (both born in U.S.) (12 Apr. 1813)

Hathcoat, Robert, age 32, arrived U.S. 1807, merchant, Boston (4 Aug. 1812)

Hawkins, Samuel, age 45, arrived in U.S. 1806, ship-joiner, Salem - wife Jane (born abroad), age 40; children: Sally, age
18, Nancy, age 15 (both born in U.S.) (6 Aug. 1812)
Haworth, Samuel, age 56, arrived U.S. June 1807, farmer, Mansfield - wife Mary, age 70 (14 Oct. 1812)
Hay, Sampson, age 23, arrived U.S. 1806, mariner, Boston (1812
or 1813)
Hayden, John, age 23, arrived U.S. Apr. 1808, labourer, Boston
(23 Feb. 1813)
Hayman, John, age 27, arrived U.S. Sept. 1804, mariner, Salem
(26 Aug. 1812)
Hays, George, age 43, carpenter, Boston - wife Martha (born in
U.S.), age 33; children: Mary, age 13, Susannah, age 11, Elea-
nor, age 10, William, age 9, Patty, age 7, George W., age 5,
Thomas, age 3 (all born in U.S.) (24 Mar. 1813)
*Healy, James, age 18, 5ft. 5in., dark complex., brown hair,
grey eyes, arrived U.S. Nov. 1812 - wife Elizabeth (born
abroad) (12 Apr. 1813)
Heath, Benjamin, age 30, arrived U.S. Jan. 1799, mariner, New
Bedford - wife Abigal (born in U.S.); child: Amelia, age 6
(18 Aug. 1812)
Heathcot, John, age 47, arrived U.S. June 1805, gardener, Waltham (7 Aug. 1812)
Heatherly, Thomas, age 70, arrived U.S. June 1774, cordwainer,
West Boylston - wife Hester (born in U.S.), age 68 (7 Sept.
1812)
Hefferman, James, age 30, arrived U.S. Aug. 1800, painter, Taunton - wife Hannah, age 38; children (probably of wife): Harriet
Prentice, age 18, Eliza Prentice, age 16, Mary Prentice, age
13 (all born in U.S.) (4 Aug. 1812)
Henderson, John, age 39, arrived U.S. June 1799, applied 1809,
boarding house (keeper), Boston - wife Sarah (born abroad),
age 35; children: John Lency, age 15, Elizabeth Lency, age 17
(13 Feb. 1813); a John Henderson, age 39, 5ft. 11in., florid
complex., dark hair, dark eyes, victualer, of Boston, on 19
Mar. 1812 was ordered to remove to Petersham, Worcester Co.
(passport no. 1 - Mass.)
Hendry, John, age 33, arrived U.S. 1804, bootmaker, Boston (21
July 1812)
Henly, Edward, age 26, arrived U.S. June 1812, labourer, Boston -
wife Catherine (born in U.S.), age 26 (23 Jan. 1813)
Henniff, Dennis, age 44, arrived U.S. Apr. 1801, gardener, Newtown, 5ft. 6in., dark complex., dark hair, grey eyes (21 Apr.
1813)
Herring, Thomas, age 57, arrived U.S. June 1806, labourer, Boston - wife Catharine (born abroad), age 69; children: Susannah,
age 9, Elizabeth, age 7 (both born in U.S.) (25 Feb. 1813)
Herring, William, age 34, arrived U.S. 1810, labourer, Boston -
wife Mary (born abroad), age 25; children: Mary, age 6, Johanna,
age 2 (both born abroad), James, age 5 mos. (born in U.S. (24
July 1812)
Hickey, John, age 44, arrived U.S. 1803, mariner, Newbury (10 Aug.
1812)
Hickley, Mark, age 30, arrived U.S. Mar. 1800, labourer, Boston -
wife Frances (born abroad); children: Andrew, age 8 (born
abroad), Mary (born in U.S.) (3 Aug. 1812)
Hicks, Phinley, age 35, arrived U.S. June 1810, trader, Boston -
wife Tracy (born abroad), age 31; children: Caroline, age 11,
Walter, age 9, Nancy, age 2 (all born abroad), infant that has
no Christian name, age 3 mos. (born in U.S.) (30 July 1812)
Hickson, John, age 25, arrived U.S. Mar. 1802, blacksmith, Boston - wife Elizabeth (born in U.S.), age 28; children: Elizabeth, age 2, Sarah, age 1 (both born in U.S.) (26 Mar. 1813)
Hickson, Thomas, age 22, arrived U.S. 1810, scrivener, Boston
(25 July 1812)

Higgins, Michael, age 30, arrived U.S. July 1805, labourer, Boston (31 July 1812)
Higgins, Terrence, age 24, arrived U.S. 1804, labourer, Boston (10 Aug. 1812)
Hill, Jas. Absolem, age 34, arrived U.S. June 1802, mariner, Boston (24 Aug. 1812)
Hills, Joseph, age 47, arrived U.S. 1807, shoemaker, Boston - wife Sarah (born abroad), age 43; children: Elizabeth, age 22, Joseph, age 23, Sarah, age 20, Richard, age 15, William, age 13, George, age 9, Hannah, age 7 (all born abroad), James, age 2 (born in U.S.); inmates: Judith Hills (sister), age 33, John Hills (Judith's son), age 2, Sarah Hills (Joseph's mother), age 85 (27 July 1812)
Hills, Joseph, Jr., age 23, arrived U.S. 1807, applied at New York 1810, shoemaker, Boston - wife Margaret (born abroad), age 29; child: Howard, age 10 weeks (born in U.S.); inmate: Sarah Hills, age 20 (21 July 1812)
Hobart, Mathew, age 36, arrived U.S. 1802, ship-carpenter, Salem - wife Sally (born in U.S.), age 30; child: Harriot, age 8 (born in U.S.) (6 Aug. 1812)
Hodshon, Richard, age 38, arrived U.S. 1801, tinplate worker, Boston - wife Mary (born abroad), age 30; children: Brooks, age 4, Eleanor, age 3, Caroline, age 9 mos. (all born in U.S.) (30 July 1812)
Hogan, Hugh, age 40, arrived U.S. 1799, labourer, Boston - wife Hanora (born abroad), age 34; children: Michael, age 12, Edward, age 7, Mary, age 6, Nancy, age 3, Catherine, age 1 (all born in U.S.) (7 Aug. 1812)
Hollings, Daniel, age 36, arrived U.S. 1793, mariner, New York - wife Jane (born in U.S.), age 30 (24 Feb. 1813)
Holman, Joseph George, age 48, arrived U.S. June 1812, comedian, Boston - inmate: Catharine Amelia Holman, age 22 (4 Jan. 1813)
Horace, Peter, age 30, arrived U.S. July 1810, mariner, Boston - wife Sarah (born in U.S.), age 26; children: Cathrine, age 6, Sarah, age 4 mos. (both born in U.S.) (3 Aug. 1812)
*Hothingham, James, age 30, 5ft. 6in., florid complex., dark hair, grey eyes (9 Apr. 1813)
Howard, Edward, age 27, arrived U.S. Sept. 1812, woolen weaver, Boston - wife Mary (born abroad), age 27; children: James, age 6, Hannah, age 5, Mary, age 3, Sarah, age 1 (all born abroad); inmate: Elizabeth Howard, age 24 (30 Sept. 1812)
Howard, John, age 29, arrived U.S. 1803, applied 1808, grocer, Boston - wife Elizabeth (born in U.S.), age 36; children: Sally, age 3, John, age 2 (both born in U.S.); inmates: Mary, John, Betsey, Sophia, Harriet and Caroline Leach (children of Mrs. Howard by a foreigner to whom she was formerly married)(29 July 1812)
Howell, James, age 27, arrived U.S. 1804, mariner, Salem - wife Margaret L. (born in U.S.), age 24 (3 Aug. 1812)
Howell, Michael, age 26, arrived U.S. 1806, checkman, Waltham - wife Mary (born in U.S.), age 25; child: James, age 1 (born in U.S.) (7 Aug. 1812)
Howes, Thomas, age 57, arrived U.S. 1803, shoemaker, Boston - wife Elizabeth (born in U.S.), age 43; children: Betsey, age 23, Thomas, age 19, William, age 17, Sally, age 16, Maria, age 13 (all born in U.S.) (27 July 1812)
Howland, Christopher, age 24, arrived U.S. Apr. 1807, mariner, Charlestown - wife Mary Ann (born abroad), age 19; child: Richard, age 3 mos. (1812 or 1813)
Hughes, Charles, age 24, arrived U.S. May 1811, woolen spinner, Boston (1 Oct. 1812)
Hug(h)es, Walter, age 29, 5ft. 11in., florid complex., dark hair, grey eyes, arrived U.S. Feb. 1813, accountant, Boston (29 May 1813)

Hughes, William, age 21, 5ft. 6in., dark complex., dark hair,
grey eyes, arrived U.S. Sept. 1804, mariner, Boston (10 Aug.
1813)
Hunt, John, age 35, arrived U.S. 1804 - wife Deliverance (born
abroad) (31 Mar. 1813)
Hunt, Timothy, age 50, arrived U.S. July 1799, gentleman, Boston -
wife Lucy (born in U.S.), age 28; children: James, age 8,
William, age 6, Bartholomew, age 6 mos., Timothy, Jr., age 6
mos. (all born in U.S.) (3 Aug. 1812)
Hurd, John, age 39, arrived U.S. 1804, distiller, Boston - wife
Mary Ann, age 39; child: Mary Ann, age 10 (born in U.S.) (30
July 1812)
Hutchinson, George, age 45, arrived U.S. June 1807, victualer,
Chelmsford - wife Eliza (born abroad), age 34; children: George,
age 9, Margret, age 7 (both born abroad), John, age 4, Hannah,
age 2, Mary Ann, age 5 mos. (last 3 born in U.S.) (10 Aug. 1812)
Hyde, James P., age 50, arrived U.S. May 1805, trader, Boston -
wife Mary (born in U.S.), age 44; children: William Grazier,
age 22, John Grazier, age 21, Mary Grazier, age 20 (all born
in U.S.) (1 Mar. 1813)
Hynes, Nicholas, age 26, in U.S. since May 1812, founder, Can-
ton (19 Apr. 1813)
Hynes, Peter, age 28, in U.S. since May 1812, founder, Canton
(19 Apr. 1813)
Ingles, Thomas, age 31, arrived U.S. 1806, labourer, Boston (23
Mar. 1813)
Irvine, Thomas, age 26, arrived U.S. May 1808, cotton weaver,
Watertown - wife Esther (born in U.S.), age 26; children: Mary
M., age 2, Susan, age 5 mos. (12 Sept. 1812)
*Isaacson, James, age 28, light complex., light hair, blue eyes -
wife Lydia (born abroad) (3 Apr. 1813)
Ivory, Edward, age 31, arrived U.S. 1805, applied 12 Mar., la-
bourer, Boston (1812 or 1813)
Jack, David, Jr., arrived U.S. 1792, tobacconist, Boston (24 July
1812)
Jack, Peter, age 23, arrived U.S. 1792, scrivener, Boston (24
July 1812)
Jackson, George K., age 34, 5ft. 4½in., florid complex., dark
hair, blue eyes, prof. of music, Boston, on 19 Mar. 1812 or-
dered to Northampton, Hampshire Co. (Mass. passport No. 3)
Jackson, James, age 23, arrived U.S. Oct. 1808, glassmaker,
Chelmsford (13 Aug. 1812)
Jacobs, John, age 49, arrived U.S. June 1804, merchant, Boston
(1812 or 1813)
Jacobs, John C., age 26, arrived U.S. Nov. 1805, copperplate
printer, Boston - wife Ann (born in U.S.), age 20; children:
George, Adeline, Charles (all born in U.S.) (5 Jan. 1813)
Jaffrey, William, age 26, arrived U.S. May 1810, gardener, Brook-
lyn (7 Jan. 1813)
James, George, age 73, arrived U.S. 1795, upholsterer, Boston -
inmate: his sister Elizabeth James, age 76 (21 July 1812)
Jefferis, George, age 49, arrived U.S. Dec. 1810, gentleman,
Boston (3 Aug. 1812)
Jerman, Roger, age 25, arrived U.S. Dec. 1800, print cutter,
Boston - wife Mercy (born in U.S.), age 25 (16 Jan. 1813)
Johnson, James, age 29, arrived U.S. 1802, stone cutter, Boston
(31 Aug. 1812)
Johnson, James, age 27, arrived U.S. Feb. 1808, labourer, Shrews-
bury (25 Aug. 1812)
Johnson, James, age 25, arrived U.S. 1811, yeoman, Boston (4 Aug.
1812)
Johnson, William, age 28, arrived U.S. 1802, mariner, Salem -
wife Deborah (born abroad) (24 Mar. 1813)
Johnston, John, age 45, arrived U.S. May 1812, weaver, Watertown -
wife Jane (born abroad), age 35 (8 Mar. 1813)

Johnston, Thomas, age 30, arrived U.S. Aug. 1812, cordwainer,
   Watertown - wife Elizabeth (born abroad), age 30 (8 Mar. 1813)
Joice, John M., age 37, arrived U.S. June 1809, scrivener, Bos-
   ton (27 July 1812)
Jones, Edward, age 37, arrived U.S. Aug. 1808, cotton spinner,
   Franklin - wife Mary (born in U.S.), age 23; child: Edward,
   Jr., age 2 (born in U.S.) (8 Aug. 1812)
Jones, Francis, age 43, arrived U.S. 1801, applied Feb. 1812,
   grocer, Boston - wife Elizabeth (born in U.S.) (18 July 1812)
Jones, James, age 41, arrived U.S. 1808, yeoman, Watertown -
   wife Elizabeth (born in U.S.), age 31 (30 July 1812)
Jones, James, age 22, arrived U.S. Sept. 1812, cabinetmaker,
   Boston (23 Sept. 1812)
Jones, John, age 45, arrived U.S. Oct. 1811, cotton weaver, Can-
   ton (12 Sept. 1812)
Jones, John, age 38, arrived U.S. 1805, innholder, Boston - wife
   Janis (born abroad), age 35; children: Thomas, age 11, James,
   age 6 (both born abroad), John Edward, age 10 mos. (born in
   U.S.); inmate: Elizabeth Lowe (sister to Mrs. Jones), an Eng-
   lish woman, age 28, who arrived U.S. 1810 (22 July 1812)
Jones, Lewis, age 29, tinplate worker, Boston - wife Elizabeth
   (born in U.S.), age 25; child: Elizah A., age 5 mos. (born in
   U.S.) (7 Aug. 1812)
Jones, Owen, age 29, arrived U.S. Nov. 1784, mariner, Boston -
   wife Elizabeth (born in U.S.), age 36; children: Elizabeth,
   age 22, Sarah, age 19, George, age 17, Catharine, age 14, Tho-
   mas, age 9, Mary, age 7, Owen, Jr., age 5, Lawry, age 3, Ann
   Maria, age 1 (all born in U.S.) (19 Apr. 1813)
Jones, Thomas, age 50, arrived U.S. Aug. 1796, minister of the
   Gospel, Gloucester - wife Sophia (born abroad), age 47;
   children: Thomas G., age 15, Sophia N., age 10, Mary H., age
   8 (all 3 born in U.S.) (19 Apr. 1813)
Jones, Thomas, age 32, arrived U.S. Aug. 1804, rigger, Boston
   (19 Apr. 1813)
Jones, William, age 35, arrived U.S. 1798, rigger, Boston - wife
   Mary (born in U.S.); children: Nancy, age 7, William, age 5,
   John (all born in U.S.) (25 Mar. 1813)
Joy, John, age 31, arrived U.S. 1807, labourer, Boston - wife
   Eleanor Fitzpatrick (born abroad), age 22 (22 Feb. 1813)
Judge, James, age 21, arrived U.S. July 1812, scrivener, Boston
   (31 July 1812)
Kavanagh, Walter, age 37, arrived U.S. 1805, applied 1809, la-
   bourer, Boston - wife Mary (born abroad), age 25; children:
   Luke, age 10, Edward, age 8 (both born abroad), James, age 5,
   John Joseph, age 6 mos. (both born in U.S.) (28 July 1812)
Kelley, Andrew, age 25, arrived U.S. Sept. 1812, linen weaver,
   Boston (30 Sept. 1812)
Kelley, John, age 45, arrived U.S. 1796, labourer, Boston - wife
   Hannah (born in U.S.), age 38; children: Nancy, age 12, John,
   age 10, Jane, age 4 (29 July 1812)
Kelley, Patrick, age 35, arrived U.S. Dec. 1807, labourer, Boyls-
   ton (28 Aug. 1812)
Kelley, Walter, age 27, arrived U.S. Aug. 1801, yeoman, Lynn (5
   Sept. 1812)
Kelley, William, age 50, arrived U.S. 1800, fisherman, Boston -
   wife Sally (born in U.S.), age 50; children: Mary (born abroad),
   age 19, child, name illegible, age 15, Elizabeth, age 11 (both
   born in U.S.) (10 Aug. 1812)
Kelly, Arthur, age 28, arrived U.S. May 1808, yeoman, Boston
   (25 Nov. 1812)
Kelly, Darby, age 36, arrived U.S. July 1800, labourer, Boston -
   wife Lucy (born in U.S.), age 38; children: Martin, age 11,
   Margaret, age 8 (both born in U.S.)

Kelly, James, age 27, arrived U.S. 1807, labourer, Boston - wife
Ann (born abroad), age 22; children: John, age 2, Ann, age 1
mo. (20 Mar. 1813)

Kennedy, James, age 32, arrived U.S. May 1812, merchant, Boston
wife Elizabeth (born abroad), age 32; child: Elizabeth (born
abroad) (24 Feb. 1813)

Kenny, Patrick, age 39, arrived U.S. June 1794, sawyer, Charlestown - wife Elizabeth (born in U.S.), age 32; children: Elizabeth, age 13, Mary, age 11, Ann, age 8, James, age 7 (27 Feb.
1813)

Kenny, Patrick, age 28, 5ft. 8in., dark complex., brown hair,
blue eyes, arrived U.S. 1812 - wife Honor (born abroad); child:
Michael (born abroad) (22 Feb. 1813)

Kenyon, William, age 23, arrived U.S. Dec. 1808, weaver, Pittsfield - wife Hannah (born in U.S.), age 19 (26 Dec. 1812)

*Keogan, Peter, age 29, 5ft. 7in., light complex., light hair,
blue eyes (6 Apr. 1813)

Keough, Edward, age 23, arrived U.S. 1804, mariner, Bristol (22
Aug. 1812)

Kerns, William, age 30, arrived U.S. 1811, whitesmith, Boston
(10 Aug. 1812)

Kerr, William, age 46, rigger, Boston - wife Sally (born in U.S.),
age 32; children: William, age 18, twins, Elizabeth & Abigel,
age 6, James, age 4, Margaret, age 8 mos. (all born in U.S.);
inmates: Sally & Mary Morris, children of Mrs. Kerr by former
marriage to a foreigner (21 July 1812)

Kerrnan, John, age 23, arrived U.S. Aug. 1812, carpenter, Quin-
cy - wife Mary (born abroad), age 22 (20 Mar. 1813)

Khalas, Thomas, age 23, arrived U.S. Oct. 1807, labourer, Boston
(31 July 1812)

Killick, Thomas, age 46, arrived U.S. Oct. 1806, glazier, Boston -
wife Ann (born abroad), age 35; child: Thomas, age 16 (born
abroad) (5 Aug. 1812)

Kilroy, John, age 37, arrived U.S. June 1811, labourer, Boston
(9 Mar. 1813)

King, Daniel, age 46, arrived U.S. 1796, labourer, Boston - wife
Mary (born abroad), age 46; children: Mary, age 12, William,
age 13, Nancy, age 7 (all born in U.S.) (17 Aug. 1812)

King, Edward, age 68, arrived U.S. 1812 on a vessel from Halifax,
Boston - wife Agness (born abroad), age 62 (24 July 1812)

*King, Richard, age 30, 5ft. 6in., dark complex., dark hair, dark
eyes (16 Apr. 1813)

Kingston, Charles H., age 17, arrived U.S. 1805, tobacconist,
Boston (28 Aug. 1812)

Knowlen, Martin, age 48, arrived U.S. May 1801, labourer, Boston -
wife Mary (born in U.S.), age 35; children: John, age 7, Margaret, age 5, Ann, age 3, James, age 1½ (all born in U.S. (21
Nov. 1812)

Koning, T.E., age 32, arrived U.S. July 1812, merchant, Boston
(28 Oct. 1812)

Lambert, John, age 32, arrived U.S. 1811, merchant, New York (21
July 1812)

Lanigan, John, age 39, arrived U.S. Sept. 1805, trader, Boston -
wife Jane (born abroad), age 35; children: Mary, age 9 (born
abroad), Joseph L., age 5, William, age 2 (both born in U.S.)
(24 Feb. 1813)

Larder, Thomas, age 33, arrived U.S. Sept. 1801, brewer, Boston -
wife Hannah (born in U.S.), age 23; children: Morris, age 5,
John, age 3, Margaret, age 2, E..in(?), age 1 (all born in U.S.)
(8 Aug. 1812)

Larkin, Ann (an Englishwoman, widow of a mariner), age 41;
children: Thos. Oliver, age 10, Ann Rogers, age 8, William M.R.,
age 5 (all born in U.S.); Mrs. Larkin arrived U.S. Feb. 1797,
trader, Charlestown (27 July 1812)

Larkin, John P., age 30, arrived U.S. Feb. 1802, hairdresser,
    Medford - wife Mary (born abroad); children: Mary, age 8,
    Samuel, age 7, Joseph, age 6, Elizabeth, age 3, John, Jr.,
    age 1 (8 Mar. 1813)
Leach, Thomas, age 58, arrived U.S. May 1800, labourer, Boston -
    wife Sarah (born in U.S.), age 37; child: Harriot, age 14 (born
    in U.S.) (19 Apr. 1813)
Leahy, William, age 36, arrived U.S. Oct. 1797, labourer, Bos-
    ton - wife Abigail (born abroad), age 27; children: David, age
    10, Margaret, age 9, Mary Ann, age 5, Thomas, age 4, Elizabeth,
    age 3, William, age 6 mos. (2 Mar. 1813)
Lee, Daniel, age 48, arrived U.S. 1779, mariner, Boston - wife
    Barbara (born abroad), age 37; inmates: Mary Campbell, age 18,
    John Campbell, age 15, James Campbell, age 12 (4 Aug. 1812)
Lee, Matthew, age 38, arrived U.S. July 1798, tallow chandler,
    Boston (19 Mar. 1813)
Lee, Robert, age 38, arrived U.S. May 1806, bellows maker, Bos-
    ton - wife Sarah (born abroad), age 33; child: Sarah, age 8
    (born abroad) (23 Nov. 1812)
Lees, John, age 30, cotton manufacturer, Newbury - wife Catha-
    rine (born abroad) (29 Aug. 1812)
Leonard, James, age 46, arrived U.S. July 1801, labourer, Bos-
    ton - wife Ann (born in U.S.), age 32; children: Mary Ann,
    age 11, James, age 4, John, age 6 mos. (1 Mar. 1813)
*Le Petit, Edmund, age 31, 6ft., light complex., dark hair, dark
    eyes (15 June 1813)
Lewis, John, age 27, arrived U.S. Oct. 1806, labourer, Boston
    (23 Feb. 1813)
*Lewis, John B., age 35, 5ft. 5in., dark complex., brown hair,
    grey eyes (5 Apr. 1813)
Lewis, Ralph, age 28, arrived U.S. 1798, mariner, Salem (8 Aug.
    1812)
Litchfield, William, age 25, arrived U.S. June 1805, yeoman,
    Dorchester - wife Hannah (born in U.S.); children: William,
    age 8, Mary, age 9 mos. (both born in U.S.) (2 Nov. 1812)
Little, William, age 31, arrived U.S. June 1801, yeoman, Abing-
    ton - wife Judith, age 38; children: James, age 8, William
    (both born in U.S.); inmate: Judith Eustis, age 16 (14 Sept.
    1812)
Lloyd, Robert B., age 36, arrived U.S. 1793, baker, Boston - wife
    Sally L., age 34; children: Ester Clark Lloyd, age 8, Robert
    B. Lloyd, age 4, Mary Ann Lloyd, age 1½ (all born in U.S.)
    (22 July 1812)
Lockwood, Joshua, age 38, arrived U.S. 1794, rigger, Charles-
    town - wife Lucy (born in U.S.), age 32; child: Abraham, age 3
    (30 July 1812)
Longhurst, John, age 30, arrived U.S. 1802, schoolmaster, Bos-
    ton (20 Mar. 1813)
Longhurst, William, age 54, arrived U.S. Oct. 1807, cordwainer,
    Boston - wife Hannah (born in U.S.), age 45; children: William
    Kirkley, age 24, John Kirkley, age 22, Robert Kirkley, age 16
    (all born in U.S.) (15 Mar. 1813)
Lord, Daniel, age 30, arrived U.S. 1807, gardener, Brighton (8
    Sept. 1812)
Low, John, age 31, dark complex., black hair, blue eyes, arrived
    U.S. Nov. 1808, mariner, Salem - wife Betsey (born abroad);
    children: John, William (both born in U.S.) (2 Apr. 1813)
Low, Philip, arrived U.S. 1804, mariner (29 Mar. 1813)
Lowden, John, age 78, brewer, Boston - wife Susan (born abroad),
    age 31; children: John, age 9 (born abroad), Susan, Mary, Fre-
    derick (all 3 born in U.S.) (18 Sept. 1812)
Lowden, John, age 58, applied 1807, tailor,
    Boston - wife Mary (born abroad), age 58 (20 July 1812)
*Livin, Benjamin, arrived U.S. 26 Mar. 1807, merchant, Boston
    (1812 or 1813)

Lud, John, age 26, arrived U.S. Apr. 1810, cotton manufacturer, West Boylston - wife Martha (born in U.S.) (15 Aug. 1812)

Lumbsden, Thomas, age 45, arrived U.S. May 1811, gentleman, Boston (7 Jan. 1813)

Lummas, Joseph, age 51, arrived U.S. 1776, applied but does not remember period, manufacturer, Andover - wife Sally (born in U.S.), age 47 (29 Aug. 1312)

Lummus, William, age 44, arrived U.S. 1810, tanner, Charlestown (4 Aug. 1812)

Lutten, Robert, age 25, arrived U.S. June 1802, mariner, Boston - wife Jane (born abroad), age 30; child: William, age 2 mos. (born in U.S.) (6 Aug. 1312)

Lynch, Thomas, age 23, 5ft. 8in., light complex., light hair, light eyes, arrived U.S. May 1813, servant, Boston (31 May 1813)

Lynn, William, age 38, arrived U.S. 1793, rigger, Boston - child: James, age 4 (born in U.S.) (25 Mar. 1813)

McAuthur, John, age 31, arrived U.S. Dec. 1811, gardener, Watertown (7 Aug. 1812)

McBaine, Wm., age 30, arrived U.S. 1805, labourer, Salem (12 Aug. 1812)

McBride, Michael, age 33, arrived U.S. 1801, applied July 1812, painter, Boston - wife Elizabeth (born abroad, arrived U.S. 1793), age 36; children: Mary Ann, age 4, John, age 19 mos. (both born in U.S.) (18 July 1812)

McCabe, John, age 60, arrived U.S. July 1805, labourer, Boston - wife Mary (born abroad), age 60; children: William, age 25, Ann, age 21, Martha, age 18, Maria, age 14, Catherine, age 9, James, age 27 (all born abroad) (7 Aug. 1812)

McCabe, Joseph, age 23, arrived U.S. Sept. 1811, yeoman, Boston (27 Nov. 1812)

McCala, Owen, age 30, arrived U.S. Aug. 1808, labourer, Boston - wife Margeret (born abroad), age 32; children: Mary Ann, age 1, James, age 3 mos. (both born in U.S.) (31 July 1812)

McCarthy, John, age 40, arrived U.S. Nov. 1797, ship-carpenter, Boston - wife Dorothy, age 45 (24 Sept. 1812)

McCartney, Robert, age 37, arrived U.S. July 1796, gunsmith, Boston - wife Elizabeth (born abroad), age 29; children: Eleanor, age 6, Robert, age 4, William, age 10 mos., John, age 8 (all born in U.S.) (15 Sept. 1812)

McCarty, Jeremiah, age 35, arrived U.S. 1805, labourer, Boston - child: William (born in U.S.), age 7 (25 July 1812)

McClary, Thomas, age 17, arrived U.S. 1811, brattaitoler, Boston (29 Aug. 1812)

McClure, William, age 45, arrived U.S. Mar. 1811, saddler, Boston - wife Rebecca, age 39; child: John, age 6 (born abroad) (25 Sept. 1812)

McCormick, Michael, age 26, 5ft. 5in., stout person, round visage, light complex., dark hair, light eyes, born in Ireland, arrived U.S. 25 Sept. 1813 in cartel Hope (T. Emery commander) from Halifax, residence Worcester (25 Sept. 1813)

McCormick, Patrick, age 26, arrived U.S. June 1804, labourer, Salem (2 Sept. 1812)

McCromack, James, arrived U.S. Sept. 1801, woolen weaver, Colrain (Coleraine?) - wife Lydia (born in U.S.), age 28; children: Nancy, age 9, Joseph, age 7, John, age 5, Lydia, age 4, Charles, age 3, Sally, age 16 days (all born in U.S.) (30 July 1812)

*McDaniel, Alexander, age 23, 5ft. 7in., dark complex., dark hair, dark eyes (11 May 1813)

McDaniel, Hugh, age 37, arrived U.S. Oct. 1801, labourer, Boston (5 Mar. 1813)

McDolen, John, age 21, arrived U.S. Dec. 1801, shoemaker, Worcester (22 Aug. 1812)

McDonald, Archibald, age 60, arrived U.S. June 1776, weaver, Paxton - wife Mary (born in U.S.), age 38 (28 Aug. 1812)

McDonald, James, age 32, arrived U.S. 1810, labourer, Boston
(18 Aug. 1812)

McDonald, Patrick, age 29, arrived U.S. 1795, labourer, Boston -
wife Ann (born in U.S.), age 23 (21 July 1812)

McDonald, William, age 53, arrived U.S. Aug. 1794, carver and
gilder, Boston - wife Elizabeth (born abroad), age 45; children: Elizabeth (born abroad), William, age 16, Susannah, age
24 (both born in U.S.) (30 July 1812)

McEarren, Andrew, age 70, arrived U.S. 1783, labourer, Sheffield -
wife Margeret (born abroad), age 35, arrived U.S. 1797 (12 Aug.
1812)

McFarland, Dennis, age 21, arrived U.S. July 1805, mariner, Boston (2 Mar. 1813)

McGarth, Philip, age 31, arrived U.S. Dec. 1811, labourer, Boston (9 Mar. 1813)

McGinnis, Thomas, age 39, arrived U.S. 1804, weaver, Boston (25
Mar. 1813)

McGonagle, Daniel, age 24, arrived U.S. Dec. 1805, labourer,
Boston - wife Margret (born abroad), age 23; children: John,
age 2, James, age 6 mos. (both born in U.S.) (3 Aug. 1812)

McGrath, Bernard, age 25, arrived U.S. Aug. 1812, weaver, Watertown (7 Oct. 1812)

McGrath, John, age 33, arrived U.S. June 1799, gardener, Rox-
bury(5 Mar. 1813); on 19 Feb. 1813 residence was Dorchester.

McGrath, John, age 32, arrived U.S. 1798 - wife Margeret (born
abroad), age 40; child: David (born in U.S.), age 5 (8 Sept.
1812)

McGrath, Patrick, age 23, arrived U.S. Sept. 1811, stone cutter,
Boston (23 Feb. 1813)

McGrath, Richard, age 29, 5ft. 9in., sandy complex., sandy hair,
dark eyes, arrived U.S. Oct. 1806, mariner, Boston (13 Apr.
1813)

Maguire, Francis, age 40, arrived U.S. 1792, shoemaker, Boston
(21 July 1812)

McGuire, Patrick, age 23, arrived U.S. Aug. 1801, painter, Boston (20 Mar. 1813)

McInevran, Patrick, age 33, arrived U.S. July 1795, hatter,
Northampton (27 July 1812)

McIntire, Archibald, age 25, arrived U.S. 1807, farmer, West
Cambridge (10 Aug. 1812)

McKagn, Daniel, age 25, labourer, Boston - wife Bridget (born
abroad), age 17; child: John, age 1 (born abroad) (29 July
1812)

Mackay, James, age 39, arrived U.S. 1805, cutler, Boston - wife
Alice (born in U.S.), age 32; inmates: James Smith, age 17,
Mary Smith, age 5 (Alice's children by a former marriage to a
foreigner) (27 Aug. 1812)

McKeachie, Thomas, age 37, arrived U.S. Oct. 1797, scrivener,
Boston (5 Jan. 1813)

McKee, Alexander, age 35, arrived U.S. June 1809, weaver, Wobourn -
wife Abigail (born abroad); child: James, age 16 mos. (27 Mar.
1813)

McKee, John, age 32, arrived U.S. Aug. 1808, yeoman, Wobourn -
wife Fanny (born abroad), age 24; children: John, age 4, Alexander, age 2, James, age 4 mos. (all born in U.S.) (27 Mar.
1813)

McKenna, Patrick, age 32, arrived U.S. Aug. 1802, labourer, Boston (23 Feb. 1813)

McKeon, Walter, age 27, labourer, Boston (27 Feb. 1813)

McKinly, John, age 21, arrived U.S. Dec. 1809, mariner, Boston
(25 Feb. 1813)

McLean, Alexander, age 40, arrived U.S. 1802, gardener, Boston -
wife Ann (born abroad), age 35; children: Joseph, age 16, Mary,
age 13 (both born abroad), Eleanor, age 8, Mary, age 4, William,
age 2 (last 3 born in U.S.) (20 Mar. 1813)

McLellan, Patrick, age 24, arrived U.S. May 1812, domestic, Roxbury (19 Jan. 1813)

McMillan, Archibald, age 44, arrived U.S. Nov. 1806, mariner, Salem - wife Hannah (born abroad); children: Margaret and Mercy (both born in U.S.) (14 Sept. 1812)

McNamara, John, age 34, arrived U.S. Sept. 1803, applied Oct. 1810, grocer, Boston (3 Aug. 1812)

*McNeil, Daniel, age 56, 5ft. 8in., florid complex., dark hair, blue eyes (20 Apr. 1813)

McNerney, Patrick, age 29, arrived U.S. Dec. 1804, trader, Boston - wife Sophia (born in U.S.), age 19; children: Eleanor, age 1, William, age 1 mo. (both born in U.S.) (27 Nov. 1812)

McNewell, Patrick, age 24, arrived U.S. Aug. 1812, weaver, Waltham (16 Sept. 1812)

McNutt, Authur, age 16, arrived U.S. Aug. 1809, shoemaker, Lynn (28 Aug. 1812)

McQueen, Archibald, age 26, 5ft. 3in., stout person, round visage, light complex., light hair, light eyes, born at Applecross, on 25 Sept. 1813 arried U.S. as passenger in cartel Hope (T. Emery commander), from Halifax, residence Worcester (9 Oct. 1813)

Madden, Mathew, age 33, arrived U.S. Oct. 1810, bookbinder, Boston (16 Nov. 1812)

Mahan, John, age 26, arrived U.S. June 1810, labourer, Boston (31 July 1812)

Major, Frederick William, age 39, arrived U.S. June 1798, blockmaker, Boston - wife Rebecca (born in U.S.), age 36; children: Eliza, age 13, Abigail, age 12, Frederick William, age 8, Rebecca, age 5, Anna, age 4, Caroline, age 2 (all born in U.S) (20 Mar. 1813)

Mallihean, John, age 28, arrived U.S. Sept. 1812, woolen weaver, Boston (30 Sept. 1812)

Malone, Richard, age 21, arrived U.S. Nov. 1810, labourer, Boston (23 Feb. 1813)

Manelly, James, age 30, arrived U.S. July 1800, labourer, Boston (19 Apr. 1813)

Manning, Phillip, age 34, 5ft. 3in., dark complex., black hair, blue eyes, arrived U.S. 1799, mariner, Salem - wife Lucy (born in U.S.); children: Susan, William, Phillip (all born in U.S.) (31 Mar. 1813)

Mare, Samuel, age 30, arrived U.S. Sept. 1807, brewer, Boston - wife Ann (born abroad), age 29; children: Samuel, age 6 (born abroad), Jane, age 4 (born in U.S.) (5 Oct. 1812)

Marrah, Edward, age 35, arrived U.S. Aug. 1802, founder, Canton - wife Esther (born in U.S.), age 26; child: Thomas, age 2 (born in U.S.) (19 Apr. 1813)

Marry, Henry, age 20, arrived U.S. 1807, apprentice to J. Odin, Boston (24 July 1812)

Marshall, James, age 39, arrived U.S. July 1798, mariner, Boston - wife Elizabeth (born abroad), age 39; children: James, age 9, John G., age 6, Jane G., age 4, Robert G., age 2 mos. (26 Mar. 1813)

Martin, Joseph, age 20, arrived U.S. June 1811, weaver, Waltham (16 Sept. 1812)

Martin, Patrick, age 29, arrived U.S. July 1806, grocer (3 Aug. 1812)

Martin, Patrick, age 29, 5ft. 4in., florid complex., brown hair, grey eyes, arrived U.S. Nov. 1808, confectioner, Boston. (10 May 1813)

Mather, James, age 42, arrived U.S. Jan. 1808, planter, Boston (30 Sept. 1812)

Mathewson, Mathew, age 37, arrived U.S. Jan. 1801, weaver, Boston (18 Sept. 1812)

Maube, Thomas, age 40, arrived U.S. 1795, blacksmith, Boston - wife Betsey (born in U.S.), age 32 (22 Mar. 1813)

Mayhr(?), Patrick, age 34, arrived U.S. 1812, labourer, Boston
  (22 Mar. 1813)
Meade, William, age 43, arrived U.S. 1807, applied Apr.
  1811, physician, Dorchester - wife Catherine (born abroad), age 29;
  inmates: Timothy Kallehan, age 25, Elizabeth Kallehan, age 20
  (30 July 1812)
Meagher, Edmund, age 47, arrived U.S. Dec. 1807, labourer, Boston (24 Feb. 1813)
Mears, Jeames, age 27, arrived U.S. Aug. 1807, applied July 1811,
  trader, Boston (27 July 1812)
Meeson, Thomas, age 14, arrived U.S. July 1804, tailor, Boston
  (20 Mar. 1813)
Meloney, John, age 26, arrived U.S. Oct. 1804, labourer, Boston -
  wife Sally (born abroad), age 28; children: Mary, age 5, John,
  age 1 mo. (26 Sept. 1812)
Melville, Luke, age 50, arrived U.S. July 1804, applied Dec.
  1811, labourer, Boston - wife Mary (born abroad); inmates:
  Michael Grant, age 7, William Grant, age 21 (children of Mrs.
  Melville) (30 July 1812)
Melville, Thomas, age 35, arrived U.S. Oct. 1804, labourer, Bos-
  ton (30 July 1812)
Meris (or Maris?), John, age 23, arrived U.S. June 1811, domestic,
  Boston (10 Aug. 1812)
Merritt, David, age 38, 5ft. 10in., dark complex., dark hair,
  dark eyes, labourer (30 Mar. 1813)
Merritt, David, age 37, arrived U.S. 1804, applied Nov. 1810,
  trader, Marblehead - wife Ann (born in U.S.); children: Eliza-
  beth and Emily (both born in U.S.) (3 Aug. 1812)
Merritt, Henry, age 4?, 5ft. 7in., dark complex., dark hair, dark
  eyes, labourer (30 Mar. 1813)
Merritt, Henry, age 40, arrived U.S. May 1805, cordwainer, Marble-
  head - wife Susanah (born in U.S.), age 30; children: David,
  age 7, Mary, age 2 (both born in U.S.) (19 Apr. 1813)
Merry, John, age 35, arrived U.S. 1793, mariner, Boston - wife
  Rebecca (born in U.S.), age 35; children: John, age 8, Mary A.,
  age 5, Eliza, age 3 (all born in U.S.) (25 Mar. 1813)
Millbourn, William, age 34, arrived U.S. 1796, mariner, Salem -
  wife Mary (born abroad), age 30; children: Margeret, age 8,
  Mary, age 6 (29 Aug. 1812)
Miller, Alexander, age 28, arrived U.S. 1805, shipwright, Boston
  (17 Aug. 1812)
Minard, Thomas A., age 37, arrived U.S. July 1801, cordwainer,
  Boston - wife Mahany (born abroad), age 35; children: Charles
  F., age 11, Lewis, age 18 (both born abroad), Sally Ann, age 8,
  Mahany, age 5, Lucina, age 3, Mary, age 5 mos. (last 4 born in
  U.S.) (19 Mar. 1813)
Montgomery, John, age 23, arrived U.S. July 1805, engraver, Bos-
  ton - wife Eleanor, age 19; child: Mary, age 13 mos. (25 Feb.
  1813)
Montgomery, Robert, age 29, arrived U.S. June 1811, ropemaker,
  Boston (19 Mar. 1813)
Montoniffe, James, age 17, arrived U.S. 1812, mariner, Boston
  (29 Aug. 1812)
Mooney, Nicholas, age 30, arrived U.S. 1800, labourer, Boston -
  wife Elizabeth (born in U.S.), age 30; children: Mary Ann, age
  7, James, age 2, Mary Cooper, age 2 (all born in U.S., the last
  two are twins) (25 July 1812)
Mooney, Patrick, age 29, arrived U.S. 1809, carpenter, Boston
  (25 July 1812)
Mooney, William C., age 25, arrived U.S. Aug. 1798, mariner, Boston (24 July 1812)
Moore, James, age 31, arrived U.S. Aug. 1801, labourer, Boston -
  wife Fanny (born abroad), age 28; children: Mary, age 6, Fanny,
  age 4, William, age 1 (all born in U.S.) (25 Feb. 1813)

Moore, Robert, age 28, arrived U.S. 1805, shoemaker, Salem (8 Aug. 1812)
Moran, Philip, age 39, arrived U.S. 1792, labourer, Salem – children: Christopher, Barbara, Ebenezer, Philip (all born in U.S.) (16 Sept. 1812)
Moreland, John, age 23, arrived U.S. 1807, cotton machine maker, Watertown – wife Delia (born in U.S.), age 20 (7 Sept. 1812)
Morey, John, age 28, arrived U.S. 1811, domestic, Boston – wife Esther (born abroad), age 23; child: James (born abroad), age 3 (22 Mar. 1813)
Morgan, Aron, age 49, arrived U.S. Sept. 1809, yeoman – children: Richard, age 22, Edmond, age 19, John, age 17, Septemius, age 15, Henry, age 13, Luke, age 20 (all born abroad) (27 Aug. 1812)
Morris, John, age 22, arrived U.S. Mar. 1810, mariner, Boston (25 Mar. 1813)
Morris, Joseph, age 40, arrived U.S. Sept. 1812, labourer, Boston – wife Jane (born abroad), age 40; children: Mary, age 11, Thomas, age 6, Christopher, age 2, Jane, age 2 mos. (all born abroad) (24 Feb. 1813)
Morris, Leonard, age 27, arrived U.S. 1806, labourer, Boston (24 Mar. 1813)
Morrison, John, age 27, arrived U.S. 1801, scrivener, Boston – wife Ellen (born abroad), age 26 (29 July 1812)
Morrisy, John, age 28, arrived U.S. 1809, labourer, Boston (22 Mar. 1813)
Mullet, William, age 26 – wife Elenor (born in U.S.), age 23; child: Mary Ann (born in U.S.), age 4 (31 July 1812)
Murphey, John, age 46, arrived U.S. Dec. 1810, labourer, Boston (27 Feb. 1813)
Murphy, Andrew, age 27, arrived U.S. May 1807, clothier, Pittsfield (30 July 1812)
Murphy, James, age 54, arrived U.S. June 1812, manufacturer, Boston (30 July 1812)
Murphy, John, age 22, arrived U.S. Oct. 1805, applied May 1812, mariner, Boston (16 Nov. 1812)
Murphy, John, age 22, arrived U.S. July 1811, clothier, Pittsfield (3 Aug. 1812)
Murphy, Machael, age 22, arrived U.S. May 1811, painter & glazier, Boston (30 July 1812)
Murphy, Martin, age 46, arrived U.S. Mar. 1796, weaver, Watertown – wife Mary (born in U.S.), age 40; children: Mary, age 14, Magal (?), age 12, Martha, age 10, Hannah, age 8, Isaack, age 6, Catherine, age 4, Jeremiah, age 8 mos. (all born in U.S.) (7 Oct. 1812)
*Murphy, Richard, age 45, 5ft. 4in., dark complex., dark hair, dark eyes – children: Mary Murphy, age 13, William Summerfield, age 18 (both born abroad) (3 Apr. 1813)
Murphy, Thomas, age 41, innholder, Concord – wife Priscilla (born in U.S.), age 44; children: Mary P., age 2, Sarah Elizabeth, age 1 (both born in U.S.) (24 July 1812)
Murray, John, age 29, arrived U.S. June 1799, tailor, Boston – wife Mary (born in U.S.), age 28; children: John, age 5, William, age 2½ (both born in U.S.) (27 July 1812)
Murray, Thomas, age 30, arrived U.S. Mar. 1806, domestic, Boston (31 July 1812)
Myles, James, age 29, arrived U.S. Mar. 1801, labourer, Boston (14 Sept. 1812)
Myshaly, John, age 49, arrived U.S. 1809, labourer, Malden – wife Betsey (born in U.S.), age 28; children: Mary, age 5, James, age 4, Edward, age 1 (all born in U.S.) (22 Aug. 1812)
Neil, Matthew, age 31, arrived U.S. Sept. 1794, mariner, Boston – wife Jane (born abroad), age 48 (2 Mar. 1813)
Nelson, William, age 58, arrived U.S. Aug. 1788, labourer, Boston – wife Jane (born abroad), age 35; children: David, age 23, Mary, age 18, John, age 8, Angus, age 2, Wm., age 3 mos.(Mar. 1813)

Nesbit, James, age 20, arrived U.S. June 1811, labourer, Boston
   (9 Mar. 1813)
Newcomb, James, age 37, 5ft. 7in., dark complex., dark hair,
   grey eyes, arrived U.S. June 1806, coachman, Boston (15 Apr.
   1813)
Newman, Charles, age 27, arrived U.S. 1810, applied June 1812,
   tailor, Boston - wife Frances (born abroad), age 28 (18 July
   1812)
Nielson, Hugh, age 30, arrived U.S. June 1801, stone cutter,
   Boston - wife Lydia (born in U.S.), age 22; children: Sarah
   Ann, age 6, Eleanor, age 2 (both born in U.S.) (27 Feb. 1813)
Nolen, James, age 49, arrived U.S. Apr. 1785, labourer, Boston -
   wife Sally (born abroad), age 43; children: James, age 6, Brid-
   get, age 4 (both born in U.S.) (27 Feb. 1813)
Nolen, William, age 24, arrived U.S. July 1807, glassmaker,
   Chelmsford (13 Aug. 1812)
Noon, Arthur, age 27, arrived U.S. June 1812, saddler, Cambridge -
   wife Sarah (born abroad), age 25 (13 Feb. 1813)
North, Stephen, age 45, arrived U.S. Aug. 1797, grocer, Boston -
   wife Caroline (born abroad); children: Martha, age 14, Betsy,
   age 12, Charlotte, age 10, James, age 8 (all born in U.S.) (19
   Mar. 1813)
Norton, William (an Italian naturalized in England), age 38, arrived U.S. 1800 - wife Mary (born abroad and arrived U.S. 1807);
   child: Thomas (born in U.S.), age 3 (20 July 1812)
*O'Brien, Alexander, age 43, 5ft. 7in., sallow complex., brown
   hair, dark eyes - wife Hannah (born abroad), age 45 (9 Apr.
   1813)
O'Brien, Dennis, age 45, arrived U.S. Dec. 1800, labourer, Boston - wife Joanna (born abroad), age 50; children: Catharine,
   age 12 (born abroad), Patrick, age 10 (born in U.S.) (19 Apr.
   1813)
O'Brien, Robert, age 31, arrived U.S. Oct. 1805, labourer, Boston (3 Aug. 1812)
O'Bryan, John, age 37, arrived U.S. July 1806, labourer, Boston
   (3 Aug. 1812)
Odber, Elias, age 48, arrived U.S. Oct. 1810, cotton spinner,
   Waltham - wife Hazaih (born abroad), age 48; child: Mary (born
   abroad), age 20 (22 Sept. 1812)
O'Kelley, Thomas, arrived U.S. Aug. 1806, tailor, Taunton (4 Aug.
   1812)
Oliver, Thomas, age 27, arrived U.S. June 1805, yeoman, Medford
   (25 Mar. 1813)
Olmstead, Aaron, age 24, arrived U.S. Mar. 1806, trader, Charlestown (4 Nov. 1812)
Olmstead, Dennis, age 27, arrived U.S. Oct. 1804, blacksmith,
   Boston - wife Elizabeth (born in U.S.), age 38; children: James,
   age 11, Dennis, age 7 (both born abroad), Ann, age 4, Elizabeth, age 2 (both born in U.S.) (16 Sept. 1812)
O'Mealy, James, age 35, arrived U.S. Oct. 1807, tailor, Boston -
   wife Joanna (born abroad), age 33; child: James (born in U.S.),
   age 1 (4 Nov. 1812)
O'Neal, Mathew, age 17, arrived U.S. 1811, trader, Boston (4 Aug.
   1812)
O'Rourke, Patrick, age 29, arrived U.S. 1802, tailor, Boston -
   wife Abigail (born in U.S.), age 23; child: James C. (born in
   U.S.), age 1 (22 Mar. 1813)
Osborne, James, age 62, arrived U.S. 1808, labourer, Groton -
   wife Mary Collet (born abroad), age 25 (21 July 1812)
Our, William, age 23, arrived U.S. Dec. 1801, carpenter, Boston -
   wife Betsy (born in U.S.), age 21; children: William, age 2,
   Thomas, age 6 mos. (both born in U.S.) (19 Apr. 1813)
Owen, William Watts, age 38, arrived U.S. June 1794, tailor, Ded-
   ham - wife Elizabeth (born abroad), age 31; children: Eliza,
   age 5, William age 3 (both born in U.S.) (4 Aug. 1812)

Pallis, Joseph, age 36, arrived U.S. 1799, blockmaker, Boston –
children: Joseph, age 9, Eliza, age 7, Mary Ann, age 1½ (all
born in U.S.) (22 Aug. 1812)

Parker, Andrew, age 32, arrived U.S. June 1798, carpenter, Boston – wife Rachael (born in U.S.), age 29; children: Nathan
B., Ann B., David and George W.H. (all born in U.S.) (1812 or
1813)

Parker, Silas, age 19, arrived U.S. 1800, student at Yale College, Boston (18 Nov. 1812)

Parker, William, age 35, arrived U.S. 1804, grocer, Boston –
wife Abigal (born in U.S.), age 32; children: Sarah Ann, age
9, Hannah, age 7 (both born abroad), William, age 4, Nancy,
age 3, John, age 3 (last 3 born in U.S.) (24 July 1812)

Parsons, Thomas, age 43, arrived U.S. Nov. 1798, dentist, Boston – wife Joanna (born abroad), age 35; children: Thomas,
age 15, Susan, age 18, Mary, age 12, George, age 9, Edwin and
Angelica (twins, age 3), Emily, age 4, Caroline, age 5, Wm.,
age 10 (all born in U.S.) (8 Aug. 1812)

Patterson, Kennith, age 30, arrived U.S. 1812, manufacturer,
Boston – wife Allice (born abroad), age 30 (30 Sept. 1812)

Patterson, William, age 25, arrived U.S. 1812, shoemaker, Salem
(17 Aug. 1812)

Paucker, Thomas, age 25, arrived U.S. 1800, mariner, New Bedford –
wife Catherin (born in U.S.), age 24 (28 Aug. 1812)

Paul, William, age 41, arrived U.S. 1808, cabinetmaker, Boston –
wife Mary (born abroad), age 29; children: Lilly, age 10 (born
abroad), Sarah, age 8, John, age 5, James, age 3, William, age
1 (last 4 born in U.S.) (1812 or 1813)

Payne, Isaac, age 44, arrived U.S. 1805, labourer, Marblehead –
wife Elizabeth (born abroad), age 40; child: Elizabeth (born
in U.S.), age 4 (3 Aug. 1812)

Peach, Daniel, age 35, arrived U.S. Apr. 1788, labourer, Boston –
wife Rebecca (born abroad), age 38 (25 Mar. 1813)

Pear, John, age 51 – wife Susan (born in U.S.), age 41; children:
Charles, age 28, Philip, age 27, Mary, age 24, Susan, age 23
(all born in U.S.) (30 July 1812)

Pear, Mathew, age 47, arrived U.S. 1801, brushmaker, Boston –
wife Sarah Ann (born abroad), age 45; children: John, age 19,
Mathew, age 16, Joseph, age 12 (all three born abroad), William,
age 9, Edward, age 7, George, age 5, Sarah Ann, age 3 (all 4
born in U.S.) (25 July 1812)

Pendergast, Thomas, age 24, arrived U.S. Aug. 1810, labourer,
Dorchester (19 Apr. 1813)

Penney, John, age 34, arrived U.S. Oct. 1804, cooper, Acton –
wife Temperance C. (born in U.S.), age 23; children: John B.,
age 3, George, age 1 (both born in U.S.) (3 Aug. 1812)

Phalen, Peter, age 45, arrived U.S. Nov. 1803, tailor, Boston –
wife Mary (born abroad), age 34; children: Jane, age 13, David,
age 10, Margaret, age 10 (all born abroad), James, age 9, Mary,
age 6, Ann, age 4, John, age 1, William, age 7 (last 5 born in
U.S.) (20 Mar. 1813)

Phealon, Patrick, age 45, arrived U.S. Nov. 1801, mason, Boston –
wife Hannah (born in U.S.), age 33; children: James, age 7,
William, age 2 (both born in U.S.) (19 Apr. 1813)

Phippen, Robert, age 37, arrived U.S. June 1812, cotton spinner,
Canton (22 Sept. 1812)

Pike, John, age 29, arrived U.S. 1804, applied July 1807, gardener, Boston (20 July 1812)

Pilkington, Henry W., age 20, arrived U.S. Sept. 1811, musician,
Boston (4 Jan. 1813)

Pitt. John, age 44, arrived U.S. Aug. 1812, gentleman, Boston
(18 Aug. 1812)

Platt, Samuel, age 36, arrived U.S. Apr. 1800, clockmaker, Concord - wife Mary (born in U.S.), age 44; children: William,
age 10, Elizabeth, age 4 (both born in U.S.) (24 July 1812)

Porter, Frederick, age 35, light complex., brown hair, grey eyes,
cordwainer, Marblehead (30 Mar. 1813)

Porter, Frederick, age 31, arrived U.S. 1797, applied Apr. 1811,
mariner, Ipswich - wife Abigail (born in U.S.), age 29 (29 Aug.
1812)

Power, James, age 25, arrived U.S. Aug. 1812, mariner, Boston
(22 Mar. 1813)

Powers, John, age 40, carpenter, Boston - wife Bridget (born in
U.S.), age 37; children: Catherine, age 3, Bridget, age 1½
(both born in U.S.) (8 Sept. 1812)

Powers, Mathew, age 22, arrived U.S. July 1812, grocer, Boston -
wife Catherine (born abroad), age 19 (31 July 1812)

Powers, Michael, age 46, arrived U.S. June 1807, labourer, Boston - wife Susan, age 50 (25 Feb. 1813)

Powers, Peter, age 35, arrived U.S. Feb. 1800, blacksmith, Boston - wife Mary (born abroad), age 35; children: Henry, age
12, Catharin, age 10, Margeret, age 2 (all born in U.S.) (30
July 1812)

Powers, Richard, age 31, arrived U.S. Oct. 1804, labourer, Boston - wife Louise (born in U.S.), age 30; child: Sarah Ann,
age 5 (4 Aug. 1812)

Powers, William, age 45, arrived U.S. Nov. 1811, labourer, Boston - wife Mary (born abroad), age 24; children: John, age 4,
Instacia, age 2 (both born abroad) (3 Aug. 1812)

Price, John, age 32, arrived U.S. 1803, mariner, Dennis - wife
Sally (born in U.S.), age 26; children: John, age 4, William,
age 5 (both born in U.S.) (7 Aug. 1812)

Price, John, age 24, arrived U.S. Jan. 1807, weaver, Dudley -
wife Ann (born in U.S.), age 23; child: George, age 18 (mos.?)
(9 Sept. 1812)

Price, Mathew, age 36, arrived U.S. 1797, labourer, Boston - wife
Margaret (born abroad), age 36; child: Richard (born in U.S.),
16 mos.; inmate: Ann Pinder, age 3 (18 Aug. 1812)

Prier, Joseph, age 43, arrived U.S. 1805, labourer, Marblehead -
wife Mary (born in U.S.), age 40; child: Joseph (born in U.S.),
age 15 (8 Apr. 1812)

Provett (?), William, age 25, arrived U.S. Jan. 1803, cotton
spinner, Taunton - wife Lydia (born in U.S.), age 23 (25 Aug.
1812)

Quigley, Edward, age 43, arrived U.S. Oct. 1806, trader, Boston -
wife Elizabeth (born abroad), age 21; child: John (born in U.S.),
age 19 mos. (31 July 1812)

Quin, James, age 30, arrived U.S. Aug. 1805, applied Apr. 1810,
labourer, Sudbury - wife Arana (born in U.S.), age 23 (13 Aug.
1812)

Quinn, Michael, age 27, arrived U.S. 1803, labourer, Boston -
wife Hannah, age 27; child: Cornelius, age 13 (27 July 1812)

Quinn, Nicholas, age 34, trader, Boston - wife Eunice (born in
U.S.), age 28; children: Nicholas, age 4, James, age 3, Mary,
age 17 (mos.) (27 July 1812)

Raddish, Thomas, age 21, arrived U.S. Sept. 1812, manufacturer,
Boston (23 Sept. 1812)

Ramsdale, John, age 43, arrived U.S. Apr. 1812, tailor, Boston
(27 July 1812)

Randal, William, age 48, arrived U.S. 1806, (tavern?)keeper, Boston - wife Mary (born in U.S.), age 48 (24 Mar. 1813)

Randale, Robert, age 42, arrived U.S. Apr. 1812, cordwainer, Boston - child: Robert, Jr. (born abroad), age 9 (14 Sept. 1812)

Randall, John, age 45, arrived U.S. 1801, grocer, Boston - wife
Elizabeth (born abroad), age 35; child: William (born abroad),
age 13 (10 Aug. 1812)

Raymur, William, age 31, gentleman, Boston - wife Eliza (born
   abroad), arrived U.S. July 1810; children: Arnold, age 9, Sarah,
   age 7 (18 July 1812)
Read, Joseph J., age 20, arrived U.S. Oct. 1806, apprentice to
   Stour(?) & Broadstreet, Boston (30 July 1812)
Redmond, William M., age 25, arrived U.S. Sept. 1810, weaver,
   Walpole (19 Mar. 1813)
Redon, Henry, age 24, arrived U.S. June 1804, spinner, Peters-
   ham (19 Apr. 1813)
Reed, Robert, age 31, arrived U.S. 1795, mariner, Salem - wife
   Mary (born abroad) (3 Apr. 1813)
Reedman, John, age 44, arrived U.S. Aug. 1807, dyer & clothier,
   West Boylston - wife Esther (born abroad), age 40; children:
   Peter, Mary, John (all born abroad), Joseph (born in U.S.)
   (17 Aug. 1812)
Reiley, William, age 35, arrived U.S. 1801, labourer, Boston -
   wife Jane (born abroad), age 35; child: John (born in U.S.),
   age 3 (17 Aug. 1812)
Renney, Edward, age 27, arrived U.S. Oct. 1811, cutler, Kings-
   ton - wife Elizabeth (born in U.S.), age 24; child: Edward
   (born in U.S.), age 3 (10 Sept. 1812)
*Richard, James, age 47, 5ft. 9in., light complex., dark hair,
   dark eyes (15 June 1813)
Rielly, James, age 43, arrived U.S. 1811, servant, Boston (22
   Feb. 1813)
Riely, James, age 38, arrived U.S. Apr. 1807, sawyer - wife Ann
   (born abroad), age 36; children: Michael, age 4, Ann, age 2,
   Julie, age 1 (all born in U.S.) (27 Feb. 1813)
Rightman, Thomas, age 52, arrived U.S. 1797, carver, Boston -
   child: Juliet (or Julia?), born in U.S. (1 Sept. 1812)
Rigley, James, age 30, arrived U.S. Nov. 1810, weaver, Pitts-
   field (31 July 1812)
Riley, James, age 44, arrived U.S. July 1812, labourer, Boston
   (9 Mar. 1813)
Riley, Thomas, age 24, arrived U.S. Aug. 1811, labourer, Cambridge (10 Aug. 1812)
Risteaux, Robert, age 36, tailor, Boston - wife Catherine (born
   abroad), age 34; children: Louisa, age 13, William, age 10,
   Catherine Matilda, age 8, Robert R., age 6, Elsie Charlotte,
   age 4 (all born in U.S.); inmates: Jona. Bradley Bellows, age
   14, Nathaniel Mason Lenge(?) (18 July 1812)
Rives, Peter, age 22, arrived U.S. Jan. 1809, seaman, Concord
   (31 July 1812)
Roan, Michael, age 26, arrived U.S. May 1812, labourer, Boston
   (19 Aug. 1812)
Roaster, George, age 28, arrived U.S. Sept. 1808, gardener, Boston - wife Cathrine (born abroad), age 20; children: Mary A.,
   age 2, John, age 1 mo. (both born in U.S.) (6 Aug. 1812)
Robbins, Thomas, age 33, 5ft. 5in., dark complex., black hair,
   brown eyes, arrived U.S. 1803, mariner, Salem - wife Mary (born
   abroad) (31 Mar. 1813)
Roberts, James, age 41, arrived U.S. Sept. 1812, manufacturer,
   Boston (23 Sept. 1812)
Roberts, William, age 40, arrived U.S. 1801, grocer, Boston -
   wife Margeret (born abroad), age 31; children: Nancy Ann, age
   4, Wm. Montgomery, age 3, Sarah Jane, age 10 mos. (all born in
   U.S.) (10 Aug. 1812)
Roberts, William, age 27, arrived U.S. Sept. 1810, comedian,
   Boston - wife Sarah Ann (born abroad), age 27; children: Eliza-
   beth, age 4, William, age 3 (both born abroad), Nancy, age 2
   (born in U.S.) (4 Jan. 1813)
Robinson, Hugh, age 21, arrived U.S. 1809, tavern(keeper?), Boston (21 July 1812)

Robinson, Joseph, age 20, arrived U.S. Jan. 1803, cotton spinner, Watertown - wife Martha (born in U.S.), age 20; children: Joseph, age 4, Lavina, age 2, Mary Ann, age 6 mos. (4 Aug. 1812)

Rogers, Mathew, age 32, arrived U.S. Nov. 1811, applied May 1812, mariner, Boston - wife Eleanor (born abroad), age 30; children: Mathew, Jr., age 9, James, age 8, Catherine, age 4, Peter, age 3, Thomas, age 1 (10 July 1812)

Rooke, William A., age 45, arrived U.S. Apr. 1809, tailor, Boston - wife Abitha (born in U.S.), age 30 (31 July 1812)

Roots, Henry, age 32, arrived U.S. 1807, manufacturer, Boston - wife Mary (born abroad), age 29; children: Rebecca (born abroad), age 8, Mary Ann, age 6, Elizabeth, age 4, Henry, age 16 mos. (last 3 born in U.S.) (26 Mar. 1813)

Rorke, Luke, age 32, arrived U.S. Aug. 1801, labourer, Boston (23 Feb. 1813)

Ross, Andrew, age 25, arrived U.S. 1804, tailor, Boston (22 July 1812)

Ross, John, age 35, arrived U.S. 1796, tailor, Boston - wife Margret (born abroad), age 30; children: Ann, age 8, Margeret, age 7 (both born in U.S.); inmates: John Barton, age 5, Elizabeth Barton, age 3, Elizabeth Barton, age 1 (25 July 1812)

Ross, Thomas, age 45, arrived U.S. Apr. 1803, whitesmith, Boston (6 Aug. 1812)

Ross, William, age 39, arrived U.S. Oct. 1804 - wife Hannah (born in U.S.), age 36 (22 July 1812)

Rowley, George, age 33, arrived U.S. Oct. 1801, manufacturer, Canton - wife Ann (born abroad), age 30; child: Eleanor, age 2 (4 Nov. 1812)

Rowse, Edward, age 43, arrived U.S. Oct. 1805, clerk, Boston (24 Feb. 1813)

Rubley, George, age 22, arrived U.S. July 1810, blacksmith, Worcester (21 Aug. 1812)

Rule, James, age 47, gardener, Cambridge - wife Bulah (born in U.S.), age 40; child: Susannah (born in U.S.), age 6 (27 Feb. 1813)

Rush, Michael, age 21, arrived U.S. Mar. 1812, mariner, Boston (24 Mar. 1813)

Russell, John, age 28, arrived U.S. 1807, labourer, Boston - wife Grace (born abroad), age 22; children: Grace (born abroad), age 6, Charles (born in U.S.), age 3 (4 Aug. 1812)

Rutter, James, age 34, arrived U.S. June 1807, cotton spinner, Dorchester - wife Allice, age 26; children: William, age 6, Ellen, age 2 (both born in U.S.) (2 Oct. 1812)

Ryan, Walter, age 33, arrived U.S. 1804, applied 1810, labourer, Boston - wife Lucy (born in U.S.), age 32 (27 July 1812)

Ryley, David, age 18, arrived U.S. 1811, labourer, Roxbury (1 Sept. 1812)

St. George, Edward, age 43, arrived U.S. 1803, baker, Boston (20 Mar. 1813)

Safferon, Joseph, age 51, arrived U.S. 1805, schoolmaster, Gloucester (25 Aug. 1812)

Sanderson, James, age 28, arrived U.S. 1805, merchant, New York (22 July 1812)

Saunders, Peter, age 20, arrived U.S. Oct. 1811, shoemaker, Lynn (19 Apr. 1813)

Savage, James R., age 21, 5ft. 11in., dark complex., dark hair, dark eyes, arrived U.S. 1801, student at law, Boston (9 July 1813)

* Scanlan, Michael, age 34, 5ft. 5in., dark complex., dark hair, dark eyes - wife Mary (born abroad), age 28; children: James, age 8, Catherine, age 6, Thomas, age 6 mos. (all born in U.S.) (3 Apr. 1813)

Schamon, George W., age 26, arrived U.S. May 1805, mariner, Boston - wife Joanna (born abroad), age 22; child: Sarah (born in U.S.), age 3 (14 Oct. 1812)

Scholfield, Isaac, age 24, arrived U.S. Oct. 1794, manufacturer
of woolen cloth, Pittsfield - wife Meloni (born in U.S.), age
19 (24 Aug. 1812)
Scholfield, Joseph, age 26, arrived U.S. 1812, woolen manufac-
turer, Boston (30 Sept.1812)
Scott, Benjamin, age 25, 5ft. 9in., light complex., brown hair,
grey eyes, arrived U.S. May 1803, yeoman, Malden (28 Apr. 1813)
Scott, Benjamin, age 23, 5ft. 6in., light complex., brown hair,
grey eyes, arrived U.S. 1803, yeoman, Malden (28 Apr. 1813)
Scott, Samuel, age 30, arrived U.S. 1809, artist, Andover (8 Aug.
1812)
Seaborn, William, age 33, arrived U.S. June 1805, carpenter,
Boston - wife Rosette (born abroad) (3 Aug. 1812)
*Seaton, Washington, age 18, 5ft. 7in., dark complex., dark hair,
dark eyes (10 Apr. 1813)
Semple, Thomas, age 50, arrived U.S. 1782, merchant, Boston -
wife Elizabeth(born in U.S.), age 45; inmate: Ann King, age 40
(25 July 1812)
Shannon, John, age 32, arrived U.S. Aug. 1812, weaver, Waltham -
wife Bridget(born abroad), age 40 (31 Mar. 1813)
Shar, James, age 60, arrived U.S. 1797, labourer, Boston (23 Mar.
1813)
Sharland, James, age 66, arrived U.S. May 1776, yeoman, Acton -
wife Nancy (born in U.S.); children: George, age 33, James,
age 28, Henry, age 24, Edmond Dana, age 22, Benjamin Hill, age
15, Joseph, age 13, Winthrop, age 18 (all born in U.S.) (29
July 1812)
Sharpe, Daniel, age 28, arrived U.S. Oct. 1805, applied July
1811, minister of a church in Boston - wife Ann (born abroad),
age 20; child Deborah Caldwell Sharpe (born in U.S.), age 7
mos. (1812 or 1813)
Sharpley, James, age 38, arrived U.S. Mar. 1803, mariner, Boston
(27 Feb. 1813)
Shea, James, age 51, arrived U.S. 1794, labourer, Boston - wife
Margeret, age 34; child: James, age 5 (18 Aug. 1812)
Shea, John, age 45, labourer, Boston - wife Mary, age 38 (29
July 1812)
Shea, John, age 30, arrived U.S. Oct. 1803, labourer, Boston (4
Mar. 1813)
Shea, Peter, age 23, arrived U.S. Aug. 1803, mason, Boston - wife
Mary (born abroad) (22 Feb. 1813)
Shea, Philip, age 33, arrived U.S. Apr. 1801, brewer, Charles-
town - wife Amy (born in U.S.), age 30; children: Lydia, age 11,
John, age 6, Margaret, age 3 (all born in U.S.) (19 Apr. 1813)
Shea, Philip, age 23, arrived U.S. Aug. 1803, tailor, Roxbury
(4 Aug. 1812)
Shea, Thomas, age 49, arrived U.S. 1798, labourer, Boston - wife
Mary (born in U.S.), age 23; children: Abigail, age 7, Mary,
age 4, Catharine, age 2 (all born in U.S.) (20 Mar. 1813)
Shea, Thomas, age 20, arrived U.S. 1802, soap boiler, Roxbury
(31 Aug. 1812)
*Shean, Darby, age 48, 5ft. 5in., florid Complex., dark hair,
blue eyes (7 Apr. 1813)
Shepperd, Joseph, age 42, arrived U.S. 1801, stocking weaver,
Watertown - wife Mary (born abroad), age 38; children: Harriot,
age 15, Thomas, age 13, Ann S., age 9, Elizabeth, age 7, Mary,
age 5 (29 Aug. 1812)
Sherlock, James, age 20, arrived U.S. July 1811, shoemaker, Fairhaven (19 Sept. 1812)
Sherridan, Charles, age 38, arrived U.S. Aug. 1801, weaver, Boston - wife Mary (born in U.S.), age 28; child: John (born in
U.S.), age 8 (19 Apr. 1813)
Shields, Charles, age 27, arrived U.S. May 1807, weaver, Watertown (16 Sept. 1812)

Shuttleworth, James, age 41, arrived U.S. Nov. 1803, scrivener,
Carbridge Port - wife Sarah (born abroad), age 37; children:
Nancy, age 14, Sophia, age 10, George, age 6, James, age 3,
Eliza, age 2 mos. (all born in U.S.) (3 Aug. 1812)

Simmons, John, age 28, arrived U.S. Dec. 1806, rigger, Boston -
wife Nancy (born in U.S.), age 26 (19 Mar. 1813)

Simpson, William, age 30, arrived U.S. 1807, trader, Boston -
wife Mary (born abroad), age 26; children: Sarah, age 4, Maria,
age 2, William, age 8 mos. (all born in U.S.) (21 July 1812)

Sindham, William, age 17, arrived U.S. Aug. 1812, gunsmith, Salem (11 Sept. 1812)

Skinner, John, age 38, arrived U.S. Aug. 1807, labourer, Watertown - wife Dorcas (born in U.S.), age 31 (10 Jan. 1813)

Skinner, John, age 38, arrived U.S. Oct. 1807, labourer, Watertown - wife Dorcas (born in U.S.), age 30 (19 Apr. 1813)

Skinner, William S., age 36, arrived U.S. 1804, merchant, Boston (21 July 1812); 5ft. 8in., dark complex., light hair, blue
eyes, on 18 Apr. 1812 ordered to Worcester, Worcester Co. (passport No. 4)

Slator, Richard, age 34, 5ft. 3in., light complex., dark hair,
light eyes, arrived U.S. July 1795, labourer, Pembroke (16 June
1813)

Slide, William S., age 33, arrived U.S. June 1803, applied Dec.
1811, mason, Pittsfield - wife Polly (born in U.S.), age 21;
child: Laura Ann, age 2 (21 Aug. 1812)

Smailes, John, age 33, arrived U.S. Aug. 1809, miller, Roxbury -
wife Mary (born abroad), age 35; child: Mary Ann (born in U.S.),
age 9 mos. (19 Sept. 1812)

Smith, Archibald, age 56, arrived U.S. Nov. 1811, ropemaker, Boston - wife Ann (born abroad); children: Ann, age 22, Jane, age
20, Margaret, age 18, Archibald, age 9 (all born abroad) (19
Mar. 1813)

Smith, James, age 27, arrived U.S. 1809, labourer, Boston (13 Aug.
1812)

Smith, James, age 26, arrived U.S. Aug. 1803, labourer, Boston
(24 Feb. 1813)

Smith, James, age 26, arrived U.S. June 1805, mariner, Boston
(11 Nov. 1812)

Smith, John, age 40, arrived U.S. 1794, applied 1798, labourer,
Boston - wife Lois (born in U.S.), age 30; children: William,
age 9, Caroline, age 7, Margaret, age 4, John, age 6 mos. (all
born in U.S.) (25 July 1812)

Smith, John, age 37, arrived U.S. 1797, mariner, Boston (23 Mar.
1813)

Smith, John, age 30, arrived U.S. 1807, cabinetmaker, Boston (17
Aug. 1812)

Smith, John M., age 17, arrived U.S. 1806, hatter, Boston (25
July 1812)

Smith, John R., age 37, arrived U.S. May 1805, painter, Boston -
wife Eliza R. (born in U.S.), age 20; children: John, age 2,
Eliza, age 1 (both born in U.S.) (5 Aug. 1812)

Smith, Joseph, age 33, arrived U.S. 1812, weaver, West Cambridge
(24 Aug. 1812)

Smith, Samuel, age 29, arrived U.S. 1812, merchant, Boston - wife
Rebecca (born in U.S.), age 25; children: Rebecca, age 6, Ann,
age 4, Jane, age 3 (all born in U.S.) (25 July 1812)

Smith, Thomas, age 31, arrived U.S. Sept. 1812, cordwainer, Boston (2 Mar. 1813)

Smith, William, age 35, arrived U.S. 1802, innholder, Boston (21
July 1812)

Snaith, William, age 28, arrived U.S. Nov. 1806, cordwainer, Boston - wife Frances (born abroad), age 28; inmates: Richard T.
Snaith, age 3, William Cock Snaith, age 2 (18 July 1812)

*Somers, William, age 44, 5ft. 8in., dark complex., dark hair,
dark eyes (14 May 1813)

Sparhawk, Nathan, age 21, arrived U.S. Dec. 1802, carpenter, Charlestown (20 Mar. 1813)

Spears, Samuel, age 45, arrived U.S. Nov. 1810, yeoman, Watertown (7 Aug. 1812)

Spencer, John, age 47, arrived U.S. 1794, merchant, Boston - wife Mary (born in U.S.), age 30 (4 Aug. 1812)

Spiller, William, age 23, arrived U.S. Apr. 1811, comedian, Boston - wife Ann (born abroad), age 22 (4 Jan. 1813)

Spring, Alexander, age 22, arrived U.S. Jan. 1813, clerk, Boston (3 Mar. 1813)

Stafford, James, age 21, arrived U.S. Aug. 1800, mariner, Boston (31 July 1812)

Stafford, Patrick, age 55, arrived U.S. 1802, labourer, Boston - wife Catherine (born abroad), age 45; children: Richard, age 17, Luke, age 15, Ann, age 13, Cathrine, age 11 (all born abroad) (3 Aug. 1812)

Steel, Thomas, age 37, arrived U.S. 1805, yeoman, Hingham - wife Rhoda, age 38; children: Thomas, age 2, Charles, age 5 mos. (both born in U.S.) (19 Mar. 1813)

Stennet, Walter Tyrell, age 22, arrived U.S. 1812, applied Mar. 1812, mechanic, Boston (20 July 1812)

Stennit, Ralph, age 28, arrived U.S. Mar. 1810, artist, Boston (3 Aug. 1812)

Stevenson, Hugh, age 31, arrived U.S. May 1800, cordwainer, Boston (5 Oct. 1812)

Stevenson, William, age 21, arrived U.S. Aug. 1812, mariner, Boston (12 Feb. 1813)

Stevison, Robert, age 20, arrived U.S. 1799, shipwright, Dartmouth (20 Aug. 1812)

Stewart, Alexander, age 30, 5ft. 6in., light complex., light hair, light eyes, arrived U.S. 1800, mariner, Salem - wife Mary (born abroad) (24 Apr. 1813)

Stiles, John B., age 18, arrived U.S. 1809, shoemaker, Marblehead (28 Aug. 1812); age 19, dark complex., brown hair, dark eyes (30 Mar. 1813)

Stiles, Samuel, age 20, arrived U.S. 1805, shoemaker, Marblehead (8 Aug. 1812)

Stocker, John, age 32, arrived U.S. Sept. 1811, trader, Boston (27 July 1812)

Strachan, Alexander, age 24, arrived U.S. 1810, blacksmith, Boston (20 July 1812)

Strawbridge, William, age 55, arrived U.S. Sept. 1807, tanner, Philadelphia (3 Aug. 1812)

Street, George, age 24, arrived U.S. 1790, shoemaker, Boston (22 Mar. 1813)

Stump, Thomas, age 32, arrived U.S. Feb. 1804, tinman, Boston - wife Jane (born abroad), age 32 (25 Sept. 1812)

Stuttard, James, age 30, arrived U.S. Sept. 1809, dyer of cloth, Mendon - wife Narcy (born abroad); child: Fanny (born abroad), age 6 (10 Nov. 1813)

Sullivan, John, age 30, arrived U.S. Sept. 1804, labourer, Boston (13 Aug. 1812)

Sullivan, Richard, age 53, arrived U.S. 1796, tailor, Boston (23 Mar. 1813)

Sullivan, Timothy, age 33, arrived U.S. 1811, whitesmith, Boston (10 Aug. 1812)

Sutton, John, age 22, arrived U.S. Sept. 1810, applied Mar. 1812, wheelwright, Worcester (12 Aug. 1812)

Sutton, Thomas, age 24, arrived U.S. Sept. 1810, applied Mar. 1812, wheelwright, Worcester (12 Aug. 1812)

Sweeney, John, age 26, arrived U.S. 1792, tobacconist, Boston (17 Aug. 1812)

Sykes, William, age 53, arrived U.S. Sept. 1801, clockmaker, Bo...(?) (9 Sept. 1812)

Symes, James, age 36, arrived U.S. Oct. 1806 - wife Elizabeth,
age 36; children: Jane, age 9, Elizabeth, age 7, Eleanor, age
5 (all born abroad), Euphemiah, age 3, Mary, age 9 mos. (both
born in U.S.) (7 Feb. 1813)

Symes, James, age 35, arrived U.S. May 1805, weaver, Pittsfield -
wife Martha (born in U.S.), age 19; child: Jacob, age 5 mos.
(10 Aug. 1812)

Tailor, Daniel, age 50, arrived U.S. June 1809, mariner, Boston
(3 Aug. 1812)

Taylor, Abraham, age 34, arrived U.S. 1797, woolen manufacturer,
Byfield (24 Aug. 1812)

Taylor, John, age 46, arrived U.S. Sept. 1812, woolen spinner,
Boston - wife Jane (born abroad), age 46; children: George,
age 4, John, age 10, Ann, age 7 (all born abroad) (2 Oct. 1812)

Taylor, John, age 40, arrived U.S. July 1805, weaver, Newbury -
wife Sarah (born abroad); children: Alice, James, Hannah, Mary,
Sarah (all born abroad), James, John (both born in U.S.) (2
Sept. 1812)

Taylor, Thomas, age 40, arrived U.S. 1801, carpenter, Boston (14
Aug. 1812)

Tenbrook, Thomas, age 22, arrived U.S. 1812, merchant, Alexandria (30 July 1812)

Thomas, Thomas, age 25, arrived U.S. June 1809, nailor, Newbury
(10 Aug. 1812)

Thomas, William, age 31, arrived U.S. Dec. 1806, mariner, Boston - wife Rachael (born abroad), age 31; children: Louisa,
age 4, Mary Ann, age 2 (both born in U.S.) (20 Mar. 1813)

Thompson, Alexander, age 32, arrived U.S. 1800, labourer, Boston - children: Jane A., age 11, Margeret, age 9, John, age 7,
Elizabeth, age 4 (18 Aug. 1812)

Thompson, William, age 40, arrived U.S. 1798, mariner, Boston
(20 Mar. 1813)

Thompson, William, age 35, arrived U.S. 1792, merchant, Boston -
children: William, age 8, Thomas, age 7 (both born in U.S.)
(20 July 1812)

Thurds, William, age 34, arrived U.S. Aug. 1802, rigger, New Bedford - wife Elizabeth (born in U.S.); children: James, age 6,
William, age 3 (both born in U.S.) (28 July 1812)

Todd, John, age 50, arrived U.S. 1794, tailor, Boston (20 July
1812)

Todd, Robert, age 32, arrived U.S. Aug. 1801, mason, Boston (26
Feb. 1813)

Trotter, Alexander, age 60, arrived U.S. Aug. 1812, weaver, Watertown - wife Frances, age 55; children: Adam, age 20, Alexander,
Jr., age 19, Mary Ann, age 16, Jane, age 12, Frances, age 21
(all born abroad)(8 Oct. 1812)

Tucker, Richard, age 25, arrived U.S. June 1807, tailor, Concord -
wife Ruth (born in U.S.), age 24; child: George (born in U.S.)
(24 July 1812)

Tue, Peter, age 31, arrived U.S. 1803, livery stable keeper, Boston (25 July 1812)

Tuohy, Michael, age 27, arrived U.S. Dec. 1807, mariner, Boston
(10 Mar. 1813)

Turner, James, age 43, arrived U.S. 1797, leather dresser, Charlestown - wife Eliza (born in U.S.); children: Anna, age
12, Eliza, age 11, Mary Ann, age 7, Horatio, age 5, George, age
3, Lucinda, age 9 mos. (all born in U.S.) (19 Feb. 1813)

Turner, James, age 43, arrived U.S. June 1803, weaver, Boston -
wife Mary (born abroad), age 37; child: Mary (born in U.S.),
age 4 (25 Jan. 1813)

Turner, James, age 19, arrived U.S. May 1811, shoemaker, Boston
(19 Mar. 1813)

Turner, John, age 34, arrived U.S. 1798, mariner, Salem - wife
Hannah (born in U.S.), age 26; child: John (born in U.S.) (7
Aug. 1812)

Turnnacliffe, George, age 49, house-carpenter, Boston - wife
Ann (born abroad), age 49 (4 Aug. 1812)
Wade, Francis, age 42, arrived U.S. Aug. 1806, stevedore, Boston - wife Rachael (born in U.S.) (3 Aug. 1812)
Wadwell, John Hunter, age 40, arrived U.S. 1812, scrivener, Boston (29 July 1812)
Wallis, Thomas, age 29, arrived U.S. 1807, cabinetmaker, Boston -
wife Mary (born abroad); children: William, age 4, Mary, age
2½, Thomas, age 5 weeks (all born in U.S.) (21 July 1812)
Wallis, William, age 28, arrived U.S. 1807, applied Mar. 1812,
grocer, Boston - wife Lucy (born in U.S.), age 29 (23 Mar.
1813)
Walsh, George, age 55, arrived U.S. Nov. 1810, shopkeeper, Boston (24 July 1812)
Walsh, Michael, age 48, arrived U.S. Nov. 1796, labourer, Boston - wife Elizabeth (born abroad), age 50 (3 Aug. 1812)
Walsh, William, age 35, arrived U.S. 1807, morocco tanner, Milton (22 Aug. 1812)
Walsh, William, age 30, arrived U.S. 1811, labourer, Boston -
wife Jane (born abroad), age 30; child: George (born abroad),
age 3; inmate: Catherine Morasey, age 25 (25 July 1812)
Walter, William, age 40, arrived U.S. Dec. 1799, rigger, Charlestown - wife Margeret (born abroad), age 45; children: Samuel,
age 21, John (both born abroad), William (born in U.S.), age
9; inmate: Margaret Perrin, age 24 (6 Aug. 1812)
Ward, Charles, age 19, arrived U.S. Aug. 1812, labourer, Boston
(20 Mar. 1813)
Ward, James, age 42, arrived U.S. 1802, applied July (1812?),
labourer, Roxbury (21 July 1812)
*Ward, Richard, age 30, 5ft. 6in., florid complex., grey hair,
grey eyes (6 Apr. 1813)
Warren, Joseph, age 25, arrived U.S. Oct. 1810, weaver, Hingham
(8 Mar. 1813)
Warren, Nicholas, age 33, arrived U.S. July 1804, labourer, Bos-
ton (31 July 1812)
Warring, Leight, age 26, arrived U.S. May 1812, comedian, Boston -
wife Susan (born abroad), age 17 (4 Jan. 1813)
Watts, Robert, age 28, arrived U.S. Oct. 1807, labourer, Boston -
wife Elizabeth, age 20; children: Joseph, age 2, Lawrence, age
9 mos. (both born in U.S.); inmate: Elanor Shadwick, age 54
(4 Aug. 1812)
Weaver, James, age 28, arrived U.S. 1808, applied 1809, labourer,
Boston (29 July 1812)
Weeks, Edmund, age 37, arrived U.S. 1806, carpenter, Boston - wife
Sarah (born abroad), age 34; child: Sarah, age 15 mos. (born
in U.S.) (21 July 1812)
Weir, William, age 24, arrived U.S. 1805, tailor, Boston - wife
Mary (born in U.S.); child: Jane (29 July 1812)
Welsh, Edmund, age 30, arrived U.S. July 1805, labourer, Boston -
wife Elizabeth (born in U.S.), age 25; child: William (born in
U.S.), age 9 mos. (3 Aug. 1812)
Welsh, Edward, age 48, arrived U.S. 1794, yeoman, Malden (22 Aug.
1812)
West, Benjamin, age 37, arrived U.S. Apr. 1805, cordwainer,
Charlestown (2 Oct. 1812)
West, Thomas, age 40, 5ft. 4in., dark complex., dark hair, grey
eyes, carpenter, Boston - child: George (born in U.S.), age 11
(13 Mar. 1813)
Weston, William, age 54, arrived U.S. Feb. 1792, trader, Boston
(27 July 1812)
Whalen, John, age 26, arrived U.S. 1797, mariner, Boston (23 Mar.
1813)
Whealon, Philip, age 48, arrived U.S. July 1807, gunsmith, Boston (6 Aug. 1812)

Wheatley, John H., age 31, arrived U.S. Apr. 1811, gentleman,
   Boston - wife Elizabeth (born abroad), age 19; child: Eliza-
   beth H. (born in U.S.), age 10 mos. (26 Feb. 1813)
Wheeler, Joseph, age 25, arrived U.S. July 1807, manufacturer,
   Boston - wife Catharine (born in U.S.), age 19 (26 Mar. 1813)
Wheildon, William, age 36, arrived U.S. May 1797, plate founder,
   Boston - wife Betsey (born in U.S.), age 36; child: Willis W.
   (born in U.S.), age 6; inmates Charles Moore, Charlotte Moore
   (children of Mrs. Wheildon) (30 July 1812)
Whelan, Nicholas, age 24, arrived U.S. July 1807, labourer, Bos-
   ton (24 Feb. 1813)
Whelar, Edward, age 45, arrived U.S. July 1812, yeoman, Boston
   (31 July 1812)
White, George Savage, age 28, arrived U.S. Jan. 1812, applied
   Mar. 1812, minister, Freetown - wife Mary (born abroad), age 27;
   children: Deborah, age 4, Mary, age 3 (both born abroad); inmate: Deborah Gregory, age 45 (3 Aug. 1812)
White, George S., age 29, arrived U.S. Jan. 1812, applied Supream
   Court R.I. Mar. 1812, minister of the Gospel, Freetown, 5ft.
   7in., dark complex., dark hair, dark eyes - wife Mary (born
   abroad), age 28 (11 May 1813)
White, John R., age 28, arrived U.S. 1812, soap boiler, Boston -
   wife Charlotte M. (born abroad), age 35 (25 Mar. 1813)
White, Miles W., age 22, arrived U.S. Aug. 1812, merchant, Boston
   (17 Aug. 1812)
Whiteaker, Samuel, age 17, arrived U.S. Aug. 1811, shoemaker,
   Boston (5 Aug. 1812)
Whitby, John, age 37, arrived U.S. 1802, labourer, Boston - wife
   Betsey (born abroad), age 39 (30 July 1812)
Whitehead, Ralph, age 45, arrived U.S. 1804, woolen manufacturer,
   Newbury - wife Abigail (his second wife, born in U.S.), age 33;
   children: Ann (born abroad), age 10, Maria (born in U.S.), age
   8 (29 Aug. 1812)
*Whittle, James, age 33, dark complex., brown hair, dark eyes -
   wife Elizabeth (born abroad); children: Lucy, James (both born
   in U.S.) (5 Apr. 1813)
Whitton, William, age 30, arrived U.S. Jan. 1800, rigger, New
   Bedford - wife Nancy (born in U.S.), age 23; children: William,
   age 5, Nancy, age 6 mos. (3 Aug. 1812)
Wickham, John, age 36, arrived U.S. 1791, trader, Boston - wife
   Elizabeth (born in U.S.), age 45; children: Mary, age 18,
   William, age 15 (both born in U.S. (24 July 1812)
Wiggin, Richard, age 33, arrived U.S. 1800, gardener, Dorchester -
   wife Waity (born in U.S.), age 30; children: Charles A., age 8,
   Thomas P., age 7, Susanah D., age 5, Richard T., age 3, Ben-
   jamin D., age 1 (all born in U.S.) (15 Mar. 1813)
Wild, David, age 32, arrived U.S. June 1807, cotton weaver, Can-
   ton - wife Betsey, age 33; children: John, age 11 (born abroad),
   Betsey, age 4 (born in U.S.) (25 Sept. 1812)
Wild, John, age 35, arrived U.S. Nov. 1811, coal miner, Canton
   (12 Sept. 1812)
Wild, John, age 33, arrived U.S. Dec. 1798, gardener, Roxbury -
   wife Susannah (born in U.S.), age 34; children: John, Jr., age
   10, Susannah, age 4, Mary, age 2 (all born in U.S. (27 Feb.
   1813)
Wilkinson, Charles, age 26, arrived U.S. 1806, blacksmith, Boston
   (25 Mar. 1813)
Willard, Charles D., age 17, arrived U.S. 1807, manufacturer,
   Boston (24 Mar. 1813)
Willard, Lewis, age 23, arrived U.S. 1812, gunsmith, Boston (20
   July 1812)
Williams, George, age 37, arrived U.S. 1790, fisherman, Boston -
   wife Harriot (born in U.S.), age 27 (19 Apr. 1813)
Williams, Henry, age 27, arrived U.S. 1811, tailor, Roxbury (1
   Sept. 1812)

Williams, James, age 22 - wife Mary (born in U.S.), age 19;
child: Mary, age 8 mos. [24 Feb. 1813)
Williams, John age 33, arrived U.S. Oct. 1807, labourer, Boston -
wife Mary (born in U.S.), age 26 (13 Aug. 1812)
Williams, John P., age 36, arrived U.S. Oct. 1810, limner, Boston
(30 July 1812)
Williams, John R., age 36, arrived U.S. Oct. 1810, scrivener,
Boston (30 July 1812)
Williams, Robert, age 48, arrived U.S. 1798, wood sawyer, Boston - wife Mary (born in U.S.), age 52; inmates: Bridget Kelley, age 18, Mary Kelley, age 14 (children of Mrs. Williams by
her first husband, a foreigner) (29 July 1812)
Willson, James, age 45, arrived U.S. July 1804, applied Aug.
1810, cordwainer, Boston (30 July 1812)
Willson, Robert, age 35, arrived U.S. 1797, slater, Boston (22
July 1812)
Wilson, Daniel, age 48, arrived U.S. June 1809, carpenter, Boston - wife Mary (born abroad), age 31; children: William, age
13, Margaret, age 10, Henry, age 7 (all born abroad), Mary,
age 1 (born in U.S.) (19 Apr. 1813)
Wilson, Daniel, age 35, arrived U.S. June 1809, grocer, Boston
(14 Sept. 1812)
Wilson, James, age 45, arrived U.S. 1798, town crier, Boston -
wife Martha (born abroad), age 35; children: John (born abroad),
age 20, Thomas, age 10, James, age 8, Elizabeth, age 3 (these
3 born in U.S.) (25 July 1812)
Wilson, James, age 30, arrived U.S. Aug. 1812, weaver, Watertown
(8 Mar. 1813)
Wilson, John, age 33, labourer, Boston - wife Mary (born in U.S.),
age 36; children: Harriot, age 5, William, age 3, Francis E.,
age 1 (all born in U.S.); inmates: Leonard Payson, age 10,
Eleen Payson, age 8, Charles Payson, age 6, Mary Payson, age 7
(10 Aug. 1812)
Wilson, John C., age 25, arrived U.S. Sept. 1812, merchant, Bos-
ton - wife Ann (born abroad), age 22; child: Mary, age 2; in-
mate: Isabella McConckley, age 25 (15 Sept. 1812)
Wilson, Mathew, age 36, arrived U.S. Aug. 1810, blacksmith, Boston (13 Mar. 1813)
Wilson, Robert, age 65, arrived U.S. June 1791, gardener, New
Bedford - wife Deborah (born abroad), age 40 (28 Oct. 1812)
Wilson, Robert, age 20, arrived U.S. Aug. 1810, weaver, Boston
(19 Apr. 1813)
Wilson, William, age 29, arrived U.S. June 1804, tailor - wife
Catherine (born abroad), age 26; children: Joseph, age 5, John,
age 4, William, age 3, Francis, age 2, Catherine, age 1 (all
born in U.S.) (24 Apr. 1813)
Woodcock, Joseph, age 38, house-carpenter, Boston - wife Ann
(born in U.S.), age 46 (3 Aug. 1812)
Woolaston, John, age 47, arrived U.S. May 1794, weaver, Boston -
wife Ann (born abroad), age 45; children: Nancy, age 20 (born
abroad), Betsey, age 16, Sally, age 14, Mary, age 13, Lydia,
age 11 (all born in U.S.) (5 Aug. 1812)
Woombell, Joseph, age 25, arrived U.S. 1810, fisherman, Boston
(22 Mar. 1813)
Worrall, Ottowell, age 41, arrived U.S. Sept. 1804, weaver, Boston - wife Ruth (born abroad), age 32; children: Jona., age 9
(born abroad), Allice, age 6, Sarah, age 3, Mary, age 1 (all 3
born in U.S.) (5 Aug. 1812)
Wrightman, Thomas, age 30, arrived U.S. 1800, grocer, Boston (10
Aug. 1812)
Wynn, John, age 30, arrived U.S. Aug. 1812, weaver, Boston - wife
Wynne, age 26; child: Mary, age 7 mos. (7 Oct. 1812)
Young, Charles, age 32, arrived U.S. Sept. 1805, comedian, Bos-
ton - wife Rebecca (born abroad), age 23 (4 Jan. 1813)

48   RHODE ISLAND

RHODE ISLAND

Ainsworth, John, age 23, 15 mos. in U.S. (13 in Dighton, Mass.
  & 2 in Providence), weaver (10-17 Aug. 1812)
Alexander, Robert, age 25, 10 mos. in U.S., Smithfield, weaver
  (10-17 Aug. 1812)
Allen, (Thom)as, age 64, 9 years in U.S., Providence, cotton
  manufacturer (17-24 Aug. 1812)
Atkinson, Joseph, age 37, 11 mos. in U.S., wife & 4 children
  (left in England), Providence, weaver (10-17 Aug. 1812)
Bain, Thomas, age 22, 9 mos. in U.S., Providence, carpenter (5-
  19 Apr. 1813)
Bakeon, Miles, age 54, 8 years in U.S. wife & 4 children, Smith-
  field, machine-maker (30 July-10 Aug. 1812)
Bakeon, William, age 22, 8 years in U.S., wife (an American),
  Smithfield, machine-maker (30 July-10 Aug. 1812)
Ball, William, age 18, 3 mos. in U.S., Providence, weaver (18
  Sept.-12 Oct. 1812)
Barker, William, age 29, 3 years in U.S. (2 years & 8 mos. in
  Leicester, Mass., & 4 in Smithfield, R.I., wire-maker; applied
  13 Apr. 1810 (30 July-10 Aug. 1812)
Bennan, John, age 25, 2½ years in U.S., Providence, weaver (30
  Dec. 1812-5 Mar. 1813)
Bentley, William, age 32, 18 mos. in U.S., Providence, weaver
  (5-19 Apr. 1813)
Bingham, Robert, age 22, 2 years in U.S. (1 in Baltimore & 1 in
  Smithfield, R.I.), weaver (30 July-10 Aug. 1812)
Boake, Richard, age 25, 7 years in U.S., wife & 3 children, New-
  port, saddler (24-31 Aug. 1812)
Brady, John C., age 35, 5 years in U.S., wife & 1 child, Cranston,
  weaver (30 Dec. 1812-5 Mar. 1813)
Bridgeford, Joseph, age 37, 17 years in U.S. (7 in N.Y. State,
  3 in Conn. & 7 in town of Smithfield, R.I.), wife & 4 children,
  cotton manufacturer (31 Aug.-18 Sept. 1812)
Bromly, Miles, age 49, 9 mos. in U.S., Providence, weaver (to 20
  July)
Callant, Thomas, age 27, 10 mos. in U.S., wife & 1 child, Pro-
  vidence, weaver (5-19 Apr. 1813)
Caral, Owen, age 51, 13 years in U.S., Portsmouth, collier (12
  Oct.-2 Nov. 1812)
Cassedy, Quintillean, age 21, 6 years in U.S., Newport, distiller
  (24-31 Aug. 1812)
Chapman, John, age 37, 10 years in U.S. (3 in Lynn, Mass., & 6
  in Cumberland, R.I.), cordwainer (30 July-10 Aug. 1812)
Cockett, John, age 35, 10 mos. in U.S., wife & 5 children, cotton
  manufacturer (10-17 Aug. 1812)
Conden, Mathew, age 31, 8 years in U.S., Portsmouth, collier
  (12 Oct.-2 Nov. 1812)
Cowburn, William, age 46, 11 mos. in U.S., Providence, weaver
  (10-17 Aug. 1812)
Crampton, John, age 28, 3 years in U.S., Smithfield, weaver (30
  July-10 Aug. 1812)
Cunliff, Joseph, age 26, 10 mos. in U.S., wife, North Providence
  (18 Sept.- 12 Oct. 1812)
Davis, William, age 22, 2 years in U.S., Smithfield, weaver (30
  July-10 Aug. 1812)
Deady, David, age 50, 11 years in U.S., Portsmouth, collier (12
  Oct.-2 Nov. 1812)
Dee, David, age 28, 7 years in U.S., wife & 1 child, Portsmouth,
  collier (12 Oct.-2 Nov. 1812)
Delahunt, Charles, age 39, 3 years in U.S., wife & 3 children,
  Smithfield, velvet cutter & dyer (10-17 Aug. 1812)
Devline, Arthur, age 20, 9 mos. in U.S. (Warwick & Providence,
  now in Providence), weaver (10-17 Aug. 1812)

Dobbin, Leonard, age 34, 1 year & 8 mos. in U.S.(9 mos. in Newport & 11 in Smithfield, R.I.), wife & 4 children, weaver (10-
17 Aug. 1812)

Dunlap, Patrick, age 25, 15 mos. in U.S., Smithfield, weaver (2
Nov. - 30 Dec. 1812)

Duxbury, (Dav)id, age 43, 2 years & 10 mos. in U.S., Smithfield,
weaver (17-24 Aug. 1812)

Ferguson, John, age 76, 6 years in U.S., 1 daughter, Newport,
tobacconist (24-31 Aug. 1812)

Ferguson, Peter, age 22, 6 years in U.S., Newport, tobacconist
(24-31 Aug. 1812)

Finch, William, age 22, 18 mos. in U.S., Smithfield, mule-spin-
ner (10-17 Aug. 1812)

Ford, Thomas, age 24, 5 mos. in U.S., Providence, weaver (31 Aug. -
18 Sept. 1812)

France, Joseph, age 20, 3 years in U.S., Smithfield, weaver (30
July - 10 Aug. 1812)

French, William, age 28, 1 year & 8 mos. in U.S., wife & 2 children, Coventry, machine-maker (30 July - 10 Aug. 1812)

Gerrard, Samuel, age 35, 1 year in U.S., wife & 5 children (he
left them in England and they are daily expected in America),
North Providence, weaver (30 July - 10 Aug. 1812)

Gill, Francis M., age 25, 5 years in U.S., wife, Johnston, weaver (18 Sept. - 12 Oct. 1812)

Gordon, Thomas, age 45, 10 mos. in U.S., wife & 6 children (he
left them in England), Providence, weaver (10-17 Aug. 1812)

Green, John, age 29, 1 year & 8 mos. in U.S., North Providence,
weaver (30 July - 10 Aug. 1812)

Greenhalgh, Samuel, age 29, 1 year & 8 mos. in U.S., wife & 5
children, Warwick, weaver (30 Dec. 1812 - 5 Mar. 1813)

Greyson, George, age 18, 1½ years in U.S., Providence, weaver
(5-19 Apr. 1813)

Handerson, Francis, age 38, 3 mos. in U.S., Newport, gentleman
(31 Aug. - 18 Sept. 1812)

Handly, Thomas, age 20, 21 mos. in U.S., Warwick, weaver (10-17
Aug. 1812)

Hardenborough, Giles, age 23, 5 years in U.S., Newport, gentleman; came to America for his education (24-31 Aug. 1812)

Harrison, Paul, age 40, 3 years in U.S., Newport, stone cutter
(24-31 Aug. 1812)

Harvey, Robert, age 26, 1 year & 8 mos. in U.S. (Warwick & Providence, now in Providence), wife & 1 child, weaver (10-17 Aug.
1812)

Heron, Thos., age 22, 3 mos. in U.S., Newport, gentleman (31 Aug.-
18 Sept. 1812)

Hilton, John, age 45, 11 years & 6 mos. in U.S. (7 years in Boston, Mass., & the 4 last years & 6 mos. in North Providence,
R.I., tailor (30 July - 10 Aug. 1812)

Hissin, Hugh, age 20, 10 mos. in U.S., Smithfield, weaver (24-
31 Aug. 1812)

Hixson, William, age 28, 15 mos. in U.S., Providence, weaver; applied Sept. 1812 (5-19 Apr. 1813)

Hoare, Henry, age 33, 7 years in U.S. (5 in Boston, Mass., 7 rest
in Coventry, R.I.), machine-maker (24-31 Aug. 1812)

Hood, Joseph, age 21, 2 years in U.S., North Providence, weaver
(30 July - 10 Aug. 1812)

Howard, William, age 44, 4 years & 3 mos. in U.S., wife & 6 children, Smithfield, warper in a cotton factory (to 20 July)

Hunt, Robert, age 25, 2 years in U.S., Cranston, weaver (30 Dec.
1812 - 5 Mar. 1813)

Jenkinson, Richard F., age 26, 15 years in U.S. (12 in N.Y. & 3
in Providence, chairmaker & gilder (served apprenticeship in
New York with Joseph Reily) (to 20 July)

Jones, John, age 33, 6 years in U.S., wife & 3 children, Warwick,
weaver & maltster (5-19 Apr. 1813)

Jones, John, age 27, 3 years in U.S., wife & 1 child, Newport,
    cordwainer (24-31 Aug. 1812)
Jones, Karl, age 20, 9 mos. in U.S. (6 mos. in Dighton, Mass.,
    3 in Providence), weaver (10-17 Aug. 1812)
Kaine, Mikel, age 25, 4 years in U.S., wife & 1 child, Smith-
    field, dyer (30 July - 10 Aug. 1812)
Kanady, Samuel, age 25, 14 years in U.S. (12 years in Pa. & 2 in
    Providence), hatter (to 20 July)
Kennedy, Archibald, age 22, 1 year & 8 mos. in U.S., North Pro-
    vidence, weaver (30 July - 10 Aug. 1812)
Kennedy, John, age 29, 1 year & 6 mos. in U.S., wife & 1 child,
    North Providence, weaver (30 July - 10 Aug. 1812)
Kerr, William, age 22, 3 years in U.S., wife, Providence, weaver
    (5-19 Apr. 1813)
Layton, John, age 31, 2 years in U.S., wife & 3 children, Warwick,
    weaver (5-19 Apr. 1813)
Leach, ..., age 40, 2 years & 10 mos. in U.S., wife & 10 children,
    (his family, left in England, is daily expected), Smithfield,
    weaver (17-24 Aug. 1812)
Lees, Randall, age 22, 2½ year in U.S., wife & 1 child, Providence,
    weaver (5-19 Apr. 1813)
Lenard, Samuel, age 28, 2 years in U.S., Portsmouth, collier (12
    Oct. - 2 Nov. 1812)
Logan, Thomas, age 37, 1 year & 6 mos. in U.S., mendicant (30
    July - 10 Aug. 1812)
Lonsdale, James, age 24, 2 years in U.S., Cranston, dyer (30 July-
    10 Aug. 1812)
Love, James, age 22, 20 mos. in U.S., wife, North Providence,
    weaver (10-17 Aug. 1812)
Low, John, age 29, 9 mos. in U.S., Providence, weaver (to 20 July)
Lowden, John, age 27, 6 years in U.S., wife & 1 child, North Pro-
    vidence, machine-maker; applied Apr. 1811 (30 July - 10 Aug.
    1812)
Loyd, (Wi)lliam, age 52, 1 year & 3 mos. in U.S., Smithfield,
    cotton spinner (17-24 Aug. 1812)
McCann, William, age 21, 8 mos. in U.S., Coventry, weaver (5-19
    Apr. 1813)
McComb, Robert, age 20, 1 year in U.S., Providence, weaver (10-
    17 Aug. 1812)
McDonnell, John, age 25, 1 year & 7 mos. in U.S., Smithfield,
    husbandman (24-31 Aug. 1812)
McGinis, (Thom)as, age 38, 4 years in U.S. (3 years & 6 mos. in
    Boston, Mass., 6 mos. in Providence, now in Providence), weaver
    (17-24 Aug. 1812)
McGough, Patrick, age 28, 6 years in U.S., wife & 2 children,
    Portsmouth, collier (12 Oct. - 2 Nov. 1812)
McKey, John, age 52, 6 years in U.S. (in Scituate, Coventry &
    Providence, now in Providence), wife & 4 children, weaver (10-
    17 Aug. 1812)
Mc Lean, (Dan)iel, age 25, 1 year & 3 mos. in U.S., Smithfield,
    weaver (17-24 Aug. 1812)
McMurray, Alexander, age 27, 20 mos. in U.S., Warwick, weaver
    (10-17 Aug. 1812)
Mackson, Noah, age 31, 9 mos. in U.S., wife & 4 children (he left
    them in England), Smithfield, weaver (10-17 Aug. 1812)
Major, James, age 42, 4 mos. in U.S., wife & 5 children, Provi-
    dence, weaver (12 Oct. - 2 Nov. 1812)
Middleton, James M., age 27, 5 mos. in U.S., Smithfield, cotton
    manufacturer (18 Sept. - 12 Oct. 1812)
Miller, James, age 23, 1 year in U.S., wife (left in England),
    Providence, weaver (to 20 July)
Miller, John, age 48, 1 year in U.S., wife & 7 children, Provi-
    dence, weaver (to 20 July)
Miller, John, age 34, 2 years in U.S., North Providence, weaver
    (5-19 Apr. 1813)

Mitchell, John, age 58, 1 mo. in U.S., 1 son, Providence, weaver
(18 Sept. - 12 Oct. 1812)
Molcom, Peter, age 32, 3 years in U.S., wife & 2 children, War-
wick, weaver (10-17 Aug. 1812)
Monks, James, age 68, 3 mos. in U.S., wife & 1 child, North Pro-
vidence, weaver (18 Sept. - 12 Oct. 1812)
Montgomery, James, age 27, 1 year & 8 mos. in U.S., Providence,
weaver (10-17 Aug. 1812)
Moorhead, John, age 25, 1 year in U.S., wife & 3 children, North
Providence, weaver (18 Sept. - 12 Oct. 1812)
Ntwisle, James, age 27, 2 years in U.S., Boston, Mass., comedian
(10-17 Aug. 1812)
Ogden, Samuel, age 43, 7 years in U.S., wife & 6 children, Pro-
vidence, machine-maker (12 Oct. - 2 Nov. 1812)
Oliver, Joseph, age 32, 8 years & 9 mos. in U.S., wife & 3 child-
ren, North Providence, husbandman (10-17 Aug. 1812)
Parkin, James, age 31, 12 years in U.S., wife & 3 children, Pro-
vidence, button maker (30 Dec. 1812 - 5 Mar. 1813)
Partington, Richard, age 40, 1 year & 6 mos. in U. S., Providence,
shuttle-maker (5-19 Apr. 1813)
Payton, James, age 22, 1 year in U.S., Cranston, weaver (30 Dec.
1812 - 5 Mar. 1813)
Pearce, James, age 20, 3 years in U.S., wife, Warwick, weaver
(5-19 Apr. 1813)
Rankan, John, age 24, 3 years in U.S., Johnston, weaver (18 Sept.-
12 Oct. 1812)
Rawson (or Ranson?), Samuel, age 32, 12 years in U.S., Newport,
mariner (24-31 Aug. 1812)
Roberts, William, age 26, 2 years in U.S., wife, 3 children & a
sister-in-law, transient, a comedian (30 July - 10 Aug. 1812)
Sands, William, age 27, 2 years in U.S., Warwick, weaver (10-17
Aug. 1812)
Seaver, John, age 36, 3 mos. in U.S., wife & 6 children (daily
expected from England), North Providence, weaver (10-17 Aug.
1812)
Sholfield, Joseph, age 53, 1 year & 8 mos. in U.S., Warwick,
bleacher (10-17 Aug. 1812)
Slater, John, age 35, 9 years in U.S., wife & 3 children, Smith-
field, manufacturer of cotton wool; applied 26 Mar. 1812 (30
July - 10 Aug. 1812)
Slatsbury, John, age 33, 6 years in U.S., wife & 3 children,
North Providence, machine-maker (5-19 Apr. 1813)
Smith, Christopher, age 29, 3 years in U.S., North Providence,
dyer (2 Nov. - 30 Dec. 1812)
Sutliffe, John, age 31, 8 mos. in U.S., wife & 4 children (they
are daily expected from England), North Providence, sley-maker
30 July - 10 Aug. 1812)
Suttall, Thomas, age 45, 1 year in U.S., North Providence, weaver
(10-17 Aug. 1812)
Thain, Charles, age 21, 6 years in U.S. (2 years in Nantucket &
4 in Smithfield), weaver (30 July - 10 Aug. 1812)
Thompson, James, age 30, 3 years in U.S., wife & 3 children, New-
port, cabinetmaker (24-31 Aug. 1812)
Thompson, John D., age 31, 11 years in U.S., wife & 5 children,
Newport, rigger (24-31 Aug. 1812)
Thornly, James, age 32, 9 mos. in U.S., wife & 2 children (left
in England), Providence, weaver (18 Sept. - 12 Oct. 1812)
Tong, John, age 40, 9 mos. in U.S., 4 children, North Providence,
weaver (5-19 Apr. 1813)
Townly, John, age 27, 14 mos. in U.S., Warwick, weaver (10-17 Aug.
1812)
Tyson, John, age 23, 1 year in U.S., North Providence, dyer (30
July - 10 Aug. 1812)
Waring, Leigh, age 25, 3 mos. in U.S., wife, Providence, comedian
(30 July - 10 Aug. 1812)

Watson, ...us, age 33, 1 year & 3 mos. in U.S., wife & 4 children,
   Smithfield, weaver (17-24 Aug. 1812)
Welch, Thomas, age 24, 7 mos. in U.S., Portsmouth, collier (12
   Oct.- 2 Nov. 1812)
Werring, Joseph, age 44, 4 years in U.S., wife & 7 children,
   Providence, button-maker; applied Mar. 1810 (30 July - 10 Aug.
   1812)
Whitehead, John, age 30, 3 years in U.S., wife & 1 child, Warwick,
   dyer (10-17 Aug. 1812)
Whites, John, age 28, 2 years in U.S., Charlestown, tailor (18
   Sept. - 12 Oct. 1812)
Wiggins, Luke, age 27, 6 years & 6 mos. in U.S. (3 years in Be-
   verly, Mass., & the three last years & 6 mos. in Warwick &
   Providence, now in Providence), wife, weaver (10-17 Aug. 1812)
Wood, Hartlay, age 49, 9 mos. in U.S., wife & 5 children, North
   Providence, weaver (18 Sept.- 12 Oct. 1812)
Young, Charles, age 32, 7 years in U.S., wife, Charleston, co-
   median (10-17 Aug. 1812)

CONNECTICUT

Allison, Samuel, age 28, 14 years in U.S., wife & 3 children,
  Middletown, tallow chandler (26 Sept. 1812)
Allwright, John, Stamford (1812-14)
Andrews, Thomas Hunt, wife, Middletown (1812-14)
Axtens, Isaac, age 32, 3 mos. in U.S., no family, Redding, car-
  penter (26 Sept. 1812)
Bailey, Wm., New Canaan (1812-14)
Baillie, Robert, age 29, 4 mos. in U.S., no family, pocketbook
  maker (16 Feb. 1813)
Baraclaugh, Wm., wife & 1 child, New Canaan (1812-14)
Barry, Wm., age unknown, resident for many years, Lyme (26 Sept.
  1812)
Barton, George, age 26, resident for 20 years, Hartford (26 Sept.
  1812)
Baxter, John, age 53, 1 year in U.S., from Grenada, no family,
  New Haven, merchant (8 Aug. 1812)
Bell, Wm. H., age 29, 12 years in U.S., wife & 1 child, Southing-
  ton, cooper (26 Sept. 1812)
Bennett, James, wife & 4 children, Derby (1812-14)
Bevan, Wm., New Canaan (1812-14)
Borgis, John, age 53, 1½ years in U.S., planter of Demerara, a
  daughter & 2 servants; has obtained passport and is presumed
  to have departed from U.S. (16 Feb. 1813)
Bowser, Robert, age 25, 6 mos. in U.S., no family, New London
  Co., itinerant Methodist preacher (8 Aug. 1812)
Boylan, James, New Haven (1812-14)
Brown, Wm., wife & 6 children, New Haven (1812-14)
Bruce, John Stuart, age 60, Tolland, State pauper (26 Sept. 1812)
Bryan, John, age 62, 1 year in U.S., 3 women & 4 servants, Middle-
  town, gentleman; applied 4 Apr. 1812 (26 Sept. 1812)
Bryan, William, age 22, 1 year in U.S, no family, Middletown,
  gentleman; applied 4 Apr. 1812; passport for John Bryan and
  family has been sent to him (26 Sept. 1812)
Bulkley, John, wife & 1 child, Derby (1812-14)
Burrell, Wm., age 20, 2 years in U.S., no family, New Canaan,
  shoemaker (8 Aug. 1812)
Bush, William, age 27, 8 years in U.S., from England, wife & 1
  child, Milford, mariner, ships as a mate (8 Aug. 1812)
Campbell, James, wife, New Haven (1812-14)
Carhart, Hacaliah, wife & 6 children, Greenwich (1812-14)
Chaplin, James, age 46, 10 years in U.S., wife, New Haven, joiner
  (16 Aug. -26 Sept. 1812)
Chapman, William T., age 24, 12 years in U.S., from England, wife,
  Norwalk, shoemaker (26 Sept. 1812)
Cole, Thomas, age 30, 7 years in U.S., from England, wife, New
  Haven, gunsmith; applied June last (8 Aug. 1812)
Collins, Patrick, age 34, 5 years in U.S., from Ireland, no family,
  Litchfield, farmer (16 Aug. 1812)
Conroy, Andrew, age 27, 5 years in U.S., from Ireland, no family,
  New London, grocer; applied 2 Dec. 1811 (8 Aug. 1812)
Cowan, George, age 30, 2 years in U.S., no family, Middletown,
  weaver (26 Sept. 1812)
Crawford, Thomas, Stratford (1812-14)
Cummerford, John, age 20, 4 mos. in U.S., from Ireland, no family,
  Stratford, laborer (26 Sept. 1812)
Davey/Davy, William, age 70, 19 years in U.S., no family, Middle-
  town, miller, "useful mechanic" (16 Aug. 1812)
Davitt, Patrick M., age 23, 1 year in U.S., from Ireland, no fa-
  mily, Milford, hatter (8 Aug. 1812)
Dawson, John, age 60, resident for 30 years, Huntington, farmer
  (26 Sept. 1812)
Deane, St. George, New Haven (1812-14)
Dobson, Peter, age 27, 9 mos. in U.S., no family, Vernon, cotton
  manufacturer (16 Aug. 1812)

Dougherty, Bryan, age 65, 30 years in U.S., wife, Hartford, la-
    borer (16 Aug. 1812)
Duffe, Robert, Stamford (1812-14)
Dunelven, Daniel, age 30, 19 years in U.S., no family, Middle-
    town, ropemaker (16 Aug. -26 Sept. 1812)
Dunkin, Daniel, age 25, 2 years in U.S., Roxbury (26 Sept. 1812)
Dunkin, David, Roxbury (1812-14)
Durnford, Elizabeth Lucas, age 45, 8 years in U.S., from Bermuda,
    3 sons (2 in college) and 1 daughter, Colchester; will not be
    naturalized lest her property in England be forfeited (8 Aug.
    1812)
Ewart, John, age 28, 14 years in U.S., wife, Farmington, tinman
    (16 Aug. 1812)
Farley, James, age 40, 1½ years in U.S., from the West Indies,
    wife, 1 son, 3 daughters & 2 servants, New London, no occupa-
    tion; intends to be naturalized (8 Aug. 1812)
Ferguson, John, age 23, 6 years in U.S., no family, New London,
    tobacconist (26 Sept. 1812)
Ferris, James, wife & 3 children, Derby (1812-14)
Ferris, Samuel, wife & 4 children, Derby (1812-14)
Floyd, John, age 28, 4 years in U.S., wife & 2 children, Danbury,
    farmer (26 Sept. 1812)
Francis, Charles, age 38, 1 year in U.S., no family, Middletown,
    no occupation (26 Sept. 1812)
Franklin, James, age 35, 5 years in U.S., from England, wife,
    New Haven, butcher (8 Aug. 1812)
Gilyard, Thomas, age 26, 5 years in U.S., from England, wife &
    1 child, Woodbridge, stocking weaver (8 Aug. 1812)
Gilyard, Thos., wife & 1 child, Derby (1812-14)
Gover, Daniel, age 24, 9 mos. in U.S., no family, Hartford, pain-
    ter (16 Aug. 1812)
Gray, John C., age 35, 22 years in U.S., wife & 2 children, Dan-
    bury, printer; born in Halifax of Tory parents who went there
    from Massachusetts; he moved to Boston in 1790; he says he was
    admitted to vote there and in this state; he claims not to be
    a British subject; he is a tool of the Federal Party to print
    libels on the government of the U.S. (26 Sept. 1812)
Green, James, age 40, 3 years in U.S., New London, merchant; his
    family is in England and the deputy marshal there is ordered
    to watch his motions (10 Feb. 1813)
Greeny, Thomas, wife & 6 children & 2 apprentices, New Canaan
    (1812-14)
Hall, Henry, wife & 1 child, New Haven (1812-14)
Heath, Edward, age 44, 9 years in U.S., wife & 1 child, Walling-
    ford, farmer (16 Aug. -26 Sept. 1812)
Hedden, Wm. L., age 19, 9 years in U.S., no family, Hartford,
    clerk (16 Aug. 1812)
Holmes, James, 2 daughters, Hartford (1812-14)
Holtham, Richard, age 42, 2 years in U.S., from England, no family,
    New Haven, accountant and clerk (8 Aug. 1812)
Honeyford, Alexander, age 40, 7 years in U.S., wife & 3 children,
    Middletown, weaver (16 Aug. 1812)
Howard, Samuel, New Haven (1812-14)
Hubbell, Nathan, age 57, born in Conn., came here from Nova Scotia
    19 years since, wife & 9 sons & 11 daughters, Huntington, far-
    mer; was in one of the associated royalists; is called major
    but receives captain's half pay; says he never took oath of al-
    legiance to King of England (8 Aug. 1812)
Huggerford, Thos., hired servants, Greenwich (1812-14)
Hughes, Micahel, Derby (1812-14)
Hutchinson, Walter, age 31, 11 years in U.S., from Scotland, wife
    & 2 children & 1 apprentice, Norwalk, shoemaker (16 Aug. 1812)
James, Richard, age 27, 6 years in U.S., from England, wife, New
    Haven, brass founder (8 Aug. 1812)

Jamieson, Wm., age 29, 2 years in U.S., from Scotland, no family,
   Norwalk, clothier and dyer (8 Aug. 1812)
Jenkinson, Richard F., Windham (1812-14)
Johnson, David, age 28, 6 years in U.S., Norfolk, clothier (26
   Sept. 1812)
Johnson, David, age 18, 6 years in U.S., from Ireland, no family,
   New London, apprentice to a tallow chandler (8 Aug. 1812)
Jones, Griffin, age 19, 11 years in U.S., from Wales, Danbury,
   hatter (16 Aug. 1812)
Jones, Hugh, age 21, 11 years in U.S., from Wales, no family,
   Danbury, hatter (16 Aug. 1812)
Jular, George, age 36, 5 years in U.S., from England, wife, New
   London, watchmaker (8 Aug. 1812)
Kennett, Thomas, age 35, 10 years in U.S., wife & 2 children,
   Norwalk, ship-carpenter (26 Sept. 1812)
Kensels, Thomas, age 26, in U.S. 7 years, Cheshire, engraver (16
   Aug.-26 Sept. 1812)
Kensett, Thomas, Cheshire (1812-14)
King, Joseph, age 53, 29 years in U.S., from England, Harwinton,
   farmer (26 Sept. 1812)
Kinier, Alexander, wife, Stratford (1812-14)
Knap, Aquila, Fairfield (1812-14)
Langon, Hugh, New Haven (1812-14)
Ledger, Wm., age 47, 5 years in U.S., Irishman, wife & 2 children,
   Litchfield, farmer (26 Sept. 1812)
Lee, Thos. Lewis, wife & 2 children, New Haven (1812-14)
Lees, James, age 33, 7 years in U.S., wife & 2 children, Middle-
   town, cotton spinner and machine maker (16 Aug. 1812)
Lees, John , age 37, 6 years in U.S., no family, Middletown,
   cotton spinner and machine maker (16 Aug. 1812)
Lees, Robert, Derby (1812-14)
Lees, Thomas, age 80, 4½ years in U.S., wife & daughter, Middle-
   town, cotton spinner and machine maker (16 Aug. 1812)
Limburner, John, age 35, 15 years in U.S., wife & 4 children, Ox-
   ford, cooper (16 Aug. -26 Sept. 1812)
Livingston, John W., age 58, born in N.Y., wife & 5 children
   (including 4 daughters), Stratford, no occupation, a British
   captain on half pay for services rendered in Conn. about 6 or
   7 years (8 Aug. 1812)
Lyster, Edward, wife & 1 child, Derby (1812-14)
McDonnell, Joel, wife & 4 children, New Haven (1812-14)
McFarlane, James, age 23, 1 year in U.S., from Ireland, no family,
   New London, currier (8 Aug. 1812)
McKay, John, age 48, 28 years in U.S., from Scotland, wife & 2
   sons & 1 daughter, Woodbury, farmer (16 Aug. 1812)
McKees, James, age 50, 17 years in U.S., Scotchman, wife & 3
   children, Washington, bricklayer (26 Sept. 1812)
McKinsey, Alexander, wife & 2 children, New Haven (1812-14)
McPherson, James, age 25, 7 mos. in U.S., no family, New London,
   merchant; deputy marshal there ordered to watch his motions
   (10 Feb. 1813)
McRae, Colin, age 36, 6 mos. in U.S., from Scotland, wife & 4
   children, New Haven, merchant; applied 20 Feb. 1812; for the
   last 12 years resided in Demerara; he made his fortune there
   and came here to enjoy it (8 Aug. 1812)
Magin, William, age 26, 12 years in U.S., wife & 2 children, Middletown, tallow chandler (16 Aug. 1812)
Manypenny, Joseph, age 37, 20 years in U.S., from Ireland, wife
   & 5 children, Danbury, weaver; said to have been convicted of
   passing counterfeit money (16 Aug. 1812)
Matthews, John, age 22, 10 mos. in U.S., from Ireland, no family,
   Norwalk, laborer (8 Aug. 1812)
Matthews, Samuel, age 20, 10 mos. in U.S., from Ireland, Norwalk,
   laborer (8 Aug. 1812)
Matthews, Thos., Bridgeport (1812-14)

May, John, age 60, 30 years in U.S., from Ireland, wife & 5 dau-
ghters & 6 sons, Woodbury, wheelwright (16 Aug. 1812)
Meadows, Robert C., age 33, 15 years in U.S., wife & 2 children,
Milford, mariner; ships as a mate (16 Aug. 1812)
Miller, Robert, age 28, 2 years in U.S., mother, 3 sisters & 3
brothers, Roxbury (26 Sept. 1812)
Morgan, Wm., age 30, in U.S. 6 years, Irishman, Litchfield (26
Sept. 1812)
Nail/Neyle, Thomas, age about 35, resident of Greenwich for about
10 years past, from England, a single man, Greenwich, school-
master (8 Aug. 1812)
Norman, Edward, age 30, 11 years in U.S., from England, wife &
3 children, Stamford, shoemaker (16 Aug. 1812)
Phillips, John, age 19, 12 years in U.S., from Wales, Danbury,
brass founder (16 Aug. 1812)
Pierce, Wm. Abbott, wife & 2 children, New Haven (1812-14)
Pratt, Edward, age 32, 13 years in U.S.. wife & 2 sons, New Lon-
don, tallow chandler (26 Sept. 1812)
Pratt, Francis, age 57, 9 years in U.S., wife, Hartford, soap
boiler; "British partisan but of little importance" (16 Aug.
1812)
Price, John, New Canaan (line drawn through item) (1812-14)
Prindle, Peter B., age unknown, Norwalk; British pensioner and
a bad inhabitant; a pilot to the enemy in the last war (26 Sept.
1812)
Reis, Frederic/Frederick, age 10, 1 year in U.S., no family,
Colchester, student (26 Sept. 1812)
Reis, Henry, age 12, 1 year in U.S., no family, Colchester, stu-
dent (26 Sept. 1812)
Richards, James, age 76, Englishman, Litchfield, laborer; a State
pauper (26 Sept. 1812)
Sangster, Wm., age 25, 3 years in U.S., from Scotland, no family,
Norwalk, dyer (26 Sept. 1812)
Simmons, James L., age 27, 5½ years in U.S., from England, wife,
Preston, cotton manufacturer (8 Aug. 1812)
Simpson, Wm. F., age 26, 5 years in U.S., from England, wife,
Bethlem, tailor (16 Aug. 1812)
Skinner, John, age 40, 11 years in U.S., from Scotland, no family,
Norwalk, shoemaker (16 Aug. 1812)
Smith, Edward, age 35, 10 years in U.S., from England, wife, New
Haven, mason (8 Aug. 1812)
Spence, Thomas, age 45, 5 years in U.S., from England, wife & 2
sons & 3 daughters, New London, grocer (8 Aug. 1812)
Spencer, Houghton, age 34, 4 years in U.S., from England, wife
& 1 daughter, New London, grocer (8 Aug. 1812)
Stevenson, Wm., age 20, 1 year & 9 mos. in U.S., no family,
Hartford, coppersmith; "attached to our government" (16 Aug.
1812)
Stewart, James, age 46, 35 years in U.S., wife & 2 sons & 4
daughters & 1 servant, New London, merchant; brought up as a
merchant in the U.S.; long a resident in New London; for many
years an agent for supplying British West India Islands; has
been British consul about 2 years; active, enterprizing and of
extensive connections (8 Aug. 1812)
Stewart, John, wife & 2 children, New Haven (1812-14)
Stroud, Joseph, age 29, 1 year in U.S., no family in U.S., Red-
ding, clothier (26 Sept. 1812)
Syres, Legar, age 34, 11 years in U.S., from Ireland, no family,
Norwalk, no trade; superintends a pottery (16 Aug. 1812)
Taylor, Samuel, age 34, 22 years in U.S., wife & 7 children,
Glastenbury, sailmaker; applied about 1808 (16 Aug. 1812)
Taylor, William, New Haven (1812-14)
Thompson, John, age 27, 11 years in U.S., no family, Hartford,
mariner (16 Aug. 1812)

Underhill, John, age 23, 12 years in U.S., from England, wife,
  Brookfield, farmer (16 Aug. 1812)
Valentine, James, age 40, 14 years in U.S., from England, wife,
  Norwalk, shoemaker (16 Aug. 1812)
Vance, William, Stratford (1812-14)
Wakefield, George, age 62, 17 years in U.S., wife, Ashford, far-
  mer; of good character; has the fee of a valuable farm (8 Aug.
  1812)
Watson, Joseph, wife & 5 children, New Canaan (1812-14)
Watson, William, age 65, 29 years in U.S., Englishman, Watertown,
  farmer (26 Sept. 1812)
Wetherel, Wm., age 18, 10 years in U.S., from London, no family,
  Danbury, hatter (16 Aug. 1812)
Wickham, Richard Straker, age 44, 4 years in U.S., from Barbados,
  wife, 4 sons, 5 daughters & 3 servants, New London, no occupation (8 Aug. 1812); on 1 Oct. 1812 passports were issued to
  Richard Straker Wickham, age 44; his wife, Mary Jane Hotherrall
  Wickham, age 40; their children, Mary Isabella, age 19, James,
  age 15, Francis, age 11, Elizabeth, age 9, Ann, age 7, Pinder,
  age 5, Isabella, age 2, and Georgiana, age 3 months; the servants, Mary Mayne, age 21, Jane Ann (black), age 22, and Caesar,
  (black), age 30; Mr. Wickham's nephew, Richard Forster Clarke,
  age 11; all were born on Barbados except Clarke, who was born
  at New London, and Georgiana Wickham, who was born at Wethers-
  field, Conn; the passports were issued that all might go to Barbados.
Wilkinson, Alexander, wife & 1 child, Derby (1812-14)
Williams, John, Coventry (1812-14)
Williams, John, age 18, 3 mos. in U.S., from Ireland, no family,
  Norwalk, hatter (8 Aug. 1812)
Winterbottom, John, wife & 4 children, Derby (1812-14)
Wood, John, age 64, 23 years in U.S., from England, wife & 6 children, Sherman, weaver (16 Aug. 1812)
Wood, John, age 37, 24 years in U.S., from Ireland, wife & 2 children, Danbury, hatter (16 Aug. 1812)
Woolsey, Benjamin M., age about 55, resident of Stratford for
  about 10 years, has wife and children; he was born in the State
  of New York and was in British service during the Revolution;
  he went to Nova Scotia but returned to the U.S. some years after
  the peace; he is called major but receives half pay of a lieutenant or captain; he claims he is not bound to report himself
  (8 Aug. 1812)
Wyman, James, age 23, 2 mos. in U.S., no family, East Windsor,
  seaman (26 Sept. 1812)

NEW YORK

Abbetson, Elihu, age 36, 6 years in U.S., 143 Chambers, tanner
(20-25 July 1812)

Abbotson, William, age 31, 6 years in U.S., Catherine St.,
leather dresser (28 July -2 Aug. 1812)

Abernethy, Abel, age 27, 2 mos. in U.S., wife & 2 children, Kingston, Ulster Co., weaver (19-24 Oct. 1812)

Abernethy, William, age 20, 2 mos. in U.S., Kingston, Ulster Co.,
weaver (19-24 Oct. 1812)

Abington, John, age 30, 5ft. 4in., light complex., dark hair,
grey eyes, Elm St. shoemaker (Navy)

Abrahams, Jacob, age 31, 10 years in U.S., wife & 6 children,
360 Water St., clothier (20-25 July 1812); 5ft. 6in., fair
complex., dark hair, dark eyes, tailor (Navy)

Absalom, William, age 36, 5 years in U.S., wife & child, 132
William St., straw hat manufacturer (20-25 July 1812); fair
complex., sandy hair, blue eyes (Navy)

Absolom, Elihu, 6ft. 2in., age 37, fair complex., black hair,
blue eyes, Chambers St., tanner (Navy)

Absolom, William, 5ft. 11in., age 31, fair complex., brown hair,
brown eyes, Chambers St., leather parer (Navy)

Achuson, Hugh, 5ft. 7in., age 26, sandy complex., red hair, blue
eyes, Orange St., cartman (Navy)

Acten, Isaac, 5ft. 4in., age 32, light complex., brown hair,
grey eyes, Beekman Slip, carpenter (Navy)

Adair, William, 5ft. 6in., age 35, dark complex., brown hair,
grey eyes, baker (Navy)

Adams, Alexander, age 22, 11 years in U.S., Amsterdam, Montgomery
Co., tailor(15 Sept. - 5 Oct. 1812); weaver (5-10 Oct. 1812)

Adams, Henry, age 32, 11 years in U.S., wife & 4 children, Johnstown, Montgomery Co., farmer (25 Aug. - 2 Sept. & 7-12 Sept.
1812)

Adams, Hugh, age 24, 5 years in U.S., 39 Cedar St., NYC, gentleman (28 July - 2 Aug. 1812)

Adams, John, age 32, 17 years in U.S., 6 persons in family,
Phelps, Ontario Co., weaver (5-15 & 24-29 Aug. 1812)

Adams, John, 5ft. 8in., age 22, dark complex., brown hair, dark
eyes, labourer (Navy)

Adams, Joseph, age 30, 7 years in U.S., wife & child, City of
Albany, currier (5-10 Oct. 1812)

Adams, Thomas, age 30, 5 years in U.S., wife, Poughkeepsie, Dutchess Co., weaver (12-17 Oct. 1812)

Adams, Thomas, age 26, 5 years in U.S., 17 Chatham St., copperplate printer (20-25 July 1812); 5ft. 5½in., fair complex.,
brown hair, blue eyes (Navy)

Adcock, John, age 37, 4 years & 10 mos. in U.S., wife & 5 children, 126 Chatham St., NYC, hatter (28 July - 2 Aug. 1812); 5ft.
8½in., dark complex., dark hair, dark eyes, Mulberry St. (Navy)

Adderly, William, 5ft. 5in., age 21, sallow complex., brown hair,
hazel eyes, gardener (Navy)

Addy, Thomas, 5ft. 9in., age 49, light complex., dark hair, blue
eyes, Murray St., hatter (Navy)

Aikin, John, age 36,4 years & 6 mos. in U.S., wife & 2 children,
NYC, carpenter (20-25 July 1812)

Aimes, Francis, age 35, 8 years in U.S., wife & 3 children, Augustus St., NYC, laborer (28 July - 2 Aug. 1812)

Ainslie, Adam, age 35 years & 6 mos., 11 years & 5 mos. in U.S.,
wife, 1 child & a bound boy, Manlius, Onondaga Co., farmer (25
Sept. - 2 Oct. 1812 & 5-10 Oct. 1812)

Ainslie, John, age 47, 7 years & 11 mos. in U.S., Manlius, Onondaga Co., farmer (28 Sept. - 3 Oct. & 18-25 Sept. 1812)

Akenhead, Robert, age 36, 11 years in U.S., 9 in family, Lyons,
Ontario Co., farmer (5-15 & 24-29 Aug. 1812)

Aldis, Charles, age 22, 7 years in U.S., 63 Nassau St., NYC,
    silversmith (20-25 July 1812); 5ft. 9in., age 23, fair complex.,
    brown hair, blue eyes, Vesey St. (Navy)
Alexander, John, age 24, 8 years in U.S., 361 Greenwich St., ap-
    plied 30 Mar. 1811, grocer (13-18 July 1812); 5ft. 7¼in., age
    25, fair complex., fair hair, grey eyes (Navy)
Alexander, Robert, age 18, 2 years in U.S., Frankfort St., mo-
    rocco dresser (Navy)
Alexander, William, age 21, 8 years in U.S., 361 Greenwich St.,
    cooper (20-25 July 1812)
Alkinson, David, age 27, 3 years in U.S., 121 Water St., seaman
    (20-25 July 1812)
Allan, George, age 26, 5 years in U.S., 370 Greenwich St., saw-
    yer (20-25 July 1812)
Allan, John, age 26, 3 days in U.S., NYC, law stationer (3-8
    Aug. 1812)
Allcock, George, age 68, 10 years in U.S., Williamson, Ontario
    Co., farmer (23-30 Aug. & 7-12 Sept. 1812)
Allcock, Nicholas, age 32, 8 years & 4 mos. in U.S., 7 in family,
    Williamson, Ontario Co., farmer (23-30 Aug. & 7-12 Sept. 1812)
Allcock, William, age 22, 10 years in U.S., Williamson, Ontario
    Co., farmer (23-30 Aug. & 7-12 Sept. 1812)
Allen, Benjamin, 5ft. 7 3/8in., age 17, light complex., dark hair,
    grey eyes, Greenwich St., blacksmith (Navy)
Allen, George, 5ft. 7in., age 30, dark complex., dark hair, grey
    eyes, Bancker St., baker (Navy)
Allen, George, 5ft. 11in., age 27, fair complex., brown hair,
    blue eyes, Gold St., sawyer (Navy)
Allen, James, age 36, 21 years in U.S., Montgomery, Orange Co.,
    schoolteacher (19-24 Oct. 1812)
Allen, James, 5ft. 4½in., age 21, light complex., brown hair,
    light eyes, Charlotte St., tobacco sp. (Navy)
Allen, John, age 50, 4 mos. in U.S., wife & 7 children, Bethel,
    Sullivan Co., farmer (31 Aug. & 19-24 Oct. 1812)
Allen, John, age 31, 9 years in U.S., wife & 3 children, Pough-
    keepsie, Dutchess Co., laborer (12-17 Oct. 1812)
Allen, John, 5ft. 4in., age 26, fair complex., light hair, blue
    eyes, potter (Navy)
Allen, Michael, age 32, 1 mo. in U.S., 98 Water St., merchant
    (20-25 July 1812)
Allen, Richard, age 25, 12 years in U.S., wife & son, hatter;
    5ft. 8in., age 27, light complex., brown hair, blue eyes, Mai-
    den Lane, hatter (20-25 July 1812 & Navy)
Allen, William, 5ft. 11in., age 50, light complex., dark hair,
    dark eyes, bellows maker (Navy)
Allen, William, age 14, 4 mos. in U.S., Bethel, Sullivan Co.,
    laborer (31 Aug. & 19-24 Oct. 1812)
Allison, James, age 37, 7 years in U.S., wife & 6 children, Mont-
    gomery, Orange Co., weaver (19-24 Oct. 1812)
Allison, William, 5ft. 8in., age 27, fair complex., dark hair,
    grey eyes, labourer (Navy)
Althouse, John, 5ft. 10in., age 20, light complex., brown hair,
    blue eyes, Hempstead, farmer (Navy)
Ames, Francis, 5ft. 8in., age 37, dark complex., black hair, blue
    eyes, labourer (Navy)
Anderson, Hamilton, age 23, 16 years & 6 mos. in U.S., wife &
    child, Shawangunk, Ulster Co., weaver (19-24 Oct. 1812)
Anderson, Hugh, 5ft. 8in., age 20, fair complex., brown hair,
    blue eyes, Catherine St., porter (Navy)
Anderson, Jacob, 5ft. 10in., age 30, brown complex., dark hair,
    hazel eyes, Brooklyn, gardener (Navy)
Anderson, James, age 30, 7 years & 8 mos. in U.S., 1 Duane St.
    (13-18 July 1812)
Anderson, James, 5ft. 7in., age 31, fair complex., brown hair,
    grey eyes, Beekman St., grocer (Navy)

Anderson, James, 5ft. 8in., age 22, fair complex., light hair,
    brown eyes, Provost St., painter (Navy)
Anderson, James B., age 42 on 2 Nov. last, 2 years in U.S. next
    May, wife & 7 children, Eaton, Madison Co., carpenter (31 Oct.
    1812); occupation given as "farmer" (30 Nov. - 5 Dec. 1812)
Anderson, John, 5ft. 8in., age 30, fair complex., brown hair,
    grey eyes, baker (Navy)
Anderson, John W., age 23, 10 years in U.S., wife, Essex Co.,
    merchant (31 Aug. - 5 Sept. 1812)
Anderson, Robert, age 20, 3 mos. in U.S., Hudson. farmer (24-29
    Aug. 1812); same, Hudson, Columbia Co. (22 Aug. 1812)
Anderson, Robert, age ?, 7 years & 7 mos. in U.S., wife & 3
    children, City of Albany (17-22 Aug. 1812)
Anderson, William, 5ft. 9in., age 37, brown complex., dark hair,
    blue eyes, Suffolk St., rigger (Navy)
Anderson, William, 5ft. 8in., age 28, fair complex., fair hair,
    blue eyes, Bancker St., labourer (Navy)
Andrew, Henry, age 26, 14 years in U.S., wife & 2 children, 78
    Maiden Lane, upholsterer, 5ft. 9in., fair complex. brown hair,
    light eyes (13-18 July 1812 & Navy)
Andrews, Charles C., age 30, 10 years in U.S., wife & child, 8
    Doyer St., teacher, applied 28 Apr. 1809 (13 -18 July 1812);
    5ft. 9½in., age 31, light complex., dark hair, grey eyes, Pearl
    St. (Navy)
Andrews, John, 5ft. 7in., age 40, dark complex., black hair,
    blue eyes, carpenter (Navy)
Andrews, John, age 32, 1 year & 7 mos. in U.S., NYC, coloring
    chemist (20-25 July 1812); 5ft. 8in., dark complex., black
    hair, blue eyes, Canon St. (Navy)
Andrews, William, age 53, 4 years in U.S., 8 children, Schenec-
    tady, preceptor of youth (10-15 Aug. 1812)
Angole, Samuel, 5ft. 7in., age 39, dark complex., light hair,
    blue eyes, Tarry Town, farmer (Navy)
Angus, David, age 26, 1 year in U.S., City of Albany, baker (17-
    22 Aug. 1812)
Angus, John, age 26, 8 years & 4 mos. in U.S., wife & child, 24
    Norfolk St., bootmaker, applied 27 June 1812 (3-8 Aug. 1812);
    5ft. 11in., light complex., light hair, grey eyes (Navy)
Ansly, Ouris (?), 5ft. 11½in., age 70, fair complex., grey hair,
    blue eyes, removed from NYC to Bedford, Westchester Co. (Navy)
Antil, Edward, said to be an officer under British pay, Goshen -
    has not reported (2 Jan. 1813)
Antil, John, said to be an officer under British pay, Goshen,
    Orange Co. - has not reported (2 Jan. 1813)
Appleby, William, 5ft. 6in., fair complex., light hair, brown
    eyes, manufacturer (Navy)
Aram, Matthias, age 39 on last 1 Jan., 6 years in U.S. on 20
    Aug. inst., wife, mother & 3 children, Whitestown, Oneida Co.,
    farmer, from Yorkshire, England (26 Aug. & 28 Sept. - 3 Oct.
    1812)
Archibald, James, age 47, 6 years in U.S., wife & 4 children,
    Charlestown, Montgomery Co., farmer (3-14 & 21-26 Sept. 1812)
Argall/Argill, William, age 25, 2 years in U.S., wife & child,
    house-carpenter(28 July - 2 Aug. 1812); 5ft. 7in., fair com-
    plex., dark hair, brown eyes, Thomas St. (Navy)
Arkins, John, age 30, 5 years & 8 mos. in U.S., wife & child,
    Fishkill, Dutchess Co., weaver (12-17 Oct. 1812)
Armstrong, Alexander, age 35, 18 years in U.S., wife & child,
    Montgomery, Orange Co., mason (19-24 Oct. 1812)
Armstrong, Andrew, 5ft. 11in., age 22, fair complex., fair hair,
    grey eyes, weaver (Navy)
Armstrong, Christopher, age 29, 6 years & 3 mos. in U.S., New
    Windsor, Orange Co., laborer (19-24 Oct. 1812)
Armstrong, Christopher, age 25, 5 years in U.S., wife & 2 child-
    ren, mason (10-15 Aug. 1812)

Armstrong, David, 5ft. 6in., age 41, dark complex., dark hair,
  black eyes, Thompson St., wheelwright (Navy)
Armstrong, Francis, age 35, 5 years & 1 mo. in U.S., wife & 3
  children, New Paltz, Ulster Co., cooper (19-24 Oct. 1812)
Armstrong, George, 5ft. 8in., age 25, dark complex., brown hair,
  brown eyes, Mulberry St., cartman, (Navy)
Armstrong, James, 5ft. 3in., age 23, black complex., dark hair,
  light eyes, Bloomingdale, labourer (Navy)
Armstrong, John, age 60, 4 years in U.S., wife, NYC, grocer (28
  July - 2 Aug. 1812)
Armstrong, John, 5ft. 6in., age 60, fair complex., grey hair,
  blue eyes, Church St., teacher (Navy)
Armstrong, John, age 50, 5 years in U.S., wife & 6 children,
  Johnsburgh, Washington Co., farmer (8 Dec. 1812)
Armstrong, John, age 20, 8 years in U.S., Montgomery, Orange Co.,
  mason (19-24 Oct. 1812)
Armstrong, John French, age 19, 1 year in U.S., 56 Pine St.,
  military sash manufacturer (13-18 July 1812); 5ft. 10in.,
  light complex., brown hair, blue eyes, Gold St. (Navy)
Armstrong, Joseph, age 50, 4 years in U.S., wife & 3 children,
  Bloomingdale (23 July - 2 Aug. 1812); 5ft. 10in.,
  dark complex., grey hair, dark eyes (Navy)
Armstrong, Mathew, 5ft. 11in., age 43, fair complex., black
  hair, grey eyes, weaver (Navy)
Armstrong, Michael, age 28, 5 years in U.S., City of Albany,
  baker (5-10 Oct. 1812)
Armstrong, Price, 5ft. 9in., age 22, fair complex., red hair,
  blue eyes, Church St., grocer (Navy)
Armstrong, Price, age 21, 4 years in U.S., NYC, teacher (28
  July - 2 Aug. 1812)
Armstrong, Thomas, 5ft. 4in., age 30, light complex., dark hair,
  blue eyes, Kips Bay, labourer (Navy)
Armstrong, Thomas, 5ft. 8in., age 22, black complex., black hair,
  grey eyes, Greenwich St., sawyer (Navy)
Armstrong, William, age 38, 8 years in U.S., wife & child, 185
  Hester St., wheelwright (28 July - 2 Aug. 1812); 5ft. 7in.,
  light complex., brown hair, blue eyes (Navy)
Arnal, William, 5ft. 6in., age 34, dark complex., brown hair,
  grey eyes, Front St., clerk (Navy)
Arnat, Hugh, age 43, 8 years & 2 mos. in U.S., Newburgh, Orange
  Co., laborer (19-24 Oct. 1812)
Arnet, William, age 43, 2 mos. in U.S., Newburgh, Orange Co.,
  laborer (19-24 Oct. 1812)
Arnold, William, age 17, 1 week in U.S., 2 Pearl St., merchant
  (14-19 Sept. 1812)
Arrowsmith, Edward, 5ft. 5in., age 20, dark complex., brown hair,
  dark eyes, Pearl St., sailmaker (Navy)
Arthevis, John, age 21, 2 years in U.S., Fishkill, Dutchess Co.,
  clerk (12-17 Oct. 1812)
Ash, Finlay, age 21, 2½ mos. in U.S., 50 South St., accountant
  (20-25 July 1812)
Ashby, William, age 50, 1 mo. in U.S., NYC, farmer (28 Sept. -
  3 Oct. 1812); 5ft. 11in., light complex., dark hair, hazel
  eyes, removed from NYC to Claverack, Columbia Co. (Navy)
Ashmale, Samuel, age 44, 24 years in U.S., wife, Westchester Co.,
  farmer (21-26 Sept. 1812)
Ashworth, John, age 29, 1 year & 9 mos. in U.S., wife & 3 children, Hudson, Columbia Co., wool spinner (17-22 Aug. 1812)
Aspin, Samuel, 5ft. 10in., age 28, fair complex., brown hair,
  brown eyes, Warren St., baker (Navy)
Atcheson, James, age 30, 10 mos. in U.S., 1 William St., teacher
  (28 July - 2 Aug. 1812)
Atcheson, John, age 21, 1 year & 3 mos. in U.S., wife & child,
  Newburgh, Orange Co., farmer (19-24 Oct. 1812)

Atcheson, William, age 41, 13 days in U.S., wife & 5 children,
150 Division St., bootmaker (21-26 Sept. 1812)
Atkins, Hugh, 5ft. 6in., age 31, light complex., brown hair,
brown eyes, baker
Atkins, William, age 36, 13 years in U.S., wife & child, corner
Livingston & First Sts., baker (28 July - 2 Aug. 1812); 5ft.
3in., fair complex., brown hair, dark eyes, Mulberry St. (Navy)
Atkinson, Abraham, 5ft. 9in., age 26, fair complex., light hair,
blue eyes, Bowery, bootmaker (Navy)
Atkinson, Thomas, 6ft., age 33, dark complex., black hair, grey
eyes, Courtland St., tavern(keeper) (Navy)
Atkinson, William, 5ft. 8in., age 42, sandy complex., brown hair,
grey eyes, Bowery, bootmaker (Navy)
Atteridge, Patrick, age 36, 5 years & 5 mos. in U.S., wife & 3
children, City of Albany (17-22 Aug. 1812)
Atwill, Richard, age 46, 15 years in U.S., wife & 3 children,
Hudson, Columbia Co., farmer (10-15 Aug. 1812)
Atwood, William, age 21, 1 year & 2 mos. in U.S., Newburgh,
Orange Co., cordwainer (19-24 Oct. 1812)
Auchincloss, Hugh, age 32, 9 years in U.S., wife & 3 children,
NYC, merchant (13-18 July 1812); 5ft. 6in., fair complex.,
dark hair, grey eyes, removed from NYC to Fishkill, Dutchess
Co. (Navy)
Auld, James, age 38, 1 year & 10 mos. in U.S., wife & 5 child-
ren, Montgomery, Orange Co., tailor; Montgomery, Orange Co.
(19-24 Oct. 1812)
Auld, James, 5ft. 10½in., age 27, brown complex., brown hair,
blue eyes, Duane St., mason (Navy)
Aylward, Pierce, age 20, 5 years in U.S., 144 Water St., clerk
(13-18 July 1812)
Aylward, Sam., 6ft. 1in., age 28, light complex., light hair,
blue eyes, Water St., clerk (Navy)
B...`k (sic!), Jonathan, 5ft. 9in., age 26, dark complex., black
hair, hazel eyes, chandler (Navy)
Babbison, Abraham, 5ft. 7½in., age 26, fair complex., fair hair,
hazel eyes, Harman St., cartman (Navy)
Bailas, William, 5ft. 7in., age 35, fair complex., light hair,
blue eyes, librarian (Navy)
Bailas, William M., age 31, 12 years in U.S., wife & child, Westchester Co., miller (14-19 Sept. 1812)
Bailey, John, age 30, 5 years in U.S., wife & 2 children, Attorney St., paver (20-25 July 1812); 5ft. 10in., fair complex.,
black hair, blue eyes (Navy)
Bailie, James, 5ft. 7in., age 45, fair complex., grey hair, blue
eyes, Vandewater St., occulist (Navy)
Bailie, Thomas, age 19, 1 year in U.S., 29 Henry St., carpenter
(28 July - 2 Aug. 1812)
Bailie, Thomas, 5ft. 8½in., age 20, fair complex., sandy hair,
blue eyes, 6th St., carman (Navy)
Baily, James, age 18, 5 years in U.S., White Hall, boatman (20-
25 July 1812)
Baker, John M., age 73, 10 years in U.S., 2 children, Chatham
St., boarding house keeper (20-25 July 1812); 5ft. 4in., fair
complex., fair hair, blue eyes (Navy)
Baker, Thomas, age 55, 16 years in U.S., wife & 2 children,
Poughkeepsie, Dutchess Co., carpenter (12-17 Oct. 1812)
Baker, Thomas, age 40, 10 years in U.S., wife & 7 children,
Crosby St., cordwainer (28 July - 2 Aug. 1812); 5ft. 9½in.,
dark complex., brown hair, black eyes (Navy)
Bakewell, Thomas, age 24, 16 years in U.S., wife & child, Broad-
way, merchant, applied 10 Nov. 1811 (20-25 July 1812); 5ft.
11in., light complex., light hair, blue eyes, china (Navy);
removed from NYC to Fishkill, Dutchess Co. (Navy)
Balderston, James, age 34, 1 year & 9 mos. in U.S., Hibernia,
N.J., superintendent iron works (3-8 Aug. 1812)

Baldwin, Benjamin, age 27 yrs. & 3 mos., 6 yrs. & 15 days in U.S., wife & 3 children, Columbiaville, Columbia Co., cotton spinner, applied at Mayor's Court in Hudson 2 Jan. 1810 (12 Aug. 1812)

Balfour, James, age 34, 8 years in U.S., wife & 3 children, Florida, Montgomery Co., farmer (18-24 Aug. & 31 Aug. - 5 Sept. 1812)

Ball, Abraham, age 45, 20 years & 6 mos. in U.S., wife, 20 Henry St., locksmith (20-25 July 1812); 5ft. 4in., age 50, fair complex., brown hair, hazel eyes (Navy)

Ball, William, age 34, 11 years in U.S., wife, 5 children, wife's sister & 1 apprentice, 31 Cedar St., harness and collar maker (13-18 July 1812)

Ball, William W., age 19, 3 years & 10 mos. in U.S., 7 Wall St., japanner (20-25 July 1812); 5ft. 10in., age 20, fair complex., brown hair, blue eyes, painter (Navy)

Ballantine/Ballentine, James, age 26, 2 years in U.S., 75 Duane St., tallow chandler (20-25 July 1812); 6ft., dark complex., black hair, blue eyes (Navy)

Ballantine, Robert, age 32, 7 years in U.S., wife & 3 children, Broadalbin, Montgomery Co., farmer (3-14 & 21-26 Sept. 1812)

Ballard, Henry, age 47, 5 years in U.S., wife & 6 children, Dryden, Tompkins Co., farmer (20-25 Oct. & 9-14 Nov. 1812)

Balster, Oliver S., age 19, 5 years in U.S., 276 Broadway, dry goods merchant (7-12 Sept. 1812); 5ft. 5in., black complex., black hair, black eyes, Chatham St., clerk (Navy); described in Navy list of persons removed as 5ft. 11in., light complex., light hair, blue eyes, removed from NYC to Fishkill, Dutchess Co.

Banaclough, John, 5ft. 9in., age 32, light complex., light hair, grey eyes, servant (Navy)

Banen, Patrick, 5ft. 9in., age 26, fair complex., fair hair, brown eyes, Elm St., labourer (Navy)

Banks, Rev. John, age 38, 16 years in U.S., wife & 5 children, Duanesburgh, Schenectady Co., minister (10-15 Aug. 1812)

Banks, John, 5ft. 2in., age 29, dark complex., brown hair, brown eyes, Mott St., grocer (Navy)

Banks, John, age 27, 9 years in U.S., wife & 2 children, 21 Mott St., merchant (20-25 July 1812); perhaps the same as the grocer.

Banks, John, 5ft. 10in., age 19, fair complex., black hair, blue eyes, cabinetmaker (Navy)

Banks, Robert, age 37, 8 years in U.S., wife & child, Catherine St., tailor, applied 7 June 1811; 5ft. 7½in., fair complex., light hair, blue eyes (13-18 July 1812 & Navy)

Bannan, Michael, age 31, 9 years in U.S., wife & 3 children, 67 Cherry St., tallow chandler, applied 24 Apr. 1811 (13-18 July 1812)

Banon, Samuel, 5ft. 8in., age 28, dark complex., black hair, hazel eyes, rigger (Navy)

Banos, Patrick, 5ft. 6in., age 27, fair complex., light hair, blue eyes, Oak St., labourer (Navy)

Baptist, Isaac, 5ft. 3in., age 35, dark complex., black hair, black eyes, Pearl St., blacksmith (Navy)

Barber, Samuel, age 44, 1 year & 3 mos. in U.S., Poughkeepsie, Dutchess Co., laborer (12-17 Oct. 1812)

Barclay, Henry, age 33, 12 years in U.S., mother, wife, 5 servants, 1 child, NYC, merchant (20-25 July 1812)

Barclay, James, age 31, 1 year & 3 mos. in U.S., New Windsor, Orange Co., weaver (19-24 Oct. 1812)

Barclay, John, age 29, 1 year & 3 mos. in U.S., New Windsor, Orange Co., weaver (19-24 Oct. 1812)

Barclay, William, age 54, 1 year & 3 mos. in U.S., wife & four children, New Windsor, Orange Co., weaver (19-24 Oct. 1812)

Bard, Joseph, age 38, 5 years & 10 mos. in U.S., 3 in family, 5 Rynders St., carpenter (3-8 Aug. 1812); 5ft. 11in., light complex., brown hair, brown eyes, Elm St. (Navy)

Bark, Francis, age 53, 12 years in U.S., 7 in family, Geneseo,
 Ontario Co., ropemaker (6-13 & 21-26 Sept. 1812)
Barker, John, 5ft. 9in., age 28, fair complex., red hair, blue
 eyes, Bowery,calico printer (Navy)
Barla(?), James, 5ft. 6in., age 27, dark complex., black hair,
 brown eyes, tailor (Navy)
Barland, William G., age 14, 11 years in U.S., Schenectady, stu-
 dent (26-31 Oct. 1812)
Barlas, William, age 55, 14 years in U.S., sister, 6 Liberty St.,
 bookseller (20-25 July 1812)
Barlas, William, 5ft. 9in., age 50, ruddy complex., light hair,
 blue eyes, Grand St., labourer (Navy)
Barlas, William, age 45, 7 years in U.S., Grand St., maltster
 (20-25 July 1812)
Barlow, John, age 26, 2 mos. in U.S., Newburgh, Orange Co., spin-
 ner (19-24 Oct. 1812)
Barnard, John, age 24, 4 years in U.S., Avon, Ontario Co., wea-
 ver (5-15 & 24-29 Aug. 1812)
Barnes, Andrew, age 25, 8 mos. in U.S., 50 Broadway, clerk (3-8
 Aug. 1812)
Barnes, Francis, age 21, 1 year in U.S., Newburgh, Orange Co.,
 carpenter (19-24 Oct. 1812)
Barnes, John, 5ft. 5in., age 40, fair complex., black hair, grey
 eyes, Crosby St., mason (Navy)
Barnet, David, 5ft. 8in., age 50, fair complex., grey hair, blue
 eyes, labourer (Navy)
Barnet, Elias, age 45, 7 mos. in U.S., wife & 3 children, 77
 Cherry St., dealer (13-18 July 1812)
Barney, John, 5ft. 6in., age 47, light complex., fair hair,
 black eyes, grocer (Navy)
Barns, Robert, age 33, 13 years in U.S., wife & 6 children, New-
 burgh, Orange Co., weaver (19-24 Oct. 1812)
Barns, William, age 59, 11 years in U.S., 5 in family, Seneca,
 Ontario Co., farmer (25 Oct. - 15 Nov. 1812)
Barns, William, Jr., age 22, 11 years in U.S., Seneca, Ontario
 Co. (25 Oct. - 15 Nov. 1812)
Barr, James, age 29, 11 years in U.S., Galway, Saratoga Co., far-
 mer (31 Aug. - 5 Sept. 1812)
Barr, James, age 25, 11 mos. in U.S., 54 Augustus St., soap boi-
 ler (20-25 July 1812)
Barr, James, age 22, 11 years & 4 mos. in U.S., Clinton, Dutchess
 Co., laborer (12-17 Oct. 1812)
Barr, James, 5ft. 11in., age 23, light complex., light hair, blue
 eyes, Augustus St., chandler (Navy)
Barr, John, age 27, 7 years in U.S., wife, child & mother-in-
 law, Ninth Ward, NYC, gardener (20-25 July 1812)
Barr, John, 5ft. 11½in., age 27, brown complex., brown hair, blue
 eyes, Bowery, gentleman (Navy)
Barr, Mathew, 5ft. 8in., age 19, fair complex., dark hair, black
 eyes, baker (Navy)
Barra, William, age 28, 8 years in U.S., Galway, Saratoga Co.,
 farmer (31 Aug. - 5 Sept. 1812)
Barradale, William, age 33, 5 years in U.S., wife, 106 Division
 St.; currier (20-25 July 1812)
Barrett, Ezekiel, age 26, 1½ years in U.S., wife, 67 Bancker St.,
 grocer (14-19 Sept. 1812); 5ft. 8in., dark complex., dark hair,
 dark eyes (Navy)
Barrett, John, age 36, 5 years & 1 mo. in U.S., wife & 5 children,
 Minisink, Orange Co., mason (19-24 Oct. 1812)
Barrett, Michael, 5ft. 9in., age 30, light complex., brown hair,
 grey eyes, Leonard St., labourer (Navy)
Barrett, Michael, age 27, 1 year & 9 mos. in U.S., wife & child,
 22 Anthony St., mason (10-15 Aug. 1812)
Barrie, Peter, age 32, 8 years in U.S., merchant(28 July - 2 Aug.
 1812); 5ft. 9in., dark complex., hair & eyes , Pearl St. (Navy)

Barrie, Peter (continued), removed from NYC to Schohary (Navy)
Barrie, George Sol., 5ft. 5in., age 24, dark complex., dark hair,
blue eyes, milkman (Navy)
Barron, Patrick, age 36, 6 years in U.S., wife, 68 Front St.,
laborer, applied 13 Mar. 1810 (28 July - 2 Aug. 1812)
Barry, James, age 30, 9 years in U.S., 46 Walker St., teacher
(20-25 July 1812)
Barry, James, 5ft. 7in., age 25, light complex., fair hair, blue
eyes, gentleman (Navy)
Barry, James, age 22, 1 year in U.S., 151 Front St., storekeeper
(20-25 July 1812)
Barry, John, 5ft. 9in., age 47, dark complex., brown hair, brown
eyes, gardener (Navy)
Barry, John, age 36, 8 years in U.S., 2 children, 151 Front St.,
storekeeper (20-25 July 1812)
Barry, John, 6ft. 1in., age 30, fair complex., brown hair, brown
eyes, Cherry St., sawyer (Navy)
Barry, Lawrence, 5ft. 10in., age 33, dark complex., black hair,
black eyes, Bowery Hill, gardener (Navy)
Barry, Moses, age 38, 10 years in U.S., Poughkeepsie, Dutchess
Co., laborer (12-17 Oct. 1812)
Barry, William, 5ft. 6in., age 28, light complex., dark hair,
blue eyes, Garden St., servant (Navy)
Barten, James, age 38, 18 years in U.S., wife & 4 children, Rome,
woolen manufacturer (3-8 Aug. 1812)
Bartis, James, age 38, 18 years in U.S., wife & 4 children, Rome,
Oneida Co., woolen manufacturer in employ of James Lynch (29
July 1812)
Bartley, Michael, age 45, 17 years in U.S., Wayne, Steuben Co.,
farmer (31 Aug. - 5 Sept. 1812)
Bartley, William, 5ft. 6in., age 52, light complex., chestnut
hair, blue eyes, labourer (Navy)
Barton, Johannes, age 37, 7 years in U.S., wife, Schenectady,
laborer (31 Aug. - 5 Sept. 1812)
Barton, Richard, 5ft. 6in., age 48, dark complex., black hair,
blue eyes, Fly Market, porter (Navy)
Barton, William, 5ft. 4in., age 27, light complex., light hair,
dark eyes, Thomas St., tanner (Navy)
Bartram, Andrew, 5ft. 10in., age 27, fair complex., fair hair,
grey eyes, Mott St., weaver (Navy)
Bascome, Cornelius, age 37, 10 mos. in U.S., City Hotel, NYC (13-
18 July 1812)
Bass, William, 6ft., age 32, fair complex., dark hair, blue eyes,
Chatham St., broker, removed from NYC to Poughkeepsie (Navy)
Bates, John, age 21 on 8 Mar. next, 7 years in U.S. on 12 Aug.
last, from Derbyshire, England, Lee, Oneida Co., farmer (29
Sept. 1812)
Bates, Joseph, age 27, 7 years in U.S., wife, City of Albany,
sawyer (5-10 Oct. 1812)
Bates, Joseph, age 25, 4 years in U.S., wife & child, 61 Pine
St., merchant (20-25 July 1812)
Bates, Joseph, 5ft. 11½in., age 24, dark complex., black hair,
grey eyes, accountant, removed from NYC to Fishkill (Navy)
Bates, Thomas, age 23 on 2 Feb. next, 7 years in U.S. on 12 Aug.
last, from Derbyshire, England, Rome, Oneida Co., farmer (29
Sept. 1812)
Baty, Robert, 5ft. 8in., age 31, fair complex., light hair, blue
eyes, Third St., sailmaker (Navy)
Baxter, John, age 18 on 12 Mar. last, 18 years in U.S. in next
Sept., from Leicestershire, England, Utica, Oneida Co., baker
(10 Aug. 1812)
Baxter, William, age 50 Feb. last, 18 years in U.S. next Sept.,
wife & 7 children, from Hogs Norton, Leicestershire, England,
Utica, Oneida Co., gardener (10 Aug. 1812)

Bayley, William P., age 22, 5 years in U.S., Shawangunk, Ulster
Co., schoolmaster (2 Jan. 1813)
Beadon, Robert, 5ft. 9in., age 23, black complex., fair hair,
blue eyes, stone cutter (Navy)
Beakey/Beaky, George Thomas, age 20, 6 mos. in U.S., NYC, pain-
ter, 5ft. 3in., dark complex., brown hair, brown eyes (2-7
Nov. 1812 & Navy)
Beatty, James, age 30, 1 year & 3 mos. in U.S., New Windsor,
Orange Co., weaver (19-24 Oct. 1812)
Beatty, James, 5ft. 7in., age 19, fair complex., fair hair, blue
eyes, Catherine St., clerk (Navy)
Beatty, John, 5ft. 9in., age 31, fair complex., dark hair, blue
eyes, Washington St., cartman (Navy)
Beatty, John, 5ft. 9in., age 21, fair complex., fair hair, grey
eyes, tallow chandler (Navy)
Beatty, Mathew, 5ft. 7in., age 21, fair complex., light hair,
Attorney St., labourer (Navy)
Beatty, Samuel, 5ft. 7in., age 44, dark complex., brown hair,
brown eyes, Broad St., labourer (Navy)
Beatty, Samuel, 5ft. 9in., age 30, fair complex., light hair,
hazel eyes, cartman (Navy)
Beatty, William, 5ft. 8in., age 31, fair complex., light hair,
blue eyes, cartman (Navy)
Beaty, James, age 17, 7 mos. in U.S., NYC, clerk (20-25 July
1812)
Beaty, Robert, age 30, 8 years in U.S., 51 Third St., sailmaker
(13-18 July 1812)
Beaumont, Joseph, age 26, 9 years in U.S., wife, Poughkeepsie,
Dutchess Co., spinner (12-17 Oct. 1812)
Beaumont, Samuel, 5ft. 6in., age 32, fair complex., brown hair,
grey eyes, Bowery, carpenter (Navy)
Beck, William, age 50, 11 years in U.S., wife & 4 children,
Bloominggrove, Orange Co., farmer (19-24 Oct. 1812)
Beers, Edward, age 32, 9 years in U.S., 5 in family, Boyle, On-
tario Co., stocking loom maker (15-22 Aug. & 31 Aug. - 5 Sept.
1812)
Beggs, John, age 24 on 29 May, 3 years in U.S. on 17 Aug., Utica,
Oneida Co., clerk (26 Aug. & 28 Sept. - 3 Oct. 1812)
Begnal, John, 5ft. 10in., age 24, dark complex., dark hair, blue
eyes, labourer (Navy)
Belden, Wilford, 5ft. 7in., age 50, light complex., dark hair,
dark eyes, sawyer (Navy)
Bell, David, 5ft. 7in., age 57, black complex., black hair, grey
eyes, Orange St., weaver (Navy)
Bell, David, 6ft., age 37, dark complex., black hair, brown eyes,
Chatham St., grocer (Navy)
Bell, Francis, age 41, 20 years in U.S., 4 children, Genoa, Cay-
uga Co., hatter, applied 1809 (14-19 Sept. & 28 Sept. -3 Oct.
1812)
Bell, George, age 28, 2 years & 9 mos. in U.S., wife & 5 child-
ren, 15 Elm St., grocer (20-25 July 1812)
Bell, George, 5ft. 8½in., age 25, fair complex., fair hair, grey
eyes, Duane St., grocer (Navy)
Bell, Hugh, age 25, 5 years in U.S., 308 Water St., shoemaker
(20-25 July 1812); 5ft. 8in., age 27, fair complex., light
hair, dark eyes (Navy)
Bell, James, age 48, 16 years in U.S., wife & 5 children, New
Scotland, Albany Co., farmer (5-10 Oct. 1812)
Bell, John, age 50, 3 years in U.S., Cornwall, Orange Co., cotton spinner (19-24 Oct. 1812)
Bell, John, age 22, 4 years & 8 mos. in U.S., Mamakating, Sullivan Co., tallow chandler (19-24 Oct. 1812)
Bell, Leonard, age 35, 1 year in U.S., wife & child, Grand St.,
cabinetmaker(13-18 July 1812); 5ft. 8in., light complex., light
hair, grey eyes, Pump St. (Navy)

Bell, Richard, age 33, 13 years in U.S., wife & 3 children, 28
  Harman St., mason (10-15 Aug. 1812); 5ft. 11in., fair complex.,
  fair hair, grey eyes, bricklayer (Navy)
Bell, Thomas, age 47, 8 years & 1 mo. in U.S., Wallkill, Orange
  Co., bootmaker (19-24 Oct. 1812)
Bell, William, age 53, 23 years in U.S., wife, Plattekill, Ul-
  ster Co., farmer (19-24 Oct. 1812)
Bell, William, age 27, 4 years in U.S., 174 William St., dyer,
  applied July 1808 (20-25 July 1812); 5ft. 5in., age 29, dark
  complex., dark hair, grey eyes, Liberty St., dyer (Navy)
Bell, William, age 20, 1 year in U.S., Montgomery, Orange Co.,
  cooper (19-24 Oct. 1812)
Bell, William, perhaps same as above, 5ft. 8in., age 20, light
  complex., fair hair, blue eyes, Water St., cooper (Navy)
Belligh, William, 5ft. 8in., age 20, light complex., light hair,
  grey eyes, Vesey St., baker (Navy)
Belton, John, age 45 last July, 2 years in U.S. on 28 Sept. last,
  wife & 10 children, Eaton, Madison Co., farmer (31 Oct. 1812)
Benford, Edward, age 52, 31 years in U.S., 6 in family, 53 East
  George St., tailor (20-25 July 1812)
Benner, John, 5ft. 5in., age 35, brown complex., brown hair,
  brown eyes, grocer (Navy)
Bennet, Alexander, 5ft. 9in., age 52, dark complex., black hair,
  brown eyes, rigger (Navy)
Bennet, Henry, age 27, 7 years in U.S., 77 Vesey St., goldsmith
  (7-19 Dec. 1812); 5ft. 6in., age 27, light complex., light
  hair, blue eyes, Bowery, goldsmith (Navy)
Bennet, James, age 28, 10 years in U.S., Geneva, joiner (19-24
  Oct. & 27 Sept. - 11 Oct. 1812)
Bennet, John M., 5ft. 10in., age 47, fair complex., fair hair,
  hazel eyes, Jay St., distiller (Navy)
Bennet, Robert, 5ft. 10in., age 30, brown complex., light hair,
  blue eyes, Greenwich St., saddler (Navy)
Bennett, James, age 24, 2 years & 6 mos. in U.S., wife, 62 Chat-
  ham St., teacher of mathematics (21 Dec. 1812- 23 Jan. 1813)
Bennett, Morris, age 46, 6 years in U.S., wife & 6 children, 8
  Jay St., distiller (20-25 July 1812)
Bennett, Reuben, age 34, 4 years & 10 mos. in U.S., wife, Man-
  lius, Onondaga Co., maltster & brewer (12-18 Sept. 1812)
Bennie, John, 5ft. 8in., age 20, dark complex., dark hair, light
  eyes, baker (Navy)
Bennis, James, 5ft. 6in., age 32, light complex., brown hair,
  grey eyes, labourer (Navy)
Bensaken, Samuel, 5ft. 5in., age 45, sallow complex., dark hair,
  hazel eyes, Phoenix, gentleman, removed from NYC to Fishkill,
  Dutchess Co. (Navy)
Benson, John, age 40, 20 years in U.S., wife & 7 children, 48
  John St., lapidary (20-25 July 1812)
Benson, Paul, age 25, 5 years in U.S., 250 William St., morocco
  dresser (10-15 Aug. 1812)
Benson, Robert, 5ft. 5in., age 24, light complex., dark hair,
  brown eyes, Read St., tanner (Navy)
Benton, Samuel, age 59, 2 years in U.S., wife & 3 children, 14
  Wall St., boot- and shoemaker, applied 3 Oct. 1810 (3-8 Aug.
  1812); 5ft. 4in., age 60, fair complex., grey hair, blue eyes,
  Wall St., bootmaker (Navy)
Benton, Thomas, age 32, 10 years in U.S., wife & child, 82 Broad-
  way, shoemaker (20-25 July 1812); 5ft. 4in., age 31, fair com-
  plex., fair hair, blue eyes, Wall St., bootmaker (Navy)
Benton, William, 5ft. 4in., age 33, fair complex., fair hair,
  blue eyes, Broadway, bootmaker (Navy)
Benton, William H., probably same as above, age 30, 6 years in
  U.S., wife, child & apprentice, 82 Broadway, boot & shoemaker
  (3-8 Aug. 1812)

Berford, Peter O., age 31, 1½ years in U.S., wife, 6 Murray St.,
    servant (13-18 July 1812)
Berry, Godfrey, age 32, 2½ years in U.S., wife, Scammel St.,
    clerk (20-25 July 1812)
Berry, Godfrey, 5ft. 8in., age 32, brown complex., brown hair,
    grey eyes, James St., tavern(keeper?) (Navy)
Beton, Thomas, age 53, 5 years in U.S., 4 children, Newtown,
    Long Island, yeoman (30 Nov. - 5 Dec. 1812)
Betty, Richard, age 45, 5 years in U.S., wife & 5 children, NYC,
    cartman (13-18 July 1812)
Bety, William, age 35, 4 years in U.S., Wallkill, Orange Co.,
    mason (19-24 Oct. 1812)
Bevan, George, age 20, 1 year in U.S., NYC, seaman (20-25 July
    1812)
Beverly, John, 5ft. 11 3/4in., age 35, brown complex., brown
    hair, blue eyes, Williamsburgh, mechanic (Navy)
Beyman, John, 5ft. 10in., age 24, dark complex., dark hair, dark
    eyes, Water St., accountant (Navy)
Beynon, John, 5ft. 10in., age 24, light complex., dark hair,
    dark eyes, removed from NYC to Whitestown (Oneida Co.) (Navy)
Beynow, John D., age 24, 1 year in U.S., 393 Pearl St., merchant
    (20-25 July 1812)
Bibby, T., age 68, 28 years in U.S., wife & 14 children, 17 Pearl
    St., commission merchant, half pay British officer (13-18 July
    1812)
Bigger, William, age 22, 1 year in U.S., Schaghticoke, Albany Co,,
    weaver (24-29 Aug. 1812)
Biggs, Alexander, age 26, 11 years in U.S., Monroe, Orange Co.,
    cooper(19-24 Oct. 1812)
Bigham, Hamilton, 5ft. 9in., age 30, dark complex., dark hair,
    hazel eyes, Harlaem, labourer (Navy)
Bilbrough, Joseph, age 27, 9 mos. in U.S., Boston, merchant (19-
    24 Oct. 1812)
Bill, John, age 38, 4 years in U.S., wife & 2 children, Newburgh,
    Orange Co., labourer (14 Aug. 1812)
Billue, John, age 20, 1 year & 4 mos. in U.S., Newburgh, cord-
    wainer (14 Aug. 1812)
Bingle, Richard, age 24, 11 years in U.S., wife, corner Mulberry
    & Hester Sts., carpenter (31 Aug. - 5 Sept. 1812); 5ft. 7½in.,
    age 27, light complex., dark hair, blue eyes, Third St., car-
    penter (Navy)
Bins (?). Joseph, 5ft. 7½in., age 32, brown complex., brown hair,
    blue eyes, cardmaker (Navy)
Bird, Joseph, age 27, 1 year in U.S., Scipio, Cayuga Co., farmer,
    "respectable & inoffensive" (7-12 Sept. 1812)
Birrel, Henry, age 29, 5 years in U.S., City of Albany, brewer
    (17-22 Aug. 1812)
Birtree, Jacob, age 26, 6 years & 4 mos. in U.S., Newburgh,
    Orange Co., tailor (14 Aug. 1812)
Bishop, John, age 25, 1 year & 8 mos. in U.S., wife, New Windsor,
    Orange Co., paper maker (19-24 Oct. 1812)
Bisset, George, age 32, 7 years in U.S., wife, Hoboken, N.J.,
    millwright (3-8 Aug. 1812)
Black, David, age 44, 20 years in U.S., wife & 6 children, Wood-
    stock, Ulster Co., merchant (7 Sept. & 19-24 Oct. 1812)
Black, Donaldson, age 22, 10 mos. in U.S., wife & child, Kings-
    ton, Ulster Co., weaver (7 Sept. & 19-24 Oct. 1812)
Black, James, age 43, 9 years in U.S., 9 in family, Manhattan-
    ville, cartman (28 July - 2 Aug. 1812); 5ft. 6in., age 45, fair
    complex., dark hair, blue eyes, Manhattanville, cartman (Navy)
Black, James, age 32, 2 years in U.S., Charleston, S.C., boot-
    maker (20-25 July 1812)
Black, James, age 27, 1 year & 6 mos. in U.S., City of Albany,
    merchant (5-10 Oct. 1812)

Black, John, age 33, 11 years in U.S., wife & 6 children, NYC,
mason (28 July - 2 Aug. 1812)
Black, John, age 31, 10 years & 8 mos. in U.S., wife & 3 Child-
ren, Wawarsing, Ulster Co., farmer (19-24 Oct. 1812)
Black, John, 5ft. 5in., age 28, fair complex., dark hair, blue
eyes, Reed St., engineer (Navy)
Blackburne, William, age 23, 8 days in U.S., Mechanic Hall, NYC,
merchant (21 -26 Sept. 1812)
Blackhall, Joseph, 5ft. 10in., age 19, light complex., brown
hair, blue eyes, Charlotte St., blacksmith (Navy)
Blackwell, John, age 23, 9 years in U.S., wife & child, City of
Albany, cartman (5-10 Oct. 1812)
Blackwood, Andrew, 5ft. 6in., age 37, dark complex., dark hair,
grey eyes, carpenter (Navy)
Blagborne, William, age 59, 3 years in U.S., 8 children & ser-
vant, Brooklyn, L.I., minister of the Gospel, applied 2 Sept.
1811 (13-18 July 1812); 5ft. 9in., light complex., grey hair,
blue eyes (Navy)
Blain, Thomas, age 31, 3 mos. in U.S., Hudson, weaver (10-15 Aug.
1812)
Blair, Ezekiel, age 30, 9 years in U.S., wife & 3 children, 47
Robinson St., cartman (20-25 July 1812); 5ft. 7in., age 33,
dark complex., brown hair, grey eyes (Navy)
Blair, Samuel, age 27, 11 mos. in U.S., wife & child, Mulberry
St., cartman (3-8 Aug. 1812)
Blair, William, age 37, 10 years in U.S., 6 in family, corner
Hester & Mulberry Sts., grocer (20-25 July 1812)
Blair, William, age 34, 8 years & 1 mo. in U.S., wife & child,
Clinton, Dutchess Co., laborer (12-17 Oct. 1812)
Blake, James, age 62, 16 years in U.S., Deerfield, Oneida Co.,
farmer (28 Sept. - 3 Oct. 1812); age given as 62 on 1 Aug.
last and residence as Western, Oneida Co. (29 Sept. 1812)
Blake, James, age 24, 11 years in U.S., 3 in family, Geneva,
Ontario Co., farmer (30 Aug. - 5 Sept. & 7-12 Sept. 1812)
Blake, William, 6ft. 1½in., age 34, red complex., dark hair,
dark eyes, teacher (Navy)
Blakely, William, 5ft. 8in., age 32, dark complex., brown hair,
grey eyes, Mulberry St., labourer (Navy)
Blakley, John, age 32, 11 years in U.S., 53 Chapel St., NYC,
clerk (20-25 July 1812)
Blakewood, Andrew, age 37, 9 years in U.S., wife & child, Crosby
St., carpenter (28 July - 2 Aug. 1812)
Bland, John, 5ft. 5in., age 30, black complex., brown hair, grey
eyes, Lumber St., blacksmith (Navy)
Bland, John, age 26, 6 years in U.S., wife & 3 children, white-
and blacksmith (28 July - 2 Aug. 1812)
Bland, Thomas, age 21, 2 years in U.S., NYC, white- and black-
smith (28 July - 2 Aug. 1812); 5ft. 6½in., age 21, light com-
plex., black hair, blue eyes, Lumber St., blacksmith (Navy)
Blandy, Thomas, age 22, 26 days in U.S., 237 Duane St. (20-25
July 1812)
Bleakley, John, 5ft. 10in., age 33, light complex., brown hair,
brown eyes, clerk, removed from NYC to Fishkill, Dutchess Co.
(Navy)
Bleakley/Blakely, Robert, age 30, 8 years & 6 mos. in U.S., wife
& 2 children, 53 Chapel St., merchant(20-25 July 1812); 5ft.
10 in., age 30, light complex., dark hair, dark eyes, removed
from NYC to Whitestown (Navy)
Bleath, John, 5ft. 8in., age 22, light complex., light hair,
brown eyes, carpenter (Navy)
Bloomer, Edward, 5ft. 6in., age 24, light complex., light hair,
grey eyes, Greenwich St., labourer (Navy)
Blue, Alexander, age 22 in Dec. last, 9 years in U.S on 1 Oct.
last, Deerfield, Oneida Co., farmer (29 Sept. 1812)

Blue, Archibald, age 22 on 10 Jan. last, 9 years in U.S. next
    Sept., wife & child, Remsen, shoemaker & tanner (26 Aug. & 28
    Sept. - 3 Oct. 1812)
Blue, Daniel, age 28 last Mar., 8 years in U.S. last Oct., Deer-
    field, Oneida Co., farmer (26 Aug. & 28 Sept. - 3 Oct. 1812)
Blue, Duncan, age 26, 8 years in U.S. last Oct., Deerfield,
    Oneida Co., farmer (26 Aug. & 28 Sept. - 3 Oct. 1812)
Blue, Malcom, age 60, 8 years in U.S. last Oct., 5 children,
    Deerfield, Oneida Co., farmer (26 Aug. & 28 Sept. - 3 Oct. 1812)
Boardman, John, age 35, 1 year in U.S., Beekman, Dutchess Co.,
    weaver (12-17 Oct. 1812)
Bodkin, George, age 22, 4 mos. in U.S., Hudson, Columbia Co.,
    labourer (28 Aug. & 31 Aug. - 5 Sept. 1812)
Bogla, James, 5ft. 10in., age 25, fair complex., brown hair,
    blue eyes, labourer (Navy)
Bogs, Francis, age 24, 2 years in U.S., wife, Poughkeepsie,
    Dutchess Co., weaver (12-17 Oct. 1812)
Boland, John, age 27, 5 years in U.S., wife, NYC, farmer (28
    July - 2 Aug. 1812)
Bolton, George, age 25, 6 years in U.S., NYC, gentleman (19-24
    Oct. 1812); 5ft. 10in., age 25, fair complex., fair hair, blue
    eyes, gentleman (Navy); called George D. in Navy report.
Bolton, John D., age 25, 4 years in U.S., wife & child, Queens
    Co., farmer (9-14 Nov. 1812)
Bonner, Alexander, age 26, 7 years & 2 mos. in U.S., wife & sis-
    ter, NYC, merchant, applied Mar. 1809 (13-18 July 1812)
Bonner, John, 6ft., age 46, fair complex., dark hair, blue eyes,
    Greenwich St., weaver (Navy)
Bonner, John, age 35, 9 mos. in U.S., wife & 3 children, 50
    South St., merchant (20-25 July 1812)
Boodle, Thomas, 5ft. 8½in., age 29, dark complex., brown hair,
    dark eyes, drayman (Navy)
Booth, James, age 43, 2 years & 9 mos. in U.S., wife & 8 child-
    ren, Poughkeepsie, Dutchess Co., cloth maker (12-17 Oct. 1812)
Booth, William, age 40, 16 years in U.S., wife & 3 children, 313
    Broadway, carpenter (20-25 July 1812); 5ft. 7in., dark complex.,
    grey hair, dark eyes, Mulberry St., carpenter (Navy)
Booth, William, age 31, 5 years in U.S., wife, NYC, sawyer (28
    July - 2 Aug. 1812); 5ft. 9in., age 32, fair complex., brown
    hair, blue eyes, Anthony St., sawyer (Navy)
Borland, Robert, 5ft. 7in., age 30, fair complex., fair hair,
    blue eyes, Chapple St., saddler (Navy)
Borthwick, John, age 61, 18 years in U.S., wife & 5 children,
    Montgomery, Orange Co., weaver (19-24 Oct. 1812)
Borthwick, John, Jr., age 23, 18 years in U.S., Montgomery,
    Orange Co., weaver (19-24 Oct. 1812)
Borthwick, William, age 21, 18 years in U.S., Montgomery, Orange
    Co., cordwainer (19-24 Oct. 1812)
Boston, Bart., age 44, 1 year in U.S., wife & 3 children, 60
    Broome St., musical instrument maker (13-18 July 1812)
Boston, Mark, 5ft. 6½in., age 36, dark complex., dark hair, dark
    eyes, coachman (Navy)
Bostwick, Benjamin S., age 23, 18 years in U.S., 3 in family, 27
    Hudson St., gentleman (20-25 July 1812)
Boulanger, Francis, age 25, 3 years & 8 mos. in U.S., Platts-
    burgh, Clinton Co., laborer, from Lower Canada (1 Sept. - 1
    Oct. & 26-31 Oct. 1812)
Boulanger, Joseph, age 17, 2 years in U.S., Plattsburgh, Clinton
    Co., laborer, from Lower Canada (1 Sept.- 1 Oct. & 26-31 Oct.
    1812)
Bower, Alexander, age 46, 8 years in U.S., wife & 12 children,
    Ulysses, Tompkins Co., farmer, applied in 1810 (28 Sept. - 3
    Oct. & 12-17 Oct. 1812)
Bower, John Plant, age 40, 1 year in U.S., wife & child, Hudson
    St., tanner & currier, applied 28 May 1811 (28 July -2 Aug. 1812)

Bowerbank, Thomas, age 71, 4 days in U.S., Brooklyn, merchant
(28 Sept. - 3 Oct. 1812)
Bowling, John, 6ft., age 35, dark complex., brown hair, grey
eyes, maltster (Navy)
Boyce, Francis, 5ft. 5in., age 32, light complex., light hair,
black eyes, Bancker St., tobacco (Navy)
Boyce, John A., age 24, 1 year in U.S., wife, Goshen, Orange Co.,
laborer (19-24 Oct. 1812.
Boyce, Robert, age 31, 8 years in U.S, 5 in family, Canandaigua,
Ontario Co., tailor, applied Feb. 1810 (21-26 Sept. 1812)
Boyd, Alexander, age 24, 1C years in U.S., 56 Bancker St., cur-
rier (28 July - 2 Aug. 1812); 5ft. 8½in., age 25, fair com-
plex., brown hair, dark eyes (Navy)
Boyd, Daniel, age 24, 4 mos. in U.S., New Windsor, Orange Co.,
weaver (19-24 Oct. 1812)
Boyd, Daniel, age 22, 10 years in U.S., 56 Bancker St., cord-
wainer (28 July - 2 Aug. 1812)
Boyd, David, 5ft. 8in., age 23, fair complex., light hair, black
eyes, Washington St., labourer (Navy)
Boyd, David, 5ft. 6in., age 22, dark complex., brown hair, grey
eyes, cordwainer (Navy)
Boyd, James, age 62, 36 years in U.S., NYC, accountant (20-25
July 1812)
Boyd, John, age 41, 7 years in U.S., wife & child, Newburgh,
Orange Co., weaver (19-24 Oct. 1812)
Boylan, Michael, 5ft. 9in., age 28, fair complex., brown hair,
grey eyes, servant (Navy)
Boyle, Bernard, age 21, 1 year in U.S., NYC, accountant (20-25
July 1812)
Boyle, Bernard, 5ft. 6in., age 22, light complex., brown hair,
blue eyes, Front St., labourer (Navy)
Boyle, Dennis, 5ft. 6in., age 22, fair complex., brown hair,
brown eyes, Mulberry St., labourer (Navy)
Boyle, Patrick, 5ft. 5in., age 32, dark complex., light hair,
black eyes, Wall St., hairdresser (Navy)
Boyle, Patrick, age 30, 13 years in U.S., wife, 304 Broadway,
hairdresser (13-18 July 1812)
Boyle, Patrick, age 28, 5 years in U.S., wife & child, Bancker
St., laborer (20-25 July 1812)
Boyle, Patrick, age 26, 5 years & 9 mos. in U.S., wife, 51 Duane
St., laborer (28 July - 2 Aug. 1812); 5ft. 10in., age 26, dark
complex., black hair, blue eyes, labourer (Navy)
Boyle, Patrick, 5ft. 5in., age 25, fair complex., brown hair,
black eyes, stone cutter (Navy)
Boyle, Richard, age 29, 7 years in U.S., wife & child, 3 James
St., hairdresser (20-25 July 1812); 5ft. 5in., age 30, fair
complex., brown hair, blue eyes, James St., hairdresser (Navy)
Boyle, Samuel, 5ft. 7in., age 35, fair complex., brown hair,
grey eyes, calico printer (Navy)
Boyle, Simeon, 5ft. 5in., age 26, fair complex., brown hair, grey
eyes, labourer (Navy)
Boyle, William Fullerton, 5ft. 6in., age 32, brown complex.,
brown hair, black eyes, William St., teacher (Navy)
Bracken, Lawrence, 5ft. 11in., age 38, dark complex., grey hair,
grey eyes, carpenter (Navy)
Bracket, William H., 5ft. 11in., age 47, dark complex., black
hair, dark eyes, Greenwich St., grocer (Navy)
Bradbury, Abraham, age 42 on 29 Nov. next, 10 years in U.S. in
last Aug., wife, child & 2 servants, Whitestown, Oneida Co.
(29 Sept. 1812)
Bradford, Henry, age 23, 19 years in U.S., 175 William St., engraver (20-25 July 1812); 5ft. 6in., dark complex., brown hair,
blue eyes (Navy)

Bradford, John, age 24, 19 years in U.S., wife & 2 children, 2
    Elm St., bookbinder (20-25 July 1812); 5ft. 5in., light com-
    plex., light hair, black eyes (Navy)
Bradish, Wheaton, age 25, 4 years in U.S., NYC, clerk, applied
    13 June 1812 (9-14 Nov. 1812); 5ft. 9in., age 26, dark com-
    plex., dark hair, dark eyes, accountant (Navy)
Bradley, Andrew, 5ft. 7in., age 20, dark complex., brown hair,
    grey eyes, Henry St., saddler (Navy)
Bradley, Francis, age 25, 1 year in U.S., 69 Front St., weaver
    (20-25 July 1812)
Bradley, Thomas, age 27, 6 years in U.S., Phelps, Ontario Co.,
    farmer (24-29 Aug. 1812)
Bradley, Thomas, age 26, 8 years in U.S., Monroe Works, Orange
    Co., cut nailer (17-22 Aug. 1812)
Bradshaw, William, age 25, 11 mos. in U.S., wife & child, Bethel,
    Sullivan Co., farmer, applied 12 Feb. 1812 (31 Aug. 1812)
Brady, Barney, 5ft. 7in., age 31, fair complex., brown hair,
    blue eyes, Elizabeth St., drayman (Navy)
Brady, Edward, 5ft. 5in., age 20, light complex., light hair,
    light eyes, Catherine St., grocer (Navy)
Brady, James, 5ft. 11in., age 30, red complex., red hair, brown
    eyes, Attorney St., labourer (Navy)
Brady, James, 5ft. 5in., age 28, s...(?) complex., brown hair,
    hazel eyes, Stagg Town, blacksmith (Navy)
Brady, James, 5ft. 6in., age 28, fair complex., black hair, brown
    eyes, Harman St., weaver (Navy)
Brady, John, 5ft. 6in., age 37, fair complex., grey hair, blue
    eyes, labourer (Navy)
Brady, Michael, age 67, 4 years & 6 mos. in U.S., 2 children, 69
    Catherine St., grocer (28 July - 2 Aug. 1812); 5ft. 1in., age
    70, sallow complex., grey hair, blue eyes Navy)
Brady, Thomas, 5ft. 8in., age 23, fair complex., fair hair, blue
    eyes, teacher (Navy)
Braine, Daniel, age 19, 6 years & 5 mos. in U.S., 44 John St.,
    clerk (3-8 Aug. 1812)
Braine, Daniel, 5ft. 8in., age 20, fair complex., brown hair,
    blue eyes, Maiden Lane, accountant (Navy)
Branden, Abraham, 5ft. 8in., age 28, dark complex., dark hair,
    black eyes, tailor (Navy)
Brannan, John, age 18, 12 years in U.S., Scipio, Cayuga Co.,
    farmer (21-26 Sept. 1812)
Brannan, Luke, 5ft. 6in., age 36, fair complex., brown hair,
    dark eyes, William St., teacher (Navy)
Brannan, Patrick, age 66, 12 years in U.S., wife & 4 children,
    Scipio, Cayuga Co., farmer, applied Jan. 1812 (7-12 Sept. 1812)
Brannan, Samuel, age 22, 12 years in U.S., Scipio, Cayuga Co.,
    farmer (21-26 Sept. 1812)
Brannon, Henry, age 27, 12 years in U.S., Scipio, Cayuga Co.,
    laborer (21-26 Sept. & 5-10 Oct. 1812)
Brannon, John, (son of Patrick), age 18, 12 years in U.S., Scipio,
    Cayuga Co., farmer (7-12 Sept. 1812)
Brannon, Michael, age 22, 5 years & 1 mo. in U.S., 45 Elm St.,
    stone cutter (28 July - 2 Aug. 1812)
Brannon, Michael, 5ft. 7in., age 22, light complex., dark hair,
    blue eyes, Anthony St., stone cutter (probably same as above)
    (Navy)
Brannon, Samuel, age 22, 12 years in U.S.(son of Patrick), Scipio,
    Cayuga Co., farmer (7-12 Sept. 1812)
Brannon, Thomas, 5ft. 9in., age 45, dark complex., brown hair,
    grey eyes, labourer (Navy)
Brark(?), James, 5ft. 6in., age 52, dark complex., grey hair,
    grey eyes, weaver (Navy)
Brawley, Thomas, age 26, 1 year in U.S., wife & 3 children, cor-
    ner Budd & Hudson Sts., weaver(28 July - 2 Aug. 1812); 5ft. 9in.,
    fair complex., black hair, dark eyes, Budd St., weaver (Navy)

Breadfoot, James, 5ft. 11 3/4in., age 33, brown complex., brown
    hair, brown eyes, brewer (Navy)
Breese, George B., 5ft. 8in,, age 23, dark complex., black hair,
    dark eyes, clerk (Navy)
Breese, Isaac, 5ft. 7in., age 43, dark complex., black hair,
    black eyes, ashman (?) (Navy)
Brenan, Edward, 5ft. 7½in., age 34, dark complex., black hair,
    grey eyes, labourer (Navy)
Brenan, Hugh, 5ft. 9in., age 26, light complex., dark hair, grey
    eyes, gardener (Navy)
Brenan, John, 5ft. 9in., age 27, dark complex., brown hair, dark
    eyes, chandler (Navy)
Brenan, John, 5ft. 7in., age 27, fair complex., light hair, blue
    eyes, teacher (Navy)
Brenan, John, 5ft. 7½in., age 26, dark complex., black hair, blue
    eyes, machine maker (Navy)
Brennan, John, age 29, 4 years in U.S., wife & child, 155 Broad-
    way, teacher, applied 20 June 1810 (13-18 July 1812)
Brennan, Lawrence, 6ft., age 25, fair complex., dark hair, grey
    eyes, hawker (Navy)
Brennan, Thomas, age 25, 9 years in U.S., 74 Wall St., barkeeper
    (17-22 Aug. 1812)
Bressiter, John, 5ft. 9in., age 31, dark complex., black hair,
    black eyes, Bancker St., carpenter (Navy)
Brett, Edmund, age 37, 5 years & 8 mos. in U.S., 3 in family, 6
    Hague St., tailor (20-25 July 1812)
Brewer, James, 5ft. 9in., age 30, light complex., light hair,
    blue eyes, coachman (Navy)
Brewer, John, age 48, 13 years in U.S., wife & 5 children, 127
    Chatham St., brewer (3-8 Aug. 1812); 5ft. 8in., age 48, brown
    complex., grey hair, blue eyes, Bloomingdale, brewer (Navy)
Brewer, John, age 36, 16 years in U.S., 6 in family, Phelps, On-
    tario Co., miller (5-15 & 24-29 Aug. 1812)
Brian, Michael, age 32, 4 years & 7 mos. in U.S., Newburgh,
    Orange Co., teacher (report of David Dill)
Brice, Archibald, age 29, 3 days in U.S., 36 Fair St., merchant
    (24-29 Aug. 1812)
Brice, Archibald, 6ft., age 27, light complex., brown hair, blue
    eyes, Fair St., clerk (Navy)
Brice, David, age 32, 6 years in U.S., 4 in family, 121 Division
    St., painter & glazier (20-25 July 1812)
Bridge, John, age 19, 1 year in U.S., 392 Pearl St., moulder (7-
    12 Sept. 1812); Bridges, John, 5ft. 7in., age 20, light com-
    plex., brown hair, blue eyes, Leonard St., moulder (Navy)
Bridge, Richard, age 24, 1 year in U.S., 39 Greenwich St., car-
    penter (31 Aug.- 5 Sept. 1812); 5ft. 6in., brown complex.,
    brown hair, light eyes, carpenter (Navy)
Bridgewood/Bridgwood, Samuel S., age 28, 2½ years in U.S., wife
    & child, 36 Dey St., merchant, applied 5 Dec. 1809 (20-25 July
    1812); 5ft. 9in., age 29, light complex., black hair, blue eyes,
    earthen(ware?) (Navy)
Bridgewood/Bridgwood, Thomas, age 18, 2½ years in U.S., 36 Dey
    St., clerk (20-25 July 1812); 5ft. 8½in., age 19, light complex.,
    dark hair, black eyes, clerk (Navy)
Brien, James, 5ft. 7in., age 45, dark complex., dark hair, brown
    eyes, William St., labourer (Navy)
Brien, William, 5ft. 8in., age 25, fair complex., brown hair,
    blue eyes, Manhattan, labourer (Navy)
Brierly, Isaac, age 21, 18 years in U.S, wife, Brooklyn, L.I.,
    cordwainer (28 July - 2 Aug. 1812)
Briggs, George, age 26, 20 years in U.S., wife & 2 children,
    plumber (20-25 July 1812)
Briggs, John, age 39, 12 years in U.S., wife & 6 children, Pulte-
    ney, Steuben Co., farmer (7-12 Sept. 1812); 4 children born in
    U.S. (25-31 Aug. & 14 Sept. 1812)

Briggs, Thomas, 5ft. 5in., age 23, dark complex., sandy hair,
light eyes, Newburgh, boatman (Navy)
Briggs, William, 5ft. 5 3/4in., age 25, fair complex., brown
hair, grey eyes, Staten Island, oysterman (Navy)
Brigham, Hamilton, age 29, 4½ years in U.S., wife & child, cor-
ner Arch St. & Broadway, laborer (20-25 July 1812)
Briscoe, William, age 38, 7 years & 1 mo. in U.S., Liberty, Sul-
livan Co., farmer (31 Aug. & 19-24 Oct. 1812)
Broadbridge/Brodbridge, James, age 36, 7 years in U.S., wife & 2
children, Newburgh, Orange Co., watchmaker (14 Aug. & 17-22
Aug. 1812)
Broderick, John, age 23, 12 years in U.S., Galway, Saratoga Co.,
merchant (14-19 Sept. 1812)
Bromell, Samuel, age 24, 9 years in U.S., 236 Water St., mariner
(12 Dec. 1812 - 23 Jan. 1813)
Bromley, William, 5ft. 4in., age 53, light complex., brown hair,
grey eyes, rigger (Navy)
Brook, John, age 25, 1 year & 3 mos. in U.S., Poughkeepsie, Dut-
chess Co., spinner (12-17 Oct. 1812)
Brook, Peter, 5ft. 7in., age 26, light complex., light hair,
light eyes, servant (Navy)
Brooks, James, 5ft. 7in., age 49, light complex., black hair,
dark eyes, Manhattan I., manufacturer (Navy)
Brooks, James, age 36, 6 years in U.S., 2 in family, 44 Cross
St., grocer (20-25 July 1812)
Brooks, Peter, 5ft. 7in., age 26, light complex., light hair,
grey eyes, servant (Navy)
Brooks, Thomas, Jr., 5ft. 7½in., age 19, fair complex., light
hair, brown eyes, accountant (Navy)
Broorn, Luke C., age 25, 12 years in U.S., wife, 82 Harman St.,
laborer (28 July - 2 Aug. 1812)
Brotherton/Brotherson, George, 5ft. 7in., age 27, fair complex.,
brown hair, blue eyes, labourer (Navy)
Broughton, John, age 26, 10 years in U.S., 92 Maiden Lane, livery
stable keeper (28 July - 2 Aug. 1812)
Brower, Thomas, age 24, 8 years in U.S., 358 Greenwich St.,
tailor (20-25 July 1812)
Brown, Alexander, 5ft. 8in., age 22, dark complex., light hair,
grey eyes, Chatham St. pedler (Navy)
Brown, David, age 50, in U.S. since 1801, wife & 4 childre', Oppenheim, Montgomery Co., wheelwright (3-14 & 21-26 Sept. 1812)
Brown, David, age 30, 8 years in U.S., wife, Brooklyn, ropemaker
(3-8 Aug. 1812); 5ft. 8in., fair complex., brown hair, blue
eyes (Navy)
Brown, David, 5ft. 5in., age 28, dark complex., brown hair, blue
eyes, Attorney St., cartman (Navy)
Brown, David, 5ft. 6 3/4in., age 21, fair complex., sandy hair,
brown eyes, Lombardy St., brass founder (Navy)
Brown, Dilworth, age 57, 7 mos. in U.S., wife & 7 children, New
Windsor, Orange Co., weaver (2 Jan. 1813)
Brown, Edward, 5ft. 2½in., age 51, fair complex., light hair,
blue eyes, Greenwich St., sawyer (Navy)
Brown, Edward, 5ft. 10in., age 30, fair complex., brown hair,
black eyes, Bowery Lane, tobacco (Navy)
Brown, Francis, age 50, 18 years in U.S., wife & 6 children, New-
burgh, Orange Co., weaver (19-24 Oct. 1812)
Brown, George, age 54, 10 days in U.S., 144 Water St., artist (21-
26 Sept. 1812)
Brown, George, age 44, 1 year & 5 mos. in U.S., wife & 8 children, Kingston, Ulster Co., weaver (7 Sept. & 19-24 Oct. 1812)
Brown, George, 5ft. 7½in., age 27, light complex., brown hair,
light eyes, Corlaers Hook, carpenter (Navy)
Brown, George, age 26, 11 years in U.S., Montgomery, Orange Co.,
weaver (19-24 Oct. 1812)

Brown, George, age 16, 7 mos. in U.S., New Windsor, Orange Co.,
  laborer (2 Jan. 1813)
Brown, Hamilton, 5ft. 5in., age 48, brown complex., brown hair,
  light eyes, 4 Milestone, furnace-man (Navy)
Brown, Jacob, age 35, 13 days in U.S., wife & child, Grand St.,
  bootmaker (21-26 Sept. 1812); 5ft. 8in., age 35, fair complex.,
  light hair, grey eyes, Murray St., bootmaker (Navy)
Brown, James, age 30, 10 years & 4 mos. in U.S., wife & 2 children, corner Grand & Rinders Sts., carpenter (20-25 July 1812);
  5ft. 8in., age 31, dark complex., brown hair, dark eyes, carpenter (Navy)
Brown, James, 5ft. 7in., age 31, light complex., light hair,
  blue eyes, Orange St., nailer (Navy)
Brown, James, age 29, 10 years in U.S., Westchester Co., laborer
  (28 July - 2 Aug. 1812)
Brown, James, age 20, 6 mos. in U.S., Argyle, Washington Co.,
  farmer (28 Sept. - 2 Oct. 1812)
Brown, James, 5ft. 9in., age 20, light complex., brown hair, blue
  eyes, Vandewater St., morocco finisher (Navy)
Brown, James V., age 23, 16 years in U.S., Schoharie Co., farmer
  (3-8 Aug. 1812)
Brown, John, age 45, 12 years in U.S., wife & 4 children, Schenec-
  tady, laborer (31 Aug. - 5 Sept. 1812)
Brown, John, 5ft. 6in., age 35, red complex., dark hair, hazel
  eyes, Barclay St., sailmaker (Navy)
Brown, John, age 30, 5ft. 9in., dark complex., brown hair, grey
  eyes, Mulberry St., pedlar (Navy)
Brown, John, age 27, 6 years in U.S., 124 Fly Market, tailor (20-
  25 July 1812)
Brown, John, 5ft. 5in., age 25, dark complex., brown hair, hazel
  eyes,Burling Slip, tailor (Navy)
Brown, John, age 24, 5 years & 3 mos. in U.S., Bethel, Sullivan
  Co., farmer, applied June 1810 (31 Aug. & 19-24 Oct. 1812)
Brown, John, 5ft. 5in., age 17, light complex., sandy hair, blue
  eyes, gardener (Navy)
Brown, Joseph, age 42, 10 years in U.S., wife & 3 children, la-
  borer (28 July - 2 Aug. 1812)
Brown, Mathew, 5ft. 11in., age 23, light complex., light hair,
  light eyes, Bowery, gardener (Navy)
Brown, Neal, age 36, 11 years in U.S., Poughkeepsie, Dutchess
  Co., laborer (12-17 Oct. 1812)
Brown, Patrick K., 5ft. 6in., age 29, fair complex., light hair,
  blue eyes, Samuel St., labourer (Navy)
Brown, Robert, age 34, 13 years in U.S., wife & 3 children, Clin-
  ton, Dutchess Co., laborer (12-17 Oct. 1812)
Brown, Robert, age 24, 6 years in U.S., 259 Broadway, merchant
  (20-25 July 1812); 6ft., age 25, fair complex., brown hair,
  blue eyes, dry goods (Navy)
Brown, Robert, age 18, 1 year & 2 mos. in U.S., Bethel, Sullivan
  Co., farmer (31 Aug. & 19-24 Oct. 1812)
Brown, Samuel, age 45, 11 years in U.S., wife & child, Schohary,
  laborer (24-29 Aug. 1812)
Brown, Samuel, 5ft. 7 3/4in., age 35, brown complex., brown hair,
  brown eyes, Broad St., grocer (Navy)
Brown, Samuel, age 30, 5 years in U.S., wife & child, Broad St.,
  grocer (Navy)
Brown, Thomas, 5ft. 8in., age 40, fair complex., dark hair, blue
  eyes, innkeeper (Navy)
Brown, Thomas, age 34, 14 years in U.S., wife & 3 children, 154
  Broadway, stone-setter & jeweller (20-25 July 1812); 5ft. 5in.,
  age 34, fair complex., brown hair, blue eyes, Broadway, engraver (Navy)
Brown, Thomas, 5ft. 7in., age 28, fair complex., dark hair, hazel
  eyes, Rose St., painter (Navy)

Brown, Thomas, age 25, 12 years & 9 mos. in U.S., wife & child,
corner Spring & Mulberry Sts., painter (20-25 July 1812)
Brown, Thomas, 5ft. 5½in., age 25, brown complex., dark hair,
grey eyes, Greenwich St., tailor (Navy)
Brown, Thomas, age 14, 4 mos. in U.S., Bethel, Sullivan Co.,
farmer (31 Aug. & 19-24 Oct. 1812)
Brown, William, age 60, 1 year in U.S., wife & 6 children,
Bethel, Sullivan Co,, weaver (31 Aug. 1812)
Brown, William, age 46, 8 years in U.S., wife & 2 children, 334
Greenwich St., laborer (28 July - 2 Aug. 1812); 5ft. 9in., age
46, pale complex., dark hair, dark eyes, Greenwich St., labou-
rer (Navy)
Brown, William, age 45, 9 years & 2 mos. in U.S., wife & 7 child-
ren, Newburgh, Orange Co., clothier, applied 29 Mar. 1810 (14
Aug. & 17-22 Aug. 1812)
Brown, William, 5ft. 5in., age 35, dark complex., brown hair,
grey eyes, Bancker St. (Navy)
Brown, William, age 32, 2 years in U.S., 3 in family, 42 Barclay
St., mathematician (20-25 July 1812)
Brown, William, 5ft. 9in., age 28, fair complex., brown hair,
blue eyes, weaver (Navy)
Brown, William, age 22, 14 days in U.S., Green St., bricklayer
(21-26 Sept. 1812)
Brown, William, age 18, 4 mos. in U.S., Newburgh, Orange Co.,
weaver (19-24 Oct. 1812)
Brown, William, age __, 1 year in U.S., wife & 6 children, Bethel,
Sullivan Co., weaver (19-24 Oct. 1812
Brown, William, age 16, 1 year & 2 mos. in U.S., Bethel, Sullivan
Co., farmer (19-24 Oct. 1812)
Browne, Edward, age 30, 40 days in U.S., wife & 3 children, 385
Bowery Lane, tobacconist (19-24 Oct. 1812)
Browne, James, age 30, 9 mos. in U.S., 104 Bowery Lane, cotton
weaver (20-25 July 1812)
Browning, William, age 20, 10 years in U.S., 356 Greenwich St.,
iron founder (3-8 Aug. 1812); 5ft. 6in., age 21, light complex.,
light hair, grey eyes, Desbrosses St., iron founder (Navy)
Bruce, Charles, age 54, 8 years in U.S., wife & 4 children, 79
Fair St., baker (31 Aug. - 5 Sept. 1812); 5ft. 4½in., age 55,
fair complex., fair hair, blue eyes, Wall St,, baker (Navy)
Bruce, George, 5ft. 7in., age 55, fair complex., grey hair, grey
eyes, looking glass maker (Navy)
Bruce, George, age 52, 8 years in U.S., wife, 156 Broadway, carver
& gilder, applied 27 July 1811 (20-25 July 1812)
Bruce, George, 5ft. 10in., age 40, light complex., light hair,
light eyes, carpenter (Navy)
Bruce, John, 5ft. 9in., age 31, fair complex., brown hair, blue
eyes, baker (Navy)
Bruce, John, 5ft. 9in., age 21, fair complex., brown hair, grey
eyes (Navy)
Bruen, William, age 37, 11 years & 2 mos. in U.S., wife & 2 child-
ren, Montgomery, Orange Co., laborer (19-24 Oct. 1812)
Brunlick, John, age 30, 7 years in U.S., wife & 4 children, 32
Henry St. (20-25 July 1812)
Bryce, Archibald, age 51, 11 years in U.S., wife & 3 children,
Mayfield, Montgomery Co., farmer (15 Sept. - 5 Oct. & 5-10 Oct.
1812)
Bryce, James, age 55, 22 years in U.S., wife & 8 children, Scipio,
Cayuga Co., farmer (14-19 Sept. & 28 Sept. - 3 Oct. 1812)
Bryers, William, age 30, 4 years in U.S., Angelica, Allegany Co.,
farmer (14 Sept. 1812)
Bryon, John, 5ft. 4in., age 20, dark complex., black hair, blue
eyes, Greenwich St., dyer (Navy)
Buchall, C., age 44, 1 mo. in U.S., 53 Nassau St., engraver (20-
25 July 1812)

Buchanan, James, 5ft. 8in., age 44, light complex., grey hair,
brown eyes, Greenwich St., sawyer (Navy)
Buchannan, Hugh, age 45, 11 years in U.S., wife & 4 children,
Montgomery, Orange Co., farmer (19-24 Oct. 1812)
Buchannan, James, age 40, 10 years in U.S., 420 Greenwich St.,
carpenter (20-25 July 1812)
Buckley, Richard, 5ft. 10in., age 25, sallow complex., blue eyes,
gardener(Navy)
Buckley, William, 5ft. 11in., age 33, fair complex., fair hair,
grey eyes, Lombardy St., weaver (Navy)
Bud, Joseph, age 27, 1 year in U.S., Scipio, Cayuga Co., farmer
(21-26 Sept. 1812)
Bud, Robert, age 51, 16 years in U.S., wife & 7 children, Gov.
Clinton's place at 3 Greenwich St., manufacturer of paper (13-
18 July 1812)
Bull, Samuel, 5ft. 8in., age 71, light complex., light hair,
light eyes, Greenwich St., glass cutter (Navy)
Bull, William, 5ft. 8in., age 33, light complex., black hair,
dark eyes, Cedar St., harness maker (Navy)
Bullen, Henry, 6ft., age 35, dark complex., black hair, brown
eyes, bricklayer (Navy)
Bullenger, Charles, 5ft. 6in., age 22, dark complex., dark hair,
dark eyes, servant (Navy)
Bullock, George, age 30, 9 years in U.S., 28 Nassau St., saddler
(20-25 July 1812); 5ft. 8in, age 30, brown complex., brown hair,
grey eyes, saddler (Navy)
Bulmer, Thomas, age 21, 1 year & 10 mos. in U.S., Newburgh,
Orange Co., hatter (14 & 17-22 Aug. 1812); 5ft. 9in., age 22,
light complex., dark hair, blue eyes, Greenwich St., hatter
(Navy)
Bumford, Edmond, 5ft. 8in., age 31, black complex., black hair,
blue eyes, Brooklyn, carpenter (Navy)
Bunsaken, Samuel, age 45, 9 years in U.S., Phoenix Coffee House
(13-18 July 1812)
Burchell, Charles, 5ft. 3in., age 42, light complex., light hair,
grey eyes, engineer (Navy)
Burck, Edward, 5ft. 5in., age 29, light complex., light hair,
blue eyes, labourer (Navy)
Burford, Joseph, age 54, 8 years in U.S., wife, sister & 1 servant, 15 Murray St., grocer (13-18 July 1812); 5ft. 7in., age
55, light complex., grey hair, blue eyes, Warren St., grocer
(Navy)
Burgess, William, age 23, 6 years in U.S., clerk (20-25 July
1812); 6ft. 1½in., age 24, dark complex., black hair, blue
eyes, Greenwich St., clerk (Navy)
Burk, Jeremiah, 5ft. 11in., age 26, dark complex., brown hair,
blue eyes, Water St., servant (Navy)
Burk, John, 5ft. 6in., age 40, dark complex., black hair, hazel
eyes, Front St., porter house (Navy)
Burk, John, 5ft. 7in., age 28, dark complex., brown hair, grey
eyes, ferryman (Navy)
Burk, Martin, 5ft. 9in., age 21, florid complex., dark hair,
blue eyes, Sugar Loaf St., servant (Navy)
Burk, Patrick, age 30, 11 years in U.S., 4 in family, 161 Bancker
St., cooper (20-25 July 1315)
Burk, Robert, 5ft. 8½in., age 21, fair complex., dark hair, grey
eyes, farmer (Navy)
Burke, David, age 30, 9 years in U.S., 42 Cross St., laborer (20-
25 July 1812)
Burke, John, age 33, 4 years in U.S., wife & child, NYC, servant
(3-8 Aug. 1812)
Burne, John, age 22, 6 years in U.S., 96 Anthony St., mason (28
July - 2 Aug. 1812)
Burneson, Andrew, age 44, 10 years in U.S., 15 Chatham St., dealer
or pedlar (7-19 Dec. 1812)

Burnett, Patrick, 5ft. 8in., age 50, dark complex., grey eyes,
  labourer (Navy)
Burnett, Reuben, age 34, 4 years & 10 mos. in U.S., wife, Manlius,
  Onondaga Co., brewer & maltster (21-26 Sept. 1812)   -
Burnett, Samuel, age 15, 9 years in U.S., corner Barclay & Green-
  wich Sts., clerk (28 July - 2 Aug. 1812)
Burns, Andrew, 5ft. 10 in., age 25, dark complex., dark hair,
  brown eyes, Broadway, clerk (Navy)
Burns, Barney, 5ft. 4in., age 47, fair complex., brown hair,
  brown eyes, labourer (Navy)
Burns, Edward, 5ft. 6in., age 30, light complex., brown hair,
  blue eyes, Pell St., coachman (Navy)
Burns, James, age 46, 19 years in U.S., wife & 7 children, Aurelius, Cayuga Co., mason (12-17 & 26-31 Oct. 1812)
Burns, James, 5ft. 9in., age 46, fair complex., grey hair, black
  eyes, Budd & Harrison Sts., mason (Navy)
Burns, John, 5ft. 6in., age 23, dark complex., black hair, brown
  eyes, Anthony St., bricklayer (Navy)
Burns, Joseph, age 34, 1 year in U.S., 33 Bancker St., card
  maker (20-25 July 1812)
Burns, Kinsey, age 32, 3 years in U.S., 61 Pine St., merchant
  (3-8 Aug. 1812)
Burns, Martin, 5ft. 6in., age 32, fair complex., sandy hair,
  blue eyes, labourer (Navy)
Burns, Martin, 5ft. 10in., age 30, fair complex., brown hair,
  grey eyes, labourer (Navy)
Burns, Michael, 5ft. 4in., age 20, dark complex., dark hair,
  grey eyes, State St., servant (Navy)
Burns, Patrick, 5ft. 8in., age 47, light complex., dark hair,
  blue eyes, cartman (Navy)
Burns, Patrick, 5ft. 5in., age 22, light complex., brown hair,
  blue eyes, Cliff St., currier (Navy)
Burns, Patrick, 5ft. 8in., age 22, fair complex., brown hair,
  black eyes, hostler (Navy)
Burns, Robert, age 22, 7 mos. in U.S., Bowery Lane, weaver of
  cotton (3-8 Aug. 1812)
Burns, Robert, 5ft. 8½in., age 22, dark complex., dark hair,
  blue eyes, Manhattan, apprentice (Navy)
Burns, Thomas, 5ft. 8in., age 46, fair complex., brown hair,
  grey eyes, labourer (Navy)
Burnside, Samuel, age 23, 13 years in U.S., 3 in family, Livonia,
  Livingston Co., farmer (25 Oct.- 15 Nov. 1812)
Burnson, James, age 26, 1 year & 11 mos. in U.S., wife & 2 child-
  ren, Shawangunk, Ulster Co., farmer (19-24 Oct. 1812)
Burr, Matthew, age 17, 1 year in U.S., 30 Pine St., baker (20-
  25 July 1812)
Burrow, William, age 47, 15 years in U.S., 10 in family, Avon,
  Ontario Co., shoemaker (5-15 & 24-29 Aug. 1812)
Burties, Jacob, age 26, 6 years & 4 mos. in U.S., Newburgh, Orange
  Co., tailor (17-22 Aug. 1812)
Burton, John, age 50, 27 years in U.S., 4 children, Schoharie,
  Schoharie Co., weaver (24-29 Aug. 1812)
Burton, John, 5ft. 9in., age 25, dark complex., dark hair, grey
  eyes, Domonick St., thread maker (Navy)
Burton, Joseph, age 55, 9 years in U.S., wife, City of Albany,
  painter (17-22 Aug. 1812)
Burton, Thomas, 5ft. 10in., age 28, dark complex., dark hair,
  dark eyes, Reed St., mason (Nqvy)
Burtrand, Andrew, 5ft. 8in., age 36, dark complex., brown hair,
  grey eyes, Augustus St., tanner (Navy)
Busby, Mathew, age 24, 5 years in U.S., Montgcmery, Orange Co.,
  laborer (19-24 Oct. 1812)
Bush, David, 5ft. 10in., age 27, fair complex., fair hair, brown
  eyes, labourer (Navy)

Butler, James, age 39, wife & child, 130 Fly Market (13-18 July 1812)

Butler, James, 5ft. 9in., age 41, fair complex., brown hair, hazel eyes, Park St., tavern (Navy)

Butler, James, age 30, 1 year & 10 mos. in U.S., brother, wife & daughter, Pearl St., Albany (28 July - 2 Aug. 1812).

Butler, Nicholas, 5ft. 6in., age 36, fair complex., brown hair, blue eyes, labourer (Navy)

Butler, William, 5ft. 7in., age 29, fair complex., brown hair, brown eyes, New St., bootmaker (Navy)

Butt, John, age 32, 4 mos. in U.S., wife & 6 children, 11 Nassau St., merchant (21 Dec. 1812 - 23 Jan. 1813)

Butt, William, age 51, wife & 3 children, NYC, coachman (3-8 Aug. 1812)

Butterworth, John, age 61, 28 years in U.S., Guilderland, Albany Co., farmer (5-10 Oct. 1812)

Buwell, Joseph, 5ft. 8in., age 34, light complex., dark hair, dark eyes, book (Navy)

Buxton, John, age 48, 11 years in U.S., 5 in family, Benton, Ontario Co., farmer (15 Nov. 1812 - 3 Jan. 1813)

Byerly, John, age 24, 3 mos. in U.S., 11 Maiden Lane, gentleman (28 July - 2 Aug. 1812)

Byers, James, 5ft. 8in., age 22, light complex., light hair, blue eyes, Elizabeth St., pedler (Navy)

Byers, William, age 30, 4 years in U.S., Angelica, Allegany Co., farmer (21-26 Sept. 1812)

Byran, James, 5ft. 6in., age 23, light complex., black hair, black eyes, hatter (Navy)

Byrd, John, age 25, 16 years in U.S., wife & 2 children, Manhattanville, manufacturer (14-19 Sept. 1812)

Byrne, Charles, age 21, 1 year in U.S., Palatine, Montgomery Co., merchant(26-31 Oct. 1812 & 17-22 Aug. 1812); age 22, 15 mos. in U.S. (11-17 Aug. 1812)

Byrne, James, 5ft. 8in., age 35, light complex., sandy hair, brown eyes, labourer (Navy)

Byrne, James, age 26, 1 year in U.S., Grand St., carpenter (28 July - 2 Aug. 1812)

Byrne, John, age 48, 1 year in U.S. on 14 May last, wife & 3 children, Eaton, Madison Co., farmer (31 Oct. & 30 Nov. - 5 Dec. 1812)

Byrne, John, 5ft. 9in., age 35, dark complex., black hair, blue eyes, Courtland St., servant (Navy)

Byrne, John, 5ft. 6in., age 28, dark complex., dark hair, blue eyes, Mulberry St., weaver (Navy)

Byrne, John, 5ft. 3 in., age 27, light complex., red hair, blue eyes, Bloomingdale, schoolmaster (Navy)

Byrne, John, 5ft. 6in., age 25, pale complex., fair hair, blue eyes, Anthony St., mason (Navy)

Byrne, Roger M., age 27, 4½ years in U.S., 51 Pine St., physician (28 July - 2 Aug. 1812); 5ft. 9in., age 27, fair complex., light hair, blue eyes, physician (Navy)

Byrne, William, age 51, 1 year in U.S., wife & 5 children, Eaton, Madison Co., farmer (30 Nov. - 5 Dec. 1812); in U.S. since 19 Oct. last, age 51 last July (31 Oct. 1812)

Byrne, William, 5ft. 7in., age 23, dark complex., dark hair, blue eyes, Mott St., weaver (Navy)

Byrns, James, 5ft. 11in., age 27, dark complex., dark hair, grey eyes, carpenter (Navy)

Byrns, John, age 57, 17 years in U.S., Schenectady, weaver (14-19 Sept. 1812)

Cade, Thomas, age 29, 11 years & 3 mos. in U.S., wife & 2 children, Poughkeepsie, Dutchess Co., laborer (12-17 Oct, 1812)

Cadman, Robert, age 38, 17 years in U.S., 2 in family, NYC, cutler (20-25 July 1812)

80   NEW YORK

Caggill, George, 5ft. 6in., age 31, dark complex., dark hair,
  grey eyes, removed from NYC to Fishkill, Dutchess Co. (Navy)
Caherty, Charles, age 25, 2 years in U.S., 38 East George St.,
  grocer (1812)
Caherty, Charles, 5ft. 6in., age 23, fair complex., fair hair,
  grey eyes, Bancker St., grocer (Navy)
Cahill, Patrick, 5ft. 8in., age 22, fair complex., brown hair,
  grey eyes, Wall St., waiter (Navy)
Cahoon, Robert, age 26, 7 years in U.S., wife, 44 Thomas St.,
  marble cutter (28 July - 2 Aug. 1812)
Cain, George, 5ft. 11in., age 32, dark complex., dark hair, hazel
  eyes, Elizabeth St., clerk (Navy)
Cain, Henry, age 32, 1 year & 9 mos. in U.S., wife & 5 children,
  Kingston, Ulster Co., weaver (19-24 Oct. 1812)
Cain, James, age 30, 1 year & 3 mos. in U.S., wife & child, Kings-
  ton, Ulster Co., weaver (19-24 Oct. 1812)
Cain, John, age 44, 1 year & 10 mos. in U.S., wife & 3 children,
  Kingston, Ulster Co., weaver (19-24 Oct. & 7 Sept. 1812)
Cain, Percival, age 19, 8 years in U.S., Goshen, Orange Co.,
  laborer (19-24 Oct. 1812)
Caine, Henry, 5ft. 8in., age 52, light complex., light hair,
  blue eyes, Gouverneur St., ship carpenter (Navy)
Cairns, John, age 36, 11 years in U.S., 376 Greenwich St., saw-
  yer (20-25 July 1812)
Cairns, William, age 48, 11 years in U.S., wife & 4 children,
  Newburgh, Orange Co., farmer (19-24 Oct. 1812)
Cairns, William, age 25, 7 years in U.S., 40 Broadway, merchant,
  applied 3 May 1809 (20-25 July 1812)
Cairns, William, 5ft. 6in., age 24, light complex., dark hair,
  blue eyes, removed from NYC (Navy)
Cakron (?), Robert, 5ft. 6in., age 26, dark complex., dark hair,
  dark eyes, Thomas St., stone cutter (Navy)
Calan/Callam, Henry, age 26, 2 years in U.S., 125 Cherry St.,
  druggist (13-18 July 1812); 5ft. 6in., age 27, dark complex.,
  dark hair, dark eyes, Cherry St., apothecary (Navy)
Calder, James, age 36, 11 years in U.S., 3 mile stone, gardener
  (28 July 2 Aug. 1812)
Calder, Thomas, age 37, 12 years in U.S., wife & 2 children,
  Goshen, Orange Co., laborer (19-24 Oct. 1812)
Caldwell, Adam, 5ft. 7in., age 20, dark complex., dark hair, dark
  eyes, carpenter (Navy)
Caldwell, Cornelius, age 42, 7 years in U.S., wife & 4 children,
  429 Pearl St., merchant (20-25 July 1812)
Caldwell, Ebenezer, 5ft. 8½in., age 21, fair complex., brown
  hair, hazel eyes, Pearl St., clerk (Navy)
Caldwell, James, age 37, 10 mos. in U.S., wife, 126 Water St.,
  umbrella maker (20-25 July 1812); 5ft. 8½in., age 38, fair
  complex., brown hair, grey eyes, Pearl St., umbrella (Navy)
Caldwell, James, age 28, 5 years in U.S., wife & 4 children,
  Wallkill, Orange Co., farmer (19-24 Oct. 1812)
Caldwell, Moore, age 20, 10 years in U.S., 6 in family, corner
  Third & Rivington Sts., grocer (20-25 July 1812)
Caldwell, Thomas E., age 24, 15 years in U.S., wife, Newburgh,
  Orange Co., laborer (19-24 Oct. 1812)
Calhoon, John, 5ft. 7in., age 31, dark complex., brown hair,
  dark eyes, Anthony St., stone cutter (Navy)
Calhoon, John, age 28, 7 years in U.S., 2 in family, 422 Pearl
  St., cotton store keeper (20-25 July 1812)
Calkrun (?), James, 5ft. 6in., age 28, fair complex., dark hair,
  blue eyes, Orange St., morocco (dresser?) (Navy)
Callaghan, Barnard, 5ft. 8in., age 30, fair complex., brown hair,
  brown eyes, labourer (Navy)
Callaghan, Charles, age 23, 1 year in U.S., wife & 2 children,
  NYC, servant (28 July - 2 Aug. 1812)

Callam, John, 5ft. 6in., age 25, fair complex., brown hair, ha-
zel eyes, Rose St., baker (Navy)
Callauger, Bartley, age 27, 10 years in U.S., 35 Duane St., la-
borer (28 July - 2 Aug. 1312)
Calloway, Arthur, age 30, 2 years in U.S., wife & 4 children,
32 Orange St., gold beater, applied 22 June 1812 (20-25 July
1812); 5ft. 7in., age 31, dark complex., dark hair, brown eyes,
Bowery, gold beater (Navy)
Calloway, Jacob, age 28, 3 mos. in U.S., wife & child, corner
Mott & Pell Sts., gold beater, applied 29 June 1812 (20-25
July 1812); 5ft. 9in., age 30, light complex., sandy hair,
grey eyes, Stuyvesant St., gold beater (Navy)
Cambell, Daniel, 5ft. 6in., age 22, fair complex., dark hair,
blue eyes, cooper (Navy)
Cameron, Angus, age 39, 11 years in U.S., wife & 4 children,
Mayfield, Montgomery Co., farmer (11-17 & 17-22 Aug. 1812)
Cameron, Daniel, age 40, 4 years in U.S., City of Albany, mer-
chant, applied 6 Aug. 1812 (17-22 Aug. 1812)
Cameron, Daniel, age 32 last May, 11 years in U.S. on 17 July
1812, wife & 2 children, Deerfield, Oneida Co., farmer (26
Aug. & 28 Sept. - 3 Oct. 1812)
Cameron, Duncan, age 49, 6 years in U.S., wife & 3 (8 in one
ref.) children, Broadalbin, Montgomery Co., farmer (18-24 Aug.
& 31 Aug. - 5 Sept. 1812)
Cameron, Duncan, age 39 May last, 27 years in U.S., wife & 3
children, Thurman, Washington Co., farmer & supervisor of town
of Thurman (24 Nov. 1812 & 21 Dec. 1812- 23 Jan. 1813)
Cameron, Duncan, age 30, 7 years in U.S., wife & 4 children,
Galway, Saratoga Co., laborer (31 Aug. - 5 Sept. 1812)
Cameron, Ewen, age 72, 7 years in U.S., Bath, Steuben Co. (25-31
Aug. & 31 Aug. - 5 Sept. & 7-12 Sept. 1812)
Cameron, Hugh, age 24, 4 mos. in U.S., Caledonia, Livingston Co.,
farmer (5-15 & 24-29 Aug. 1812)
Cameron, James, age 48, 11 years in U.S., wife & 6 children,
Smithfield, Madison Co., farmer (1 Aug. & 10-15 Aug. 1812)
Cameron, James C., age 34, 27 years in U.S. in May last, Thurman,
Washington Co., farmer (24 Nov. 1812 & 21 Dec. 1812 - 23 Jan.
1813)
Cameron, James, J., age 31 on 25 Jan. next, 27 years in U.S. in
Sept. last, wife & 3 children, Thurman, Washington Co., far-
mer (24 Nov. 1812 & 21 Dec. 1812 - 23 Jan. 1813)
Cameron, John, age 61, 28 years in U.S., wife & 7 children,
Schenectady, farmer (17-22 Aug. 1812)
Cameron, John, age 61, 28 years in U.S., wife & 10 children,
Broadalbin, Montgomery Co, farmer (15 Sept. - 5 Oct. 1812);
wife & 1 child recorded (5-10 Oct. 1812)
Cameron, John, age 34, 8 years in U.S. 6 in family, Caledonia,
Livingston Co., merchant (5-15 Aug. & 25-29 Aug. 1812)
Cameron, Owen, age 72, 7 years in U.S., Bath, Steuben Co. (24
Aug. 1812); see Cameron, Ewen above.
Cammack, James, 5ft. 6in., age 27, fair complex., fair hair,
blue eyes, Catherine St., shoemaker (Navy)
Cammoran, Michael, 5ft. 8in., age 40, dark complex., brown hair,
hazel eyes, painter (Navy)
Campbell, Alexander, 5ft. 5in., age 22, fair complex., brown
hair, grey eyes, Chapple St., sailmaker (Navy)
Campbell, Archibald, age 35, 14 years in U.S., wife & 3 child-
ren, 103 Lombard St., shipwright (13-18 July 1812); 5ft. 7in.,
light complex., light hair, light eyes (Navy)
Campbell, Archibald, age c. 27, c. 6 years in U.S., Geauga Co.,
Ohio, merchant (31 Oct. & 30 Nov. - 5 Dec. 1812)
Campbell, Charles, age 20, 3 mos. in U.S., 121 Chamber St., tai-
lor; 5ft. 6in., age 21, dark complex., dark hair, dark eyes,
Greenwich St., tailor (3-8 Aug. 1812 & Navy)

Campbell, D., age 56, 26 years in U.S., wife & 4 servants, Staten
Island, farmer (20-25 July 1812); probably Donald Campbell, a
half pay British officer, 5ft. 9in., age 56, fair complex.,
dark hair, blue eyes, removed from NYC to Fishkill, Dutchess
Co. (Navy)

Campbell, Daniel, age 38, 12 years in U.S., 16 Broadway, merchant (3-8 Aug. 1812)

Campbell, Duncan, age 37, in U.S. since 1 Aug. 1812, Manlius,
Onondaga Co,, scene painter (16-25 Nov. & 30 Nov. - 5 Dec.
1812)

Campbell, Edward, physician, removed from NYC to Schenectady
(Navy)

Campbell, Hugh, age 31, 250 Broadway, laborer (28 July - 2 Aug.
1812)

Campbell, James, age 18, 42 days in U.S., Montgomery, Orange Co.,
laborer (19-24 Oct. 1812)

Campbell, John, 5ft. 6in., age 41, dark complex., brown hair,
blue eyes, labourer (Navy)

Campbell, John, age 33, 9 years & 11 mos. in U.S., wife & 2
children, Mamakating, Ulster Co., cooper (19-24 Oct. 1812)

Campbell, John, 5ft. 8in., age 31, dark complex., dark hair,
grey eyes, wheelwright (Navy)

Campbell, John, 5ft. 7in., age 30, dark complex., dark hair,
grey eyes, Spring St., sawyer (Navy)

Campbell, John, age 26, 11 years in U.S., wife, Wallkill, Orange
Co., cooper (19-24 Oct. 1812)

Campbell, John, age 21, 16 mos. in U.S., Broadalbin, Montgomery
Co., tailor (6 Oct. - 4 Nov. & 9-14 Nov. 1812)

Campbell, John, age 19, 2 years in U.S., NYC, clerk (20-25 July
1812); 5ft. 7in., age 20, fair complex., dark hair, dark eyes,
Liberty St., clerk (Navy)

Campbell, Malcolm, age 31 on 10 Sept. next, 5 years in U.S. on
13 Sept. next, wife & 5 children, Russia, Herkimer Co., farmer,
from Argyle, Scotland (29 Sept. & 28 Sept. - 3 Oct. 1812)

Campbell, Nicholas, age 33, 8 years & 10 mos. in U.S., 2 children, 13 Hague St., NYC, cooper (20-25 July 1812); 5ft. 8in.,
age 33, fair complex., grey hair, blue eyes, James St., cooper
(Navy)

Campbell, Peter, age 31, 6 years in U.S., wife & 3 children,
Broadalbin, Montgomery Co., farmer (21-26 Sept. 1812)

Campbell, Peter, 5ft. 6in., age 20, light complex., light hair,
blue eyes, stone cutter (Navy)

Campbell, Philip, 5ft. 9in., age 30, dark complex., dark hair,
brown eyes, labourer (Navy)

Campbell, Robert, 5ft. 8in., age 21, light complex., dark hair,
brown eyes, Dover St., blacksmith (Navy)

Campbell, Thomas, age 30, 7 years in U.S., Greenwich Lane, farmer (10-15 Aug. 1812)

Campbell, William, age 32, 11 years in U.S., Chatham St., carpenter (20-25 July 1812); 5ft. 5in., age 32, dark complex.,
dark hair, brown eyes, Catherine St,, carpenter (Navy)

Campbell, William, age 18, 1 year & 4 mos. in U.S., 197 Broadway, clerk (13-18 July 1812)

Campble, John, age 29, 9 years in U.S., wife, Desbrosses St.,
sawyer (20-25 July 1812); see Campbell, John, above.

Campzlan (?). J.H., age 21, 2 mos. in U.S., 94 Pearl St., wheelwright (last word, wheelwright, crossed out) (20-25 July 1812)

Canchran, Alex., age 47, 8 years in U.S., 11 in family, Chautau-
qua Co., farmer (15 Nov. 1812 - 3 Jan. 1813)

Cane, William, 6ft., age 26, light complex., brown hair, brown
eyes, Harrison St., distiller (Navy)

Canlin, Michael, age 21, 7 years in U.S., NYC, cooper (20-25
July 1812)

Cannin, John, 5ft. 6in., age 21, light complex., black hair,
blue eyes, Greenwich St., dyer (Navy)

Cannon, John, 6ft. 1½in., age 31, light complex., sandy hair,
blue eyes, Bowery, cartman (Navy)
Cannon, Michael, 5ft. 7in., age 51, dark complex., dark hair,
dark eyes, Catherine Lane, labourer (Navy)
Cannon, Robert, 5ft. 7½in., age 30, dark complex., dark hair,
blue eyes, Bancker St., painter (Navy)
Canonon (?), Patrick, age 23, 1 year & 1 mo. in U.S., Goshen,
Orange Co., laborer (19-24 Oct. 1812)
Canott (?), Christopher, 5ft. 7in., age 45. dark complex., dark
hair, grey eyes, Broadway, waiter (Navy)
Canuck, James, age 26, 11 years in U.S., wife & child, corner
Pump & Orange Sts., shoemaker (28 July - 2 Aug. 1812)
Cardinn, George, 5ft. 11in., age 36, brown complex., brown hair,
blue eyes, Washington St., gun flint (Navy)
Carew, Edward, age 30, 10 years in U.S., New Paltz, Ulster Co.,
laborer (19-24 Oct. 1812)
Carlan, Alexander, 5ft. 10in., age 29, fair complex., brown hair,
blue eyes, North Moore St., cartman (Navy)
Carlin, Francis M., 5ft. 6in., age 48, dark complex., grey hair,
blue eyes, laborer (Navy)
Carlin, Henry, age 21, 1 year & 1 mo. in U.S., 64 Cedar St.,
laborer (3-8 Aug. 1812)
Carlin, William, 5ft. 9in., age 24, light complex., brown hair,
black eyes, 124 Water St., grocer (Navy)
Carlisle, John, age 15, 2 mos. in U.S., 124 Water St., NYC (20-
25 July 1812)
Carlisle, Samuel, age 48, 17 years in U.S., wife & 5 children,
Galway, Saratoga Co., mason (31 Aug. - 5 Sept. 1812)
Carlisle, Samuel, age 26, 12 years & 3 mos. in U.S., wife & 3
children, Newburgh, Orange Co., carpenter (14 Aug. 1812 & 17-
22 Aug. 1812)
Carlisle, William, age 24, 6 years in U.S., 124 Water St., gro-
cer (20-25 July 1812)
Carlow, Alexander, age 28, 6 years in U.S., wife & 2 children,
North Moore St., NYC, cartman (28 July - 2 Aug. 1812)
Carman, Thomas H., age 19, 5 years in U.S., 31 Hudson St., clerk
(20-25 July 1812); 5ft. 8in., age 20, dark complex., black
hair, brown eyes, Chatham St., clerk, removed to Fishkill in
Dutchess Co. (Navy)
Carne, Henry, age 50, 7 years in U.S., wife & 2 children,Gouver-
neur St., ship chandler (20-25 July 1812)
Carner (or Cainer?), Neal, 5ft. 7in., age 27, light complex.,
dark hair, blue eyes, Liberty St., blacksmith (Navy)
Carnes, William, 5ft. 11in., age 24, light complex., brown hair,
blue eyes, removed from NYC to Dutchess & Columbia (Navy)
Carney, Charles, 5ft. 8in., age 25, light complex., black hair,
blue eyes, labourer (Navy)
Carney, John, age 30, 7 years in U.S., Minisink, Orange Co., la-
borer (19-24 Oct. 1812)
Carr, Daniel, 5ft. 6in., age 28, dark complex., dark hair, black
eyes, Ann St., tailor (Navy)
Carr, George, age 32, 7 years & 6 mos. in U.S., 5 in family,
Elizabeth St., NYC, clerk (20-25 July 1812)
Carr, Henry, 5ft. 9in., age 27, dark complex., black hair, brown
eyes, Catherine Lane, labourer (Navy)
Carr, Henry William, age 26, 6 weeks in U.S., NYC, bootmaker (9-
14 Nov. 1812)
Carr, John, 5ft. 9in., age 27, fair complrx., dark hair, grey
eyes, Harman St., bootmaker (Navy)
Carr, John, 5ft. 8½in., age 24, light complex., dark hair, light
eyes, Cherry St., carpenter (Navy)
Carr, Joseph, 5ft. 11in., age 25, light complex., dark hair,
brown eyes, sawyer (Navy)
Carr, Morgan, 5ft. 5in., age 35, fair complex., brown hair,
black eyes, Catherine Lane, labourer (Navy)

Carrel, Dennis, age 31, 11 years in U.S., Monroe Works, Orange
    Co., cut nailer (17-22 Aug. 1812)
Carrew (or Cancer?), Andrew, 5ft. 8in., age 20, dark complex.,
    brown hair, grey eyes, Attorney St., labourer (Navy)
Carrigan, William, age 43, 1 year & 10 mos. in U.S., wife & 5
    children, weaver (19-24 Oct. 1812)
Carrigon, Neal, age 30, 9 years in U.S., Clinton, Dutchess Co.,
    laborer (12-17 Oct. 1812)
Carroll, Charles, age 20, 17 years in U.S., Poughkeepsie, Dut-
    chess Co., potter (12-17 Oct. 1812)
Carroll, Christopher, age 38, 1 mo. in U.S., Amboy, N.J., ser-
    vant, applied 18 June 1812 (20-25 July 1812)
Carroll, Dennis, 6ft., age 25, fair complex., brown hair, grey
    eyes, 4 Mile Stone, Gospel preacher (Navy)
Carroll, Edward, 5ft. 6in., age 24, fair complex., fair hair,
    brown eyes, stone cutter (Navy)
Carroll, John, 5ft. 8in., age 25, brown complex., brown hair,
    brown eyes, labourer (Navy)
Carroll, John, 5ft. 3in., age 20, dark complex., dark hair,
    black eyes, Cherry St., ship carpenter (Navy)
Carroll, John S., age 31, 8 years in U.S., wife & 3 children,
    42 Barclay St., fife major N.Y. Artillery (20-25 July 1812);
    6ft. 1in., age 31, light complex., brown hair, blue eyes, fife
    major (Navy)
Carroll, Lawrence, 5ft. 5in., age 33, dark complex., dark hair,
    dark eyes, mariner (Navy)
Carroll, Matthew, age 28, 9 years & 8 mos. in U.S., 23 Ferry St.,
    trader & accountant, applied 13 Apr. 1812 (20-25 July 1812);
    Carroll, Mathew, 5ft. 10in., age 29, fair complex., dark hair,
    blue eyes, book (Navy)
Carroll, Patrick, age 26, 2 years in U.S., wife & child, 26 Skin-
    ner St., carpenter (20-25 July 1812)
Carroll, Peter, 5ft. 10in., age 35, dark complex., black hair,
    grey eyes, cartman (Navy)
Carroll, Thomas, 5ft. 7½in., age 26, fair complex., brown hair,
    blue eyes, painter (Navy)
Carse, William, age 26, 1 year & 3 mos. in U.S., 26 Harrison St.,
    distiller (20-25 July 1812)
Carson, James, 5ft. 5in., age 35, dark complex., dark hair, light
    eyes, shoemaker (Navy)
Carson, James, age 34, 9 years in U.S., wife & 6 children, 104
    Chatham St., shoe store keeper, applied 15 Mar. 1810 (20-25
    July 1812)
Carson, John M., 5ft. 4in., age 26, dark complex., dark hair,
    black eyes, Chatham St., shoemaker (Navy)
Carson, Johnson, 5ft. 4in., age 36, light complex., brown hair,
    light eyes, cartman (Navy)
Carson, Samuel, age 48, 16 years in U.S., wife & 8 children,
    Virgil, Cortland Co., farmer (25 Nov. - 7 Dec. & 7-19 Dec.
    1812)
Carson, Thomas, 5ft. 11in., age 19, brown complex., light hair,
    hazel eyes, Grand & Rynder St., servant (Navy)
Carter, J.C., 5ft. 5½in., age 18, fair complex., brown hair,
    grey eyes, clerk (Navy)
Carter, Joseph, 5ft. 7in., age 30, light complex., brown hair,
    dark eyes, Mulberry St., teacher (Navy)
Carter, Thomas, age 51, 7 years & 3 mos. in U.S., wife & 4 child-
    ren, 30 Roosevelt St., shipwright (3-8 Aug. 1812); 5ft. 6in.,
    dark complex., brown hair, grey eyes, Roosevelt St., shipwright
    (Navy)
Carter, William, 5ft. 9in., age 47, dark complex., brown hair,
    grey eyes, Spring St., slater (Navy)
Carven, Owen, 5ft. 5in., age 23, light complex., brown hair,
    grey eyes, labourer (Navy)

Carvertt, John, age 37, 17 years in U.S., wife & 4 children,
  Homer, Cortland Co., farmer (28 Dec. 1812 - 3 Feb. 1813)
Cascaden, Alexander, age 35, 9 years in U.S., 4 children, 33
  Lombard St., cartman (20-25 July 1812)
Case, Dennis, 5ft., age 34, fair complex., black hair, blue eyes,
  labourer (Navy)
Casey, James, age 31, 2 years in U.S., wife & child, 21 Orange
  St., tailor (28 July - 1 Aug. 1812); 5ft. 7in., age 31, dark
  complex., dark hair, blue eyes, Orange St., tailor (Navy)
Casey, Patrick, age 39, 5 years in U.S., carpenter (20-25 July
  1812); 5ft. 7in., age 39, fair complex., black hair, brown
  eyes, Mott St., carpenter (Navy)
Cashman, Charles, age 25, 6 years in U.S., Water St., grocer
  (20-25 July 1812); 5ft. 5¼in., age 26, fair complex., black
  hair, dark eyes, Water St., grocer (Navy)
Cashman, Daniel, age 23, 6 years in U.S., 55 Chatham St., clerk
  (20-25 July 1812); 5ft. 5½in., age 24, fair complex., light
  hair, black eyes, clerk (Navy)
Cassady, Murray, 6ft., age 29, dark complex., black hair, black
  eyes, farmer (Navy)
Cassaly, Owen, 5ft. 7in., age 24, light complex., brown hair,
  blue eyes, Pump St., weaver (Navy)
Cassedy, Andrew, 5ft. 4in., age 40, light complex., brown hair,
  dark eyes, labourer (Navy)
Cassedy, George, age 58, 12 years in U.S., wife & 5 children,
  Montgomery, Orange Co., innkeeper (19-24 Oct. 1812)
Cassedy, George, Jr., age 16, 12 years in U.S., Montgomery,
  Orange Co., innkeeper (19-24 Oct. 1812)
Cassin, Richard, age 24, 2 years in U.S., wife & child, New-
  burgh, Orange Co., laborer (19-24 Oct. 1812)
Caughay, Michael, 5ft. 11in., age 23, dark complex., dark hair,
  blue eyes, Greenwich St., sawyer (Navy)
Cauldwell (see Caldwell), Cornelius, 5ft. 6½in., age 43, light
  complex., brown hair, grey eyes (Navy)
Cauldwell (see Caldwell), Ebenezer, 5ft. 8in., age 21, pale com-
  plex., brown hair, hazel eyes, removed from NYC to Goshen,
  Orange Co. (Navy)
Cavan, William, 5ft. 5in., age 26, fair complex., dark hair,
  brown eyes, Little George St., servant (Navy)
Cavenagh, Bernard, 5ft. 6½in., age 23, fair complex., fair hair,
  blue eyes, Kips Bay, stone cutter (Navy)
Cavenagh, John, 5ft. 7½in., age 30, light complex., brown hair,
  black eyes, labourer (Navy)
Cavenagh, Patrick, 5ft. 5in., age 27, brown complex., fair hair,
  grey eyes, labourer (Navy)
Cavon, John, 5ft. 4in., age 41, light complex., black hair, dark
  eyes, labourer (Navy)
Cavon, Johnson, 5ft. 4in., age 36, light complex., brown hair,
  grey eyes, cartman (Navy)
Cawen, Thomas, age 34, 20 years in U.S., wife & 4 children,
  Scipio, Cayuga Co., farmer (7-12 Sept. 1812)
Cawin, James, 5ft. 4in., age 29, dark complex., dark hair, blue
  eyes, carpenter (Navy)
Chaffey, Richard, age 18, 5 mos. in U.S., City of Albany, clerk
  (17-22 Aug. 1812)
Chalmers, Mathew, age 33, 9 years in U.S., wife & child, Galway,
  Saratoga Co., farmer (31 Aug. - 5 Sept. 1812)
Chalmers, Stewart, age 30, 10 years in U.S., wife & child, Sche-
  nectady, weaver (24-29 Aug. 1812)
Chalmers, William, age 68, 11 years in U.S., wife & 4 children,
  Broadalbin, Montgomery Co., farmer (7-12 Sept. 1812)
Chalmer, William, age 39, 8 years in U.S., wife & 4 children,
  Galway, Saratoga Co., farmer (31 Aug. - 5 Sept. 1812)
Chamberlain, Thomas, age 27, 7 years in U.S., wife & 2 children,
  61 Chapel St., carpenter (20-25 July 1812)

Chambers, David, age 30, 3 years in U.S., wife & 3 children,
City of Albany, laborer (17-22 Aug. 1812)
Chambers, James, 5ft. 7in., age 24, dark complex., dark hair,
blue eyes, grocer (Navy)
Chambers, James T., age 22, 2 years in U.S., 33 Lombard St.,
grocer (20-25 July 1812); James/James T., 5ft. 7in., age 23,
dark complex., brown hair, grey eyes, grocer, removed from
NYC to Goshen, Orange Co. (Navy)
Chambers, John, 5ft. 4½in., age 37, light complex., brown hair,
blue eyes, Bowery, retailer dry goods, removed from NYC to
Goshen, Orange Co. (Navy)
Chambers, John, age 34, 6 years in U.S., wife & 2 children,
Water St., boat builder (20-25 July 1812)
Chambers, William, age 29, 6 years in U.S., wife & child, 26
Second St., boat builder, applied Nov. (13-18 July 1812)
Chambers, William E., 5ft. 11in., dark complex., black hair,
black eyes, Brooklyn, boat builder - perhaps same as the Wil-
liam Chambers above - (Navy)
Chambers, William, 4ft. 1in., age 29, light complex., light hair,
grey eyes, mariner (Navy)
Chandler, James, 5ft. 5in., age 46, light complex., brown hair,
brown eyes, Orange St., sawyer (Navy)
Chandler, Joseph, age 46, 8 years in U.S., 447 Greenwich St.,
sawyer (20-25 July 1812)
Chapman, Charles, 5ft. 9in., age 40, dark complex., dark hair,
brown eyes, Fourth St., teacher (Navy)
Chapman, Joseph, age 52, 7 years in U.S., wife & 3 children, 205
Greenwich St., general store keeper (13-18 July 1812)
Chapman, Joseph, 5ft. 6in., age 53, dark complex., dark hair,
dark eyes, Greenwich St., tailor (Navy)
Chapman, William, age 32 on 5 Oct. next, 2 years in U.S. on 3
Oct. next, wife & 3 children, Whitestown, Oneida Co., cord-
wainer (26 Aug. & 28 Sept. - 3 Oct. 1812)
Chapman, William, age 29, 4 years & 10 mos. in U.S., 18 Broad-
way, merchant, applied 15 Mar. 1811 (20-25 July 1812); 5ft.
6in., age 29, light complex., light hair, grey eyes, removed
from NYC to Fishkill, Dutchess Co. (Navy)
Chappell, Thomas, 5ft. 6in., age 20, fair complex., dark hair,
light eyes, Provoost St., baker (Navy)
Chard, Edward, 5ft. 5½in., age 26, Lombardy St., dark complex.,
dark hair, dark eyes, shipwright (Navy)
Charlmbers, James, age 29, 8 years in U.S., Schenectady, mill-
wright (10-15 Aug. 1812)
Charlton, John, age 30, 11 years in U.S., 2 in family, Seneca,
Ontario Co., farmer (5-15 & 24-29 Aug. 1812)
Charlton, Robert, age 32, 5 years in U.S., wife & child, Orange
St., cartman (28 July - 2 Aug. 1812)
Charnock, Hugh, 5ft. 7in., age 35, dark complex., dark hair,
light eyes, theatrical performer (Navy)
Chavel/Chevelle, George, age 30, 8 years in U.S., 27 James St.,
porterhouse keeper (20-25 July 1812)
Chevelle, George, 5ft. 2in., age 30, fair complex., brown hair,
grey eyes, Fair St., barkeeper (Navy)
Cheesman, William, age 31, 7 years in U.S., wife & 3 children,
5 Charlotte St., sailmaker (21 Dec. 1812 - 23 Jan. 1813)
Cheesman, William, 5ft. 11in., age 30, dark complex., dark hair,
brown eyes, sailmaker (Navy)
Cheetham, James, age 24, 16 years in U.S., wife & 3 children, 8
Canal St., coachmaker (28 July - 2 Aug. 1812)
Cheney, George, 5ft. 8in., age 20, fair complex., dark hair,
dark eyes, Republican Alley, cartman (Navy)
Cheny, Lother, 5ft. 4in., age 18, fair complex., brown hair,
brown eyes, labourer (Navy)
Cherry, Christoper, 5ft. 10in., age 35, fair complex., dark hair,
dark eyes, Republican Alley, cartman (Navy)

Chevin, William, 5ft. 10½in., age 32, light complex., brown hair,
   brown eyes, Harrison St., ship carpenter (Navy)
Chietien (or Chietier), Antoine, age 42, 3 years & 10 mos. in
   U.S., wife & 7 children, Plattsburgh, Clinton Co., carter,
   from Lower Canada (1 Sept. - 1 Oct. & 26-31 Oct. 1812)
Chitlick, Archibald, age 35, 11 years in U.S., wife & 3 child-
   ren, New Paltz, Ulster Co., clothier (19-24 Oct. 1812.)
Christian, Alexander, 5ft. 11in., age 35, dark complex., brown
   hair, grey eyes, Greenwich St., gardener (Navy)
Christian, Mathew, 5ft. 10in., age 35, fair complex., black hair,
   grey eyes, Mulberry St., cartman (Navy)
Christian, Mathias, 5ft. 9in., age 31, brown complex., black
   hair, light eyes, clerk (Navy)
Christian, Matthias, age 30, 7 years & 11 mos. in U.S., wife & 4
   children, 27 Chapel St., auctioneer (13-18 July 1812)
Christian, William, 5ft. 7in., age 25, dark complex., black hair,
   blue eyes, Harman St., labourer (Navy)
Christie, Colin, age 46, in U.S. since 3 July 1802, wife & 5
   children, Mayfield, Montgomery Co., farmer (11-17 & 17-22 Aug.
   1812)
Christie, Duncan, age 26, 8 years in U.S., wife, Johnstown, Montgomery Co., farmer (18-24 Aug. & 31 Aug. - 5 Sept. 1812)
Christie, John, age 30, in U.S. since Oct. 1803, Johnstown, Montgomery Co., farmer (18-24 & 31 Aug. - 5 Sept. 1812)
Christie, Thomas, age 27, 13 years in U.S., wife & child, Shawangunk, Ulster Co., millwright (19-24 Oct. 1812)
Christie, William, age 36, 12 years in U.S., 2 children, New
   Windsor, Orange Co., wire drawer (19-24 Oct. 1812)
Church, George, age 29, 1 year & 4 mos. in U.S., Manlius, Onon-
   daga Co., tallow chandler and soap boiler (12-18 & 21-26 Sept.
   1812)
Church, James, 5ft. 10in., age 24, fair complex., brown hair,
   blue eyes, labourer (Navy)
Church, Robert, 5ft. 8in., age 30, dark complex., brown hair,
   grey eyes, Manhattan I., ship carpenter (Navy)
Churcholm, William, age 30, 16 years in U.S., Schenectady, farmer (24-29 Aug. 1812)
Cire, Michael, 5ft. 5in., age 42, dark complex., dark hair,
   black eyes, baker (Navy)
Clanahan, David, age 22, 3 years in U.S., Newburgh, Orange Co.,
   carpenter (14 & 17-22 Aug. 1812); 5ft. 10in., age 22, black
   complex., dark hair, blue eyes, carpenter (Navy)
Clarey, William, age 34, 28 years in U.S., wife & child, Pala-
   tine, Montgomery Co., farmer (3-14 & 21-26 Sept. 1812)
Clark, Andrew, 5ft. 9in., age 35, fair complex., dark hair, grey
   eyes, Reed St., storekeeper (Navy)
Clark, Andrew, age 34, 2 years & 3 mos. in U.S., wife & child,
   78 Bayard St., baker (7-19 Dec. 1812)
Clark, Cornelius, 5ft. 6in., age 52, dark complex., brown hair,
   grey eyes, Sixth St., mason (Navy)
Clark, Cornelius, age 38, 11 years in U.S., wife & 4 children,
   Catskill, Greene Co., hatter (10-15 Aug. 1812)
Clark, Edward, age 25, 1 year in U.S., Orange Co., laborer (10-
   15 Aug. 1812)
Clark, Edward Hyde, age 16, 1 year in U.S., City of Albany, stu-
   dent, applied 5 Aug. 1811 (17-22 Aug. 1812)
Clark, Edward Robert, age 22, 1 year & 4 mos. in U.S., Claremont,
   Westchester Co., gentleman (20-25 July 1812); 5ft. 8½in., age
   23, dark complex., brown hair, brown eyes, Bloomingdale, gentle-
   man (Navy)
Clark, George, age 48, 7 years in U.S., wife & 3 children, 4 Peck
   slip, hairdresser, applied 16 Apr. 1810 (13-18 July 1812)
Clark, George, age 44, 8 years in U.S., 2 sons & 1 servant, City
   of Albany, superintends property (17-22 Aug. 1812)

Clark, George Hyde, age 17, 1 year in U.S., City of Albany, student, applied 5 Aug. 1811 (17-22 Aug. 1812)

Clark, Henry, age 53, 23 years in U.S., wife & 8 children, Colonie, Albany Co., gardener (17-22 Aug. 1812)

Clark, Hugh, 5ft. 7in., age 36, fair complex., dark hair, brown eyes, gardener (Navy)

Clark, James, age 48, 7 years in U.S., wife & 2 children, NYC, cartman (28 July - 2 Aug. 1812)

Clark, James, age 45, 19 years in U.S., wife & 2 children, Montgomery, Orange Co., farmer (21 Dec. 1812 - 23 Jan. 1813)

Clark, James, age 45, 11 years in U.S., wife & 6 children, Newburgh, Orange Co., tanner (19-24 Oct. 1812)

Clark, James, 5ft. 8in., age 41, fair complex., brown hair, blue eyes, Delancey St., cartman (Navy)

Clark, James, age 34, 8 years in U.S., wife & child, Kingston, Ulster Co., dyer (7 Sept. & 19-24 Oct. 1812)

Clark, James, age 31, 7 years in U.S., wife, 12 Suffolk St., blacksmith, applied 13 Feb. 1812 (14-19 Sept. 1812)

Clark, John, 5ft. 6in., age 35, fair complex., brown hair, black eyes, Wall St., soda water (Navy)

Clark, John, age 30, 5 years & 9 mos. in U.S., Cornwall, Orange Co., farmer (19-24 Oct. 1812)

Clark, John, 4 years & 8 mos. in U.S., 82 Broadway, shoemaker (28 July - 2 Aug. 1812); 5ft. 8in., age 20, dark complex., dark hair, grey eyes, shoemaker (Navy)

Clark, Nathan, 5ft. 8in., age 26, light complex., brown hair, light eyes, Yonkers, gardener (Navy)

Clark, Smyth/Smith, age 27, 1 year & 8 mos. in U.S., 439 Greenwich St., weaver (28 July - 2 Aug. 1812); 5ft. 8in., age 28, light complex., dark hair, blue eyes, Greenwich St., weaver (Navy)

Clark, Terrence, age 23, 4 years in U.S., coachman (5-10 Oct. 1812)

Clark, William, age 37, 11 years in U.S., wife & 6 children, Newburgh, Orange Co., farmer (19-24 Oct. 1812)

Clarke, John, age 35, 6 years in U.S., wife & child, 3 Broad St., NYC, grocer (28 July - 2 Aug. 1812)

Clarke, Thomas, age 27, 1 mo. in U.S., wife, Brooklyn, L.I. (28 July - 2 Aug. 1812)

Clarkson, David, age 43, 7 years in U.S., 4 in family, Avon, Ontario Co., mason (5-15 & 24-29 Aug. 1812)

Clarkson, John, 5ft. 8in., age 20, fair complex., brown hair, black eyes, Greenwich St., weaver (Navy)

Clarkson, William, age 28, 1 year in U.S., wife, Clinton, Dutchess Co., weaver (12-17 Oct. 1812)

Claydon, Thomas, age 31, 6 years in U.S., City of Albany, servant (17-22 Aug. 1812)

Clayton, Thomas B., age 20, 8 mos. in U.S., Hurley, Ulster Co., miller (19-24 Oct. 1812)

Cleland, Thornton, 5ft. 10in., age 21(or 24?), fair complex., fair hair, blue eyes, Mott & Grand Sts., jeweller (Navy)

Clements, David, age 32, 9 years & 2 mos. in U.S., wife & 2 children, Thompson, Sullivan Co., farmer (19-24 Oct. 1812)

Clements, James, age 38, 9 years & 9 mos. in U.S., 2 children, Partition St. veterinary surgeon (28 July - 2 Aug. 1812); 5ft. 10in., age 38, light complex., brown hair, brown eyes, Partition St., veterinary (Navy)

Clendinning, Archibald, age 30, 4 years in U.S., wife & 2 children, Wallkill, Orange Co., cooper (19-24 Oct. 1812)

Clifton, William, age 54, 19 years in U.S., wife & child, Johnstown, Montgomery Co., farmer (25 Aug.- 2 Sept. & 7-12 Sept. 1812)

Clone, John, 5ft. 8in., age 25, fair complex., sandy hair, blue eyes, labourer (Navy)

Clowney, Robert, age 46, 1 year in U.S., wife & 4 children, Newburgh, Orange Co., weaver (19-24 Oct. 1812)
Clugstan, George, 5ft. 7in., age 25, fair complex., fair hair,
  blue eyes, Greenwich St., weaver (Navy)
Clyde, John, age 24, 8 years in U.S., wife & 2 children, 50 Duane
  St., stone cutter (20-25 July 1812); Clyd, John, 5ft. 7in.,
  age 25, fair complex., fair hair, hazel eyes, Washington St.,
  stone cutter (Navy)
Clyde, William, 5ft. 7in., age 18, fair complex., fair hair,
  blue eyes, stone cutter (Navy)
Coates, Edward, age 31, 9 years in U.S., wife & 4 children, Ba-
  tavia Lane, NYC, mariner (28 July - 2 Aug. 1812)
Coates, James, age 41, 7 years in U.S., 6 in family, Lyons, On-
  tario Co., farmer (31 Aug. - 5 Sept. 1812)
Coats, Edward, 5ft. 5in., age 30, brown complex., dark hair,
  black eyes, Roosevelt St., rigger (Navy)
Coats/Coates, James, Jr., age 14, 7 years in U.S., Lyons, Onta-
  rio Co., farmer (15-22 Aug. & 31 Aug. - 5 Sept. 1812)
Coats, John, Jr., age 39, 10 years in U.S., 6 in family, Geneseo,
  Ontario Co., farmer (6-13 & 21-26 Sept. 1812)
Coburn, Samuel, age 33, 6 years in U.S., Rose Hill, mason (3-8
  Aug. 1812); probably the same - Coburn, Samuel, 5ft. 10½in.,
  age 35, fair complex., light hair, light eyes, Cross Road, ma-
  son (Navy)
Cobut, Frederick, 5ft. 6in., age 64, fair complex., grey hair,
  black eyes, teacher (Navy)
Cochlan, William, age 45, 10 years in U.S., wife & 5 children,
  Bergen, N.J., servant (28 July - 2 Aug. 1812)
Cochran, Daniel, age 28, 13 years in U.S., NYC, distiller (3-8
  Aug. 1812)
Cochran, Henry, age 27, 1 year & 4 mos. in U.S., 40 Cross St.,
  NYC, musician (20-25 July 1812)
Cochran, Michael, age 21, 1 year & 7 mos. in U.S., 143 Washington
  St., NYC, waiter (28 July - 2 Aug. 1812)
Cochran, Robert, 5ft. 8in., age 27, fair complex., brown hair,
  hazel eyes, weaver (Navy)
Cochran, Robert, age 23, 1½ years in U.S., 56 Anthony St., musi-
  cian (20-25 July 1812)
Cochran, Thomas, age 33, 1 year in U.S., wife & 2 children, 363
  Greenwich St., NYC (20-25 July 1812)
Cochran, William, age 26, 1 year & 4 mos. in U.S., 40 Cross St.,
  trader (20-25 July 1812); perhaps the same as above - Cochran,
  William, 5ft. 10 in., age 27, fair complex., fair hair, hazel
  eyes, pedler (Navy)
Cockrane, Thomas, 5ft. 10in., age 24, sandy complex., brown hair,
  dark eyes, Greenwich St., watchmaker (Navy)
Cockrin, Mathew, age 47, 10 years in U.S., 36 Gold St., NYC,
  porter (28 July - 2 Aug. 1812)
Cockrin, Michael, 5ft. 7in., age 47, fair complex., brown hair,
  blue eyes, Gold St., porter (Navy)
Codd, William, age 23, 1 year & 2 mos. in U.S., 382 Pearl St.,
  cabinetmaker (20-25 July 1812); 5ft. 8in., age 24, fair complex.,
  brown hair, dark eyes, cabinetmaker (Navy)
Coen, Owen, 5ft. 5in., age 23, fair complex., brown hair, grey
  eyes, Duane St., labourer (Navy)
Coffee, Andrew, age 21, 11 mos. in U.S., Bethel, Sullivan Co.,
  laborer (19-24 Oct. 1812)
Coffee, James, age 29, 7 years in U.S., wife & 2 children, City
  of Albany, gardener (17-22 Aug. 1812)
Coffeland, Edward, age 22, 7 years in U.S., 14 Greenwich St.,
  NYC, servant (28 July - 2 Aug. 1812)
Coffrey, James, 5ft. 8in., age 36, fair complex., brown hair,
  grey eyes, gardener (Navy)
Coggill, George, age 30, wife & 2 children, corner Broadway &
  Murray Sts., merchant, applied 21 Mar. 1812 (7-12 Sept. 1812)

Coghlan, James, age 39, 3 years in U.S., wife & child, 4 Warren
St., NYC, clerk, applied 22 June 1812 (20-25 July 1812); Cogh-
lin, James, 5ft. 6in., age 39, ruddy complex., fair hair, blue
eyes, Broome St., clerk (Navy)
Cogley, David, 5ft. 9in., age 25, brown complex., brown hair,
blue eyes, turner (Navy)
Coher, Nicholas, 5ft. 7in., age 60, dark complex., grey hair,
grey eyes, Manhattanville, farmer (Navy)
Coher, Peter, age 23, 5 years in U.S., Manhattanville, manufacturer of woolen (31 Aug. -5 Sept. 1812); Coher, Peter, 5ft.
8½in., age 23, dark complex., dark hair, black eyes, Manhattanville, manufacturer (Navy)
Coinighaway, Darby, 5ft. 6in., age 31, dark complex., dark hair,
blue eyes, Anthony St., labourer (Navy)
Colbart/Colbert, Robert, age 54, 12 years in U.S., wife & child,
Bloomingdale, gardener & grocer (20-25 July 1812); 5ft. 7in.,
age 55, dark complex., brown hair, brown eyes, Bloomingdale,
gardener (Navy)
Colden, Thomas, said to be officer in British pay, Montgomery,
Orange Co., has not reported (2 Jan. 1813)
Cole, Charles, age 34, 5 years in U.S., wife & 3 children, Clare-
mont, Westchester Co., laborer (20-25 July 1812)
Cole, Charles, 5ft. 8½in., age 34, fair complex., brown hair,
blue eyes, Stanton St., sawyer (Navy)
Cole, Patrick, age 30, 5 years in U.S., wife, 11 Henry St., NYC,
laborer (7-12 Sept. 1812)
Cole, William, age 30, 3 mos. in U.S., wife & 3 children, Mama-
kating, Ulster Co., farmer (19-24 Oct. 1812)
Coleman, David, 5ft. 10in., age 33, dark complex., dark hair,
hazel eyes, farmer (Navy)
Coleman, James, age 31, 8 years & 6 mos. in U.S., Newburgh,
Orange Co., shoemaker (19-24 Oct. 1812)
Coleman, William, age 31, 5 years in U.S., wife & 3 children,
Norfolk St., NYC, baker (20-25 July 1812); 5ft. 9½in., age 32,
light complex., dark hair, dark eyes, baker (Navy)
Colgin, William, 5ft. 7in., age 31, light complex., brown hair,
blue eyes, Elm St., tanner (Navy)
Colhoun, Joseph, 5ft. 6in., age 20, brown complex., brown hair,
blue eyes, shoemaker (Navy)
Collard, Felix, age 24, 2 mos. in U.S., Newburgh, Orange Co.,
laborer (19-24 Oct. 1812)
Collingwood, Charles, age 29, 8 years in U.S., wife & 2 child-
ren, Elmira, Tioga Co., tailor (26-31 Oct. 1812)
Collins, Bartholomew, age 48, 13 years in U.S., Riverhead, Suf-
folk Co., iron manufacturer (20-25 July 1812)
Collins, Bartholomew, 5ft. 10in., age 44, fair complex., dark
hair, blue eyes, Brooklyn (Navy)
Collins, Henry, 5ft. 8in., age 52, dark complex., brown hair,
blue eyes, blacksmith (Navy)
Collins, James, 5ft. 9in., age 33, light complex., brown hair,
hazel eyes, Jefferson St., painter (Navy)
Collins, James, 5ft. 5in., age 26, dark complex., black hair,
brown eyes, Temple St., labourer (Navy)
Collins, John, age 28, 5 years in U.S., Newburgh, Orange Co.,
laborer (14 Aug. & 17-22 Aug. 1812)
Collins, Patrick, 5ft. 8½in., age 24, fair complex., dark hair,
blue eyes, Brooklyn (Navy)
Collins, William, 5ft. 7in., age 65, dark complex., grey hair,
grey eyes, Jefferson St., glazier (Navy)
Coltro, Benjamin, age 28, 10 years in U.S., wife & 3 children,
Blooming Grove, Orange Co., farmer (21 Dec. 1812 - 23 Jan.
1813 & 2 Jan. 1813)
Con, George, age 37, 21 years in U.S., wife & 4 children, Ovid,
Seneca Co., farmer (28 Sept. - 3 Oct. & 12-17 Oct. 1812)

Concklin, William, 5ft. 10in., age 23, dark complex., brown hair,
dark eyes, Ferry St., tanner (Navy)

Coner (or Coney?), Michael, 5ft. 5in., age 29, dark complex.,
brown hair, blue eyes, Banker St., labourer (Navy)

Conin, Joseph, 5ft. 10in., age 39, light complex., light hair,
grey eyes, Roosevelt St., rigger (Navy)

Connelly, Charles, age 56, 7 years in U.S., 3 in family, 180
William St., NYC, grocer (20-25 July 1812)

Connelly, Charles, 5ft. 6in., age 26, dark complex., brown hair,
brown eyes, Reed & Chapple Sts., grocer (Navy)

Connelly, James, age 38, 8 years in U.S., wife & 2 children, 48
Duane St., laborer (28 July - 2 Aug. 1812)

Connelly, James, 5ft. 8in., age 30, dark complex., brown hair,
blue eyes, labourer (Navy)

Connelly, James, 5ft. 8in., age 24, "o" complex., dark hair,
blue eyes, labourer (Navy)

Connelly, John, age 30, 8 years in U.S., wife, 26 Stone St.,
waterman (20-25 July 1812); 5ft. 5in., age 30, light complex.,
dark hair, grey eyes, boatman (Navy)

Connely, John, 67 Nassau St., NYC, cordwainer (10-15 Aug. 1812)

Connelly, Peter, 5ft. 8in., age 28, dark complex., black hair,
grey eyes (Navy)

Connelly, Walter, 5ft. 8in., age 29, dark complex., brown hair,
dark eyes, Grand St., accountant (Navy)

Connelly, William, age 34, 7 years & 11 mos. in U.S., wife & 2
children, 15 Henry St., NYC, ship-carpenter (28 July - 2 Aug.
1812)

Conning, William, age 43, 17 years in U.S., wife & 4 children,
Wallkill, Orange Co., carpenter (19-24 Oct. 1812)

Connolly, James, 5ft. ½in., age 36 (or 31?), dark complex., brown
hair, brown eyes (or dark eyes?), Duane St., lamplighter (Navy)

Connolly, Patrick, 5ft. 8in., age 48, dark complex., dark hair,
grey eyes, gardener (Navy)

Connolly, William, 5ft. 8in., age 32, fair complex., brown hair,
blue eyes, carpenter (Navy)

Connor, Edward, age 41, 6 years in U.S., Newburgh, Orange Co.,
laborer (19-24 Oct. 1812)

Connor, Jacob, age 50, 11 years in U.S., wife & 6 children, Montgomery, Orange Co., farmer (19-24 Oct. 1812)

Connor, James, age 50 last May, 2 years in U.S. last Sept., 5
children, Eaton, Madison Co., farmer (31 Oct. & 30 Nov. - 5
Dec. 1812)

Connor, Joseph, age 56, 24 years in U.S., wife & 6 children,
Wallkill, Orange Co., weaver (19-24 Oct. 1812)

Conway, Charles, age 23, 1 year & 1 mo. in U.S., Fishkill, Dutchess Co., weaver (12-17 Oct. 1812)

Conway, Patrick, 5ft. 2in., age 50, light complex., grey hair,
blue eyes, Pearl St., labourer (Navy)

Conway, Patrick, age 44, 5 years & 9 mos. in U.S., wife & 6
children, NYC, hatter, applied 10 Apr. 1810 (20-25 July 1812);
probably the same - Conway, Patrick, 5ft. 5in., age 46, light
complex., brown hair, grey eyes, Grand St., hatter (Navy)

Cook, James, 5ft. 5in., age 31, light complex., dark hair, grey
eyes, Jay St., milkman (Navy)

Cook, Thomas, 5ft. 3in., age 34, brown complex., brown hair,
blue eyes, Cherry St., tailor (Navy)

Cook, Thomas, age 28, 4 years in U.S., wife & 2 children, 50
Frankfort St., NYC, merchant, applied 10 Apr. 1812 (20-25 July
1812); Cook, Thomas, 5ft. 8in., age 29, light complex., dark
hair, black eyes, Frankfort St., dealer in glass, (Navy)

Cook, Thomas, 5ft. 8in., age 29, light complex., dark hair, blue
eyes, removed from NYC to Fishkill, Dutchess Co. (Navy)

Cook, William, age 34, 8 years in U.S., wife, 6 children, brother
and sister, 63 James St., carver & gilder (20-25 July 1812); 5
ft. 5in., brown complex. & hair, grey eyes (Navy)

Cooke, Hugh, 5ft. 10in., age 41, "s" complex., sandy hair, grey
eyes, weaver (Navy)
Cooke, James, age 35, 7 years in U.S., wife & child, 14 Jay St.,
NYC, milkman (28 July - 2 Aug. 1812)
Cooke, Thomas, age 33, 4½ years in U.S, wife & 6 children, 183
Cherry St., NYC, tailor (20-25 July 1812) - perhaps the same
as the Thomas Cook, tailor, above.
Cooney, Michael, age 28, 9 years in U.S., wife & 2 children,
Bancker St., NYC, laborer (20-25 July 1812)
Cooper, Allen/Allan, age 37, 1 year in U.S., wife & 4 children,
129 William St., NYC, shoemaker (20-25 July 1812); 5ft. 8in.,
age 37, dark complex., black hair, blue eyes, William St.,
shoemaker (Navy)
Cooper, Benjamin, 5ft. 5 3/4in., age 33, light complex., brown
hair, grey eyes, Church St., gunmaker (Navy)
Cooper, Charles, age 23, 2 years & 10 mos. in U.S., Poughkeepsie,
Dutchess Co., clothier (12-17 Oct. 1812)
Cooper, John, age 31, 7 years in U.S., wife & 4 children, Westchester Co., blacksmith (28 July - 2 Aug. 1812)
Cooper, John, 5ft. 8in., age 31, dark complex., dark hair, grey
eyes, labourer (Navy)
Cooper, Robert, 5ft. 9in., age 55, fair complex., dark hair,
blue eyes, baker (Navy)
Cooper, Thomas, 5ft. 7in., age 45, dark complex., brown hair,
dark eyes, Henry St., tailor (Navy)
Copland, Edward, 5ft. 10 in., age 23, light complex., dark hair,
brown eyes, Greenwich St., servant (Navy)
Copland, James, 5ft. 5in., age 25, light complex., brown hair,
grey eyes, clerk (Navy)
Copland, Thomas, 5ft. 6in., age 23, light complex., dark hair,
blue eyes, Greenwich St., servant (Navy)
Coppinger, Joseph, age 55, 10 years in U.S., wife & 4 children,
corner Oliver & Cherry Sts., NYC, clothing store keeper (13-18
July 1812); 5ft. 10in., age 57, fair complex., grey hair, light
eyes, Cherry St., shopkeeper (Navy)
Corbet, Francis, age 60, 12 years in U.S., 4 children, 110 Broad-
way, NYC, teacher (17-22 Aug. 1812)
Corbly, Christopher, 5ft. 6in., age 31, fair complex., dark hair,
brown eyes, Sharff (?) St., cartman (Navy)
Corbly/Corbley, Thomas, age 45, light complex., brown hair, blue
eyes, Charlotte St., paver (Navy)
Corbley, Thomas, age 38, 12 years in U.S., wife & 2 children,
corner Charlotte & Bancker Sts., NYC, paver (20-25 July 1812)
Corcoran, David, 5ft. 6in., age 28, light complex., brown hair,
brown eyes, distiller (Navy)
Corcoran, James, 5ft. 8in., age 20, light complex., brown hair,
brown eyes, blacksmith (Navy)
Corcoran, Michael, 5ft. 7in., age 22, light complex., dark hair,
hazel eyes, Hudson Square, butler (Navy)
Cormick, Alexander, age 24, 4 years in U.S., Schenectady, farmer
(10-15 Aug. 1812)
Cornell, James, age 28, 1 year & 9 mos. in U.S., wife & child,
NYC, carpenter (28 July - 2 Aug. 1812)
Cornell, James, 5ft. 8in., age 30, brown complex., fair hair,
brown eyes, Augustus St., house-joiner (Navy) - perhaps the
same as the carpenter above.
Cornell, Walter, age 30, 2 years in U.S., wife & child, Water St.,
NYC, grocer (28 July - 2 Aug. 1812)
Cornochan, Samuel, 5ft. 5in., age 36, fair complex., brown hair,
grey eyes, carpenter (Navy)
Cornwell, Charles M., age 17, 4 years in U.S., NYC, shopkeeper
(26-31 Oct. 1812); Cornwell, Charles M., 5ft. 5in., age 17,
fair complex., brown hair, black eyes, Maiden Lane, clerk
(Navy)

Cornwell/Cornwall, Thomas R., age 27, 11 years in U.S., 87 Maiden
Lane, NYC, dry goods merchant (17-22 Aug. 1812); 5ft. 9in.,
age 28, light complex., brown hair, hazel eyes, removed from
NYC to Goshen, Orange Co. (Navy)
Correy, Owen, 5ft. 6in., age 24, fair complex., brown hair, blue
eyes, Duane St., labourer (Navy)
Corrican, James, 5ft. 7in., age 52, dark complex., brown hair,
brown eyes, Cheapside, paver (Navy)
Corrican, James, 5ft. 6in., age 22, dark complex., black hair,
black eyes, Cheapside, weaver (Navy)
Corrigan, William, 5ft. 4in., age 43, fair complex., light hair,
blue eyes, cartman (Navy)
Corry, Bernard, age 30, 5 years in U.S., 26 Duane St., NYC,
wheelwright (20-25 July 1812)
Cortland, Owen, 5ft. 6in., age 39, dark complex., dark hair,
grey eyes, labourer (Navy)
Cosgrove, Barnard, age 21, 10 mos. in U.S., Clinton, Dutchess
Co., weaver (12-17 Oct. 1812)
Cotes, Richard, age 42, 10 years in U.S., wife, 809 Washington
St., NYC, boarding house keeper (10-15 Aug. 1812)
Cothell, Hugh, age 22, 1 year & 2 mos. in U.S., 30 Pine St.,
NYC, baker (20-25 July 1812); 5ft. 7½in., age 24, brown com-
plex., brown hair, brown eyes, Pine St., baker (Navy)
Cotter, Michael, age 20, 7 mos. in U.S., 316 Pearl St., clerk
(20-25 July 1812)
Cotton, Charles, age 23, 7 years & 2 mos. in U.S., New Paltz,
Ulster Co., farmer (19-24 Oct. 1812)
Coughey, Robert, age 44, 2 years in U.S., wife & 3 children,
Newburgh, Orange Co., miller (19-24 Oct. 1812)
Coughran, John, age 40, 11 years in U.S., 2 in family, 40 Cross
St., NYC, laborer (20-25 July 1812); 5ft. 8in., age 41, dark
complex., black hair, brown eyes, Cross St., labourer (Navy)
Coughran, William, 5ft. 6in., age 35, fair complex., brown hair,
blue eyes, labourer (Navy)
Courtney, Lord Vincent, age 43, 1 year & 4 mos. in U.S., Clare-
mont, gentleman (20-25 July 1812); 5ft. 7½in., age 44, fair
complex., grey hair, fair eyes, Bloomingdale, gentleman (Navy)
Cowan, George, 5ft. 8in., age 51, fair complex., sandy hair,
blue eyes, Augustus St., mason (Navy)
Cowan, James, age 48, 5 years in U.S., wife & 2 children, 468
Pearl St., tallow chandler (3-8 Aug. 1812)
Cowan, John, age 45, 21 years in U.S., Phelps, Ontario Co., far-
mer (24-29 Aug. 1812)
Cowan, John, age 20, 15 years in U.S., City of Albany, clerk (17-
22 Aug. 1812)
Cowan, William, 5ft. 5½in., age 42, dark complex., light hair,
black eyes, gilder (Navy)
Coward, George, age 36, 7 years in U.S., 10 in family, Seneca,
Ontario Co., farmer, applied Feb. 1812 (5-15 & 24-29 Aug. 1812)
Cowin, Dennis, 5ft. 8in., age 27, light complex., brown hair,
blue eyes, labourer (Navy)
Cowling, Joseph, 6ft., age 48, red complex., grey hair, blue eyes,
combmaker (Navy)
Cox, William, age 33, 1 year & 6 mos. in U.S., wife & 4 child-
ren, Pompey, Onondaga Co., farmer (5-11 & 14-19 Sept. 1812)
Cox, William, age 27, 7 years in U.S., wife & 3 children, Rose
Hill, Seneca Co., farmer (28 July - 2 Aug. 1812)
Cox, William, 5ft. 9½in., age 27, light complex., sandy hair,
grey eyes, 3 Mile Stone, wagoner (Navy)
Cox, William Collins, age 22, 3 years in U.S., 6 Warren St.,
merchant (26-31 Oct. 1812)
Coyle, Daniel, age 30, 5 years & 1 mo. in U.S., Minisink, Orange
Co. (19-24 Oct. 1812)
Coyle, Dennis, 5ft. 6in., age 30, fair complex., black hair,
grey eyes, porter (Navy)

Crabtree, James, age 48, 15 years & 2 mos. in U.S., wife & 6
  children, Plattsburgh, Clinton Co., farmer, from Halifax (1
  Sept. - 1 Oct. & 26-31 Oct. 1812)
Crabtree, Joseph, age 41, 1 year & 10 mos. in U.S., Rhinebeck,
  Dutchess Co., clothier (12-17 Oct. 1812)
Cracken, John, age 28, 10 years in U.S., wife & 3 children,
  Schenectady, weaver (17-22 Aug. 1812)
Craft, Alexander, age 33, 6 years in U.S., wife & 2 children,
  Livingston, Columbia Co., applied July 1808 (12 Sept. 1812)
Craig, David, 5ft. 7½in., age 37, sandy complex., brown hair,
  grey eyes, blacksmith (Navy)
Craig, Edward, age 32, 6 years in U.S., 26 Henry St., NYC, ped-
  lar & dealer (7-19 Dec. 1812)
Craig, Gordon, age 31, 12 years & 10 mos. in U.S., wife & child,
  Marbletown, Ulster Co., farmer (19-24 Oct. 1812)
Craig, James, 5ft. 4in., age 43, dark complex., brown hair, grey
  eyes, Grand St., cartman (Navy)
Craig, James, age 32, 17 years in U.S., 3 sons, Greenwich St.,
  NYC, farmer (14-19 Sept. 1812)
Craig, Mathias, age 26, 3 years in U.S., 4 Bancker St., NYC,
  tanner & currier (28 July - 2 Aug. 1812)
Craig, Robert, age 22, 6 mos. in U.S., NYC, labourer (20-25 July
  1812)
Craig, Robert, 5ft. 8in., age 22, dark complex., dark hair, black
  eyes, Greenwich St., sawyer (Navy)
Craig, Samuel, age 63, 5 years & 1 mo. in U.S., wife & child,
  Montgomery, Orange Co., weaver (19-24 Oct. 1812)
Craighton, Daniel, age 48, in U.S. since 9 Sept. 1785, wife & 9
  children, Broadalbin, Montgomery Co., farmer (11-17 & 17-22
  Aug. 1812)
Crane, Solomon, age 22, 1 year & 3 mos. in U.S., wife, Beekman,
  Dutchess Co., weaver (12-17 Oct. 1812)
Cranston, William, age 25, 11 years in U.S., 428 Greenwich St.,
  NYC, grocer (20-25 July 1812)
Crawford, Aaron, 5ft. 11in., age 32, fair complex., brown hair,
  grey eyes, Duane & Elm Sts., thread fac(tory) (Navy)
Crawford, David, age 36, 18 years in U.S., wife & 5 children,
  139 Harman St., NYC, drayman (20-25 July 1812); 5ft. 9in.,
  age 36, fair complex., dark hair, grey eyes, Harman St,, dray-
  man (Navy)
Crawford, Hayes, age 55, 11 years in U.S., wife & 7 children,
  Coeymans Patent, Albany Co., farmer (5-10 Oct. 1812)
Crawford, Hugh, age 21, 6 weeks in U.S., 44 Pine St., NYC, gen-
  tleman (20-25 July 1812)
Crawford, John, age 45, 11 years in U.S., wife & child, student
  physick (24-29 Aug. 1812)
Crawford, John, 5ft. 9in., age 21, light complex., "c" hair,
  dark eyes, cordwainer (Navy)
Crawford, John, 5ft. 5in., age 21, dark complex., black hair,
  dark eyes, gardener (Navy)
Crawford, William, age 35, 10 years in U.S., wife, Montgomery,
  Orange Co., farmer (19-24 Oct. 1812)
Crawford, William, age 21, 4 years & 4 mos. in U.S., wife, Beek-
  man, Dutchess Co., weaver (12-17 Oct. 1812)
Cray, John D., age 28 next 4 Dec., 12 years in U.S. on 26 Dec.
  next, wife (an American) & child, Utica, Oneida Co., copper-
  smith, from Essex Co., Canada (10 & 17-22 Aug. 1812)
Crean, Michael, age 32, 4 years & 7 mos. in U.S., Newburgh, Orange
  Co., teacher (14 & 17-22 Aug. 1812)
Criard (?), Bernard, 5ft. 8in., age 25, brown complex., brown
  hair, brown eyes, Henry St., joiner (Navy)
Creighton, John, age 34, 15 years in U.S., wife, Lenox, Madison
  Co., farmer (3 Aug. & 10-15 Aug. 1812)
Creighton, John, age 20, 1 year & 3 mos. in U.S., Wallkill,
  Orange Co., laborer (19-24 Oct. 1812)

Crew, Francis, 5ft. 9in., age 32, dark complex., black hair, brown eyes, grocer (Navy)

Crichton, James, age 28, 8 years & 2 mos. in U.S., wife & 3 children, 157 Reed St., NYC, stone cutter, applied 24 Mar. 1810 (28 July - 2 Aug. 1812)

Crichton, John, age 24, 6 weeks in U.S., wife & child, 157 Reed St., stone cutter (28 July - 2 Aug. 1812)

Crighton, David, 5ft. 9½in., age 40, fair complex., sandy hair, blue eyes, White St., stone cutter (Navy)

Crighton, James, age 35, 11 years in U.S., 30 Gold St., NYC, bookbinder (20-25 July 1812)

Crighton, James, Jr., 5ft. 11in., age 28, light complex., light hair, grey eyes, Reed St., storekeeper (Navy)

Crighton, James, Sr., 5ft. 8in., age 32, fair complex., light hair, blue eyes, Beach St., stone cutter (Navy)

Criler, James, 5ft. 8in., age 47, dark complex., black hair, brown eyes, blacksmith (Navy)

Crimless (?), John, 5ft. 7in., age 30, dark complex., brown hair, hazel eyes, lamplighter (Navy)

Critchley/Crichley, Michael, age 37, 1 year in U.S. on 29 May last, wife & child, Eaton, Madison Co., farmer (31 Oct. & 30 Nov. - 5 Dec. 1812)

Crockett, John, age 30, 6 years in U.S., merchant, NYC, applied 15 Sept. 1809 (28 July - 2 Aug. 1812); 5ft. 8in., age 28, ruddy complex., brown hair, grey eyes, removed from NYC to Goshen, Orange Co. (Navy)

Croft, Samuel, 5ft. 5½in., age 23, brown complex., brown hair, brown eyes, William St., carpenter (Navy)

Crofton, Thomas, age 47, 5 years in U.S., wife & child, NYC, innkeeper (20-25 July 1812)

Crofts, Alexander, age 33, 6 years in U.S., wife & 2 children, Livingston, Columbia Co., farmer, applied July 1808 (14- 19 Sept. 1812) - see Craft, Alexander, the same.

Cromwell, Isaac, age 22, 2 years in U.S., Clinton, Dutchess Co., weaver (12-17 Oct. 1812)

Cronolein (?), David, 5ft. 10in., age 25, fair complex., brown hair, grey eyes, clerk (Navy)

Crosbie, Peter, 5ft. 7in., age 35, red complex., brown hair, blue eyes, potter (Navy)

Crosby, James, age 35, 11 years in U.S., wife & child, 13 Gold St., NYC, accomptant, applied Oct. 1801 (13-18 July 1812); 5ft. 11½in., age 35, light complex., brown hair, blue eyes, removed from NYC to Goshen, Orange Co. (Navy)

Crosby, John, age 54, 17 years in U.S., wife, Scipio, cooper (12-17 Oct. 1812)

Crosier, Richard, 5ft. 7in., age 20, dark complex., brown hair, blue eyes, Bancker St., labourer (Navy)

Cross, James, 5ft. 7in., age 47, dark complex., dark hair, blue eyes, Bowery Lane, blacksmith (Navy)

Cross, James, age 31, 7 years in U.S., wife & 2 children, Hudson, weaver (10-15 Aug. 1812)

Cross, James, Jr., 5ft. 8in., age 23, light complex., brown hair, grey eyes, Liberty St., blacksmith (Navy)

Cross, Richard, 5ft. 5½in., age 32, light complex., brown hair, grey eyes, hostler (Navy)

Cross, William, 6ft., age 43, dark complex., dark hair, brown eyes (Navy)

Cross, William, age 41, 11 years in U.S., wife & 4 children, Rhinebeck, Dutchess Co., glove maker (12-17 Oct. 1812)

Crosset, James, age 27, 7 years in U.S., Geneseo, Ontario Co., farmer (11-15 & 26-31 Oct. 1812)

Crosset, John, age 48, 7 years in U.S., Sparta, Ontario Co., farmer (11-25 & 26-31 Oct. 1812)

Crosset, Wilson, age 29, 7 years in U.S., Geneseo, Ontario Co., farmer (11-25 & 26-31 Oct. 1812)

Crotchett, John, 5ft. 8in., age 28, ruddy complex., brown hair,
  grey eyes, 79 Front St., grocer (Navy)
Crowly, Edward, age 33, 9 years in U.S., wife & 2 children, City
  of Albany, sailmaker (5-10 Oct. 1812)
Crowther, David, age 24, 2 years in U.S., NYC, merchant (19-24
  Oct. 1812); 5ft. 11in., age 25, fair complex., brown hair,
  grey eyes, removed from NYC to Fishkill, Dutchess Co. (Navy)
Crozer, George, age 28, 11 years in U.S., Seneca, Ontario Co.,
  farmer (5-15 & 24-29 Aug. 1812)
Crozier, Archibald, age 21, 10 years in U.S., New Paltz, Ulster
  Co., cooper (19-24 Oct. 1812)
Crozier, Samuel, age 35, 15 years & 1 mo. in U.S., New Paltz,
  Ulster Co., weaver (19-24 Oct. 1812)
Crozier, William, age 25, 10 years in U.S., New Paltz, Ulster
  Co., laborer (19-24 Oct. 1812)
Crumby, John, 5ft. 6in., age 25, dark complex., brown hair,
  grey eyes, Fair & Gold Sts., blacksmith (Navy)
Crumby, Joseph, 5ft. 9in., age 23, fair complex., brown hair,
  dark eyes, Broad St., tobacco (Navy)
Cruthers, James, age 53, 1 year & 11 mos. in U.S., wife & 2
  children, New Windsor, Orange Co., weaver (19-24 Oct. 1812)
Cruthers, Samuel, age 21, 1 year & 11 mos. in U.S., New Windsor,
  Orange Co., weaver (19-24 Oct. 1812)
Cuddy, Michael, 5ft. 11in., age 26, fair complex., brown hair,
  brown eyes, Manhattan, sawyer (Navy)
Culbert (or Culbut?), John, 5ft. 6in., age 32, fair complex.,
  brown hair, blue eyes, Mulberry St., weaver (Navy)
Culbert, Thomas, age 27, 5 years in U.S. last Dec., wife & 3
  children, Eaton, Madison Co., farmer (31 Oct. & 30 Nov. - 5
  Dec. 1812)
Cull, Felix, age 30, 12 years in U.S., wife, Goshen, Orange Co.,
  farmer (19-24 Oct. 1812)
Cullen, Patrick, age 27, 6 years in U.S., 21 Little George St.,
  NYC, grocer (28 July - 2 Aug. 1812)
Cullen, Patrick, 5ft. 2in., age 26, light complex., brown hair,
  blue eyes, Anthony St., mason (Navy)
Cumberland, Stephen, age 29, 6 years in U.S., wife & 3 children,
  Westchester Co. (12-17 Oct. 1812)
Cummings, James, age 52, 7 years in U.S., wife & 5 children,
  Schenectady, farmer (24-29 Aug. 1812)
Cummings/Cumings, James, age 20½, 4 years & 7 mos. in U.S., 26
  Front St., NYC, clerk (28 July - 2 Aug. 1812); 5ft. 7in., age
  21, light complex., brown hair, brown eyes, Water St., clerk
  (Navy)
Cummings, John, 5ft. 6in., age 35, light complex., dark hair,
  grey eyes, Hell Gate, gardener (Navy)
Cummings, Thomas, 5ft. 5in., age 23, fair complex., brown hair,
  grey eyes, labourer (Navy)
Cummings, William, 5ft. 6in., age 33, dark complex., light hair,
  grey eyes, farmer (Navy)
Cummins, James, Jr., age 20, 7 years in U.S., Schenectady, far-
  mer (24-29 Aug. 1812)
Cummins, Matthew, age 32, 14 years in U.S., wife & 3 children,
  North East, Dutchess Co., farmer (12-17 Oct. 1812)
Cummins, William, age 18, 7 years in U.S., Schenectady, farmer
  (24-29 Aug. 1812)
Cunningham, Arthur, age 38, 9 mos. in U.S., 11 in family, 104
  Bowery Lane, NYC, cotton manufacturer (28 July - 2 Aug. 1812)
Cunningham, Coney, 5ft. 5in., age 22, dark complex., dark hair,
  black eyes, Mulberry St., labourer (Navy)
Cunningham, Connel, age 18, 1 year & 1 mo. in U.S., corner Cross
  & Duane Sts., NYC, blacksmith (28 July - 2 Aug. 1812)
Cunningham, Daniel, age 22, 1 year in U.S., 75 Mulberry St., NYC,
  laborer (28 July - 2 Aug. 1812)

Cunningham, David, 5ft. 6in., age 28, light complex., brown hair, blue eyes, Bloomingdale, blacksmith (Navy)

Cunningham, David, 5ft. 6in., age 25, dark complex., dark hair, black eyes, Fourth St., blacksmith (Navy)

Cunningham, David, age 20, 8 mos. in U.S., Rivington St., NYC, hemp dresser (3-8 Aug. 1812)

Cunningham, David, 5ft. 8in., age 19, fair complex., fair hair, blue eyes, Ridge St., hemp dresser (Navy) - perhaps the same as the David above.

Cunningham, George, age 38, 1 year & 10 mos. in U.S., Hudson, Columbia Co., weaver (rep. c. Sept. 1812) - perhaps Cunningham, George, age 33, 1 year & 10 mos. in U.S., wife & 4 children, Hudson, weaver (3-8 Aug. 1812)

Cunningham, James, age 23, 1 year in U.S., 75 Mulberry St., NYC, laborer (28 July - 2 Aug. 1812); 5ft. 6in., age 24, fair complex., brown hair, grey eyes, Mulberry St., labourer (Navy)

Cunningham, James, 5ft. 6in., age 21, dark complex., brown hair, grey eyes, labourer (Navy)

Cunningham, John, age 50, 19 years in U.S., wife & 7 children, Johnstown, Montgomery Co., farmer (25 Aug. -2 Sept. & 7-12 Sept. 1812)

Cunningham, John, 5ft. 6in., age 30, light complex., brown hair, grey eyes, Bowery, blacksmith (Navy)

Cunningham, John, age 28, 9 years in U.S., wife & child, NYC, blacksmith (28 July - 2 Aug. 1812)

Cunningham, Michael, 5ft. 4½in., age 27, light complex., brown hair, blue eyes, Pearl St., labourer (Navy)

Cunningham, Robert, age 25, 18 years in U.S., wife, New Windsor, Orange Co., farmer (19-24 Oct. 1812)

Cunningham, Robert, 5ft. 10in., age 22, fair complex., brown hair, grey eyes, flax dresser (Navy)

Cunningham, William, age 49, 23 years in U.S., wife & 9 children, New Windsor, Orange Co., farmer (19-24 Oct. 1812)

Cupher, Henry Joseph, 5ft. 7in., age 22, light complex., brown hair, blue eyes, Water St., musician (Navy)

Curphew, Henry Joseph, age 21 on 19 Aug. inst., in U.S. since 18 July 1811, Utica, Oneida Co., musical preceptor, from Isle of Man (10 & 17-22 Aug. 1812)

Curr, John, age 58, 18 years in U.S., Schoharie, Onondaga Co., millwright (14-19 Sept. 1812)

Curran, James, age 25, 5years & 3 mos. in U.S., wife & 2 children, Woodstock, Ulster Co., laborer (19-24 Oct. 1812)

Curran, William, age 27, 17 years in U.S., wife & child, Hurley, Ulster Co., carpenter (19-24 Oct. 1812)

Currey, John, age 23, 1 year in U.S., 110 Reed St., NYC, laborer (20-25 July 1812)

Currey, Michael, 5ft. 5in., age 29, dark complex., brown hair, blue eyes, William St., mason (Navy)

Currie, Bernard, 5ft. 9in., age 27, sandy complex., dark hair, brown eyes, labourer (Navy)

Currie (or Curris?), Thomas, age 28, 18 years in U.S., wife & 2 children, Schoharie, Onondaga Co, farmer (14-19 Sept. 1812)

Curry, John, 5ft. 11in., age 30, dark complex., brown hair, brown eyes, grocer (Navy)

Curry, Thomas, 5ft. 10in., age 25, fair complex., brown hair, grey eyes, labourer (Navy)

Curtis, John, age 48, 14 years in U.S., wife, Utica, Oneida Co., grocer, from Gloucestershire, Eng. (10 & 17-22 Aug. 1812)

Cushing, Thomas, age 29, 5 years & 3 mos. in U.S., Fishkill, Dutchess Co., miller (12-17 Oct. 1812)

Cuthell, John, 5ft. 6in., age 30, fair complex., dark hair, grey eyes, Church St., cabinetmaker (Navy)

Dabron, John, age 47 on 8 Aug. last, 8 years in U.S. on 13 Dec. last, wife & child, Whitestown, Oneida Co., farmer (26 Aug. 1812)

Dagherty, Dudley, 5ft. 8in., age 28, dark complex., dark hair,
grey eyes, labourer (Navy)
Dale, James, age 26, 3 days in U.S., wife & son, Water St., NYC,
manufacturer (28 Sept. - 3 Oct. 1812)
Dailes(or Daile?), John, 5ft. 7in., age 43, fair complex., brown
hair, brown eyes, Spring St., carman (Navy)
Dales, John, age 41, 5 years in U.S., wife & 3 children, 8 Ryn-
ders St., NYC, cartman (3-8 Aug. 1812)
Dallace, Alexander, 5ft. 8in., age 29, dark complex., dark hair,
dark eyes, carpenter (Navy)
Dalmage, Adam, 6ft.; age 26, dark complex., black hair, black
eyes, Elizabeth St., tallow chandler (Navy)
Dalmage, John, 5ft. 7in., age 24, fair complex., black hair,
blue eyes, labourer (Navy)
Dalton, Andrew, 5ft. 6in., age 25, dark complex., black hair,
brown eyes, Ferry St., labourer (Navy)
Dalton, John, age 36, 4 years & 8 mos. in U.S., wife & child, 6
Lombardy St., NYC, accountant (28 July - 2 Aug. 1812)
Daly, Charles, 5ft. 5½in., age 47, sandy complex., light hair,
dark eyes, Orange St., labourer (Navy)
Damerum (?), William, age 46, 4 mos. in U.S., 20 Beekman St.,
NYC, carpenter (20-25 July 1812)
Dann, William, age 35, 10 years in U.S., wife, mother-in-law,
brother-in-law, 112 Broad St., NYC, grocer, applied Apr. 1810
(20-25 July 1812)
Darke, Richard, age 40, 8 years in U.S., wife & 5 children,
Bloomingdale (17-22 Aug. 1812)
Darling, James, age 38, 11 years in U.S., wife & child, Shandaken,
Ulster Co., farmer (19-24 Oct. 1812)
Dash, Richard, 5ft. 5in., age 40, ruddy complex., dark hair,
light eyes, Bloomingdale, butcher (Navy)
Davenport, Christopher, age 22, 16 years in U.S., wife & child,
Clinton, Dutchess Co., clothier (12-17 Oct. 1812)
Davenport, John, age 40, 6 years in U.S., Dr. Forbes (age 70,
his father-in-law), a niece & 3 servants, Brooklyn, Long Island,
merchant (13-18 July 1812); 5ft. 6½in., age 41, fair complex.,
light hair, blue eyes, Brooklyn, gentleman (Navy)
David, John, age 36, 5 years in U.S., NYC, pedlar, applied 13
July 1812 (20-25 July 1812)
Davidson, Alexander, age 30, 1 year in U.S., Monroe Works, Orange
Co., cut nailor (17-22 Aug. 1812)
Davidson, John, 5ft. 7in., age 23, dark complex., black hair,
dark eyes, Partition St., stone cutter (Navy)
Davidson, John Elmer, 5ft. 9in., age 21, dark complex., dark
hair, black eyes, William St. seaman (Navy)
Davidson, Samuel, age 26, 3 years in U.S., 64 Murray St., NYC,
carpenter (28 July - 2 Aug. 1812); 5ft. 9in., age 26, fair com-
plex., brown hair, brown eyes, Warren St., carpenter (Navy)
Davidson, Thomas, 5ft. 8½in., age 35, dark complex., dark hair,
dark eyes, removed from NYC to Fishkill, Dutchess Co. (Navy)
Davidson, William, age 25, 1 mo. in U.S., Monroe Works, Orange
Co., cut nailor (17 -22 Aug. 1812)
Davidson, William, age 25, 2 mos. in U.S., Water St., barkeeper
(20-25 July 1812); probably the same, Davidson, William, 5ft.
7in., age 27, fair complex., fair hair, hazel eyes, Water St.,
barkeeper (Navy)
Davie, John, 5ft. 5in., age 61, fair complex., grey hair, blue
eyes, brass founder (Navy)
Davie/Davey, Teghe (or Tighe?), age 18, 1 year & 9 mos. in U.S.,
NYC, carpenter (17-22 Aug. 1812); 5ft. 9in., age 19, fair complex., sandy hair, blue eyes, carpenter (Navy)
Davis, Aaron, age 20, 5 years in U.S., 79 Cherry St., NYC, broker
(20-25 July 1812)
Davis, Alexander, age 45 c̲. Feb. last, 27 years in U.S. 3 Sept.,
wife & child, Lee, Oneida Co., farmer , from Tyrone (27 Sept. 1812)

Davis, Alexander, age 45, 2 years in U.S., wife & child, Deer-
field, Oneida Co., farmer (28 Sept. - 3 Oct. 1812)
Davis, Daniel, age 22, 5 years in U.S., wife & child, Mamakating,
Sullivan Co., carpenter (19-24 Oct. 1812)
Davis, David, age 29, 1 year in U.S., 79 Cherry St., NYC, sale-
man (20-25 July 1812)
Davis, David, age 28, 10 years in U.S., wife & 3 children, Clin-
ton, Dutchess Co., laborer (12-17 Oct. 1812)
Davis, David A., age 24, 11 years in U.S., New Windsor, Orange
Co., farmer (21 Dec. 1812 - 23 Jan. 1813 & 2 Jan. 1813)
Davis, Hugh, 5ft. 11in., age 32, black complex., dark hair, grey
eyes, Cherry St., sawyer (Navy)
Davis, Jabez, 5ft. 10in., age 30, fair complex., light hair,
hazel eyes, Grand St., tailor (Navy)
Davis, James, age 42, 14 years in U.S., New Paltz, Ulster Co.,
weaver (19-24 Oct. 1812)
Davis, James, age 40, 1 year in U.S., wife & 2 children, Pro-
vost St., NYC, grocer (20-25 July 1812)
Davis, James, age 24, 3 years in U.S., 3 in family, Avon, On-
tario Co., farmer (21-26 Sept. 1812)
Davis, James, age 16, 11 years in U.S., Seneca, Ontario Co.,
farmer (5-15 & 24-29 Aug. 1812)
Davis, John, age 45, 11 years in U.S., 3 in family, Seneca, On-
tario Co., farmer (5-15 & 24-29 Aug. 1812)
Davis, John, age 42, 7 years in U.S., wife & 5 children, 318
Washington St., clerk (13-18 July 1812); 5ft. 5in., dark com-
plex., dark hair, hazel eyes, Washington St., clerk (Navy)
Davis, John, 5ft. 10in., age 34, light complex., light hair,
light eyes, teacher (Navy)
Davis, Joseph, 5ft. 7in., age 31, fair complex., fair hair, grey
eyes, Gold St., grocer (Navy)
Davis, Luke, age 24, 15 years in U.S., wife, 126 Chatham St.,
NYC, physician (28 July - 2 Aug. 1812)
Davis, Nathaniel S., age 19, 16 years in U.S., 149 Broadway, NYC,
perfumer (20-25 July 1812)
Davis, Richard, age 36, 5 years in U.S., wife & 4 children, Ma-
making, Sullivan Co., weaver (19-24 Oct. 1812)
Davis, Richard Edward, age 30, 10 years in U.S., wife & 4 child-
ren, Saratoga, Saratoga Co., laborer (17-22 Aug. 1812)
Davis, Solomon, age 24, 1 year & 4 mos. in U.S., 79 Cherry St.,
NYC, tailor (20-25 July 1812); 4ft. 10in., age 23, dark com-
plex., dark hair, hazel eyes, Cherry St., tailor (Navy)
Davis, William, 5ft. 3in., age 41, light complex., dark hair,
grey eyes, clerk (Navy)
Davis, William, 5ft. 8in., age 22, light complex., dark hair,
dark eyes, Birmingham, cordwainer (Navy)
Davison, John, age 26, 1 year & 2 mos. in U.S., Manlius, Ononda-
ga Co., farmer (28 Sept. - 3 Oct. 1812); 1 in family (18-25
Sept. 1812)
Dawson, Patrick, 5ft. 10in., age 22, light complex., brown hair,
brown eyes, hatter (Navy)
Dawson, Thomas, age 39, 9 years in U.S., wife & 3 children, City
of Albany, merchant, applied 6 Apr. 1812 (24-29 Aug. 1812)
Dawson, William, age 59, 1 day in U.S., City Hotel, NYC, merchant
(21-26 Sept. 1812)
Day, Patrick, age 30, 2 years in U.S., wife, 8 Dover St., NYC,
tavern-keeper (20-25 July 1812)
Day, Patrick, 5ft. 7 3/4in., age 31, fair complex., black hair,
brown eyes, Henry St., labourer (Navy)
Day, Thomas, age 38, 11 years in U.S., wife & 7 children, 10 Reed
St., NYC, ropemaker (20-25 July 1812); 5ft. 8in., age 39, light
complex, light hair, blue eyes, Reed St., ropemaker (Navy)
Dayley, Pat, 5ft. 8in, age 35, light complex., brown hair, blue
eyes, Liberty St., hostler (Navy)

Dean, George, 5ft. 4in., age 26, fair complex., brown hair, blue
eyes, Fair St., hatter (Navy)
Dean, Hugh, age 30, 7 years in U.S., 32 Vesey St., NYC, umbrella
manufacturer, applied 23 Apr. 1810 (13-18 July 1812)
Dean, Jonathan, 5ft. 11in., age 22, fair complex., fair hair,
grey eyes, Corlears Hook, cartman (Navy)
Dean, Joseph, age 28, 1 year in U.S., Kings Co., teacher (3-8
Aug. 1812)
Debbs, Benjamin, age 32, 18 years in U.S., wife & child, 9 Water
St., cut nailor (7-12 Sept. 1812); see Dibbs, Benjamin, below.
Decker, James T., 5ft. 11in., age 21, brown complex., light hair,
grey eyes, hairdresser (Navy)
Delaney, Moses, age 28, 10 years in U.S., wife & 2 children, Mi-
nisink, Orange Co., farmer (19-24 Oct. 1812)
Delap, Aaron, age 22, 3 years in U.S., Athens, Greene Co., mer-
chant (17-22 Aug. 1812)
Delvin, Arthur, 5ft. 5in., age 21, dark complex., dark hair,
blue eyes, Hester St., weaver (Navy)
Delvin, Thomas, 5ft. 7in., age 20, fair complex., fair hair,
blue eyes, coachman (Navy)
Demaien, William, 6ft., age 47, dark complex., dark hair, black
eyes, Washington St., sawyer (Navy)
Dempsey, Francis, age 47, 2 years in U.S., wife, son & daughter,
49 Broad St., NYC, teacher, applied 18 Sept. 1810 (13-18 July
1812); 5ft. 7in., age 48, light complex., dark hair, grey eyes,
teacher (Navy)
Dempsey, Joseph, age 26, 6 years in U.S., 7 Division St., NYC,
chandler (20-25 July 1812); 5ft. 8in., age 26, fair complex.,
fair hair, blue eyes, Division St., chandler (Navy)
Dempsey, Peter, age 24, 8 years in U.S., NYC, student-at-law (20-
25 July 1812); 5ft. 7in., age 24, fair complex., brown hair,
grey eyes, Division St., student (Navy)
Denham, Alexander, age 37, 8 years in U.S., wife & 6 children,
Hebron, Washington Co. (31 Aug. - 5 Sept. 1812)
Denham, John D,, age 28, 3 mos. in U.S., NYC, merchant (17-22
Aug. 1812)
Denis, Donovan, 5ft. 7in., age 61, light complex., brown hair,
blue eyes, Oak St., gentleman (Navy)
Denman, William, age 48, 17 years in U.S., wife & 9 children,
Neversink, Sullivan Co., farmer (19-24 Oct. 1812)
Denman, William, Jr., age 19, 17 years in U.S., Neversink, Sul-
livan Co., farmer (19-24 Oct. 1812)
Dennison, Michael, age 23, 2 years in U.S., Botanic Garden, NYC,
botanist (20-25 July 1812); 5ft. 11in., age 24, brown complex.,
dark hair, grey eyes, Botanic Garden, botanist (Navy)
Dennison, Samuel, age 37, 15 years in U.S., 7 in family, Phelps,
Ontario Co., farmer(5-15 Aug. 1812)
Dennison, Thomas, age 24, 3½ years in U.S., Pine St., NYC, ac-
countant (20-25 July 1812); 5ft. 8in., age 25, dark complex.,
dark hair, hazel eyes, accountant (Navy); removed from NYC to
Goshen, Orange Co. (Navy)
Denniston, James, age 28, 1 year in U.S., Montgomery, Orange Co.,
weaver (19-24 Oct. 1812)
Denniston, Ralph, age 30, 2 years in U.S., wife & 2 children,
Montgomery, Orange Co., wheelmaker (19-24 Oct. 1812)
Denton, Charles, age 34, 9 years in U.S., NYC, merchant (3-8 Aug.
1812); 5ft. 10in., age 34, fair complex., dark hair, grey eyes,
removed from NYC to Fishkill, Dutchess Co. (Navy)
Dergan (?), John, age 37, 18 years in U.S., NYC, laborer (20-25
July 1812)
Derry, John, age 48, 9 years in U.S., wife & 6 children, West-
chester Co., farmer (28 July - 2 Aug. 1812)
Derry, Valentine, age 45, 5 years in U.S., Bloomingdale, applied
23 May 1809 (20-25 July 1812)

Dibbs, Benjamin, 5ft. 8in., age 32, dark complex., dark hair,
  hazel eyes, Water St., nailor (Navy) - see Debbs, Benjamin.
Dick, Benjamin, age 28, 7 years & 3 mos. in U.S., wife, New Wind-
  sor, Orange Co., farmer (19-24 Oct. 1812)
Dick, George, 5ft. 5in., age 26, dark complex., black hair, blue
  eyes, labourer (Navy)
Dick, George, age 25, 5 mos. in U.S., 306 Broadway, NYC, clerk
  (20-25 July 1812)
Dick, James, age 29, 8 years, 11 mos. & 20 days in U.S., wife &
  4 children, Plattsburgh, Clinton Co., tanner & currier, applied
  May Term of Common Pleas, from Scotland (1 Oct. & 26-31 Oct.
  1812)
Dickens, Samuel, age 46 on 13 July last, 2 years in U.S. on 5
  July last, wife & 10 children, Whitestown, Oneida Co., turner
  (26 Aug. & 28 Sept. - 3 Oct. 1812)
Dickers (or Dickens?), Henry, 5ft. 4in., age 26, light complex.,
  light hair, grey eyes, milkman (Navy)
Dickey, Adam, age 35, 3 mos. in U.S., Newburgh, Orange Co., joi-
  ner (19-24 Oct. 1812)
Dickinson, John, 5ft. 8in., age 46, dark complex., dark hair,
  blue eyes, New St., labourer (Navy)
Dickinson, Thomas, age 49, 9 mos. in U.S., NYC, teacher (13-18
  July 1812)
Dickson, Adam, age 60, 8 years in U.S., wife, Colonie, Albany
  Co., cutter (31 Aug. - 5 Sept. 1812)
Dickson (or Dirckson?), James, 5ft. 10in., age 26, fair complex.,
  brown hair, grey eyes, Thomas St., cartman (Navy)
Dickson, John, age 22, 9 years in U.S., Colonie, Albany Co.,
  maker of surgical instruments (24-29 Aug. 1812)
Dickson, Samuel, 5ft. 10in., age 39, dark complex., black hair,
  black eyes, Orange St., labourer (Navy)
Diemon, James, 5ft. 9¾in., age 31, sandy complex., brown hair,
  grey eyes, Duane St., labourer (Navy)
Dilly, Alexander, age 62, 32 years in U.S., wife & 7 children,
  Deerpark, Orange Co., farmer (19-24 Oct. 1812)
Din, Walter, 5ft. 5in., age 22, brown complex., brown hair, grey
  eyes, Bancker St., coachman (Navy)
Dirkin, Alexander, age 19, 1 year & 3 mos. in U.S., 127 corner
  James & Chatham Sts., NYC, cotton spinner (28 July - 2 Aug.
  1812)
Disney, Thomas, 5ft. 8in., age 54, red complex., grey hair, blue
  eyes, Henry St., chandler (Navy)
Ditchet, John, age 40, 8 years in U.S., wife & child, 142 William
  St., NYC, draper, applied 1809 (28 July - 2 Aug. 1812); 5ft.
  7½in., age 41, dark complex., dark hair, blue eyes, William
  St., tailor (Navy)
Ditty, Thomas, 5ft. 10in., age 26, fair complex., fair hair,
  blue eyes, labourer (Navy)
Divine, Stephen, age 20, 1 year in U.S., Rome, Oneida Co., wea-
  ver (3-8 Aug. 1812)
Divine, William, age 19, 1 year & 3 mos. in U.S., 34 Augustus St.,
  NYC, gardener (28 July - 2 Aug. 1812)
Dixon, Henry, age 39, 5 years in U.S., wife & child, 189 Harman
  St., NYC, ship chandler (28 July - 2 Aug. 1812)
Dixon, Henry, 5ft. 9in., age 37, light complex., light hair,
  grey eyes, Harman St., ship carpenter (Navy) - same as above?
Dixon, James, 5ft. 9in., age 60, fair complex., brown hair, brown
  eyes, Jay St., soap (boiler) (Navy)
Dixon, John, age 53, 2 years in U.S., 140 Cherry St., NYC, regy.
  & intelge. office (20-25 July 1812)
Dixon, Mathew, age 27, 10 mos. in U.S., 116 Broad St., NYC, grocer (20-25 July 1812); 5ft. 3 3/4in., age 27, fair complex.,
  dark hair, grey eyes, Broad St., grocer (Navy)
Dixson, Edward, age 42, 12 years in U.S., Seneca, Ontario Co.,
  teacher (24-29 Aug. 1812)

Doath, David, 5ft. 7in., age 22, light complex., brown hair,
   dark eyes, John St., baker (Navy)
Dodd, Adam, age 18, 11 years in U.S., Seneca, Ontario Co., far-
   mer (5-15 & 24-29 Aug. 1812)
Dodd, Anthony, age 43, 11 years in U.S., 6 in family, Seneca,
   Ontario Co., farmer (5-15 & 24-29 Aug. 1812)
Dodd, William, age 45, 8 years in U.S., wife & 4 children, 186
   Bowery, NYC, grocer (20-25 July 1812)
Doddrell, James, age 38, 1 year & 1 mo. in U.S., wife & 6 child-
   ren, 69 Warren St., NYC, dyer (28 July - 2 Aug. 1812)
Dodgson, Enoch, age 33, 4 years & 8 mos. in U.S., wife & 2 child-
   ren, 40 Bowery Lane, merchant, applied 14 Mar. 1810 (10-15 Aug.
   1812); 5ft. 8in., age 34, dark complex., brown hair, brown
   eyes, removed from NYC to Fishkill, Dutchess Co. (Navy)
Dogherty, Anthony, 5ft. 8in., age 45, fair complex., brown hair,
   brown eyes, Catherine St., hostler (Navy)
Dogherty, James, 5ft. 6in., age 34, fair complex., dark hair,
   blue eyes, Greenwich St., labourer (Navy)
Doig, Perry, age 62, 28 years in U.S., wife & 3 children, City
   of Albany, tailor (17-22 Aug. 1812)
Doige, Thomas, age 34, 2 years in U.S., wife, Albany St., NYC,
   clerk, applied Feb. 1812 (28 July - 2 Aug. 1812)
Donaldson, Benjamin, age 22, 7 years in U.S., Argyle, Washington
   Co., student at physick, applied Aug. 1811 (28 Sept. - 3 Oct.
   1812)
Donaldson, David, age 35, 8 years in U.S., wife & 6 children,
   Ballstown, Saratoga Co., gardener (14-19 Sept. 1812)
Donaldson, James, age 32, 1 year in U.S., wife, NYC, saddler (3-
   8 Aug. 1812)
Donaldson, James, age 30, 7 years in U.S., Argyle, Washington
   Co., merchant, applied Aug. 1812 (28 Sept. - 3 Oct. 1812)
Donaldson, Peter, age 52, 15 years in U.S., wife & 4 children,
   Neversink, Sullivan Co., farmer (19-24 Oct. 1812)
Donaldson, Robert, 5ft. 5in., age 34, brown complex., brown hair,
   grey eyes, seaman (Navy)
Donaldson, Samuel, age 26, 6 years in U.S., wife, Argyle, Washing-
   ton Co., merchant, applied Aug. 1811 (28 Sept. - 3 Oct. 1812)
Donally, Patrick, 5ft. 8in., age 46, light complex., grey hair,
   blue eyes, Harman St., bricklayer (Navy)
Donalson, James, 5ft. 5in., age 54, dark complex., dark hair,
   blue eyes, cartman (Navy)
Donavan, Henry, 5ft. 7in., age 41, brown complex., brown hair,
   grey eyes, rigger (Navy)
Doner (?), John, 5ft. 4in., age 40, dark complex., brown hair,
   dark eyes, Jay St., mariner (Navy)
Donien, Thomas, 5ft. 9in., age 32, fair complex., sandy hair,
   grey eyes, William St., currier (Navy)
Donnan, Alexander, age 51, 28 years in U.S., wife & 8 children,
   Amsterdam, Montgomery Co., farmer (18-24 Aug. & 31 Aug. - 5
   Sept. 1812)
Donnelly, Adam, 5ft. 8in., age 22, brown complex., brown hair,
   blue eyes, Stanton St., sawyer (Navy)
Donnelly, John, 5ft. 7in., age 29, light complex., brown hair,
   blue eyes, Mulberry St., labourer (Navy)
Donnin, Thomas, 5ft. 7½in., age 34, dark complex., dark hair,
   grey eyes, Cherry St., sawyer (Navy)
Donovan, Daniel, age 45, 14 years in U.S., wife & 4 children,
   Claverack, Columbia Co., farmer (28 Aug. & 31 Aug. - 5 Sept.
   1812)
Donovan, Edward, age 30, 7 years in U.S., wife & child, Bloomingdale, labourer (20-25 July 1812)
Doolett, Abraham, age 33, 15 years & 6 mos. in U.S., wife & 5
   children, Pompey, Onondaga Co., carpenter (2-11 Nov. & 30 Nov.-
   5 Dec. 1812)

Doran, James, 5ft. 5in., age 38, brown complex., grey hair, grey
  eyes, labourer (Navy)
Doran, William, age 42, 7 years in U.S., wife & 3 children, 81
  Hester St., woolen manufacturer, applied Dec. 1808 (28 July -
  2 Aug. 1812); 5ft. 4in., age 42, fresh complex., grey hair,
  grey eyes (Navy)
Dorin, Arthur, age 40, 17 years in U.S., wife & 3 children, New
  Paltz, Ulster Co., miller (19-24 Oct. 1812)
Dorin, Patrick, age 21, 3 mos. in U.S., Newburgh, Orange Co.,
  laborer (19-24 Oct. 1812)
Dorman, William, 5ft. 2in., age 15, light complex., sandy hair,
  blue eyes, Water St., labourer (Navy)
Dornin, Thomas, age 33, 11 years in U.S., wife & 4 children,
  NYC, sawyer (28 July - 2 Aug. 1812)
Dornin, Thomas, age 31, 1 year in U.S., wife & 2 children, 32
  Bancker St., NYC, currier (28 July - 2 Aug. 1812)
Doudall, James, age 47 on 17 Aug., 22 years in U.S. next Oct.,
  wife & adopted son, Utica, Oneida Co., farmer (26 Aug. & 28
  Sept. - 3 Oct. 1812)
Doughan, John, 5ft. 6in., age 36, dark complex., dark hair, grey
  eyes, grocer (Navy)
Dougherty, Dennis, age 32, 5 years in U.S., wife & child, 44
  East George St., NYC, grocer (20-25 July 1812)
Dougherty, Dudley, age 28, 1 year in U.S., 99 Anthony St., NYC,
  laborer (28 July - 2 Aug. 1812)
Dougherty, Edward, age 20, 4 mos. in U.S., Clinton, Dutchess
  Co., weaver (12-17 Oct. 1812)
Dougherty, George, age 38, 14 years in U.S., Northeast, Dutchess
  Co., tailor (12-17 Oct. 1812)
Dougherty, Henry, 5ft. 9in., age 34, dark complex., brown hair,
  blue eyes, weaver (Navy)
Dougherty, Henry, age 30, 9 mos. in U.S., wife & 2 children,
  Republican Alley, NYC, laborer (20-25 July 1812)
Dougherty, Michael, age 27, 2 mos. in U.S., New Windsor, Orange
  Co., laborer (19-24 Oct. 1812)
Dougherty, Neal, age 28, 22 years in U.S., Bloominggrove, Orange
  Co., farmer (19-24 Oct. 1812)
Dougherty, Peter, age 40, 21 years in U.S., wife & 6 children,
  Platakill, Ulster Co., farmer (19-24 Oct. 1812)
Dougherty, Quinton, age 26, 3 years in U.S., wife, Wallkill,
  Orange Co., laborer (19-24 Oct. 1812)
Dougherty, William, 5ft. 8in., age 31, dark complex., brown hair,
  dark eyes, shoemaker (Navy)
Douglass, Alexander, age 31, 11 years in U.S., wife & 2 children,
  Smithfield, Madison Co., farmer (4 Aug. & 10-15 Aug. 1812)
Douglass, Daniel, age 34, 11 years in U.S., wife & 3 children,
  Smithfield, Madison Co., farmer (4 Aug. & 10-15 Aug. 1812)
Douglass, James, 5ft. 4in., age 23, fair complex., fair hair,
  brown eyes, Elm St., labourer (Navy)
Douglass, James, age 21, 16 years in U.S., 15 Reed St., NYC,
  trowel maker (28 July - 2 Aug. 1812); 5ft. 9in., age 22, light
  complex., light hair, brown eyes, Reed St. (Navy)
Douglass, John, age 36, 11 years in U.S., wife & 5 children,
  Smithfield, Madison Co., farmer (1 Aug. & 10-15 Aug. 1812)
Douglass, Joseph, age 21, 1 year & 6 mos. in U.S., Montgomery,
  Orange Co., weaver (19-24 Oct. 1812)
Doure (or Douie?), Henry, age 44, 1 year in U.S., wife & four
  children, 6 Chesnut St., NYC, merchant (28 July - 2 Aug. 1812)
Douie, Henry, 5ft. 3in., age 45, dark complex., dark hair, dark
  eyes, Nassau St., tailor (Navy)
Dow, Daniel, age 37, 2 years & 9 mos. in U.S., Johnstown, Mont-
  gomery Co., distiller of whiskey (11-17 & 17-22 Aug. 1812)
Dow, James, age 36 in Oct. last, 11 years in U.S. in May last,
  wife & 4 children, Thurman, Washington Co., farmer, was naturalized but lost certificate (24 Nov. 1812)

Dowd, John, 5ft. 6in., age 36, light complex., fair hair, blue
  eyes, Barclay St., pedler (Navy)
Dowd, Theophilus, 5ft. 11in., age 47, dark complex., brown hair,
  blue eyes, Cherry St., sawyer (Navy)
Dowland, Michael, age 34, 11 years in U.S., wife & child, Mont-
  gomery, Orange Co., farmer (19-24 Oct. 1812)
Dowley, Timothy, 5ft. 7in., age 47, light complex., sandy hair,
  blue eyes, gardener (Navy)
Dowling, James, age 36, 20 years in U.S., wife & 2 children,
  Ulysses, Tompkins Co., schoolmaster, applied in 1798 (28 Sept. -
  3 Oct. & 12-17 Oct. 1812)
Dowling, William, 5ft. 8in., age 40, dark complex., brown hair,
  blue eyes, grocer (Navy)
Downy, James, 5ft. 9½in., age 46, dark complex., dark hair, brown
  eyes, Front St., seaman (Navy)
Downy, Patrick, age 28, 4 years in U.S., Phoenix Coffee House,
  NYC, cook (28 July - 2 Aug. 1812); 5ft. 4in., age 30, fair
  complex., fair hair, brown eyes, Tontine Coffee House, cook
  (Navy)
Doyle, Edward, age 49, 1 year in U.S., 5 children, 37 Cross St.,
  NYC, laborer (28 July - 2 Aug. 1812)
Doyle, Edward, age 35, 1½ years in U.S., wife & 4 children,
  Orange St., NYC, carpenter (20-25 July 1812)
Doyle, Edward, 5ft. 1½in., age 30, dark complex., brown hair,
  grey eyes, carpenter (Navy)
Doyle, John, age 36, 9 years in U.S., NYC (9-14 Nov. 1812)
Doyle, John, 5ft. 8in., age 37, fair complex., brown hair, light
  eyes, Manhattanville, farmer (Navy)
Doyle, Lawrence, 5ft. 9in., age 47, dark complex., black hair,
  blue eyes, East George St., labourer (Navy)
Doyle, Philip, age 31, 1 year & 7 mos. in U.S., 21 Fayette St.,
  NYC, shoemaker (20-25 July 1812)
Drabble, James, age 28, 1 year & 4 mos. in U.S., 44 Pine St.,
  NYC, merchant (20-25 July 1812)
Draddy, Patrick, age 30, 1 year in U.S., 57 White Hall, NYC,
  laborer (20-25 July 1812)
Draddy, Patrick, 5ft. 7in., age 30, fair complex., light hair,
  brown eyes, Bancker St., labourer (Navy)
Drake, Henry, age 24, 1 year & 2 mos. in U.S., Greenwich St.,
  NYC, merchant (28 July - 2 Aug. 1812)
Drayton, John, age 47, 8 years in U.S., wife & 5 children, 156
  Bowery, NYC, hairdresser (20-25 July 1812)
Drennan, Alexander, age 37, 1 year & 3 mos. in U.S., wife & 6
  children, 37 Charlotte St., NYC, distiller (28 July - 2 Aug.
  1812)
Drennan, James, age 35, 9 years in U.S., wife & child, 13 Elm
  St., NYC, fireman (20-25 July 1812)
Drew, A., age 21, 7½ years in U.S., 69 Washington St., NYC, com-
  mercial pursuits (13-18 July 1812)
Drew, Robert, age 48, 4 years in U.S., 1 child, Greenwich St.,
  NYC, nailer, applied 23 Apr. 1810 (13-18 July 1812)
Drummond, James, age 52, 23 years in U.S., Rockland Co., farmer
  (31 Aug. - 5 Sept. 1812)
Drummond, John, 5ft. 7in., age 21, light complex., brown hair,
  hazel eyes, Bowery Lane, brass (founder) (Navy)
Drummond, Thomas, age 45, 1 year & 2 mos. in U.S., wife & 5
  children, Clinton, Dutchess Co., weaver (12-17 Oct. 1812)
Duait (or Duart?), John, 5ft. 9in., age 32, fair complex., brown
  hair, brown eyes, Bowery, weaver (Navy)
Dudley, Edward, age 43, 5 years in U.S., wife & 4 children, NYC,
  merchant, applied 6 Feb. 1810 (13-18 July 1812); 6ft., age 43,
  light complex., grey hair, grey eyes, removed from NYC to Claverack, Columbia Co. (Navy)
Duer, Stephen, age 20, 1 year in U.S., Rome, Oneida Co., weaver,
  employed in factory of James Lynch (29 July 1812)

Duff, Alexander, age 31, 8 years in U.S., City of Albany, mason
(17-22 Aug. 1812)
Duff, Anthony D., age 30, 7 years in U.S., wife & 3 children,
69 Washington St., NYC, merchant (20-25 July 1812); 5ft. 10in.,
fair complex., light hair, brown eyes, removed from NYC to
Goshen, Orange Co. (Navy)
Duff, Peter, 5ft. 7in., age 36, dark complex., dark hair, blue
eyes, lamplighter (Navy)
Duff, William, age 50, 17 years in U.S., Newburgh, Orange Co.,
weaver (19-24 Oct. 1812)
Duffie, Owen, 5ft. 1 3/4in., age 21, fair complex., red hair,
blue eyes, Nassau St., coachman (Navy)
Duffy, John, 5ft. 8in., age 22, light complex., sandy hair,
brown eyes (Navy)
Duffy, Peter, age 50, 2 years in U.S., wife & 3 children, Eliza-
beth St., NYC, merchant (20-25 July 1812)
Duffy, Philip, 5ft. 7in., age 45, light complex., brown hair,
blue eyes, Elizabeth St., cartman (Navy)
Duggan, Daniel, age 33, 1 year & 1 mo. in U.S., wife & 2 children, 34 Augustus St., NYC, cabinetmaker (28 July - 2 Aug. 1812)
Duggan (or Dugnan?), Michael, 5ft. 4in., age 60, pale complex.,
grey hair, grey eyes, pedler (Navy)
Duke, James, 5ft. 4½in., age 32, dark complex., dark hair, dark
eyes, Bancker St., painter (Navy)
Duke, William, age 27, 9 years in U.S., wife & 2 children, 16
Thomas St., NYC, carpenter (20-25 July 1812); 5ft. 8in., age
27, light complex., dark hair, blue eyes, Thomas St., carpen-
ter (Navy)
Dunbar, George, age 39, 17 years in U.S., wife & 4 children,
Schenectady, schoolmaster (17-22 Aug. 1812)
Dunbar, George, 5ft. 8in., age 30, fair complex., brown hair,
grey eyes, tailor (Navy); 3 years in U.S., 273 Greenwich St.,
tailor (3-8 Aug. 1812)
Dunbar, James, 5ft. 11in., age 22, fair complex., dark hair,
blue eyes, Christopher St., calico (printer?) (Navy)
Dummer, Peter, 5ft. 6in., age 22, dark complex., dark hair, grey
eyes, labourer (Navy)
Duncan, Alexander, age 41, 5ft. 5½in., fair complex., fair hair,
grey eyes, Barclay St., tailor (Navy)
Duncan, Alexander, age 38, 1 year in U.S., wife & 2 children,
131 Chamber St., NYC, merchant tailor (20-25 July 1812)
Duncan, Daniel, age 28, 6 years in U.S., wife, 15 Lower Robin-
son St., NYC, rigger, applied 4 years since (3-8 Aug. 1812)
Duncan, James, 5ft. 7in., age 36, dark complex., dark hair,
brown eyes, Elm St., engineer (Navy)
Duncan, James, age 32, 11 years in U.S., wife & 3 children, Marbletown, Ulster Co., sawmaker (19-24 Oct. 1812)
Duncan, James, age 28, 1 year in U.S., wife & 2 children, 47 Beaver St., NYC, brewer (28 July - 2 Aug. 1812)
Duncan, James, 5ft. 9in., age 25, dark complex., brown hair,
dark eyes, baker(?) (Navy)
Duncan, Richard, age 67, 47 years in U.S., 7 in family, British
captain on half pay (17-22 Aug. 1812)
Dunham, Henry, 5ft. 8½in., age 32, light complex., brown hair,
blue eyes, Oliver St., rigger (Navy)
Dunlap, Abraham, age 48, 23 years in U.S., Wallkill, Orange Co.,
weaver (21 Dec. 1812 - 23 Jan. 1813 & 2 Jan. 1813)
Dunlap, Hugh, age 35, 4 mos. in U.S., wife & 2 children, Bethel,
Sullivan Co., farmer (31 Aug. 7 19-24 Oct. 1812)
Dunlap, William, age 54, 17 years & 10 mos. in U.S., Montgomery,
Orange Co., laborer (19-24 Oct. 1812)
Dunlevy, Servence Mack, 5ft. 4in., age 30, dark complex., brown
hair, brown eyes, Anthony St., labourer (Navy)
Dunn, David, 5ft. 9in., age 30, dark complex., brown hair,
brown eyes, labourer (Navy)

Dumond, William V., age 60, 20 years in U.S., wife & 9 children,
   Coeymans, (British) lieutenant on half pay (2-7 Nov. 1812)
Dunn, Edward, 5ft. 11in., age 34, fair complex., light hair,
   grey eyes, carpenter (Navy)
Dunn, James, age 45, 5ft. 10in., fair complex., grey hair, dark
   eyes, Fair St., carpenter (Navy)
Dunn, James, age 40, 8 years in U.S., wife & 6 children, 36 Gold
   St., NYC, grocer (28 July - 2 Aug. 1812)
Dunn, James, 5ft. 9in., age 40, dark complex., brown hair, grey
   eyes, Gold St., porter (Navy)
Dunn, John, age 26, 4 years in U.S., wife, Saratoga, farmer (17-
   22 Aug. 1812)
Dunn, Joseph, age 72, 29 years in U.S., 514 Pearl St., NYC (20-
   25 July 1812)
Dunn, Maus, age 34, 9 years in U.S., 2 in family, NYC, laborer
   (28 July - 2 Aug. 1812)
Dunn, Robert, age 28, 2 weeks in U.S., City Hotel, NYC, merchant
   (12-17 Oct. 1812)
Dunn, William, 5ft. 7in., age 36, light complex., dark hair,
   light eyes, Broad St., clerk (Navy)
Dunnield, James, 5ft. 9in., age 25, dark complex., brown hair,
   grey eyes, Brooklyn, calico (printer) (Navy)
Dunseeth, James, age 46, 31 years in U.S., wife & 4 children,
   NYC, physician (20-25 July 1812)
Dunston, Charles, 5ft. 10in., age 34, fair complex., dark hair,
   grey eyes, gentleman (Navy)
Dury, Valentine, 5ft. 6in., age 46, fair complex., dark hair,
   blue eyes, Bloomingdale, professor (?) (Navy)
Duvant, John, 5ft. 6in., age 47, fair complex., brown hair, grey
   eyes, Manhattanville, gardener (Navy)
Dwyer, Thomas, age 27, 4 mos. in U.S., 17 Bancker St., NYC, tai-
   lor (20-25 July 1812)
Dwyer, William, age 21, 1 year & 8 mos. in U.S., Mount Pleasant,
   coachman (10-15 Aug. 1812)
Dwyer, William, 5ft. 5in., age 21, fair complex., brown hair,
   grey eyes, Desbrosses St., cartman (Navy)
Dyer, Daniel, age 31, 9 years in U.S. wife, 2 Orange St., NYC,
   money collector & wine cooper (13-18 July 1812)
Dyer, Samuel, age 20, 1 year & 1 mo., in U.S., 132 Water St.,
   NYC, brushmaker, applied 25 June 1812 (28 July - 2 Aug. 1812)
Dyson, Henry, 5ft. 5in., age 22, dark complex., black hair, brown
   eyes, First St., printer (Navy)
Dyson, James Smith, 5ft. 9in., age 17, fair complex., light hair,
   blue eyes, Broadway, weaver (Navy)
Eagar, Charles, 5ft. 9in., age 24, fair complex., sandy hair,
   grey eyes, Reed St., stone cutter (Navy)
Eaken, English, age 21, 5 years in U.S., Augustus St., NYC, currier (28 July - 2 Aug. 1812); 5ft. 5in., age 22, light complex.,
   brown hair, dark eyes, Augustus St., currier (Navy)
Eakin, John, 5ft. 5in., age 34, brown complex., brown hair, brown
   eyes, Hester St., carpenter (Navy)
Earl, John, age 31, 6 years & 2 mos. in U.S., wife & 2 children,
   360 Pearl St., NYC, brushmaker (14-19 Sept. 1812); 5ft. 2in.,
   age 32, light complex., dark hair, grey eyes, Pearl St., brushmaker (Navy)
Easingwood, Mathew, age 38, 2 years in U.S., wife, NYC, printer
   (13-18 July 1812); 5ft. 8in., age 39, dark complex., dark hair,
   dark eyes (Navy)
Eastmond, John, 5ft. 7in., age 41, light complex., black hair,
   grey eyes, Bowery, clerk (Navy)
Eddy, James, 5ft. 5in., age 32, light complex., brown hair, blue
   eyes, Brooklyn, hatter (Navy)
Eddy, John, 5ft. 8 3/4in., age 35, dark complex., black hair,
   black eyes, carpenter (Navy)

Edgecomb, John, age 36, 4 mos. in U.S., 1 son, 150 Broadway,
NYC, merchant (20-25 July 1812)
Edgson, William, age 37, 6 years in U.S., wife & 4 children, 116
Cherry St., NYC, cordwainer (20-25 July 1812)
Edmeston, Andrew, age 29, 1 year in U.S., Otsego Co., applied
4 Feb. 1812 (13 -18 July 1812)
Edmonds, Bogert, 5ft., 6 3/4in., age 28, dark complex., brown
hair, grey eyes, Greenburgh, Westchester Co. (Navy)
Edson, William, 5ft. 6in., age 36, fair complex., brown hair,
brown eyes, Mott St., shoemaker (Navy)
Edwards, Daniel, age 54, 6 years in U.S., wife, Corlears Hook,
livery stable keeper (21-26 Sept. 1812) - perhaps the same:
Edward, Daniel, 5ft. 10in., age 54, light complex., sandy hair,
grey eyes, flour dealer (Navy)
Edwards, Richard, age 30, 7 years in U.S., wife & 3 children,
Amenia, Dutchess Co., miller (12-17 Oct. 1812)
Edwards, Thomas, 5ft. 9in., age 38, dark complex., dark hair,
grey eyes, Bloomingdale, labourer (Navy)
Edwards, Thomas age 27 on 1 June last, 11 years in U.S. in Aug.
inst., Whitestown, Oneida Co., farmer (29 Sept. & 28 Sept. -
3 Oct. 1812)
Egenton, William, age 24, 6 years in U.S., 505 Pearl St., NYC,
carpenter (28 July - 2 Aug. 1812)
Egeran/Egern, Joshua, age 31, 3 years in U.S., wife, Prince St.,
NYC, ropemaker (20-25 July 1812); 5ft. 4½in., age 32, brown
complex., brown hair, grey eyes, Sullivan St., ropemaker (Navy)
Egerton, John, 5ft. 5in., age 22, light complex., light hair,
grey eyes, burr mill (Navy)
Elder, John, age 30, 2 years in U.S., corner Chapel & Robinson
Sts., NYC, grocer (28 July - 2 Aug. 1812)
Elder, Stewart, age 26, 6 years in U.S., wife & child, 13 Robin-
son St., NYC, grocer, applied 2 Nov. 1810 (13-18 July 1812)
Elexander, Samuel, age 26, 7 years in U.S., Saugerties, Ulster
Co., tanner (19-24 Oct. 1812)
Elkins, James, age 39, 16 years in U.S., 5 in family, 192 Wa-
shington St., mason (20-25 July 1812); 5ft. 8in., age 39, dark
complex., dark hair, black eyes, Barclay St., mason (Navy)
Elkins, William, age 57, 6 years in U.S., 89 Front St., NYC, la-
bourer (20-25 July 1812)
Elkins/Elkin, William, 5ft. 6in., age 55, light complex., light
hair, grey eyes, labourer (Navy)
Ellicot (?), William, 5ft. 7in., age 21, fair complex., fair
hair, grey eyes, Cross St., blacksmith (Navy)
Elliot, George, age 32, 14 years in U.S., wife & 4 children,
Schoharie, tanner (24-29 Aug. 1812)
Elliot, John, 5ft. 8½in., age 45, pale complex., grey hair, grey
eyes, Anthony St., teacher (Navy)
Elliot, John, 5ft. 9½in., age 28, dark complex., dark hair,
black eyes, grocer (Navy)
Elliot, Moses, 5ft. 10in., age 30, fair complex., light hair,
light eyes, tanner (Navy)
Elliot, William, 5ft. 5½in., age 49, brown complex., dark hair,
dark eyes, Oyster Bay, schoolmaster (Navy)
Ellipson, John, age 30, 4 years & 5 mos. in U.S., Poughkeepsie,
Dutchess Co., brickmaker (12-17 Oct. 1812)
Ellis, Alexander, 5ft. 7½in., age 27, fair complex., brown hair,
light eyes, Anthony St., cartman (Navy)
Ellis, John, 5ft. 6in., age 24, red complex., brown hair, blue
eyes, Cedar St., coachman (Navy)
Ellis, John, Jr., age 25, 18 years in U.S., wife & 2 children,
Essex St., NYC, ship carver (28 July - 2 Aug. 1812); 5ft. 3 in.,
fair complex., brown hair, brown eyes, ship carver (Navy)
Ellis, Thomas, age 30, 1 year & 8 mos. in U.S., NYC, carpenter
(28 July - 2 Aug. 1812)

Elsworth, John, 5ft. 8in., age 24, light complex., brown hair,
    dark eyes, William St., maltster (Navy)
Emerson, James, age 22, 1 year & 2 mos. in U.S., Hudson, Columbia
    Co., weaver (10-15 Aug. 1812)
English, Edward, 5ft. 6½in., age 28, light complex., brown hair,
    grey eyes, Front St., stevedore (Navy)
English, John, age 27, 7 years in U.S., wife & child, NYC, ship-
    wright (20-25 July 1812); 5ft. 7in., age 28, dark complex.,
    dark hair, dark eyes, Bancker St., shipwright (Navy)
English, Richard, age 32, 10½ years in U.S., wife & 3 children,
    Stafford, Genesee Co., carpenter (10 Dec. 1812 - 15 Feb. 1813)
English, William, age 25, 1 year & 4 mos. in U.S., Newburgh,
    Orange Co., tailor (19-24 Oct. 1812)
Enwer, Nicholas, age 66, 5 years in U.S., wife & child, Moore
    St., NYC, grocer (28 July - 2 Aug. 1812); 5ft. 5in., age 66,
    light complex., grey hair, brown eyes, Moore St., grocer (Navy)
Enwer, Patrick, age 23, 11 years in U.S., Front St., NYC, grocer
    (28 July - 2 Aug. 1812); 5ft. 4½in., age 23, fair complex.,
    brown hair, brown eyes, Cherry St., grocer (Navy)
Erwin, Jared, age 31, 7 years & 2 mos. in U.S., Bethel, Sullivan
    Co., farmer (31 Aug. & 19-24 Oct. 1812)
Erret, Henry, age 24, 1 year & 10 mos. in U.S., 3 in family, 8
    Warren St., NYC, accountant (13-18 July 1812)
Eulis, James, age 23, 1 year & 10 mos. in U.S., Montgomery,
    Orange Co., weaver (19-24 Oct. 1812)
Evans, Daniel, age 23, 1 year & 11 mos. in U.S., Hudson, Colum-
    bia Co., weaver (10-15 Aug. 1812)
Evans, James, 5ft. 9in., age 36, fair complex., sandy hair,
    blue eyes, carver (Navy)
Evans, John, age 35, 6 years in U.S., wife & 5 children, 186
    Broadway, carver & gilder (20-25 July 1812)
Evans, Joseph, 5ft. 10in., age 25, fair complex., red hair, blue
    eyes, Provost St., coachman (Navy)
Evans, Robert, age 35 on 14 July last, 11 years in U.S. on 2 Aug.
    last, wife, Steuben, Oneida Co., farmer (29 Sept. & 28 Sept. -
    3 Oct. 1812)
Evans, Robert, 5ft. 9in., age 29, fair complex., fair hair, dark
    eyes, Pearl St., cordwainer (Navy)
Evans, Robert, 5ft. 9in., age 27, fair complex., fair hair, dark
    eyes, sawyer (Navy)
Evans, Thomas, 5ft. 8in., age 30, florid complex., brown hair,
    blue eyes, gardener (Navy)
Evans, Thomas Edward, age 19, 15 days in U.S., 110 Greenwich St.,
    NYC, merchant (5-10 Oct. 1812)
Evatt, John, age 20, 5 years in U.S., Canandaigua, Ontario Co.,
    farmer (5-15 & 24-29 Aug. 1812)
Evens, Ezekiel, age 25, 1 year & 2 mos. in U.S., wife & 2 child-
    ren, Cornwall, Orange Co., weaver (19-24 Oct. 1812)
Evens, George, age 21 last Feb., 9 years in U.S. this Aug., a
    single man, Utica, Oneida Co., blacksmith, from Tenbury, Eng.
    (10 Aug. 1812) - same save that he has a wife (17-22 Aug. 1812)
Everard, Ebenezer, age 41, 5 years in U.S., wife & 7 children,
    Bethel, Sullivan Co., farmer (31 Aug. 1812)
Everard, Thomas, age 29, 10 years 7 10 mos. in U.S., wife & 3
    children, Elmira, Tioga Co., nailor (to 20 Oct. & 26- 31 Oct.
    1812)
Everend, Ebenezer, age 51, 5 years in U.S., wife & 7 children,
    Bethel, Sullivan Co., farmer (19-24 Oct. 1812)- possible con-
    fusion with Everard, Ebenezer, above?
Everson, Nicholas, age 34, 4 years & 4 mos. in U.S., wife & 2
    children, Poughkeepsie, Dutchess Co., laborer (12-17 Oct. 1812)
Ewelt, Henry, 6ft., age 24, fair complex., brown hair, blue eyes,
    Warren St., accountant (Navy)
Fagan, Charles, age 26, 4 years in U.S., Monroe Works, Orange
    Co., cut nailor (17-22 Aug. 1812)

Fagan, Edward, 5ft. 6in., age 24, light complex., light hair,
blue eyes, Provost St., stone cutter (Navy)

Fagan, James, 5ft. 6in., age 45, dark complex., brown hair,
brown eyes, labourer (Navy)

Fagan, Patrick, 5ft. 5in., age 35, light complex., brown hair,
brown eyes, Manhattanville, blacksmith (Navy)

Fague (?), William, 5ft. 9in., age 26, fair complex., light hair,
light eyes, boatman (Navy)

Faigy (?), Samuel, 5ft. 8in., age 32, light complex., grey hair,
blue eyes, Henry St., weaver (Navy)

Fairbairn, James, age 57, 28 years in U.S., wife & 2 children,
Northumberland, Saratoga Co., tailor (31 Aug.- 5 Sept. 1812)

Fairbanck, Jonathan, age 45, 9 years in U.S., Rhinebeck, Dutchess
Co., clothier (12-17 Oct. 1812)

Falconer, George, age (illegible), 7 mos. in U.S., wife, 33 Dey
St., NYC, commercial pursuits (13-18 July 1812)

Falconer, Patrick, age 34, 18 years in U.S., 13 Broadway, NYC,
merchant (20-25 July 1812)

Falconer, William, age 22, 21 years in U.S., 336 Greenwich St.,
Venetian blind maker, applied 8 June 1812 (20-25 July 1812)

Farley, James, 5ft. 5in., age 35, dark complex., grey hair, brown
eyes, Attorney St., cartman (Navy)

Farquha, Roderick M., 5ft. 5in., age 44, fair complex., dark
hair, blue eyes, cooper (Navy)

Farrell, Francis, age 43, 2 years in U.S., 29 Chatham Row, NYC,
storekeeper, applied 22 June 1812 (20-25 July 1812)

Farrell, John, age 30, 7 years in U.S., 32 Barclay St., NYC, labourer (28 July - 2 Aug. 1812)

Farrell, John, age 24, 6 years in U.S., 14 Frankford St., NYC,
tailor (20-25 July 1812)

Farrell, John /John J.O. (for O'Farrell?), age 27, 1 year & 7
mos. in U.S., wife & child, Newark, N.J., merchant (10-15 Aug.
1812)

Farrell, Michael, age 26, 2 years in U.S., Goshen, Orange Co.,
laborer (19-24 Oct. 1812)

Farrell, Patrick, 5ft. 8in., age 35, light complex., light hair,
blue eyes, Rye, Westchester Co., labourer (Navy)

Farren, Barney, 5ft. 7in., age 22, light complex., brown hair,
brown eyes, hatter (Navy)

Farren, Daniel, age 28, 15 years in U.S., Goshen, Orange Co.,
laborer (19-24 Oct. 1812)

Farren, John, 5ft. 7in., age 28, fair complex., brown hair, blue
eyes, weaver (Navy)

Farwell, Roger, 5ft. 8in., age 25, brown complex., fair hair,
blue eyes, William St., tailor (Navy)

Faulkner, Thomas, age 38, 19 years in U.S., wife & 6 children,
Roxbury, Delaware Co., shoemaker (7-12 Sept. 1812)

Faulkner, William, 5ft. 9in., age 26, light complex., brown hair,
blue eyes, Duane St., chandler (Navy)

Fawcet/Fawsit, William, age 43, 7 years in U.S., wife & 3 children, 1 Liberty St., NYC, blacksmith (28 July - 2 Aug. 1812);
5ft. 7½in., age 43, dark complex., black hair, brown eyes,
Warren St., blacksmith (Navy)

Feagan, Edward, age 48, 1 year in U.S., wife, 41 Cross St., NYC,
laborer (20-25 July 1812)

Fearon, George, age 31 on 15 July last, 1 year in U.S. on 12 Aug.
last, wife, mother, 3 children & 1 servant, Eaton, Madison Co.,
farmer (31 Oct. & 30 Nov. - 5 Dec. 1812)

Feaser, John C., age 22, 2 years in U.S., Bancker St., NYC, baker
(20-25 July 1812)

Featherstonhaugh, G.W., age 32, 5 years in U.S., wife & child,
Duanesburgh, Schenectady Co., farmer (28 July - 2 Aug. 1812)

Feeney, Dennis, 5ft. 7in., age 30, fair complex., fair hair,
blue eyes, Cross St., labourer (Navy)

Feeny (or Furey?), Andrew, 5ft. 6in., age 29, dark complex., dark
  hair, blue eyes, Vandewater St., currier (Navy)
Fegan, Edward, 5ft. 7in., age 48, fair complex., fair hair, blue
  eyes, Cross St., labourer (Navy)
Fegan, Francis, age 22, 5 years in U.S., NYC, stone cutter (14-
  19 Sept. 1812)
Fegan, Henry, age 30, 5 years in U.S., 130 Chamber St., NYC,
  butcher (14-19 Sept. 1812)
Fegan, James, 5ft. 6in., age 25, dark complex., brown hair, dark
  eyes, Bowery Lane, butcher (Navy)
Fegan, Patrick, age 23, 5 years in U.S., NYC, cooper (14-19 Sept.
  1812); 5ft. 5½in., age 24, dark complex., black hair, grey
  eyes, cooper (Navy)
Fehe(?)ligh, John, 5ft. 8in., age 35, dark complex., brown hair,
  grey eyes, Bowery, gardener (Navy)
Fennell, James, age 31, 5 mos. in U.S., wife & 4 children, 37
  Cross St., NYC, stone cutter (20-25 July 1812); 5ft. 4in.,
  age 32, fair complex., sandy hair, blue eyes, stone cutter
  (Navy)
Fenner, Thomas, age 62, 9 years in U.S., 3 children, Poughkeepsie,
  Dutchess Co., farmer (12-17 Oct. 1812)
Fenningham, Martin, 5ft. 5in., age 27, fair complex., brown hair,
  grey eyes, Duane & Cross Sts., labourer (Navy)
Fenton, James, 5ft. 10 in., age 28, fair complex., black hair,
  brown eyes, Greenwich St., gardener (Navy)
Ferguson, Alexander, age 45, 8 years in U.S., wife & 3 children,
  Johnsburgh, Washington Co., farmer (21 Dec. 1812 - 23 Jan.
  1813); wife Margaret & children Isabella, Jane & Alexander,
  Johnsburgh, Washington Co., farmer (30 Dec. 1812)
Ferguson, Alexander, age 41, 8 years in U.S., 1 daughter, NYC
  (13-18 July 1812); 5ft. 5in., age 42, dark complex., brown hair,
  dark eyes, fan sash maker (Navy)
Ferguson, Daniel, 5ft. 7½in., age 41, dark complex., brown hair,
  grey eyes, Duane St., nailor (Navy)
Ferguson, Hugh, 5ft. 8in., age 40, light complex., brown hair,
  grey eyes, labourer (Navy)
Ferguson, James, age 40, 15 years in U.S., 440 Greenwich St.,
  NYC, grocer (20-25 July 1812); 5ft. 7in., age 40, fair com-
  plex., brown hair, blue eyes, storekeeper (Navy)
Ferguson, James, age 34, 3 years in U.S., Caledonia, Genesee Co.,
  mason (24-29 Aug. 1812)
Ferguson, James, 5ft. 6in., age 33, fair complex., sandy hair,
  brown eyes, Charlotte St., ship carpenter (Navy)
Ferguson, James, 5ft. 6in., age 18, light complex., brown hair,
  grey eyes, Bowery, labourer (Navy)
Ferguson, John, age 33, 2½ years in U.S., wife & child, Bancker
  St., NYC, no status given (20-25 July 1812)
Ferguson, John, 5ft. 9in., age 30, dark complex., dark hair,
  grey eyes, Bancker St., maltster (Navy)
Ferquand, Paul Leonard, 5ft. 3¼in., age 35, fair complex., dark
  hair, brown eyes, Broome St., schoolmaster (Navy)
Ferran, James, 5ft. 10in., age 28, fair complex., fair hair,
  blue eyes, cartman (Navy)
Ferris, Robert, 5ft. 10in., age 24, light complex., sandy hair,
  blue eyes, Pecks Slip, labourer (Navy)
Ferris, Thomas, age 46, 2 years in U.S., wife, 8 Liberty St.,
  NYC, grocer (13-18 July 1812)
Ferris, Thomas, 5ft. 5in., age 45, dark complex., dark hair,
  blue eyes, Greenwich St., innkeeper (Navy)
Ferry, Daniel, 5ft. 6 3/4in., age 35, dark complex., dark hair,
  grey eyes, Courtland St., servant (Navy)
Ferry, Philip, 5ft. 8in., age 44, light complex., dark hair,
  blue eyes, pedler (Navy)
Ferryth (?), Alexander, 5ft. 10in., age 23½, fair complex., light
  hair, hazel eyes, Division St., ship carpenter (Navy)

Fewley, John, 5ft. 6in., age 29, fair complex., brown hair,
blue eyes, preacher (Navy)
Field, Isaac D., age 31, 2 years in U.S., Newark, N.J., store-
keeper (28 Sept. - 3 Oct. 1812)
Field, William, 5ft. 7in., age 41, brown complex., fair hair,
grey eyes, Water St., labourer (Navy)
Fife, John, age 28, 5 years in U.S., Clinton, Dutchess Co.,
labourer (12-17 Oct. 1812)
Fife, Thomas, age 27, 9 years & 6 mos. in U.S., Bloominggrove,
Orange Co., laborer (21 Dec. 1812- 23 Jan. 1813)
Fife, Thomas, age 27, 9 years in U.S., Orange Co., weaver (10-
15 Aug. 1812) - the same as Thomas above?
Finch, James, age 28, 3 years in U.S. on 7 Sept. last, wife (an
American), Whitestown, Oneida Co., carder & spinner (26 Aug.
& 28 Sept. - 3 Oct. 1812)
Finean, Martin, age 48, 6 years in U.S., wife, corner Duane &
Augustus Sts., NYC, laborer (28 July - 2 Aug. 1812)
Finegan, John, 5ft. 9in., age 25, brown complex., brown hair,
grey eyes, Broome St., weaver (Navy)
Finey, James, 5ft. 5½in., age 22, light complex., brown hair,
grey eyes, Front St., cooper (Navy)
Finlay, John, age 28, 8 years in U.S., wife & child, Haverstraw,
Rockland Co., minister of the Gospel (28 July - 2 Aug. 1812)
Finley, David, 5ft. 7in., age 38, fair complex., fair hair, blue
eyes, Leonard St. (Navy)
Finley, James, age 32, 2 years & 9 mos. in U.S., wife & 5 child-
ren, Newburgh, Orange Co., laborer (19-24 Oct. 1812)
Finn, Martin, 5ft. 8in., age 49, fair complex., dark hair, dark
eyes, Moore St., labourer (Navy)
Fiphily, John, age 33, 5 years in U.S., NYC, laborer (7-12 Sept.
1812)
Firkins, George, age 46, 19 years in U.S., wife & 5 children,
Cato, Cayuga Co., tailor, marched as a volunteer in Captain
Woodruff's company (5-10 & 19-24 Oct. 1812)
Fisher, Alexander Duff, age 36, 2 years in U.S., wife & child,
Jay St., NYC, comedian (20-25 July 1812);
Fisher, Allen Duff Clark, 5ft. 4in., age 38, fair complex., light
hair, blue eyes, comedian (Navy)
Fisher, Andrew, age 42, 10 years in U.S., wife & 4 children, 5
Elizabeth St., NYC, butcher (20-25 July 1812); 5ft. 8in., age
44, fair complex., fair hair, blue eyes, Division St., butcher
(Navy)
Fisher, Andrew, 5ft. 7½in., age 30, light complex., light hair,
blue eyes, steam boat coaster (Navy)
Fisher, James, 5ft. 7½in., age 21, fair complex., red hair, glass
manufacturer (Navy)
Fisher, John, age 52, 6 years in U.S., wife & 4 children, Johnstown, Montgomery Co., merchant (11-17 & 17-22 Aug. 1812)
Fisher, John, age 24, 2½ years in U.S., 43 Partition St., NYC,
waiter (20-25 July 1812); 5ft. 2½in., age 24, light complex.,
light hair, blue eyes, Greenwich St., waiter (Navy)
Fisher, Joshua, 5ft. 9in., age 34, ruddy complex., dark hair,
hazel eyes, Broadway, physician (Navy)
Fisher, Robert, age 32, 7 years in U.S., Coffee House Slip, NYC,
grocer (28 July - 2 Aug. 1812)
Fitchpatrick (sic!), Patrick, age 32, 6 years in U.S., wife & 5
children, NYC, blacksmith (20-25 July 1812)
Fitzsimmons, John, age 30, 12 years in U.S., New Windsor, Orange
Co., farmer (2 Jan. 1813 & 21 Dec. 1812 - 23 Jan. 1813)
Fitzgerald. Morris, age 22, 11 years in U.S., 56 Beaver St.,
NYC, dyer (3-8 Aug. 1812)
Fitzgerald, William, 5ft. 6in., age 37, fair complex., fair hair,
blue eyes, Division St., tailor (Navy)
Fitzpatrick, J., 5ft. 9in., age 22, fair complex., fair hair,
grey eyes, labourer (Navy)

Fitzpatrick, John, age 27, 3 years in U.S., 53 East George St.,
    NYC, grocer (2-7 Nov. 1812)
Fitzpatrick, William, age 30, 1 year in U.S., 16 William St.,
    NYC, sawyer (28 July - 2 Aug. 1812)
Fitzpatrick, William, 5ft. 8in., age 27, fair complex., brown
    hair, brown eyes, Hamilton Square, labourer (Navy)
Fitzreade, William C., age 26, 1 year & 3 mos. in U.S., wife &
    2 children, Kingston, Ulster Co., merchant (19-24 Oct. 1812)
Fitzsimmons, David, age 24, 1 year in U.S., Montgomery, Orange
    Co., farmer (19-24 Oct. 1812)
Fitzsimmons, John, age 21, 1 year & 2 mos. in U.S., Wallkill,
    Orange Co., weaver (19-24 Oct. 1812)
Fitzsimmons, Martin, age 56, 24 years in U.S., Fort Ann, Washing-
    ton Co., farmer, disabled from rheumatism (16 Oct. & 26-31 Oct.
    1812)
Flagherty, James, age 36, 7 years & 3 mos. in U.S., wife & 6
    children, Montgomery, Orange Co., weaver (19-24 Oct. 1812)
Flagherty, John, age 16, 5 years in U.S., Montgomery, Orange Co.,
    weaver (19-24 Oct. 1812)
Flanagan, Michael, 7 years in U.S., wife & 3 children, NYC, saw-
    yer (18 July - 2 Aug. 1812); 5ft. 7½in., age 34, fair complex.,
    brown hair, grey eyes, sawyer (Navy)
Flanagan, Peter, age 26, 6 years in U.S., 48 Lombardy St., NYC,
    clerk (20-25 July 1812); 5ft. 7½in., age 26, dark complex.,
    dark hair, bkue eyes, Lombardy St., clerk (Navy)
Flanrey, Thomas, age 25, 15 years in U.S., Johnstown, Montgomery
    Co., tailor (18-24 Aug. & 31 Aug. - 5 Sept. 1812)
Fleming, John, 5ft. 3in., age 25, light complex., sandy hair,
    grey eyes, labourer (Navy)
Fleming, John B., age 25, 7 years & 2 mos. in U.S., wife & 3
    children & 2 servants, 77 Broad St., NYC, merchant (13-18 July
    1812); 5ft. 10in., age 26, fair complex., brown hair, blue eyes,
    removed from NYC (Navy)
Fleming, William, 5ft. 6in., age 40, light complex., sandy hair,
    grey eyes, Greenwich St., labourer (Navy)
Fleming, William, 5ft. 7in., age 36, sandy complex., dark hair,
    blue eyes, carpenter (Navy)
Fletcher, John, 5ft. 9in., age 20, light complex., brown hair,
    grey eyes, baker (Navy)
Fletcher, Joseph, age 37, 12 years in U.S., wife & 4 children,
    41 Barclay St., NYC, carpenter (28 July - 2 Aug. 1812); 5ft.
    7½in., age 37, brown complex., brown hair, blue eyes, Thomas
    St., carpenter (Navy)
Flinn, Christopher, 5ft. 8in., age 40, dark complex., brown hair,
    grey eyes, carpenter (Navy)
Flinn, John, age 46, 11 years in U.S., 4 males & 1 female in his
    family, corner Barclay & Church Sts., NYC (20-25 July 1812);
    5ft. 6in., age 46, dark complex., light hair, brown eyes, Bar-
    clay St., tailor (Navy)
Flood, Patrick, age 35, 5 years in U.S., Monroe Works, Orange
    Co., cut nailor (18 - 22 Aug. 1812)
Flynn, John, age 22, 9 years in U.S., Scipio, Cayuga Co., labo-
    rer, "peaceable & inoffensive" (7-12 & 21-26 Sept. 1812)
Flynn, Michael, age 40, 8 years in U.S., wife & 4 children, NYC,
    wheelwright (13-18 July 1812); 5ft. 5in., age 40, dark complex.,
    brown hair, blue eyes, Mulberry St., wheelwright (Navy)
Fogerty, Jeremiah, age 27, 1 year & 6 mos. in U.S., Washington,
    Dutchess Co., weaver (12-17 Oct. 1812)
Foley, Bartholomew, age 46, 16 years in U.S., wife & 5 children,
    Minisink, Orange Co., schoolmaster (19-24 Oct. 1812)
Foley, Bartholomew, age 35, 6 years in U.S., wife, 39 Augustus
    St., NYC, laborer (28 July - 2 Aug. 1812); 5ft. 9½in., age 35,
    fair complex., brown hair, grey eyes, labourer (Navy)
Foley, Edward, 5ft. 6in., age 27, light complex., dark hair,
    dark eyes, William St., nailor (Navy)

Foley, James, age 33, 6 years in U.S., NYC (20-25 July 1812)
Foley, Philip, 5ft. 7in., age 45, sandy complex., brown hair,
  grey eyes, labourer (Navy)
Folingsby/Follensby, William G., age 18, 1 year & 6 mos. in U.S.,
  NYC, clerk (20-25 July 1812); 5ft. 9in., age 19, brown com-
  plex., dark hair, blue eyes, clerk (Navy)
Follington, James, 5ft. 7in., age 35, dark complex., dark hair,
  grey eyes, Hell Gate, gardener (Navy)
Foly, Michael, 5ft. 3in., age 35, light complex., dark hair,
  blue eyes, Augustus St., nailor (Navy)
For, Henry, 5ft. 7½in., age 35, fair complex., dark hair, hazel
  eyes, burns stone (Navy)
For, Patrick, 5ft. 8in., age 45, fair complex., brown hair, grey
  eyes, labourer (Navy)
Forbes, Daniel, age 22, 11 years in U.S., Lenox, Madison Co.,
  farmer (3 Aug. & 10-15 Aug. 1812)
Forbes, Duncan, age 29, 9 years in U.S., City of Albany, tobac-
  conist (17-22 Aug. 1812)
Forbes, James, age 20, 1 year & 9 mos. in U.S., Cornwall, Orange
  Co., weaver (19-24 Oct. 1812)
Forbes, John, 5ft. 6in., age 46, brown complex., brown hair,
  brown eyes, Elm St., carpenter (Navy)
Forbes, John, 5ft. 7in., age 45, fair complex., dark hair, grey
  eyes, North Moore St., servant (Navy)
Forbes, John, age 29, 11 years in U.S., wife, Lenox, Madison Co.,
  farmer (3 Aug. & 10-15 Aug. 1812)
Forbes, Peter, age 26, 6 years in U.S., Lenox, Madison Co., farmer (3 Aug. & 10-15 Aug. 1812)
Ford, George, 5ft. 7in., age 49, dark complex., black hair, grey
  eyes, weaver (Navy)
Ford, John, age 45, 19 years in U.S., 395 Greenwich St., NYC,
  thread manufacturer (28 July - 2 Aug. 1812); 5ft. 3½in., black
  complex., black hair, grey eyes, Greenwich St., thread manufacturer (Navy)
Ford, William, age 64, 13 years in U.S., NYC, cabinetmaker (20-
  25 July 1812); 5ft. 8in., age 66, light complex., grey hair,
  blue eyes, cabinetmaker (Navy)
Forrest, Robert, age 44, 10 years in U.S., wife, Delaware Co.,
  minister, applied 2 June 1812 (17-22 Aug. 1812)
Forrest, William, age 22, 11 years in U.S., Dominick St., NYC,
  usher (20-25 July 1812); 5ft. 9in., age 22, fair complex.,
  brown hair, brown eyes, Varick St., teacher (Navy)
Forsyth, Alexander, age 22, 21½ years in U.S., wife, NYC, shipwright (28 July - 2 Aug. 1812)
Forsyth, James, age 29, 7 years in U.S., Greenwich St., NYC,
  weaver (10-15 Aug. 1812)
Forsyth, Joseph, age 28, 6 years & 2 mos. in U.S., Bethel, Sul-
  livan Co., farmer, applied June 1810 (31 Aug. & 19-24 Oct.
  1812)
Forsyth, Robert, age 27, 1 year & 6 mos. in U.S., 49 Pearl St.,
  NYC, tailor (20-25 July 1812); 5ft. 8in., age 28, light com-
  plex., fair hair, grey eyes, Water St., tailor (Navy)
Fortune, Henry, 5ft. 6in., age 47, dark complex., dark hair, dark
  eyes, Broadway, waiter (Navy)
Foster, Arthur, age 22, 1 year & 2 mos. in U.S., Montgomery,
  Orange Co., farmer (19-24 Oct. 1812)
Foster, George S., age 27, 4½ years in U.S., 30 Thames St., co-
  median (20-25 July 1812)
Foster, James, age 29, 1 year in U.S., wife & 2 children, Mont-
  gomery, Orange Co., farmer (19-24 Oct. 1812)
Foster, John, age 42, 8 years in U.S., 4 in family, NYC, groom
  (3-8 Aug. 1812)
Foster, Robert, 6ft., age 30, fair complex., brown hair, grey
  eyes, Stagg Town, labourer (Navy)

Foster, William, 5ft. 5in., age 40, light complex., fair hair,
  blue eyes, cartman (Navy)
Foundling, William, 5ft. 6in., age 35, dark complex., dark hair,
  brown eyes, weaver (Navy)
Fowle, Daniel, age 32, 13 years in U.S., 5 in family, Seneca,
  Ontario Co., farmer (15-22 Aug. & 31 Aug. - 5 Sept. 1812)
Fowle, James, age 43, 8 years in U.S., Geneva, Ontario Co.,
  brewer (15-22 Aug. & 31 Aug. - 5 Sept. 1812)
Fowler, John, 5ft. 5in., age 55, light complex., light hair,
  brown eyes, Pump St., tailor (Navy)
Fowler, Jonathan, age 57, born in State of N.Y., wife, Westches-
  ter Co., farmer, half pay British officer (13-18 July 1812)
Fowler, Samuel, 5ft. 6in., age 32, dark complex., dark hair,
  black eyes, shoemaker (Navy)
Fowler, William, age 24, 4 years in U.S., wife & child, 17
  Spring St., NYC, baker (3-8 Aug. 1812)
Fox, Patrick, age 18, 1½ years in U.S., Minisink, Orange Co.,
  shoemaker (19-24 Oct. 1812)
Francis, James, 5ft. 2in., age 36, light complex., brown hair,
  grey eyes, Walnut St., chemist (Navy)
Francis, Patrick, 5ft. 8in., age 33, dark complex., black hair,
  blue eyes, Ferry St., labourer (Navy)
Franklin, Joseph, age 25, 1½ years in U.S., 1 Clark St., NYC,
  merchant (28 July - 2 Aug. 1812)
Franklyn, Joseph, 5ft. 10 in., age 27, fair complex., dark hair,
  grey eyes, grocer, removed from NYC to Fishkill, Dutchess Co.
  (Navy) - Navy in one record gives color of hair as red.
Fraser, Donald, age 40, 6 years in U.S., City of Albany (17-22
  Aug. 1812)
Fraser, James, carver & gilder (17-22 Aug. 1812)
Frasher, Charles, 5ft. 8in., age 29, ruddy complex., dark hair,
  grey eyes, John St., painter (Navy)
Frashur, John, 5ft. 8in., age 50, dark complex., grey hair, dark
  eyes, weaver (Navy)
Frasher, John, 5ft. 3½in., age 25, fair complex., brown hair,
  grey eyes, Bancker St., baker (Navy)
Frasher, Robert, 5ft. 11in., age 31, fair complex., fair hair,
  brown eyes, Lombardy St., cartman (Navy)
Frasier, Daniel, 5ft. 6in., age 35, ruddy complex., red hair,
  grey eyes, Batavia Lane, labourer (Navy)
Frazer, James, age 24, 8 years in U.S., Bethel, Sullivan Co.,
  farmer (31 Aug. & 19-24 Oct. 1812)
Frazer, Robert, age 27, 8 years in U.S., Bethel, Sullivan Co.,
  farmer, applied June 1811 (31 Aug. & 19-24 Oct. 1812)
Frazer, William, age 23, 4 years in U.S., wife & 2 children,
  Bethel, Sullivan Co., farmer (19-24 Oct. 1812); wife & four
  children, applied June 1810 (31 Aug. 1812)
Freeland, William, 5ft. 8in., age 29, dark complex., dark hair,
  brown eyes, North Moore St., stone cutter (Navy)
Freeman, Daniel, 5ft. 3in., age 27, brown complex., dark hair,
  brown eyes, Greenwich St,, servant (Navy)
French, John, 5ft. 7in., age 48, fair complex., brown hair,
  brown eyes, Duane St., drayman (Navy)
Frewny, Patrick, 5ft. 8in., age 25, brown complex., dark hair,
  grey eyes, labourer (Navy)
Frith, John, age 22, 1 year & 9 mos. in U.S., 23 Chatham St.,
  NYC, maker of musical instruments (20-25 July 1812)
Frost, James, age 59, 18 years in U.S., wife & 9 children, Green-
  wich St., NYC, grocer & gardener (28 July - 2 Aug. 1812);
  5ft., age 59, dark complex., brown hair, dark eyes, Greenwich
  St., gardener (Navy)
Froud, William, 5ft. 7½in., age 36, brown complex., brown hair,
  grey eyes, Pearl St., cordwainer (Navy)
Fullalove, Richard, age 27, 5 years & 6 mos. in U.S., Barclay
  St., NYC, tailor (20-25 July 1812)

Fulton, John, age 45, 1 year & 2 mos. in U.S., wife & 5 child-
ren, Newburgh, Orange Co., farmer (19-24 Oct. 1812)
Fulton, Joseph, age 30, 11 years in U.S., wife & 3 children,
Montgomery, Orange Co., shoemaker (19-24 Oct. 1812)
Fulton, William, age 30, 10 mos. in U.S., wife & child, Kingston,
weaver (7 Sept. & 19-24 Oct. 1812)
Gaffany, Lawrence, age 25, 9 years in U.S., Scipio, Cayuga Co.,
labourer (7-12 Sept. 1812)
Gaffinnee/ Gaffennee, Edward, age 23, 2 mos. in U.S., wife & 2
children, Newburgh, Orange Co., weaver (14 Aug. & 17-22 Aug.
1812)
Gailaspe, Hugh, 5ft. 8in., age 31, light complex., light hair,
blue eyes, Bancker St., brewer (Navy)
Gailey, James, age 24, 1 year & 11 mos. in U.S., Montgomery,
Orange Co., farmer (19-24 Oct. 1812)
Gainor, Barnard, age 48, 18 years in U.S., wife & 7 children,
Aurelius, Cayuga Co., farmer (12-17 Oct. & 26-31 Oct. 1812)
Galbrath, Humphry, 5ft., 8in., age 35, fair complex., fair hair,
brown eyes, Cross St., shoemaker (Navy)
Gallagher, Andrew, 5ft. 5in., age 25, dark complex., dark hair,
brown eyes, cordwainer (Navy)
Gallagher, Bartholomew, 5ft. 6in., age 24, fair complex., brown
hair, grey eyes, labourer (Navy)
Gallagher, Hugh, 5ft. 7in., age 30, dark complex., brown hair,
blue eyes, labourer (Navy)
Gallagher, John, age 29, 11 years in U.S., NYC, tailor (28 July-
2 Aug. 1812)
Gallagher, John, 5ft. 6in., age 29, dark complex., dark hair,
blue eyes, Park St., grocer (Navy)
Gallagher, John, 5ft. 3in., age 27, fair complex., fair hair,
brown eyes, Augustus St., labourer (Navy)
Gallagher, John, 5ft. 7in., age 24, fair complex., brown hair,
blue eyes (Navy)
Gallagher, John, 5ft. 1in., age 19, fair complex., fair hair,
brown eyes, Augustus St., labourer (Navy)
Gallagher, Michael, age 30, 9 years in U.S., 7 Republican Alley
(20-25 July 1812)
Galla(g)her, Michael, 5ft. 6½in., age 24, dark complex., black
hair, blue eyes, Murray St., labourer (Navy)
Gallagher, Patrick, 5ft. 10in., age 23, fair complex., dark hair,
blue eyes, Garden St., morocco (dresser) (Navy)
Gallagher, Patrick, age 23, 5 years in U.S., NYC, groom (3-8 Aug.
1812); - probably the same - 5ft. 5in., age 24, light complex.,
flax(en?) hair, blue eyes, Partition St., stable keeper (Navy)
Gallaugher, Edward, age 30, 7 years in U.S., wife & child, Pough-
keepsie, Dutchess Co., laborer (12-17 Oct. 1812)
Gallaugher, James, age 32, 11 years in U.S., Monroe Works, Orange
Co., cut nailor (17-22 Aug. 1812)
Gallaugher, John, age 27, 7 years in U.S., Poughkeepsie, Dutchess
Co., laborer (12-17 Oct. 1812)
Gallaugher, John, age 18, 1 year in U.S., Monroe Works, Orange
Co., cut nailor (17-22 Aug. 1812)
Galleher, Hugh, 5ft. 8in., age 20, brown complex., brown hair,
grey eyes, Broome St., weaver (Navy)
Gally, John, age 35, 1 year & 1 mo. in U.S., Wallkill, Orange
Co., weaver (19-24 Oct. 1812)
Galvin, Peter, 5ft. 6in., age 36, dark complex., brown hair, blue
eyes, Grand St., skinner (Navy)
Gamble, John, age 28, 1 year in U.S., NYC, saddler (3-8 Aug. 1812);
probably the same - 6ft., age 27, fair complex., fair hair,
black eyes, saddler (Navy)
Gamble, William, age 24, 10 years in U.S., 49 Cross St., blacksmith (20-25 July 1812)
Ganandan, John, age 32, 6 years in U.S., wife & child, Poughkeep-
sie, Dutchess Co., merchant (12-17 Oct. 1812)

Gancy, Peter, 5ft. 6in., age 30, brown complex., fair hair, grey
  eyes, Bancker St., grocer (Navy)
Ganet, James, 5ft. 8in., age 31, light complex., brown hair,
  blue eyes, labourer (Navy)
Gange, William, age 54, 12 years in U.S., wife, Schenectady,
  laborer (24-29 Aug. 1812)
Gannon, William R., 5ft. 9in., age 29, fair complex., red hair,
  grey eyes, tallow chandler (Navy)
Gardiner, George, 5ft. 9in., age 35, light complex., brown hair,
  hazel eyes, Mulberry St., grocer (Navy)
Gardner, George, (no age given), 15 days in U.S., 197 Broadway,
  NYC, iron merchant (10-15 Aug. 1812)
Gardner, George, age 49, 9 years in U.S., 10 Little George St.,
  NYC, tailor (28 July - 2 Aug. 1812)
Gardner, George, age 35, 1 year & 8 mos. in U.S., 27 James St.,
  NYC, gentleman (20-25 July 1812)
Garland, John, age 45, 1 year in U.S., wife & 2 children, 175
  Water St., NYC, confectioner (20-25 July 1812); 5ft. 5in., age
  48, dark complex., dark hair, brown eyes, Water St., confec-
  tioner (Navy)
Garner, Daniel, 5ft. 8½in., age 47, light complex., grey hair,
  grey eyes, rigger (Navy)
Garner, John, age 32, 11 years in U.S., Long Island, teacher
  (28 July - 2 Aug. 1812); 5ft. 8in., age 32, light complex.,
  dark hair, blue eyes, Hempstead, Queens Co., teacher (Navy)
Garner, William, age 25, 1 year in U.S., Utica, Oneida Co.,
  carriage maker (17-22 Aug. 1812); age 25 last Dec. 29, in U.S.
  since 12 Aug. 1811, Utica, Oneida Co., carriage maker, from
  Tewkesbury, Gloucestershire, Eng. (10 Aug. 1812)
Garnison, Samuel, age 38, 1 year & 6 mos. in U.S., wife & 2
  children, Newburgh, Orange Co., weaver (19-24 Oct. 1812)
Garrett, James, age 45, 14 years in U.S., wife & 6 children,
  Johnstown, Montgomery Co., laborer (21-26 Sept. 1812)
Garrie, Thomas, 5ft. 10in., age 40, dark complex., dark hair,
  brown eyes, Hempstead, Long Island (Navy); but also Garrie,
  Thomas, 5ft. 10in., age 34, fair complex., dark hair, brown
  eyes, Queens Cö., physician (Navy)
Garsed, John, 6ft. age 28, brown complex., brown hair, grey eyes,
  removed from NYC to Claverack (Navy)
Garsed, John, age 23, 1 year & 7 mos. in U.S., 68 Greenwich St.,
  NYC, manufacturer (21 Dec. 1812 - 23 Jan. 1813)
Garside, Thomas, age 38, 10 mos. in U.S., wife & 2 children, Hud-
  son, Columbia Co., weaver (17-22 Aug. 1812)
Garvey, Peter, age 28, 4 years in U.S., 30 East George St., NYC,
  grocer (20-25 July 1812)
Garwood, James, age 73 on 17 May last, 16 years in U.S. on 25
  July last, wife, son, grandson & daughter, Lee, Oneida Co.,
  farmer, applied about 3 years ago (29 Sept. 1812)
Gascoein, George, 5ft. 5½in., age 28, dark complex., brown hair,
  black eyes (Navy)
Gasham, Mundiger (?), age 13, 5 years in U.S. 79 Barclay St.,
  NYC, yeoman (28 July - 2 Aug. 1812)
Gasley, John, age 40, 22 years & 10 mos. in U.S., New Windsor,
  Orange Co., farmer (19-24 Oct. 1812)
Gasley, Joseph, age 52, 28 years in U.S., wife & 2 children,
  Newburgh, Orange Co., grocer (19-24 Oct. 1812)
Gaty, Michael, 5ft. 5in., age 32, fair complex., light hair,
  grey eyes, Henry St., labourer (Navy)
Gawin, Alexander, age 24, 14 years in U.S., Republican Alley,
  NYC, labourer (20-25 July 1812); 5ft. 11in., age 24, dark com-
  plex., dark hair, hazel eyes, Harlaem, labourer (Navy)
Gawley, Andrew, age 22, 2 years in U.S., brother, 2 sisters &
  mother, Lee, Oneida Co. (28 Sept. - 3 Oct. 1812); age nearly
  22, 2 years in U.S. on 3 inst. Sept., brother, 2 nephews &
  mother, Lee, farmer, from Tyrone, Ire. (29 Sept. 1812)

Gawley, Joseph, age 36, 2 years in U.S., wife & 2 children, Lee,
   farmer (28 Sept. - 3 Oct. 1812); age 36 about last March, 27
   years in U.S. on 20 Nov. next, wife & 2 children, Lee, Oneida
   Co., farmer, from Tyrone, Ireland (29 Sept. 1812)
Gaynor, John, age 40, 14 years in U.S., wife & 6 children, Mont-
   gomery, Orange Co., schoolmaster (19-24 Oct. 1812)
Gaynor, John, age 28, 9 years in U.S., wife, 89 Anthony St.,
   NYC, yeoman (28 July - 2 Aug. 1812)
Geauld, George, age 35, 11 years in U.S., Partition St., NYC,
   shoemaker (20-25 July 1812)
Geery, James, 5ft. 7in., age 38, fair complex., fair hair, grey
   eyes, Mulberry St., grocer (Navy)
Geery, Joseph, 5ft. 7in., age 22, fair complex., fair hair, dark
   eyes, Bowery, mason (Navy)
Geery, Samuel, 5ft. 8in., age 28, fair complex., brown hair,
   blue eyes, Broome St., grocer (Navy)
Geesely (or Geenly?), Henry, 5ft. 6in., age 52, fair complex.,
   brown hair, grey eyes (Navy)
Gelaspie, James, 5ft. 6in., age 25, dark complex., dark hair,
   brown eyes, tailor (Navy)
Gelan, Martin, 5ft. 4in., age 38, light complex., light hair,
   brown eyes, Elm St., labourer (Navy)
Geller, Michael, 5ft. 7in., age 21, fair complex., brown hair,
   blue eyes, Elm St., baker (Navy)
Geller, William, 5ft. 9in., age 30, dark complex., brown hair,
   brown eyes, Elm St., founder (Navy)
Gelman, John, 5ft. 8in., age 37, dark complex., black hair,
   brown eyes, Bancker St., stone cutter (Navy)
Gelston, George, age 28, 5 years in U.S., wife & child, Castle-
   town, Richmond Co., cooper (31 Aug. - 5 Sept. 1812)
Gelston, James, 5ft. 4in., age 21, fair complex., fair hair,
   grey eyes, Elizabeth St., mason (Navy)
Gelston, Thomas, age 31, 11 years in U.S., 5 in family, Canandaigua, Ontario Co., laborer ((5-15 & 24-29 Aug. 1812)
Gely, John, age 30, 19 years in U.S., wife, Schenectady, carpenter (17-22 Aug. 1812)
Gentle, Andrew, age 35, 7 years in U.S., wife & 3 children, NYC,
   gardener (13-18 July 1812); 5ft. 9in., age 36, fair complex.,
   brown hair, light eyes, Maiden Lane, gardener (Navy)
Geon (or Gion or Gron?), Pat, 5ft. 6in., age 24, dark complex.,
   brown hair, dark eyes, Walnut St., grocer (Navy)
George, Samuel, age 46, 3 years in U.S., 171 Harman St., NYC,
   merchant (20-25 July 1812); 5ft. 4in., age 46, brown complex.,
   brown hair, blue eyes, Harman St., broker (Navy); light com-
   plex., light hair, blue eyes, removed from NYC to Fishkill
   (Navy)
George, William, age 56, 15 years in U.S., wife & 3 children,
   Courtlandt Town, farmer (10-15 Aug. 1812)
Gerear (?), Thomas, 5ft. 6in., age 44, dark complex., brown hair,
   grey eyes, labourer (Navy)
German, William, 5ft. 5in., age 40, dark complex., dark hair,
   dark eyes, Water St., tobacco (Navy)
Gibben (or Gibbon), Michael, 6ft., age 35, fair complex., dark
   hair, grey eyes, Mulberry St., labourer (Navy)
Gibbons, John, age 33, 1½ years in U.S., wife & child, Rome,
   Oneida Co., woolen manufacturer (3-8 Aug. & 29 July 1812)
Gibbons, John, 5ft. 8in., age 28, fair complex., brown hair,
   dark eyes, tanner (Navy)
Gibbons, William, age 27, 9 years in U.S., wife & 3 children,
   89 Front St., grocer (20-25 July 1812); 5ft. 8in., age 28,
   dark complex., black hair, brown eyes, Bancker St., grocer
   (Navy)
Gibbs, John, age 30, 10 years & 1 mo. in U.S., wife, Newburgh,
   Orange Co., carpenter (14 Aug. & 17-22 Aug. 1812)

Gibbs, Joseph, 5ft. 10in., age 27, light complex., brown hair,
blue eyes, bellows maker (Navy)
Gibbs, Robert, age 28, 10 years in U.S., wife & child, 16 Char-
lotte St., NYC, labourer (13-18 July 1812)
Gibbs, Robert, 5ft. 6in., age 26, light complex., light hair,
grey eyes, labourer (Navy)
Gibbs, Thomas, age 34, 10 years & 1 mo. in U.S., wife & child,
Mamakating, Sullivan Co., laborer (19-24 Oct. 1812)
Gibson, David, age 34, 10 years in U.S., Goshen, Orange Co., la-
borer (19-24 Oct. 1812)
Gibson, John, age 67, 9 years in U.S., 4 in family, Bancker St.,
NYC, hosier (20-25 July 1812)
Gibson, John, 5ft. 6in., age 33, dark complex., brown hair, dark
eyes, Beekman St., cordwainer (Navy)
Gibson, John, 5ft. 5in., age 30, fair complex., dark hair, brown
eyes (Navy)
Gibson, Joseph, age 28, 1 year & 1 mo. in U.S., Hudson, Columbia
Co., weaver (fall of 1812)
Gibson, Robert, age 19, 2 years in U.S., Angelica, Allegany Co.,
laborer (26-31 Oct. 1812)
Gibson, Samuel, 5ft. 8in., age 50, light complex., light hair,
light eyes, Hudson St., labourer (Navy)
Gibson, Samuel, 5ft. 6in., age 49, light complex., dark hair,
blue eyes, labourer (Navy)
Gibson, Thomas, age 22, 1 year in U.S., Rome, Oneida Co., clothier
(3-8 Aug. 1812)
Gibson, William, 5ft. 6in., age 26, fair complex., brown hair,
grey eyes, New St., cordwainer (Navy)
Gibson, William, age 20, 7 years in U.S., Schenectady, shoemaker
(17-22 Aug. 1812)
Gibson, Wood, 5ft. 5 3/4in., age 20, fair complex., brown hair,
grey eyes, Front St., coach trimmer (Navy)
Gilbert, John, age 30 on 3 July last, 16 years in U.S. in Oct.
next, wife & child, Utica, Oneida Co., starch & fig blue manufacturer, from London (10 Aug. & 17-22 Aug. 1812)
Gilchrist, Robert, age 21, 6 years in U.S., 146 Water St., grocer
(20-25 July 1812); 5ft. 11in., age 22, dark complex., brown
hair, brown eyes, grocer, removed from NYC to Poughkeepsie
(Navy)
Gilfort, John, 5ft. 7in., age 37, brown complex., brown hair,
blue eyes, gardener (Navy)
Gilgan, Daniel, 5ft. 6in., age 30, fair complex., dark hair,
brown eyes, labourer (Navy)
Gilgan, Mathew, 5ft. 7in., age 47, fair complex., brown hair,
brown eyes, Anthony St., labourer (Navy)
Gill, Joseph, age 39, 10 years in U.S., Maiden Lane, NYC, livery
stable keeper (28 July - 2 Aug. 1812)
Gill, Joseph, 5ft., age 40, dark complex., brown hair, dark eyes,
Washington St., coachman (Navy)
Gill, Patrick, age 19, 8 years in U.S., 47 Elm St., NYC, stone
cutter (28 July - 2 Aug. 1812)
Gill, Roger, age 47, 8 years in U.S., wife & 2 children, corner
Cannon & Delancy Sts., NYC, cartman (20-25 July 1812)
Gill, Thomas, age 27, 3 years in U.S., 14 Frankford St., NYC,
accountant (20-25 July 1812); 5ft. 9in., age 29, dark complex.,
brown hair, blue eyes, Frankfort St., clerk (Navy)
Gillan, George, 5ft. 9in., age 30, light complex., brown hair,
grey eyes, removed from NYC to Goshen, Orange Co. (Navy)
Gillan, John, age 25, 5 years in U.S., Monroe Works, Orange Co.,
cut nailor (17-22 Aug. 1812)
Gillen, Thomas, age 47, 9 years in U.S., Poughkeepsie, Dutchess
Co., laborer (12-17 Oct. 1812)
Gillespie, David, 6ft., age 25, fair complex., brown hair, brown
eyes, brewer (Navy)

Gillespie, Dennis, age 18, 4 mos. in U.S., 78 Bayard St., NYC,
baker (7-19 Dec. 1812)
Gillespie, Edward, age 36, 3 years & 8 mos. in U.S., NYC, editor
of a paper(20-25 July 1812)
Gillespie, Francis, 5ft. 10in., age 29, dark complex., black
hair, grey eyes, shoemaker (Navy)
Gillespie, John, age 23, 18 years in U.S., wife & child, Bowery
Lane, NYC, blacksmith (10-15 Aug. 1812); 6ft., age 23, dark
complex., brown hair, grey eyes, Bowery, blacksmith (Navy)
Gillespie, Joseph, age 25, 16 years in U.S., wife, Schenectady,
laborer (17-22 Aug. 1812)
Gillespie, Robert, 5ft. 10in., age 22, fair complex., fair hair,
dark eyes, Delancey Mills, cordwainer (Navy)
Gillespie, Thomas, age 37, 4 years in U.S., wife & 2 children,
10 Bancker St., NYC, laborer (20-25 July 1812); 5ft. 11in.,
age 37, brown complex., brown hair, blue eyes, Henry St., labourer (Navy)
Gillespy, Edward, 5ft. 9in., age 35, light complex., dark hair,
grey eyes (Navy)
Gillespy, George, 5ft. 3 3/4in., age 30, fair complex., light
hair, brown eyes, William St., printer (Navy)
Gilley, W.B., 5ft. 8in., age 27, dark complex., dark hair, dark
eyes, Lumber St., bookbinder (Navy); age 27, 4½ yrs.in U.S.(Jy'12)
Gillin, James, 5ft. 6in., age 28, brown complex., brown hair,
dark eyes, Augustus St., labourer (Navy)
Gillon, James, 5ft. 4in., age 50, dark complex., dark hair, grey
eyes, Duane St., blacksmith (Navy)
Gillon, John, 5ft. 9in., age 32, dark complex., black hair, blue
eyes, mason (Navy)
Gillow, William, age 28, 12 years in U.S., Montgomery, Orange
Co., weaver (19 - 24 Oct. 1812)
Gilmartin, Charles, 5ft. 5in., age 34, fair complex., brown hair,
brown eyes, labourer (Navy)
Gilmartin, John, 5ft. 8in., age 25, light complex., dark hair,
blue eyes, labourer (Navy)
Gilmartin, Patrick, 5ft. 11in., age 27, light complex., brown
hair, grey eyes, Augustus St., labourer (Navy)
Gilmer, John, 5ft. 11in., age 27, dark complex., dark hair, dark
eyes, Suffolk St., blacksmith (Navy)
Gilmore, Robert, age 53, 2 mos. in U.S., wife & 6 children, New-
burgh, Orange Co., cooper (19-24 Oct. 1812)
Gilroy, Charles, age 19, 12 years in U.S., 17 Little George St.,
NYC, fig blue manufacturer (28 July - 2 Aug. 1812)
Gilson, Thomas, age 22, 1 year in U.S., Rome, Oneida Co., clothier
(29 July 1812)
Gilstans, Patrick, age 25, 1 year & 2 mos. in U.S., Montgomery,
Orange Co., laborer (19-24 Oct. 1812)
Gimmel, Thomas, age 38, 14 years in U.S., wife & 7 children,
farmer (19-24 Oct. 1812)
Ginn, John, 5ft. 4in., age 48, brown complex., brown hair, grey
eyes, Bayard St., cartman (Navy)
Glancey, Dailey, 5ft. 5in., age 25, fair complex., dark hair,
brown eyes, labourer (Navy)
Glass, James, Sr., age 73, 4 years & 4 mos. in U.S., wife & 3
children, Camillus, Onondaga Co., farmer, applied 27 Jan. 1813
(28 Dec. 1812 - 3 Feb. 1813)
Glass, James, age 24, 10 mos. in U.S., NYC, copper- & tin smith
(20-25 July 1812)
Glass, John, age 30, 10 years in U.S., wife & child, Fishkill,
Dutchess Co., weaver (12-17 Oct. 1812)
Glass, William, age 31, 5 years & 6 mos. in U.S., Camillus, Onondaga Co., farmer, applied 27 Jan. 1813 (28 Dec. 1812 - 3 Feb.
1813)
Glaze, William, age 33, 1 year & 1 mo. in U.S., wife & 3 children, father & mother, Greenwich St., glass maker (28 Jy.-2 Au.'12)

Glaze, William, 5ft. 10in., age 33, dark complex., brown hair,
   blue eyes, Greenwich St., glass maker (Navy) - same as above.
Glazebrook, George age 40, 17 years in U.S., wife & 5 children,
   Plattsburgh, Clinton Co., farmer (1 Sept. - 1 Oct., 26-31 Oct.
   1812)
Glenie, Patrick, 5ft. 8in., age 28, light complex., sandy hair,
   blue eyes, Greenwich St., coachman (Navy)
Glenny, John, age 67, 16 years in U.S., wife & 2 children, Vir-
   gil, Cortland Co., farmer (25 Nov.- 7 Dec. & 7-19 Dec. 1812)
Glory, Frederick, age 50, 11 years in U.S., wife & child, Pough-
   keepsie, Dutchess Co., baker (12-17 Oct. 1812)
Glover, James, age 33, 5 years in U.S., wife & 2 children, 10
   Hanson St., baker (20-25 July 1812); 5ft. 6¼in., age 34, dark
   complex., black hair, black eyes, Hanson St., baker (Navy)
Glover, Thomas, 5ft. 8in., age 33, fair complex., brown hair,
   blue eyes, painter (Navy)
Godley, John, age 28, 5 years & 1 mo. in U.S., Colonie, Albany
   Co., miller, applied 5 Aug. 1812 (17-22 Aug. 1812)
Goldsmith, Richard, age 23, 10 years in U.S., wife, mother and
   sister, Beekman St., NYC, cabinetmaker (28 July - 2 Aug. 1812)
Golloway, Zaccariah (his family resides in Upper Canada,and he
   in New Windsor, Orange Co.), has not reported (2 Jan. 1813)
Gomes, Isaac, age 16, 2 years in U.S., 79 Barclay St., NYC, yeo-
   man (28 July - 2 Aug. 1812)
Gonell, James, 5ft. 7in., age 40, dark complex., dark hair, dark
   eyes, Liberty St., teacher (Navy)
Goodfellow, James, age 24, 5 years in U.S., millwright (28 July -
   2 Aug. 1812)
Goorly, David, age 23, 2 years in U.S., Newburgh, Orange Co.,
   grocer (19-24 Oct. 1812)
Goorly, Thomas, age 52, 2 years in U.S., wife & child, Newburgh,
   Orange Co., farmer (19-24 Oct. 1812)
Goorly, William, age 22, 1 year & 3 mcs. in U.S., Wallkill, Orange
   Co., farmer (19-24 Oct. 1812)
Gordon, Frederick, age 22, 5 mos. in U.S., 50 Oak St., musician
   (28 July - 2 Aug. 1812)
Gordon, Frederick, 5ft. 8in., age 26, light complex., dark hair,
   grey eyes, John St., fifer - probably same as above(Navy)
Gordon, John, age 50, 11 years in U.S., wife & daughter, 6 Cherry
   St., shoemaker (13-18 July 1812); 5ft. 7in., age 52, light com-
   plex., dark hair, hazel eyes, Cherry St., shoemaker (Navy)
Gordon, John, age 27, 1 year & 7 mos. in U.S., wife & child, New
   Windsor, Orange Co., laborer (19-24 Oct. 1812)
Gordon, John, age 20, 7 years in U.S., Newburgh, Orange Co.,
   watchmaker (19-24 Oct. 1812)
Gordon, Thomas, age 38, 18 years & 3 mos. in U.S., wife & 2 child-
   ren, Montgomery, Orange Co., weaver (19-24 Oct. 1812)
Gordon, William, age 25, 1 year & 9 mcs. in U.S., wife & 2 child-
   ren, Fishkill, Dutchess Co., laborer (12-17 Oct. 1812)
Gore, Arthur, age 25, 4 mos. in U.S., wife & 2 servants, Staten
   Island, gentleman, has been or now is a British major and aid
   to General Barrisford in the British service (28 July - 2 Aug.
   1812)
Gorgill, Charles, 5ft. 6in., age 22, fair complex., fair hair,
   blue eyes, labourer (Navy)
Gorman, James, 5ft. 5in., age 30, fair complex., sandy hair,
   brown eyes, labourer (Navy)
Gorman, Patrick, age 26, 2 years & 4 mos. in U.S., Poughkeepsie,
   Dutchess Co., laborer (12-17 Oct. 1812)
Gorrell, James, age 39, 10 years in U.S., wife & servant, NYC,
   teacher (20-25 July 1812)
Gospell, Thomas, age 27, 1½ years in U.S., 439 Greenwich St.,
   carpenter (20-25 July 1812); 5ft. 10in., age 28, dark complex.,
   brown hair, brown eyes, Warren St., carpenter (Navy)

Gould, William, 5ft. 8in., age 19, light complex., dark hair,
grey eyes, Maiden Lane, apprentice (Navy)
Goundry, Francis, age 43, 10 years in U.S., 2 in family, Benton,
Ontario Co., farmer (15 Nov. 1812 - 3 Jan. 1813)
Gourley, William, age 26, 10 years in U.S., 10 Little George St.,
NYC, tailor (20-25 July 1812)
Gourly, Thomas, age 20, 4 years & 3 mos. in U.S., wife, Mont-
gomery, Orange Co., laborer (19-24 Oct. 1812)
Gow, Pat, 5ft. 7in., age 28, light complex., brown hair, blue
eyes, Duane St., labourer (Navy)
Gowan, John, age 28, 4 years in U.S., Water Works, NYC, engineer
(20-25 July 1812)
Gowan, John, 5ft. 5in., age 30, fair complex, brown hair, blue
eyes, millwright (Navy)
Gowen, Thomas, age 34, 20 years in U.S., wife & 4 children, Sci-
pio, Cayuga Co., farmer (21-26 Sept. 1812)
Grace, Samuel, age 36, 10 years in U.S., wife & child, 37 Maiden
Lane, NYC, clerk (20-25 July 1812)
Grace, Solomon, 5ft. 1in., age 26, fair complex., brown hair,
grey eyes, clerk (Navy)
Graham, Arthur, 5ft. 11in., age 46, dark complex., dark hair,
blue eyes, gardener (Navy)
Graham, Barnard/Bernard, age 22, 3 years in U.S., Bloomingdale,
laborer (17-22 Aug. 1812); 5ft. 9in., age 23, dark complex.,
black hair, blue eyes, Dutch St., labourer (Navy)
Graham, Bontine N., age 32, 3½ mos. in U.S., Lewis Hotel, Albany
(13-18 July 1812)
Graham, Bryan, age 34, 11 years in U.S., Monroe, Orange Co.,
clerk (20-25 July 1812)
Graham, Duncan, age 42, 8 years in U.S., 5 in family, 62 Morris
St., NYC, grocer (20-25 July 1812); 5ft. 9½in., age 45, fair
complex., fair hair, brown eyes, Murray St., grocer (Navy)
Graham, George, 5ft. 8in., age 30, fair complex., brown hair,
brown eyes, Mulberry St., carpenter (Navy)
Graham, George, 5ft. 6in., age 24, fair complex., light hair,
grey eyes, Mulberry St., carpenter (Navy)
Graham, George, age 21, 6 years in U.S., 92 Maiden Lane, NYC,
coachman (28 July - 2 Aug. 1812)
Graham, George, age 19 on 16 Sept. last, 1 year in U.S. last
June, Whitestown, Oneida Co., counterpain weaver (26 Aug. &
28 Sept. - 3 Oct. 1812)
Graham, James, age 52, in U.S. 2 years, wife & 6 children, NYC,
manufacturer (20-25 July 1812)
Graham, James, 5ft. 5½in., age 40, fair complex., brown hair,
blue eyes, Orange St., butcher (Navy)
Graham, James, 5ft. 4½in., age 38, fair complex., light hair,
brown eyes, Thompson St., ropemaker (Navy)
Graham, James, age 27, 3 years in U.S., wife & child, Wallkill,
Orange Co., weaver (19-24 Oct. 1812)
Graham, John, 5ft. 11in., age 45, fair complex., light hair,
light eyes, Broadway, gardener (Navy)
Graham, John, 5ft. 8in., age 40, fair complex., brown hair, grey
eyes, Hammond St., weaver (Navy)
Graham, John, 5ft. 8in., age 29, dark complex., dark hair, grey
eyes, clerk (Navy)
Graham, John, age 24 years & 8 mos., about 19 years in U.S.,
wife Perlina, Hartford, Washington Co., farmer, came to U.S.
with his parents at about age of 5; his father was naturalized
about 2 years ago (16 Oct. 1812)
Graham, John B., age 27, 5 years in U.S., Chenango Co., brewer
(10-15 Aug. 1812)
Graham, Joseph, 5ft. 6in., age 40, dark complex., dark hair,
dark eyes, mason (Navy)
Graham, Peter, 5ft. 6in., age 21, fair complex., fair hair, grey
eyes, Harlaem, servant (Navy)

Graham, Phelix, age 21, 2 years in U.S., wife, 300 Bowery, NYC,
     weaver (20-25 July 1812)
Graham, Robert, age 43, 18 years in U.S., wife & 2 children, 481
     Greenwich St., NYC, shoemaker (3-8 Aug. 1812)
Graham, Robert, age 24, 1 year & 2 mos. in U.S., Wallkill,
     Orange Co., farmer (19-24 Oct. 1812)
Graham, Thomas, 5ft. 8in., age 45, dark complex., dark hair,
     blue eyes, Water St., tinsmith (Navy)
Graham, Thomas, 5ft. 10in., age 35, dark complex., dark hair,
     dark eyes, Stagg Town, cartman (Navy)
Gram, Hugh, 5ft. 6½in., age 48, fair complex., dark hair, blue
     eyes, Henry St., labourer (Navy)
Gramsley/Gramsly, Hugh, age 16, 12 years in U.S., Bethel, Sul-
     livan Co., farmer (31 Aug. 7 18-24 Oct. 1812)
Grant, James, 5ft. 7in., age 47, dark complex., dark hair, blue
     eyes, Spring St., nailor (Navy)
Grant, James, 5ft. 11in., age 34, brown complex., brown hair,
     blue eyes, Lombardy St., shipwright (Navy)
Grant, John, 5ft. 5in., age 40, light complex., sandy hair, grey
     eyes, Henry St., tailor (Navy)
Grant, John, 5ft. 7in., age 25, dark complex., brown hair, brown
     eyes, stone cutter (Navy)
Gratram (or Gratiam?), John, age 24, 19 years in U.S., wife,
     Hartford, Washington Co., farmer (26-31 Oct. 1812)
Gray, Adam, age 28, 5 years in U.S., 439 Greenwich St., NYC,
     sawyer (20-25 July 1812); 5ft. 7in., age 28, fair complex.,
     light hair, brown eyes, Greenwich St., sawyer (Navy)
Gray, Charles, age 20, 1½ years in U.S., Pearl St., NYC, merchant
     (20-25 July 1812); 5ft. 9in., age 21, dark complex., brown
     hair, blue eyes, Pearl St., accountant (Navy)
Gray, John, age 21, 17 years & 2 mos. in U.S., New Windsor,
     Orange Co., farmer (19-24 Oct. 1812)
Gray, William, age 70, 22 years in U.S., 4 in family, Westches-
     ter Co., farmer (28 July - 2 Aug. 1812); 5ft. 5in., age 71,
     light complex., grey hair, blue eyes, farmer (Navy)
Gray, William, age 30, 6 years in U.S., 160 Greenwich St., mer-
     chant (20-25 July 1812)
Grecan (?), John, 5ft. 8½in., age 27, light complex., dark hair,
     grey eyes, Pearl St., pedler (Navy)
Grecoven (?), William, 5ft. 8in., age 35, "s" complex., brown
     hair, blue eyes, Bloomingdale, labourer (Navy)
Green, James, age 41, 1½ years in U.S., 247 Broadway, merchant
     (20-25 July 1812); 5ft. 10in., age 41, sandy complex, brown
     hair, brown eyes, gentleman (Navy); removed from NYC to Pough-
     keepsie, Dutchess Co. (Navy)
Green, John, age 45, 11 years & 2 mos. in U.S., wife & 7 child-
     ren, Poughkeepsie, Dutchess Co., weaver (12-17 Oct. 1812)
Green, John, age 30, 5 years in U.S., 208 Greenwich St., NYC,
     tallow chandler (28 July - 2 Aug. 1812); 5ft. 9in., fair com-
     plex., light hair, blue eyes, Greenwich St., soap boiler (Navy)
Green, John, 5ft. 3½in., age 30, fair complex., brown hair, grey
     eyes, Water St., tailor (Navy)
Green, Joseph, age 19, 5 weeks in U.S., Pine St., NYC, merchant
     (7-12 Sept. 1812); 5ft. 10 3/4in., age 19, light complex., dark
     hair, blue eyes, Washington St., clerk (Navy); removed from
     NYC to Fishkill, Dutchess Co. (Navy)
Green, Knowles, age 40, 8 mos. in U.S., NYC, merchant (19-24
     Oct. 1812)
Green, Mathew, 5ft. 10½in., age 22, fair complex., dark hair,
     grey eyes, bricklayer (Navy)
Green, William, age 46, 20 years in U.S., NYC, cotton broker
     (20-25 July 1812); 5ft. 8in., fair complex., dark hair, black
     eyes, removed from NYC to Stanton Hill at John Lawton's,
     Greene Co. (Navy)

Green, William, age 44, 10 years in U.S., wife & 5 children, New
York Hospital, clerk (13-18 July 1812); 5ft. 10in., age 45,
fair complex., brown hair, blue eyes, N.Y. Hospital, clerk
(Navy)

Greenwood, Richard, age 35, 11 years in U.S., wife & 5 children,
39 Maiden Lane, NYC, seed store keeper (13-18 July 1812); 5ft.
8in., age 36, light complex., brown hair, hazel eyes, removed
from NYC to Goshen, Orange Co. (Navy)

Gregory, Michael, age 38, 1 year & 3 mos. in U.S., 5 in family,
36 Charlotte St., NYC, weaver (28 July - 2 Aug. 1812)

Grier, James, age 26, 4 mos. in U.S., wife & 4 children, Kingston, Ulster Co., weaver (19-24 Oct. 1812)

Grier, Joseph, age 24, 2 mos. in U.S., wife, Kingston, Ulster
Co., weaver (19-24 Oct. 1812)

Grier, Joseph, age 20, 3 years in U.S., mother, Kingston, Ulster
Co., weaver (19-24 Oct. 1812)

Grier, Robert, age 33, 4 mos. in U.S., wife & 3 children, Kingston, weaver (7 Sept. & 19-24 Oct. 1812)

Griffin, Benjamin Pitt, age 27, 4 years in U.S., wife & 2 children, Desbrosses St., NYC, gold beater (20-25 July 1812); 5ft.
8in., age 29, dark complex., dark hair, dark eyes, Desbrosses
St., gold beater (Navy)

Griffin, Jeremiah, age 35, 9 years in U.S., wife & 2 children,
9 Broad St., intelligence office keeper (20-25 July 1812); 5ft.
7in., age 36, black complex., dark hair, hazel eyes, Broad St.,
register (Navy)

Griffin, Thomas, age 35, 5 years in U.S., girl, 47 Greenwich St.,
NYC, bookseller (20-25 July 1812); 5ft. 9in., age 36, fair
complex., brown hair, hazel eyes, Greenwich St., bookseller
(Navy)

Griffin, Thomas, age 28, 1 year in U.S., wife & child, 20 Vandewater St., NYC, slater (28 July - 2 Aug. 1812)

Griffith, Griffith, 5ft. 7½in., age 32, dark complex., grey hair,
blue eyes, ferryman (Navy)

Griffith, Meredith, age 35, 12 years in U.S., wife & 4 children,
Poughkeepsie, Dutchess Co., tailor (12-17 Oct. 1812)

Griffith, Thomas, 5ft. 9in., age 30, light complex., light hair,
blue eyes, Gold St., currier (Navy)

Griffiths, John, age 23, 3 years in U.S., Schenectady, hostler
(24-29 Aug. 1812)

Grillin, Patrick, age 30, 11 years in U.S., wife & child, Poughkeepsie, Dutchess Co., laborer (12-17 Oct. 1812)

Grimble, William, 5ft. 6in., age 24, fair complex., dark hair,
brown eyes, Cross St., blacksmith (Navy)

Grimes, John, 5ft. 7in., age 24, light complex., sandy hair,
brown eyes, Bowery (Navy)

Grimshaw, Isaac, age 40, 7 years in U.S., wife & 2 children, NYC,
teacher, applied 3 or 4 years ago (28 Sept. - 3 Oct. 1812);
5ft. 9in., age 41, brown complex., dark hair, grey eyes, White
St., teacher (Navy)

Grimshaw, John, age 48, 10 years in U.S., wife & 6 children,
Washington, Dutchess Co., woolen manufacturer (12-17 Oct. 1812)

Griner, Casper, age 34 on 12 Mar. last, 14 years in U.S. in Aug.
last, wife, Deerfield, Oneida Co., crown glass blower (29 Sept.
& 28 Sept. - 3 Oct. 1812)

Griswold, Thomas, age 43, 8 years in U.S., 6 in family, Seneca,
Ontario Co., farmer (5-15 & 25-29 Aug. 1812)

Gruger, A.E., age 21, 7 years in U.S., mother, 65 Warren St.,
dancing master (20-25 July 1812)

Grundy, Samuel, age 27, 6 years in U.S., 20 Nassau St., porter,
applied 22 May 1811 (13-18 July 1812); 5ft. 8 3/4in., age 27,
fair complex., sandy hair, brown eyes, Nassau St., porter (Navy)

Gubbin, Michael, age 35, 2 mos. in U.S., wife & child, 67 Mulberry St., farmer (28 July - 2 Aug. 1812)

Guess, Francis, age 23, 12 years in U.S., Johnstown, Montgomery
Co., farmer (7-19 Dec. 1812)
Guess, James, age 36, 12 years in U.S., wife, 5 children & an
apprentice, Johnstown, Montgomery Co., farmer (5-9 & 7-19 Dec.
1812)
Guess, John, age 34, 12 years in U.S., wife & child, Johnstown,
Montgomery Co., farmer (5 Nov. - 9 Dec. & 7-19 Dec. 1812)
Guest, Thomas R., age 21, 3 days in U.S., NYC, merchant (14-19
Sept. 1812)
Gulon, Patrick, 5ft. 3in., age 30, fair complex., fair hair,
blue eyes, Duane St., labourer (Navy)
Gumbleton, Robert, age 20, 3 years in U.S., 159 Pearl St., NYC,
printer (28 July - 2 Aug. 1812)
Gumshaw (or Grimshaw?), Joseph, age 49, 6 years in U.S., 12 in
family, Oneida Co., clothier (3-8 Aug. 1812)
Gunn, John, age 19, 1 year in U.S., 141 Water St., NYC, saddler
(13-18 July 1812)
Gurrel, Patrick, age 22, 6 years in U.S., wife & child, Monroe
Works, Orange Co., cut nailor (17-22 Aug. 1812)
Gurrie (?), James S., age 30, 18 years in U.S., 3 children, 75
William St., NYC, dyer (30 Nov. - 5 Dec. 1812)
Guthrie, James, age 46, 5 years in U.S., wife & 5 children, Gal-
way, Saratoga Co., farmer (24-29 Aug. 1812)
Guy, Darby, age 32, 6 years & 9 mos. in U.S., City of Albany,
tailor, applied May 1810 (17-22 Aug. 1812)
Habersham, Martin, age 36, 9 years in U.S., wife & 1 son, 173
Elm St., NYC, tailor (20-25 July 1812); 5ft. 5in., age 36,
dark complex., brown hair, dark eyes, William St., tailor
(Navy)
Haddan, William, age 31, 21 years in U.S., wife & 2 children,
Montgomery, Orange Co., farmer (19-24 Oct. 1812)
Hadden, David, age 39, 6 years in U.S., wife & 2 children, 81
Greenwich St., NYC, merchant (24-29 Aug. 1812); 5ft. 5in.,
dark complex., dark hair, blue eyes, removed from NYC to Co-
lumbia & Dutchess Counties (Navy)
Hadden, John, age 63, 21 years in U.S., wife & child, Montgomery,
Orange Co., farmer (19-24 Oct. 1812)
Hagan, Barnabas, age 35, 6 years & 2 mos. in U.S., Kingston,
Ulster Co., weaver (19-24 Oct. 1812)
Hagen, James, 5ft. 5in., age 43, light complex., brown hair,
grey eyes, Catherine St., NYC, shoemaker (Navy)
Hagen, John, age 43, 11 years in U.S., wife & 6 children, 80
Catherine St., NYC, shoemaker (20-25 July 1812)
Hagerty, James, 5ft. 5in., age 22, light complex., light hair,
grey eyes, segar (maker) (Navy)
Haggart, Daniel, age 19, 18 mos. in U.S., Johnstown, Montgomery
Co., shoemaker (6 Oct. - 4 Nov. & 9-14 Nov. 1812)
Haggart, James, age 22, 17 mos. in U.S., Johnstown, Montgomery
Co., wheelwright (3-14 & 21-26 Sept. 1812)
Haggen, Thomas, 5ft. 9in., age 49, fair complex., dark hair,
brown eyes, Greenwich St., bleacher (Navy)
Hagins, Thomas, 5ft. 9in., age 28, dark complex., dark hair,
dark eyes, cartman (Navy)
Haie, Opekim (?), 5ft. 7in., age 48, fair complex., fair hair,
blue eyes, mason (Navy)
Hains, William, age 40, 15 years in U.S., wife, William St.,
NYC, mariner, applied Dec. 1807 (28 July - 2 Aug. 1812)
Halder, Charles, age 32, 1 year in U.S., wife & 2 children, Sara-
toga, weaver (17-22 Aug. 1812)
Hall, Adam, age 25 last July, in U.S. since 11 June 1801, Utica,
Oneida Co., blacksmith, from Scotland (10 Aug. & 17-22 Aug.
1812)
Hall, Bryan, 5ft. 5in., age 45, light complex., dark hair, light
eyes, Vandewater St., currier (Navy)

Hall, Charles, age 30, 2 years in U.S., wife & 2 children, 56
Stone St., NYC, teacher (20-25 July 1812)
Hall, Charles, age 26, 2 years in U.S., wife, 22 Bancker St.
NYC, sawyer (28 July - 2 Aug. 1812); 5ft. 11 3/4in., age 26,
brown complex., brown hair, blue eyes, Greenwich St., sawyer
(Navy)
Hall, George, 5ft. 7½in., age 27, fair complex., light hair,
grey eyes, Lumber St., servant (Navy)
Hall, John, age 28, 12 years in U.S., town & county of West-
chester, merchant (20-25 July 1812)
Hall, John, 6ft. 1in., age 25, light complex., brown hair, grey
eyes, grocer (Navy)
Hall, Joseph, age 45, 11 years in U.S., wife, town of Colonie,
gardener (5-10 Oct. 1812)
Hall, Joseph, 5ft. 5in., age 45, fair complex., brown hair, blue
eyes, gardener (Navy)
Hall, Joseph, 5ft. 3½in., age 24, light complex., brown hair,
blue eyes, Greenwich St., labourer (Navy)
Hall, Richard, age 24 years & 8 mos., 2 years & 8 mos. in U.S.,
wife, Hudson, Columbia Cc., weaver (12 Aug. & 17-22 Aug. 1812)
Hall, Robert, 5ft. 8in., age 37, light complex., brown hair,
brown eyes, Lombardy St., carpenter (Navy)
Hall, Roger, age 18, 11 years in U.S., Seneca, Ontario Co., far-
mer (15 Nov. 1812 - 3 Jan. 1813)
Hall, Samuel, age 24, 6 years & 3 mos. in U.S., New Windsor,
Orange Co., schoolmaster (19-24 Oct. 1812)
Hall, William, age 47, 18 years in U.S., wife & 4 children, City
of Albany, carpenter (17-22 Aug. 1812)
Hall, William, 5ft. 7½in., age 30, fair complex., brown hair,
grey eyes, Sixth St., labourer (Navy)
Hallam, Stephen, 5ft. 9in., age 54, fair complex., dark hair,
grey eyes, labourer (Navy)
Halliday, James, age 27, 11 years in U.S. wife & child, 113
Front St., NYC, grocer (20-25 July 1812); 5ft. 5in., age 27,
light complex., black hair, light blue eyes, removed from NYC
to Goshen, Orange Co. (Navy)
Halliday, Thomas, age 40, 9 years in U.S., wife & 4 children,
Whitestown, Oneida Co., overseer of carding manufactory (28
Sept. - 3 Oct. 1812)
Halligan, Richard, 5ft. 8in., age 27, fair complex., brown hair,
blue eyes, labourer (Navy)
Hamilton, Alexander, 5ft. 6in., age 65, pale complex., dark hair,
grey eyes, Chesnut St., baker (Navy)
Hamilton, Alexander, 5ft. 9in., age 47, fair complex., dark hair,
grey eyes, Norfolk St., ropemaker (Navy)
Hamilton, Archibald, age 66, 3 years in U.S., wife & 3 children,
NYC, baker (20-25 July 1812)
Hamilton, Archibald, 5ft. 7in., age 20, light complex., sandy
hair, grey eyes, baker (Navy)
Hamilton, David, age 37, 13 years & 10 mos. in U.S., Shawangunk,
Ulster Co., weaver (19-24 Oct. 1812)
Hamilton, Girvin, age 23, 1 year in U.S., Newburgh, Orange Co.,
house-carpenter (19-24 Oct. 1812)
Hamilton, Henry, 5ft. 6½in., age 35, sandy complex., dark hair,
blue eyes, Mulberry St., cartman (Navy)
Hamilton, Henry, 5ft. 8in., age 19, light complex., sandy hair,
grey eyes, Chesnut St., baker (Navy)
Hamilton, James, 5ft. 9in., age 35, light complex., dark hair,
brown eyes, Chamber St., coachman (Navy)
Hamilton, James, age 32, 5 years in U.S., Greenwich St., coachman (28 July - 2 Aug. 1812); 5ft. 10in., age 32, fair complex.,
brown hair, black eyes, Greenwich St., coachman (Navy)
Hamilton, James, 5ft. 10in., age 22, light complex., light hair,
grey eyes, Lombardy St., cartman (Navy)

Hamilton, James, age 20, 9 days in U.S., 40 Broadway, gentleman
  (17-22 Aug. 1812)
Hamilton, James, 5ft. 10in., age 18, dark complex., sandy hair,
  grey eyes, Chesnut St., baker (Navy)
Hamilton, John, 5ft. 10in., age 52, light complex., brown hair,
  grey eyes, cartman (Navy)
Hamilton, John, 5ft. 6in., age 28, light complex., brown hair,
  blue eyes, Lumber St., labourer (Navy)
Hamilton, John, age 25, 2 mos. in U.S., 2 in family, 104 Bowery
  Lane, cotton weaver (20-25 July 1812)
Hamilton, John, 5ft. 6in., age 24, fair complex., brown hair,
  blue eyes, Fourth St., weaver (Navy)
Hamilton, John, 5ft. 11in., age 24, dark complex., brown hair,
  black eyes, Christopher St., type founder (Navy)
Hamilton, Jonathan, age 40, 16 years in U.S., Schoharie (24-29
  Aug. 1812)
Hamilton, Robert, 5ft. 7in., age 38, dark complex., brown hair,
  blue eyes, labourer (Navy)
Hamilton, Robert, 5ft. 7½in., age 36, dark complex., brown hair,
  grey eyes, Corlaers Hook, labourer (Navy)
Hamilton, Samuel, 5ft. 10in., age 27, fair complex., brown hair,
  blue eyes, Christopher St., type founder (Navy)
Hamilton, Thomas, 5ft. 9½in., age 32, light complex., brown hair,
  blue eyes, manufacturer (Navy)
Hamilton, William, age 38, 10 mos. in U.S., corner Hester & 3rd
  . Sts., NYC, grocer(20-25 July 1812); 5ft. 10in., age 38, light
  complex., brown hair, grey eyes, Third St., small grocer (Navy)
Hammill, William, 5ft. 4in., age 23, light complex., light hair,
  light eyes, Batavia Lane, sailmaker (Navy)
Han, Henry, age 28, 3 years in U.S., wife & child, 32 Henry St.,
  NYC, shoemaker (28 July - 2 Aug. 1812)
Hancock, Thomas, 5ft. 8in., age 23, light complex., brown hair,
  brown eyes, Lumber St., saddler (Navy)
Hancock, William, age 30, 2 mos. in U.S., 75 Duane St., NYC,
  tallow chandler (20-25 July 1812)
Hancock, William, 5ft. 11in., age 26, dark complex., brown hair,
  brown eyes, chandler (Navy)
Hanely, Barnard, 5ft. 1in., age 30, fair complex., fair hair,
  brown eyes, Bowery, labourer (Navy)
Hanen, John, 5ft. 9in., age 22, fair complex., brown hair, dark
  eyes, East George St., labourer (Navy)
Hanen, Mathew, 5ft. 6in., age 42, fair complex., fair hair, grey
  eyes, labourer (Navy)
Haney, John, 5ft. 9in., age 44, light complex., sandy hair, grey
  eyes, Norfolk St., shipwright (Navy)
Haney, William, 5ft. 4in., age 31, fair complex., dark hair, grey
  eyes, Jamaica, Queens Co., farmer (Navy)
Hankinson, Francis, age 26, 6 years in U.S., wife & child, Johns-
  town, Montgomery Co., farmer (6 Oct - 4 Nov. & 9-14 Nov. 1812)
Hanley, John, age 15, 8 years in U.S., Seneca, Ontario Co., (24-
  28 Aug. 1812)
Hanley, Mathew, 5ft. 9in., age 47, fair complex., dark hair,
  blue eyes, Greenwich St., labourer (Navy)
Hanley, William, age 41, 8 years in U.S., 8 in family, Seneca,
  Ontario Co., farmer (5-15 & 24-29 Aug. 1812)
Hanley, William, Jr., age 17, 8 years in U.S., Seneca, Ontario
  Co., farmer (5-15 & 24-29 Aug. 1812)
Hanna, Alexander, 5ft. 7in., age 31, brown complex., brown hair,
  blue eyes, labourer (Navy)
Hanna, James, age 26, 10 years in U.S., Newburgh, Orange Co.,
  grocer (19-24 Oct. 1812)
Hanna, James, 5ft. 6in., age 20, dark complex., dark hair, dark
  eyes, Catherine Lane, tanner (Navy)
Hannah, Henry, 5ft. 10in., age 23, dark complex., dark hair,
  brown eyes, skinner, painter (<u>sic</u>!) (Navy)

Hannah, John, 5ft. 8in., age 20, dark complex., dark hair, brown
eyes, Water St., coppersmith (Navy)
Hannah/Hanna, Lawrence, age 48, 6 years in U.S., wife & 4 children, Talbot St., NYC, laborer (20-25 July 1812); 5ft. 2in.,
age 49, dark complex., black hair, grey eyes, Talbot St., brass
founder (Navy)
Hannah, Robert, age 51, 15 years in U.S., wife & 4 children,
Half Moon, Saratoga Co., weaver (26-31 Oct. 1812)
Hannah, William, age 35, 6 years in U.S., wife & 5 children, 89
Fair St., NYC, tailor (20-25 July 1812); 5ft. 11in., age 36,
dark complex., grey hair, grey eyes, Gold St., tailor (Navy)
Hannan, Henry, 5ft. 8in., age 30, dark complex., brown hair,
hazel eyes, cordwainer (Navy)
Hannigan, Dennis, 5ft. 5 3/4in., age 20, dark complex., dark
hair, light eyes, George St., grocer (Navy)
Hanterly, Peter, 5ft. 7in., age 24, fair complex., dark hair,
grey eyes, Cherry St., labourer (Navy)
Hansen, Michael, 5ft. 8in., age 30, brown complex., dark hair,
dark eyes, William St., Labourer (Navy)
Harbart (or Harburt?), Daniel, age 41, 11 years & 4 mos. in U.S.,
Clinton, Dutchess Co., laborer (12-17 Oct. 1812)
Hardie, George, 5ft. 7½in., age 28, fair complex., brown hair,
light eyes, Greenwich St., tailor (Navy)
Harden/Hardin, William, age 58, 35 years in U.S., wife & 1 son,
Palatine, Montgomery Co., weaver (25 Aug. - 2 Sept. & 7-12
Sept. 1812)
Hardy, Edward, age 18, 8 years in U.S., family of Jas. Hardy &
wife, Johnstown, Montgomery Co., farmer (28 July - 2 Aug. 1812);
he lives with his father (5 Nov. - 9 Dec. 1812)
Hardy, George, age 40, 8 years in U.S., wife & 8 children, 222
Greenwich St., tailor (20-25 July 1812)
Hardy, John, age 65, 19 years in U.S., wife & 5 children, Mont-
gomery Co., farmer (10-15 Aug. 1812)
Hardy, Thomas, 5ft. 6½in., age 24, fair complex., sandy hair,
brown eyes, Front St., labourer (Navy)
Hare, Andrew, age 27, 6 years in U.S., 2 in family, 41 Cheap-
side St., brewer (20-25 July 1812)
Hare, John, age 21, 1 year in U.S., Hudson, Columbia Co., weaver
(3-8 Aug. 1812)
Harkness, James, 5ft. 10in., age 25, light complex., brown hair,
light eyes, weaver (Navy)
Harley, Charles, age 26, 13 years in U.S., Mamakating, Sullivan
Co., farmer (19-24 Oct. 1812)
Harley, Thomas, age 30, 6 years in U.S., wife & child, 439 Pearl
St., NYC, saddler (26-31 Oct. 1812)
Harman, Henry, age 23, 10 mos. in U.S., Scammel St., NYC, chemist
(20-25 July 1812)
Harman, Thomas, 5ft. 5½in., age 40, dark complex., dark hair,
dark eyes, Pearl St., morocco dresser (Navy)
Haron (?), Andrew, 5ft. 11in., age 60, brown complex., brown
hair, grey eyes, Bancker St., grocer (Navy)
Harper, Richard, 5ft. 6in., age 47, dark complex., brown hair,
grey eyes, Bowery, grocer (Navy)
Harper, Thomas, age 35, 2 years in U.S., Manhattanville, carpen-
ter (14-19 Sept. 1812)
Harpham, Henry, age 20 years & 11 mos., 8 years & 5 mos. in U.S.,
Cicero, Onondaga Co., farmer (7-28 Dec. 1812 & 21 Dec. 1812 -
23 Jan. 1813)
Harpham, Septibah, age 20, 7 years in U.S., Whitestown, Oneida
Co., joiner, from Lancashire, Eng. (26 Aug. & 28 Sept. - 3 Oct.
1812)
Harriman, Thomas, age 50, 14 years in U.S., 6 in family, Cale-
donia, Genesee Co., farmer (5-15 & 24-29 Aug. 1812)
Harrington, John, age 27, 6 years in U.S., Fishkill, Dutchess
Co., weaver (12-17 Oct. 1812)

Harris, George, age 27, 2 years in U.S., Livingston, Columbia
    Co., clothier (17-22 Aug. 1812)
Harris, George, age 24, 3 mos. in U.S., Minisink, Orange Co.,
    cooper (19-24 Oct. 1812)
Harris, John, age 18, 17 years in U.S., Duanesburgh, Schenectady
    Co., laborer (26-31 Oct. 1812)
Harris, Thomas, age 46, 5 years in U.S., wife, 172 Water St.,
    NYC, tavern-keeper (20-25 July 1812)
Harris, Thomas, 5ft. 9in., age 46, dark complex., brown hair,
    dark eyes, Flushing St., storekeeper (Navy)
Harriss, Thomas, 5ft. 7½in., age 38, dark complex., dark hair,
    brown eyes, labourer (Navy)
Harrison, Francis, age 29, 8 years in U.S., wife & 2 children,
    Cherry St., NYC, cartman (20-25 July 1812); 5ft. 9in., age 30,
    dark complex., brown hair, dark eyes, Cherry St., cartman (Navy)
Harrison, James, age 29, 5 mos. in U.S., Columbiaville, Columbia
    Co., cotton spinner (17-22 Aug. 1812)
Harrison, James, age 29, 7 years in U.S., wife & child, 10 Ferry
    St., NYC, morocco dresser (20-25 July 1812)
Harrison, Thomas, age 40, 8 years in U.S., wife, 63 Liberty St.,
    NYC, dyer, applied Nov. 1811 (20-25 July 1812); 5ft. 7½in.,
    age 40, light complex., light hair, light eyes, Liberty St.,
    dyer (Navy)
Harrison, William, age 34, 19 years in U.S., New Windsor, Orange
    Co., weaver (19-24 Oct. 1812)
Harrison, William, 5ft. 9½in., age 27, dark complex., dark hair,
    grey eyes, painter (Navy)
Harrott, William, age 36, 8 years in U.S., Minisink, Orange Co.,
    laborer (19-24 Oct. 1812)
Hart, Andrew, 5ft. 7in., age 45, fair complex., brown hair, blue
    eyes, Anthony St., labourer (Navy)
Hart, Hugh, 5ft. 7in., age 35, fair complex., fair hair, grey
    eyes, Elm St., labourer (Navy)
Hart, James, 5ft. 11in., age 30, dark complex., brown hair, grey
    eyes, waiter (Navy)
Hart, Michael, age 37, 9 years in U.S., wife, 43 Cross St., NYC,
    laborer (28 July - 2 Aug. 1812)
Hart, William, 5ft. 8in., age 36, fair complex., dark hair, blue
    eyes, Washington St., rigger (Navy)
Harvey, John, age 44, 17 years in U.S., 1 boy, Norfolk St., NYC,
    shipwright (20-25 July 1812)
Harvey, Samuel, age 30, 8 years in U.S., wife, Mamakating, Sul-
    livan Co., weaver (19-24 Oct. 1812)
Harvey, William, no age given, 7 mos. in U.S., wife & 2 servants,
    Jamaica, Long Island, farmer (20-25 July 1812)
Hasket, John, age 38, 9 years in U.S., 1 son, 141 Water St., NYC,
    saddler, applied 2 or 3 years since (13-18 July 1812); 5ft.
    7in., age 39, light complex., dark hair, blue eyes, Water St.,
    saddler (Navy)
Hasket, Maysey, age 45, 1 year in U.S., 4 children, Woodstock,
    Ulster Co., shoemaker (13-18 July 1812)
Haskin, Roger, 5ft. 5in., age 35, dark complex., brown hair,
    brown eyes, Bancker St., cordwainer (Navy)
Haskin, Simon, 5ft. 8in., age 38, dark complex., brown hair,
    black eyes, labourer (Navy)
Hasler, George, 5ft. 3in., age 29, dark complex., dark hair,
    grey eyes, Chatham St., carver (Navy)
Hasselt, Michael, 5ft. 4in., age 27, fair complex., light hair,
    blue eyes, Richmond Co., teacher (Navy)
Hastie (or Haster?), Robert, 5ft. 10in., age 24, light complex.,
    light hair, light eyes, clerk, removed from NYC to Fishkill,
    Dutchess Co. (Navy)
Hastings, Alexander, 5ft. 6in., age 33, fair complex., sandy
    hair, blue eyes, Budd St., preacher (Navy)

Haswell, Walter, age 41, 6 mos. in U.S., Chamber St., NYC,
  gentleman (28 July - 2 Aug. 1812)
Hathwell, George H. age 34, 1 year in U.S., wife & 3 children,
  Bedford St., NYC, carver & gilder (3-8 Aug. 1812)
Hawkes, George, 5ft. 8in., age 30, fair complex., light hair,
  blue eyes, removed from NYC (Navy)
Hawkins, James, age 30, 12 years in U.S., New Windsor, Orange
  Co., laborer (19-24 Oct. 1812)
Hawthorn, John, age 44, 11 years in U.S., 15 Chatham St., NYC,
  dealer & pedlar (7-19 Dec. 1812)
Hay, Lionel, age 43, 9 years in U.S., wife & 9 children, Whites-
  town, Oneida Co., farmer (30 Nov. - 5 Dec. 1812)
Haycock, Thomas, 5ft. 9in., age 32, dark complex., brown hair,
  grey eyes, Manhattan, weaver (Navy)
Hayes, Samuel, age 45, 5 mos. in U.S., Hudson, Columbia Co.,
  farmer (19-22 Aug. 1812)
Haynes, John, 5ft. 7½in., age 38, light complex., brown hair,
  grey eyes, Bancker St., grocer (Navy)
Haynes, Thomas, 5ft. 8in., age 46, fair complex., grey hair,
  hazel eyes, Spring St., pin maker (Navy); age 47, 2 years in
  U.S., wife & 2 children, 157 Spring St., NYC, pin manufacturer
  (28 July - 2 Aug. 1812)
Hays, James, age 22, 11 years in U.S., Saratoga, Saratoga Co.,
  weaver (17-22 Aug. 1812)
Hays, John, 5ft. 10in., age 37, fair complex., light hair, blue
  eyes, Hammond St., weaver (Navy)
Hays, Joseph, age 26, 4 years & 4 mos. in U.S., Mamakating, Sul-
  livan Co., weaver (19-24 Oct. 1812)
Hays, Mathew, 5ft. 10in., age 28, fair complex., brown hair,
  grey eyes, Hagen St., skinner (Navy)
Hays, Samuel, age 39, 23 years in U.S., wife & 5 children, New-
  burgh, Orange Co., laborer (19-24 Oct. 1812)
Hays, Walter, 5ft. 10¼in., age 41, florid complex., brown hair,
  blue eyes, Vandewater St., labourer (Navy)
Haythorn, James, age 33, 10 days in U.S., 401 Pearl St., NYC,
  leather dresser (26-31 Oct. 1812)
Hayton, John, age 27, 2 years & 9 mos. in U.S., Newburgh, Orange
  Co., weaver (19-24 Oct. 1812)
Hayver, James, 5ft. 11in., age 35, fair complex., dark hair,
  grey eyes, gardener (Navy)
Heafield, John, age 24, 1 year & 10 mos. in U.S., 9 Leonard St.,
  NYC, whitesmith (3-8 Aug. 1812)
Heaily, Thomas, 5ft. 9in., age 28, fair complex., sandy hair,
  brown eyes, cartman (Navy)
Heainey, Thomas, 5ft. 11in., age 25, fair complex., sandy hair,
  blue eyes, Arch St., labourer (Navy)
Heal, William, 5ft. 6in., age 45, light complex., brown hair,
  grey eyes, Water St., bellows man (Navy)
Healey, Thomas, 5ft. 5in., age 20, light complex., brown hair,
  blue eyes, Pearl St., saddler (Navy)
Healy, Paul, age 35, 5 years in U.S., wife, 1 child, 1 girl, 27
  Augustus St., NYC, laborer (20-25 July 1812)
Hearfield, John, 5ft. 10½in., age 24, light complex., dark hair,
  light eyes, Leonard St., blacksmith (Navy)
Hearn, John, age 33, 8 years in U.S., wife & 3 children, Lumber
  St., NYC, laborer (20-25 July 1812)
Heath, Joseph, 5ft. 7½in., age 25, light complex., fair hair,
  blue eyes, clerk (Navy)
Heather, William, age 20, 2 mos. in U.S., Kingston, Ulster Co.,
  weaver (7 Sept. & 19-24 Oct. 1812)
Heathington, James, 5ft. 10in., age 30, fair complex., dark hair,
  brown eyes, Bayard St., grocer (Navy)
Heaton, Edward, 5ft. 6in., age 32, brown complex., brown hair,
  blue eyes, bricklayer (Navy)

Heely, James, 5ft. 9in., age 29, fair complex., brown hair, blue
    eyes, Wall St. accountant (Navy)
Heely, Paul, 5ft. 9in., age 30, light complex., sandy hair, light
    eyes, Duane St., labourer (Navy)
Heeman, Philip, 5ft. 10in., age 29, "s" complex., "s"(andy) hair,
    brown eyes, Liberty St., blacksmith (Navy)
Heffernan, John, age 30, 6 years in U.S., wife, Kips Bay, grocer
    (10-15 Aug. 1812); 5ft. 10in., age 30, dark complex., dark hair,
    grey eyes, grocer (Navy)
Helley, James, 5ft. 6in., age 26, dark complex., light hair, blue
    eyes, removed from NYC (Navy)
Helly, James, 5ft. 6in., age 21, dark complex., light hair, blue
    eyes (Navy)
Helly, William, 5ft. 6in., age 33, fair complex., brown hair,
    brown eyes, labourer (Navy)
Helm, Henry Anthony, age 27, 10 mos. in U.S., 30 Vesey St., NYC,
    dancing master (28 Sept. - 3 Oct. 1812)
Helston, Thomas, 5ft. 6in., age 24, fair complex., dark hair,
    dark eyes, comedian (Navy)
Hencey, John, 5ft. 5in., age 48, fair complex., brown hair, hazel
    eyes, paver (Navy)
Hend, Thomas, 5ft. 6in., age 25, dark complex., brown hair, grey
    eyes, Broadway, weaver (Navy)
Henderson, Andrew, age 27, 7 years & 9 mos. in U.S., Wallkill,
    Orange Co., weaver (19-24 Oct. 1812)
Henderson, Archibald, 5ft. 5in., age 38, light complex., light
    hair, black eyes, baker (Navy)
Henderson, Archibald, 5ft. 6in., age 25, brown complex., dark
    hair, grey eyes, Orange St., painter (Navy)
Henderson, David, 5ft. 11in., age 30, fair complex., brown hair,
    grey eyes, Bloomingdale, labourer (Navy)
Henderson, John, age 30, 1 year & 1 mo. in U.S., wife & 3 child-
    ren, Wallkill, Orange Co., weaver (19-24 Oct. 1812)
Henderson, John, 5ft. 11in., age 23, brown complex., brown hair,
    brown eyes, blacksmith (Navy)
Henderson, John, 5ft. 6in., age 21, light complex., brown hair,
    blue eyes, Bancker St., cartman (Navy)
Henderson, Robert, age 35, 7 years in U.S., wife & 6 children,
    270 Pearl St., NYC, pocketbook manufacturer (20-25 July 1812)
Henderson, Robert, 5ft. 5in., age 34, dark complex., dark hair,
    blue eyes, Bloomingdale, manufacturer (Navy)
Henderson, Samuel, 5ft. 8in., age 25, brown complex., black hair,
    grey eyes, Attorney St., cartman (Navy)
Hendict (?), Andrew, 5ft. 10in., age 38, light complex., brown
    hair, blue eyes (Navy)
Hening, George, age 68, 5 years in U.S., 257 Bowery Lane, NYC,
    tailor (20-25 July 1812); 5ft. 11in., age 68, dark complex.,
    grey hair, grey eyes, Leonard St., tailor (Navy)
Hening, James, age 39, 7 years in U.S., wife & son, Rivington
    St., NYC, brewer, applied 16 Aug. 1811 (20-25 July 1812); 5ft.
    2in., age 40, dark complex., dark hair, grey eyes, Rivington
    St., brewer (Navy)
Hening, James, Jr., 5ft. 4in., age 19, dark complex., black hair,
    grey eyes, Delancy St., brewer (Navy)
Hennel, Andrew, age 38, 10 years in U.S., wife & 2 children, 12
    Harman St., NYC, shipwright (31 Aug. - 5 Sept. 1812)
Hennelly, Andrew, 5ft. 3in., age 29, fair complex., brown hair,
    blue eyes, labourer (Navy)
Hennesalty (?), Bernard, 5ft. 11in., age 30, fair complex., fair
    hair, grey eyes, sawyer (Navy)
Henrietta, Barnaby, age 26, 8 years in U.S., wife & 2 children,
    NYC, sawyer (28 July - 2 Aug. 1812)
Henrietta, Francis, age 21, 1 year & 2 mos. in U.S., NYC, sawyer
    (28 July - 2 Aug. 1812)

Henrietta, James, age 28, 4 years in U.S., wife, NYC, tallow
    chandler (20-25 July 1812); 5ft. 8in., age 30, dark complex.,
    black hair, grey eyes, Greenwich St., soap boiler (Navy)
Henry, Augustus, age 19, 1 year in U.S., Monroe Works, Orange
    Co., cut nailor (17-22 Aug. 1812)
Henry, Bernard, 5ft. 8½in., age 26, dark complex., brown hair,
    blue eyes, mason (Navy)
Henry, James, 5ft. 8in., age 21, brown complex., dark hair,
    brown eyes, Greenwich St., sawyer (Navy)
Henry, John, age 28, 4 years in U.S., NYC, seaman (3-8 Aug. 1812)
Henry, John, age 21, 3 mos. in U.S., Montgomery, Orange Co.,
    weaver (19-24 Oct. 1812)
Henry, John, 5ft. 9in., age 22, fair complex., brown hair, grey
    eyes, blacksmith (Navy)
Henry, Samuel, age 25, 3 mos. in U.S., City of Albany, clerk
    (17-22 Aug. 1812)
Henryett, Bennet, age 25, 3 years in U.S., 4 in family, Boyle,
    Ontario Co., laborer (15 Nov. 1812 - 3 Jan. 1813)
Heow, Richard, age 39, 18 years in U.S., wife & 5 children, Sha-
    wangunk, Ulster Co., shoemaker (19-24 Oct. 1812)
Hepwell, Abraham, 5ft. 5in., age 56, light complex., grey hair,
    grey eyes, East George St., labourer (Navy)
Hepwell, Abraham, 5ft. 7in., age 28, light complex., light hair,
    black eyes, blacksmith (Navy)
Hepwell, James, age 29, 7 years in U.S., wife & child, 12 Fayette
    St., NYC, morocco dresser (20-25 July 1812); 5ft. 7in., age 28,
    fair complex., brown hair, grey eyes, Fayette St., morocco
    (Navy)
Hepwell, John, 5ft. 6½in., age 25, fair complex., dark hair,
    brown eyes, coachman (Navy)
Hepwell, Wesley, 5ft. 8in., age 22, fair complex., fair hair,
    brown eyes, blacksmith (Navy)
Herlson, Thomas, age 23, 1 year & 4 mos. in U.S., 13 Dey St.,
    NYC, comedian (17-22 Aug. 1812)
Herring, James, age 46, 20 years in U.S., wife & 4 children,
    Woodstock, Ulster Co., schoolmaster (19-24 Oct. 1812)
Hewett, Thomas, age 35, 11 years in U.S., 7 in family, 198 Wil-
    liam St., NYC, tailor (20-25 July 1812); 5ft. 3in., age 37 dark
    complex., dark hair, light eyes, William St., tailor (Navy)
Hewit, Thomas, 5ft. 6in., age 28, light complex., brown hair,
    brown eyes, weaver (Navy)
Hewitt, Josephus, age 34, 9 years in U.S., 4 in family, 29 Hes-
    ter St., NYC, tailor, applied 27 June 1812 (3-8 Aug. 1812);
    Hewitt, Joseph, 5ft. 4in., age 34, fair complex., dark hair,
    dark eyes, Hester St., tailor (Navy)
Hewitt, Thomas, age 28, 4 years & 4 mos. in U.S., Bethlehem,
    Albany Co., carder (17-22 Aug. 1812)
Hick, Robert, 5ft. 5in., age 50, light complex., light hair,
    blue eyes, Sixth St., manufacturer of thread (Navy)
Hickenbottom, William, age 34, 8 years in U.S., 3 in family,
    2 Mile Stone, coachman (20-25 July 1812)
Hickey, Andrew, age 28, 4 mos. in U.S., NYC, laborer (28 July -
    2 Aug. 1812)
Hickman, Samuel, 5ft. 7in., age 26, brown complex., brown hair,
    brown eyes, labourer (Navy)
Higgenbotham, (no surname given), 5ft. 10in., age 36, fair com-
    plex., brown hair, blue eyes, Broadway, servant (Navy)
Higgins, Charles, 5ft. 2in., age 47, fair complex., red hair,
    blue eyes, Broome St., labourer (Navy)
Higgins, James, 5ft. 6in., age 29, fair complex., brown hair,
    blue eyes, Elm St., maltster (Navy)
Higgins, Patrick, age 20, 1 year in U.S., 75 Mulberry St., NYC,
    laborer (28 July - 2 Aug. 1812); 5ft. 8in., age 20, light com-
    plex., brown hair, blue eyes, labourer (Navy)

Higgins, Peter, age 27, 5 years in U.S., wife & child, 43 Cross
St., NYC, grocer (20-25 July 1812)
Higgins, Peter, 5ft. 9in., age 28, fair complex., sandy hair,
grey eyes, Cross St., bricklayer (Navy)
Higgins, Thomas, age 28, 5 years in U.S., Duane St., cartman
(28 July - 2 Aug. 1812)
Higgins, William, age 40, 8 years in U.S., wife & 3 children,
NYC, tallow chandler, applied 29 Aug. 1804 (20-25 July 1812)
Higgins, William, 5ft. 6in., age 37, fair complex., brown hair,
blue eyes, Bancker St., chandler (Navy)
Higgins, William, 5ft. 8in., age 22, fair complex., brown hair,
grey eyes, labourer (Navy)
Higginson, Samuel, Sr., 5ft. 9in., age 66, fair complex., grey
hair, hazel eyes, rushmaker (or brushmaker?) (Navy)
Higginson, Samuel, Jr., 5ft. 9in., age 29, fair complex., brown
hair, blue eyes, shoemaker (Navy)
Higham, Thomas, age 39, 6 years & 10 mos. in U.S., wife & 2
children, Charleston, S.C., merchant (28 July - 2 Aug. 1812)
Hill, Alexander, age 36, 2 years in U.S., wife & boy, Kips Bay,
NYC, tanner (3-8 Aug. 1812); 5ft. 7½in., age 35, dark complex.,
brown hair, grey eyes, tanner (Navy)
Hill, Hugh, age 21, 3 years in U.S., 15 Courtlandt St., NYC,
clerk (20-25 July 1812); 5ft. 11in., age 21, light complex.,
brown hair, black eyes, clerk (Navy)
Hill, Isaac, age 31, 5 years & 4 mos. in U.S., wife & 4 children, Camillus, Onondaga Co., merchant, applied 27 Jan. 1813
(28 Dec. 1812 - 3 Feb. 1813)
Hill, James, age 48, 2 years in U.S., wife & 6 children, Bethel,
Sullivan Co., farmer (19-24 Oct. 1812); applied 12 Feb. 1812
(31 Aug. 1812)
Hill, Jeremiah, 5ft. 8in., age 32, light complex., dark hair,
grey eyes, Chatham St., broker (Navy); removed from NYC to
Poughkeepsie, Dutchess Co. (Navy)
Hill, John, age 42, 10 years in U.S., wife & 3 children, NYC,
blacksmith (28 July - 2 Aug. 1812); 5ft. 6in., "s" complex.,
sandy hair, blue eyes, Orchard St., blacksmith (Navy)
Hill, John, age 19, 2 years in U.S., Bethel, Sullivan Co., far-
mer (31 Aug. & 19-24 Oct. 1812)
Hill, John Watson, age 40, 11 years in U.S., wife & 2 children,
City of Albany, millwright (24-29 Aug. 1812)
Hill, Robert, age 20, 2 mos. in U.S., Kingston, Ulster Co., wea-
ver (7 Sept. 1812)
Hill, William, age 34, 9 years in U.S., 5 in family, Boyle, Ontario Co., farmer, applied Feb. 1810 (5-15 & 24-29 Aug. 1812)
Hill, William, age 22, 2 years in U.S., Montgomery, Orange Co.,
weaver (19-24 Oct. 1812)
Hillock/Hillich, Humphry, age 28, 2 years in U.S., Tontine Coffee House, waiter (20-25 July 1812); 5ft. 8½in., age 32, dark
complex., brown hair, blue eyes, Water St., servant (Navy)
Hilton, Robert, age 48, 6 mos. in U.S., wife & 8 children, Mamaroneck, Westchester Co., cotton spinner (28 Sept. - 3 Oct.
1812); 5ft. 10in., age 48, light complex., grey hair, blue
eyes, cotton spinner (Navy)
Hind, James, age 25, 1 year in U.S., 187 Bowery Lane, NYC (20-
25 July 1812)
Hind, Thomas, age 47, 7 years in U.S., 4 children, Hudson, Columbia Co., brewer (10-15 Aug. 1812)
Hine (?), Redmond, 5ft. 11in., age 22, fair complex., brown hair,
hazel eyes, butcher (Navy)
Hines, Felix, 5ft. 8in., age 22, fair complex., fair hair, blue
eyes, bootmaker (Navy)
Hing, Robert, 5ft. 8in., age 24, dark complex., dark hair, blue
eyes, instrument (maker) (Navy)
Hippon, William, age 21, 3 days in U.S., NYC, woolen manufacturer (26-31 Oct. 1812)

Hirst, George, age 27, 1 year & 2 mos. in U.S., Manhattanville, NYC, manufacturer (14-19 Sept. 1812)

Hodges, Iyzack, age 38, 9 years in U.S., wife & 2 children, NYC, accountant (20-25 July 1812); 5ft. 7½in., dark complex., dark hair, dark eyes, Chatham St., clerk (Navy)

Hodgkinson, Thomas, age 37, 8 years in U.S., wife & 2 children, 53 Nassau St., innkeeper, applied Jan. 1809 (20-25 July 1812); 5ft. 8in., age 35, light complex., dark hair, brown eyes, innkeeper (Navy)

Hodgson, George, age 70, 23 years in U.S., Johnsburgh, Washington Co., farmer (7-19 Dec, 1812)

Hodgson, George, age 30, 24 years in U.S., 8 in family, NYC, cartman (20-25 July 1812)

Hodgson, John, age 34, 20 years in U.S., wife, Johnsburgh, Washington Co., farmer (21 Dec. 1812 - 23 Jan. 1813); age 34 on 22 Aug. last, 20 years in U.S. in July last (24 Nov. 1812)

Hodgson, William, 5ft. 5½in., age 23, light complex., brown hair, blue eyes, Greenwich St., bookkeeper (Navy)

Hoe, Robert, 5ft. 6in., age 28, fair complex., brown hair, brown eyes, Pearl St., carpenter (Navy)

Hogarth, William, 5ft. 8in., age 26, dark complex., brown hair, blue eyes, pedler (Navy)

Hogg, John, age 35, 12 years in U.S., wife & 3 children, Schoharie, tailor (24-29 Aug. 1812)

Holding, William, age 35, 7 mos. in U.S., 155 Bancker St., NYC, weaver (20-25 July 1812)

Holland, Charles, 5ft. 4in., age 25, ruddy complex., dark hair, grey eyes, Greenwich St., gardener (Navy)

Holland, Henry, 5ft. 6in., age 26, fair complex., brown hair, blue eyes, Cherry St., physician (Navy)

Holland, Stephen, age 54, 3 years in U.S., corner Mott & North Sts., NYC, dealer (20-25 July 1812)

Holliday, John, age 42, 19 years in U.S., 4 in family, physician (24-29 Aug. 1812); Phelps, Ontario Co. (5-15 Aug. 1812)

Holliday, Thomas, age 40 last Oct., 9 years in U.S. on 25 May last, wife & 4 children, Whitestown, Oneida Co., overseer of carding manufactory (26 Aug. 1812)

Hollin, Charles, age 29, 1 year & 2 mos. in U.S., Wallkill, Orange Co., farmer (19-24 Oct. 1812)

Hollinghead, Thomas, 5ft. 7in., age 20, light complex., light hair, dark eyes, Cedar St., hatter (Navy)

Hollinsworth, Samuel, age 29, 2 years in U.S. on 29 May next, wife & child, Eaton, Madison Co., farmer (31 Oct. & 30 Nov. - 5 Dec. 1812)

Hollis, Humphrey, 3 mos. in U.S., Butternuts, Otsego Co.(30 Nov. - 5 Dec. 1812)

Holly, John, 5ft. 3½in., age 29, dark complex., brown hair, grey eyes, Ferry St., labourer (Navy)

Holly, William, 5ft. 5¼in., age 33, brown complex., dark hair, light eyes, accountant (Navy)

Holma, Joseph George, age 48, 4 days in U.S., NYC, comedian (14-19 Sept. 1812); 5ft. 9in., age 48, theatre (Navy)

Holmes, Absalom, age 54, 9 years in U.S., wife & 6 children, Westchester Co., cordwainer (3-8 Aug. 1812)

Holmes, James, age 21, 5 years in U.S., Rome, Oneida Co., weaver (29 July & 3-8 Aug. 1812)

Holwick, John N., age 47, 32 years in U.S., wife & 8 children, Shawangunk, Ulster Co,, farmer (19-24 Oct. 1812)

Hood, George, age 21, 2 years in U.S., 164 Greenwich St., NYC, English agent for manufacturing houses (20-25 July 1812)

Hood, Thomas, age 32, 10 years in U.S., wife, 64 Cherry St., painter & glazier, applied Nov. 1810 (20-25 July 1812); 5ft. 9in., age 32, light complex., brown hair, light eyes, painter (Navy)

Hope, David, 5ft. 10in, age 45, dark complex., brown hair, black
  eyes, Greenwich Lane, weaver (Navy)
Hope, Robert, age 51, 8 years in U.S. wife & 7 children, Green-
  wich Lane, grocer (20-25 July 1812)
Hope, Robert, 5ft. 10in., age 52, fair complex., brown hair,
  grey eyes, Greenwich, weaver (Navy) - same as above?
Hopkins, Benjamin, age 58, 20 years in U.S., wife & 2 children,
  NYC, laborer (14-19 Sept, 1812)
Hopkins, Henry, age 32, 1 year & 3 mos. in U.S., wife & 3 child-
  ren, Thompson, Sullivan Co., farmer (19-24 Oct. 1812)
Hopkins, John, 5ft. 10in., age 46, fair complex., brown hair,
  grey eyes, Reed St., labourer (Navy)
Hopkins, William, 5ft. 8in., age 53, brown complex., dark hair,
  grey eyes, tobacco (for tobacconist?) (Navy)
Hore, Andrew, 5ft. 6in., age 26, dark complex., black hair,
  blue eyes, Cheapside, brewer (Navy)
Horlor, George, age 28, 7 years in U.S., wife & 4 children, 23
  Pell St., NYC, carver & gilder (13-18 July 1812)
Horne, Simon, 5ft. 6in., age 31, dark complex., brown hair,
  dark eyes, labourer (Navy)
Horrick, William Rhodes, 5ft. 5in., age 32, light complex.,
  sandy hair, hazel eyes, Christopher St., weaver (Navy)
Horton, James, 5ft. 7in., age 27, light complex., dark hair,
  hazel eyes, comedian (Navy)
Horton, Joseph, age 25, 11 years in U.S., wife, 44 Leonard St.,
  NYC, comedian (20-25 July 1812)
Hosking, John, age 52, 16 years in U.S., 3 children, Gouverneur
  St., NYC, ship-carpenter (10-15 Aug. 1812); 5ft. 5in., age 53,
  light complex., light hair, dark eyes, Greenwich St., ship-
  carpenter (Navy)
Houlding, William, 5ft. 6in., age 35, dark complex., dark hair,
  brown eyes, Henry St., weaver (Navy)
Housedellen, Henry, 5ft. 8in., age 30, dark complex., brown hair,
  grey eyes, joiner (Navy)
Houston, James, age 28, 9 years in U.S., corner Wall & Front Sts.,
  grocer (28 July - 2 Aug. 1812); 5ft. 8¼in., age 25, light complex., brown hair, black eyes, Wall St., grocer (Navy)
Houston, John, age 32 on 7 Aug. last, in U.S. since 14 May 1803,
  wife & child, Utica, Oneida Co., joiner, from Nottinghamshire,
  Eng. (26 Aug. & 28 Sept. - 3 Oct. 1812)
Hovel, John S., age 33, 10 years in U.S., wife, Anthony St., NYC,
  comedian (20-25 July 1812)
Howard, Charles, 5ft. 9in., age 34, ruddy complex., black hair,
  light eyes, Peekskill, cotton manufacturer (Navy)
Howard, George, age 50, 2 years in U.S., Manhattanville, manu-
  facturer (21-26 Sept. 1812); 5ft. 7in., age 50, pale complex.,
  black hair, brown eyes, Manhattanville, manufacturer (Navy)
Howard, Hugh, age 46, 11 years in U.S., wife & 2 children, Clinton, Dutchess Co., laborer (12-17 Oct. 1812)
Howard, Richard, 5ft. 5in., age 47, dark complex., dark hair,
  light eyes, Lumber St., shoemaker (Navy)
Howard, Thomas, age 30, 6 years in U.S., wife & child, Hudson,
  Columbia Co., farrier (22 Aug. & 24-29 Aug. 1812)
How, Samuel, 5ft. 5in., age 20, light complex., dark hair, blue
  eyes, Temple St., mariner (Navy)
Howe, William, age 25, 1 year & 4 mos. in U.S., wife, Claremont,
  servant (20-25 July 1812); 5ft. 7in., age 26, light complex.,
  dark hair, dark eyes, City Hotel, waiter (Navy)
Howel, John, 5ft. 9in., age 40, dark complex., dark hair, grey
  eyes, Greenwich St., maltster (Navy)
Howell, James, age 23, Oneida Co., farmer (28 July - 2 Aug. 1812)
Hoy, David, age 33, 8 years in U.S., wife & 2 children, 70 Bayard
  St., NYC, cartman (28 July - 2 Aug. 1812); 5ft. 10¼in., age 34,
  ruddy complex., brown hair, blue eyes, cartman (Navy)

Hoye, Michael, 5ft. 5in., age 25, light complex., brown hair,
blue eyes, William St., labourer (Navy)
Hubbard, Beevis (?), 5ft. 6in., age 25, light complex., light
hair, brown eyes, City Hotel, waiter (Navy)
Hubbard, John, age 26, 7 years in U.S., 77 John St., NYC, mechanic (13-18 July 1812)
Hubbs, John, 5ft. 9in., age 25, dark complex., dark hair, brown
eyes, Arundle St., weaver (Navy)
Huchinson, Robert, 5ft. 9in., age 29, fair complex., fair hair,
grey eyes, removed from NYC to Goshen, Orange Co. (Navy)
Hugh, Michael, 5ft. 7in., age 27, light complex., dark hair,
blue eyes, Bowery, shoemaker (Navy)
Hughes, Arthur, 5ft. 6in., age 40, dark complex., brown hair,
grey eyes, Chamber St., Labourer (Navy)
Hughes, Arthur, 5ft. 5½in., age 23, fair complex., dark hair,
brown eyes, Pump St., wheelwright (Navy)
Hughes, Bernard, 5ft. 7in., age 26, fair complex., brown hair,
brown eyes, Broadway, labourer (Navy)
Hughes, Christopher, age 30, 6 years in U.S., 5 in family, Mulberry St., NYC, laborer (20-25 July 1812)
Hughes, David, 5ft. 5in., age 42, fair complex., brown hair,
brown eyes, cooper (Navy)
Hughes, Edward, age 20, 1½ years in U.S., 4 Bancker St., NYC,
teacher (13-18 July 1812); 5ft. 10in., age 20, fair complex.,
brown hair, blue eyes, teacher (Navy)
Hughes, Herman, age 30, 15 years in U.S., wife & child, NYC,
merchant (28 July - 2 Aug. 1812); 5ft. 10in., age 30, fair
complex., sandy hair, blue eyes, removed from NYC to Fishkill,
Dutchess Co. (Navy)
Hughes, Hugh, age 30, 11 years in U.S., wife & 2 children, Rem-
sen, Oneida Co., farmer (29 Sept. & 28 Sept. - 3 Oct. 1812)
Hughes, James, 5ft. 10in., age 56, fair complex., brown hair,
blue eyes, clockmaker (Navy)
Hughes, James, 5ft. 6in., age 30, dark complex., dark hair, dark
eyes, Lombardy St., labourer (Navy)
Hughes, Peter, 5ft. 8in., age 30, brown complex., dark hair,
brown eyes, Grand St., weaver (Navy)
Hughes, Robert, age 56 on 21 inst. Oct., 1 year in U.S. on 1
July last, wife & 4 children, Eaton, Madison Co., farmer (31
Oct. & 30 Nov. - 5 Dec. 1812)
Hughes, Walter, 6ft., age 30, dark complex., brown hair, blue
eyes, gentleman (Navy); 5ft., age 30, light complex., brown
hair, blue eyes, removed from NYC to Whitestown (Navy)
Hullard, John, 5ft. 7in., age 24, dark complex., dark hair, black
eyes, jeweler (Navy)
Hullsy, William, age 33, 10 years in U.S., 11 Wall St., NYC,
merchant (31 Aug. - 5 Sept. 1812)
Hume, William, age 40, 7 years in U.S., wife & 4 children, Manhattan Is., blacksmith (17-22 Aug. 1812); 5ft. 11in., age 43,
light complex., brown hair, blue eyes, blacksmith (Navy)
Humphreys/Humphrys, Joseph, age 26 on 12 Mar. last, 5 years in
U.S. on 12 Nov. next, wife & child, Whitestown, Oneida Co.,
carpenter & joiner (26 Aug. & 28 Sept. - 3 Oct. 1812)
Humphry, Moses Chamb., 5ft. 10½in., age 25, ruddy complex., sandy
hair, brown eyes, Cross St., morocco dresser (Navy)
Hunt, Benjamin, 5ft. 8in., age 54, dark complex., grey hair,
brown eyes, New Town, farmer (Navy)
Hunt, Charles, 5ft. 6in., age 40, light complex., light hair,
grey eyes, brass founder (Navy)
Hunt, John, age 31, 5 years in U.S., wife & 2 children, 35 Bayard
St., NYC, shoemaker (20-25 July 1812); 5ft. 5in., age 31, light
complex., brown hair, grey eyes, Pine St., cordwainer (Navy)
Hunter, Adam, age 27, 9 years in U.S., 98 William St., NYC, merchant (9-14 Nov. 1812); 5ft. 10in., age 27, fair complex.,
light hair, grey eyes, removed to Salisbury, Orange Co. (Navy)

Hunter, Alexander, age 46, 23 years & 2 mos. in U.S., wife & 11
    children, Virgil, Cortland Co., farmer (30 Nov. - 5 Dec. 1812
    & 2-11 Nov. 1812)
Hunter, David, age 30, 10 years in U.S., wife & 3 children, NYC,
    rigger (20-25 July 1812); 5ft. 7 3/4in., age 31, fair complex.,
    brown hair, light eyes, Washington St., rigger (Navy)
Hunter, James, 5ft. 5½in., age 29, light complex., brown hair,
    grey eyes, New Slip, labourer (Navy)
Hunter, John, age 33, 10 years in U.S., wife & child, NYC, school-
    master (26-31 Oct. 1812); 5ft. 6in., age 34, dark complex.,
    brown hair, brown eyes, Division St., schoolmaster (Navy)
Hunter, John, 5ft. 8in., age 24, dark complex., brown hair, dark
    eyes, Catherine St., brewer (Navy)
Hunter, John, 5ft. 9 3/4in., age 24, light complex., light hair,
    blue eyes, labourer (Navy)
Hunter, Robert, 5ft. 7in., age 28, light complex., brown hair,
    blue eyes, Reed St., soap boiler (Navy)
Hunter, Samuel, 5ft. 8in., age 39, fair complex., dark hair,
    light eyes, Chamber St., weaver (Navy)
Huntington, Edward, 5ft. 7in., age 45, fair complex., brown hair,
    light eyes, Staten Island (Navy)
Hurley, William, 5ft. 10in., age 24, dark complex., dark hair,
    grey eyes, Greenwich St., potter (Navy)
Hussy, Dennis, 5ft. 9in., age 28, dark complex., brown hair,
    blue eyes, Sixth St., tailor (Navy)
Hutchings, William, 5ft. 5½in., age 39, dark complex., brown
    hair, hazel eyes, Lombardy St., carpenter (Navy)
Hutchinson, George, age 33, 5 years in U.S., corner Pearl & Broad
    Sts., NYC, porter (3-8 Aug. 1812)
Hutchinson, Henry, age 19, 4 mos. in U.S., Clinton, Dutchess Co.,
    weaver (12-17 Oct. 1812); 5ft. 10in., age 20, light complex.,
    brown hair, grey eyes, Clinton Town, weaver (Navy)
Hutchinson, James, age 24, 3 years in U.S., 90 Maiden Lane, NYC,
    merchant, applied 2 Feb. 1811 (20-25 July 1812)
Hutchinson, James, 5ft. 8in., age 23, light complex., light hair,
    blue eyes, leather (dresser) (Navy)
Hutchinson, Michael, age 40, 8 years in U.S., wife & child, cor-
    ner Pearl & Elm Sts. (20-25 July 1812); 5ft. 6in., age 41, fair
    complex., fair hair, grey eyes, grocer (Navy)
Hutchinson, Thomas, 5ft. 10½in., age 24, dark complex., dark hair,
    dark eyes, removed from NYC to Goshen, Orange Co. (Navy)
Hutchinson, Robert, age 29, 4 years in U.S., 143 Pearl St., NYC,
    merchant, applied 13 Nov. 1811 (7-12 Sept. 1812); 5ft. 9in.,
    age 29, fair complex., fair hair, grey eyes, agent (Navy)
Hutton, Isaac G., age 21, 1 year in U.S., City of Albany (17-22
    Aug. 1812)
Hutton, Richard, age 43, 9 years in U.S., wife & 2 servants, 167
    Bancker St., NYC, rigger (28 July - 2 Aug. 1812); 5ft. 6in.,
    age 39, dark complex., dark hair, dark eyes, Bancker St., rig-
    ger (Navy)
Hyde, Robert, age 30, 9 years in U.S., wife & child, 171 Hester
    St., NYC (28 July - 2 Aug. 1812); 5ft. 6in., age 32, dark com-
    plex., brown hair, grey eyes, Hester St., labourer (Navy)
Hyman, Henry, age 30, 7 years in U.S., 4 in family, First St.,
    NYC, jeweler (20-25 July 1812); 5ft. 4in., age 31, dark com-
    plex., dark hair, black eyes, Barclay St., speculator (Navy)
Hynes, John, age 34, 2 years in U.S., wife, 2 Bancker St., NYC,
    grocer (20-25 July 1812)
Hynes, John, 5ft. 11in., age 30, fair complex., fair hair, grey
    eyes, Duane St., carpenter (Navy)
Innes, William, age 23, 6 years in U.S., wife & 4 children, Cor-
    laers Hook, chemist (20-25 July 1812); 5ft. 8in., age 30, light
    complex., brown hair, blue eyes, Walnut St., chemist (Navy)
Innet, Edward, age 26, 9 years in U.S., wife & child, 126 Broad
    St., 5ft. 10in., light com., dark hair & eyes, grocer (Jy. & Navy)

Ireland, Henry, Sr., 5ft. 7in., age 58, dark complex., black
    hair, blue eyes, Murray St., copper(smith) (Navy)
Ireland, Henry, Jr., 5ft. 8in., age 20, light complex., dark
    hair, dark eyes, cooper (Navy)
Irish, Charles, age 27, 7 years in U.S., 1 child, 5 Wall St.,
    watchmaker, applied 27 June 1812 (13-18 July 1812); 5ft. 7in.,
    age 30, fair complex., light hair, light eyes, Wall St., watch-
    maker (Navy)
Ironside, George, age 38, 5 years in U.S., wife & 2 children,
    18 Nassau St., NYC, teacher of languages (20-25 July 1812); 5
    ft. 6in., age 39, fair complex., light hair, blue eyes, Nassau
    St., teacher (Navy)
Irven, George, age 26, 1 year & 5 mos. in U.S., wife & 2 child-
    ren, Kingston, Ulster Co., weaver (7 Sept. & 19-24 Oct. 1812)
Irvin, George, 6ft. 1in., age 38, fair complex., brown hair,
    blue eyes, Oyster Bay, teacher (Navy)
Irvin, James, age 21, 3 years in U.S., Greenwich St., calico
    printer (28 July - 2 Aug. 1812)
Irvin, John, 5ft. 10in., age 28, dark complex., black hair,
    brown eyes, Lumber St., saddler (Navy)
Irvin, Joseph, 5ft. 5½in., age 30, light complex., brown hair,
    grey eyes, tailor (Navy)
Irvin, Thomas, age 50, 7 years in U.S., wife & 3 children, 100
    Front St., NYC, merchant, applied 1797 (13-18 July 1812)
Irvine, John, age 24, 10 years in U.S., Stratford, Montgomery
    Co., cordwainer (16 Feb. - 8 Mar. 1813)
Irvine, William, age 21, 10 years in U.S., Stratford, Montgomery
    Co., farmer (5 Nov. - 9 Dec. & 7-19 Dec. 1812)
Irvine, William, Sr., age 65, 10 years in U.S., wife & 6 children,
    Stratford, Montgomery Co., farmer (16 Feb. - 8 Mar. 1813)
Isaacks (?), J., age 24, 2½ mos. in U.S., 11 Rose St., NYC, mer-
    chant (26-31 Oct. 1812)
Ives, John, 5ft. 4in., age 40, light complex., dark hair, grey
    eyes, Chapple St., tailor (Navy)
Jackes, William, age 43, 3 years in U.S., wife & 3 children,
    Greenwich St., NYC, asst. keeper St. Prison (20-25 July 1812)
Jackson, Charles, age 24, 14 years in U.S., Bloominggrove, Orange
    Co., cabinetmaker (19-24 Oct. 1812)
Jackson, Charles, 5ft. 7in., age 17, fair complex., fair hair,
    grey eyes, ship(wright) (Navy)
Jackson, G.K., age 55, 16 years in U.S., wife & 5 children, 380
    Bowery Lane, NYC, professor of music (20-25 July 1812)
Jackson, Henry, age 22, 7 years in U.S., 18 Broadway, NYC, mer-
    chant, applied 5 June 1812 (20-25 July 1812)
Jackson, James, 5ft. 6in., age 38, fair complex., brown hair,
    blue eyes, Spring St., cabinetmaker (Navy)
Jackson, James, age 37, 7 years in U.S., corner Varick & Budd
    Sts., NYC, sandpaper & emery maker (20-25 July 1812); 5ft. 7in.,
    age 38, fair complex., brown hair, grey eyes, emery maker (Navy)
Jackson, James, age 36, 9 years in U.S., wife & 5 children,
    Spring St., NYC, cabinetmaker, applied 3 July 1803 (20-25 July
    1812) - same as James the cabinetmaker above.
Jackson, James, 5ft. 11in., age 26, fair complex., light hair,
    blue eyes, gardener (Navy)
Jackson, Joseph, age 20, 11 days in U.S., wife, 13 Front St.,
    NYC, accountant (14-19 Sept. 1812)
Jackson, Martin, 5ft. 5½in., age 22, light complex., dark hair,
    brown eyes, South St., stone cutter (Navy)
Jackson, Matthias, age 28, 5 years & 9 mos. in U.S., Camillus,
    Onondaga Co., carpenter (5-11 & 14-19 Sept. 1812)
Jackson, Richard, 5ft. 7in., age 41, light complex., sandy hair,
    dark eyes, Greenwich, hatter (Navy)
Jackson, Robert, age 45, 9 years in U.S., wife & 5 children, 78
    Thames St., NYC, hostler (20-25 July 1812)

Jackson, Robert, 5ft. 10in., age 45, red complex., brown hair,
blue eyes, Cedar St., labourer (Navy)

Jackson, William, age 31, 7 years in U.S., Cornwall, Orange Co.,
farmer (19-24 Oct. 1812)

Jacobs, John, age 26, 7 years in U.S., wife & 2 children, 19
Anthony St., NYC, comedian (20-25 July 1812)

Jaffray, John R., age 27, 7 days in U.S., daughter, 127 Pearl
St., NYC, merchant (24-29 Aug. 1812)

James, Daniel, age 39, 9 years in U.S., wife & 4 children, Desbrosses St., NYC, carpenter (20-25 July 1812); 5ft. 5½in.,
age 40, brown complex., brown hair, blue eyes, Desbrosses St.,
carpenter (Navy)

James, James, age 38 on 23 Oct. 1812, 11 years in U.S. on 16
July 1812, Utica, Oneida Co., shoemaker (26 Aug. & 28 Sept. -
3 Oct. 1812)

James, John, age 44 in Oct. next., 12 years in U.S. on 15 July
next, wife & 6 children, Remsen, Oneida Co., farmer (29 Sept.
& 28 Sept. - 3 Oct. 1812)

James, Richard, age 34, 6 years in U.S., wife & child, Dutchess
Co., farmer (3-8 Aug. 1812)

James, Samuel, 5ft. 4in., age 20, light complex., brown hair,
light eyes, Nassau St., bookbinder (Navy)

Jameson, Alexander, age 50, 17 years & 7 mos. in U.S., wife &
5 children (Thomas, Eleanor, Alexander, Sarah-Ann, Priscilla),
Dryden, Tompkins Co., farmer (20-25 Oct. & 9-14 Nov. 1812)

Jameson, Charles, age 30, 2 years in U.S., Johnstown, Montgomery
Co., clothier (25 Aug. - 2 Sept. & 7-12 Sept. 1812)

Jameson, Robert H., 5ft. 6in., age 24, fair complex., brown hair,
blue eyes, Greenwich St., grocer (Navy)

Jameson, Thomas, age 18, 7 (or 17?) years in U.S., Dryden, Tompkins Co., farmer (20-25 Oct. & 6-14 Nov. 1812)

Jamison, Andrew, age 21, 6 mos. in U.S., Bowery, NYC, marine
(20-25 July 1812)

Jaques, John, age 33, 10 years in U.S., 55 Liberty St., NYC,
grocer, applied 25 Aug. 1809 (13-18 July 1812); 5ft. 7½in.,
age 35, dark complex., dark hair, hazel eyes, Liberty St.,
grocer (Navy)

Jason, John, age 46, 18 years in U.S., 9 in family, Honeoye,
Ontario Co., distiller (5-15 & 24-29 Aug. 1812)

Jay, John, 5ft. 10in., age 45, light complex., dark hair, black
eyes, Bloomingdale, accountant (Navy)

Jefferson, James, 5ft. 6in., age 27, light complex., brown hair,
blue eyes, mechanic (Navy)

Jeffreies, John, age 43, 10 mos. in U.S., wife & child, Montgomery, Orange Co., weaver (19-24 Oct. 1812)

Jeffron, Joseph, age 35, 10 years in U.S., Monroe, Orange Co.,
clerk (21 Dec. 1812 - 23 Jan. 1813 & 2 Jan. 1813)

Jemison, Andrew, 5ft. 6¼in., age 22, fair complex., black hair,
black eyes, Hudson St., cotton spinner (Navy)

Jenkins, Benjamin, age 55 last May, 11 years in U.S. last June,
wife & 3 children, Whitestown, Oneida Co., farmer (26 Aug. &
28 Sept. - 3 Oct. 1812)

Jenkins, David, 5ft. 9in., age 28, light complex., light hair,
blue eyes, soldier (Navy)

Jenkins, Richard, age 20, 11 years in U.S., Clinton, Dutchess
Co., laborer (12-17 Oct. 1812)

Jenkins, Thomas, age 62 on 15 June last, 11 years in U.S. on 26
July last, wife, Deerfield, Oneida Co., farmer/carpenter (29
Sept. & 28 Sept. - 3 Oct. 1812)

Jenkins, Thomas, age 41, 11 years in U.S., wife & 3 children,
Clinton, Dutchess Co., laborer (12-17 Oct. 1812)

Jenkins, Thomas, 5ft. 8in., age 39, ruddy complex., brown hair,
blue eyes, Cold Spring, dyer (Navy)

Jenkins, Thomas, 5ft. 4½in., age 23, light complex., brown hair,
blue eyes, Sixth St., brass (founder) (Navy)

Jenkins, Thomas D., age 17, 11 years in U.S., Clinton, Dutchess
Co., laborer (12-17 Oct. 1812)
Jenkinson, Isaac, Sr., age 60, 1½ years in U.S., wife & 7 child-
ren, Hester St., NYC, gardener (3-8 Aug. 1812)
Jenkinson, Isaac, Jr., 5ft. 7in., age 21, red complex., brown
hair, blue eyes, Hester St., painter (Navy)
Jenkinson, James, 5ft. 8in., age 24, dark complex., black hair,
blue eyes, Crosby St., printer (Navy)
Jenkinson, Joseph, age 29, 5 years in U.S., wife & 2 children,
Hester St., NYC, painter & glazier (20-25 July 1812); 5ft. 7in.,
age 29, pale complex., black hair, black eyes, Hester St.
painter (Navy)
Jenkinson, William, age 43, 4 years in U.S., wife & 3 children,
70 Cedar St., NYC, bookkeeper (13-18 July 1812); 5ft. 8in.,
age 44, fair complex., light hair, light eyes, accountant
(Navy); removed from NYC to Goshen, Orange Co. (Navy)
Jewson, George, age 41, 16 years in U.S., wife & child, Henry
St., NYC, printer (26-31 Oct. 1812); 5ft. 8in., age 42, light
complex., light hair, blue eyes, printer (Navy)
John, Simon, age 35 on 30 Nov. last, 11 years in U.S. on 30 July
last, wife & 3 children, Deerfield, Oneida Co., farmer, from
South Wales (26 Aug. & 28 Sept. - 3 Oct. 1812)
Johnson, Alexander, age 25, 6 years in U.S., wife & child, 18
Bancker St., NYC, tailor (20-25 July 1812); 5ft. 8in., age 26,
light complex., brown hair, blue eyes, tailor (Navy)
Johnson, Arthur, age 25, 10 years in U.S., wife, Montgomery,
Orange Co., farmer (19-24 Oct. 1812)
Johnson, Bryan, 5ft. 7in., age 25, fair complex., light hair,
blue eyes, coachman (Navy)
Johnson, Edward, 5ft. 5in., age 27, light complex., light hair,
hazel eyes, Mulberry St., tinplate (worker) (Navy)
Johnson, George, 5ft. 8in., age 39, dark complex., dark hair,
dark eyes, cordwainer (Navy)
Johnson, George, 5ft. 8in., age 30, light complex., brown hair,
brown eyes, Liberty St., teacher (Navy)
Johnson, George, Jr., 5ft. 4in., age 25, fair complex., light
hair, blue eyes, Liberty St., mariner (Navy)
Johnson, Henry, 5ft. 5in., age 28, light complex., brown hair,
blue eyes, accountant (Navy)
Johnson, Henry, age 25, 1 year & 3 mos. in U.S., wife & child,
NYC, shoemaker (20-25 July 1812)
Johnson, James, age 28, 18 years in U.S., wife & child, City of
Albany, baker (31 Aug. - 5 Sept. 1812)
Johnson, John, age 29, 8 years in U.S., 25 Liberty St., NYC,
merchant, applied 10 May 1809 (20-25 July 1812); 5ft. 10½in.,
age 29, fair complex., light hair, grey eyes, removed from NYC
to Fishkill, Dutchess Co. (Navy)
Johnson, Malcom, age 38 to 40, 8 years in U.S. last Oct., wife &
2 children, Deerfield, Oneida Co., farmer (26 Aug. & 28 Sept. -
3 Oct. 1812)
Johnson, Mathew, 5ft. 9in., age 45, dark complex., black hair,
grey eyes, Reed St., grocer (Navy)
Johnson, Nathan Perry, age 31, 5 years & 9 mos. in U.S., wife,
City of Albany, grocer (17-22 Aug. 1812)
Johnson, Richard, 5ft. 8in., age 32, fair complex., fair hair,
light eyes, labourer (Navy)
Johnson, Richard, age 26, 2 years in U.S., 2 in family, Front
St., NYC, blacksmith (20-25 July 1812)
Johnson, Robert, age 45, 5 years in U.S., wife & 2 children,
Hudson, Columbia Co., merchant, applied Mar. 1812 (10-15 Aug.
1812)
Johnson, Robert, 5ft. 11in., age 23, light complex., dark hair,
blue eyes, Grand St., cartman (Navy)
Johnson, Thomas, age 29, 2 years in U.S., wife & child, 140 Cha-
pel St., NYC, tallow chandler (13-18 July 1812) -see following

Johnson, Thomas, 5ft. 6in., age 29, light complex., brown hair,
brown eyes, Harlaem, chandler (Navy)- see last item.
Johnson, Thomas, 5ft. 5in., age 21, sandy complex., light hair,
blue eyes, Chatham St., clerk (Navy)
Johnson, William, age 44, 6 years & 6 mos. in U.S., wife & 4
children, 102 John St., NYC, engraver, applied Jan. 1811 (20-
25 July 1812); 5ft. 6in., age 45, red complex., brown hair,
blue eyes, John St., engraver (Navy)
Johnson, William, age 26, 6 years in U.S., Goshen, Orange Co.,
laborer (19-24 Oct. 1812)
Johnson, William M., age 48, 25 years in U.S., Montgomery, Orange
Co., laborer (19-24 Oct. 1812)
Johnson, George, age 49, 4 years in U.S., 32 White Hall St.,
NYC, merchant (24-29 Aug. 1812)
Johnston, George, age 38, 10 years in U.S., 7 in family, NYC,
cordwainer (20-25 July 1812)
Johnston, Henry, 5ft. 8in., age 25, fair complex., light hair,
blue eyes, Henry St., shoe(maker) (Navy)
Johnston, James, 5ft. 7in., age 36, red complex., dark hair,
grey eyes, cartman (Navy)
Johnston, James, age 31, 14 years in U.S., wife & child, West-
chester Co., farmer (3-8 Aug. 1812)
Johnston, James W., age 21, 33 days in U.S. (20-25 July 1812)
Johnston, Michael, age 37, 8 years & 3 mos. in U.S., 6 in family,
Sparta, Ontario Co. (25 Oct. - 15 Nov. 1812)
Johnston, Robert, age 45, 5 years in U.S., wife & 2 children,
Hudson, Columbia Co., merchant, applied Mar. 1812 (n.d.)
Johnston, William, 5ft. 10in., age 30, dark complex., brown hair,
brown eyes, Mulberry St., blacksmith (Navy)
Jolly, Job Henry, age 21, 1 year & 9 mos. in U.S., Rhinebeck,
Dutchess Co., teacher (12-17 Oct. 1812)
Jolly, Patterson, 6ft., age 29, light complex., brown hair, grey
eyes, Bancker St., labourer (Navy)
Jones, Anthony, 5ft. 9¼in., age 28, dark complex., black hair,
brown eyes, Christopher St., calico (printer) (Navy)
Jones, Anthony W., 5ft. 8in., age 21, fair complex., brown hair,
dark eyes, pianoforte (maker) (Navy)
Jones, Benjamin, 5ft. 9in., age 30, light complex., light hair,
blue eyes, waterman (Navy)
Jones, David, 5ft. 5in., age 48, dark complex., brown hair, grey
eyes, Orange St., mason (Navy)
Jones, David, age 35, 11 years in U.S., wife & 6 children, Clinton, Dutchess Co., laborer (12-17 Oct. 1812)
Jones, David, 5ft. 9in., age 21, fair complex., grey hair, light
eyes, Bancker St., maltster (Navy)
Jones, Edward, age 35, 5 years in U.S., wife, Greenwich St., NYC,
gardener (28 July - 2 Aug. 1812); 5ft. 7in., age 35, fair com-
plex., brown hair, brown eyes, Greenwich St., gardener (Navy)
Jones, Edward, 5ft. 6in., age 24, light complex., brown hair,
black eyes, stone cutter (Navy)
Jones, Enoch, 5ft. 5½in., age 25, dark complex., brown hair, dark
eyes, Crosby St., mason (Navy)
Jones, Griffith, 5ft. 2in., age 30, dark complex., dark hair,
dark eyes, Bayard St., carpenter (Navy)
Jones, Griffith G., age 36 on 15 Aug. last, 11 years in U.S. in
May last, wife & 4 children, Trenton, Oneida Co., farmer (29
Sept. & 28 Sept. - 3 Oct. 1812)
Jones, Griffith J., age 45, 11 years in U.S., wife & child, Rem-
sen, Oneida Co., farmer (29 Sept. & 28 Sept. - 3 Oct. 1812)
Jones, Henry, age 21, 14 years in U.S., City of Albany, student
at law (31 Aug. - 5 Sept. 1812)
Jones, Hugh G., age 25 on 12 Nov. next, 11 years in U.S. on 15
Oct. last, Steuben, Oneida Co., carpenter (29 Sept. & 28 Sept.-
3 Oct. 1812)

Jones, Jeremiah, 5ft. 5½in., age 31, sandy complex., brown hair, grey eyes, William St., distiller (Navy)

Jones, John, age 56, 11 years in U.S., wife & 5 children, 110 Greenwich St., NYC, merchant (2-7 Nov. 1812)

Jones, John, 5ft. 8in., age 58, brown complex., grey hair, grey eyes, Greenwich St., boarding (house keeper?), removed from NYC to Goshen, Orange Co. (Navy)

Jones, John, age 46, 3 mos. in U.S., wife & 3 children, 269 Broadway, NYC, cordwainer (3-8 Aug. 1812)

Jones, John, 5ft. 5in., age 46, dark complex., dark hair, light eyes, manufacturer, from Boston (Navy)

Jones, John, age 45, 11 years in U.S., wife & 6 children, Eaton, Madison Co., farmer (26 Aug. & 28 Sept. - 3 Oct. 1812)

Jones, John, 5ft. 6in., age 36, dark complex., black hair, grey eyes, Pearl St., gardener (Navy)

Jones, John, 5ft. 6in., age 25, dark complex., black hair, grey eyes, Kips Bay NYC, mason (Navy)

Jones, John R., age 40 last Mar., 12 years in U.S. last July, wife & 3 children, Remsen, Oneida Co., farmer (29 Sept. & 28 Sept. - 3 Oct. 1812)

Jones, Lewis, age 54, 20 years in U.S., 7 in family, Boyle, Ontario Co., shoemaker (11-25 & 26-31 Oct. 1812)

Jones, Michael, 5ft. 5in., age 27, fair complex., fair hair, blue eyes, Reed St., labourer (Navy)

Jones, Moses, age 24 on 14 last Nov., 11 years in U.S. on 23 July last, Remsen, Oneida Co., farmer (29 Sept. & 28 Sept. - 3 Oct. 1812)

Jones, Owen, 5ft. 8in., age 48, fair complex., brown hair, grey eyes, Broadway, shoemaker (Navy)

Jones, Owen P., age 20, 6 years in U.S., Fitzroy Road, coachman (10-15 Aug. 1812)

Jones, Owen P., 5ft. 9in., age 21, sandy complex., brown hair, brown eyes, milkman (Navy) - same as above?

Jones, Richard, age 23 on 1 Apr. last, 11 years in U.S. on 10 May last, Utica, Oneida Co., mason (26 Aug. & 28 Sept. - 3 Oct. 1812)

Jones, Robert G., age 22 on 28 Jan. last, 11 years in U.S. on 15 Oct. last, Steuben, Oneida Co., carpenter (29 Sept. & 28 Sept. - 3 Oct. 1812)

Jones, Thomas, 5ft. 4½in., age 31, fair complex., light hair, blue eyes, Chapple St., tailor (Navy)

Jones, Thomas, age 30, 14 years in U.S., wife, Steuben, Madison Co., farmer (31 Oct. & 30 Nov. - 5 Dec. 1812)

Jones, Thomas, 5ft. 6in., age 22, fair complex., brown hair, dark eyes, carpenter (Navy)

Jones, Thomas, age 20, 11 years in U.S., Clinton, Dutchess Co., laborer (12-17 Oct. 1812)

Jones, Timothy, age 22, 1 year & 1 mo. in U.S., 269 Broadway, NYC, cordwainer (3-8 Aug. 1812); 5ft. 8½in., age 23, fair complex., grey hair, brown eyes, Bowery, cordwainer (Navy)

Jones, William, age 44, 6 years in U.S., 2 apprentices, corner Hester & Elm Sts., NYC, brass founder (20-25 July 1812); 6ft., age 45, fair complex., grey hair, light eyes, Hester St., brass (founder) (Navy)

Jones, William, age 36, 2 years in U.S., wife & 6 children, 15 Van Dam St., NYC, gold beater, applied 13 Sept. 1811 (13- 18 July 1812); 5ft. 8in., age 36, fair complex., dark hair, brown eyes, Broad St., gold beater (Navy)

Jones, William, 5ft. 7in., age 31, dark complex., dark hair, blue eyes, Brooklyn, milkman (Navy)

Jones, William, 5ft. 9in., age 27, fair complex., brown hair, dark eyes, Henry St., butcher (Navy)

Jones, William, age 27, 16 years in U.S., Clinton, Dutchess Co., laborer (12-17 Oct. 1812)

Jones, William, 5ft. 1in., age 25, light complex., black hair, dark eyes, 4th stone, tailor (Navy)

Jones, William G., age 20 next Christmas, 11 years in U.S. on 15 Oct. last, Steuben, Oneida Co., carpenter (29 Sept. & 28 Sept. - 3 Oct. 1812)

Jones, William R., age 42 last June, 12 years in U.S. last July, wife & 4 children, Steuben, Oneida Co., mason (29 Sept.); he is also called farmer & joiner (28 Sept. - 3 Oct. 1812)

Jordan, John, age 49, 1 mo. in U.S., wife & 2 children, Greenwich St., NYC, weaver (28 July - 2 Aug. 1812) - probably the same is, Jordan, John, 5ft. 11in., age 50, dark complex., brown hair, brown eyes, Washington St., weaver (Navy)

Jordan, John, 5ft. 4½in., age 18, fair complex., red hair, blue eyes, John St., baker (Navy)

Joyce, James, age about 27 next Apr., in U.S. since 15 of last Aug., Little Falls, Herkimer Co., minister of the Gospel, from Ireland (26 Aug. & 28 Sept. - 3 Oct. 1812)

Jubb, Thomas, age 23, 2 years & 9 mos. in U.S., 3 in family, 85 Second St., NYC, tailor (28 July - 2 Aug. 1812); 5ft. 7½in., age 23, light complex., dark hair, blue eyes, Grand St., tailor (Navy)

Kafe (?), Thomas, 5ft. 4in., age 49, dark complex., brown hair, grey eyes, labourer (Navy)

Kain, George, 5ft. 9in., age 45, fair complex., dark hair, grey eyes, Corlaers Hook, cartman (Navy)

Kalin, Abraham, 5ft. 8½in., age 23, light complex., brown hair, blue eyes, Middle Road, labourer (Navy)

Kanada, Alexander, age 48, 12 years in U.S., wife & 5 children, Hadly, Saratoga Co., farmer (14-19 Sept. 1812)

Kane, James, age 35, 18 years in U.S., wife, Catskill, weaver (17-22 Aug. 1812)

Karr, William, age 24, 2 mos. in U.S., 3 in family, 44 Mulberry St., NYC, laborer (20-25 July 1812)

Kaster, Albert H., 5ft. 4½in., age 30, brown complex., brown hair, blue eyes, hatter (Navy)

Kavanagh, Patrick, age 50, 7 years in U.S., sister & 1 son, 152 Front St., NYC, grocer (20-25 July 1812); 5ft. 6in., age 51, pale complex., grey hair, blue eyes, grocer (Navy)

Kavenagh, Patrick, 5ft. 9in., age 52, light complex., grey hair, grey eyes, Elm St., dealer in rags (Navy)

Kavenagh, James, 5ft. 6½in., age 43, fair complex., fair hair, fair eyes, Cheapside, carpenter (Navy)

Kavenagh, Patrick, 5ft. 6in., age 28, dark complex., dark hair, brown eyes, Old Slip, grocer (Navy)

Kavaneaugh, Dennis/Denis, age 40 next Dec., 3 years in U.S. on 1 Nov. next, wife & 4 children, Eaton, Madison Co., farmer, applied Jan. 1812 (31 Oct. & 30 Nov. - 5 Dec. 1812)

Kaveny, Patrick, age 60, 7 years in U.S., wife & 3 children, NYC, dealer (13-18 July 1812)

Kay, Thomas, age 30, 1 year & 8 mos. in U.S., wife & child, Clinton, Dutchess Co., spinner (12-17 Oct. 1812)

Keagan, Michael, 5ft. 5in., age 20, dark complex., brown hair, brown eyes, teacher (Navy)

Kealey, Edmond, 5ft. 10in., age 25, fair complex., light hair, light eyes, Pearl St., currier (Navy)

Kear, John, 5ft. 5in., age 33, fair complex., light hair, light eyes, Greenwich St., gardener (Navy)

Kearn, Allen, age 62 on 4 Jan. next, 6 years in U.S. on 1 June last, Eaton, Madison Co., farmer (31 Oct. & 30 Nov. - 5 Dec. 1812)

Kearn, Edward, age 24, 6 years in U.S. on 27 May last, wife & child, Eaton, Madison Co., farmer (31 Oct. & 30 Nov. - 5 Dec. 1812)

Kearns, James, age 35, 5 years in U.S., wife & 3 children, Johnstown, Montgomery Co., blacksmith (3-14 & 21-26 Sept. 1812)

Kearns, Patrick, 5ft. 11in., age 24, dark complex., dark hair,
dark eyes, waiter (Navy)
Kearsing, John, 5ft. 8in., age 35, light complex., grey hair,
brown eyes, Bowery, piano (Navy)
Kearsing, John, Jr., age 25, 8 years & 10 mos. in U.S., wife &
2 children, 281 Bowery Lane, NYC, pianoforte manufacturer (20-
25 July 1812)
Kearsing, Thomas, age 37, 5 years & 9 mos. in U.S., 7 children,
NYC, pianoforte manufacturer, applied 4 Feb. 1811 (20-25 July
1812); 5ft. 5in., age 40, brown complex., fair hair, grey eyes,
Bowery, pianoforte (Navy)
Kearsing, William, age 30, 9 years & 8 mos. in U.S., 279 Bowery,
NYC, pianoforte manufacturer (20-25 July 1812); 5ft. 9in., age
30, light complex., grey hair, brown eyes, Bowery, piano (Navy)
Keating, Barney, 5ft. 9in., age 25, fair complex., brown hair,
brown eyes, Bowery, thread manufacturer (Navy)
Keefe, Michael, 5ft. 4in., age 25, light complex., dark hair,
blue eyes, labourer (Navy)
Keely, Edmund, age 24, 9 years & 8 mos. in U.S., wife & 2 sons,
NYC, currier (20-25 July 1812)
Keely. William, age 33, 5 years & 9 mos. in U.S., wife, 3 Ann
St. (20-25 July 1812)
Keegan, Michael, age 19, 1 year & 3 mos. in U.S., 6 Mile Stone,
teacher (20-25 July 1812)
Keegan, Timothy, age 30, 9 years in U.S., wife & 3 children, 28
Augustus St., NYC, cartman (3-8 Aug. 1812); 5ft. 6in., age 32,
fair complex., fair hair, grey eyes, cartman (Navy)
Keenan, Hugh, age 37, 11 years in U.S., wife & 5 children, New
Paltz, Ulster Co., farmer (19-24 Oct. 1812)
Keenan, John, age 37, 11 years in U.S., wife & 6 children, New
Paltz, Ulster Co., farmer (19-24 Oct. 1812)
Keenan, Michael, 5ft. 5in., age 30, light complex., dark hair,
brown eyes, weaver (Navy)
Keenan, Patrick, age 31, 10 mos. in U.S., wife & 2 children, 17
Hester St., NYC, founder (20-25 July 1812)
Keenen, Patrick, age 22, 1 year & 10 mos. in U.S., Kingston,
Ulster Co., weaver (19-24 Oct. 1812)
Keese, James, 5ft. 11in., age 26, light complex., sandy hair,
grey eyes, Broadway, coachman (Navy)
Kehoe, Cornelius, 5ft. 9in., age 28, fair complex., light hair,
blue eyes, labourer (Navy)
Kehoe, John, age 21, 1 year & 2 mos. in U.S., 17 Bancker St.,
NYC, morocco dresser (20-25 July 1812); 5ft. 9in., age 21,
fair complex., light hair, brown eyes, Cherry St., morocco
(Navy)
Kehoe, Joseph, age 35, 3 mos. in U.S., Claremont, Westchester
Co., laborer (20-25 July 1812)
Kehoe, Joseph, 5ft. 9in., age 37, red complex., brown hair, blue
eyes, Manhattan, labourer (Navy)
Kelaspeek (for Gelaspie?), Patrick, 5ft. 5in., age 45, sandy
complex., dark hair, blue eyes, Duane St., labourer (Navy)
Kelbreath, Stuart, age 26, 2 years in U.S., wife & 2 children,
73 Duane St., NYC, millwright (20-25 July 1812); Kelbreath,
Stewart, 5ft. 11in., age 28, light complex., light hair, grey
eyes, millwright (Navy)
Kelland, Philip, 5ft. 8in., age 40, light complex., brown hair,
grey eyes, Henry St., brass founder (Navy); 9 years & 8 mos.
in U.S., wife & 3 children, 15 Bancker St., brass founder (3-
18 July 1812)
Kellett, John, age 32, 6 years in U.S., wife & 3 children, Scipio, Cayuga Co., farmer, "opposed to the present administration
of the government" (7-12 & 21-26 Sept. 1812)
Kelly, Andrew, 5ft. 9in., age 24, fair complex., dark hair, brown
eyes, Mott St., labourer (Navy)

Kelly, Bernard, 5ft. 6½in., age 31, dark complex., brown hair,
    hazel eyes, labourer (Navy)
Kelly, George, 5ft. 5in., age 21, fair complex., dark hair,
    grey eyes, chane (?) bearer (Navy)
Kelly, Henry, 5ft. 9in., age 25. light complex., light hair,
    grey eyes, Bloomingdale, labourer (Navy)
Kelly, Hugh, age 25, 1 year & 6 mos. in U.S., Newburgh, Orange
    Co., weaver (19-24 Oct. 1812)
Kelly, James, age 33, 8 years in U.S., wife & 3 children, NYC,
    paver (10-15 Aug. 1812)
Kelly, Jo., 5ft. 8in., age 33, dark complex., brown hair, blue
    eyes (Navy)
Kelly, John, age 32, 5 years in U.S., wife & child, Saratoga,
    merchant (17-22 Aug. 1812)
Kelly, John, 5ft. 6in., age 29, dark complex., brown hair,
    brown eyes, Stanton St., miller (Navy)
Kelly, John, age 28, 3 years in U.S., wife, Marcellus, Ononda-
    ga Co., farmer (12-18 & 21-26 Sept. 1812)
Kelly, John, 5ft. 5in., age 26, light complex., brown hair,
    dark eyes, Elizabeth St., comb maker (Navy)
Kelly, John, 6ft., 1½in., age 24, light complex., light hair,
    blue eyes, servant (Navy)
Kelly, Mark, 5ft. 10in., age 50, fair complex., grey hair, grey
    eyes, blacksmith (Navy)
Kelly, Patrick, age 46, 4 years in U.S., New Windsor, Orange
    Co., laborer (19-24 Oct. 1812)
Kelly, Patrick, 5ft. 5in., age 36, light complex., dark hair,
    blue eyes, Duane St., nailor (Navy)
Kelly, Patrick, 5ft. 11in., age 36, light complex., brown hair,
    light complex., baker (Navy)
Kelly, Patrick, age 33, 1 year in U.S., Plattekill, Ulster Co.,
    weaver (19-24 Oct. 1812)
Kelly, Patrick, age 20, 5 years in U.S., 89 Warren St., NYC,
    painter (20-25 July 1812); 5ft. 8in., age 21, light complex.,
    brown hair, blue eyes, Chapple St., painter (Navy)
Kelly, Patrick, 5ft. 10in., age 23, sandy complex., brown hair,
    blue eyes, iron (Navy)
Kelly, Peter, 5ft. 3in., age 41, sandy complex., brown hair,
    blue eyes, Robeson St., grocer (Navy)
Kelly, Peter, age 40, 11 years in U.S., wife & child, NYC, gar-
    dener (20-25 July 1812)
Kelly, Peter, age 26, wife & 2 children, 249 William St., NYC,
    shoemaker (30 Nov. - 5 Dec. 1812)
Kelly, William, 5ft. 5in., age 21, dark complex., brown hair,
    grey eyes, Grand St., skinner (Navy)
Kelso, Joseph, age 20, 11 mos. in U.S., Bloominggrove, Orange
    Co., weaver (19-24 Oct. 1812)
Kemp, James, 5ft. 7½in., age 47, light complex., light hair,
    black eyes, Chamber St., waiter (Navy)
Kempshall, Thomas, age 17, 6 years in U.S., Boyle, Ontario Co.,
    laborer (15-22 Aug. & 31 Aug. - 5 Sept. 1812)
Kempshall, Timothy, age 15, 6 years in U.S., Boyle, Ontario Co.,
    laborer (15-22 Aug. & 31 Aug. - 5 Sept. 1812)
Kempshall, William, age 14, 6 years in U.S., Palmyra, Ontario
    Co., laborer (15-22 Aug. 1812); age given as 15 (31 Aug. - 5
    Sept. 1812)
Kempshall, Willis, age 22, 6 years in U.S., Boyle, Ontario Co.,
    joiner, applied Feb. 1812 (15-22 Aug. & 31 Aug. - 5 Sept. 1812)
Kenan, John, 5ft. 8in., age 50, light complex., pattern (Navy)
Kenard, Charles, 5ft. 7in., age 23, light complex., light hair,
    brown eyes, waiter (Navy)
Kench, James, 5ft. 6in., age 35, fair complex., black hair,
    grey eyes, Bancker St., labourer (Navy)
Kench, Thomas, 5ft. 7in., age 26, light complex., light hair,
    brown eyes, Pearl St., grocer (Navy)

Kench, William, 5ft. 7in., age 32, dark complex., brown hair,
grey eyes, Bancker St., grocer (Navy)
Kendrick, Walter, age 47, 16 years in U.S., wife & 5 children,
65 Nassau St., NYC, hatter (20-25 July 1812)
Kenedy, Edward, 5ft. 10in., age 23, fair complex., dark hair,
grey eyes, Orange St., labourer (Navy)
Kenedy, Henry, 5ft. 9in., age 48, fair complex., fair hair, grey
eyes, weaver (Navy)
Kenedy, Hugh, 5ft. 7in., age 58, fair complex., fair hair, blue
eyes, mason (Navy)
Kenedy, James, 5ft. 5in., age 34, dark complex., brown hair,
brown eyes, Chatham St., maltster (Navy)
Kenedy, John, 5ft. 8in., age 45, sandy complex., brown hair,
grey eyes, labourer (Navy)
Kenedy, John, 5ft. 6in., age 26, light complex., fair hair, light
eyes, tailor (Navy)
Kenedy, Robert, 5ft. 8in., age 28, black complex., black hair,
brown eyes, Division St., cartman (Navy)
Kelly, William, 5ft. 6in., age 33, fair complex., brown hair,
hazel eyes, labourer (Navy)
Kenkade, William, 5ft. 8½in., age 30, fair complex., fair hair,
grey eyes, Love Lane, gardener (Navy)
Kennan, John, 5ft. 9in., age 20, light complex., dark hair, brown
eyes, servant (Navy)
Kennedy, David S., age 21, 5 years & 2 mos. in U.S., 14 Greenwich
St., NYC, clerk (9-14 Nov. 1812); 5ft. 11in., age 21, light
complex., light hair, blue eyes, clerk (Navy)
Kennedy, Dennis, 5ft. 6in., age 48, light complex., light hair,
blue eyes, Hoorns Hook, gardener (Navy)
Kennedy, Robert, 5ft. 8in., age 34, fair complex., dark hair,
grey eyes, Church St., carpenter (Navy)
Kennedy, Robert, age 33, 9 years in U.S., City of Albany, laborer
(17-22 Aug. 1812)
Kennie, Robert, 5ft. 7½in., age 30, fair complex., fair hair,
blue eyes, Elizabeth St., mason (Navy)
Kensley, Thomas, 5ft. 9in., age 48, dark complex., grey hair,
blue eyes, Pine & Front Sts., grocer (Navy)
Kent, John, age 26, 5 years & 6 mos. in U.S., NYC, butcher (26-
31 Oct. 1812); 5ft. 7in., age 26, fair complex., brown hair,
hazel eyes, Grand St., butcher (Navy)
Keogan, Daniel, age 50, 11 years & 3 mos. in U.S., wife & 4 child-
ren, Plattekill, Ulster Co., weaver (19-24 Oct. 1812)
Kepock, Alexander, 6ft., age 27, dark complex., light hair, grey
eyes, Nyack, Rockland Co., quarryman (Navy)
Kerdolff, John, age 27, 15 years in U.S., Orchard St., NYC, baker
(21 Dec. 1812 - 23 Jan. 1813)
Kergen, Peter, age 27, 2 mos. in U.S., New Windsor, Orange Co.,
weaver (19-24 Oct. 1812)
Kerighorn, John, age 44, 16 years in U.S., Angelica, Allegany
Co., tanner & shoemaker (7-12 Sept. 1812)
Kerly, Patrick, 5ft. 8in., age 38, light complex., brown hair,
dark eyes, Maiden Lane, porter (Navy)
Kernan, John, 5ft. 8in., age 25, light complex., brown hair, blue
eyes, pedler (Navy)
Kernan, Patrick, 5ft. 7½in., age 31, sandy complex., brown hair,
hazel eyes, iron founder (Navy)
Kerney, Patrick, 5ft. 6½in., age 27, fair complex., brown hair,
grey eyes, Harman St., locksmith (Navy)
Kerr, Alexander, age 54, 1 year & 9 mos. in U.S., Deerpark,
Orange Co., farmer (19-24 Oct. 1812)
Kerr, Hamilton, age 23, 8 years in U.S., 124 Water St., NYC,
chandler (20-25 July 1812); 5ft. 6in., age 23, fair complex.,
dark hair, grey eyes, chandler (Navy)
Kerr, Hugh, age 27, 6 years in U.S., wife & 2 children, City of
Albany, nailor (17-22 Aug. 1812)

Kerr, James, 5ft. 8½in., age 30, dark complex., brown hair, brown
   eyes, Elm St. (Navy)
Kerr, James, age 20, 1 year & 9 mos. in U.S., wife & 2 children,
   93 Elm St., NYC, carpenter (28 July - 2 Aug. 1812)
Kerr, John Eliot, 5ft. 10½in., age 21, brown complex., brown
   hair, blue eyes, clerk (Navy)
Kerr, Joseph, age 28, 8 years in U.S., 124 Water St., NYC, grocer (20-25 July 1812); 6ft., age 29, fair complex., brown hair,
   blue eyes, grocer (Navy)
Kerr, Robert, age 24, 1 year & 9 mos. in U.S., Deerpark, Orange
   Co., merchant (19-24 Oct. 1812)
Kerr, Thomas, 5ft. 9in., age 47, dark complex., dark hair, grey
   eyes, Greenwich St., gardener (Navy)
Kerr, William, 5ft. 8in., age 32, dark complex., brown hair,
   blue eyes, Duane St., burr mill (Navy)
Kerr, William, 5ft. 5in., age 28, fair complex., dark hair, grey
   eyes, Greenwich St., gardener (Navy)
Kerr, William, age 25, 5 years in U.S., wife & child, NYC, tailor
   (28 July - 2 Aug. 1812)
Kerr, William, age 23, 21 years in U.S., Newburgh, Orange Co.,
   merchant (19-24 Oct. 1812)
Kerrigan, James, 5ft. 6in., age 22, dark complex., black hair,
   grey eyes, leather dresser (Navy)
Kerrigan, Patrick, 5ft. 7in., age 26, fair complex., brown hair,
   grey eyes, skinner (Navy)
Kerrigan, William, 5ft. 6in., age 33, dark complex., light hair,
   brown eyes, Anthony St., labourer (Navy)
Ketchum, John J., age 41, 7 mos. in U.S., wife & 7 children, 21
   Suffolk St., NYC, "no occupation" (13-18 July 1812)
Keten, Bernard, age 26, 3½ years in U.S., wife & 2 children,
   300 Bowery, NYC, thread maker (20-25 July 1812)
Kevan, John, 5ft. 8in., age 27, fair complex., dark hair, brown
   eyes, labourer (Navy)
Keys, William, 5ft. 8in., age 35, fair complex., sandy hair,
   blue eyes, cartman (Navy)
Kighley, George, age 32, 7 years in U.S., 68 Greenwich St., NYC,
   merchant (13-18 July 1812)
Kighley, George, 6ft., age 32, brown complex., brown hair, grey
   eyes, removed from NYC to Claverack, Columbia Co. (Navy) -
   same as above.
Kilby, Christopher, age 50, 8 years in U.S., wife & 8 children,
   Hadley, Saratoga Co., innkeeper (14-19 Sept. 1812)
Kilby, Felix, age 18, 8 years in U.S., NYC, paver (10-15 Aug.
   1812)
Killkreest, Alexander, age 22, 3 mos. in U.S., Newburgh, Orange
   Co., block & pump maker (19-24 Oct. 1812)
Killmartin, Daniel, 5ft. 9in., age 44, pale complex., brown hair,
   hazel eyes, labourer (Navy)
Kilpatrick, Joseph, 5ft. 6in., age 28, dark complex., brown hair,
   brown eyes, Harlaem, blacksmith (Navy)
Kilpatrick, Robert, 5ft. 8in., age 50, dark complex., brown hair,
   dark eyes, Harlaem, blacksmith (Navy)
Kilpatrick, William, 5ft. 1in., age 19, dark complex., black
   hair, dark eyes, Harlaem, blacksmith (Navy)
Kinch, Thomas, age 26, 1 year & 2 mos. in U.S., wife & 2 child-
   ren, NYC, grocer (20-25 July 1812)
Kinch, William, age 33, 6 years in U.S., wife & 4 children, 116
   Bancker St., NYC, grocer (20-25 July 1812)
Kinchelsa (?), Stephen, age 23, 6 mos. in U.S., 304 Water St.,
   NYC (28 July - 2 Aug. 1812)
King, David, age 36, 2½ mos. in U.S., 98 Broad St., NYC (20-25
   July 1812)
King, James, 5ft. 10½in., age 37, pale complex., black hair,
   blue eyes, Cliff St., cooper (Navy); age 36, 9 years in U.S.,
   41 Cliff St., NYC, cooper (28 July - 2 Aug. 1812)

King, Lawrence, 5ft. 6in., age 21, light complex., brown hair,
blue eyes, iron (Navy)

King, Robert, 5ft. 8½in., age 24, dark complex., dark hair, blue
eyes, Elm St., musical instrument (maker) (Navy)

King, Samuel, 4ft. 10in., age 22, dark complex., dark hair, dark
eyes, apprentice (Navy)

King, Thomas, 5ft. 3in., age 22, dark complex., dark hair, dark
eyes, Pearl St., instrument (Maker) (Navy)

King, William, age 37, 7 years in U.S., wife & 2 children, Schenectady, Schenectady Co., weaver (17-22 Aug. 1812)

Kinghorn, John, age 44, 16 years in U.S., Angelica, Allegany Co.,
tanner & shoemaker (25-31 Aug. 1812)

Kinkaid, James, age 22, 5 years in U.S., 23 Bridge St., NYC,
chandler (24-29 Aug. 1812)

Kinlock, Stewart, 5ft. 8in., age 25, fair complex., brown hair,
blue eyes, Greenwich St., confectioner (Navy)

Kinnier, Robert, age 29, 8 years in U.S., wife & 2 children,
corner Elizabeth & Grand Sts., NYC, cotton manufacturer (28
July - 2 Aug. 1812)

Kinsley, Thomas, age 27, 8 mos. in U.S., Newburgh, Orange Co.,
laborer (19-24 Oct. 1812)

Kirby, John, age 33, 7 years in U.S., 93 Broadway, NYC, saddler
(3-8 Aug. 1812); 5ft. 10in., age 36, light complex., brown
hair, grey eyes, saddler (Navy)

Kirk, Robert, age 13, 2 mos. in U.S., Bancker St., NYC, baker
(28 July - 2 Aug. 1812); 5ft. 6in., red complex., light hair,
blue eyes, baker (Navy)

Kirk, William, age 24, 1 year & 10 mos. in U.S., 146 Water St.,
NYC, accountant (20-25 July 1812); 5ft. 10in., age 25, fair
complex., sandy hair, blue eyes, Broadway, accountant (Navy)

Kirkland, John, age 34, 2 years in U.S., Bayard St., NYC, baker
(28 July - 2 Aug. 1812); 5ft. 8in., age 35, dark complex.,
brown hair, dark eyes, Bayard St., baker (Navy)

Kirkpatrick, William, 5ft. 7in., age 27, fair complex., brown
hair, black eyes, weaver (Navy)

Kitlick, William, age 47, 3 years in U.S., wife & 2 children,
Rome, Oneida Co., weaver (3-8 Aug. 1812); also (29 July 1812)

Kilkenny, Edward, age 27, 13 years & 6 mos. in U.S., wife & 2
children, City of Albany, laborer (17-22 Aug. 1812)

Knapp, Edward, age 24, 9 years & 1 mo. in U.S., wife & 2 children, Montgomery, Orange Co., cabinetmaker (19-24 Oct. 1812)

Knight, Abraham, age 25, 6 years in U.S., wife, NYC, merchant
tailor (20-25 July 1812); 5ft. 6½in., age 26, dark complex.,
dark hair, grey eyes, Ann St., tailor (Navy)

Knight, Joseph, age 34, 9 years in U.S., wife & 6 children, Broadway, NYC, confectioner, applied 1810 (20-25 July 1812); 5ft.
8in., age 35, light complex., brown hair, blue eyes, Broadway,
confectioner (Navy)

Knowlton, Thomas, age 47, 7 years in U.S., wife & 6 children,
City of Albany, carpenter (5-10 Oct. 1812)

Knox, John, age 23, 2 years in U.S., NYC, clerk, applied 26 Nov.
1811 (20-25 July 1812); 5ft. 6in., age 23, light complex.,
dark hair, grey eyes, Pearl St., accountant (Navy)

Knox, William, age 29, 6 years in U.S., wife & child, corner
Mott & Pump Sts., NYC, grocer, applied 14 Sept. 1809 (13-18
July 1812); 5ft. 8in., age 29, brown complex., black hair,
brown eyes, Church St,, clerk (Navy)

Koke, James, 5ft. 7in., age 20, fair complex., brown hair, brown
eyes, sawyer (Navy)

Korter, Albert Henry, age 30, 5 years & 8 mos. in U.S., wife &
3 children, 15 Frankfort St., NYC, hatter (3-8 Aug. 1812)

Korter, Henry, 5ft. 8in., age 30, fair complex., brown hair,
grey eyes, carpenter (Navy)

Kumerly, Thomas, age 40, 1 year & 3 mos. in U.S., Clinton, Dutchess Co., weaver (12-17 Oct. 1812)

Kyle, Alexander, age 21, 10 mos. in U.S., Poughkeepsie, Dutchess
   Co., laborer (12-17 Oct. 1812)
Kyle, Hamilton, age 21, 1 year & 1 mo. in U.S., Montgomery,
   Orange Co., farmer (19-24 Oct. 1812)
La Flesh, Peter, age 32, 12 years in U.S., wife & 5 children
   born in U.S., Bath, Steuben Co., cabinetmaker (25-31 Aug. 1812)
La Flesh, Rene, age 32, 12 years in U.S., wife & 5 children,
   Bath, Steuben Co., cabinetmaker (7-12 Sept. 1812)
Lafferty, John, 5ft. 6in., age 43, dark complex., dark hair, grey
   eyes, labourer (Navy)
Laidlaw, John, age 21, 17 years in U.S., 25 Liberty St., NYC,
   merchant (20-25 July 1812)
Lake, James, age 45, 17 years in U.S., wife & 7 children, 131
   Greenwich St., NYC, tailor (20-25 July 1812)
Lambert, Edward, 5ft. 4in., age 35, light complex., dark hair,
   brown eyes, Spring St., cordwainer (Navy)
Lambert, John, age 32, 1 year & 6 mos. in U.S., City Hotel, NYC,
   merchant (13-18 July 1812)
Lambert, Robert, 5ft. 10in., age 37, brown complex., dark hair,
   light eyes, Spring St., cordwainer (Navy)
Lambert, Robert, age .25, 6 years in U.S., wife & 2 children,
   Spring St., NYC, grocer (20-25 July 1812)
Lamond, John, age 39, 11 years in U.S., wife & 5 children, Pala-
   tine, Montgomery Co., farmer (3-14 & 21-26 Sept. 1812)
Lang, Nathaniel, 5ft. 8in., age 36, light complex., brown hair,
   grey eyes, Greenwich St., sawyer (Navy)
Lang, Thomas, age 27 in Dec. last, 9 years in U.S. in July last,
   wife, Utica, Oneida Co., mason (26 Aug. & 28 Sept. - 3 Oct.
   1812)
Lanman, John, age 31, 2 years in U.S., Beekman, Dutchess Co.,
   weaver (12-17 Oct. 1812)
Lappin, Edward, 5ft. 6in., age 23, light complex., fair hair,
   blue eyes, Pearl St., tailor (Navy)
Larcomb, Richard, age 28, 8 years in U.S., wife & child, 224
   William St., NYC, machinist (20-25 July 1812)
Larkin, John, age 20, 3 years in U.S., 5 Wall St., NYC, watchmaker (20-25 July 1812); 5ft. 10in., age 20, light complex.,
   dark hair, light eyes, watchmaker (Navy)
Larose, Lewis, age 44, 11 years in U.S., wife, 133 Mott St., NYC,
   laborer (20-25 July 1812)
Larry, John, 5ft. 7in., age 50, fair complex., light hair, blue
   eyes, New St., coachman (Navy)
Larry, William Barry, 5ft. 6in., age 16, fair complex., brown
   hair, blue eyes (Navy)
Latham, William, age 27, 1 year in U.S., 40 Broadway, NYC, mer-
   chant (20-25 July 1812)
Lathersdale, William, age 36, 9 years in U.S., wife, Princeton,
   Schenectady Co., farmer & shoemaker (17-22 Aug. 1812)
Lauderdale, Robert, age 35, 3 mos. in U.S., Washington Co.,
   schoolmaster (3-8 Aug. 1812)
Laugheny, Barney, 5ft. 7in., age 23, fair complex., brown hair,
   blue eyes, Grand St., skinner (Navy)
Laughin, Patrick, 5ft. 9in., age 28, brown complex., brown hair,
   dark eyes, George St., grocer (Navy)
Laughlin, Alexander, age 28, 4 mos. in U.S., Newburgh, Orange
   Co., weaver (14 & 17-22 Aug. 1812)
Laughlin, Andrew, age 25, 1 year in U.S., Newburgh, Orange Co.,
   laborer (19-24 Oct. 1812)
Laughlin, John, age 37, 10 years in U.S., wife & 2 children,
   Wallkill, Orange Co., farmer (21 Dec. 1812 - 23 Jan. 1813)
Laughlin, William, age 38, 18 years in U.S., wife & 4 children,
   Shawangunk, Ulster Co., farmer (19-24 Oct. 1812)
Laughlin, William, age 27, 2 years in U.S., wife & child, New-
   burgh, Orange Co., weaver (14 & 17-22 Aug. 1812)

Laughman, John, 5ft. 5in., age 32, brown complex., brown hair,
  grey eyes, Greenwich St., gardener (Navy)
Laurie, George, age 30, 8 years in U.S., NYC, merchant, applied
  22 May 1812 (20-25 July 1312)
Laurie, John, age 26, 5 years in U.S., NYC, merchant (20-25 July
  1812)
Lavin, Lawrence, age 25, 5 years in U.S., 43 Cross St., NYC,
  morocconist (10-15 Aug. 1312)
Law, James, age 38, 10 years in U.S., Schenectady, farmer & carpenter, applied 3 years ago (17-22 Aug. 1812)
Law, William, 5ft. 5in., age 26, dark complex., dark hair, blue
  eyes, Cherry St., nailor (Navy)
Lawrence, George, age 34, 5 years in U.S., wife & child, Broadway, cabinetmaker (20-25 July 1812); 5ft. 6½in., age 35, light
  complex., dark hair, blue eyes, Crosby St., cabinetmaker (Navy)
Lawrence, Nathaniel, age 30, 4½ years in U.S., 92 Greenwich St.,
  NYC, merchant, applied 9 Jan. 1809 (20-25 July 1812); 5ft. 6½
  in., age 30, dark complex., brown hair, black eyes, removed
  from NYC to Schenectady (Navy)
Lawrie, George, 5ft. 10in., age 30, light complex., light hair,
  light eyes, removed from NYC (Navy) - see Laurie, George, above
Lawrie, John, 6ft., age 26 light complex., light hair, brown
  eyes, removed from NYC (Navy) - see Laurie, John, above
Lawson, John, age 47, 7 years & 2 mos. in U.S., Rhinebeck, Dut-
  chess Co., clothier (12-17 Oct. 1812)
Lawson, Joseph, age 30, 1 year in U.S., wife & child, Schoharie,
  Schoharie Co., weaver (24-29 Aug. 1812)
Lawson, Peter, age 42, 11 years in U.S., wife & 4 children,
  Clinton, Dutchess Co., laborer (12-17 Oct. 1812)
Lawson, Robert, age 34, 7 years in U.S., wife & child, Mont-
  gomery, Orange Co., weaver (19-24 Oct. 1812)
Lawther, John, age 33, 4 years in U.S., wife & 2 children, Scho-
  harie, Schoharie Co., blacksmith (24-29 Aug. 1812)
Leary, Alexander, age 45, 11 years in U.S., Wallkill, Orange Co.,
  weaver (19-24 Oct. 1812)
Leary, John, 5ft. 6in., age 25, fair complex., black hair, blue
  eyes, Crosby St., cartman (Navy)
Leary, William H., age 26, 5 years in U.S., wife & 6 children,
  NYC, innkeeper, applied 28 Aug. 1811 (20-25 July 1812)
Leary, William Barry, age 16, 1 year in U.S., 46 Walker St.,
  NYC, teacher (20-25 July 1812)
Le Breton, Pierre, age 22, 1 year & 3 mos. in U.S., Johnstown,
  Montgomery Co., printer (7-12 Sept. 1812 & 25 Aug. - 2 Sept.
  1812)
Leckie, Robert, age 36, 8 years in U.S., wife & 3 children,
  Governors Island, stone mason (21 Dec. 1812 - 23 Jan. 1813)
Ledd (or Ledel?), George, 5ft. 10in., age 29, fair complex.,
  light hair, grey eyes, John St., cordwainer (Navy)
Leddell, Alexander, age 36, 27 years in U.S., wife & 5 children,
  Duanesburgh, Schenectady Co., farmer (17-22 Aug. 1812)
Ledgebury, James, age 25, 7 years in U.S., wife, 2 Mile Stone,
  gardener (10-15 Aug. 1812)
Ledlie, James B., age 30, 8 years in U.S., wife & 3 children,
  14 Skinner St., NYC, tallow chandler (20-25 July 1812); 5ft.
  6in., age 30, dark complex., brown hair, light eyes, Skinner
  St., chandler (Navy)
Lee, Allen, 6ft., age 35, dark complex., black hair, blue eyes,
  gardener (Navy)
Lee, Charles, age 35, 18 years in U.S., wife & 4 children, 71
  John St., NYC, tailor (13-18 July 1812); 5ft. 11in., age 38,
  light complex., light hair, blue eyes, tailor (Navy)
Lee, Charles S., age 27, 10 years in U.S., sister, Lispenard
  St., NYC, clerk (20-25 July 1812)
Lee, Christopher, age 30, 2½ years in U.S., 36 Charlotte St.,
  cooper (28 July - 2 Aug. 1812)

Lee, Christopher, 5ft. 4in., age 31, fair complex., black hair,
   grey eyes, Bancker St., labourer (Navy)
Lee, Ephraim, age 30, 9 years in U.S., 19 Roosevelt St., NYC,
   merchant, applied 6 May 1812 (20-25 July 1812)
Lee, Kavin, 5ft. 8in., age 23, fair complex., brown hair, light
   eyes, coachman (Navy)
Lee, Moore, age 23, 4 years & 10 mos. in U.S., 100 Chatham St.,
   NYC, merchant (20-25 July 1812); 6ft., age 24, fair complex.,
   brown hair, blue eyes, removed from NYC to Salisbury, Orange
   Co. (Navy)
Lee, Patrick, 5ft. 6in., age 25, brown complex., brown hair,
   grey eyes, Anthony St., cartman (Navy)
Lee, Richard Leonard, age 27, 9 years in U.S., 68 Greenwich St.,
   merchant, applied 30 May 1812 (20-25 July 1812); 5ft. 11 in.,
   age 28, light complex., dark hair, light eyes, removed from
   NYC to Fishkill, Dutchess Co. (Navy)
Lee, Terence, 5ft. 6in., age 53, fair complex., brown hair, grey
   eyes, Mulberry St., labourer (Navy)
Lee, William, age 27, 5 years in U.S., Leonard St., NYC, painter
   & glazier, applied 25 Apr. 1811 (20-25 July 1812); 5ft. 11 in.,
   age 27, fair complex., light hair, dark eyes, Harrison St.,
   painter (Navy)
Leedel, George, age 28, 4 years in U.S., wife & child, 76 John
   St., NYC, cordwainer (20-25 July 1812)
Leedy, James, 5ft. 6in., age 36, fair complex., brown hair, blue
   eyes, Anthony St., labourer (Navy)
Lees, Randall, age 21, 1 year & 10 mos. in U.S., wife, Hudson,
   Columbia Co., weaver (3-8 Aug. & Sept. 1812)
Leete, John, age 36, 8 years in U.S., wife & 3 children, Rockland Co., farmer (3-8 Aug. 1812); 5ft. 8¼in., age 37, dark complex., brown hair, brown eyes, Haverstraw, Rockland Co., far-
   mer (Navy)
Lefrancis, Lewis, 5ft. 5in., age 33, dark complex., dark hair,
   black eyes, brass founder (Navy)
Legget, James, 5ft. 9in., age 30, dark complex., dark hair, brown
   eyes, weaver (Navy)
Leggett/Legget, Joseph R., age 40, 9 years in U.S., wife & 2
   children, 231 Bowery Lane, NYC, teacher (31 Aug. -5 Sept. 1812);
   5ft. 6in., age 43, dark complex., brown hair, grey eyes, Bowery,
   teacher (Navy)
Legget, William, age 42, 18 years in U.S., 10 in family, Honeoye,
   Ontario Co., distiller (5-15 & 24-29 Aug. 1812)
Leigh, Sir Egerton, age 52, 2 days in U.S., Mechanic Hall, NYC,
   gentleman (19-24 Oct. 1812)
Lendrey, David, 5ft. 10in., age 22, fair complex., brown hair,
   blue eyes, Barclay St., laborer (Navy)
Lendrum/Landrum, George, 6 years & 4 mos. in U.S., Argyle, Washing-
   ton Co., house-carpenter, applied 20 Sept. 1811 (5-10 Oct. 1812)
Lenen, Robert, 5ft. 6in., age 46, dark complex., dark hair, blue
   eyes, Catherine St., shoemaker (Navy)
Leney, William S., age 40, 7 years in U.S., wife & 6 children,
   384 Broadway, NYC, engraver, applied 28 June 1809 (13-18 July
   1812); 5ft. 5in., age 44, fair complex., brown hair, blue eyes,
   Bowery, engraver (Navy)
Lennon, Edward, age 28, 5 years & 2 mos. in U.S., 36 Augustus
   St., NYC, cordwainer (28 July - 2 Aug. 1812); 5ft. 7in., age
   26, dark complex., brown hair, dark eyes, Augustus St., cord-
   wainer (Navy)
Lennon, Henry, age 17, 1 year & 2 mos. in U.S., 36 Augustus St.,
   NYC, cordwainer (28 July - 2 Aug. 1812)
Lennon, James, 5ft. 8in., age 23, dark complex., fair hair, grey
   eyes, Augustus St., shoemaker (Navy)
Leonard, Davis, 5ft. 7in, age 22, fair complex., fair hair, brown
   eyes, cooper (Navy)

Leonard, Dennis, age 22, 4 mos. in U.S., Montgomery, Orange Co.,
  carpenter (19-24 Oct. 1812)
Leonard, Edward, 5ft. 10in., age 45, dark complex., brown hair,
  hazel eyes, oysterman (Navy)
Leonard, Edward, 5ft. 8in., age 24, light complex., brown hair,
  blue eyes, farmer (Navy)
Leonard, Manwaring, age 29, 5 years & 11 mos. in U.S., wife & 5
  children, Mamakating, Sullivan Co., saddler (19-24 Oct. 1812)
Lerd, James, age 29, 11 years in U.S., wife, Saratoga, weaver
  (24-29 Aug. 1812)
Leri, Benjamin, age 20, 1 year & 4 mos. in U.S., 183 Greenwich
  St., NYC, watchmaker (20-25 July 1812)
Leslie, Alexander, age 55, 11 years in U.S., Schoharie, farmer
  (14-19 Sept. 1812)
Leslie, Robert, age 20, 5 years in U.S., 205 Front St., NYC,
  mariner (13-18 July 1812)
Levi, Benjamin, 5ft. 2in., age 21, dark complex., black hair,
  black eyes, watchmaker (Navy)
Lewis, Arthur, age 34, 12 years in U.S., 2 in family, Seneca,
  Ontario Co., cordwainer (23-30 Aug. 1812)
Lewis, Christian, age 32, 9 years in U.S., NYC, watchmaker (20-
  25 July 1812)
Lewis, David, age 58 on 10 Apr. last, 12 years in U.S. in Oct.
  next, wife & 5 children, Trenton, Oneida Co., farmer (29 Sept.
  & 28 Sept. - 3 Oct. 1812)
Lewis, David, age 35, 12 years in U.S., wife & 7 children, Pough-
  keepsie, Dutchess Co., laborer (12-17 Oct. 1812)
Lewis, Edward, age 22, 13 years in U.S., Junius, Seneca Co.,
  joiner (25 -31 Oct. 1812); age given as 24 (9-14 Nov. 1812)
Lewis, Lucas, age 24, 11 years in U.S., Montgomery, Orange Co.,
  carpenter (19-24 Oct. 1812)
Lewis, Peter, age 48, 11 years in U.S., 2 in family, Avon, On-
  tario Co., shoemaker (15 Nov. 1812 - 3 Jan. 1813)
Lewis, Thomas, age 51, 12 years in U.S., Bloominggrove, Orange
  Co., farmer (19-24 Oct. 1812)
Leyden, Hugh, age 44, 11 years in U.S., wife & 2 children, Clin-
  ton, Dutchess Co., farmer (12-17 Oct. 1812)
Liberty, Joseph, age 24, 12 years in U.S., Saugerties, Ulster
  Co., brickmaker (19-24 Oct. 1812)
Liddal, Alexander, age 56, 27 years in U.S., wife & 5 children,
  Duanesburgh, Schenectady Co., farmer (8-15 Aug. 1812)
Liddal, Thomas, age 41, 27 years in U.S., wife & 3 children,
  Duanesburgh, Schenectady Co., farmer (10-15 Aug. 1812)
Lightbody, James, age 37, 6 years in U.S., wife & 3 children,
  33 Bancker St., NYC, dyer (20-25 July 1812); 5ft. 10in., age
  39, dark complex., dark hair, blue eyes, Bancker St., dyer
  (Navy)
Lightborn, William, age 59, 6 years in U.S., 11 in family, 27
  Hudson St., NYC, gentleman (20-25 July 1812)
Lightbourn, Nathaniel, age 26, 6 years in U.S., wife & child,
  237 Duane St., NYC, merchant (20-25 July 1812)
Lindon, Michael, age 24, 1 year in U.S., Bloomingdale, teacher
  (10-15 Aug. 1812); 5ft. 7in., age 24, dark complex., brown
  hair, grey eyes, Bloomingdale, teacher (Navy)
Lindsay/Lindsey, George, age 34, 5 years in U.S., wife & 3 child-
  ren, Arundle St., NYC, morocco leather dresser (20-25 July
  1812); 6ft., age 36, fair complex., fair (?) hair, blue eyes,
  Arundle St., morocco (Navy)
Lindsey, George, 5ft. 7in., age 26, dark complex., dark hair,
  labourer (Navy)
Lindsey, Richard, 5ft. 9in., age 42, dark complex., grey hair,
  dark eyes, removed from NYC to Cooperstown, Otsego Co. (Navy)
Linen, Robert, age 46, 17 years in U.S., 16 Catherine St., NYC,
  shoemaker (20-25 July 1812)

Linford, John, 5ft. 8in., age 30, light complex., brown hair,
   brown eyes, carpenter (Navy)
Linnard, Roger, age 38, 2 mos. in U.S., corner Barclay & Church
   Sts., NYC, cooper (28 July - 2 Aug. 1812)
Linnen, Joseph, age 47, 1 year & 2 mos. in U.S., wife & child,
   Newburgh, Orange Co., weaver (19-24 Oct. 1812)
Linnon, James, age 23, 1½ years in U.S., NYC, shoemaker (2-7
   Nov. 1812)
Linton, Robert, age 46, 12 years in U.S., Vesey St., NYC, sawyer
   (20-25 July 1812); 5ft. 8in., age 48, fair complex., grey hair,
   blue eyes, Greenwich St., sawyer (Navy)
Linton, Thomas, age 30, 5 years in U.S., wife & child, Pough-
   keepsie, Dutchess Co., currier (12-17 Oct. 1812)
Linus, Arthur, age 34, 12 years in U.S., 2 in family, Seneca,
   Ontario Co., cordwainer (7-12 Sept. 1812)
Lipsey, John, age 22, 1 year & 10 mos. in U.S., Newburgh, Orange
   Co., laborer (19-24 Oct. 1812)
Little, H.O., 5ft. 8½in., age 31, fair complex., dark hair,
   brown eyes (Navy)
Little, William, age 31, 12 years in U.S., wife & 5 children,
   Montgomery, Orange Co., laborer (19-24 Oct. 1812)
Little, William, age 26, 3 mos. in U.S., Newburgh, Orange Co.,
   weaver (14 Aug. 1812)
Little, William, age 20, 3 mos. in U.S., Newburgh, Orange Co.,
   weaver (19-22 Aug. 1812)
Littleboy, William, 5ft. 9in., age 35, dark complex., brown hair,
   brown eyes, Chatham St., comb maker (Navy)
Livingston, John, age 40 in Nov. last, in U.S. since 1 May 1811,
   wife & 2 children, Whitestown, Oneida Co., bolter spinner/ cot-
   ton spinner, from near Glasgow, Scotland (26 Aug. & 28 Sept. -
   3 Oct. 1812)
Lloyd, John, 5ft., age 30, fair complex., brown hair, blue eyes,
   Pine St., baker (Navy)
Lloyd, Joseph, 5ft. 5in., age 45, light complex., light hair,
   grey eyes, Bowery, sleuth(?) (Navy)
Loague, Robert, age 27, 5 years in U.S., wife & 2 sons, Kips
   Bay (20-25 July 1812)
Lock, William, age 33, 7 years in U.S., wife & 2 children, Bloom-
   ingdale, shoemaker (20-25 July 1812); 5ft. 6in., age 34, dark
   complex., brown hair, brown eyes, Bloomingdale, shoemaker (Navy)
Lockhard, George, age 40, 12 years in U.S., wife & 4 children,
   Montgomery, Orange Co., weaver (19-24 Oct. 1812)
Lockhard, John, age 22, 11 years in U.S., Galway, Saratoga Co.,
   farmer (31 Aug. - 5 Sept. 1812)
Lockhart, Thomas, 5ft. 10in., age 26, fair complex., dark hair,
   brown eyes, Greenwich St., carpenter (Navy)
Lockhead, Robert, 5ft. 10in., age 33, fair complex., brown hair,
   blue eyes, Greenwich St., sawyer (Navy)
Logan, George, age 28, 8 years in U.S., Spring St., NYC, sawyer
   (26-31 Oct. 1812)
Logue, Robert, 5ft. 6in., age 27, light complex., grey hair,
   hazel eyes, sawyer (Navy) - same as Loague, Robert, above
Lombard, Patrick, age 43, 5 years in U.S., wife & 3 children,
   306 Water St., NYC, laborer (28 July - 2 Aug. 1812)
Long, George, age 30, 6 years in U.S., wife & child, 71 Pearl
   St., NYC, printer & bookseller, applied 10 Jan. 1812 (20-25
   July 1812); 5ft. 10in., age 32, dark complex., dark hair, blue
   eyes, Pearl St., printer (Navy)
Long, Matthew, age 35, 12 years in U.S., wife & 4 children, Mini-
   sink, Orange Co., farmer (19-24 Oct. 1812)
Lord, Henry, age 30, 11 years in U.S., wife & 2 children, Sche-
   nectady, teacher (31 Aug. - 5 Sept. 1812)
Lorin, Alexander, 5ft. 1½in., age 36, dark complex., black hair,
   black eyes (Navy)

Lough, Joseph, age 27, 6 years in U.S., Champlain, steamboat
    maker, from Scotland (1 Sept. - 1 Oct. & 26-31 Oct. 1812)
Loughan, Patrick, age 26, 2 years in U.S., corner Bancker & East
    George Sts., NYC, yeoman (28 July - 2 Aug. 1812)
Lougheed, John, age 57, 4 years in U.S., wife & 7 children,
    Dryden, Tompkins Co., farmer (2-7 Nov. & 30 Nov. - 5 Dec. 1812)
Loughead, John, age 26, 4 years & 3 mos. in U., Wallkill, Orange
    Co., farmer (19-24 Oct. 1812)
Loughead, John, age 21, 10 years in U.S., Montgomery, Orange
    Co., cooper (19-24 Oct. 1812)
Loughead, Robert, age 23, 9 years & 2 mos. in U.S., wife, Wall-
    kill, Orange Co., farmer (19-24 Oct. 1812)
Love, John, age 45, 22 years in U.S., wife & 6 children, Cats-
    kill, Greene Co., sawyer (17-22 Aug. 1812)
Love, Samuel, age 35, 2 years in U.S., Warwick, Orange Co., wea-
    ver (2 Jan. 1813 & 21 Dec. 1812 - 23 Jan. 1813)
Love, Samuel, 5ft. 8½in., age 28, light complex., brown hair,
    grey eyes, Fourth St., gardener (Navy)
Love, William, 5ft. 9in., age 26, light complex., brown hair,
    black eyes, Glass House, Rensselaer Co., farmer (Navy)
Low, Richard, age 36, 11 mos. in U.S., wife & 2 children, Mont-
    gomery Co., manufacturer of woolen cloth (10-15 Aug. 1812)
Lowery, Henry, age 17, 2 years & 6 mos. in U.S., Newburgh, Orange
    Co., farmer (19-24 Oct. 1812)
Lowery, Hugh, age 28, 1 year & 2 mos. in U.S., wife & 6 children,
    New Windsor, Orange Co., laborer (19-24 Oct. 1812)
Lowery, James, age 55, 28 years in U.S., wife & 3 children, Au-
    relius, Cayuga Co., farmer (12-17 & 26-31 Oct. 1812)
Lowin, Dennis, 5ft. 6in., age 28, brown complex., dark hair,
    brown eyes, Gold St., blacksmith (Navy)
Lowin, John, 5ft. 8in., age 50, dark complex., black hair, dark
    eyes, Duane St., blacksmith (Navy)
Lowrie, Alexander, 5ft. 8in., age 25, fair complex., sandy hair,
    blue eyes, Depeyster St., tobacco (Navy)
Lowrie, James, 5ft. 8in., age 28, dark complex., brown hair,
    brown eyes, Greenwich St., carpenter (Navy)
Lowry, Robert, age 37, 15 years in U.S., wife & 6 children,
    City of Albany, baker (24-29 Aug. 1812)
Lucas, Archibald, age 30, 11 mos. in U.S., wife & child, Kings-
    ton, Ulster Co., carpenter (19-24 Oct. 1812)
Lucas, Samuel, 5ft. 8in., age 26, light complex., brown hair,
    grey eyes, Henry St., cooper (Navy)
Lucas, William, age 43, 2 years in U.S., wife & 1 son, 175 Water
    St., NYC, druggist & grocer (20-25 July 1812)
Luccock, Thomas, age 49, 2 years in U.S., Hannibal, Onondaga
    Co., mason (18-25 Sept. 1812)
Lucie, Charles, age 28, 23 years in U.S., wife & 2 children,
    Chazy, Clinton Co., farmer, from St. Dennis, Lower Canada
    (1 Sept. - 1 Oct. & 26-31 Oct. 1812)
Luckie, Robert, 5ft. 10in., age 37, fair complex., fair hair,
    blue eyes, Beach St., mason (Navy)
Lucy, William, 5ft. 4in., age 42, dark complex., black hair,
    dark eyes, Provost St., painter (or printer?) (Navy)
Luke, James, 5ft. 6in., age 46, light complex., brown hair,
    blue eyes, Chatham St., corset (Navy)
Lumby, Benjamin, 5ft. 3in., age 48, light complex., light hair,
    grey eyes, labourer (Navy)
Lumby, Benjamin, age 38, 7 years in U.S., wife & 4 children, 2
    Mile Stone, NYC, farmer (28 July - 2 Aug. 1812)
Lumby, Thomas, age 21, 6 years & 11 mos. in U.S., wife, corner
    Spring & Crosby Sts., NYC, shoemaker (28 July - 2 Aug. 1812);
    5ft. 5in., age 22, dark complex., dark hair, dark eyes, Spring
    St., shoemaker (Navy)

Lumsden, John, age 35, 9 years & 9 mos. in U.S., wife & 3 children, 139 Chamber St., NYC, tailor (3-8 Aug. 1812)

Lumsden, John, 5ft. 11in., age 31, light complex., brown hair, blue eyes, Chamber St., tailor (Navy)

Lush, John, 5ft. 8in., age 37, dark complex., light hair, brown eyes, Water St., carpenter (Navy)

Lutherdale, John, age 65, 17 years in U.S., Princetown, Schenectady Co., teacher (26-31 Oct. 1812)

Lyde, John, age 34, 8 years in U.S., wife, Wallkill, Orange Co., weaver (19-24 Oct. 1812)

Lyle, James, age 29, 1 year & 3 mos. in U.S., Clinton, Dutchess Co., weaver (12-17 Oct. 1812)

Lyman, Francis, age 48, 9 mos. in U.S., wife, 6 Warren St., NYC, merchant (13-18 July 1812); 5ft. 7in., age 46, dark complex., dark hair, dark eyes, removed from NYC to Goshen, Orange Co. (Navy)

Lynch, Barnard, age 30, 5 years & 8 mos. in U.S., wife & 2 children, Minisink, Orange Co., farmer (19-24 Oct. 1812)

Lynch, Dennis, 5ft. 8in., age 40, dark complex., brown hair, grey eyes, Pearl St., labourer (Navy)

Lynch, Hugh, 5ft. 10in., age 50, fair complex., grey hair, grey eyes, Bancker St., labourer (Navy)

Lynch, James, age 34, 1 year & 6 mos. in U.S., 128 Water St., NYC, accountant, applied 2 June 1812 (3-8 Aug. 1812)

Lynch, James, 5ft. 4in., age 21, light complex., fair hair, blue eyes, Broad St., clerk (Navy)

Lynch, John, age 62, 1 year in U.S., wife & child, Bancker St., NYC, laborer (20-25 July 1812)

Lynch, John, 5ft. 4in., age 62, fair complex., grey hair, grey eyes, Bancker St., weaver (Navy)

Lynch, Patrick, age 36, 8 years in U.S., wife, Newburgh, Orange Co., laborer (19-24 Oct. 1812)

Lynch, Tarans, age 28, 13 years in U.S., wife & 2 children, Eaton, Madison Co., farmer (30 Nov. - 5 Dec. 1812); 13 years in U.S. last June (31 Oct. 1812)

Lynch, Thomas, age 30, 7 years in U.S., wife & child, 3 Broad St., NYC, grocer (28 July - 2 Aug. 1812)

Lynch, Thomas, 5ft. 4in., age 30, dark complex., black hair, blue eyes, Wall St., soda water (Navy)

Lynch, Thomas, 5ft. 8in., age 23, light complex., light hair, light eyes, Broadway, servant (Navy)

Lynch, Thomas, age 22, 1 year in U.S., 33 Nassau St., NYC, laborer (21-26 Sept. 1812)

Lynn, Eneas, 5ft. 6in., age 64, sandy complex., brown hair, grey eyes, Bowery, teacher (Navy)

Lynn, Mathew, 5ft. 10in., age 40, sandy complex., brown hair, grey eyes, Fourth St., labourer (Navy)

Lyon (or Lyons?), George, 5ft. 9in., age 25, fair complex., fair hair, grey eyes, Front St., labourer (Navy)

Lyons, Lawrence B., 5ft. 2in., age 38, fair complex., red hair, light eyes, Elizabeth St., weaver (Navy)

Lyon (or Lyons?), Thomas, 5ft. 6in., age 28, dark complex., light hair, dark eyes, Broadway, paper (maker?) (Navy)

McAlice, George, 5ft. 8in., age 30, dark complex., dark hair, brown eyes, Hester St., cartman (Navy)

McAlla, Robert, 5ft. 10in., age 33, dark complex., dark hair, blue eyes, Broadway, weaver (Navy)

McAllister, Alexander, 5ft. 10in., age 26, light complex., red hair, blue eyes, blacksmith (Navy)

McAllister, James, age 29, 17 years in U.S., wife & child, 164 Walker St., NYC, hatter (20-25 July 1812); 5ft. 6in., age 30, dark complex., dark hair, black eyes, Cedar St., hatter (Navy)

McAllum, John, 5ft. 6½in., age 27, dark complex., black hair, dark eyes, Liberty St., clerk (Navy)

McAlpin, James, age 29, 1 year & 3 mos. in U.S., wife & 2 children, Clinton, Dutchess Cc., weaver (12-17 Oct. 1812)

McAlpin, John, age 21 last Mar., 17 years in U.S., New Hartford, Oneida Co., cordwainer (26 Aug. 1812); age 21, 17 years in U.S., Trenton, Oneida Co., cordwainer (28 Sept. -3 Oct. 1812)

McAlroy, William, age 20 on 12 July last, 1 year in U.S. on 17 Sept. last, Whitestown, Cneida Co., sattinet weaver (26 Aug. 1812)

McAnnesser, Andrew, age 40, 8 years in U.S., wife & 3 children, NYC, laborer (28 July - 2 Aug. 1812)

McAnulty (or McAnully?), James, 5ft. 9in., age 26, brown complex., light hair, grey eyes, ferryman (Navy)

McArdle, John, age 30, 6 years & 4 mos. in U.S., New Windsor, Orange Co., laborer (19-24 Oct. 1812)

McArdle, John, age 27, 1 year & 6 mos. in U.S., 3 children, Newburgh, Orange Co., weaver (14 Aug. 1812)

McArdle, Philip, age 13 (error for probably 33), 13 years in U.S., New Windsor, Orange Co., laborer (19-24 Oct. 1812)

McArthur, Archibald, age 25 on 27 May, 11 years in U.S. last June, wife & 3 children, Utica, Oneida Co., farmer (26 Aug. & 28 Sept. - 3 Oct. 1812)

McArthur, Charles, age 20, 10 mos. in U.S., 9 James St., NYC, dyer (10-15 Aug. 1812)

McArthur, Colin, age 48, 9 years in U.S., wife & 3 children, 275 Greenwich St., NYC, dyer (17-22 Aug. 1812)

McArthur, Daniel, age 48, 1 year in U.S., 7 children, Dryden, Tompkins Co., farmer (25-31 Oct. & 9-14 Nov. 1812)

McArthur, Daniel, age 14, 1 year in U.S., Dryden, Tompkins Co., farmer (25-31 Oct. & 9-14 Nov. 1812)

McArthur, John, age 50, 5 years in U.S., wife, daughter & 2 apprentices, 9 James St., NYC, dyer (20-25 July 1812); 5ft. 8in., age 50, light complex., grey hair, blue eyes, James St., dyer (Navy)

McArthur, John, age 20, 1 year in U.S., Dryden, Tompkins Co., farmer (25-31 Oct. & 9-14 Nov. 1812)

McArthur, Peter, age 23, 10 mos. in U.S., 33 Bancker St., NYC, dyer (10-15 Aug. 1812); 5ft. 10 in. age 22, fair complex., black hair, black eyes, dyer (Navy)

McAuley, Samuel, age 34, 6 years in U.S., wife, 521 Pearl St., NYC, physician (30 Nov. - 5 Dec. 1812)

McAulle, John, age 27, 1 year & 6 mos. in U.S., 3 children. Newburgh, Orange Co., weaver (17-22 Aug. 1812)

McAvoy, James, age 30, 1 year in U.S., wife & 3 children, Newburgh, Orange Co., laborer (19-24 Oct. 1812)

McAvoy, Richard, age 30, 5 years in U.S., Newburgh, Orange Co., farmer (19-24 Oct. 1812)

McBarlas, William, 5ft. 10½in., age 30, light complex., fair hair, grey eyes, Greenwich St., manufacturer of thread (Navy)

McBarnet, Donald, age 28, 1 year & 3 mos. in U.S., City of Albany, laborer (17-22 Aug. 1812)

McBeth, Mathew, 5ft. 7in., age 33, dark complex., brown hair, grey eyes, bricklayer (Navy)

McBotts, John, age 29, 4 years in U.S., City of Albany, shoemaker (5-10 Oct. 1812)

McBrair, James, age 31, 9 years in U.S., wife & 3 children, 63 Maiden Lane, NYC, tailor, applied 21 Apr. 1810 (13-18 July 1812); 5ft. 7in., age 32, dark complex., brown hair, brown eyes, Maiden Lane, tailor (Navy)

McBrair, John, 6ft., age 22, light complex., light hair, blue eyes, labourer (Navy)

McBrian, Francis, age 41, 11 years & 2 mos. in U.S., New Paltz, Ulster Co., weaver (19-24 Oct. 1812)

McBridge, William, 5ft. 11in., age 27, fair complex., dark hair, blue eyes, Mulberry St., cartman (Navy)

McCab, Patrick, 5ft. 7½in., age 23, light complex., brown hair,
    blue eyes, John St., hostler (Navy)
McCabe, Charles, 5ft. 5in., age 45, light complex., brown hair,
    blue eyes, Augustus St., mariner (Navy)
McCabe, Linus, age 27, 13 years in U.S., wife & 2 children, New
    Windsor, Orange Co., farmer (19-24 Oct. 1812)
McCabe, Michael, age 31, 11 years in U.S., Schenectady, farmer
    & brewer (8-15 & 17-22 Aug. 1812)
McCabe, Owen, 5ft. 10 3/4in., age 30, dark complex., brown hair,
    brown eyes, hostler (Navy)
McCafferty, John, age 29, 6 years in U.S., wife, 2 sons & sister,
    6 Ann St., NYC, grocer, applied 31 Jan. 1812 (28 July - 2 Aug.
    1812)
McCafferty, John, 5ft. 5in., age 27, fair complex., fair hair,
    blue eyes, Ann St., tailor (Navy)
McCain, John, age 18, 4 mos. in U.S., City of Albany, coachman
    (5-10 Oct. 1812)
McCall, Dugall, age 46, 21 years in U.S., wife & 5 children,
    Johnstown, Montgomery Co., farmer (3-14 Sept. 1812)
McCall, James, age 21, 10 years in U.S., 98 William St., NYC,
    dry good merchant (20-25 July 1812)- probably the same, McCall,
    James, 5ft. 11in., age 23, fair complex., brown hair, light
    eyes, removed from NYC to Fishkill, Dutchess Co. (Navy)
McCall, John, age 18, 5 years & 8 mos. in U.S., 173 Pearl St.,
    clerk (20-25 July 1812)
McCalla, John, age 22, 1 year in U.S., Montgomery, Orange Co.,
    carpenter (19-24 Oct. 1812)
McCallagh, Patrick, age 45, 8 years in U.S., wife & 5 children,
    33 Chatham St., NYC, laborer (20-25 July 1812)
McCallam, Charles, 5ft. 11in., age 33, fair complex., light hair,
    dark eyes, maltster (Navy)
McCallam, Peter, 5ft. 7½in., age 38, light complex., brown hair,
    blue eyes, steam boat, mariner (Navy)
McCallum, Duncan, 5ft. 7in., age 28, light complex., brown hair,
    blue eyes, blacksmith (Navy)
McCallun, Neil, age 39, 1 year in U.S., wife & child, Dryden,
    Tompkins Co., farmer, applied 1812 (25-31 Oct. & 9-14 Nov.
    1812)
McCalm, Henry, age 30, 3 years in U.S., wife & 3 children, Mon-
    roe Works, Orange Co., cut nailor (17-22 Aug. 1812)
McCam (?), Peter, 5ft. 10in., age 32, fair complex., fair hair,
    blue eyes, Orange St. labourer (Navy)
McCanat, James, 5ft. 10in., age 35, fair complex., fair hair,
    grey eyes, Cherry St., cartman (Navy)
McCandley, Hugh, 5ft. 7in., age 32, light complex., brown hair,
    dark eyes, labourer (Navy)
McCandy, Daniel, 5ft. 8in., age 25, fair complex., fair hair,
    grey eyes, weaver (Navy)
McCanly, John, age 34, 11 years in U.S., wife & 3 children, Mon-
    roe Works, Orange Co., cut nailor (17-22 Aug. 1812)
McCanly, Thomas, age 26, 4 years in U.S., Monroe Works, Orange
    Co., cut nailor (17-22 Aug. 1812)
McCann, Patrick, 5ft. 7in., age 45, dark complex., dark hair,
    blue eyes, Mulberry St., labourer (Navy)
McCarthy, John, age 45, 11 years in U.S., 112 Bancker St., NYC,
    grocer (20-25 July 1812); 5ft. 7in., age 45, sandy complex.,
    brown hair, blue eyes, Bancker St., grocer (Navy)
McCarthy, Thomas, age 24, 4½ years in U.S., wife, Salina, Onon-
    daga Co., salt manufacturer (12-18 & 21-26 Sept. 1812)
McCartney, Samuel, 5ft. 6in., age 20, fair complex., black hair,
    blue eyes, Broadway, shoemaker (Navy)
McCarty, Andrew, 5ft. 8in., age 24, light complex., red hair,
    light eyes, Water St., coachman (Navy)
McCarty, Arthur, age 35, 3 mos. in U.S., Bloomingdale, NYC, far-
    mer (28 July - 2 Aug. 1812)

McCarty, Dennis, 5ft. 7in., age 19, fair complex., fair hair,
    hazel eyes, grocer (Navy)
McCarty, John, age 51, 16 years in U.S., Rochester, Ulster Co.,
    weaver (19-24 Oct. 1812)
McCarty, Miles, age 37, 12 years in U.S., 63 East George St.,
    sawyer (28 July - 2 Aug. 1812)
McCashland, John, 5ft. 6in., age 55, fair complex., pale hair,
    grey eyes, Bowery, calico (Navy)
McCaskin, Patrick, age 53, 7 years in U.S., wife & 5 children,
    New Windsor, Orange Co., laborer (19-24 Oct. 1812)
McCauly, John, 5ft. 6in., age 20, dark complex., brown hair,
    blue eyes, stone cutter (Navy)
McCauly, Samuel, 5ft. 11in., age 34, dark complex., dark hair,
    dark eyes, Pearl St., physician (Navy)
McCay, John, age 19, 4 years in U.S., 127 Water St., NYC, clerk
    (20-25 July 1812)
McCellen, George, 5ft. 10in., age 36, pale complex., brown hair,
    blue eyes, tobacco (Navy)
McClanahan, John, age 25, 7 years & 2 mos. in U.S., New Windsor,
    Orange Co., weaver (19-24 Oct. 1812)
McClanen, Alexander, 5ft. 7in., age 35, dark complex., brown
    hair, grey eyes, Greenwich St., labourer (Navy)
McClatchy, Richard, age 35, 2 mos. in U.S., Newburgh, Orange
    Co., farmer (19-24 Oct. 1812)
McClave, James, age 45, 18 years in U.S., New Windsor, Orange
    Co., chairmaker (19-24 Oct. 1812)
McClay, Archibald, age 34, 6½ years in U.S., wife & 6 children,
    7 Mott St., minister of the Gospel, applied Apr. 1811(28 July-
    2 Aug. 1812); 5ft. 8in., age 34, fair complex., black hair,
    blue eyes, Gospel (Navy)
McClean, John, 5ft. 10½in., age 22, fair complex., fair hair,
    blue eyes, Maiden Lane, clerk (Navy)
McClean, Patrick, age 27, 6 years in U.S., 4 in family, 25 Au-
    gustus St., NYC, laborer (28 July - 2 Aug. 1812)
McCleary/McClary, John, age 34, 6 years in U.S., wife & 3 child-
    ren, NYC, house-carpenter (10-15 Aug. 1812); 5ft. 6in., age
    35, dark complex., dark hair, grey eyes, Thomas St., carpen-
    ter (Navy)
McClee, Joseph, age 20, 1 year in U.S., Newburgh, Orange Co.,
    weaver (19-24 Oct. 1812)
McClelan, Patrick, 5ft. 5in., age 22, light complex., brown
    hair, blue eyes, Murray St., labourer (Navy)
McCleland/McClelland, John, age 25, 1 year in U.S., Lyons, On-
    tario Co., farmer (5-15 & 24-29 Aug. 1812)
McCleland, William, 5ft. 8in., age 50, light complex., light
    hair, blue eyes, Barclay St., tailor (Navy)
McClosky, Robert, 5ft. 6in., age 20, fair complex., dark hair,
    dark eyes, Maiden Lane, accountant (Navy)
McCluny, Mathew, 5ft. 6in., age 20, fair complex., fair hair,
    blue eyes, Orange St., weaver (Navy)
McClure, George, age 22, 10 years in U.S., 63 Ann St., NYC,
    cabinetmaker (20-25 July 1812); 5ft. 3in., age 23, light com-
    plex., fair hair, blue eyes, cabinetmaker (Navy)
McClure, John, age 45, 7 years in U.S., wife & 4 children, Bethel,
    Sullivan Co., applied June 1810 (31 Aug. & 19-24 Oct. 1812)
McClure, Patrick, 5ft. 7in., age 45, dark complex., dark hair,
    blue eyes, Mulberry St., labourer (Navy)
McClure, Thomas, age 23, 3 years in U.S., 93 Beekman St., NYC,
    cabinetmaker (20-25 July 1812)
McClure, William, age 52, 18 years in U.S., New Windsor, Orange
    Co., mason (19-24 Oct. 1812)
McColl, Dugall, age 46, 21 years in U.S., wife & 5 children,
    Johnstown, Montgomery Co., farmer (21-26 Sept. 1812)
McCollough, James, age 29, 5 years & 3 mos. in U.S., wife &
    child, Newburgh, Orange Co., farmer (19-24 Oct. 1812)

McCollough, William, age 24, 13 mos. in U.S., wife, Newburgh,
Orange Co., cooper (14 Aug. & 17-22 Aug. 1812)
McColter (?), James, 5ft. 9in., age 27, dark complex., brown
hair, blue eyes, Augustus St., pedler (Navy)
McComb, John, age 27, 8 years in U.S., wife & 3 children, 116
Reed St., NYC, grocer (20-25 July 1812)
McComb, John, 5ft. 8in., age 27, brown complex., brown hair,
brown eyes, Chamber St., grocer (Navy) - probably same as the
above
McComb, Robert, age 35, 1 year & 3 mos. in U.S., wife & 3 child-
ren, Cornwall, Orange Co., weaver - time in U.S. also given
as 1 year & 1 mo. (19-24 Oct. 1812)
McComb, Thomas, age 30, 3 years in U.S., wife & 3 children,
Schenectady, brewer (10-15 Aug. 1812)
McCombs, James, 5ft. 9in., age 32, fair complex., black hair,
grey eyes, Guanis, Kings Co., teacher (Navy) - also given as
5ft. 8in., age 32, fair complex., brown hair, blue eyes, a
teacher (Navy)
McConkey, Thomas, age 26, 1 year & 4 mos. in U.S., Wallkill,
Orange Co., laborer (19-24 Oct. 1812)
McConn, Charles, age 22, 1 year in U.S., wife & child, Wallkill,
Orange Co., weaver (19-24 Oct. 1812)
McConnell, David, 5ft. 6in., age 30, fair complex., fair hair,
grey eyes, shoemaker (Navy)
McConnell, Barney, age 40, 10 years in U.S., 92 Maiden Lane,
NYC, hostler (28 July - 2 Aug. 1812); 5ft. 10in., age 40,
fair complex., dark hair, brown eyes, hostler (Navy)
McConnell, James, 5ft. 6in., age 26, light complex., light hair,
blue eyes, weaver (Navy)
McConnell, John, age c. 60, in U.S. since Aug. last, 2 children,
Deerfield, Oneida Co., farmer, from Ireland (26 Aug. & 28 Sept. -
3 Oct. 1812)
McConnell, John, 6ft. 1in., age 37, fair complex., brown hair,
brown eyes, tobacco (Navy)
McConnell, Michael, 5ft. 10in., age 37, fair complex., brown
hair, grey eyes, Cross St., labourer (Navy)
McConnell, Michael, age 32, 3 years in U.S., 2 in family, 25
William St., NYC, laborer (20-25 July 1812)
McConnell, Patrick, age 37, 15 years in U.S., 7 in family, Se-
neca, Ontario Co., farmer (5-15 & 24-29 Aug. 1812)
McConnell, Robert, age 19½, 19 years in U.S., Florida, Montgo-
mery Co., farmer (25 Aug. - 2 Sept. & 7-12 Sept. 1812)
McConnell, Tarry (or Terry?), age 31, 8 years & 11 mos. in U.S.,
Wallkill, Orange Co., laborer (19-24 Oct. 1812)
McCoon, Moses, age 20, 10 mos. in U.S., wife, Wallkill, Orange
Co., laborer (19-24 Oct. 1812)
McCoppin, William, age 44, 8 years & 10 mos. in U.S., 2 child-
ren, New Windsor, Orange Co., physician (19-24 Oct. 1812)
McCormack, Bernard, age 26, 1 year & 4 mos. in U.S., 25 Old Slip,
NYC, clerk (20-25 July 1812)
McCormick, Charles, 5ft. 9in., age 33, fair complex., fair hair,
blue eyes, weaver (Navy)
McCormick, Edward, age 34, 6 years in U.S., wife & 4 children,
Republican Alley, NYC, laborer (20-25 July 1812)
McCormick, James, age 33, 7 years in U.S., wife & 3 children,
Newburgh, Orange Co., weaver (19-24 Oct. 1812)
McCormick, John, age 19, 1 year & 1 mo. in U.S., Bloominggrove,
Orange Co., weaver (19-24 Oct. 1812)
McCormick, Robert, age 27, 5 years in U.S., 96 Front St., NYC,
clerk (28 July - 2 Aug. 1812); 5ft. 6in., age 28, light com-
plex., fair hair, blue eyes, clerk (Navy)
McCormick, Samuel, age 19, 12 years in U.S., Newburgh, Orange
Co., brickmaker (19-24 Oct. 1812)
McCormick, William, age 26, 11 years & 3 mos. in U.S., wife & 4
children, Monroe, Orange Co., cooper (19-24 Oct. 1812)

McCormick, William, 5ft. 8in., age 22, dark complex., brown hair,
  black eyes, mariner (Navy)
McCoskey, Robert, age 20, 2 years in U.S., 111 Maiden Lane, NYC,
  broker (20-25 July 1812)
McCotter, James, age 27, 2 years in U.S., NYC, pedler (26-31 Oct.
  1812)
McCotton, John, age 21, 2 years & 11 mos. in U.S., wife, Mama-
  kating, Sullivan Co., carpenter (19-24 Oct. 1812)
McCoun, James, age 28, 6 weeks in U.S., wife & 2 children, Mont-
  gomery, Orange Co., mason (19-24 Oct. 1812)
McCour, Andrew, age 27, 11 years in U.S., Poughkeepsie, Dutchess
  Co., weaver (12-17 Oct. 1812)
McCowbray, Robert, age 28, 5 years & 1 mo. in U.S., Blooming-
  grove, Orange Co., cabinetmaker (19-24 Oct. 1812)
McCowlin (or McConlin?), Patrick, 5ft. 8in., age 35, light com-
  plex., dark hair, light eyes (Navy)
McCown, William, age 30, 8 years in U.S., wife & child, Monroe
  Works, Orange Co., cut nailor (17-22 Aug. 1812)
McCoy, Alexander, age 29, 8 years in U.S., wife, 1 child &
  mother, NYC, shipwright (20-25 July 1812); 5ft. 10in., age 30,
  light complex., light hair, grey eyes, Charlotte St., ship-
  carpenter (Navy)
McCoy, Bryan, 5ft. 7in., age 32, fair complex., red hair, grey
  eyes, labourer (Navy)
McCoy, Daniel, age 31, 1 year in U.S., wife & 5 children, Mon-
  roe Works, Orange Co., cut nailor (17-22 Aug. 1812)
McCoy, Dennis, 6ft. 2in., age 34, dark complex., dark hair,
  brown eyes, sawyer (Navy)
McCoy (spelled McKoy), George, 5ft. 8in., age 36, fair complex.,
  brown hair, grey eyes, carpenter (Navy)
McCoy, James, 5ft. 9½in., age 30, fair complex., brown hair,
  brown eyes, ship-carpenter (Navy)
McCoy, John, 5ft. 10in., age 35, light complex., fair hair,
  brown eyes, paver (Navy)
McCoy, John, age 35, 14 years in U.S., wife, 422 Greenwich St.,
  NYC, grocer (28 July - 2 Aug. 1812)
McCoy, Neil, 5ft. 11in., age 32, light complex., dark hair,
  brown eyes, gardener (Navy)
McCracken, John, age 72, 1 year in U.S., wife & 3 sons, 503
  Greenwich St., NYC, machinist (28 July - 2 Aug. 1812); 5ft.
  8in., age 72, fair complex., fair hair, grey eyes, Greenwich
  St., mechanic (Navy)
McCrea, John, age 33, 1 year & 9 mos. in U.S., wife & child,
  Mamakating, Sullivan Co., weaver (19-24 Oct. 1812)
McCredy, Anthony, age 49, 5 years in U.S., 7 in family, 21 Ban-
  cker St., NYC, laborer (20-25 July 1812)
McCroskey, James, age 26, 1 year & 3 mos. in U.S., Mamakating,
  Sullivan Co., tailor (19-24 Oct. 1812)
McCrosson, Jas., age 36, 19 years in U.S., 4 in family, Honeoye,
  Ontario Co., distiller (25 Oct. - 15 Nov. 1812)
McCrulate (?), Francis, 5ft. 6in., age 25, dark complex., brown
  hair, grey eyes, labourer (Navy)
McCrum, James, 5ft. 7½in., age 41, light complex., dark hair,
  dark eyes, Greenwich St., sawyer (Navy)
McCrum, Robert, 5ft. 10in., age 22, fair complex., brown hair,
  grey eyes, John St., labourer (Navy)
McCullagh, Patrick, 5ft. 8in., age 46, fair complex., dark hair,
  dark eyes, Mott St., labourer (Navy)
McCullen, Robert, 5ft. 5in., age 47, light complex., dark hair,
  grey eyes, Grand St., weaver (Navy)
McCulloch, John, 5ft. 7in., age 35, dark complex., brown hair,
  black eyes, stone cutter (Navy)
McCullough, Samuel, age 22, 16 years in U.S., New Paltz, Ulster
  Co., farmer (19-24 Oct. 1812)

McCullum, James, 5ft. 7in., age 24, fair complex., red hair,
  grey eyes, Manhattan, sawyer (Navy)
McCully, Robert, 5ft. 7in., age 27, light complex., dark hair,
  grey eyes, sawyer (Navy)
McCully, William, 5ft. 7in., age 32, light complex., fair hair,
  light eyes, farmer (Navy)
McCune, Robert, 5ft. 8in., age 27, dark complex., dark hair,
  grey eyes, Pine St., baker (Navy)
McCune, William, 5ft. 8in., age 17, fair complex., dark hair,
  blue eyes, Greenwich St., hos . . . (perhaps hostler?) (Navy)
McCunn, Thomas, age 22, 6 years in U.S., 337 Greenwich St., NYC,
  stone cutter (28 July - 2 Aug. 1812); 5ft. 11 3/4in., age 24,
  light complex., fair hair, grey eyes, Greenwich St., stone
  cutter (Navy)
McCutchin/McCutchan, William, age 37, 5 years & 11 mos. in U.S.,
  wife & 7 children, Bethel, Sullivan Co., farmer (31 Aug. &
  19-24 Oct. 1812)
McDade, Cornelius, 5ft. 8in., age 49, brown complex., black hair,
  grey eyes, milkman (Navy)
McDermond, John, 5ft. 7in., age 25, dark complex., brown hair,
  brown eyes, weaver (Navy)
McDermott, Cornelius, 5ft. 5in., age 28, fair complex., brown
  hair, blue eyes, Greenwich St., stone cutter (Navy)
McDermott, Henry, age 23, 8 years in U.S., wife & child, NYC,
  tobacconist (9-14 Nov. 1812)
McDermott, John, age 25, 5 years in U.S., corner Duane St., NYC,
  laborer (3-8 Aug. 1812)
McDerrveed (?), John, 5ft. 7in., age 25, fair complex., fair
  hair, brown eyes, Augustus St., labourer (Navy)
McDinnott (?), Charles, age 23, 10 years in U.S., 3 in family,
  Benton, Ontario Co., farmer (25 Oct. - 15 Nov. 1812)
McDinnott (?), John, age 46, 19 years in U.S., 2 in family, Ben-
  ton, Ontario Co., farmer (25 Oct. - 15 Nov. 1812)
McDonah, Malac, 5ft. 6in., age 25, fair complex., fair hair,
  blue eyes, Catherine St., book (?)
McDonagh, Michael, 5ft. 6in., age 25, red complex., light hair,
  grey eyes, Prince (?) St., stone cutter (Navy)
McDonagh, Michael, 5ft. 7in., age 23, light complex., brown hair,
  blue eyes, Corlaers Hook, stone cutter (Navy)
McDonagh, Pat, 5ft. 5in., age 21, fair complex., fair hair, blue
  eyes, Catherine St., currier (Navy)
McDonah, Peter, 5ft. 7in., age 27, red complex., brown hair,
  grey eyes, Elm St., labourer (Navy)
MacDonah, Thomas, 5ft. 7in., age 24, fair complex., brown hair,
  brown eyes, Vesey St., clerk (Navy)
McDonald, Alexander, 5ft. 8in., age 22, fair complex., fair hair,
  brown eyes, clerk (Navy)
McDonald, Alexander, 5ft. 5½in., age 22, fair complex., fair
  hair, blue eyes, removed from NYC to Fishkill, Dutchess Co.
  (Navy)
McDonald, Daniel, 5ft. 5in., age 38, dark complex., dark hair,
  dark eyes, Lumber St., cooper (Navy)
McDonald, Duncan, age 32, 27 years in U.S., wife & 4 children,
  Thurman, Washington Co., farmer (21 Dec. 1812 - 23 Jan. 1813);
  he was 32 in Feb. last and was 27 years in U.S. in Aug. last
  (24 Nov. 1812)
McDonald, Edward, 5ft. 9in., age 30, light complex., brown hair,
  brown eyes, Water St., tavern-keeper (Navy)
McDonald, James, age 36, 1 year in U.S., wife & 4 children, 28
  Harman St., NYC, house-carpenter (20-25 July 1812); 5ft. 8in.,
  age 37, light complex., sandy hair, blue eyes, Harman St.,
  carpenter (Navy)
McDonald, James Peter, 5ft. 3in., age 37, fair complex., brown
  hair, blue eyes, Sugar Loaf, manufacturer (Navy)

McDonald, John, age 60, 27 years in U.S. in Aug. last, wife & 4
children, Thurman, Washington Co., farmer (24 Nov. 1812 & 21
Dec. 1812 - 23 Jan. 1813)

McDonald, John, age 39, 2 mos. in U.S., wife & 2 children, Amsterdam, Montgomery Co., farmer(18-24 Aug. & 31 Aug. - 5 Sept.
1812)

McDonald, John, 5ft. 8in., age 27, light complex., dark hair,
brown eyes, Hester St., machine maker (Navy)

McDonald, Lawrence, age 65, 9 mos. in U.S., wife & 3 sons, 127
James St., cotton manufacturer (28 July - 2 Aug. 1812); 5ft.
10 in., age 67, fair complex., fair hair, brown eyes, cotton
manufacturer (Navy)

McDonald, Lawrence, 5ft. 9in., age 19, fair complex., dark hair,
light eyes, machine maker (Navy)

McDonald, Mathew, 5ft. 8in., age 22, fair complex., fair hair,
grey eyes, labourer (Navy)

McDonald, Patrick, 5ft. 9in., age 28, light complex., fair hair,
grey eyes, Greenwich St., farmer (Navy)

McDonald, William, 5ft. 2½in., age 28, light complex., light
hair, brown eyes, Bowery Hill, servant (Navy)

McDonald, William, age 22, 13 years in U.S., Johnstown, Montgomery Co., carpenter (7-12 Sept. 1812)

McDonnell, Alexander, age 22, 1 year in U.S., 32 Bancker St.,
NYC, currier, applied 27 July 1812 (10-15 Aug. 1812); tanner &
currier (13-18 July 1812)

McDonnell, Alexander, age 49, 9 days in U.S., wife & 3 children,
40 Broadway, NYC, gentleman (17-22 Aug. 1812)

McDonnell, Hugh, age 30, 11 years in U.S., Mamakating, Sullivan
Co., weaver (19-24 Oct. 1812)

McDonnell, John, age 30, 3 years in U.S., 32 Bancker St., NYC,
clerk, applied 27 Aug. 1810 (10-15 Aug. 1812)

McDonnell, John, age 30, 4 years in U.S., 32 Bancker St., NYC,
applied 23 Dec. 1809 (13-18 July 1812)

McDonnell, Mathew, 5ft. 6½in., age 48, light complex., light
hair, brown eyes, Front St., mason (Navy)

McDonnell, Patrick, 5ft. 4½in., age 25, light complex., sandy
hair, brown eyes, tailor (Navy)

McDonnell, Patrick, age 21, 1 year in U.S., Newburgh, Orange Co.,
laborer (19-24 Oct. 1812)

McDonough, Hugh, age 21, 9 years & 2 mos. in U.S., Shawangunk,
Ulster Co., slate dresser (19-24 Oct. 1812)

McDonough, James, age 28, 5 years in U.S. wife & 3 children,
Montgomery Co., cooper (17-22 Aug. 1812)

McDonough, James, age 25, 9 years & 2 mos. in U.S., Shawangunk,
Ulster Co., clothier (19-24 Oct. 1812)

McDonough, John, age 36, 11 years & 2 mos. in U.S., wife & 6
children, Shawangunk, Ulster Co., farmer (19-24 Oct. 1812)

McDonough, John, age 32, 9 years in U.S., 50 Cross St., NYC, laborer (20-25 July 1812)

McDonough, Michael, age 24, 8 years in U.S., wife & 3 children,
Orange St., NYC, stone cutter (20-25 July 1812)

McDonough, Richard, age 20, 9 years & 2 mos. in U.S., Shawangunk,
Ulster Co., farmer (19-24 Oct. 1812)

McDonough, Thomas, age 61, 9 years & 2 mos. in U.S., wife & 5
children, Shawangunk, Ulster Co., farmer (19-24 Oct. 1812)

McDonough, Thomas, age 30, 11 years & 2 mos. in U.S., wife, Shawangunk, Ulster Co., farmer (19-24 Oct. 1812)

McDougall, Allen, age 29, 8 years in U.S., wife & child, 384
Pearl St., NYC, cooper (20-25 July 1812); 5ft. 7½in., age 29,
dark complex., brown hair, dark eyes, Pearl St., cooper (Navy)

McDougall, James, age 31, 1 year in U.S., Beekman, Dutchess Co.,
weaver (12-17 Oct. 1812)

McDougall, John, age 27, 7 years in U.S., 342 Greenwich St., NYC,
sawyer (20-25 July 1812)

McDouglass, Charles, 5ft. 8in., age 24, dark complex., dark
  hair, black eyes, Greenwich St., sawyer (Navy)
McDowal, Alexander, age 45,1 year & 1 mo. in U.S., 2 in family,
  Washington Co., shoemaker (3-8 Aug. 1812)
McDowell, John, age 18, 1 year & 4 mos. in U.S., Montgomery,
  Orange Co., weaver (19-24 Oct. 1812)
McDowell, Thomas, age 20, 17 mos. in U.S., Kingston, Ulster Co.,
  weaver (7 Sept. & 19-24 Oct. 1812)
McDowell, William, age 23, 1 year & 10 mos. in U.S., wife & 3
  children, Montgomery, Orange Co., weaver (19-24 Oct. 1812)
McDuff, Andrew, age 21, 4½ years in U.S., Chatham St., NYC, clerk,
  applied 4 May 1812 (28 July - 2 Aug. 1812); 5ft. 7in., age 22,
  dark complex., brown hair, dark eyes, clerk (Navy); removed
  from NYC to Goshen, Orange Co. (Navy)
McEaden (?), Francis, 5ft. 6in., age 48, dark complex., grey
  hair, blue eyes, labourer (Navy)
McEkin, John, age 30, 1 year in U.S., Newburgh, Orange Co,, storekeeper (19-24 Oct. 1812)
McElhany, Peter, age 33, 16 years & 11 mos. in U.S. wife & child,
  Shawangunk, Ulster Co., farmer (19-24 Oct. 1812)
McElroy, Alexander, age 52 on 10 Feb. last, in U.S. since 4 Aug.
  1810, wife & 6 children, Trenton, Oneida Co., weaver (29 Sept.
  & 28 Sept. - 3 Oct. 1812)
McElroy, Peter, 5ft. 5in., age 25, fair complex., sandy hair,
  grey eyes, labourer (Navy)
McElvanny, Charles, age 37, 12 years & 3 mos. in U.S., wife & 3
  children, Montgomery, Orange Co., farmer (19-24 Oct. 1812)
McElve, John, age 36, 14 years & 10 mos. in U.S., wife & 4 child-
  ren, Shawangunk, Ulster Co., wheelmaker (19-24 Oct. 1812)
McEndle, John, 5ft. 4in., age 36, light complex., dark hair,
  grey eyes, Henry St., grocer (Navy)
McEnere, Gerald, 5ft. 9in., age 28, dark complex., dark hair,
  b (for brown or blue?),eyes, Ann St., comedian (Navy)
McEver, Thomas H., 6ft., age 25, fair complex., fair hair, blue
  eyes, mason (Navy)
McEvery, Patrick, 5ft. 2in., age 30, fair complex., light hair,
  grey eyes, servant (Navy)
McEwan, Duncan, age 56 in May last, 27 years in U.S. in Aug.
  last, wife & 7 children, Thurman, Washington Co., farmer (24
  Nov. 1812 & 21 Dec. 1812 - 23 Jan. 1813)
McEwan, Hugh, age 47 , 12 years in U.S. in Aug. last, wife &
  child, Thurman, Washington Co., farmer, applied for naturali-
  zation 4 or 5 years ago last winter (24 Nov. 1812 & 21 Dec.
  1812 - 23 Jan. 1813)
McEwan, John, age 21 in Apr. last, 9 years in U.S., Thurman,
  Washington Co., farmer (24 Nov. 1812 & 21 Dec. 1812 - 23 Jan.
  1813)
McFadden, Edward, 5ft. 4in., age 27, dark complex., brown hair,
  brown eyes, Elm St., tailor (Navy)
McFaddon, John, age given as 40 and 44, 15 years in U.S., wife
  & child, Newburgh, segar maker (14 Aug. & 17-22 Aug. 1812)
McFarlan, Andrew, age 47, 19 years in U.S., Schenectady, laborer
  (31 Aug. - 5 Sept. 1812)
McFarlan, Archibald, age 25, 3 years in U.S., 156 Chamber St.,
  NYC, clerk (3-8 Aug. 1812)
McFarlan, John, age 49, 8 years in U.S., wife & 2 children,
  Greenwich St., NYC, teacher, applied 26 Apr. 1809 (28 July -
  2 Aug. 1812) - perhaps the same, McFarlan, John, 5ft. 9in.,
  age 50, fair complex., brown hair, black eyes, Bank St., orphan assy (Navy)
McFarland, Alexander, 5ft. 7in., age 27, dark complex., dark
  hair, brown eyes, Desbrosses St., stone cutter (Navy)
McFarland, Andrew, 5ft. 8in., age 38, light complex., dark hair,
  blue eyes, Second St., shoemaker (Navy)

McFarland, Daniel, 5ft. 3in., age 46, light complex., grey hair,
grey eyes, saddler (Navy)

McFarland, Donald, 5ft. 8in., age 23, fair complex., light hair,
brown eyes, Mott St., tailor (Navy)

McFarland, Francis, 5ft. 10½in., age 29, fair complex., dark
hair, dark eyes, Chatham St., comedian (Navy)

McFarland Frederick, 5ft. 7in., age 50, ruddy complex., grey
hair, blue eyes, Garden St., teacher (Navy)

McFarland, Michael, 5ft. 7in., age 26, fair complex., brown hair,
grey eyes, grocer (Navy)

McFarland, William, 5ft. 6½in., age 20, fair complex., dark hair,
brown eyes, Cedar St., labourer (Navy)

McFarland, William, 5ft. 9in., age 20, dark complex., brown hair,
brown eyes, Desbrosses St., stone cutter (Navy)

McFarland, William, 5ft. 9in., age 18, fair complex., fair hair,
grey eyes, labourer (Navy)

McFarlane, Daniel, age 55, 6 years in U.S., wife & 7 children,
Broadalbin, Montgomery Co., farmer (15 Sept. - 5 Oct. & 5 Oct.-
10 Oct. 1812)

McFarlane, Donald, age 27, 4 years & 8 mos. in U.S., 4 in family,
8 Mott St., NYC, tailor (28 July - 2 Aug. 1812)

McFarlane, Duncan, age 51, 5 years in U.S., wife & 5 children,
Broadalbin, Montgomery Co., farmer (3-14 & 21-26 Sept. 1812)

McFarlane, Henry, 5ft. 9in., age 26, dark complex., dark hair,
grey eyes, Second St., carpenter (Navy)

McFarquhar, Redk., age 44, 10 years in U.S., wife & 2 children,
90 Washington St., NYC, cooper (28 July - 2 Aug. 1812)

McFerron, William, age 35, 15 years in U.S., wife & 5 children,
Salina, Onondaga Co., cooper (2-11 Nov. & 30 Nov. - 5 Dec.
1812)

McGah, William, age 23, 1 year in U.S., Greenwich St., NYC,
weaver (28 July - 2 Aug. 1812)

McGahan, Andrew, 5ft. 9in., age 29, dark complex., dark hair,
blue eyes, Lombardy St., drayman (Navy)

McGahey, John, age 30, 6 years in U.S., wife & 2 children, 58
Pearl St., NYC, laborer (20-25 July 1812)

McGahey, Owen, age 35, 12 years in U.S., 1 child, Newburgh,
Orange Co., grocer (19-24 Oct. 1812)

McGaehy (for McGahey?), Owen, 5ft. 10in., age 36, fair complex.,
fair hair, blue eyes, Newburgh, Orange Co., farmer (Navy) - may
be the same as the above

McGahey (or McGahry?), Patrick, age 30, 11 years in U.S., wife
& child, Newburgh, Orange Co., grocer (14 & 17-22 Aug. 1812)

McGaley, John, 5ft. 6in., age 32, fair complex., brown hair,
light eyes, Dey St., servant (Navy)

McGan, James, age 55 on 25 July last, 15 years in U.S. this 15th
inst., wife & 5 children, Whitestown, Oneida Co., weaver (26
Aug. 1812)

McGanigle, John, 5ft. 5in., age 49, light complex., grey hair,
brown eyes, Beekman Slip, cork cutt (Navy)

McGaraghy, John, age 27, 6 years in U.S., wife & 2 children,
NYC, laborer (20-25 July 1812)

McGarrah (?), George, 5ft. 8in., age 35, light complex., brown
hair, blue eyes, labourer (Navy)

McGarry, Peter, 5ft. 6in., age 37, fair complex., brown hair,
brown eyes, labourer (Navy)

McGavan, Dennis, age 24, 6 years in U.S., wife & child, Monroe
Works, Orange Co., cut nailor (17-22 Aug. 1812)

McGee, David, 5ft. 6in., age 19, light complex., light hair,
light eyes, boot (Navy)

McGee, James, age 21, 6 mos. in U.S., Goshen, Orange Co., weaver
(19-24 Oct. 1812)

McGee, John C., 5ft. 8in., age 25, light complex., light hair,
blue eyes, boot (Navy)

Magee, Patrick, age 23, 7 years in U.S., wife & child, 84 Front
  St., NYC, cooper (20-25 July 1812); McGee, Patrick, 5ft. 5in.,
  age 24, dark complex., brown hair, black eyes, Water St.,
  cooper (Navy)
McGhie, Alexander, age 24, 2 mos. in U.S., 156 Chamber St., NYC,
  merchant (28 July - 2 Aug. 1812)
McGill, James, age 36, 17 years in U.S., wife & 5 children, Wall-
  kill, Orange Co., farmer (19-24 Oct. 1812)
McGill, Patrick, age 26, 2 years in U.S., Newburgh, Orange Co.,
  carpenter (14 & 17-22 Aug. 1812)
McGillivray, William, age 25, in U.S. since Oct. 1802, Broadal-
  bin, Montgomery Co., schoolmaster (18-24 Aug. 1812)
McGimpsy, William, age 31, 1 year in U.S., wife & child, 173
  Bowery Lane, NYC, weaver (20-25 July 1812); McJimsey, William,
  5ft. 6in., age 31, light complex., brown hair, grey eyes, Third
  St., weaver (Navy)
McGinley, John, 5ft. 4in., age 20, dark complex., light hair,
  dark eyes, labourer (Navy)
McGinly, Edward, age 23, 1 year & 2 mos. in U.S., Schenectady,
  laborer (31 Aug. - 5 Sept. 1812)
McGinnis, Edward, 5ft. 7in., age 34, fair complex., dark hair,
  grey eyes, Bancker St., labourer (Navy)
McGinnis, Edward, age 30, 1 year in U.S., 32 Bancker St., NYC,
  currier, applied 27 July 1812 (10-15 Aug. 1812); 5ft. 10in.,
  age 30, light complex., dark hair, brown eyes, Roosevelt St.,
  currier (Navy)
McGinnis, James, age 25, 1 year in U.S., New York, farrier &
  smith (17-22 Aug. 1812); 5ft. 7in., age 26, dark complex., dark
  hair, black eyes, blacksmith (Navy)
Maginis, James, 5ft. 7in., age 24, fair complex., brown hair,
  blue eyes, engraver (Navy)
McGinnis, James, age 21, 1 year & 10 mos. in U.S., wife & child,
  68 William St., NYC, barkeeper (28 July - 2 Aug. 1812)
McGinnis, John, age 45, 6 years in U.S., wife, 104 Bowery Lane,
  NYC, pedler, applied 18 Apr. 1812 (20-25 July 1812)
McGinnis, John, age 42, 7 years in U.S., wife & 6 children,
  Marbletown, Ulster Co., farmer (19-24 Oct. 1812)
McGinnis, John, 5ft. 7in., age 22, light complex., brown hair,
  blue eyes, Corlaers Hook, stone (Navy)
McGinniss, Samuel, age 23, 1 year in U.S., NYC, farrier (3-8 Aug.
  1812); 5ft. 9in., age 24, fair complex., brown hair, brown
  eyes, blacksmith (Navy)
McGir, Arthur, 5ft. 5in., age 20, fair complex., black hair,
  brown eyes, Duane St., servant (Navy)
McGlade, Thomas, 5ft. 6in., age 46, dark complex., dark hair,
  brown eyes, Middle Road, gardener (Navy)
McGlaughlin, James, 5ft. 9½in., age 20, fair complex., brown
  hair, blue eyes, stone cutter (Navy)
McGleon, Farrell, 5ft. 7in., age 40, fair complex., fair hair,
  grey eyes, Augustus St., labourer (Navy)
McGohan, Daniel, age 32, 5 years in U.S., wife, 21 Bancker St.,
  NYC, drayman (20-25 July 1812)
McGonnigle, Peter, 5ft. 11in., age 27, light complex., sandy
  hair, grey eyes, Augustus St., bricklayer (Navy)
McGoughey, Farrell, age 27, 2 years in U.S., Goshen, Orange Co.,
  farmer (19-24 Oct. 1812)
McGourney, Peter, 5ft. 6in., age 30, fair complex., black hair,
  blue eyes, weaver (Navy)
McGovern, Christopher, 5ft. 7in., age 37, pale complex., light
  hair, brown eyes, Hague St., tailor (Navy)
McGovern, Mathew, age 36, 12 years in U.S., Minisink, Orange Co.,
  laborer (19-24 Oct. 1812)
McGowan, Daniel, 5ft. 9in., age 28, fair complex., black hair,
  blue eyes, labourer (Navy)

McGowan, Farrel, 5ft. 4in., age 43, dark complex., brown hair,
grey eyes, labourer (Navy)
McGowan, Hugh, age 29, 6 years in U.S., 3 Maiden Lane, NYC,
hatter (20-25 July 1812); 5ft. 7in., age 29, light complex.,
fair hair, blue eyes, Maiden Lane, hatter (Navy)
McGowan, James, 5ft. 5in., age 42, fair complex., fair hair,
blue eyes, labourer (Navy)
McGowan, James, age 35, 15 years in U.S., wife & 5 children,
Whitestown, Oneida Co., weaver (28 Sept. - 3 Oct. 1812)
McGowan, John, 5ft. 6in., age 38, ruddy complex., brown hair,
dark eyes, ashman (Navy)
McGowan, John, 5ft. 8in., age 22, light complex., brown hair,
blue eyes, Augustus St., labourer (Navy)
McGowan, Michael, age 27, 6 years in U.S., Broadway, NYC, coach-
man (17-22 Aug. 1812); 5ft. 8in., age 28, fair complex., dark
hair, grey eyes, coachman (Navy)
McGowan, Michael, 5ft. 8in., age 22, fair complex., fair hair,
dark eyes, labourer (Navy)
McGowan, Patrick, age 28, 3 years in U.S., wife & child, Division St., NYC, gardener (28 July - 2 Aug. 1812)
McGowan, Patrick, 5ft. 5½in., age ? 9, fair complex., dark hair,
grey eyes, labourer (Navy)
McGowan, Terrence, 5ft. 8in., age 46, dark complex., dark hair,
brown eyes, Anthony St., labourer (Navy)
McGowan, Thomas, 5ft. 5in., age 47, light complex., brown hair,
blue eyes, Anthony St., Labourer (Navy)
McGowen, Christopher, age 35, 10 years in U.S., wife & 3 child-
ren, 61 Bancker St., NYC, tailor (20-25 July 1812)
McGowen, Daniel, age 25, 8 years in U.S., 17 Augustus St., NYC,
laborer (28 July - 2 Aug. 1812)
McGowin, Daniel, age 30, 9 years in U.S., wife & 2 children,
Monroe Works, Orange Co., cut nailor (17-22 Aug. 1812)
McGown, George, age 40, 15 years in U.S., wife & 2 children,
Wayne, Steuben Co., farmer (14 Sept. & 21-26 Sept. 1812)
McGowra (?), Peter, 5ft. 8in., age 28, fair complex., dark hair,
grey eyes, labourer (Navy)
McGrain, Thomas, age 34, 33 days in U.S., 2 children, 3 South
St., NYC, farmer (13-18 July 1812)
McGrath, James, 5ft. 7½in., age 28, fair complex., brown hair,
grey eyes, Brooklyn, labourer (Navy)
McGrath, Patrick, 5ft. 6½in., age 29, fair complex., dark hair,
brown eyes, servant (Navy)
McGrath, Patrick, age 23, 1 year in U.S., NYC, accountant (20-
25 July 1812)
McGrathy (?), John, 5ft. 8½in., age 27, fair complex., dark hair,
grey eyes, Orange St., maltster (Navy)
McGraw, Joseph, age 30, 11 years in U.S., wife & 4 children,
Dryden, Tompkins Co., weaver (9-14 Nov. 1812)
McGredie (?), Anthony, 5ft. 6in., age 56, dark complex., brown
hair, brown eyes, Batavia Lane, labourer (Navy)
McGreeiry, John, age 30, 5 years in U.S., 16 Duane St., NYC,
wheelwright (20-25 July 1812)
McGregor, Duncan, age 55, 10 years in U.S., wife & 5 children,
Galway, Saratoga Co., farmer (31 Aug. - 5 Sept. 1812)
McGregor, Gregor, age 33, 11 years in U.S., Johnstown, Montgomery
Co. (15 Sept. - 5 Oct. & 5-10 Oct. 1812)
McGregor, John, age 46, 8 years in U.S., wife & child, Mayfield,
Montgomery Co., weaver (25 Aug. - 2 Sept. & 7-12 Sept. 1812)
McGregor, Malcom, age 32, 3½ years in U.S., wife & 2 children,
Amsterdam, Montgomery Co., laborer (15 Sept. - 5 Oct. & 5-10
Oct. 1812)
McGregor, Renold, age 36, 23 years in U.S., wife & 2 children,
Northumberland, Saratoga Co., farmer (14-19 Sept. 1812)
McGregor, William, age 44, 14 years in U.S., wife & 4 children,
Johnstown, Montgomery Co., weaver (11-17 & 17-22 Aug. 1812)

McGruy (?), John, 5ft. 5in., age 30, dark complex., brown hair, grey eyes, Duane St., wheelwright (Navy)

Maguire, James, age 26, 3 years in U.S., Greenwich St., NYC, type founder (28 July - 2 Aug. 1812)

McGuire, John, age 43, 6 years in U.S., 15 Chatham St., NYC, dealer & pedler (7-19 Dec. 1812)

McGuire, Michael, 5ft. 10in., age 24, fair complex., brown hair, grey eyes, tailor (Navy)

McGuire, Ross, 5ft. 7in., age 21, fair complex., fair hair, blue eyes, Cross St., mason (Navy)

McGune (?), Thomas, 5ft. 7in., age 37, dark complex., brown hair, blue eyes, Catherine St., labourer (Navy)

McGunigle, Patrick, age 21, 6 years in U.S., 102 Duane St., NYC, distiller (28 July - 2 Aug. 1812); 5ft. 8in., age 23, fair complex., fair hair, blue eyes, Augustus St., distiller (Navy)

McGunn, Mathew, 5ft. 8in., age 28, dark complex., dark hair, light eyes, farmer (Navy)

McGurgen, Terrence, age 21, 1 year & 2 mos. in U.S., Blooming-grove, Orange Co., farmer (19-24 Oct. 1812)

McHackney, Ducking (or Disching?), 5ft. 10in., age 29, light complex., dark hair, blue eyes, Cliff St., cooper (Navy)

McHector, McLeod, 5ft. 6in., age 60, light complex., grey hair, grey eyes, Newburgh, Orange Co. (Navy)

McHollin (?), Barney, 5ft. 8½in., age 26, brown complex., dark hair, dark eyes, West Farms, potter (Navy)

McIleon (?), William, 5ft. 6in., age 31, fair complex., fair hair, blue eyes, labourer (Navy)

McIllow, Daniel, 5ft. 4in., age 35, brown complex., brown hair, blue eyes, Talbot St., labourer (Navy)

McIlmoyl, James, age 26, 7 mos. in U.S., Salina, Onondaga Co., farmer (25 Sept. - 2 Nov. & 9-14 Nov. 1812)

McIlveron (?), Andrew, 5ft. 8in., age 25, fair complex., light hair, blue eyes, currier (Navy)

McIlvin, Mathew, 5ft. 9in., age 26, fair complex., sandy hair, blue eyes, Orange St., nailor (Navy)

McIlwain, John, age 21, 7 mos. in U.S., Broome St., laborer (28 July - 2 Aug. 1812)

McIlwain/McIlvain, Robert, age 42, 11 years in U.S., 2 in family, 485 Pearl St., NYC, grocer (28 July - 2 Aug. 1812); 5ft. 8in., age 41, light complex., brown hair, grey eyes, grocer (Navy)

McIlvarie (?), David, 5ft. 11½in., age 22, dark complex., dark hair, dark eyes, Harman St., painter (Navy)

McIlwink, Gilbert, age 35, 8 years & 2 mos. in U.S., wife & 2 children, Minisink, Orange Co., cotton weaver (19-24 Oct. 1812)

McIntire, James, 5ft. 7in., age 24, light complex., brown hair, blue eyes, Mulberry St., labourer (Navy)

McIntosh, Allen, age 51, 9 years in U.S., 5 in family, 60 Chamber St., NYC, tailor (28 July - 2 Aug. 1812); 5ft. 2in., age 48, dark complex., fair hair, blue eyes, Chamber St., tailor (Navy)

McIntosh, Angus, age 31, 9 years in U.S., 333 Pearl St., clerk (20-25 July 1812); 5ft. 7½in., age 32, light complex., sandy hair, blue eyes, Pearl St., clerk (Navy)

McIntosh, David, age 33, 11 years in U.S., City of Albany, hostler (24-29 Aug. 1812)

McIntosh, James, age 31 on 15 Nov. next, 10 years in U.S. on 12 Dec. next, wife & 2 children, Eaton, Madison Co., farmer (31 Oct. & 30 Nov. - 5 Dec. 1812)

McIntosh, John, age 50, in U.S. since 9 Sept. 1785, wife & 2 children, Mayfield, Montgomery Co., farmer (11-17 & 17-22 Aug. 1812)

McIntosh, William, age 29, 1 year in N.Y., Troy, joiner (17-22 Aug. 1812)

McIntyre, John, age 52, in U.S. since 1 Nov. 1805, wife & 5 children, Johnstown, Montgomery Co., farmer (11-17 Aug. 1812)

McIntyre, Mark, age 27, 1 year & 2 mos. in U.S., wife & child,
  Clinton, Dutchess Co., weaver (12-17 Oct. 1812)
McIntyre, Murdock, age 34, 2 years & 8 mos. in U.S., wife & 2
  children, Bloominggrove, Orange Co., farmer (19-24 Oct. 1812)
McIntyre, Peter, Jr., age 44, in U.S. since Oct. 1803, wife & 4
  children, Johnstown, Montgomery Co., farmer (18-24 Aug. & 31
  Aug. - 5 Sept. 1812)
McIvery, Barnard, age 27, 1 year in U.S., Newburgh, Orange Co.,
  laborer (19-24 Oct. 1812)
McJohnson, William, age 26, 8 years in U.S., wife & 3 children,
  Minisink, Orange Co., laborer (19-24 Oct. 1812)
McKay, Alexander, age 53, 29 years in U.S., wife & 6 children,
  Galway, Saratoga Co., farmer (24-29 Aug. 1812)
Mackay, Andrew, age 46, 5 years in U.S., 276 Front St., NYC,
  seaman (20-25 July 1812)
McKay, Archibald, age 25, 2 years in U.S., 372 Greenwich St.,
  NYC, sawyer (20-25 July 1812)
Mackay, Daniel, age 19, 5 years in U.S., wife & child, Clinton,
  Dutchess Co., machine maker (12-17 Oct. 1812)
McKay, Edward, 5ft. 7in., age 31, fair complex., brown hair,
  grey eyes (Navy)
McKay, George, age 30, 2 years & 11 mos. in U.S., Newburgh,
  Orange Co., carpenter (19-24 Oct. 1812)
Makay, James, age 26, 1 year in U.S., 124 Fly Market, NYC, tailor
  (20-25 July 1812)
McKay, John, 5ft. 10in., age 35, light complex., fair hair,
  brown eyes (Navy)
McKay, John, 5ft. 6in., age 31, fair complex., light hair, blue
  eyes, brass (Navy)
McKay, John, Jr., age 21, 8 years in U.S., Columbiaville, Colum-
  bia Co., cotton manufacturer (3-8 Aug. 1812)
McKean, Alexander, age 20, 6 weeks in U.S., corner Mulberry &
  Hester Sts., weaver (28 July -2 Aug. 1812)
McKee, Andrew, age 28, 7 years & 6 mos. in U.S., NYC, carpenter
  (28 July - 2 Aug. 1812)
McKee, Bernard, age 27, 6 years in U.S., Philadelphia, laborer
  (7-12 Sept. 1812)
McKee, Charles, age 25, 7 years in U.S., wife & child, NYC, stone
  cutter (28 July - 2 Aug. 1812); 5ft. 8in., age 26, light com-
  plex., fair hair, grey eyes, Chapple St., stone cutter (Navy)
McKee, Henry, age 30, 11 years in U.S., 6 in family, 304 Water
  St., NYC, painter (20-25 July 1812)
McKee, James, age 54, 9 years in U.S., wife & 6 children, Dryden,
  Tompkins Co., weaver (12-17 Oct. 1812)
McKee, James, age 54, 9 years in U.S., wife & 6 children, Scipio,
  Cayuga Co., weaver (25-31 Oct. 1812) - perhaps the same as the
  above?
McKee, James, 5ft. 11in., age 30, fair complex., grey hair, grey
  eyes, Harman St., mason (Navy)
McKee, James, age 21, 2 mos. in U.S., wife Newburgh, Orange Co.,
  weaver (19-24 Oct. 1812)
McKee, James, age 20, 9 years in U.S., Dryden, Tompkins Co.,
  farmer (25-31 Oct. & 9-14 Nov. 1812)
McKee, John, age 21, 2 mos. in U.S., 2 in family, Broome St.,
  NYC, carpenter (28 July - 2 Aug. 1812)
McKee, John, age 15, 9 years in U.S., Dryden, Tompkins Co.,
  farmer (25-31 Oct. & 9-14 Nov. 1812)
McKee, Joseph, age 23, 2 years in U.S., Clinton, Dutchess Co.,
  weaver (12-17 Oct. 1812); 5ft. 6in., age 23, fair complex.,
  fair hair, grey eyes (Navy)
McKee, Michael, age 20, 4 years in U.S., 130 Chamber St., NYC,
  stone cutter (7-12 Sept. 1812); 5ft. 8in., age 20, fair complex., brown hair, blue eyes, stone (Navy)
McKee, Nathaniel, age 20, 2 mos. in U.S., 173 Bowery, NYC, weaver (20-25 July 1812)

McKee, Robert, age 44, 6 years in U.S., wife & 7 children, Dryden, Tompkins Co., farmer (25-31 Oct. & 9-14 Nov. 1812)

McKee, Thomas, 5ft. 6in., age 27, dark complex., black hair,
grey eyes, Vandewater St., morocco (Navy)

McKee, Thomas, age 21, 2 years in U.S., New Windsor, Orange Co.,
weaver (19-24 Oct. 1812)

McKee, Thomas, age 20, 1 year in U.S., New Paltz, Ulster Co.,
farmer (19-24 Oct. 1812)

McKeen, Robert, 5ft. 9in., age 40, black complex., black hair,
brown eyes, Charlotte St. (Navy)

McKellan, Archibald, age 29, 8 years in U.S., 41 Cliff St., NYC,
cooper (28 July - 2 Aug. 1812); McKella, Archibald, 5ft. 6in.,
age 30, p (for "pale") complex., grey eyes, Cliff St., cooper
(Navy)

McKelvey/McKelvy, John, age 27, 10 years in U.S., wife & child,
260 William St., NYC, cooper (20-25 July 1812); 5ft. 10½in.,
age 27, dark complex., brown hair, grey eyes, cooper (Navy)

McKendry, Daniel, age 26, 2 years & 9 mos. in U.S., Greenwich
St., NYC, weaver (20-25 July 1812)

McKenna, Hugh, 5ft. 6in., age 20, fair complex., sandy hair,
light eyes, Tontine, servant (Navy)

McKenna, James, 5ft. 6½in., age 25, light complex., brown hair,
blue eyes, labourer (Navy)

McKenney, John, age 21, 16 years in U.S., Galway, Saratoga Co.,
farmer (14-19 Sept. 1812)

McKennie, James, 5ft. 7in., age 40, light complex., light hair,
blue eyes, William St., hairdresser (Navy)

McKenny, Massias, age 56, 13 years in U.S., wife & 2 children,
Saratoga, storekeeper (19-22 Aug. 1812)

McKenty, Bernard, age 50, 3 mos. in U.S., wife & 5 children, 42
Charlotte St., NYC, laborer (20-25 July 1812)

McKenzie, Alexander, age 36, 11 years in U.S., wife & child, 25
Vesey St., NYC, grocer (20-25 July 1812); 5ft. 6in., age 37,
light complex., dark hair, hazel eyes, Vesey St., grocer (Navy)

McKenzie, Alexander George, age 26, 11 years in U.S., wife,Sci-
pio, Cayuga Co., farmer, a volunteer in Capt. Richmond's company of exempts(5-10 & 19-24 Oct. 1812)

McKenzie, James, age 38, 8 years in U.S., wife & 4 children,
141 Pearl St., NYC, hairdresser (13-18 July 1812)

McKeog (?), Robert, 5ft. 3½in., age 22, dark complex., dark
hair, brown eyes, cartman (Navy)

McKeon, Felix, age 28, 11 years in U.S., Monroe Works, Orange
Co., cut nailor (17-22 Aug. 1812)

McKeon, Patrick, age 21, 1 mo. in U.S., Mulberry St., NYC, clerk
(20-25 July 1812); probably the same as McKeon, Pat, 5ft. 9in.,
age 22, fair complex., brown hair, grey eyes, Water St., clerk
(navy)

McKeon, Robert, age 38, 9 mos. in U.S., wife, NYC, laborer (20-
25 July 1812)

McKeon, Roger, 5ft. 8in., age 48, fair complex., grey hair,
light eyes, Greenwich St., gardener (Navy)

McKercher, John, age 30, 5 years in U.S., wife & 3 children,
Galway, Saratoga Co., laborer (31 Aug. - 5 Sept. 1812)

McKercher, John, age 29, 3 years in U.S., Charlton, Saratoga
Co., laborer (26-31 Oct. 1812)

McKercher, John, Jr., age 26, 14 years in U.S., wife & child,
Amsterdam, Montgomery Co., laborer (25 Aug. - 2 Sept. & 7-12
Sept. 1812)

McKevell (?), Henry, 5ft. 7in., age 25, fair complex., brown
hair, blue eyes, grocer (Navy)

McKever, Charles, age 37, 17 years in U.S., 3 children, Schoharie,
farmer (24-29 Aug. 1812)

Mackey, William, age 32, 4 years in U.S., 15 Elm St., NYC (20-
25 July 1812)

McKibbin, Adam, 5ft. 10in., age 28, light complex., brown hair,
blue eyes, Bellvue, bricklayer (Navy)
McKibbon, George, age 45, 5 years in U.S., wife & 6 children,
21 Old Slip, NYC, grocer, applied 22 Mar. 1810 (20-25 July
1812); 5ft. 8in., age 46, dark complex., brown hair, brown
eyes, Rose St., grocer (Navy)
McKichnie, Duncan, age 27, 8 years in U.S., wife & child, 60
Catherine St., NYC, cooper (28 July - 2 Aug. 1812)
McKie, Alexander, 5ft. 5in., age 45, light complex., fair hair,
blue eyes, Bancker St., cartman (Navy)
McKie, Andrew, 5ft. 4in., age 29, light complex., brown hair,
dark eyes, Warren St., carpenter (Navy)
Mackie, George, 5ft. 7in., age 25, light complex., brown hair,
hazel eyes, removed from NYC to Balston, Saratoga Co. (Navy)
McKie, Henry, 5ft. 8in., age 30, fair complex., fair hair, blue
eyes, printer (Navy)
McKie, Thomas, age 51, 6 years in U.S., Neversink, Sullivan Co.,
laborer (19-24 Oct. 1812)
McKinlay, John, age 55, 5 years in U.S., wife, Mayfield, Mont-
gomery Co., shoemaker (25 Aug. - 2 Sept. & 7-12 Sept. 1812)
McKinlay, Peter, age 54, 28 years in U.S., wife & 11 children,
Mayfield, Montgomery Co., farmer (11-17 & 17-22 Aug. 1812)
McKinly, Barnaby, 5ft. 6in., age 27, ruddy complex., dark hair,
light eyes, labourer (Navy)
McKinney, William, age 46, 20 years in U.S., wife & 10 children,
Painted Post, Steuben Co., weaver (25-31 Aug. & 7-12 Sept. 1812
McKinney, William, age 41, 20 years in U.S., wife & 9 children,
Painted Post, Steuben Co., farmer (14 Sept. & 21-26 Sept. 1812)
McKissock, William, 5ft. 7in., age 62, light complex., fair hair,
grey eyes, grocer (Navy)
McKitchnie, Duncan, 5ft. 6in., age 28, dark complex., brown hair,
brown eyes, Nassau St., mason (Navy)
McKnight, John, 5ft. 8in., age 22, fair complex., brown hair,
blue eyes, Bloomingdale, manufacturer (Navy)
McKone, Hugh, 5ft. 10in., age 22, light complex., brown hair,
blue eyes, Fly Market, porter (Navy)
McLachlan, Fergus, age 65, 5 years in U.S., wife & 2 children,
Palatine, Montgomery Co., farmer (3-14 Sept. 1812)
McLachlan, James, age 30, 8 years in U.S., wife & 4 children,
Palatine, Montgomery Co., farmer (3-14 Sept. 1812)
McLachlan, Peter, age 28, 11 years in U.S., wife & 2 children,
Amsterdam, Montgomery Co., miller (25 Aug. - 2 Sept. 1812)
McLachlin, Daniel, age 25, 8 years in U.S., wife, Saratoga, shoe-
maker (17-22 Aug. 1812)
McLane (or McLaine?), Patrick, 5ft. 7in., age 25, light complex.,
dark hair, blue eyes, nailor (Navy)
McLaren, Robert, age 35, 5 years in U.S., wife & 6 children,
Amsterdam, Montgomery Co., blacksmith (3-14 & 21-26 Sept. 1812)
McLash, George, age 37, 4 years in U.S., City of Albany, brewer
(17-22 Aug. 1812)
McLaughlin, Dennis, age 25, 3 mos. in U.S., wife & child, Wall-
kill, Orange Co., laborer (19-24 Oct. 1812)
McLaughlin Duncan, age 31, 5 years in U.S., Schenectady, laborer
(17-22 Aug. 1812)
McLaughlin, Hugh, 5ft. 3in., age 22, fair complex., fair hair,
blue eyes, accountant (Navy)
McLaughlin, James, age 60, 28 years in U.S., Scipio, Cayuga Co.,
weaver (14-19 Sept. & 28 Sept. - 3 Oct. 1812)
McLaughlin, James, 5ft. 10in., age 27, fair complex., brown hair,
blue eyes, miller (Navy)
McLaughlin, James, age 21, 3 mos. in U.S., Wallkill, Orange Co.,
laborer (19-24 Oct. 1812)
McLaughlin, James, Jr., age 35, 17 years in U.S., wife & 4 children, Scipio, Cayuga Co., farmer (14-17 Sept. & 28 Sept. -3 Oct.
1812)

McLaughlin, John, 5ft. 4in., age 51, light complex., brown hair,
  blue eyes, Greenwich St., servant (Navy)
McLaughlin, John, 5ft. 9in., age 28, fair complex., fair hair,
  blue eyes, Duane St., labourer (Navy)
McLaughlin, John, age 27, 3 mos. in U.S., Wallkill, Orange Co.,
  laborer (19-24 Oct. 1812)
McLaughlin, John, 5ft. 6in., age 23, fair complex., brown hair,
  black eyes, Collect St., currier (Navy)
McLaughlin, John P., age 21, 1 year in U.S., Monroe Works, Orange
  Co., cut nailor (17-22 Aug. 1812)
McLaughlin, Patrick, age 28, 5 years in U.S., wife & child, Sci-
  pio, Cayuga Co., distiller,(7-14 & 21-26 Sept. 1812)
McLaughlin, Peter, age 28, 11 years in U.S., wife & 2 children,
  Amsterdam, Montgomery Co., miller (7-12 Sept. 1812)
McLaughlin, Philip, 5ft. 10in., age 23, light complex., fair
  hair, blue eyes, sawyer (Navy)
McLaughlin, Samuel, 5ft. 7½in., age 21, light complex., sandy
  hair, brown eyes, currier (Navy)
McLaughlin, William, 5ft. 8in., age 22, dark complex., brown
  hair, dark eyes, Lombardy St., labourer (Navy)
McLean, Duncan, age 31, 3 years & 2 mos. in U.S., Cornwall,
  Orange Co., weaver (19-24 Oct. 1812)
McLean, Hector, age 23, 9 years in U.S., Johnstown, Montgomery
  Co., turner (7-12 Sept. 1812)
McLean, James, Sr., 5ft. 7in., age 45, pale complex., brown hair,
  grey eyes, cartman (Navy)
McLean, James, 5ft. 10in., age 35, fair complex., fair hair,
  grey eyes, carpenter (Navy)
McLean, James, age 24, 5 years in U.S., Monroe Works, Orange Co.,
  cut nailor (17-22 Aug. 1812)
McLean, John, 5ft. 6in., age 30, dark complex., brown hair, dark
  eyes, Water St., servant (Navy)
McLean, Owen, age 26, 6 years in U.S., Monroe Works, Orange Co.,
  cut nailor (17-22 Aug. 1812)
McLeod, John, age 45, 14 years in U.S., wife & 3 children, Bushwick, Long Island, manufacturer (20-25 July 1812)
McLeod, John, 5ft. 9in., age 46, light complex., light hair, grey
  eyes, Gold St., cotton manufacturer (Navy) - perhaps same as
  the above
McLoughlin, John, 5ft. 6in., age 29, fair complex., brown hair,
  grey eyes, grocer (Navy)
McLymont, Peter, age 36, 7 years & 5 mos. in U.S., Montgomery,
  Orange Co., schoolmaster (21 Dec. 1812 - 13 Jan. 1813 & 2 Jan.
  1813)
McMaher, Patrick, 5ft. 5in., age 32, dark complex., brown hair,
  blue eyes, Bancker St., grocer (Navy)
McMarns, William, age 21, 4 years in U.S., Fishkill, Dutchess Co.,
  weaver (12-17 Oct. 1812)
McMartin, Finlay, age 46, 3 years in U.S., wife & 6 children,
  Amsterdam, Montgomery Co., farmer, applied 2 years ago (3-14
  & 21-26 Sept. 1812)
McMenomy, J., 5ft. 8in., age 24, light complex., black hair,
  grey eyes, Front St., boatman (Navy)
McMenomy, James, age 24, 2 years in U.S., wife & 2 children,
  speculator (20-25 July 1812)
McMillan, Andrew, age 67, 28 years in U.S., wife & 3 children,
  Schenectady, farmer (17-22 Aug. 1812)
McMillan, Thomas, age 32, 28 years in U.S., wife & 5 children,
  Schenectady, farmer (17-22 Aug. 1812)
McMillin, William, age 52, 21 years in U.S., Scipio, Cayuga Co.,
  farmer (7-12 & 21-26 Sept. 1812)
McMonagal, William, age 42, 15 years & 10mos. in U.S., wife & 3
  children, Wallkill, Orange Co., distiller (19-24 Oct. 1812)
McMullen, James, age 43, 1 year & 3 mos. in U.S., wife & 4 child-
  ren, Clinton, Dutchess Co., weaver (12-17 Oct. 1812)

McMullen, John, age 35, 15 years in U.S., wife & 2 children,
Wayne, Steuben Co., farmer (24 Aug. & 31 Aug. - 5 Sept. 1812)
McMullin, Joseph, 5ft. 6in., age 22, fair complex., brown hair,
blue eyes, Westchester, farmer (Navy)
McMurdy, Anthony, age 25, 21 years in U.S., wife, City of Albany,
laborer (5-10 Oct. 1812)
McMurray, James, age 46, 8 years in U.S., wife & 6 children,
NYC, hairdresser (20-25 July 1812)
McMurray, James, 5ft. 7in., age 45, fair complex., brown hair,
blue eyes, Peck Slip, hairdresser (Navy)
McMurray, James, 5ft. 8in., age 31, Varick St., carpenter (Navy)
McMurray, James, 5ft. 8in., age 30, light complex., brown hair,
grey eyes, Cherry St., jeweler (Navy)
McMurray, James F., age 24, 5 years in U.S., wife, 10 Chatham
St., physician, applied 4 Apr. 1811 (20-25 July 1812)
McNab, Andrew, age 26, 6 years in U.S., Geneva, Ontario Co.,
brewer (3-8 Aug. 1812)
McNab, Archibald, age 29, in U.S. since Dec. 1802, Johnstown,
Montgomery Co., farmer (13-24 Aug. & 31 Aug. - 5 Sept. 1812)
McNab, John, 5ft. 7in., age 31, light complex., brown hair, grey
eyes, Greenwich St., gardener (Navy)
McNabb, John, age 30, 1 year & 2 mos. in U.S., wife & 2 children,
Greenwich St., NYC, merchant (20-25 July 1812)
McNab, Peter, age 38, 8 years in U.S., wife & 2 children, May-
field, Montgomery Co., farmer ((11-17 & 17-22 Aug. 1812)
McNair, James, age 61, 34 years in U.S., wife & 9 children, town
& co. of Onondaga, laborer; his family is dispersed through
N.Y. & Conn.; his children were all born in Conn. (24-29 Aug.
& 31 Aug. - 5 Sept. 1812)
McNair, John, age 53, 7 years in U.S., NYC, blacksmith (28 July -
2 Aug. 1812); 5ft. 9in., age 54, dark complex., grey hair,
blue eyes, blacksmith (Navy)
McNally, Henry, age 32, 4 years in U.S., NYC (20-25 July 1812);
5ft. 5in., age 32, fair complex., fair hair, grey eyes, Henry
St., cartman (Navy)
McNally, James, age 20, 1 year & 7 mos. in U.S., 67 Cherry St.,
NYC, soap boiler (20-25 July 1812)
McNally, John, 5ft. 6in., age 23, fair complex., dark hair, blue
eyes, clerk (Navy)
McNally, Mathew, 5ft. 10in., age 30, dark complex., grey hair,
grey eyes, cartman (Navy)
McNassan, Patrick, 5ft. 8in., age 35, light complex., light hair,
grey eyes, Bloomingdale, labourer (Navy)
McNaughton, John, 5ft. 8in., age 43, light complex., grey hair,
hazel eyes, waiter (Navy)
McNaughton, Malcom, 5ft. 4in., age 35, fair complex., brown hair,
black eyes, Spring St., hairdresser (Navy)
McNeal, Thomas, age 25, 3 mos. & 2 days in U.S., corner Fitzroy
Road, NYC, farmer (28 July - 2 Aug. 1812)
McNee, John, age 38, 7 years in U.S., wife & 3 children, Sche-
nectady, shoemaker (10-15 Aug. 1812)
McNeigh, Hugh, 5ft. 8in., age 52, dark complex., dark hair, dark
eyes, Manhattan, tailor (Navy)
McNeill, Charles, age 56, 22 years in U.S., wife & 7 sons, Ja-
maica, Long Island (20-25 July 1812)
McNeill, Daniel, 5ft. 6in., age 51, florid complex., dark hair,
blue eyes (Navy)
McNeilly (?), John, 5ft. 10in., age 28, fair complex., chestnut
hair, blue eyes, Augustus St., grocer (Navy)
McNeirk (?), John, 5ft. 8in., age 36, fair complex., brown hair,
blue eyes, clockmaker (Navy)
McNesser (?), Andrew, 5ft. 8in., age 41, fair complex., fair
hair, grey eyes, Anthony St., labourer (Navy)
McNevin, William, 5ft. 5in., age 40, light complex., light hair,
blue eyes, Stagg Town, gardener (Navy)

McNiel, James, age 35, 16 years in U.S., wife & 2 children, Catskill, Greene Co., bookbinder (17-22 Aug. 1812)

NcNiesh, John, age 35, 9 mos. in U.S., wife, 5 in family, 110
Water St., NYC, clock- and watchmaker (20-25 July 1812)

McNoughton, John, age 44, 7 years in U.S., Saratoga (17-22 Aug.
1812)

McNoughton, Malcom, age 34, 6 years in U.S., wife & 4 children,
NYC, flax dresser (20-25 July 1812)

McNully, Andrew, 5ft. 9in., age 29, fair complex., brown hair,
blue eyes, Stagg Town, blacksmith (Navy)

McNutt, James, age 33, 21 years in U.S., Farmington, Ontario
Co., distiller (6-15 & 24-29 Aug. 1812)

McPherson, Daniel, age 44, 6 years in U.S., wife & 2 children,
Broadalbin, Montgomery Co., farmer (18-24 Aug. & 31 Aug. - 5
Sept. 1812)

McPherson, George, age 20, 2 years & 6 mos. in U.S., 20 Henry
St., NYC, whitesmith (28 Sept. - 3 Oct. 1812)

McPherson, George, 5ft. 8in., age 21, dark complex., dark hair,
blue eyes, Grand St., blacksmith (Navy)

McPherson, Walter, age 38, 19 years in U.S., 4 in family, Phelps,
Ontario Co., farmer (5-15 & 24-29 Aug. 1812)

McQuaid, Edward, 5ft. 5in., age 27, brown complex., brown hair,
brown eyes, labourer (Navy)

McQuaid, James, 5ft. 7in., age 40, dark complex., black hair,
grey eyes, Chapple St., labourer (Navy)

McQuaid, James, 5ft. 6in., age 23, fair complex., brown hair,
blue eyes, Mulberry St., carpenter (Navy)

McQuaid, Patrick, 5ft. 7in., age 30, fair complex., dark hair,
brown eyes, blacksmith (Navy)

McQueen, Alexander, 5ft. 10in., age 45, light complex., sandy
hair, blue eyes, Ridge St., labourer (Navy)

McQueen, Archibald, age 35, 15 years in U.S., wife & 2 children,
Amsterdam, Montgomery Co., farmer (5 Nov. - 9 Dec. & 7-19 Dec.
1812)

McQuig, Dougal, age 23, 3 years in U.S., City of Albany, laborer
(5-10 Oct. 1812)

McQuillen, John, age 26, 2 years in U.S., Lombardy St., NYC,
mason (28 July - 2 Aug. 1812)

McQuinten, James, 5ft. 8in., age 27, fair complex., light hair,
brown eyes, Greenwich St., cotton manufacturer (Navy)

McQuoid, William, age 28, 5 in family, corner Hester & Rynders
Sts., drayman (20-25 July 1812); 5ft. 11in., age 28, dark
complex., dark hair, light eyes, Hester St., drayman (Navy)

McReaile, George, 5ft. 7in., age 24, fair complex., black hair,
black eyes, labourer (Navy)

McSealy, Edward, 5ft. 7in., age 32, fair complex., brown hair,
fair eyes, mason (Navy)

McSteer, Peter, age 62, 2 years in U.S. on 3 Oct., Eaton, Madison Co., farmer (31 Oct. & 30 Nov. - 5 Dec. 1812)

McTavush, Alexander, age 29, 6 years in U.S., City of Albany,
merchant (17-22 Aug. 1812)

McTeer, Barnet, age 42, 12 years in U.S., wife & 4 children,
tailor (19-24 Oct. 1812)

McTerren (?), Bayan , 5ft. 11in., age 24, fair complex., dark
hair, grey eyes, Pump & Mott Sts., labourer (Navy)

McVea, David, 5ft. 11in., age 27, light complex., brown hair,
grey eyes, Clinton, weaver (Navy)

McVean, Henry, age 20, 3 mos. in U.S., NYC, baker (3-8 Aug. 1812)

McVean, Peter, age 29, 11 years in U.S., Johnstown, Montgomery
Co., laborer (7-12 Sept. 1812)

McVean, James, 5ft. 6in., age 26, dark complex., black hair,
black eyes, Burling Slip, tailor (Navy)

McVey, Hugh, 5ft. 8in., age 24, fair complex., fair hair, grey
eyes, Greenwich St., labourer (Navy)

McVey, Thomas, 5ft. 7in., age 27, fair complex., fair hair, grey
   eyes, Greenwich St., stone cutter (Navy)
McVickar, James, age 28, 11 years & 8 mos. in U.S., Shawangunk,
   Ulster Co., carpenter (19-24 Oct. 1812)
McVicker, James, age 39, 6 years in U.S., 135 Chatham St., NYC,
   grocer (20-25 July 1812)
McVicker, James, 5ft. 7½in., age 36, dark complex., dark hair,
   brown eyes, Henry St., weaver (Navy)
McVie, David, age 27, 1 year & 9 mos. in U.S., Clinton, Dutchess
   Co., laborer (12-17 Oct. 1812)
McWatters (?), William, 5ft. 6in., age 30, dark complex., dark
   hair, grey eyes, cordwainer (Navy)
McWhelan, Joseph, age 25, 7 years in U.S., Johnstown, Montgomery
   Co., farmer (15 Sept. - 5 Oct. 1812)
McWilliams, David, age 17, 2 years in U.S., Schenectady, laborer
   (14-19 Sept. 1812)
McWilliams, William, age 30, 3 years in U.S., wife & 3 children,
   Schenectady, brewer (10-15 Aug. 1812)
Maben, George, age 67, 15 years in U.S., wife & 5 children,
   Duanesburgh, Schenectady Co., farmer (10-15 Aug. 1812)
Maben, James, age 30, 15 years in U.S., Duanesburgh, Schenectady
   Co., farmer (10-15 Aug. 1812)
Machan, Bernard, 5ft. 7in., age 45, dark complex., black hair,
   blue eyes, Third St., labourer (Navy)
Madden, Edward, age 29, 16 years in U.S., Wallkill, Orange Co.,
   laborer (19-24 Oct. 1812)
Magerus, James, age 23, 40 days in U.S., Bowery Lane, NYC, pain-
   ter & engraver (19-24 Oct. 1812)
Mahan, John, 6ft. 2in., age 40, fair complex., brown hair, blue
   eyes, manufacturer (Navy)
Mahan, Pat, 5ft. 10in., age 34, ruddy complex., fair hair, blue
   eyes, labourer (Navy)
Maher, Thomas, age 35, 9 years in U.S., wife & 4 children, Mon-
   roe Works, Orange Co., cut nailor (17-22 Aug. 1812)
Maher, William, age 40, 1 year & 11 mos. in U.S., wife, NYC,
   laborer (28 July - 2 Aug. 1812)
Maher (?), William, age 23, 20 years in U.S., Schoharie, farmer
   (24-29 Aug. 1812)
Mahon, Charles, age 26, 1 year & 8 mos. in U.S., Greenwich St.,
   NYC, gardener, applied 22 June 1812 (20-25 July 1812)
Maiben (?), Richard, 5ft. 3in., age 40, fair complex., light
   hair, blue eyes, Spring St., chemist (Navy)
Main, Alexander, age 24, 5 years in U.S., 93 Nassau St., NYC,
   mariner (20-25 July 1812)
Mair (?), Charles, 5ft. 6in., age 28, dark complex., light hair,
   dark eyes, teacher (Navy)
Maitland, Archibald, age 25, 4 years in U.S., wife & child, 144
   Bancker St., NYC, shoemaker (20-25 July 1812)
Makimson, Hugh, age 42, 17 years in U.S., NYC, drayman (10-15
   Aug. 1812)
Malcom, David, age 36, 7 years in U.S., Colonie, Albany Co.,
   tobacconist (17-22 Aug. 1812)
Malcom, John, 5ft. 7in., age 22, fair complex., dark hair, coach
   painter (Navy)
Malcomsen, James, age 46, 5 years in U.S., wife, Clinton, Dutchess
   Co., weaver (12-17 Oct. 1812)
Malcomsen, John, age 17, 5 years in U.S., Clinton, Dutchess Co.,
   weaver (12-17 Oct. 1812)
Maliod, Hector, age 65, 6 years & 9 mos. in U.S., wife & 3 child-
   ren, Newburgh, Orange Co. (19-24 Oct. 1812)
Malloch/Mallock, Andrew, age 37, 9 years in U.S., wife, 53 Li-
   berty St., NYC, teacher, applied 8 July 1809 (13-18 July 1812);
   5ft. 5 3/4in., age 37, ruddy complex., grey hair, blue eyes,
   Liberty St., teacher (Navy)

Mallon, P., age 38, 17 years in U.S., 72 Duane St., NYC, accoun-
    tant (13-18 July 1812)
Malloy, Robert, age 47, 8 years in U.S., wife & 5 children, 45
    Charlotte St., NYC, grocer, applied Apr. 1809 (20-25 July 1812)
Manager, T.J.G.W., 5ft. 6in., age 19, fair complex., fair hair,
    blue eyes, accountant (Navy)
Manahan (or Manaham?), James, 5ft. 7in., age 32, fair complex.,
    dark hair, blue eyes, Catherine St., painter (Navy)
Managhan, James, age 27, 18 years in U.S., wife & 2 children,
    Scipio, Cayuga Co., farmer (12-17 Oct. 1812)
Manahan, James, age 24, 5 years in U.S., 2 children, NYC, tobac-
    conist (2-7 Nov. 1812); 5ft. 6in., age 25, fair complex., brown
    hair, brown eyes, Water St., tobacco (Navy)
Manahan, Patrick, 5ft. 7in., age 37, fair complex., light hair,
    blue eyes, mason (Navy)
Manks, William, age 21, 1 year & 10 mos. in U.S., NYC, importer
    (14-19 Sept. 1812)
Mann, James, 5ft. 9in., age 47, dark complex., dark hair, blue
    eyes, grocer (Navy)
Mann, James, 5ft. 7in., age 20, dark complex., dark hair, blue
    eyes, servant (Navy)
Mansfield, Charles, age 53, 18 years in U.S., wife & 7 children,
    Shawangunk, Ulster Co., weaver (19-24 Oct. 1812)
Mansfield, Charles, age 20, 6 mos. in U.S., 41 Roosevelt St.,
    NYC, carpenter (28 July - 2 Aug. 1812)
Mansfield, Samuel, 5ft. 7in., age 37, fair complex., dark hair,
    black eyes, innkeeper (Navy)
Manuel, David, age 46, 11 years in U.S., wife & 5 children,
    Remsen, Oneida Co., farmer (29 Sept. & 28 Sept. - 3 Oct. 1812)
Marben, Richard, age 39, 10 years in U.S., wife & 7 children,
    NYC, chemist (31 Aug. - 5 Sept. 1812) - doubtless the same as
Maiben (?), Richard, above.
Marcier, John, 5ft. 8in, age 46, dark complex., dark hair, dark
    eyes, Oak St., jeweler (Navy)
Marden, John, age 32, 3 years in U.S., 5 in family, Geneva, On-
    tario Co., weaver (31 Aug. - 5 Sept. 1812)
Margarry, Henry J., 5ft. 8in., age 30, fair complex., dark hair,
    dark eyes, Maiden Lane, stationer (Navy)
Markham, William, 5ft. 5in., age 50, light complex., brown hair,
    blue eyes, labourer (Navy)
Markimson, Gorvin, age 39, 18 years in U.S., wife & 6 children,
    Shawangunk, Ulster Co., farmer (19-24 Oct. 1812)
Markison, Hugh, 5ft. 9in., age 36, fair complex., black hair,
    blue eyes, Duane St., drayman (Navy)
Marks, John, age 30, 1 year in U.S., 7 in family, corner Hester
    & Mulberry Sts., NYC, laborer (20-25 July 1812)
Marks, Robert, 5ft. 8in., age 27, sandy complex., dark hair,
    grey eyes, cartman (Navy)
Marks, William, 5ft. 10½in., age 22, light complex., brown hair,
    dark eyes, removed from NYC to Fishkill, Dutchess Co. (Navy)
Marley, John, 5ft. 6 3/4in., age 33, fair complex., dark hair,
    brown eyes, William St., rigger (Navy)
Marlow, Christian, 5ft. 8½in., age 25, dark complex., dark hair,
    brown eyes, baker (Navy)
Marlow, William, 5ft. 2in., age 23, fair complex., light hair,
    blue eyes, Broadway, servant (Navy)
Marren, Patrick, age 25, 6 years & 2 mos. in U.S., Goshen, Orange
    Co., laborer (19-24 Oct. 1812)
Marriott, Samuel, age 32, 10 years in U.S., wife & 2 children,
    Claverack, Columbia Co., farmer, applied Apr. 1809 (5 Sept. &
    7-12 Sept. 1812)
Marsden, John, age 34, 3 mos. in U.S., wife & 3 children, Green-
    wich St., NYC, Methodist minister (20-25 July 1812)
Marsden, Joshua, 5ft. 8in., age 35, light complex., brown hair,
    blue eyes, Greenwich St., teacher (Navy)

Marsh, Robert, 5ft. 7in., age 65, dark complex., dark hair,
   hazel eyes, Little George St., labourer (Navy)
Marshall, James, age 46, 10 years in U.S., Montgomery, Orange
   Co., weaver (19-24 Oct. 1812)
Marshall, James, age 42, 7 years in U.S., wife, 109 Lombardy St.,
   NYC, brass founder, applied 7 Feb. 1812 (20-25 July 1812); 5ft.
   9in., age 43, dark complex., dark hair, grey eyes, Lombardy
   St., founder (Navy)
Marshall, James, age 26, 8 years in U.S., wife & 3 children, 358
   Greenwich St., NYC, shoemaker (20-25 July 1812); 5ft. 9½in.,
   age 27, fair complex., dark hair, dark eyes, Greenwich St.,
   shoemaker (Navy)
Marshall, John, age 45, 1 mo. in U.S., wife & 4 children, far-
   mer (19-24 Oct. 1812)
Marshall, John, age 40, 10 years in U.S., wife, 36 Cedar St.,
   NYC, harness maker (20-25 July 1812); 6ft. 1in., age 43, light
   complex., light hair, brown eyes, Cedar St., harness (Navy)
Marshall, John, age 23, 9 years in U.S., NYC, merchant (28 July -
   2 Aug. 1812)
Marshall, John, 6ft., age 23, fair complex., fair hair, grey
   eyes, grocer (Navy) - probably same as above
Marshall, William, age 56, 6 years in U.S., 7 in family, 42
   Cross St., shoemaker (28 July - 2 Aug. 1812)
Marshall, William, age 25, 8 years in U.S., 42 Cross St., NYC,
   millwright (28 July - 2 Aug. 1812)
Marshall, William, 5ft. 3 3/4in., age 23, dark complex., black
   hair, dark eyes, Cross St., millwright (Navy) - perhaps same
   as the above
Martain, James, age 42, 12 years in U.S., wife & 4 children,
   Scipio, Cayuga Co., farmer, a cripple, applied 1812 (28 Sept. -
   3 Oct. & 12-17 Oct. 1812)
Martain, James, age 42, 8 years in U.S., wife, Montgomery, Orange
   Co., farmer (19-24 Oct. 1812)
Martin, Alexander, age 40, 11 mos. in U.S., wife & 6 children,
   Kingston, Ulster Co., weaver (19-24 Oct. 1812)
Martin, Alexander, age 29, 8 years in U.S., wife & 2 children,
   25 Augustus St., NYC, stone cutter (17-22 Aug. 1812); 5ft. 6in.,
   age 29, dark complex., dark hair, brown eyes, stone cutter
   (Navy)
Martin, Andrew, 5ft. 7in., age 19, fair complex., brown hair,
   grey eyes, Warren St., chair (Navy)
Martin, Daniel, 5ft. 7in., age 29, dark complex., dark hair,
   black eyes, Anthony St., labourer (Navy)
Martin, George, 5ft. 8in., age 35, light complex., brown hair,
   brown eyes, labourer (Navy)
Martin, George, age 30, 6 years in U.S., 470 Greenwich St., NYC,
   sawyer (20-25 July 1812)
Martin, George, age 26, 12 years in U.S., Richmond, Va., merchant
   (3-8 Aug. 1812)
Martin, George, 5ft. 7in., age 25, light complex., brown hair,
   hazel eyes, Maiden Lane, clerk (Navy)
Martin, James, age 27, 1 year in U.S., Greenwich St., NYC, mus-
   lin weaver (28 July - 2 Aug. 1812)
Martin, James, 5ft. 8in., age 26, light complex., light hair,
   blue eyes, weaver (Navy)
Martin, James R., age 31, 12 years in U.S., wife, Saratoga,
   cooper (17-22 Aug. 1812)
Martin, John, age 41, 6 years in U.S., Montgomery, Orange Co.,
   farmer (19-24 Oct. 1812)
Martin, John, age 34, 1 year in U.S., wife & child, 44 Hudson
   St., NYC, tailor (20-25 July 1812)
Martin, John, 5ft. 5in., age 36, dark complex., brown hair,
   brown eyes, Thomas St., tailor (Navy) - perhaps same as above
Martin, John, 5ft. 10in., age 23, brown complex., brown hair,
   blue eyes, Stanton St., sawyer (Navy)

Martin, John, 5ft. 10in., age 18, fair complex., fair hair, blue
  eyes, blacksmith (Navy)
Martin, Joseph, age 39, 2 years in U.S., 8 in family, Beaver St.,
  NYC, watchmaker (20-25 July 1812); 5ft. 7in., age 40, dark
  complex., dark hair, brown eyes, Catherine St., clockmaker
  (Navy)
Martin, Leonard, 5ft. 11in., age 36, dark complex., brown hair,
  blue eyes, carpenter (Navy)
Martin, Morris, 5ft. 8½in., age 28, light complex., fair hair,
  blue eyes, grocer (Navy)
Martin, Samuel, age 43, 12 years in U.S., wife & 2 children,
  Dryden, Tompkins Co., farmer (26-31 Oct. 1812)
Martin, Samuel, age 43, 12 years in U.S., wife & 2 children,
  Cato, Cayuga Co., farmer (12-17 Oct. 1812)
Martin, Stephen, 5ft. 6in., age 38, fair complex., black hair,
  blue eyes, Elm St., carpenter (Navy)
Martin, Thomas, age 24, 19 years in U.S., 232 Hester St., NYC,
  cordwainer (20-25 July 1812)
Marvereald, Richard, age 34, 10 years in U.S., wife & 3 child-
  ren, Stamford, Delaware Co., wool carder (12-17 Oct. 1812)
Mason, Thomas, age 29, 4 years in U.S., Connecticut, seaman (12-
  17 Oct. 1812)
Masey (?), John, 5ft. 7in., age 45, light complex., grey hair,
  blue eyes, Bowery, shoe (Navy)
Massey, Mathew, age 23, 10 mos. in U.S., Mamakating, Sullivan
  Co., tallow chandler (19-24 Oct. 1812)
Masterton, Henry, age 29, 1 year in U.S., wife & child, Goshen,
  Orange Co., laborer (19-24 Oct. 1812)
Masterton, Owen, 5ft. 8in., age 45, fair complex., fair hair,
  brown eyes, Anthony St., labourer (Navy)
Mathew, Edward, 5ft. 5in., age 42, dark complex., black hair,
  blue eyes, labourer (Navy)
Mathews, John, age 29, 2 years in U.S., wife & child, 9 Maiden
  Lane, NYC, boot- & shoemaker, applied 11 Aug. 1810 (13-18 Aug.
  1812); 5ft. 9½in., age 30, fair complex., dark hair, light
  eyes, Maiden Lane, boot (Navy)
Mathews, Patrick, age 19, 1 year in U.S., Monroe Works, Orange
  Co., cut nailor (17-22 Aug. 1812)
Mathews, Stephen, age 24, 1 year in U.S., wife & child, Kips
  Bay, laborer (3-8 Aug. 1812); 5ft. 8in., age 24, fair complex.,
  brown hair, grey eyes, Kips Bay, labourer (Navy)
Maurice, Thomas, 5ft. 7in., age 23, red complex., brown hair,
  brown eyes, Mercer St., ink (Navy)
Maxwell, James, 6ft. 3in., age 36, dark complex., brown hair,
  light eyes, gentleman (Navy)
Maxwell, John, Jr., age 32, 16 years in U.S., Charlton, Saratoga
  Co., farmer (31 Aug. - 5 Sept. 1812)
Maxwell, Thomas, age 31, 60 Courtlandt St., NYC, merchant (13-
  18 July 1812)
May, George, 5ft. 8½in., age 31, fair complex., dark hair, blue
  eyes, Read St., mason (Navy)
May, Lionel, age 43 on 6 July last, 9 years in U.S. on 2 Feb.
  next, wife & 5 children, Whitestown, Oneida Co., farmer (31
  Oct. 1812)
Mayer, Stephen, 5ft. 6in., age 38, dark complex., brown hair,
  grey eyes, Pearl St., tailor (Navy)
Mayo, Samuel, age 32, 20 years in U.S., wife & 4 children, 63
  Chatham St., NYC (20-25 July 1812)
Mayo, Samuel, 5ft. 7½in., age 33, dark complex., dark hair, dark
  eyes, Catherine St., upholsterer (Navy) - probably same as
  above
Mead, Owen, 5ft. 10in., age 34, dark complex., brown hair, brown
  eyes, gardener (Navy)
Meahan, Charles, 5ft. 9in., age 26, fair complex., brown hair,
  blue eyes, Greenwich St., gardener (Navy)

Meaghin, Michael, 5ft. 6in., age 35, ruddy complex., black hair, blue eyes, gardener (Navy)

Meahen, James, 5ft. 7in., age 29, dark complex., brown hair, dark eyes, Elm St., paver (Navy)

Mealy, John, age 18, 15 years in U.S., 17 Chatham St., NYC, copperplate printer (20-25 July 1812)

Mearns, Alexander, age 26, 6 years & 10 mos. in U.S., wife, Newburgh, Orange Co., mariner (14 Aug. & 17-22 Aug. 1812)

Medell, John, 5ft. 11 3/4in., age 25, light complex., brown hair, blue eyes, Mamaroneck, weaver (Navy)

Meek, Robert, age 27, 1 year & 4 mos. in U.S., wife & 2 children, Kingston, Ulster Co., weaver (19-24 Oct. 1812)

Megarey, Henry J., age 30, 11 years in U.S., wife & child, 103 Maiden Lane, NYC, stationer (20-25 July 1812)

Megivey, John, 5ft. 7in., age 20, light complex., dark hair, brown eyes, Bayard St., cordwainer (Navy)

Meigan (?), William, 5ft. 8in., age 43, fair complex., dark hair, blue eyes, Harman St., tailor (Navy)

Meighan, Mathew, age 20, 8 mos. in U.S., NYC, clerk (26-31 Oct. 1812); 5ft. 5in., age 20, fair complex., fair hair, dark eyes, labourer (Navy)

Mejiness, Edward, age 34, 1½ years in U.S., wife & 2 children, NYC (20-25 July 1812)

Meloy (?), Robert, age 49, 5ft. 5in., dark complex., dark hair, dark eyes, Charlotte St., tailor (Navy)

Mentland, William, 5ft. 7in., age 26, dark complex., brown hair, light eyes, Pump St., cordwainer (Navy)

Menugh (?), Martin, 5ft. 6in., age 38, dark complex., brown hair, brown eyes, Manhattan, labourer (Navy)

Menzies, James, age 19, 4 years in U.S., Johnstown, Montgomery Co., farmer (15 Sept. - 5 Oct. & 5-10 Oct. 1812)

Menzies, John, age 48, nearly 5 years in U.S., 5 children, Johnstown, Montgomery Co., stone mason (16 Feb. - 8 Mar. 1813)

Menzies, Robert, age 49, 10 years in U.S., wife & 7 children, Johnstown, Montgomery Co., farmer (11-17 & 17-22 Aug. 1812)

Mercer, John, 5ft. 10in., age 53, light complex., brown hair, blue eyes, Coffee House, oyster (Navy)

Merc...(illeg.), John, age 45, 3 years in U.S., wife & child, corner Oak & Roosevelt Sts., NYC, jeweler (20-25 July 1812)

Merchison, John, 5ft. 4in., age 24, light complex., dark hair, light eyes, West Farms, tailor (Navy)

Meredith, Hugh, age 52 Oct. next, 12 years in U.S. last July, wife & 6 children, Steuben, Oneida Co., farmer (29 Sept. & 28 Sept. - 3 Oct. 1812)

Meredith, John, age 44, 16 years in U.S., City of Albany, shoemaker (17-22 Aug. 1812)

Meredith, Richard, age 36, 3 years in U.S., 26 Elm St., NYC, carpenter (28 July - 2 Aug. 1812)

Merkel/Merkle, Jacob, age 72, 3 years in U.S., Manheim, Montgomery Co., gentleman (6 Oct. - 4 Nov. & 9-14 Nov. 1812)

Mervin, Alexander, 5ft. 11in., age 26, light complex., dark hair, grey eyes, Newburgh, Orange Co., boatman (Navy)

Meving, Mathew, age 20, 1 year & 6 mos. in U.S., Washington, Dutchess Co., spinner (12-17 Oct. 1812)

Miers, John, age 28, 2 years in U.S., wife, City of Albany, laborer, applied 1 Aug. 1811 (17-22 Aug. 1812)

Milbourne, Charles Cotton, age 56, 20 years in U.S., wife & 2 children, 45 Sugar Loaf St., NYC, artist (26-31 Oct. 1812); 5ft. 4in., age 58, ruddy complex., dark hair, dark eyes, Sugar Loaf St., painter (Navy)

Mill, John, 5ft. 11in., age 30, light complex., light hair, grey eyes, Greenwich St., schoolmaster (Navy)

Millen, James, age 26, 1 year in U.S., wife, 6 Greenwich St., NYC, weaver (2-7 Nov. 1812)

Millar, John, age 29, 8 years in U.S., Troy, Rensselaer Co.,
   grocer (20-25 July 1812)
Millen (possibly Miller?), William, 5ft. 10in., age 28, dark
   complex., brown hair, grey eyes, Pearl St., labourer (Navy)
Miller, Alexander, age 45, 1 year & 5 mos. in U.S., 9 children,
   93 Church St., NYC, cotton manufacturer (20-25 July 1812)
Miller, Alexander, 5ft. 8 3/4in., age 28, fair complex., sandy
   hair, grey eyes (Navy)
Miller, Andrew, age 31 next Sept., 2 years in U.S. on 1 Aug.
   last, Whitestown, Oneida Co., weaver (26 Aug. & 28 Sept. - 3
   Oct. 1812)
Miller, Andrew, age 30, 11 years in U.S., wife & child, corner
   Catherine & Bancker Sts., NYC, grocer (20-25 July 1812)
Miller, Church, 5ft. 7in., age 20, fair complex., dark hair,
   brown eyes, Oak St., tailor (Navy)
Miller, David, age 27 last Sept., 27 years in U.S. on 1 Aug.
   last, Whitestown, Oneida Co., weaver, from Scotland (26 Aug.
   & 28 Sept. - 3 Oct. 1812)
Miller, David, age 24, 5 years & 10 mos. in U.S., corner Elm &
   Anthony Sts., NYC, ship-carpenter (7-19 Dec. 1812)
Miller, Frederick, age 27, 5 mos. in U.S., NYC, merchant (26-31
   Oct. 1812)
Miller, George, 5ft. 10in., age 45, dark complex., black hair,
   black eyes, Henry St., grocer (Navy)
Miller, George, age 41, 1 year & 1 mo. in U.S., wife & child,
   NYC, grocer (10-15 Aug. 1812)
Miller, James, 5ft. 8in., age 48, dark complex., black hair,
   brown eyes, Greenwich St., marble (Navy)
Miller, James, 5ft. 10in., age 26, dark complex., dark hair,
   blue eyes, William St., weaver (Navy)
Miller, John, age 50, 7 years in U.S., 4 in family, 33 Chatham
   St., NYC, cabinetmaker (20-25 July 1812); 5ft. 7in., age 50,
   dark complex., dark hair, dark eyes, Harman St., cabinetmaker
   (Navy)
Miller, John, age 30, 10 years in U.S., wife & 2 children, Prince-
   ton, Schenectady Co., farmer (10-15 Aug. 1812)
Miller, John, age 30, 22 years in U.S., wife & 3 children, Bath,
   Steuben Co., farmer (25-31 Aug. & 7-12 Sept. 1812)
Miller, John, 5ft. 8in., age 20, light complex., light hair,
   grey eyes, Harman St., cabinetmaker (Navy)
Miller, John S., age 40, 5 years in U.S., wife, Chatham St., NYC,
   broker (20-25 July 1812); 5ft. 5½in., age 41, fair complex.,
   brown hair, black eyes, Chatham St., broker (Navy)
Miller, Robert, age 43, 22 years in U.S., Bath, Steuben Co.,
   laborer (25-31 Aug. & 7-12 Sept. 1812)
Miller, Robert, age 29 on 2 Oct. last, 8 years in U.S. on 12
   Nov. last, wife & 2 daughters, Utica, Oneida Co., cordwainer
   (26 Aug. & 28 Sept. - 3 Oct. 1812)
Miller, Simon, age 44, 23 years in U.S., wife & child, Newburgh,
   Orange Co., tallow chandler (19-24 Oct. 1812)
Miller, Thomas, age 33, 9 years in U.S., wife & 2 children, 334
   Greenwich St., NYC, cartman (20-25 July 1812); 5ft. 7in., age
   33, dark complex., brown hair, brown eyes, Greenwich St., cart-
   man (Navy)
Miller, William, 5ft. 6½in., age 40, brown complex., brown hair,
   blue eyes, Chew (?) St., rigger (Navy)
Milligan, Samuel, 5ft. 7in., age 19, fair complex., light hair,
   blue eyes, shoemaker (Navy)
Milligan, Thomas, 5ft. 9in., age 28, dark complex., dark hair,
   grey eyes, Manhattan, labourer (Navy)
Millikin, David, 5ft. 7in., age 30, fair complex., brown hair,
   blue eyes, weaver (Navy)
Mills, George, 5ft. 7in., age 39, fair complex., fair hair,
   brown eyes, schoolmaster (Navy)

Mills, George, age 38, 7 years in U.S., wife & 4 children, Tap-
pan, Rockland Co., teacher (31 Aug. - 5 Sept. 1812)
Mills, Henry, age 31, 8 years in U.S., 2 in family, 93 Broad St.,
NYC, cartman (31 Aug. - 5 Sept. 1812); 5ft. 9in., age 31, dark
complex., brown hair, brown eyes, cartman (Navy)
Mills, Richard, age 18, 5 years in U.S., Charlotte St., NYC,
seaman (20-25 July 1812)
Mills, William, age 32, 18 years in U.S., 2 children, Saratoga,
shoemaker (17-22 Aug. 1812)
Millwood, Samuel, age 35, 5 years in U.S., wife & 3 children,
Brooklyn, Long Island, master armourer at the navy yard (20-
25 July 1812)
Mingham, Rob., 5ft. 8in., age 29, dark complex., black hair,
black eyes, cartman (Navy)
Minnen, Hugh, age 42, 7 years in U.S., wife & child, Montgomery,
Orange Co., weaver (19-24 Oct. 1812)
Minus, David, age 36, 7 years in U.S., wife & child, 72 Wall St.,
NYC, grocer (13-18 July 1812); 5ft. 10in., age 36, fair com-
plex., light hair, blue eyes, Wall St., grocer (Navy)
Missey, Henry, age 21, 5 years in U.S., Newburgh, Orange Co.,
laborer (19-24 Oct. 1812)
Missing, John, age 39, 10 years in U.S., wife & 6 children, Henry
St., NYC, teacher (20-25 July 1812); 5ft. 4in., age 40, dark
complex., dark hair, dark eye, Henry St., teacher (Navy)
Mitchell, Francis, 5ft. 9in., age 35, light complex., brown hair,
blue eyes, Orange St., baker (Navy)
Mitchell, John, age 33, 17 years in U.S., wife & 6 children, NYC,
sawyer (28 July - 2 Aug. 1812)
Mitchell, John, age 23, 5 years in U.S., wife, Orange St., NYC,
painter & glazier (20-25 July 1812)
Mitchell, John D., age 33, 8 years in U.S., NYC, schoolmaster
(9-14 Nov. 1812)
Mitchell, Robert, age 34, 5 years in U.S., wife & 2 children,
25 Bowery Lane, NYC, thread manufacturer (20-25 July 1812);
5ft. 11in., age 33, fair complex., grey hair, light eyes,
thread manufacturer (Navy)
Mitchell, Thomas, age 26, 6 years in U.S., wife, 24 Harman St.,
NYC, cooper (9-14 Nov. 1812); 5ft. 10in., age 26, fair complex.,
sandy hair, blue eyes, cooper (Navy)
Mitchell, William, 5ft. 9in., age 27, brown complex., dark hair,
blue eyes, Mulberry St., blacksmith (Navy)
Mitchell, William, 5ft. 8in., age 27, light complex., light hair,
blue eyes, removed from NYC (Navy) - probably same as the
above
Mitchell, William, age 25, 11 years in U.S., NYC, coach maker
(28 July - 2 Aug. 1812)
Mitchell, William, 5ft. 7½in., age 26, red complex., brown hair,
brown eyes, John St., coachman (Navy) - perhaps same as the
above
Moffat, Henry, 5ft. 6in., age 55, brown complex., brown hair,
brown eyes, Greenwich St., weaver (Navy)
Moffat, Patrick, 5ft. 8in., age 30, fair complex., brown hair,
blue eyes, Division St., music (Navy)
Moffat, Richard, 5ft. 7in., age 18, fair complex., dark hair,
blue eyes, labourer (Navy)
Moffet, William, age 29, 5 years in U.S., wife, 376 Greenwich
St., NYC, cartman (28 July - 2 Aug. 1812); 5ft. 10in., age 30,
fair complex., fair hair, blue eyes, cartman (Navy)
Moffet, William, age 29, 5 years in U.S., 109 Washington St.,
NYC boarding house keeper (10-15 Aug. 1812)
Moffit, William, 5ft. 8 3/4in., age 29, dark complex., dark hair,
grey eyes, Washington St., victualer (Navy) - perhaps the same
as the above
Moffitt, John, age 29, 11 years in U.S., Mayfield, Montgomery
Co., weaver (3-14 & 21-26 Sept. 1812)

Moffitt, William, age 63, 11 years in U.S., wife, Mayfield, Montgomery Co., weaver (18-24 Aug. & 31 Aug. - 5 Sept. 1812)
Mollan, William J., age 19 on 29 Dec. 1812, in U.S. since 15
Dec. 1809, Utica, Oneida Co., from Monaghan, Ireland (10 Aug.
& 17-22 Aug. 1812)
Mollery, Patrick, 5ft. 5in., age 20, fair complex., dark hair,
blue eyes, stone cutter (Navy)
Mollock, William, age 34, 10 years in U.S., wife & child, Sche-
nectady, farmer (24-29 Aug. 1812)
Monagan, William, age 42, 15 years & 10 mos. in U.S., wife & 3
children, Wallkill, Orange Co,, distiller (21 Dec. 1812 - 23
Jan. 1813)
Monaghan, James, age 27, 18 years in U.S., wife & 2 children,
Scipio, Cayuga Co., farmer (28 Sept. - 3 Oct. 1812)
Monahan, Patrick, 5ft. 6in., age 49, light complex., light hair,
blue eyes, Front St., grocer (Navy)
Monahan, Patrick, age 35, 7 years in U.S., wife & 4 children,
116 Lombardy St., NYC, tobacconist (20-25 July 1812)
Monclaw (?), George, Sr., 5ft. 8in., age 57, dark complex., dark
hair, dark eyes, Duane St., grocer (Navy)
Monegan, Patrick, 5ft. 6in,, age 47, light complex., light hair,
blue eyes, grocer (Navy)
Montcraf (?), William, 5ft. 9in., age 30, dark complex., brown
hair, black eyes, sawyer (Navy)
Monell, Edward, age 28, 3 years in U.S., wife & 2 children, City
of Albany, laborer (17-22 Aug. 1812)
Monghan, Richard, 5ft. 7in., age 39, light complex., light hair,
blue eyes, labourer (Navy)
Monighan, Patrick, age 48, 5 years in U.S., wife & 2 children,
153 Front St., NYC, grocer (20-25 July 1812) - apparently the
same as the Patrick Monahan, grocer, above
Monilaw/Monilaws, George, age 27, 4 years in U.S., 269 Greenwich St., NYC, grocer, applied 31 Mar. 1810 (20-25 July 1812);
5ft. 7in., age 28, fair complex., dark hair, light eyes, Hudson St., grocer (Navy)
Monnegan, William, age 42, 15 years & 10 mos. in U.S., wife & 3
children, Wallkill, Orange Co., distiller - same as the Wm.
Monagan above
Monson, Robert, 4ft. 4in., age 33, light complex., black hair,
grey eyes, Greenwich St., grocer (Navy)
Montgomery, Andrew, 5ft. 9in., age 26, light complex., dark hair,
brown eyes, weaver (Navy)
Montgomery, Henry, age 26, 11 mos. in U.S., wife & child, Mamakating, Sullivan Co., wheelwright (19-24 Oct. 1812)
Montgomery, James, age 32, 7 years & 9 mos. in U.S., wife & 2
servants, merchant, applied 24 Aug. 1807 (3-8 Aug. 1812)
Montgomery, James, 5ft. 6in., age 32, fair complex., red hair,
grey eyes, Henry St., harness cleaner (Navy)
Montgomery, James, 5ft. 11in., age 28, dark complex., dark hair,
blue eyes, Hester St., weaver (Navy)
Montgomery, John, 5ft. 8in., age 52, dark complex., brown hair,
dark eyes, tinman, Union Air Furnace (Navy)
Montgomery, John B., age 27, 2 years in U.S., 160 William St.,
NYC, grocer (20-25 July 1812); 5ft. 5in., age 27, fair complex.,
brown hair, grey eyes, Maiden Lane, grocer (Navy)
Montgomery, Robert, age 27, 1 year & 9 mos. in U.S., wife & 2
children, Newark, N.J., tanner, applied 1 June 1811 (3-8 Aug.
1812)
Montgomery, Samuel, age 38, 10 mos. in U.S., Schenectady, physician (31 Aug. - 5 Sept. 1812)
Montgomery, William, age 17, 4 mos. in U.S., 160 William St.,
clerk, applied 6 Apr. 1812 (13-18 July 1812); 5ft. 5½in., age
18, dark complex., brown hair, grey eyes, Maiden Lane, accountant (Navy); removed from NYC to Catskill, Greene Co. (Navy)

NEW YORK 181

Mooney, Charles, age 30, 7 years in U.S., wife & 3 children, 83
Mott St., NYC, grocer (20-25 July 1812)
Mooney, James, 5ft. 3in., age 60, fair complex., grey hair, la-
bourer (Navy)
Mooney, James, 5ft. 6in,, age 34, fair complex., fair hair, Elm
St., labourer (Navy)
Mooney, Larance, age 45, 14 years in U.S., Greenwich St., NYC,
farmer (14-19 Sept. 1812)
Mooney, Thomas, 5ft. 7in., age 26, fair complex., dark hair,
dark eyes, Chapple St., coachman (Navy)
Mooney, William, 5ft. 10in., age 38, light complex., brown hair,
grey eyes, Greenwich St., saddler (Navy)
Moor, William, age 22, 8 mos. in U.S., Montgomery, Orange Co.,
laborer (19-24 Oct. 1812)
Moore, Adam, age 28, 6 mos. in U.S., wife & 2 children, 98 Murray St., NYC, laborer (20-25 July 1812)
Moore, Arthur, age 37, 9 years in U.S., 5 in family, corner Hudson & Anthony Sts., NYC, house-carpenter, applied 5 July 1810
(3-8 Aug. 1812); 5ft. 7½in., age 37, dark complex., dark hair,
blue eyes, Lespinard St., carpenter (Navy)
Moore, Francis, 5ft. 7in., age 28, dark complex., dark hair,
dark eyes, labourer (Navy)
Moore, John, 5ft. 6½in., age 42, dark complex., black hair, grey
eyes, Water St., grocer (Navy)
Moore, John, 5ft. 8in., age 39, light complex., light hair, blue
eyes, North Hempstead, Queens Co., weaver (Navy)
Moore, John, 5ft. 11in., age 32, light complex., brown hair,
blue eyes, Bloomingdale, farmer (Navy)
Moore, Joseph, (age not given), 2½ years in U.S., Bowery, NYC,
shoemaker (3-8 Aug. 1812); 5ft. 7in., age 26, dark complex.,
brown hair, grey eyes, Bowery, shoemaker (Navy)
Moore, Mark, age 45, 12 years in U.S., wife & 5 children, 24
Harman St., NYC, grocer, applied July 1812 (10-15 Aug. 1812);
6ft. 1in., age 46, brown complex., brown hair, brown eyes,
Harman St., hatter - are these two men the same?
Moore, Parker, 5ft. 7 3/4in., age 38, red complex., fair hair,
grey eyes, mason (Navy)
Moore, Richard, 5ft. 7in., age 30, dark complex., dark hair,
dark eyes, gardener (Navy)
Moore, Thomas, age 32, 7 years & 3 mos. in U.S., wife & 3 child-
ren, Colonie, Albany Co., slater (17-22 Aug. 1812)
Moore, Thomas H., age 37, 12 years in U.S., wife & 2 children,
17 Anthony St., NYC, carpenter (20-25 July 1812); 5ft. 6in.,
light complex., dark hair, blue eyes, Anthony St., carpenter
(Navy)
Moore, William, 5ft. 8½in, age 28, dark complex., dark hair,
blue eyes, sawyer (Navy)
Moore, William, 5ft. 8in., age 27, fair complex., dark hair,
blue eyes, Bloomingdale, labourer (Navy)
Moore, William, 5ft. 5in., age 25, dark complex., brown hair,
blue eyes, engineer (Navy)
Moorhead, John, age 35, 2 years & 6 mos. in U.S., wife & 6 children, Montgomery, Orange Co., blacksmith (19-24 Oct. 1812)
Moorhead, John, age 26, 5 years in U.S., wife, NYC, cartman (28
July - 2 Aug. 1812); 5ft. 11in., age 26, light complex., flax.
hair, blue eyes, Broome St., cartman (Navy)
Morehead, John, 5ft. 10in., age 52, light complex., flax. hair,
brown eyes, cartman (Navy)
Morehead, Robert, age 37, 10½ years in U.S., 30 Pine St., NYC,
baker (20-25 July 1812); 5ft. 8in., age 39, fair complex.,
brown hair, blue eyes, Pine St., baker (Navy)
Moran, John, age 35, 3 years in U.S., NYC, tobacconist (2-7 Nov.
1812); 5ft. 9in., age 37, fair complex., dark hair, brown eyes,
Water St., tobacco (Navy)

Moran, Michael, age 46, 1 year in U.S., 245 William St., NYC,
  carpenter (28 July - 2 Aug. 1812)
Moran, Nicholas, 5ft. 10in., age 46, fair complex., brown hair,
  brown eyes, brush (Navy)
Moran, Richard, 5ft. 11½in., age 22, fair complex., dark hair,
  brown eyes, Pump St., paver (Navy)
Mordick (?), Mathew, 5ft. 8in., age 22, light complex., brown
  hair, grey eyes, Clinton Town, Dutchess Co., weaver (Navy)
Moreland, Henry, 5ft. 5in., age 34, light complex., grey hair,
  brown eyes, grocer (Navy) - see Henry Morland below.
Morewood, Alexander, 6ft., age 45, dark complex., brown hair,
  dark eyes, Greenwich St., marble (Navy)
Morgan, Alexander, 5ft. 9in., age 45, dark complex., dark hair,
  dark eyes, blacksmith (Navy)
Morgan, Alexander, age 24, 1 year & 8 mos. in U.S., 4 Lumber St.,
  blacksmith (28 July - 2 Aug. 1812)
Morgan, Charles, age 28 on 2 Dec. last, 8 years in U.S. on 10
  Nov. last, wife, Utica, Oneida Co., cordwainer (26 Aug. 1812);
  same, except that residence is given as Whitestown (28 Sept. -
  3 Oct. 1812)
Morgan, Felix, age 46, 11 years in U.S., wife & 5 children, New
  Windsor, Orange Co., laborer (19-24 Oct. 1812)
Morgan, Hugh, age 28, 4 years in U.S., Newburgh, Orange Co.,
  joiner (19-24 Oct. 1812)
Morgan, Patrick, age 47, 11 years in U.S., wife & 2 children,
  Newburgh, Orange Co., weaver (19-24 Oct. 1812)
Morgan, Patrick, age 31, 11 years in U.S., Newburgh, Orange Co.,
  laborer (19-24 Oct. 1812)
Morgan, Thomas, age 47, 11 years in U.S., 9 in family, Rhinebeck,
  Dutchess Co., gardener (28 July - 2 Aug. 1812)
Morgan, William, age 43, 5 years in U.S., wife & 2 children, 83
  Harman St., NYC, tailor (28 July - 2 Aug. 1812)
Morland, Henry, age 33, 8 years in U.S., wife & child, 1 Oliver
  St., NYC, storekeeper, applied May 1810 (13-18 July 1812)
Morland, James, age 42, 18 years in U.S., Seneca, Ontario Co.,
  weaver (5-25 & 24-29 Aug. 1812)
Morni (?), John, 5ft. 8½in., age 50, fair complex., brown hair,
  grey eyes, Porter House (Navy)
Morno, Peter J., age 24, 3 years in U.S., 144 Water St., clerk
  (13-18 July 1812)
Morris, Edward, age 42, 9 years in U.S., wife, NYC, innkeeper
  (20-25 July 1812)
Morris, James, age 38, 8 years in U.S., wife & 3 children, Clin-
  ton, Dutchess Co., weaver (12-17 Oct. 1812)
Morris, John, age 48, 8 years in U.S., wife & 2 children, NYC,
  grocer, applied 29 Aug. 1804 (20-25 July 1812)
Morris, John, age 30, 15 years in U.S., Hamilton, Madison Co.,
  hatter (26-31 Oct. 1812)
Morris, John, age 27, 2 years in U.S., wife, Bloomingdale, farmer (10-15 Aug. 1812)
Morris, Morris W., 5ft. 7½in., age 24, fair complex., fair hair,
  brown eyes, Division St., turner (Navy)
Morriss (?), William, 5ft. 6in., age 46, dark complex., dark
  hair, blue eyes, Fourth St., baker (Navy)
Morris, William, 5ft. 4½in., age 21, fair complex., fair hair,
  grey eyes, painter (Navy)
Morrison, Andrew, age 46, 15 years & 1 mo. in U.S., wife & 3
  children, Goshen, Orange Co., weaver (19-24 Oct. 1812)
Morrison, Benjamin, 5ft. 2½in., age 23, light complex., dark
  hair, brown eyes, saddler (Navy)
Morrison, Daniel, age 33, 10 years in U.S., Clinton, Dutchess
  Co., laborer (12-17 Oct. 1812)
Morrison, Daniel, age 33, 10 years in U.S., wife & 3 children,
  NYC, cut nail manufacturer (28 July - 2 Aug. 1812); 5ft. 9in.,
  dark complex., brown hair, grey eyes, Hester St., nailor (Navy)

Morrison, James, 5ft. 7in., age 46, fair complex., brown hair,
grey eyes, tobacco (Navy)

Morrison, John, 5ft. 7in., age 40, light complex., grey hair,
grey eyes, Jones St., calico (Navy)

Morrison, John, age 20, 17 years in U.S., NYC, watchmaker (20-
25 July 1812); 5ft. 4½in., age 21, light complex., light hair,
light eyes, Cherry St., watchmaker (Navy)

Morrison, Neal, age 28, 7 years in U.S., wife, corner Bancker
& East George Sts., NYC, grocer; 5ft. 8in., age 28, grocer
(Navy)

Morrison, Neal, 5ft. 8in., age 25, brown complex., black hair,
blue eyes, grocer (Navy)

Morrison, Robert, age 31, 11 years in U.S., wife & child, 386
Greenwich St., NYC, grocer (17-22 Aug. 1812)

Morrison, Samuel, age 36, 7 years in U.S., wife & 4 children,
corner Water & Walnut Sts., NYC, grocer (13-18 July 1812)

Morrison, Samuel, 5ft. 5in., age 34, fair complex., dark hair,
light eyes, Walnut St., carpenter (Navy)

Morrison, Samuel, 5ft. 8in., age 28, brown complex., brown hair,
black eyes, Middle Road, labourer (Navy)

Morrison, William, 5ft. 8in., age 23, dark complex., dark hair,
grey eyes, leather dresser (Navy)

Morrisy, William, age 29, 5½ years in U.S., NYC, merchant (28
July - 2 Aug. 1812); 5ft. 6in., age 29, fair complex., brown
hair, dark eyes, Greenwich St., clerk (Navy)

Morrow, George, age 30, 7 years in U.S., wife, Montgomery, Orange
Co., farmer (19-24 Oct. 1812)

Morrow, James, age 35, 1 year & 3 mos. in U.S., wife, New Windsor, Orange Co., whitesmith (19-24 Oct. 1812)

Morrow, John, age 68, 19 years in U.S., wife & 5 children, Milton, Saratoga Co., farmer (24-29 Aug. 1812)

Morrow, John, age 24, 1 year in U.S., Newburgh, Orange Co., laborer (19-24 Oct. 1812)

Morrow, John, age 22, 3 mos in U.S., Cross St., NYC, cotton
manufacturer (28 July - 2 Aug. 1812); 5ft. 8in., age 22, red
complex., brown hair, blue eyes, manufacturer (Navy)

Morrow, Robert, 5ft. 7½in., age 19, fair complex., brown hair,
light eyes, dyer (Navy)

Morrow, William, age 35, 6 years in U.S., Wallkill, Orange Co.,
laborer (19-24 Oct. 1812)

Morrow, William, age 23, 1 year & 3 mos. in U.S., New Windsor,
Orange Co., shoemaker (19-24 Oct. 1812)

Mortimer, Benjamin, 5ft. 11¼in., age 45, fair complex., dark
hair, dark eyes, preacher (Navy)

Motley, Peter, 5ft. 5in., age 21, dark complex., brown hair,
brown eyes, stone (Navy)

Mowbray, Philip, age 30, 6 years & 2 mos. in U.S., wife, Montgomery, Orange Co., schoolmaster (19-24 Oct. 1812)

Muir, Robert, age 22, 6 years in U.S., Aurelius, Washington Co.,
clerk to a merchant (21-27 Dec. 1812 & 21 Dec. 1812 - 23 Jan.
1813)

Muirs, Henry, age 56, 20 years in U.S., wife & 7 children, Schoharie, farmer (24-29 Aug. 1812)

Mulden (or Muldon), Michael, age 34, 6 years in U.S., wife & 2
sons, Hudson, Columbia Co., merchant, applied May 1808 (17-22
Aug. 1812)

Mulhearn (?), Peter, age 39, fair complex., brown hair, blue
eyes, labourer, 5ft. 10in. (Navy)

Mulholm, Peter, 5ft. 9in., age 23, sandy complex., red hair,
grey eyes, weaver (Navy)

Mullen, Michael, age 58, 33 years in U.S., wife & 6 children,
Shawangunk, Ulster Co., farmer (19-24 Oct. 1812)

Mullender, Isaac, Jr., age 30, 18 years in U.S., 4 in family,
Seneca, Ontario Co., farmer (28 July - 2 Aug. 1812)

Mulligan, Archibald, age 47, 11 years in U.S., wife, New Windsor,
    Orange Co., shoemaker (19-24 Oct. 1812)
Mulligan, J., 5ft. 6in., age 34, fair complex., brown hair, brown
    eyes, John St., shoemaker (Navy)
Mulligan, Owen, 5ft. 7in., age 26, brown complex., brown hair,
    brown eyes, Henry St., labourer (Navy)
Molonny, John, 5ft. 8in., age 37, dark complex., dark hair,
    brown eyes, Augustus St., labourer (Navy)
Mullowney, John, age 36, 5 years in U.S., wife & 3 sons in Bal-
    timore, 48 Duane St., NYC, laborer (28 July - 2 Aug. 1812) -
    possibly the same as the above.
Mullony, Owen, 5ft. 8in., age 40, dark complex., dark hair, grey
    eyes, Broadway, coachman (Navy)
Mulnix, James, age 21, 1 year & 2 mos. in U.S., Newburgh, Orange
    Co., carpenter (14 Aug. & 17-22 Aug. 1812)
Mulock, Benjamin, age 38, 11 years in U.S., wife & 4 children,
    Fishkill, Dutchess Co., farmer (12-17 Oct. 1812)
Mulvey, Roger, age 43, 8 years in U.S., wife, 15 Fayette St.,
    NYC, grocer (20-25 July 1812); 5ft. 8in., age 44, florid com-
    plex., white hair, hazel eyes, Fayette St. grocer (Navy)
Mulvin, Johnson, 5ft. 8in., age 26, fair complex., fair hair,
    grey eyes, Henry St., cartman (Navy)
Mulyneaux, Daniel, age 34, 3 mos. in U.S., wife & 2 children,
    Newburgh, Orange Co., carpenter (19-24 Oct. 1812)
Mumford, George, age 32, 3 years in U.S., Geneva, Ontario Co.,
    brewer (3-8 Aug. 1812)
Munell (?), Robert, 5ft. 5in., age 24, fair complex., fair hair,
    brown eyes, Bancker St., grocer (Navy)
Munn, David, age 43, 2 years in U.S., wife & 5 children, Mama-
    kating, Sullivan Co., farmer (19-24 Oct. 1812)
Munrow, Archibald, age 44, 12 years in U.S., Schenectady, labo-
    rer (31 Aug. - 5 Sept. 1812)
Munson, John, 5ft. 8in., age 28, dark complex., dark hair, brown
    eyes, Greenwich St. (Navy)
Munson, Thomas, 6ft., age 30, fair complex., dark hair, brown
    eyes, Cherry St., grocer (Navy)
Murchison, John, age 34, 1 year in U.S., Westchester Co., tailor
    (20-25 July 1812)
Murdock, John, age 29, 4 mos. in U.S., Kingston, Ulster Co.,
    weaver (7 Sept. & 19-24 Oct. 1812)
Murdock, Philip, 5ft. 6in., age 27, brown complex., brown hair,
    grey eyes, Catherine St., maltster (Navy)
Murloue (?), Christian, age 24, 1 year & 9 mos. in U.S., Bayard
    St., NYC, baker (28 July - 2 Aug. 1812)
Murphy, Anthony, 5ft. 11½in., age 26, brown complex., dark hair,
    blue eyes, labourer (Navy)
Murphy, Bernard, age 29, 5 years in U.S., wife & 3 children, West
    Farms, Westchester Co., stone mason (7-19 Dec. 1812)
Murphy, Bernard, 5ft. 7in., age 26, light complex., dark hair,
    dark eyes, Elm St., baker (Navy)
Murphy, Edward, age 32, 8 years in U.S., wife & 4 children, 26
    Stone St., NYC, carpenter (20-25 July 1812)
Murphy, G., 5ft. 6½in., age 28, fair complex., brown hair, brown
    eyes, Water St., chandler (Navy)
Murphy, Hugh, 5ft. 8in., age 25, fair complex., red hair, blue
    eyes, mechanic (Navy)
Murphy, James, age 35, 9 years in U.S., Ellies (?) Island or West
    Harford (Harford in Cortland Co.?), laborer (20-25 July 1812)
Murphy, John, age 39, 9 years in U.S., wife & 2 children, Clin-
    ton, Dutchess Co., laborer (12-17 Oct. 1812)
Murphy, John, age 27, 3 years in U.S., NYC, blacksmith (20-25
    July 1812)
Murphy, John, age 23, 6 years in U.S., 204 Bancker St., NYC,
    clerk (20-25 July 1812)

Murphy, John, age 20, 3 mos. in U.S., wife, Hudson, Columbia Co.,
    weaver (3-8 Aug. 1812)
Murphy, Lawrence, age 37, 3 years in U.S., 6 children, 75 Bancker
    St., NYC, grocer (28 July - 2 Aug. 1812)
Murphy, Michael, age 34, 13 years in U.S., Clermont, Columbia
    Co., teacher, applied July 1808 (12 Sept. & 14-19 Sept. 1812)
Murphy, Owen, 5ft. 10½in., age 37, fair complex., brown hair,
    grey eyes, grocer (Navy)
Murphy, William, 6ft. 1in., age 54, light complex., light hair,
    blue eyes, Burling Slip, labourer (Navy)
Murran, Thomas, age 29, 1½ years in U.S., wife & 2 children, 71
    Cherry St., NYC, tea & wine store (13-18 July 1812)
Murray, Alexander, age 30, 6 years in U.S., Duane St., NYC,
    grocer (20-25 July 1812); 6ft., age 31, dark complex., brown
    hair, black eyes, Duane St., grocer (Navy)
Murray, John, age 35, 16 years in U.S., Hudson, Columbia Co.,
    shoemaker (10-15 Aug. 1812)
Murray, John, age 33, 8 years in U.S., wife, 305 Broadway, NYC,
    merchant, applied 18 July 1812 (3-8 Aug. 1812)
Murray, John, age 28, 6½ years in U.S., wife, NYC, shipwright
    (20-25 July 1812)
Murray, John, 5ft. 6½in., age 28, fair complex., brown hair,
    blue eyes, servant (Navy)
Murray, John, 5ft. 8in., age 25, fair complex., light hair, blue
    eyes, Division St., shipwright (Navy)
Murray, John, age 22, 9 mos. in U.S., Duanesburgh, Schenectady
    Co., carpenter (10-15 Aug. 1812)
Murray, John, 5ft. 4½in., age 19, light complex., brown hair,
    blue eyes, Greenwich St., clerk (Navy)
Murray, John, age 18, 16 years in U.S., 40 Barclay St., NYC,
    accountant (20-25 July 1812)
Murray, Robert, 5ft. 11in., age 24, fair complex., fair hair,
    brown eyes, Pump St., labourer (Navy)
Murray, S., 5ft. 8in., age 34, fair complex., dark hair, brown
    eyes, retail (Navy)
Murray, Terence, age 28, 9 years in U.S., wife, 84 Fair St.,
    NYC, cordwainer (20-25 July 1812)
Murray, William, 5ft. 8in., age 27, light complex., auburn hair,
    blue eyes, shoe (Navy)
Murrell, Robert, age 25, 9 years in U.S., corner Charlotte &
    Bancker Sts., NYC, grocer (20-25 July 1812)
Murtock, William, 5ft. 10in., age 35, fair complex., black hair,
    blue eyes, labourer (Navy)
Myers, John, 5ft. 9½in., age 23, fair complex., brown hair, blue
    eyes, Cherry St., brass (Navy)
Myers, Stephen, age 38, 15 years in U.S., wife, 361 Pearl St.,
    NYC, tailor (3-8 Aug. 1812)
Myher, John, 6ft., age 33, light complex., brown hair, blue eyes,
    statuary (Navy)
Nail, James, age 19, 11 weeks in U.S., Newburgh, Orange Co.,
    laborer (19-24 Oct. 1812)
Napier, William, age 23, 9 years in U.S., 64 Chapel St., NYC,
    mariner, applied 9 June 1812 (20-25 July 1812)
Naren, Mathew, 5ft. 8in., age 48, dark complex., dark hair,
    black eyes, labourer (Navy)
Nattrass, John, 6 years in U.S., wife & 2 children, Swartekill
    (?), Ulster Co., farmer (21 Dec. 1812 - 23 Jan. 1813)
Naylor, Robert, age 50, 6 mos. in U.S., NYC, merchant (20-25
    July 1812)
Neadless, Francis, 5ft. 7in., age 25, light complex., light hair,
    grey eyes, Catherine Lane, labourer (Navy)
Neilson, James, 5ft. 6½in., age 26, fair complex., dark hair,
    grey eyes, Mott St., labourer (Navy)
Neilson, John, age 50, 15 mos. in U.S., wife & 8 children, Hud-
    son, Columbia Co., weaver (10-15 Aug. 1812)

Neilson, John, 5ft. 5in., age 39, dark complex., dark hair, blue
  eyes, William St., tailor (Navy)
Neilson, John, 5ft. 10in., age 34, dark complex., dark hair,
  grey eyes, Reed St., grocer (Navy)
Neilson, Joseph, 5ft. 7in., age 27, light complex., brown hair,
  blue eyes, teacher (Navy)
Neilson, Thomas, 5ft. 9in., age 32, dark complex., dark hair,
  grey eyes, Reed St., grocer (Navy)
Neilson, William, 5ft. 4½in., age 51, dark complex., dark hair,
  black eyes, butcher (Navy)
Neing (?), James, 5ft. 11in., age 37, pale complex., brown hair,
  brown eyes, cooper (Navy)
Nelis, Joseph, 5ft. 6in., age 30, fair complex., brown hair,
  brown eyes, Anthony St., labourer (Navy)
Nelson, John, age 23, 8 years & 10 mos. in U.S., wife & 2 child-
  ren, New Windsor, Orange Co., farmer (19-24 Oct. 1812)
Nelson, John, 5ft. 6in., age 19, light complex., light hair,
  grey eyes, Maiden Lane, tailor (Navy)
Nelson, Joseph, age 30, 1 day in U.S., wife, Tontine Coffee
  House, NYC, merchant (21-26 Sept. 1812)
Nelson, Robert, age 28, 18 years in U.S., wife & 3 children,
  Dryden, Tompkins Co., farmer (20-25 Oct. & 9-14 Nov. 1812)
Nelson, William, age 60, 18 years in U.S., wife & 2 children,
  Dryden, Tompkins Co., farmer (20-25 Oct. & 9-14 Nov. 1812)
Nelson, William, age 51, 12 years in U.S., wife & child, 150
  Division St., NYC, butcher (14-19 Sept. 1812)
Nelson, William, Jr., age 18, 18 years in U.S., Dryden, Tompkins
  Co., farmer (20-25 Oct. & 9-14 Nov. 1812)
Nelus (?), Barney, 5ft., age 28, light complex., brown hair,
  grey eyes, Anthony St., mason (Navy)
Nesbit, Robert, age 37, 5ft. 3in., dark complex., brown hair,
  brown eyes, Nassau St., chandler (Navy)
Nesbit, Robert, age 31, 12 years in U.S., 4 in family, 108 Beek-
  man St., NYC, tallow chandler & grocer (20-25 July 1812)
Nesbitt, Hugh, 5ft. 6in., age 26, dark complex., black hair,
  blue eyes, Orange St., grocer (Navy)
Neville, Peter, 5ft. 9½in., age 23, fair complex., brown hair,
  blue eyes, Exchange (Navy)
Nevin, Archibald, 5ft. 3in., age 25, fair complex., light hair,
  brown eyes, tavern (Navy)
Nevins, John, age 22, 3 years in U.S., 63 Greenwich St., NYC,
  merchant, applied June 1812 (20-25 July 1812)
Newhouse, John, age 22, 16 years & 5 mos. in U.S., wife & child,
  Poughkeepsie, Dutchess Co., cooper (12-17 Oct. 1812)
Newland, John, age 39 on 18 Apr. last, 5 years in U.S. on 15
  Sept. 1812, wife & 8 children, Utica, Oneida Co., cordwainer,
  naturalized 5 Aug. 1812 in Justices Court in New York (26 Aug.
  & 28 Sept. - 3 Oct. 1812)
Newland, Ridgeway, age 47, 2 mos. in U.S., wife & 3 children,
  Newburgh, Orange Co., farmer (19-24 Oct. 1812); 5ft. 6in.,
  fair complex., dark hair, blue eyes, Newburgh, gardener (Navy)
Newman, Charles, age 29, 1 year & 9 mos. in U.S., Hudson, Colum-
  bia Co., wool manufacturer (17-22 Aug. 1812)
Newman, John P., age 30, 6 years in U.S., 66 Cedar St., NYC,
  grocer, applied 18 July 1808 (20-25 July 1812)
Newport, George, 5ft. 8in., age 38, fair complex., brown hair,
  blue eyes, removed from NYC to Red Hook, Dutchess Co. (Navy)
Newport, George, age 30, 8 years & 10 mos. in U.S., wife & child,
  NYC, merchant & grocer (20-25 July 1812)
Newport, George, 5ft. 9in., age 30, fair complex., brown hair,
  brown eyes, clerk (Navy)
Newton, John, 5ft. 9½in., age 40, fair complex., brown hair,
  grey eyes, brick (Navy)
Neyle, Thomas Alward, 9 years in U.S., NYC, teacher (20-25 July
  1812); 5ft. 10in., age 25, light complex., brown hair, blue(Navy)

Niblo, John, 5ft. 3in., age 25, fair complex., brown hair, blue
   eyes, labourer (Navy)
Nice, Archibald, 5ft. 9in., age 36, fair complex., brown hair,
   grey eyes, potter (Navy)
Nicholls, Anthony Edward, age 29, 9 years in U.S., wife & 2 children, 163 William St., NYC, shipwright (20-25 July 1812);
   Nicholls, Edward, 5ft. 6½in., age 29, dark complex., brown
   hair, brown eyes, Cheapside, shipwright (Navy)
Nichols, John, age 35, 1 year in U.S., 1 son, 146 Broadway, NYC,
   hairdresser (20-25 July 1812); 5ft. 11in., age 37, dark complex., dark hair, black eyes, hairdresser (Navy)
Nichols, Thomas, 5ft. 8in., age 30, fair complex., light hair,
   grey eyes, victualer (Navy)
Nicholson, Charles, 5ft. 8in., age 27, fair complex., fair hair,
   blue eyes, farmer (Navy)
Nicholson, J.M., age 21, 6 mos. in U.S., 26 Garden St., NYC,
   soap boiler (20-25 July 1812)
Nicholson, Thomas, age 25, 2 years in U.S., New Windsor, Orange
   Co., weaver (19-24 Oct. 1812)
Nicholson, William, 5ft. 9in., age 34, "aub" complex., brown
   hair, blue eyes, labourer (Navy)
Nicholson, William, 5ft. 9in., age 27, sandy complex., sandy
   hair, brown eyes, labourer (Navy)
Niles, Michael, 5ft. 6in., age 22, fair complex., brown hair,
   grey eyes, Anthony St., stone cutter (Navy)
Nixon, George, age 45, 1 year & 3 mos. in U.S., wife & 2 child-
   ren, Hudson, Columbia Co., weaver (10-15 Aug. 1812)
Nixon, James, age 18, 2 years in U.S., NYC, accountant, applied
   7 Dec. 1810 (20-25 July 1812); 5ft. 10in., age 19, fair complex., fair hair, grey eyes, Pearl St., accountant (Navy)
Noble, Archibald, age 44 on 7 June 1812, 17 years in U.S., wife
   & 4 children, Johnsburgh, Washington Co., farmer (8 Dec. & 7-
   19 Dec. 1812)
Noble, Brabazon/Brabison, age 77, 17 years in U.S., Westchester
   Co. (3-8 Aug. 1812); 5ft. 9½in., age 77, fair complex., white
   hair, dark eyes, Yonkers, gentleman (Navy)
Noble, David, age 33, 16 years in U.S., wife named Prudence,
   Johnsburgh, Washington Co., farmer (8 Dec. & 7-19 Dec. 1812)
Noble, Edward, age 40 on 12 Oct. last, 17 years in U.S. in June
   last, wife & 7 children, Johnsburgh, Washington Co., farmer
   (24 Nov. 1812 & 21 Dec. 1812 - 23 Jan. 1813)
Noble, John, age 41, 11 years in U.S., wife & 2 more women, 63
   Stone St., NYC, merchant, applied 17 Sept. 1810 (13-18 July
   1812); 5ft. 6in., age 41, fair complex., brown hair, grey eyes,
   removed from NYC to Goshen, Orange Co. (Navy)
Noble, John, age 25, 17 years in U.S., wife & child, Johnsburgh,
   Washington Co., farmer (8 Dec. & 7-19 Dec. 1812)
Noble, John, age 24, 1 year & 2 mos. in U.S., wife & child, Mont-
   gomery, Orange Co., farmer (19-24 Oct. 1812)
Noble, William, 5ft. 9in., age 21, light complex., light hair,
   blue eyes, Water St., tanner (Navy)
Norman, John, age 32, 10 years in U.S., wife & 3 children, Hud-
   son, Columbia Co., baker (17-22 Aug. 1812)
Norris, Edward, age 32, 2 years & 7 mos. in U.S., wife & 3 child-
   ren, 154 Reed St., NYC, marble cutter (28 July - 2 Aug. 1812);
   5ft. 7in., age 33, sandy complex., brown hair, blue eyes, Reed
   St., marble (Navy)
Northam, Mathew, age 63, 9 years in U.S., wife & child, 300 Bowery
   Lane, NYC, carpenter (10-15 Aug. 1812); 5ft. 6in., age 64,
   light complex., grey hair, blue eyes, Bowery, gentleman (Navy)
Noud, George, 5ft. 4in., age 24, fair complex., brown hair, blue
   eyes, George St., grocer (Navy)
Noulan, Michael, 5ft. 9in., age 31, fair complex., brown hair,
   blue eyes, William St., black(smith) (Navy)

Nowden, Alexander, 5ft. 4in., age 19, sandy complex., dark hair,
   dark eyes, stone cutter (Navy)
Noye, Richard, age 21, 4 years in U.S., Brooklyn, Long Island,
   miller (7-19 Dec. 1812); 5ft. 8½in., age 22, light complex.,
   sandy hair, light eyes, Brooklyn, miller (Navy)
Nugent, Edward, 5ft. 9in., age 43, fair complex., fair hair,
   blue eyes, Rose St., labourer (Navy)
Nugent, William George, age 24, 2 years in U.S., wife, 258 William
   St., NYC (26-31 Oct. 1812); 5ft. 8in., age 25, fair complex.,
   red hair, brown eyes, Prince St., clerk in Superior Court, removed from NYC to Goshen, Orange Co. (Navy)
Oats, Patrick, 5ft. 7in., age 26, fair complex., brown hair,
   grey eyes, Augustus St., labourer (Navy)
O'Bail (?), Hugh, 5ft. 6in., age 28, light complex., light hair,
   blue eyes, cartman (Navy)
O'Brien, Daniel, 5ft. 4½in., age 43, dark complex., dark hair,
   grey eyes, coachman (Navy)
O'Brien, James, 5ft. 8in., age 35, fair complex., fair hair,
   brown eyes, Water St. (Navy)
O'Brien, James, age 34, 2½ years in U.S., mother, wife & 4 children, Catharine Slip, NYC, grocer & stone cutter (28 July - 2
   Aug. 1812)
O'Brien, James Slater, 5ft. 6in., age 26, light complex., light
   hair, blue eyes, Beekman St., weaver (Navy)
O'Brien, Terrly, 5ft. 6in., age 28, fair complex., brown hair,
   grey eyes, tailor (Navy)
O'Brien, Timothy, 5ft. 6in., age 40, dark complex., dark hair,
   blue eyes, labourer (Navy)
O'Brien, William, age 35, 15 years in U.S., wife & child, NYC,
   insurance broker (20-25 July 1812); 5ft. 8in., age 35, fair
   complex., dark hair, blue eyes, Greenwich St., clerk (Navy)
O'Brion, John, age 56, 26 years in U.S., 6 in family, Benton,
   Ontario Co., tailor (25 Oct. - 15 Nov. 1812)
O'Bryen, Patrick, age 56, 17 years in U.S., wife & child, City
   of Albany, gardener (17-22 Aug. 1812)
O'Callaghan, James, 5ft. 10in., age 31, fair complex., fair hair,
   blue eyes, Brooklyn, chandler (Navy)
O'Car, William, age 25, 4 years in U.S., Scipio, Cayuga Co.,
   chairmaker (12-17 Oct. 1812)
O'Carr, William, age 21, 4 years in U.S., Scipio, Cayuga Co.,
   chairmaker, applied 4 Jan. 1811 (26-31 Oct. 1812)
O'Challaghan, Jeremiah, age 40, 15 years in U.S., wife & 2 children, Scipio, Cayuga Co., mason, applied in 1802 (21-26 Sept. &
   5-10 Oct. 1812)
O'Conner, Barnard, 5ft. 8¼in., age 33, fair complex., dark hair,
   blue eyes, Bayard St., grocer (Navy)
O'Conner, Edward, 5ft. 10½in., age 32, brown complex., brown
   hair, grey eyes, Elm St., clerk (Navy)
O'Conner, James, 5ft. 9in., age 45, light complex., light hair,
   blue eyes, labourer (Navy)
O'Conner, James, 5ft. 8in., age 25, fair complex., light hair,
   blue eyes, Ferry St., tanner (Navy)
O'Conner, Michael, 5ft. 9in., age 52, light complex., brown hair,
   blue eyes, labourer (Navy)
O'Conner, Michael, 5ft. 10in., age 30, fair complex,, fair hair,
   blue eyes, James Slip, grocer (Navy)
O'Conner, Thomas, 5ft. 7in., age 33, sandy complex., brown hair,
   blue eyes, slater (Navy)
O'Connor, James, age 48, 8 years in U.S., 2 in family, 21 Stone
   St., NYC, laborer, applied 6 Mar. 1809 (20-25 July 1812)
O'Connor, John, age 30, 8 years in U.S., wife & 3 children, Sche-
   nectady (31 Aug. - 5 Sept. 1812)
O'Connor, Miles, age 32, 8 years in U.S., Goshen, Orange Co.,
   laborer (9-24 Oct. 1812)

Ocdoty/Octoby, Robert, age 30, 9 years in U.S., 4 in family,
    Benton, Ontario Co., farmer (5-15 & 24-29 Aug. 1812)
O'Donald, Hugh, age 25, 9 years in U.S., Clinton, Dutchess Co.,
    laborer (12-17 Oct. 1812)
O'Donald, Robert, age 30, 5 years in U.S., wife & 2 children,
    445 Greenwich St., NYC, sawyer (20-25 July 1812)
O'Donnel, Barney, 5ft. 6in., age 20, dark complex., brown hair,
    brown eyes, Grand St., hatter (Navy)
O'Donnel, Hugh, 5ft. 8in., age 37, dark complex., dark hair,
    grey eyes, Rockland, Sullivan Co., weaver (Navy)
O'Donnel, James, 5ft. 8½in., age 30, dark complex., black hair,
    dark eyes, labourer (Navy)
O'Donnel, John, 5ft. 7½in., age 27, light complex., brown hair,
    brown eyes, labourer (Navy)
O'Donnel, John, 5ft. 4in., age 25, light complex., grey hair,
    brown eyes, Mulberry St., labourer (Navy)
O'Donnel, John, age 22, 5 years in U.S., 96 Anthony St., NYC,
    laborer (28 July - 2 Aug. 1812)
O'Donnel, Michael, 5ft. 6in., age 22, light complex., brown
    hair, blue eyes, Mulberry St., labourer (Navy)
O'Donnell, Andrew, age 22, 6 years in U.S., 18 East Rutgers St.,
    NYC, waiter (28 July - 2 Aug. 1812); 5ft. 3½in., age 23, light
    complex., brown hair, light eyes, waiter (Navy)
O'Donnell, Barney, age 19, 1 year & 1 mo. in U.S., Grand St.,
    NYC, laborer (28 July - 2 Aug. 1812)
O'Donnell, Dennis, 5ft. 6in., age 26, light complex., dark hair,
    blue eyes, labourer (Navy)
O'Donnell, John, age 27, 7 years in U.S., wife, Minisink, Orange
    Co., weaver (19-24 Oct. 1812)
O'Donnell, Michael, age 22, 1 year in U.S., wife & child, 96
    Anthony St., NYC, laborer (28 July - 2 Aug. 1812)
O'Hara, Charles P.F., age 31, 1 mo. in U.S., 72 Wall St., NYC,
    teacher of music (13-18 July 1812)
O'Hara, John, age 42, 10 years in U.S., Poughkeepsie, Dutchess
    Co., laborer (12-17 Oct. 1812)
O'Harra, James, age 35, 7 years in U.S., wife & 5 children,
    Goshen, Orange Co. (19-24 Oct. 1812)
O'Keefe, Henry, age 25, 6 years in U.S., Onondaga, Onondaga Co.,
    tailor (5-11 & 14-19 Sept. 1812)
O'Lalahan, James, 5ft. 6in., age 26, light complex., light hair,
    blue eyes, farmer (Navy)
Olay, James, age 30, 3 years in U.S., Fishkill, Dutchess Co.,
    weaver (12-17 Oct. 1812)
Olding, Josep, age 35, 8 years in U.S., 3 in family, 124 Fly
    Market, NYC, cordwainer (20-25 July 1812)
Oldrin, William, age 39, 18 years in U.S., wife, Suffolk Co.,
    farmer (9-14 Nov. 1812)
Oliff, William, 5ft., age 26, fair complex., brown hair, grey
    eyes, Thomas St., prompter (Navy)
Oliphont, John, age 41, 1 year in U.S., 1 son, Cayuga, tailor
    (24-29 Aug. 1812)
Oliver, Benjamin, 5ft. 8in., age 29, fair complex., fair hair,
    brown eyes, Greenwich St., stone cutter (Navy)
Oliver, James, 5ft. 8in., age 34, light complex., brown hair,
    black eyes, Broadway, distiller (Navy)
Oliver, James, age 30, 11 years in U.S., wife & 2 children, Sche-
    nectady, teacher (17-22 Aug. 1812)
Olliff, William, age 25, 11 years in U.S., wife, NYC, prompter,
    N.Y. Theatre (20-25 July 1812) - same as Oliff, Wm., above
O'Neal, Barnard, age 23, 3 mos. in U.S., wife & child, Newburgh,
    Orange Co., laborer (19-24 Oct. 1812)
O'Neal, Mathew, 5ft. 7½in., age 45, light complex., brown hair,
    grey eyes, labourer (Navy)

O'Neal/O'Neil, Roger, age 34, 7 years in U.S., wife & child, 3
  Catharine Lane, NYC, laborer (28 July - 2 Aug. 1812); 5ft.
  10in., age 35, fair complex., brown hair, brown eyes, labourer
  (Navy)
O'Neel, Hugh, age 38, 1 year in U.S., 15 James St., NYC, schoolmaster (3-8 Aug. 1812)
O'Neil, Edward, age 30, 17 years in U.S., Kingston, Ulster Co.,
  teacher (19-24 Oct. 1812)
O'Neil, Hugh, age 42, 6 mos. in U.S., wife & 5 children, NYC,
  carpenter (20-25 July 1812); 5ft. 10in., age 44, fair complex.,
  brown hair, blue eyes, Henry St., carpenter (Navy)
O'Neil, James, age 55, 17 years in U.S., wife & 4 children, Hurley, Ulster Co., schoolmaster (19-24 Oct. 1812)
O'Neil, James, 5ft. 10in., age 45, fair complex., light hair,
  grey eyes, tanner (Navy)
O'Neil, John, age 63, 17 years in U.S., wife & 3 children, Hurley, Ulster Co., farmer (19-24 Oct. 1812)
O'Neil, John, 5ft. 3in., age 38, dark complex., dark hair, grey
  eyes, retailer (Navy)
O'Neil, Thomas, 5ft. 10in., age 22, fair complex., fair hair,
  blue eyes, flax dresser (Navy)
O'Neil, William, age 21, 17 years in U.S., Hurley, Ulster Co.,
  farmer (19-24 Oct. 1812)
O'Neill, John, age 31, 1 year & 10 mos. in U.S., Harlaem, boatman (20-25 July 1812)
O'Pray, Hugh, age 30, 1 year & 2 mos. in U.S., Newburgh, Orange
  Co., laborer (19-24 Oct. 1812)
O'Ranna, Patrick, age 27, 8 years in U.S., wife & child, Mama-
  kating, Sullivan Co., tailor (19-24 Oct. 1812)
O'Reilly, Edward, age 24, 1 year & 2 mos. in U.S., wife & child,
  180 Bowery Lane, NYC, flax manufacturer (20-25 July 1812); 5ft.
  11in., age 25, fair complex., brown hair, blue eyes, Bowery,
  thread (Navy)
Oriel (?), James, 5ft. 6½in., age 38, dark complex., brown hair,
  dark eyes, Hempstead, Long Island (Navy)
O'Riley, Hugh, age 26, 19 years in U.S., wife, 18 Bancker St.,
  NYC, gardener (28 July - 2 Aug. 1812)
O'Roke, Bryan, 5ft. 7in., age 25, fair complex., brown hair,
  brown eyes, labourer (Navy)
O'Roke, Patrick, 5ft. 4in., age 25, fair complex., light hair,
  grey eyes, Staten Island, teacher (Navy)
Orr, David, age 31, 10 years in U.S., 2 in family, Gorham, Ontario Co., farmer, applied Feb. 1809 (27 Sept. - 11 Oct. &
  19-24 Oct. 1812)
Orr, James, age 45, 2 mos. in U.S., wife & 5 children, NYC, weaver (10-15 Aug. 1812); 5ft. 8in., age 46, light complex., sandy
  hair, blue eyes, Greenwich St., weaver (Navy)
Osborn/Osburn, James, age 32, 7 years in U.S., wife & child,
  205 Greenwich St., NYC, tailor (13-18 July 1812); 5ft. 10in.,
  age 32, pale complex., dark hair, dark eyes, Greenwich St.,
  tailor (Navy)
Osburn, Michael, 5ft. 6in., age 36, light complex., brown hair,
  blue eyes, Th... St., mariner (Navy)
O'Sullivan, Sylvester, age 21, 9 years in U.S., NYC, hairdresser
  (20-25 July 1812)
Othwell, David, age 22, 17 years in U.S., 7 Hague St., NYC,
  morocco dresser (20-25 July 1812)
Otis, Patrick, age 30, 9 years in U.S., wife & 4 children, Clin-
  ton, Dutchess Co., laborer (12-17 Oct. 1812)
Ottley, Thomas/Thomas, Jr., age 23, 6 years in U.S., Phelps, On-
  tario Co., farmer (5-15 & 24-29 Aug. 1812)
Ottley, William, age 60, 6 years in U.S., 3 in family, Phelps,
  Ontario Co., farmer (5-15 & 24-29 Aug. 1812)
Ottley, William, Jr., age 25, 6 years in U.S., Phelps, Ontario
  Co., farmer (5-15 & 24-29 Aug. 1812)

Overend, William, age 21, 1 year & 9 mos. in U.S., Wallkill,
    Orange Co., weaver (19-24 Oct. 1812)
Owen, David, age nearly 44, 11 years in U.S. on 30 July last,
    wife & 5 children, Deerfield, Oneida Co., farmer (26 Aug. &
    28 Sept. - 3 Oct. 1812)
Owen, Hugh, age 42, 11 years in U.S., wife & 5 children, Trenton,
    Oneida Co., farmer (29 Sept. & 28 Sept. - 3 Oct. 1812)
Owen, Humphrey, age 48, 16 years in U.S., 1 child, Clinton, Dut-
    chess Co., laborer (12-17 Oct. 1812)
Owen, John D., age 57 on 16 Aug. inst., 11 years in U.S., wife,
    Steuben, Oneida Co., farmer, from South Wales (26 Aug. & 28
    Sept. - 3 Oct. 1812)
Owen, William, 5ft. 4in., age 35, fair complex., brown hair,
    blue eyes, milkman (Navy)
Owens, Alexander, 5ft. 11in., age 37, dark complex., dark hair,
    grey eyes, Sag Harbour (Navy)
Owens, John, 5ft. 3½in., age 32, light complex., brown hair,
    grey eyes, West Farms, teacher (Navy)
Owens, John, age 27, 6 years in U.S., Sag Harbour, storekeeper
    (20-25 July 1812)
Owens, John, 5ft. 11½in., age 28, light complex., light hair,
    grey eyes, pedler (Navy)
Owens, Richard, 5ft. 8½in., age 27, fair complex., dark hair,
    dark eyes, Rose St., painter (Navy)
Owens, Thomas, 5ft. 8in., age 26, light complex., light hair,
    blue eyes, Division St., painter (Navy)
Oxenham, Thomas, 5ft. 5in., age 22, fair complex., dark hair,
    blue eyes, labourer (Navy)
Oxtoby, William, age 52, 11 years in U.S., wife & 2 children,
    Bloomingdale, farmer (10-15 Aug. 1812); 5ft. 6in., age 55,
    brown complex., dark hair, grey eyes, farmer (Navy)
Padley, Moses, age 39, 7 years in U.S., 2 in family, Ontario,
    Ontario Co., farmer, applied 15 Oct. 1812) (11-15 Oct. 1812)
Page, Job, age 36, 8 years in U.S., wife & child, 110 Broad St.,
    NYC, grocer (13-18 July 1812)
Page, Joel, 5ft. 9in., age 37, fair complex., brown hair, hazel
    eyes, Broad St., labourer (Navy)
Page, John, age 16, 2 years in U.S., Scipio, Cayuga Co., laborer,
    bound apprentice to Wm. S. Burling of Scipio (21-16 Sept. &
    5-10 Oct. 1812)
Page, Joseph, age 51, 6 years in U.S., wife & 3 children, Washing-
    ton St., NYC, shoemaker (13-18 July 1812); 5ft. 6in., age 51,
    light complex., grey hair, light eyes, Duane Mark., shoe (Navy)
Page, Richard, age 54, 11 years & 1 mo. in U.S., wife & 2 child-
    ren, Mamakating, Sullivan Co., farmer (19-24 Oct. 1812)
Palmer, Edward, age 26, 6 years in U.S., Henry St., chairmaker
    (20-25 July 1812); 5ft. 6in., age 26, dark complex., brown
    hair, blue eyes, Wall St., chair (Navy)
Palmer, Henry, age 26, 14 years in U.S., wife & child, 125 Banc-
    ker St., NYC, waterman (20-25 July 1812)
Palmer, Henry, age 19, 8 years in U.S., 53 Partition St., NYC,
    clerk (20-25 July 1812)
Palmer, James, age 26, 12 years in U.S., wife & 2 children, Hud-
    son, Columbia Co., stone cutter (10-15 Aug. 1812)
Palmer, Joseph, age 38, 13 years in U.S., wife & 7 children,
    Poughkeepsie, Dutchess Co., clothier (12-17 Oct. 1812)
Palmer, Joseph, age 18, 2 mos. in U.S., 253 Pearl St., NYC, yeo-
    man (20-25 July 1812)
Palmer, Robert, age 46, 5 years in U.S., wife & 2 children, Fish-
    kill, Dutchess Co., shoemaker (12-17 Oct. 1812)
Palmer, Robert, 6ft., age 27, dark complex., dark hair, grey eyes,
    stone cutter (Navy)
Pander, Lawrence, 6ft., age 30, fair complex., brown hair, grey
    eyes, Bancker St., brewer (Navy)

Park, Andrew, 5ft. 9in., age 22, fair complex., fair hair, grey
  eyes, weaver (Navy)
Park, David, age 25, 2 years & 2½ mos. in U.S., corner Cross &
  Pearl Sts., NYC, saddler (28 July - 2 Aug. 1812); 5ft. 6in.,
  age 26, brown complex., dark hair, grey eyes, Anthony St.,
  saddler (Navy)
Park, James, age 26, 1 year & 11 mos. in U.S., New Haven, wea-
  ver (26-31 Oct. 1812)
Park, John, 5ft. 6in., age 30, fair complex., sandy hair, blue
  eyes, labourer (Navy)
Parker, George, age 24, 15 years in U.S., Oppenheim, Montgomery
  Co., farmer (3-14 & 21-16 Sept. 1812)
Parker, George, age 24, 9 years in U.S., Boyle, Ontario Co.,
  farmer, applied Feb. 1810 (30 Aug. - 5 Sept. & 7-12 Sept. 1812)
Parker, James, age 22, 16 years in U.S., Genoa, Cayuga Co., far-
  mer (2-7 Nov. & 30 Nov. - 5 Dec. 1812)
Parker, John, age 47, 5 years in U.S., 177 William St., mechanic,
  applied 26 Apr. 1810 (20-25 July 1812)
Parker, John, 5ft. 7in., age 35, fair complex., dark hair, dark
  eyes, Sullivan St., steel manufacturer (Navy)
Parker, John, age 26, 2 mos. in U.S., 2 Bancker St., NYC, sad-
  dler (20-25 July 1812)
Parker, Michael, age 29, 9 years in U.S., Boyle, Ontario Co.,
  farmer, applied Feb. 1810 (30 Aug. - 6 Sept. & 7-12 Sept. 1812)
Parker, William, age 65, 9 years in U.S., 4 in family, Boyle,
  Ontario Co., farmer, applied Feb. 1809 (30 Aug. - 6 Sept. &
  7-12 Sept. 1812)
Parker, William, age 57, 5 years in U.S., 46 Greenwich St., NYC,
  servant (3-8 Aug. 1812)
Parker, William, 5ft. 8in., age 42, light complex., light hair,
  dark eyes, ...per St., butcher (Navy)
Parker, William, age 28, 15 years in U.S., wife & 2 children,
  Oppenheim, Montgomery Co., farmer (3-14 & 21-26 Sept. 1812)
Parker, William, Jr., age 27, 9 years in U.S., Boyle, Ontario
  Co., farmer, applied Feb. 1810 (30 Aug. - 5 Sept. & 7-12 Sept.
  1812)
Parkin, William, 5ft. 7in., age 20, fresh complex., dark hair,
  dark eyes, steel manufacturer (Navy)
Parks, James, 5ft. 8in., age 26, fair complex., fair hair, blue
  eyes, Greenwich St., weaver (Navy)
Parks, John, 5ft. 10in., age 47, fair complex., brown hair,
  grey eyes, Greenwich St., diesinker (Navy)
Parks, John, 5ft. 9in., age 33, fair complex., dark hair, light
  eyes, Harman St., drayman (Navy)
Parks, Thomas, age 33, 11 years in U.S., wife & child, Catharine
  St., NYC, mason (3-8 Aug. 1812); 5ft. 8in., age 33, dark com-
  plex., brown hair, blue eyes, Front St., bricklayer (Navy)
Parks, Thomas, 5ft. 10in., age 23, light complex., dark hair,
  dark eyes, Elizabeth St., brewer (Navy)
Parks, Thomas, age 18, 2½ years in U.S., 28 Nassau St., NYC,
  refiner of iron (20-25 July 1812)
Parmeter, John, 5ft. 5in., age 32, dark complex., light hair,
  blue eyes, Pearl St., shoemaker (Navy)
Parr, Samuel, 5ft. 10 3/4in., age 25, brown complex., brown hair,
  brown eyes, Duane St., brewer (Navy)
Parrot, Edward, age 52, 10 years in U.S., 5 in family, Boyle,
  Ontario Co., farmer, applied Feb. 1811 (15-22 Aug. 1812)
Parrot, George, age 52, 10 years in U.S., 5 in family, Boyle,
  Ontario Co., farmer, applied Feb. 1811 (31 Aug. - 5 Sept. 1812)
Parry, John, 5ft. 5in., age 54, dark complex., dark hair, dark
  eyes, tobacco (Navy)
Passmer, William, 5ft. 8in., age 34, fair complex., grey hair,
  blue eyes, labourer (Navy)

Paten/Paton, George, age 30, 7 years in U.S., wife, 16 Beaver
St., NYC, dyer (20-25 July 1812); 5ft. 8½in., age 27, dark
complex., brown hair, blue eyes, dyer (Navy)
Patten, Henry, 5ft. 11in., age 27, fair complex., dark hair,
blue eyes, Desbrosses St., sawyer (Navy)
Patten, John, 5ft. 9in., age 28, light complex., brown hair,
blue eyes, Sandy Hill, labourer (Navy)
Patten, William, 5ft. 7in., age 48, light complex., light hair,
dark eyes, Yonkers, farmer (Navy)
Patterson, Adam, 6ft., age 30, fair complex., fair hair, blue
eyes, Greenwich St., tailor (Navy)
Patterson, Arthur, age 44, 8 years in U.S., 8 in family, 15 Water
St., NYC, cartman (20-25 July 1812); 5ft. 5in., age 45, dark
complex., brown hair, grey eyes, Water St., cartman (Navy)
Patterson, David, age 27, 1 year & 6 mos. in U.S., wife & 2
children, Newburgh, Orange Co., weaver (19-24 Oct. 1812)
Patterson, Dennis, 5ft. 4in., age 30, light complex., dark hair,
blue eyes, weaver (Navy)
Patterson, Dennis, age 28, 6 years in U.S., 250 Bowery, NYC, cut
nailor (3-8 Aug. 1812)
Patterson, Edward, 5ft. 10in., age 30, fair complex., light hair,
light eyes, Orange St., trader (Navy)
Patterson, Hugh, 5ft. 9in., age 24, light complex., brown hair,
blue eyes, mason (Navy)
Patterson, James, 5ft. 7½in., age 35, fair complex., brown hair,
light eyes, State Prison, weaver (Navy)
Patterson, James, 5ft. 9in., age 27, fair complex., dark hair,
brown eyes, Thames St., cooper (Navy)
Patterson, James, age 20, 9 years in U.S., 15 Water St., NYC,
wood sawyer (20-25 July 1812)
Patterson, James W., age 25, 4 years in U.S., State of Ohio,
trader (20-25 July 1812)
Patterson, Michael, 5ft. 6in., age 24, light complex., fair hair,
blue eyes, cooper (Navy)
Patterson, Peter, age 56, 2 years in U.S., wife & daughter, Greenwich St., NYC, physician (20-25 July 1812); 5ft. 3in., age 57,
fair complex., fair hair, grey eyes, physician (Navy)
Patterson, Robert, age 32, 3 years in U.S., wife & 3 children,
Hudson, Columbia Co., grocer, applied Mar. 1812 (10-15 Aug.
1812)
Patterson, Robert, age 25, 2 years in U.S., Greenwich St., NYC,
weaver (28 July - 2 Aug. 1812)
Patterson, Thomas, age 34, 8 years in U.S., wife, NYC, cartman
(28 July - 2 Aug. 1812); 5ft. 10in., age 33, fair complex.,
brown hair, blue eyes, Sixth St., cartman (Navy)
Patterson, Thomas, 5ft. 8½in., fair complex., dark hair, blue
eyes, weaver (Navy)
Patterson, William, age 32, 10 years in U.S., wife, Columbia-
ville, Columbia Co., millwright (24-29 Aug. 1812)
Patterson, William, 5ft. 9in., age 32, dark complex., dark hair,
grey eyes, Christopher St., carpenter (Navy)
Patterson, William, age 30, 9 years in U.S., wife & 2 children,
Greenwich St., NYC, carpenter & grocer (28 July - 2 Aug. 1812)
Patterson, William, age 30, 6 years & 4 mos. in U.S., Onondaga,
Onondaga Co., weaver (30 Nov. - 5 Dec. 1812)
Patterson, William, 5ft. 2in., age 28, fair complex., brown hair,
brown eyes, Murray St., grocer (Navy)
Patterson, William, age 23, 8 years in U.S., 2 in family, 1 Ba-
tavia Lane, NYC, tin- and sheet iron worker (20-25 July 1812);
5ft. 6in., age 23, dark complex., brown hair, blue eyes, Ba-
tavia Lane, tinsmith (Navy)
Patton, Andrew, age 27, 6 years in U.S., wife & 2 children, Desbrosses St., sawyer (20-25 July 1812)
Patton, John, age 30, 5 years in U.S., 171 Hester St., NYC (10-
15 Aug. 1812)

Patton, Patrick, 5ft. 9in., age 28, fair complex., dark hair,
grey eyes, Water St., labourer (Navy)
Patton, William, 5ft. 8in., age 22, light complex., brown hair,
grey eyes, mason (Navy)
Paul, Alexander, age 22, 2 years in U.S., 121 Chamber St., NYC,
weaver (3-8 Aug. 1812)
Paul, James, age 35, 2½ mos. in U.S., wife & 2 children, 47 Bea-
ver St., NYC, brewer (28 July - 2 Aug. 1812); 5ft. 9in., age
35, dark complex., brown hair, grey eyes, Thames St., brewer
(Navy)
Paul, James, 5ft. 6in., age 28, dark complex., brown hair, grey
eyes, labourer (Navy)
Paul, Robert, 5ft. 9in., age 23, brown complex., brown hair,
brown eyes, coachman (Navy)
Pay, William, age 28, 5 years in U.S., wife & child, City of
Albany, parchment maker (17-22 Aug. 1812)
Peacock, Jonathan, Jr., 5ft. 11in., age 30, fair complex., sandy
hair, blue eyes, Bloomingdale, farmer (Navy)
Peacock, Thomas, 5ft. 5in., age 22, dark complex., brown hair,
brown eyes, weaver (Navy)
Pearce, William, age 49, 8 years in U.S., wife & 5 children, 20
Division St., NYC, missioner Baptist Society (20-25 July 1812)
Pearsall, William, 5ft. 4in., age 22, fair complex., light hair,
grey eyes, Sixth St., tobacco (Navy)
Pearse, William, 5ft. 3in., age 45, light complex., light hair,
grey eyes, Division St., tailor (Navy)
Pearson, Thomas, age 28, 5 years in U.S., Genoa, Cayuga Co.,
farmer (7-12 & 21-16 Sept. 1812)
Pedan, James, 5ft. 6in., age 24, dark complex., brown hair, dark
eyes, tailor (Navy)
Pedley, Moses, age 39, 7 years in U.S., 2 in family, Ontario,
Wayne Co., farmer, applied 15 Oct. 1812 (26-31 Oct. 1812)
Peedlar, John, 5ft. 11½in., age 31, brown complex., brown hair,
grey eyes, New Slip, weaver (Navy)
Pelles, John, 5ft. 9in., age 32, light complex., brown hair,
blue eyes, Newtown, Queens Co., gardener (Navy)
Pellington, James, 5ft. 6in., age 34, light complex., light hair,
blue eyes, Dominick St., silver plater (Navy)
Pendaget, John, 5ft. 7 3/4in., age 46, dark complex., dark hair,
brown eyes, labourer (Navy)
Pendegrass, Michael, 5ft. 7½in., age 29, light complex., red
hair, light eyes, coachman (Navy)
Penin, John, 5ft. 7½in., age 41, dark complex., black hair,
black eyes, farmer (Navy)
Penner, John, 5ft. 11in., age 22, light complex., light hair,
grey eyes, Cherry St., distiller (Navy)
Penny, John, age 19, 2½ years in U.S., NYC, coppersmith (20-25
July 1812)
Penry, Thomas, age 39, 11 years in U.S., City of Albany, grocer,
applied 4 Aug. 1812 (31 Aug. - 5 Sept. 1812)
Pensain, James, age 31, 2 years in U.S., 3 in family, Geneva,
Ontario Co., butcher (6-13 Sept. 1812)
Pepper, Edward, 5ft. 5in., age 30, fair complex., brown hair,
blue eyes, blacksmith (Navy)
Pepper, Hipolite, age 18, 1 mo. in U.S., City of Albany, shoe-
maker (17-22 Aug. 1812)
Pepper, James, 5ft. 8in., age 28, fair complex., brown hair, blue
eyes, Hester St., blacksmith (Navy)
Percival, Joseph, age 23, 2 years in U.S., Rome, Oneida Co.,
weaver (29 July & 3-8 Aug. 1812)
Percival, Samuel, age 43 on 4 Feb. last, 2 years in U.S. on 6
Oct., wife & 4 children, Eaton, Madison Co., farmer (31 Oct. &
30 Nov. - 5 Dec. 1812)
Perine, John, age 24, 1 year in U.S., 80 Front St., NYC, clerk
(20-25 July 1812)

Perrin, Mathew, age 27, 11 years in U.S., wife, 29 Chatham Row,
NYC, merchant (20-25 July 1812)

Perrot, John, 5ft. 8in., age 46, fair complex., brown hair, blue
eyes, painter (Navy)

Perry, Samuel, 5ft. 7in., age 28, light complex., fair hair,
blue eyes, sawyer (Navy)

Pesko, Daniel, age 36, 16 years in U.S., wife & 3 children, City
of Albany, laborer (17-22 Aug. 1812)

Petcherd (or Pitchard), Samuel, 5ft. 9in., age 20, fair complex.,
sandy hair, blue eyes, butcher (Navy)

Peters, Benjamin L., age 22, 7 years in U.S., 7 Fair St., clerk
(20-25 July 1812)

Phair, Thomas, age 30, 1 year & 2 mos. in U.S., wife & 3 children, Newburgh, Orange Co., weaver (19-24 Oct. 1812)

Phelan, Patrick, 5ft. 3in., age 39, dark complex., black hair,
hazel eyes, stevedore (Navy)

Phelon, John, 5ft. 8in., age 24, dark complex., brown hair, blue
eyes, labourer (Navy)

Philips, Henry, age 42, 1 year & 9 mos. in U.S., 2 in family,
70 Henry St., NYC, tailor (20-25 July 1812)

Phillips, James, 5ft. 6in., age 46, fair complex., fair hair,
brown eyes, Downing St., labourer (Navy)

Phillips, John, 5ft. 8in., age 43, fair complex., sandy hair,
brown eyes, labourer (Navy)

Phillips, John, age 38, 11 years in U.S., 68 Ann St., NYC, manufacturer of copper and tin ware (20-25 July 1812)

Phillips, John, 5ft. 10in., age 28, dark complex., dark hair,
grey eyes, waiter (Navy)

Phillips, Thomas, 5ft. 8in., age 42, fair complex., brown hair,
blue eyes, Harman St., tailor (Navy)

Phillips, Thomas, 5ft. 6½in., age 33, dark complex., dark hair,
dark eyes, carpenter (Navy)

Philpot, William, age 46, 3 years in U.S., wife & 6 children,
Eaton, Madison Co., farmer (31 Oct. & 30 Nov. - 5 Dec. 1812)

Picket, William, 5ft. 7in., age 36, fair complex., brown hair,
dark eyes, Talbot St., labourer (Navy)

Pickford, Isaac, 5ft. 8in., age 28, fair complex., brown hair,
hazel eyes, carpenter's mate (Navy)

Pierce, Edward, 5ft. 8in., age 27, fair complex., brown hair,
blue eyes, labourer (Navy)

Pierce, William G., age 43 in Oct. last, 17 years in U.S. last
June, wife & 7 children, Steuben, Oneida Co., farmer (29 Sept.
& 28 Sept. - 3 Oct. 1812)

Pierpont, Thomas, 5ft. 9in., age 51, dark complex., grey hair,
dark eyes, Broome St., tobacco (Navy)

Pierson, Jacob, 5ft. 6in., age 34, red complex., red hair, brown
eyes, Greenwich St., weaver (Navy)

Pierson, William, 5ft. 8in., age 46, dark complex., dark hair,
brown eyes, rigger (Navy)

Pigg, Roger, age 33, 8 years in U.S., wife & 4 children, 51 Maiden Lane, NYC, tailor, applied Aug. 1811 (13-18 July 1812);
5ft. 7in., age 33, fair complex., sandy hair, blue eyes, Maiden Lane, tailor (Navy)

Pigot, Simeon, 5ft. 7in., age 20, fair complex., light hair,
grey eyes, Hagen (?) St., skinner (Navy)

Pike, Benjamin, age 38, 14 years in U.S., wife & 3 children, 12
Wall St., NYC, optician (23 July - 2 Aug. 1812); 5ft. 2in.,
age 39, dark complex., dark hair, dark eyes, Wall St., optician
(Navy)

Pike, Samuel, age 28, 3 years in U.S., 65 Chatham St., spectacle
maker (20-25 July 1812); 5ft. 3in., age 29, dark complex.,
dark hair, brown eyes, Chatham St., watch (Navy)

Pilgrim, Nathaniel, age 36, 11 years in U.S., wife, 26 Elm St.,
NYC, plane maker (13-18 July 1812)

Pine, William, age 46, 3 years in U.S., wife & 8 children, 248
    Pearl St., NYC, merchant (17-22 Aug. 1812)
Pinkerton/Pinckerton, James, age 23, 2 years in U.S., 15 Henry
    St., NYC, bricklayer (28 July - 2 Aug. 1812); 5ft. 8in., age
    23, sandy complex., brown hair, black eyes, Henry St., brick
    (Navy)
Pinkey, Robert, 5ft. 10in., age 36, dark complex., black hair,
    grey eyes, Pearl St., tanner (Navy); Pinkney, Robert, age 36,
    2 years in U.S., 142 William St., tanner (28 July - 2 Aug.
    1812)
Pinsam, James, age 31, 2 years in U.S., 3 in family, Geneva,
    Ontario Co., butcher (21-26 Sept. 1812)
Pinser, Thomas, age 42, 8 years in U.S., wife & 2 children, New-
    burgh, Orange Co., farmer, applied 19 Feb. 1810 (14 Aug. 1812)
Pitcairn, Robert, age 24, 18 years in U.S., Poughkeepsie, Dutchess
    Co., currier (12-17 Oct. 1812)
Planter, Anthony, age 36, 16 years in U.S., wife & 2 children,
    City of Albany, blacksmith, applied 5 Aug. 1812 (17-22 Aug.
    1812)
Plasket/Plaskit, William, age 69, 4 years & 10 mos. in U.S.,
    wife, Bowery, NYC, cordwainer, applied 16 July 1810 (3-8 Aug.
    1812); 5ft. 7½in., age 70, dark complex., dark hair, dark eyes,
    Mulberry St., shoe (Navy)
Plomedon, Ennis, 5ft. 7½in., age 38, dark complex., brown hair,
    blue eyes, Greenwich St., labourer (Navy)
Plume, John, age 45, 4 years & 9 mos. in U.S., wife & 2 child-
    ren, 259 William St., innkeeper (3-8 Aug. 1812); 5ft. 10in.,
    age 45, dark complex., brown hair, brown eyes, William St.,
    tavern-keeper (Navy)
Pluncket/Plunkitt, Brien/Bryan, age 23, 2 years in U.S., Repub-
    lican Alley, NYC, carpenter; 5ft. 6in., age 23, dark complex.,
    brown hair, dark eyes, Read St., carpenter (Navy)
Pocock, John, age 40 on 11 Nov. next, 10 years in U.S. on 8 Nov.
    next, wife & daughter, Whitestown, Oneida Co., tinplate worker
    (29 Sept. & 28 Sept. - 3 Oct. 1812)
Pogue, William, 5ft. 7in., age 27, light complex., brown hair,
    brown eyes, Broome St., labourer (Navy)
Pollock, Samuel, 5ft. 9in., age 25, light complex., light hair,
    blue eyes, Liberty St., grocer (Navy)
Pollock, William, 5ft. 8½in., age 30, light complex., light hair,
    blue eyes, grocer (Navy)
Polson, Daniel, age 36, 8 years & 11 mos. in U.S., wife & 3 child-
    ren, Onondaga, Onondaga Co., joiner & carpenter (5-11 & 14-19
    Sept. 1812)
Pool, Edmond, 5ft. 6in., age 35, fair complex., brown hair, grey
    eyes, Chapple St., carpenter (Navy)
Poole, James, 5ft. 7in., age 28, fair complex., light hair, grey
    eyes, Harman St., labourer (Navy)
Pootly, John, age 24, 4 years in U.S., NYC, cooper (10-15 Aug.
    1812)
Popham, Thomas F., age 49, 2 years in U.S., 231 Church St., NYC,
    mason (20-25 July 1812); 5ft. 7in., age 50, light complex.,
    brown hair, grey eyes, Church St., mason (Navy)
Poppleton, Thomas H., 5ft. 4½in., age 47, fair complex., brown
    hair, hazel eyes, Bowery, surveyor (Navy)
Port, George, age 25, 12 years in U.S., wife & child, Johnstown,
    Montgomery Co., farmer (5 Nov. - 9 Dec. & 17-19 Dec. 1812)
Port, John, age 59, 14 years in U.S. wife & 2 children, Johns-
    town, Montgomery Co., farmer (11-17 Aug. 1812)
Port, William, age 31, 7½ years in U.S., wife & child, Johnstown,
    Montgomery Co., farmer (6 Oct. - 4 Nov. & 9-14 Nov. 1812)
Porter, Alexander, age 29, 3 years in U.S., wife, 11 Jefferson
    St., NYC, grocer (17-22 Aug. 1812); 6ft. 1in., age 30, brown
    complex., sandy hair, blue eyes, Jefferson St., grocer (Navy)

Porter, James, age 28, 14 years in U.S., wife & 5 children,
Schenectady, barker (31 Aug. - 5 Sept. 1812)
Porter, John, 5ft. 9in., age 34, dark complex., black hair, blue
eyes, Hubbard St., pit sawyer (Navy)
Porter, Moses, 5ft. 6in., age 32, dark complex., dark hair, dark
eyes, Augustus St., tanner (Navy)
Porter, Robert, 18 years in U.S., 4 in family, Naples, Ontario
Co., wheelwright (15 Nov. 1812 - 3 Jan. 1813)
Porter, Samuel, 5ft. 6in., age 34, fair complex., brown hair,
grey eyes, paper (Navy)
Portley, John, 5ft. 8in., age 25, dark complex., dark hair,
brown eyes, Coffee House Slip, cooper (Navy)
Post, John, age 59, 14 years in U.S., wife & 2 children, Johnstown, Montgomery Co., farmer (17-22 Aug. 1812)
Pott, Gideon, age 26, 7 years & 4 mos. in U.S., wife & child &
2 servants, 2 Stone St., NYC, merchant, applied 7 Sept. 1810
(13-18 July 1812); 6ft. 1in., age 27, dark complex., brown
hair, black eyes, removed from NYC (Navy)
Pott, John, age 36, 10 years in U.S., Long Island, miller (20-
25 July 1812)
Potter, Oliver, 5ft. 7in., age 26, light complex., sandy hair,
blue eyes, Bloomingdale (Navy)
Potter, Robert, age 24, 6 years in U.S., Water St., NYC, boat
builder (10-15 Aug. 1812)
Potts, Robert, age 28, 1 year & 6 mos. in U.S., wife, Newburgh,
Orange Co., laborer (19-24 Oct. 1812)
Pounds, Robert R., age 28, 7 years & 10 mos. in U.S., wife &
child, NYC, tailor (28 July - 2 Aug. 1812)
Pover, James, 5ft. 8in., age 48, fair complex., brown hair, grey
eyes, Rips Hill, maltster (Navy)
Powell, David N., age 20, 11 years in U.S. Phelps, Ontario Co.,
farmer (5-15 & 24-29 Aug. 1812)
Powell, Howell R., age 52, 11 years in U.S. 2 in family, Phelps,
Ontario Co., clergyman (5-15 & 24-29 Aug. 1812)
Powell, John, age 49, 11 years in U.S., wife & 7 children, Le-
banon, Madison Co., farmer (26 Aug. & 28 Sept. - 3 Oct. 1812)
Powell, Jonathan L., age 23, 11 years in U.S., 2 in family, Phelps,
Ontario Co., schoolmaster (5-15 & 24-19 Aug. 1812)
Powell, William, age 24, 5 years in U.S., wife & 3 children,
Orange Co., minister of the Gospel (3-8 Aug. 1812)
Power, John, age 30, 8 years in U.S., wife & 2 children, 16 Wil-
liam St., NYC, grocer (20-25 July 1812)
Powers, James, 5ft. 9in., age 30, light complex., light hair,
blue eyes, Broadway, coachman (Navy)
Powers, John, 5ft. 10in., age 35, dark complex., black hair,
black eyes, William St., mariner (Navy)
Powers, Patrick, 5ft. 6in., age 38, fair complex., brown hair,
grey eyes, Harlaem, coachman (Navy)
Pownell/Pownal, George, age 37, 4 mos. in U.S., wife & 3 child-
ren, Fair St., NYC, cabinetmaker, applied 21 Oct. 1812 (26-31
Oct. 1812); 5ft. 7in., age 37, brown complex., brown hair,
brown eyes, Church St., joiner (Navy)
Prakins, Thomas, age 46, 11 years in U.S., wife & 5 children,
Newburgh, Orange Co., weaver (12 Aug. & 17-22 Aug. 1812)
Preston, Michael, 5ft. 3in., age 33, light complex., brown hair,
grey eyes, labourer (Navy)
Preswick, Henry W., age 28, 7 years in U.S., Mount Pleasant,
Westchester Co., farmer (3-8 Aug. 1812); 5ft. 6in., age 28,
dark complex., dark hair, dark eyes, Mount Pleasant, farmer
(Navy)
Price, David, 5ft. 6in., age 23, light complex., brown hair,
dark eyes, painter (Navy)
Price, William, 5ft. 10in., age 45, light complex., brown hair,
light eyes, John St., manufacturer (Navy)

Price, William, 5ft. 6in., age 36, dark complex., black hair,
blue eyes, South St., sawyer (Navy)
Priestle, Richard, age 31, 10 years in U.S., Boyle, Ontario Co.,
farmer, applied Feb. 1810 (5-15 & 24-29 Aug. 1812)
Priestly, Samuel, age 26, 6 years in U.S., wife & child, Brook-
lyn, musician (20-25 July 1812)
Priestly, William, age 38, 5 years in U.S., wife, Schenectady,
shoemaker (10-15 Aug. 1812)
Prince, James, age 37, 10 years in U.S., wife, laborer (24-29
Aug. 1812)
Pringle, Thomas, age 33, 9 years in U.S., wife & 4 children,
village of Greenwich, clerk (13-18 July 1812)
Pringle, Thomas, 5ft., 9in., age 34, light complex., brown hair,
grey eyes, teller Bank of New York (Navy)
Pritchard, Henry, age 49, 9 years in U.S., wife, 159 Greenwich
St., NYC, baker (20-25 July 1812); 5ft. 6in., age 49, red com-
plex., light hair, hazel eyes, Greenwich St., confectioner
(Navy)
Pritchard, James, age 24, 1 year & 7 mos. in U.S., wife, NYC,
comedian (13-18 July 1812); 5ft. 7in., age 25, fair complex.,
brown hair, hazel eyes, West St., comedian (Navy)
Pritchard, John, 5ft. 9in., age 35, dark complex., brown hair,
blue eyes, Duane St., rigger (Navy)
Proper, John, 5ft. 9in., age 25, light complex., light hair,
dark eyes, Warren St., coachman (Navy)
Prosser, John, age 27, 16 years in U.S., 67 Murray St., NYC,
coach maker (28 July - 2 Aug. 1812)
Prout, Roger, age 46, 6 years in U.S., wife & 4 children, Spring
St., NYC, manufacturer of printer's ink, applied 20 Nov. 1808
(13-18 July 1812); 5ft. 10in., age 46, fair complex., brown
hair, grey eyes, Spring St., manufacturer (Navy)
Prowitt, Thomas, age 39, 12 years in U.S., wife & 2 children,
Hudson, Columbia Co., teacher (10-15 Aug. 1812)
Pugh, John, 5ft. 6in., age 22, dark complex., black hair, grey
eyes, Robinson St., cordwainer (Navy)
Purcel, William, 5ft. 7in., age 28, fair complex., brown hair,
blue eyes, Broadway, shoemaker (Navy)
Purdie, Samuel, age 46, (illegible) years & 9 mos. in U.S., wife
& child, City of Albany, joiner (24-29 Aug. 1812)
Purdy, David, age 58, 28 years in U.S., 13 in family, Queens Co.,
farmer (26-31 Oct. 1812)
Purdy, Gilbert, age 24, 3 mos. in U.S., Newburgh, Orange Co.,
laborer (19-24 Oct. 1812)
Purgil, William, 5ft. 4in., age 30, brown complex., brown hair,
grey eyes, carpenter (Navy)
Purser, Thomas, age 42, 8 years in U.S., wife & 2 children, Newburgh, Orange Co., farmer (17-22 Aug. 1812)
Purves, Francis, age 26, 1 day in U.S., NYC, merchant (28 Sept. -
3 Oct. 1812)
Purves, William, age 36, 11 years in U.S., 44 Barclay St., NYC,
carpenter (28 July - 2 Aug. 1812)
Purvis, William, 5ft. 7½in., age 32, light complex., brown hair,
brown eyes, Barclay St., carpenter (Navy) - perhaps same as
above.
Pye, John, age 38, 9 years in U.S., wife & child, NYC, locksmith
(20-25 July 1812); 5ft. 6in., age 39, fair complex., brown
hair, grey eyes, Bowery, locksmith (Navy)
Pye, Thomas, age 62, 3 years in U.S., Rome, Oneida Co., weaver,
employed in factory of James Lynch (29 July 1812)
Pye, Thomas, 5ft. 8in., age 31, light complex., light hair, light
eyes, milkman (Navy)
Pye, William, age 32, 11 years in U.S., wife & 2 children, 45
Pearl St., NYC, locksmith (20-25 July 1812); 5ft. 9in., age 32,
fair complex., brown hair, brown eyes, Pearl St., locksmith
(Navy)

Pyke, Thomas, age 62, 3 years in U.S., Rome, Oneida Co., weaver
(3-8 Aug. 1812)
Quick, Cornelius, 5ft. 9½in., age 26, fair complex., black hair,
hazel eyes, Robinson St., servant (Navy)
Quick, Edward, age 38, 17 years in U.S., wife & 7 children, 162
Broadway, hairdresser (20-25 July 1812); 5ft. 7in., age 38,
fair complex., brown hair, dark eyes, Broadway, hairdresser
(Navy)
Quigley, Andrew, 5ft. 9in., age 46, light complex., brown hair,
blue eyes, gardener (Navy)
Quigley, John, age 28, 5 years & 3 mos. in U.S., wife & child,
Deerpark, Orange Co., shoemaker (19-24 Oct. 1812)
Quin, Edward, 5ft. 11in., age 24, brown complex., brown hair,
hazel eyes, labourer (Navy)
Quin, Edward C., 5ft. 9in., age 27, fair complex., brown hair,
brown eyes, clerk (Navy)
Quin, John, age 42, 9 years in U.S., Bath, Steuben Co., laborer
(25-31 Aug. & 7-12 Sept. 1812)
Quin, John, age 30, 8 years in U.S., wife, 37 Catherine St.,
NYC, merchant tailor, applied Apr. 1808 (20-25 July 1812)
Quin, John, 5ft. 5in., age 29, fair complex., dark hair, blue
eyes, Cherry St., tailor (Navy)
Quin, John, 5ft. 7in., age 26, dark complex., dark hair, grey
eyes, Church St., teacher (Navy)
Quin, Nicholas, 5ft. 4in., age 27, red complex., brown hair,
grey eyes, Church St., stone cutter (Navy)
Quin, Patrick, age 24, 19 years in U.S., 3 in family, Benton,
Ontario Co., farmer (25 Oct. - 15 Nov. 1812)
Quinn, Michael, age 29, 7 years in U.S., wife & 3 children, Wall-
kill, Orange Co., teacher (19-24 Oct. 1812)
Quinten, Allen, 5ft. 8in., age 30, fair complex., brown hair,
blue eyes, Front St., cartman (Navy)
Racey, Charles, age 33, 5 years in U.S., wife & 2 children, 13
James St., NYC, brewer (20-25 July 1812); 5ft. 8in., age 35,
dark complex., dark hair, dark eyes, James St., brewer (Navy)
Racey, James, age 31, 2 years in U.S., Hudson, Columbia Co.,
brewer (3-8 Aug. 1812)
Racey, Thomas, age 52, 8 years in U.S., wife & 5 children, 19
Henry St., NYC, tallow chandler (20-25 July 1812)
Radforth, Thomas, 5ft. 10in., age 20, brown complex., brown hair,
blue eyes, Washington St., weaver (Navy)
Rafferty, James, age 30, 5 years in U.S., mother, 11 Dutch St.,
NYC, bunting manufacturer (31 Aug. - 5 Sept. 1812)
Rafferty, John, age 28, 1 year in U.S., Newburgh, Orange Co.,
laborer (19-24 Oct. 1812)
Rafferty, Patrick, 6ft. 1in., age 21, fair complex., fair hair,
blue eyes, De Peyster St., cooper (Navy)
Rafferty, Patrick, 5ft. 7in., age 20, fair complex., brown hair,
grey eyes, Jacob St., morocco (Navy)
Rafferty, Rev. Wm., age 28, 9 mos. in U.S., Bloominggrove, Orange
Co., minister of the Gospel (19-24 Oct. 1812)
Raisbeck, William, 5ft. 8in., age 30, dark complex., dark hair,
dark eyes, Brookhaven, saddler (Navy)
Ralph, John Rhodes, age 26, 1 year & 3 mos. in U.S., 68 Green-
wich St., NYC, merchant (20-25 July 1812)
Ramsay, John, 5ft. 10in., age 27, dark complex., dark hair, blue
eyes, Greenwich St., pit sawyer (Navy)
Ramsey, Alexander, age 22, 10 years & 2 mos. in U.S., Bethel,
Sullivan Co., carpenter (31 Aug. & 19-24 Oct. 1812)
Ramsey, John, age 30, 6 years in U.S., Greenwich St., NYC, saw-
yer (20-25 July 1812)
Ramsey, Samuel, age 31, 8 mos. in U.S., wife & child, New Wind-
sor, Orange co., weaver (19-24 Oct. 1812)
Randolph, Lewis, age 28, 5 years in U.S., wife, Desbrosses St.,
NYC, sawyer (28 July - 2 Aug. 1812)

Rankin, Alexander, 5ft. 11 3/4in., age 38, fair complex., fair
hair, blue eyes, labourer (Navy)
Rankin, Thomas, age 31, 8 years & 9 mos. in U.S., wife, Deerpark,
Orange Co., farmer (19-24 Oct. 1812)
Rankin, William, age 44, 9 years in U.S., wife & 2 children, 58
Cedar St., NYC, saddler (20-25 July 1812); 5ft. 7in., age 46,
light complex., dark hair, blue eyes, saddler (Navy)
Ransford, Samuel B., age 36, 9 years in U.S., wife & 4 children,
6 Mile Stone, innkeeper (20-25 July 1812); Ransford, Samuel,
5ft. 7in., age 37, florid complex., dark hair, black eyes,
asst. keeper State Prison (Navy)
Rapelye, George F., age 25, 22 years in U.S. Newtown, Long Island,
farmer (21-26 Sept. 1812); 5ft. 11in., age 27, light complex.,
light hair, blue eyes, yeoman (Navy)
Ratchford, John, 5ft. 5½in., age 28, fair complex., fair hair,
blue eyes, baker (Navy)
Raven, Richard, age 43, 8 years in U.S., assistant keeper of the
State Prison (20-25 July 1812)
Raven, Richard, 5ft. 6½in., age 35, fair complex., brown hair,
blue eyes, Bloomingdale, tanner (Navy)
Raven, Thomas, 5ft. 8in., age 30, fair complex., brown hair,
Brookhaven, saddler (Navy)
Rawlinson, Thomas W., age 27, 6 years in U.S., City (probably of
Albany, illegible because of ink blot), merchant (20-25 July
1812)
Ray, Francis, age 32, 11 years in U.S., wife & child, Newburgh,
Orange Co., mason (19-24 Oct. 1812)
Ray, Thomas, 5ft. 8in., age 74, fair complex., fair hair, grey
eyes, labourer (Navy)
Rea, David, age 96, 1 year & 6 mos. in U.S., wife, Athens, Greene
Co., weaver (3-8 Aug. 1812)
Rea, David, age 21, 1 year & 2 mos. in U.S., Poughkeepsie, Dut-
chess Co., weaver (12-17 Oct. 1812)
Rea, James, age 22, 1 year & 3 mos. in U.S., wife, Poughkeepsie,
Dutchess Co., weaver (12-17 Oct. 1812)
Rea, Robert, age 30, 1 year in U.S., wife & 3 children, City of
Albany, merchant (5-10 Oct. 1812)
Read, James, age 29, 6 years in U.S., NYC, cartman (28 July - 2
Aug. 1812); 5ft. 8in., age 30, light complex., fair hair, grey
eyes, Bayard St., cartman (Navy)
Read, John, age 24, 2 years in U.S., Richmond Co., basket maker
(10-15 Aug. 1812)
Read, Sampson, age 27, 9 years in U.S., Richmond Co., basket
maker, applied 13 Apr. 1811 (10-15 Aug. 1812); 5ft. 6in., age
28, fair complex., brown hair, grey eyes, basket (Navy)
Read, William A., 5ft. 5in., age 32, fair complex., brown hair,
brown eyes, Essex St., clerk, removed from NYC to Goshen, Orange
Co. (Navy)
Reaman, John, age 20, 1 year in U.S., City of Albany, laborer
(5-10 Oct. 1812)
Reaman, Moses, age 22, 1 year in U.S., City of Albany, laborer
(5-10 Oct. 1812)
Reamond, Peter, age 16, 1 year in U.S., City of Albany, servant
(5-10 Oct. 1812)
Reanny, Anthony, 5ft. 3½in., age 30, fair complex., fair hair,
dark eyes, Middle Road, labourer (Navy)
Reath, Michael, 5ft. 6in., age 45, fair complex., brown hair,
blue eyes, clerk (Navy)
Reben, Patrick, 5ft. 6in., age 26, fair complex., brown hair,
grey eyes, cartman (Navy)
Reddell, William, 5ft. 7in., age 34, dark complex., dark hair,
dark eyes, Varick St., stone cutter (Navy)
Reddy, Timothy, age 34, 15 years in U.S., wife & 6 children,
Scipio, Cayuga Co., tailor (7-12 & 21-26 Sept. 1812)

Redmond, Thomas, age 35, 9 years & 9 mos. in U.S., NYC, accountant (20-25 July 1812)

Redshaw, William, age 25, 11 mos. in U.S., wife & child, Bethel, Sullivan Co., farmer (19-24 Oct. 1812)

Redstone, Henry, 5ft. 3in., age 19, fair complex., dark hair, hazel eyes, organ (Navy)

Redstone, Thomas, 5ft. 6in., age 22, fair complex., brown hair, dark eyes organ b(uilder) (Navy)

Redstone, William, Sr., 5ft. 7½in., age 64, fair complex., grey hair, hazel eyes, organ (Navy)

Redstone, William, 5ft. 5in., age 29, fair complex., black hair, grey eyes, gardener (Navy)

Reed, John, age 29, 6 years in U.S., White Hall, Washington Co., merchant (21-16 Sept. 1812)

Reed, John, 5ft. 9in., age 28, light complex., light hair, blue eyes, stone cutter (Navy)

Reed, John, 5ft. 5in., age 23, light complex., light hair, brown eyes, George St. (Navy)

Reed, John, Jr., age 23, 16 years in U.S., Rensselaer Co., farmer (5-10 Oct. 1812)

Reed, Samuel, 5ft. 7in., age 35, fair complex., dark hair, grey eyes, Stagg Town, sawyer (Navy)

Reed, Stephen, age 45, 21 years in U.S., New Windsor, Orange Co., laborer (19-24 Oct. 1812)

Reed, Thomas, age 34, 2 years in U.S., wife & 4 children, corner Reed St. & Broadway, NYC, grocer (13-18 July 1812); 5ft. 6in., age 35, fair complex., brown hair, grey eyes, Broadway, grocer (Navy)

Reed, Thomas, age 30, 10 years in U.S., 2 in family, Mendon, Ontario Co., farmer (30 Aug. - 5 Sept. & 7-12 Sept. 1812)

Reed, William, age 73, 10 years in U.S., 2 in family, Boyle, Ontario Co., well digger, applied Nov. 1811 (13-27 Sept. & 28 Sept. - 3 Oct. 1812)

Reed, William, 5ft. 9in., age 47, light complex., brown hair, grey eyes, Bloomingdale, gardener (Navy)

Rees, John, 5ft. 9in., age 33, light complex., brown hair, black eyes, Cheapside, drayman (Navy)

Reeves, Charles, 5ft. 8½in., age 37, fair complex., dark hair, grey eyes, grocer (Navy)

Reeves, William, age 22, 1 year in U.S., 110 Greenwich St., NYC (20-25 July 1812); Reeves, William P.T., 5ft. 7½in., age 23, fair complex., light hair, blue eyes, Greenwich St. (Navy)

Reid, Hugh, 6ft. 2in., age 25, dark complex., black hair, grey eyes, Barclay St., painter (Navy)

Reid, James, age 31, 7 years in U.S., wife & child, NYC, cordwainer (28 July - 2 Aug. 1812)

Reid, James, 5ft. 5½in., age 29, brown complex., brown hair, light eyes, Hester St., boot (Navy)

Reid, Robert, 5ft. 6in., age 29, dark complex., brown hair, grey eyes, Thomas St., boot (Navy)

Reid, Robert, age 26, 6 years in U.S., wife & 2 children, NYC, cordwainer (28 July - 2 Aug. 1812)

Reid, William, age 30, 10 years in U.S., wife & 3 children, Amsterdam, Montgomery Co., merchant (11-17 & 17-22 Aug. 1812)

Reilly, Hugh, age 19, 12 years in U.S., Newburgh, Orange Co., laborer (19-24 Oct. 1812)

Reily, James, age 36, 10 years in U.S., wife, Newburgh, Orange Co., laborer (17-22 Aug. 1812)

Reilly, Patrick, 5ft. 9in., age 25, fair complex., fair hair, light eyes, Water St., tobacco (Navy)

Reily, Thomas, 5ft. 8in., age 32, fair complex., fair hair, brown eyes, Mott St., cartman (Navy)

Reilly/Reily, Thomas, age 17, 9 mos. in U.S., Newburgh, Orange Co., labourer (14 Aug. & 17-22 Aug. 1812)

Remel, Joseph, 5ft. 7½in., age 46, fair complex., dark hair,
dark eyes, Reed St., smith (Navy)
Rench, Patrick, 5ft. 10in., age 27, light complex., brown hair,
brown eyes, Catherine St., nailor (Navy)
Renwick, Adam, age 18, 11 years in U.S., Seneca, Ontario Co.,
farmer (5-15 & 24-29 Aug. 1812)
Renwick, George, age 58, 11 years in U.S., 4 in family, Gorham,
Ontario Co., farmer (13-27 Sept. & 28 Sept. - 3 Oct. 1812)
Renwick, George, age 22, 11 years in U.S., Gorham, Ontario Co.,
farmer (15-22 Aug. & 31 Aug. - 5 Sept. 1812)
Renwick, James, age 15, 11 years in U.S., Gorham, Ontario Co.,
farmer (13-27 Sept. & 28 Sept. - 3 Oct. 1812)
Renwick, John, age 51, 11 years in U.S., 6 in family, Seneca,
Ontario Co., farmer (5-15 & 24-29 Aug. 1812)
Reymes (?), Patrick, age 32, 5 years in U.S., 53 Cross St., NYC,
laborer (20-25 July 1812)
Reynold, Joseph, age 40, 1 year in U.S., 3 children, Cornwall,
Orange Co., weaver (21 Dec. 1812 - 23 Jan. 1813 & 2 Jan. 1813)
Reynolds, James, age 60, 1 year in U.S., wife & 3 children, 15
Water St., NYC, laborer (13-18 July 1812)
Reynolds, James, 5ft. 8in., age 60, dark complex., brown hair,
blue eyes, weaver (Navy)
Reynolds, James, 5ft. 8in., age 33, brown complex., brown hair,
grey eyes, Greenwich St., cartman (Navy)
Reynolds, James A., 5ft. 7in., age 18, dark complex., brown hair,
grey eyes, Frankfort St., clerk (Navy)
Reynolds, Lackey, age 32, 10 years in U.S., Queens Co., farmer
(31 Aug. - 5 Sept. 1812)
Reynolds, Thomas, 5ft. 9in., age 24, fair complex., brown hair,
blue eyes, Anthony St., labourer (Navy)
Reynolds, William, 5ft. 1 3/4in., age 46, dark complex., light
hair, dark eyes, Harman St., mariner (Navy)
Reynolds, William, age 37, 11 years in U.S., 1 child, Bulls Head,
drover (30 Nov. - 5 Dec. 1812)
Reynolds, William, 5ft. 7in., age 24, dark complex., dark hair,
grey eyes, Henry St., file cutter (Navy)
Reynoldson, Thomas, 5ft. 4in., age 33, dark complex., black hair,
brown eyes, mechanic (Navy)
Rhey, Thomas, 5ft. 7in., age 22, fair complex., fair hair, grey
eyes, Cow Bay, weaver (Navy)
Ribbons, Robert, age 34, 16 years in U.S., wife & 5 children,
142 Duane St., NYC, cooper (20-25 July 1812); 5ft. 6in., age
35, dark complex., dark hair, dark eyes, Reed St., cooper (Navy)
Rice, David, age 28, 6 years & 11 mos. in U.S., wife, 112 Reed
St., NYC (20-25 July 1812); 5ft. 10in., age 30, light complex.,
brown hair, dark eyes (Navy)
Rice, Edward, 5ft. 8in., age 52, dark complex., brown hair, blue
eyes, labourer (Navy)
Rice, Joseph James, age 28, 21 years in U.S., wife & 2 children,
30 Barclay St., NYC, gunsmith (28 July - 2 Aug. 1812); 5ft.
3in., age 29, fair complex., dark hair, grey eyes, Chamber St.,
gun maker (Navy)
Richard, Joseph, 5ft. 4in., age 28, light complex., light hair,
blue eyes, Bowery, druggist (Navy)
Richards, John, 5ft. 9in., age 37, fair complex., dark hair,
dark eyes, brewer (Navy)
Richards, Richard, age 46, 5 years in U.S. on 24 June last, wife
& 6 children, Eaton, Madison Co., farmer (31 Oct. & 30 Nov. -
5 Dec. 1812)
Richards, William, age 63, 16 years in U.S., wife, Steuben, Oneida Co., farmer (29 Sept. & 28 Sept. - 3 Oct. 1812)
Richards, William, age 37, 5 years in U.S., wife & child, corner
Garden & New Sts., NYC, tallow chandler (20-25 July 1812)

Richards, William, age 29 on 9 Feb. last, 11 years in U.S. on
27 July last, 1 girl, Utica, Oneida Co., cordwainer (26 Aug.
& 28 Sept. - 3 Oct. 1812)
Richards, William, age 24, 19 years in U.S., 140 Front St., NYC,
tobacconist (20-25 July 1812); 5ft. 6in., age 24, dark complex.,
black hair, dark eyes, Front St., tobacco (Navy)
Richardson, James, age 29, 6 years in U.S., wife & 2 children,
New Windsor, Orange Co., laborer (19-24 Oct. 1812)
Richardson, John, age 52, 3 mos. in U.S., 4 in family, Fayette
St., NYC, teacher (20-25 July 1812); 5ft. 10in., age 52, dark
complex., dark hair, dark eyes, Beekman Slip, teacher (Navy)
Richardson, John, 6ft., age 45, fair complex., light hair, blue
eyes, teacher (Navy)
Richardson, Joseph, age 51, 6 years in U.S., 8 in family, Geneva,
Ontario Co., farmer (25 Oct. - 15 Nov. 1812)
Riche, Alexander, 5ft. 9in., age 26, fair complex., brown hair,
grey eyes, Arundle St., weaver (Navy)
Richie (?), John, 5ft. 8in., age 42, dark complex., black hair,
black eyes, mariner (Navy)
Richmond, Archibald, age 28, 2 years & 8 mos. in U.S., wife & 3
children, 37 Charlotte St., NYC, distiller (28 July - 2 Aug.
1812)
Richard, Joseph, age 27, 17 years in U.S., 184 Bowery Lane, NYC,
druggist (20-25 July 1812); see Richard, Joseph, above.
Ricketts, George A., age 22, 9 years in U.S., 203 Broadway, NYC
(13-18 July 1812)
Rickets, George H., 5ft. 11in., age 23, dark complex., sandy
hair, brown eyes, cabinetmaker (Navy)
Rickets, George H., 5ft. 11in., age 23, sandy complex., sandy
hair, blue eyes, Harlaem, innkeeper (Navy)
Riddle, Christopher, 6ft., age 30, dark complex., black hair,
black eyes, Lumber St., blacksmith (Navy)
Riddle, Samuel, age 12, 1 year & 6 mos. in U.S., Schaghticoke,
Albany Co., weaver (24-29 Aug. 1812)
Riley, Edward, 5ft. 6in., age 40, fair complex., dark hair, dark
eyes, music inst. maker (Navy)
Ring, Thomas, age 24, 5 years in U.S., wife & child, Schenectady,
laborer & grocer (17-22 Aug. 1812)
Riorden, Dennis, age 25, 13 years in U.S., Phelps, Ontario Co.,
cooper (5-15 & 24-29 Aug. 1812)
Ripley, Thomas B., age 21, 1 year in U.S., Columbiaville, Colum-
bia Co., machine maker (22 Aug. & 24-29 Aug. 1812)
Ritchie, Alexander, age 26, 1 year & 4 mos. in U.S., Greenwich
St., NYC, weaver (28 July - 2 Aug. 1812)
Ritchie, John, 5ft. 9in., age 27, fair complex., dark hair, grey
eyes, Henry St., weaver (Navy)
Roach, James, 5ft. 4½in., age 48, fair complex., dark hair, blue
eyes, gardener (Navy)
Roach, James, age 40, 2 years in U.S., Westchester Co., gardener
(10-15 Aug. 1812)
Roach, James, 5ft. 10in., age 33, fair complex., brown hair, grey
eyes, labourer (Navy)
Roach, John, 5ft. 4in., age 30, light complex., light hair, blue
eyes, Elizabeth St., mason (Navy)
Roach, Patrick, age 26, 5 years in U.S., Montgomery, Orange Co.,
farmer (21 Dec. 1812 - 23 Jan. 1813 & 2 Jan. 1813)
Robb, Alexander, age 53, 18 years in U.S., 6 Water St., NYC, tai-
lor (3-8 Aug. 1812); 5ft. 6in., age 52, dark complex., dark
hair, brown eyes, Water St., tailor (Navy)
Robb, Alexander, 5ft. 8½in., age 35, dark complex., brown hair,
blue eyes, Stagg Town, sawyer (Navy)
Robb, Alexander, age 30, 8 years in U.S., 2 in family, Rivington
St., sawyer (28 July - 2 Aug. 1812)
Robb, John, age 29, 10 mos. in U.S., wife & child, New Windsor,
Orange Co., mason (19-24 Oct. 1812)

Roberts, James, age 59 on 12 Dec. next, 12 years in U.S. on 12
Sept. next, wife & 8 children, Lee, Oneida Co., farmer, from
Lancashire, England (29 Sept. 1812)

Roberts, John, age 46, 6 years in U.S., Seneca, Ontario Co.,
laborer (15-22 Aug. & 31 Aug. - 5 Sept. 1812)

Roberts, John, age 35, 11 years in U.S., wife & 4 children,
Poughkeepsie, Dutchess Co., laborer (12-17 Oct. 1812)

Roberts, John, age 30, 8 years in U.S., wife & 3 children, 395
Greenwich St., NYC, stone cutter (26-31 Oct. 1812); 5ft. 8¼in.,
age 33, fair complex., fair hair, grey eyes, Greenwich St.,
stone cutter (Navy)

Roberts, Thomas, age 40 last summer, 11 years in U.S., wife & 2
children, Whitestown, Oneida Co., farmer (26 Aug. & 18 Sept. -
3 Oct. 1812)

Roberts, Thomas, age 29 on 12 June last, 8 years in U.S. last
Oct., wife & 3 children, Trenton, Oneida Co., cooper (26 Aug.
& 28 Sept. - 3 Oct. 1812)

Roberts, William, age 37, 10 years in U.S., Pearl St., NYC,
gentleman (20-25 July 1812)

Roberts, William, 5ft. 5in., age 24, light complex., light hair,
blue eyes, Elizabeth St., maltster (Navy)

Robertson, Alexander, age 37, 8 years in U.S., wife & 5 children, Johnsburgh, Washington Co., farmer(21 Dec. 1812 - 23 Jan.
1813); wife is Elizabeth and children are Daniel, Alexander,
Charles, Margaret, Elizabeth (30 Dec. 1812)

Robertson, Alexander, age 36, 12 years in U.S., wife & 3 children, 420 Greenwich St., NYC, sawyer (20-25 July 1812); 5ft.
6in., age 37, fair complex., light hair, blue eyes, Greenwich
St., pit sawyer (Navy)

Robertson, Alexander, age 35 in Dec. last, 8 years in U.S. in
Sept. last, wife & 4 children, Thurman, Washington Co., farmer
(24 Nov. 1812 & 21 Dec. 1812 - 23 Jan. 1813)

Robertson, Daniel, age 46, 2 years in U.S., wife & 5 children,
Smithfield, Madison Co., farmer (1 Aug. & 10-15 Aug. 1812)

Robertson, David, age 44, 1 year in U.S., wife & 6 children,
Greenwich Lane, NYC, clerk (20-25 July 1812); 5ft. 6in., age
44, fair complex., dark hair, grey eyes, bank (Navy)

Robertson, Donald, age 30, 8 years in U.S. in Sept. last, wife
& 2 children, Thurman, Washington Co., farmer (24 Nov. 1812 &
21 Dec. 1812 - 23 Jan. 1813)

Robertson, Gilbert, age 50, 27 years in U.S., wife & 3 children,
NYC, merchant (13-18 July 1812)

Robertson, James, age 32, 9 years in U.S., wife & 2 children,
City of Albany, stone cutter, applied 7 Aug. 1812 (17-22 Aug.
1812)

Robertson, James, age 22, 9 mos. in U.S., corner Mott & Grand
Sts., NYC, merchant (28 July - 2 Aug. 1812); 5ft. 5in., age
23, fair complex., dark hair, brown eyes, James St., pedler
(Navy)

Robertson, John, age 49, 11 years in U.S., wife & child, Smithfield, Madison Co., farmer (1 Aug. & 10-15 Aug. 1812)

Robertson, John, age 48, 9 years in U.S., 6 children, Greenwich
Lane, NYC, farmer, applied 26 Apr. 1809 (10-15 Aug. 1812); 5ft.
7in., age 50, fair complex., brown hair, grey eyes, Greenwich
Lane, gardener (Navy)

Robertson, John, age 30, 11 years in U.S., wife & 4 children,
Johnstown, Montgomery Co., laborer (6 Oct. - 4 Nov. & 9-14
Nov. 1812)

Robertson, John, age 25, 2 years & 10 mos. in U.S., 12 Dutch St.,
NYC, printer (20-25 July 1812)

Robertson, Robert, age 26, 11 years in U.S., Smithfield, Madison
Co., farmer (1 Aug. & 10-15 Aug. 1812)

Robertson, Robert S., age 19, 13 years in U.S., Newburgh, Orange
Co., carpenter (14 Aug. & 17-22 Aug. 1812)

Robins, Nathaniel, 5ft. 7in., age 60, dark complex., dark hair,
    brown eyes, Richmond Co., farmer (Navy)
Robinson, Gilbert, 5ft. 10in., age 50, fair complex., grey hair,
    blue eyes, removed from NYC to Columbia (Navy)
Robinson, John, age 33, 3 years in U.S., 44 Thomas St., NYC,
    mason (20-25 July 1812)
Robinson, John, 5ft. 9in., age 29, fair complex., black hair,
    grey eyes, Cherry St., brushmaker (Navy)
Robinson, John, 5ft. 8in., age 27, fair complex., sandy hair,
    brown eyes, Pine St., printer (Navy)
Robinson, Thomas, age 40, 11 years in U.S., wife & 6 children,
    Mount Pleasant, Westchester Co., farmer (7-19 Dec. 1812)
Robinson, William, 5ft. 5½in., age 29, dark complex., dark hair,
    dark eyes, Oak St., rigger (Navy)
Robison, William, age 19, 14 mos. in U.S., Amsterdam, Montgomery
    Co., wheelwright (15 Sept. - 5 Oct. 1812)
Roble (name blotted, possibly Robb), James, age 25, 10 mos. in
    U.S., wife & child, Newburgh, Orange Co., weaver (19-24 Oct.
    1812)
Robson, Gowen, age 19, 11 years in U.S., Seneca, Ontario Co.,
    farmer (5-15 & 24-29 Aug 1812)
Robson, James, age 14, 11 years in U.S., Seneca, Ontario Co.,
    farmer (5-15 & 24-29 Aug. 1812)
Robson, John, age 21, 11 years in U.S., Seneca, Ontario Co.,
    farmer (5-15 & 24-29 Aug. 1812)
Robson, John, age 18, 6 years in U.S., Gorham, Ontario Co., far-
    mer (15-22 Aug. & 31 Aug. - 5 Sept. 1812)
Robson, Robert, age 17, 11 years in U.S., Seneca, Ontario Co.,
    farmer (24-29 Aug. 1812)
Robson, William, age 19, 1 year & 2 mos. in U.S., Amsterdam,
    Montgomery Co., wheelwright (5-10 Oct. 1812) - obviously the
    same as Robison, William, above.
Roburt, James, age 59, 12 years in U.S., wife & 8 children, Lee,
    Oneida Co., farmer (28 Sept. - 3 Oct. 1812) - obviously the
    same as Roberts, James, above.
Roby, Thomas, age 47, 1½ years in U.S., wife & child, Rockland,
    teacher (20-25 July 1812); 5ft. 8in., age 47, brown Complex.,
    brown hair, dark eyes, Slaughter's Landing, Rockland Co.,
    teacher (Navy)
Rochfort, James, age 24, 8 years in U.S., wife & child, 251
    William St., NYC, grocer (20-25 July 1812)
Rock, James, age 29, 1 year & 2 mos. in U.S., wife, Republican
    Alley, NYC, weaver (20-25 July 1812)
Rodgers, James, age 43, 11 years in U.S., wife & 7 children,
    City of Albany, millwright (24-29 Aug. 1812)
Rodgers, James, Jr., age 15, 11 years in U.S., City of Albany,
    apprentice (24-29 Aug. 1812)
Rodgers, Thomas, age 24, 11 years in U.S., NYC, cooper (17-22
    Aug. 1812)
Roe, John H., age 24, 3 mos. in U.S., Mamakating, Sullivan Co.,
    teacher (19-24 Oct. 1812)
Roe, Peter, 6ft., age 24, fair complex., fair hair, brown eyes,
    shipwright (Navy)
Roger, Allen, age 46, 18 years in U.S., wife & 3 children, West-
    chester Co., baker (28 July - 2 Aug. 1812)
Rogers, Andrew, age 32, 11 years in U.S., wife & 2 children,
    Grand St., NYC, confectioner (20-25 July 1812)
Rogers, James, age 48, 2 years & 8 mos. in U.S., 2 sons, Bethel,
    Sullivan Co., carpenter (31 Aug. & 19-24 Oct. 1812)
Rogers, James, age 32, 25 years in U.S., Schenectady, farmer
    (17-22 Aug. 1812)
Rogers, James, 5ft. 11in., age 30, fair complex., brown hair,
    grey eyes, Reed St., musician (Navy)

Rogers, John, 5ft. 4½in., age 32, light complex., dark hair,
dark eyes, jeweler (Navy)
Rogers, John, age 22, 12 years in U.S., 45 Nassau St., NYC,
jeweler (10-15 Aug. 1812) - can he be the same as the John
above through some error in age?
Rogers, John, 6ft., age 20, fair complex., fair hair, Elm St.,
labourer (Navy)
Rogers, John H., age 26, 17 years in U.S., Saugerties, Ulster
Co., currier (19-24 Oct. 1812)
Rogers, Joseph, age 28, 8 years & 9 mos. in U.S., City of Albany,
stone cutter (17-22 Aug. 1812)
Rogers, Joseph, age 28, 9 years in U.S., wife & child, 63 Chatham St., NYC, storekeeper (20-25 July 1812); 5ft. 7in., age 28,
fair complex., fair hair, black eyes, Chatham St., grocer (Navy)
Rogers, Samuel, age 28, 7 mos. in U.S., NYC, sawyer (21-26 Sept.
1812)
Rogers, Thomas, 5ft. 6in., age 24, dark complex., brown hair,
blue eyes, Read St., cooper (Navy)
Rogers, Thomas H., age 27, 3 years in U.S., 7 Maiden Lane, NYC,
plumber & glazier (20-25 July 1812)
Rogers, William, age 38, 9 years in U.S., wife, Charlton, Sara-
toga Co., farmer (31 Aug. - 5 Sept. 1812)
Rogerson, Thomas, age 35, 9 years in U.S., wife & 4 children,
64 Barclay St., NYC, merchant (20-25 July 1812)
Rogerson, Thomas, 5ft. 10½in., age 35, fair complex., brown hair,
blue eyes, Greenwich St., currier (Navy)
Rollston, Andrew, age 44, 1 year in U.S., Newburgh, Orange Co.,
laborer (19-24 Oct. 1812)
Roodman, Michael, age 41, 11 mos. in U.S., wife & 2 children,
Schenectady, tanner & shoemaker (10-15 Aug. 1812)
Rooke, William, age 50 on 3 Jan. last, 1 year & 11 mos. & 14
days in U.S., Whitestown, Oneida Co., schoolmaster, from York-
shire, England (26 Aug. & 28 Sept. - 3 Oct. 1812)
Rooney, Alexander, age 29, 2 years & 10 mos. in U.S., wife & 3
children, Kingston, Ulster Co., weaver (19-24 Oct. 1812)
Rooney, Felam, 5ft. 10in., age 32, light complex., dark hair,
blue eyes, Duane St., labourer (Navy)
Rooney, John, age 31, 3 years in U.S., 124 Chamber St., NYC,
teacher (20-25 July 1812)
Rooney, Lawrence, 5ft. 11in., age 40, fair complex., grey hair,
blue eyes, Orange St., labourer (Navy)
Rooney, Owen, age 30, 6 years in U.S., Livingston, Columbia Co.,
teacher (28 Aug. & 31 Aug. - 5 Sept. 1812)
Rose, Philip, 5ft. 6in., age 28, fair complex., dark hair, blue
eyes, removed from NYC to Utica, Oneida Co. (Navy)
Rositer, John, age 31, 8 years in U.S., 165 Bancker St., NYC,
shipwright (20-25 July 1812)
Ross, Caleb, age 27, 1 mo. in U.S., wife, 73 Stone St., NYC,
tinman (26-31 Oct. 1812); 5ft. 8in., age 28, dark complex.,
dark hair, dark eyes, Chamber St., tinplate worker (Navy)
Ross, George, age 24, 3 mos. in U.S., 28 Nassau St., NYC, business (20-25 July 1812)
Ross, John, age 44, 24 years in U.S., wife & 3 children, painter
(20-25 July 1812)
Ross, John, 5ft. 8in., age 23, dark complex., black hair, black
eyes, Greenwich St., sawyer (Navy & 28 July - 2 Aug. 1812)
Ross, Robert, age 21, 9 years & 10 mos. in U.S., Montgomery,
Orange Co., weaver (19-24 Oct. 1812)
Ross, Thomas, age 42, 2 years in U.S., 9 State St., NYC, merchant,
"mercantile speculator," lately a surgeon in the British Army;
he came here 14 May 1810 and boards at Gen. Bloomfield's head-
quarters (13-18 July 1812)
Ross, William, 5ft. 6in., age 28, fair complex., fair hair, blue
eyes, Arundle St., rock blow (Navy)

Rothgangal/Rothgangol, John, age 26, 10 years in U.S., Rose Hill,
tallow chandler (28 July -2 Aug. 1812); 5ft. 4in., age 27,
brown complex., brown hair, blue eyes, Bowery, tallow (Navy)
Rowe, Peter, age 23, 11 mos. in U.S., 303 Water St., NYC, shipwright (28 July - 2 Aug. 1812)
Rowe, Robert, age 32, 11 years in U.S., wife & 3 children, Broadway, NYC, cabinetmaker (20-25 July 1812); 5ft. 6in., age 34,
light complex., brown hair, brown eyes, Wooster St., cabinetmaker (Navy)
Rowland, William, age 28, 10 years in U.S., wife, Fitzroy Road,
NYC, gardener (20-25 July 1812)
Roy, William, age 21, 2 years in U.S., 28 Wall St., NYC, shoe-
maker (10-15 Aug. 1812); 5ft. 6in., age 21, brown complex.,
brown hair, blue eyes, cordwainer (Navy)
Royce, Allen, 5ft. 8in., age 47, fair complex., brown hair, blue
eyes, Mount Pleasant, Westchester Co., miller (Navy)
Royce, Amos, age 25, 8 years in U.S., City of Albany, shoemaker
(17-22 Aug. 1812)
Royce, Robert, age 31, 8 years in U.S., 5 in family, Canandaigua,
Ontario Co., tailor, applied Feb. 1810 (6-13 Sept. 1812)
Ruckel, William, age 23, 11 years & 5 mos. in U.S., 72 Warren
St., NYC, baker (9-14 Nov. 1812)
Rudd, Charles, 5ft. 10in., age 27, dark complex., brown hair,
grey eyes, Mulberry St., carpenter (Navy)
Ruddick, William, age 24, 3 mos. in U.S., Wallkill, Orange Co.,
weaver (19-24 Oct. 1812)
Ruggles, Joseph, age 20, 4 years in U.S., sister, Mrs. Keese's
boarding house (13-18 July 1812)
Rulloff, Hamilton, 5ft. 7in., age 21, fair complex., fair hair,
grey eyes, Bowery Lane, weaver (Navy)
Rulye, James, age 36, 5 years in U.S., wife, Newburgh, Orange
Co., labourer (14 Aug. 1812)
Russ, Charles, age 26, 2 weeks in U.S., 341 Pearl St., NYC, merchant (19-24 Oct. 1812)
Russel, John, 5ft. 7in., age 32, brown complex., brown hair,
black eyes, Harman St., cooper (Navy)
Russell, Henry, age 22, 4 years in U.S., 263 Pearl St., NYC,
clerk (26-31 Oct. 1812); 5ft. 5in., age 23, light complex.,
light hair, blue eyes, Spring St., accountant (Navy); removed
from NYC to Goshen, Orange Co. (Navy)
Russell, John, age 38, 10 years in U.S., wife & 5 children, Saratoga, Saratoga Co., weaver (17-22 Aug. 1812)
Rutherford, James, age 40, 11 years in U.S., 6 in family, Benton,
Ontario Co., farmer (25 Oct. - 15 Nov. 1812)
Ryan, James, 5ft. 7in., age 35, light complex., light hair, blue
eyes, chandler (Navy)
Ryan, James, age 30, 8 years in U.S., 24 Stone St., NYC, chandler
(10-15 Aug. 1812); 5ft. 7in., age 30, light complex., light
hair, blue eyes, Stone St., chandler (Navy)
Ryan, John, 5ft. 6in., age 28, fair complex., brown hair, grey
eyes, Whitehall, coachman (Navy)
Ryan, John, 5ft. 6in., age 26, light complex., fair hair, grey
eyes, Mott St., carpenter (Navy)
Ryan, John C., 5ft. 9½in., age 32, brown complex., brown hair,
blue eyes, distiller (Navy)
Ryan, Patrick, 5ft. 5in., age 48, dark complex., dark hair, dark
eyes, mason (Navy)
Ryan, Patrick, 5ft. 8in., age 46, fair complex., brown hair, grey
eyes, grocer (Navy)
Ryan, Robert, 5ft. 8in., age 25, light complex., dark hair, blue
eyes, Greenwich St., labourer (Navy)
Ryan, Thomas, 5ft. 8in., age 25, pale complex., fair hair, brown
eyes, Anthony St., mason (Navy)
Ryan, Thomas, age 22, 1 year in U.S., 4 Bancker St., NYC, teacher
(20-25 July 1812)

Ryley, Edward, age 45, 7 years in U.S., wife & 6 children, 23
    Chatham St., music publisher (20-25 July 1812)
Sadler, Hugh Baker, age 19, 1 year in U.S., Johnstown, (no status
    given) (28 July - 2 Aug. 1812)
Sails, John, age 24, 11 years in U.S., Poughkeepsie, Dutchess
    Co., boatman (24-29 Aug. 1812)
St. Ledger, John, age 29, 2 years in U.S., wife & child, Green-
    wich St., NYC, weaver (28 July - 2 Aug. 1812)
Salemon, John, 5ft. 10½in., age 35, light complex., dark hair,
    blue eyes, Catherine Lane, blacksmith (Navy)
Salmon (or Salmer?), Joseph, 5ft. 5¼in., age 19, fair complex.,
    light hair, blue eyes, Pearl St., student (Navy)
Salridge, Robert, 5ft. 5½in., age 25, fair complex., brown hair,
    dark eyes, Manhattan, domestic (Navy)
Sample, Richard, age 23, 8 years in U.S., Newburgh, Orange Co.,
    laborer (19-24 Oct. 1812)
Sampson, Henry, age 26, 6 years in U.S., 5 in family, Lyons,
    Ontario Co., farmer (15-22 Aug. & 31 Aug. - 5 Sept. 1812)
Sampson, Samuel, age 16, 6 years in U.S., Lyons, Ontario Co.,
    farmer (15-22 Aug. & 31 Aug. - 5 Sept. 1812)
Sampson, Thomas, age 19, 6 years in U.S., Lyons, Ontario Co.,
    farmer (15-22 Aug. & 31 Aug. - 5 Sept. 1812)
Sangham (?), Waburton, 5ft. 8in., age 30, dark complex., brown
    hair, blue eyes, Greenwich St. (Navy)
Sanley, William, age 30, 9 years in U.S., wife & child, City of
    Albany, gilder (17-22 Aug. 1812)
Saunders, James, 5ft. 6in., age 45, freckles, brown hair, blue
    eyes, Bowery, gardener (Navy)
Saunders, John, 5ft. 4½in., age 33, dark complex., dark hair,
    grey eyes, seaman (Navy)
Savage, Crosfield, age 22, 1 year & 10 mos. in U.S., 79 Cherry
    St., NYC, carpenter (28 July - 2 Aug. 1812); 5ft. 9in., age
    22, light complex., dark hair, blue eyes, Cherry St., carpen-
    ter (Navy)
Savage, William, age 24, 1 day in U.S., Tontine Coffee House,
    NYC (21-26 Sept. 1812)
Saxton, William, 5ft. 6in., age 35, light complex., brown hair,
    blue eyes, Brookhaven, Suffolk Co., coaster (Navy)
Scanlan, John, 5ft. 10in., age 34, fair complex., dark hair,
    grey eyes, Front St., nail cutter (Navy)
Scanlan, Peter, age 33, 10 years in U.S., wife & 6 children (5
    born in U.S.), Wayne, Steuben Co., farmer (24 Aug. & 31 Aug. -
    5 Sept. 1812)
Schieffelin, Thomas, age 43, 7 years in U.S., mother, sister,
    wife & 5 children, NYC, merchant (20-25 July 1812)
Schefflin, Thomas, 5ft. 11in., age 44, fair complex., dark hair,
    grey eyes, Cleff St., bank clerk (Navy)
Scholfield, John, 5ft. 3in., age 29, fair complex., dark hair,
    light eyes, Sandy Hill, labourer (Navy)
Schoon, John, age 21, 13 years in U.S., City of Albany, merchant
    (17-22 Aug. 1812)
Scofield, Joseph, age 58, 4 mos. in U.S., Love Lane, NYC, farmer
    (28 July - 2 Aug. 1812)
Scoon, William, age 56, 13 years in U.S., wife & 3 children,
    City of Albany, laborer (17-22 Aug. 1812)
Scotford, Joseph, age 32 on 14 Nov. next, 8 years in U.S. on 9
    May last, wife & 3 children, Whitestown, Oneida Co., tinplate
    worker (29 Sept. & 28 Sept. - 3 Oct. 1812)
Scott, Adam, age 24, 2 years in U.S., Columbiaville, Columbia
    Co., millwright (28 Aug. & 31 Aug. - 5 Sept. 1812)
Scott, Alexander, 5ft. 7in., age 54, dark complex., brown hair,
    dark eyes, James St., labourer (Navy)
Scott, Alexander, 5ft. 9in., age 29, fair complex., brown hair,
    grey eyes, Augustus St., baker (Navy)

Scott, Charles, age 44, 1 year in U.S., wife & 3 children, Church
    St., NYC, cordwainer (20-25 July 1812)
Scott, Charles, age 26, 22 years in U.S., Clinton, Dutchess Co.,
    laborer (12-17 Oct. 1812)
Scott, David, age 28, 8 years in U.S., Newburgh, Orange Co.,
    farmer (19-24 Oct. 1812)
Scott, Henry, 5ft. 10in., age 24, dark complex., dark hair, dark
    eyes, Lumber St., blacksmith (Navy)
Scott, Isaac, age 65, 3 years in U.S., 284 Bowery Lane, NYC,
    farmer (13-18 July 1812)
Scott, James, age 52, 2 years & 11 mos. in U.S., wife & 7 child-
    ren, Mamakating, Sullivan Co., laborer (19-24 Oct. 1812)
Scott, James, age 42 on 17 Sept. 1812, 7 years in U.S., wife &
    3 daughters, Deerfield, Oneida Co., baker, applied in Utica
    2 years since, from Cambridge, England (10 Aug. & 17-22 Aug.
    1812)
Scott, James, 5ft. 9in., age 24, light complex., light hair,
    brown eyes, Elm St., millwright (Navy)
Scott, John, age 55, 16 years in U.S., wife & child, Johnstown,
    Montgomery Co., farmer (5 Nov. - 9 Dec. & 7-19 Dec. 1812)
Scott, John, age 40, 1 year & 3 mos. in U.S., wife & 4 children,
    Flatbush, Long Island, tailor (3-8 Aug. 1812); 5ft. 6in., age
    40, brown complex., black hair, brown eyes, tailor (Navy)
Scott, John, age 37, 2 years & 9 mos. in U.S., 3 children, cor-
    ner Crosby & Broome Sts., NYC, carpenter (28 July - 2 Aug.
    1812)
Scott, John, age 31, 9 years in U.S., wife & 2 children, 1 Banc-
    ker St., NYC, bookbinder (28 Sept. - 3 Oct. 1812); 5ft. 2½in.,
    age 31, fair complex., brown hair, blue eyes, Pump St., book
    (Navy)
Scott, John, age 21, 11 years in U.S., City of Albany, clerk
    (5-10 Oct. 1812)
Scott, John, 5ft. 11in., age 22, light complex., brown hair,
    brown eyes, clerk (Navy)
Scott, Robert, 5ft. 10in., age 24, dark complex., black hair,
    black eyes, Orange St., labourer (Navy)
Scott, Stephen, age 27, 22 years in U.S., Clinton, Dutchess Co.,
    laborer (12-17 Oct. 1812)
Scott, William, 5ft. 4in., ruddy complex., brown hair, brown
    eyes, cooper (Navy)
Scott, William, 5ft. 4in., age 26, fair complex., fair hair,
    grey eyes, dyer (Navy)
Scott, William, 5ft. 9in., age 26, dark complex., dark hair,
    brown eyes, Henry St., cartman (Navy)
Scott, William, age 17, 2 years & 11 mos. in U.S., Mamakating,
    Sullivan Co., farmer (19-24 Oct. 1812)
Scumgoni, Rev. James, age 53, 9 years & 11 mos. in U.S., wife &
    child, New Windsor, Orange Co., minister of the Gospel, applied
    Sept. 1812 (19-24 Oct. 1812)
Searle, Thomas, age 19, 4 years in U.S., 434 Greenwich St., NYC,
    apprentice to a gold beater (20-25 July 1812); 5ft. 7½in., age
    20, fair complex., light hair, blue eyes, Greenwich St., gold
    beater (Navy)
Season, George, age 29, 1 year in U.S., wife, 139 Chamber St.,
    NYC, harness maker (20-25 July 1812); 5ft. 10in., age 28,
    light complex., light hair, grey eyes, Water St., harness maker
    (Navy)
Seavey, Francis A., 5ft. 8in., age 30, light complex., black
    hair, dark eyes, removed from NYC to Goshen, Orange Co. (Navy)
Sedgebeer, William, age 32, 7 years in U.S., wife & child, NYC,
    brewer (28 July - 2 Aug. 1812); 5ft. 5in., age 32, fair com-
    plex., light hair, blue eyes, Reed St., brewer (Navy)
Sedgebury, James, 5ft. 7in., age 25, fair complex., black hair,
    blue eyes, Bowery, gardener (Navy)

Sedgwick, Harry Lethfield, age 22, 2 years & 6 mos. in U.S.,
    teacher (31 Aug. - 5 Sept. 1812)
Seeds, John, age 23, 13 years in U.S., Goshen, Orange Co., car-
    penter (19-24 Oct. 1812)
Seeds, Moses, age 20, 13 years in U.S., Goshen, Orange Co., car-
    penter (19-24 Oct. 1812)
Segar,Richard Holt, age 26, 5 years in U.S., NYC, merchant (2-
    7 Nov. 1812)
Segar/Seger, William, age 40, 14 years in U.S., wife & 3 child-
    ren, NYC, merchant, applied 15 Jan. 1799 (20-25 July 1812);
    5ft. 10in., age 41, light complex., brown hair, grey eyes,
    Ferry St., bookkeeper (Navy); removed from NYC to Hurley,
    Ulster Co. (Navy)
Selby, William, age 33, 10 years in U.S., wife & 4 children,
    Colonie, Albany Co., tailor (17-22 Aug. 1812)
Sellery, William R., 5ft. 9½in., age 23, fair complex., brown
    hair, brown eyes, Guanis, Long Island, teacher (Navy)
Sevell, John, 5ft. 3in., age 54, light complex., dark hair, blue
    eyes, Cherry St. (Navy)
Sewart, Walter, 5ft. 2in., age 45, dark complex., dark hair,
    grey eyes, Liberty St., cordwainer (Navy)
Sewell, George N., age 21, 11 years in U.S., 125 Water St., NYC,
    accountant (13-18 July 1812); 5ft. 4in., age 22, light com-
    plex., brown hair, blue eyes, Water St., clerk (Navy); removed
    from NYC to Goshen, Orange Co. (Navy)
Sexton, John, age 30, 22 years in U.S., wife & 2 children, Sha-
    wangunk, Ulster Co., laborer (19-24 Oct. 1812)
Sexton, Michael, 5ft. 3in., age 26, fair complex., light hair,
    brown eyes, Beaver St., coachman (Navy)
Shains, Robert, age 22, 8 mos. in U.S., Montgomery, Orange Co.,
    weaver (19-24 Oct. 1812)
Shalcross, John, 5ft. 10in., age 36, dark complex., dark hair,
    black eyes, cotton spinner (Navy)
Shane/Shene, John, age 26, 5 years in U.S., wife, Elizabeth St.,
    NYC, butcher (20-25 July 1812); 5ft. 6in., age 28, dark com-
    plex., black hair, blue eyes, Essex St., butcher (Navy)
Shanklin, James, age 22, 1 year & 1 mo. in U.S., Montgomery,
    Orange Co., farmer (19-24 Oct. 1812)
Shanks, William, age 46, 8 mos. in U.S., 187 Bowery Lane, NYC
    (20-25 July 1812); 5ft. 6in., age 46, dark complex., grey hair,
    dark eyes, Brooklyn, weaver (Navy)
Shannon, Samuel, age 30, 2 years in U.S., wife & 2 children,
    Greenwich St., NYC, weaver (28 July - 2 Aug. 1812); 5ft. 10in.,
    age 30, fair complex., light hair, blue eyes, weaver (Navy)
Sharen, Daniel, age 28, 8 years in U.S., wife & child, Schenec-
    tady, laborer (24-29 Aug. 1812)
Sharp, Luke, 5ft. 7in., age 20, light complex., light hair,
    hazel eyes, steamboat waiter (Navy)
Sharp, Samuel, age 35, 10 years in U.S., wife & 6 children, 40
    Dey St., NYC, cabinetmaker (20-25 July 1812); 5ft. 7½in., age
    36, fair complex., dark hair, blue eyes, Dey St., cabinet-
    maker (Navy)
Sharp, William, 5ft. 5in., age 50, dark complex., dark hair,
    dark eyes, gardener (Navy)
Shaw, Edward, 5ft. 9in., age 23, fair complex., fair hair, blue
    eyes, labourer (Navy)
Shaw, John, 5ft. 8in., age 45, fair complex., grey hair, brown
    eyes, labourer (Navy)
Shaw, John, age 39, 10 years in U.S., wife & 4 children, 15 Henry
    St., NYC, morocco dresser (20-25 July 1812); 5ft. 7in., age 39,
    fair complex., light hair, light eyes, leather dresser (Navy)
Shaw, Joseph, 5ft. 8in., age 20, fair complex., brown hair, grey
    eyes, shipwright (Navy)

Shaw, Matthew, age 31, 11 years in U.S., wife & child, 407 Greenwich St., NYC, sawyer (20-25 July 1812); 5ft. 8in., age 34,
brown complex., red hair, grey eyes, Henry (?) St., sawyer
(Navy)

Shaw, Moses, age 30, 1 year & 4 mos. in U.S., wife & 2 children,
Greenwich St., NYC, muslin manufacturer (28 July - 2 Aug. 1812)

Shaw, Thomas, age 32, 9 years in U.S., wife & 3 children, NYC,
stable keeper, applied 12 Jan. 1809 (20-25 July 1812); 5ft.
6in., age 33, dark complex., dark hair, blue eyes, Nassau St.,
hackney (Navy)

Shaw, William, age 33, 4 years & 6 mos. in U.S., wife & 5 children, Westchester Co., blacksmith (3-8 Aug. 1812); 5ft. 8½in.,
age 34, light complex., brown hair, grey eyes, West Farms,
Westchester Co., blacksmith (Navy)

Shaw, William, 5ft. 8in., age 30, fair complex., light hair,
blue eyes, Mulberry St., cartman (Navy)

Sheales, John, age 65, 11 years in U.S., wife & 5 children,
Johnstown, Montgomery Co., weaver (15 Sept. - 5 Oct. & 5-10
Oct. 1812)

Shean, David, 5ft. 8in., age 31, brown complex., dark hair, blue
eyes, Bloomingdale, gardener (Navy)

Shean, Robert, 5ft. 7in., age 33, fair complex., brown hair,
grey eyes, Harman St., cartman (Navy)

Shean, William, 5ft. 8½in., age 22, fair complex., dark hair,
blue eyes, labourer (Navy)

Sheareard, T.S., age 28, 1 year in U.S., Coffee House Slip, NYC
(13-18 July 1812)

Sheldon, Joseph, age 28, 5 years & 5 mos. in U.S., Williamson,
Ontario Co., farmer (7-12 Sept. 1812 & 23-30 Aug.)

Sheldon, Richard, age 45, 3 mos in U.S., 55 William St., merchant
(28 July - 2 Aug. 1812)

Shelton, William, age 33 on 19 Aug. inst., 10 years in U.S. on
28 Sept. next, wife & 2 children, Deerfield, Oneida Co., butcher (26 Aug. & 28 Sept. - 3 Oct. 1812)

Shepherd, Hugh R., 5ft. 6in., age 37, dark complex., brown hair,
grey eyes, ropemaker (Navy)

Sheriff, Adam D., age 30, 7 days in U.S., City Hotel, NYC, distiller (24-29 Aug. 1812); 5ft. 11 3/4in., age 29, fair complex.,
light hair, blue eyes, Frankfort St., distiller (Navy)

Shernden (?), Thomas, 5ft. 5in., age 27, dark complex., brown
hair, blue eyes, Bowery, thread (Navy)

Sherry, Patrick, 5ft. 7in., age 25, dark complex., fair hair,
brown eyes, Front St., labourer (Navy)

Shield, Francis, 5ft. 9in., age 28, fair complex., dark hair,
brown eyes, First St., printing (Navy)

Shield, Terence, age 34, 1 year & 8 mos. in U.S., wife & 3 children, 16 Spring St., NYC, weaver (20-25 July 1812)

Shields, Henry, age 28, 2 years in U.S., wife & 4 children,
corner Arundle & Rivington Sts., NYC, saddler (28 July - 2 Aug.
1812)

Shields, Robert, 5ft. 8in., age 22, light complex., light hair,
grey eyes (Navy)

Shiers, Dudley, age 37 on 30 Jan. last, 7 years in U.S. on 3
June last, wife, Utica, Oneida Co., gardener (29 Sept. & 28
Sept. -3 Oct. 1812)

Shinnon, John, age 23, 4 mos. in U.S., Clinton, Dutchess Co.,
laborer (12-17 Oct. 1812)

Shorland, Thomas, age 42, 4 years in U.S., wife, Spring St., NYC,
grocer (20-25 July 1812)

Shorland, Thomas, 5ft. 9in., age 34, light complex., light hair,
blue eyes, Spring St., painter (Navy)

Short, John, 5ft. 7in., age 26, light complex., light hair, grey
eyes, Bloomingdale, labourer (Navy)

Shub, Terrence, 5ft. 10in., age 32, pale complex., brown hair,
grey eyes, Elizabeth St., weaver (Navy)

Shub, William, 5ft. 8in., age 60, dark complex., black hair,
grey eyes, farmer (Navy)
Shulick, Patrick, 5ft. 8in., age 32, florid complex., dark hair,
grey eyes, tallow (Navy)
Shumpton, Thomas, age 41, 16 years in U.S., wife & child, Albany
Co., paper mould maker (3-8 Aug. 1812)
Sillery (or Sellery), William R., age 22, 1 year & 6 mos. in
U.S., Jamaica, Long Island, teacher of mathematics (14-19 Sept.
1812) - same as Sellery, William R., above.
Simon, Nicol, age 27, 6 years in U.S., Manhattanville, carpenter
(31 Aug. - 5 Sept. 1812)
Simpson, Daniel, age 24, 8 years in U.S., Colonie, Albany Co.,
miller, applied 5 Aug. 1812 (17-22 Aug. 1812)
Simpson, Edward, age 28, 3 years in U.S., 13 Dey St., comedian,
applied 19 Jan. 1810 (20-25 July 1812); 5ft. 8in., age 28, fair
complex., light hair, blue eyes, comedian (Navy)
Simpson, George, age 35, 11 years in U.S., wife & 4 children,
Florida, Montgomery Co., farmer (18-24 Aug. & 31 Aug. - 5 Sept.
1812)
Simpson, Martin, age 24, 5 years in U.S., 300 Bowery, NYC, manu-
facturer (19-24 Oct. 1812); 5ft. 11in., age 24, fair complex.,
brown hair, grey eyes, Bowery, thread (Navy)
Simpson, Robert, 5ft. 10in., age 23, fair complex., brown hair,
brown eyes, Hammond St., weaver (Navy)
Sinclair, David, 5ft. 7in., age 49, light complex., light hair,
blue eyes, Corlaers Hook, cork cutter (Navy)
Sinclair, Hugh, age 24, 4 years & 3 mos. in U.S., City of Albany,
paver (17-22 Aug. 1812)
Sinclair, Joseph, age 42, 7 years in U.S., wife & child, Richmond
Co., weaver (7-19 Dec. 1812)
Sinclair, Thomas, age 29, 2 years in U.S., Hurley, Ulster Co.,
weaver (17-24 Oct. 1812)
Skinner, Alexander, age 28 years & 2 mos., 5 years & 10 mos. in
U.S., wife & child, Argyle, Washington Co., house-carpenter,
applied about 20 Sept. 1811 (5-10 Oct. 1812)
Skinner, James, age 26, 2 years in U.S., wife & child, 14 Beek-
man St., NYC, blacksmith (10-15 Aug. 1812); 5ft. 8 3/4in., age
27, fair complex., fair hair, light eyes, Pecks Slip, black-
smith (Navy)
Skuse, Charles, age 46, 17 years in U.S., Phelps, Ontario Co.,
cooper (5-15 & 24-29 Aug. 1812)
Slane, Manus, 5ft. 6in., age 40, light complex., fair hair, blue
eyes, Augustus St., labourer (Navy)
Slater, George, age 37, 5 years in U.S., wife & 2 children, 42
Vandewater St., NYC, morocco dyer (20-25 July 1812); 5ft. 8in.,
age 37, light complex., light hair, blue eyes, Ferry St., mo-
rocco (Navy)
Slater, George, age 34, 17 years in U.S., wife & 4 children,
Newburgh, Orange Co., shoemaker (19-24 Oct. 1812)
Slater, William, age 39, 18 years in U.S., wife & 4 children,
New Windsor, Orange Co., shoemaker (19-24 Oct. 1812)
Slattery, Edmund, age 19, 8 years in U.S., Johnstown, Montgomery
Co., merchant (5 Aug. - 2 Sept. & 7-12 Sept. 1812)
Slattery, Edmund, age 17, 8 years in U.S., Johnstown, Montgomery
Co., clerk (28 July - 2 Aug. 1812)
Slattery, Joseph, 5ft. 4in., age 24, light complex., dark hair,
brown eyes, Lombardy St., shipwright (Navy)
Sloan, Charles, age 22, 6 years in U.S., Fishkill, Dutchess Co.,
weaver (12-17 Oct. 1812)
Sloan, James, age 33, 11 years in U.S., wife & 3 children, Wall-
kill, Orange Co., weaver (19-24 Oct. 1812)
Sloan, James, age 20, 2 mos. in U.S., Newburgh, Orange Co., la-
borer (19-24 Oct. 1812)
Sloan, Thomas, 5ft. 9in., age 31, fair complex., brown hair,
grey eyes, Read St., bricklayer (Navy)

Sloat, Thomas, age 21, 13 years in U.S., Beekman St., NYC, cabi-
netmaker (28 July - 2 Aug. 1812)
Sloboy, William, 5ft. 9in., age 26, fair complex., brown hair,
dark eyes, Partition St., livery (Navy)
Slowley, William, age 26, 3 years in U.S., wife & child, 43 Par-
tition St., NYC, grocer (20-25 July 1812)
Sluckland, Frederick, 5ft. 9in., age 24, fair complex., brown
hair, light eyes, servant (Navy)
Sly, George, age 37, 1 year in U.S., wife & 2 children, Colonie,
Albany Co., shoemaker (17-22 Aug. 1812)
Smart, Robert, age 39, 8 years in U.S., wife & 3 children, 9
Lombard St., NYC, applied 13 Nov. 1809 (20-25 July 1812); 5ft.
5½in., age 40, dark complex., dark hair, hazel eyes, Lombardy
St., grocer (Navy)
Smart, Walter, age 45, 4 years & 8 mos. in U.S., wife & 3 child-
ren, 76 Liberty St., NYC, shoemaker (20-25 July 1812)
Smiley, James, age 48, 1 year & 2 mos. in U.S., Wallkill, Orange
Co., farmer (19-24 Oct. 1812)
Smiley, James, age 28, 8 years in U.S., Wallkill, Orange Co.,
farmer (19-24 Oct. 1812)
Smiley, Samuel, age 35, 2 years in U.S., wife & 4 children, 45
Cherry St., NYC, shoemaker (28 July - 2 Aug. 1812); 5ft.
7 3/4in., age 34, fair complex., sandy hair, blue eyes, cord-
wainer (Navy)
Smilie, Alexander, 5ft. 6in., age 23, light complex., brown hair,
grey eyes, Hague St., morocco (Navy)
Smith, Alexander, age 25, 2 years in U.S., wife & child, Schoharie,
laborer (24-29 Aug. 1812)
Smith, Archibald, 5ft. 8in., age 30, light complex., brown hair,
brown eyes, Mulberry St., paver (Navy)
Smith, Charles, 5ft. 10in., age 23, light complex., brown hair,
grey eyes, Anthony St., labourer (Navy)
Smith, Donald, age 50, 7 years in U.S., 8 in family, 7 Catharine
Lane, NYC, laborer (20-25 July 1812)
Smith, Duncan, age 38 last Mar., 5 years in U.S. in last July,
wife & 5 children, Russia, Herkimer Co., farmer (26 Aug. & 28
Sept. - 3 Oct. 1812)
Smith, George, age 25, 9 mos. in U.S., wife & child, 25 Thomas
St., NYC, cordwainer (3-8 Aug. 1812); 5ft. 8in., age 27, fair
complex., brown hair, light eyes, cordwainer (Navy)
Smith, Henry, 5ft. 3in., age 23, fair complex., fair hair, grey
eyes, weaver (Navy)
Smith, Hugh, 5ft. 2in., age 28, fair complex., brown hair, grey
eyes, Second St., cartman (Navy)
Smith, James, age 47, 1 year & 9 mos. in U.S., 5 children, New-
burgh, Orange Co., weaver (19-24 Oct. 1812)
Smith, James, age 33, 8 years in U.S., wife & child, Schoharie,
tanner (24-29 Aug. 1812)
Smith, James, age 33, 10 years in U.S., wife & 6 children, 89
Bancker St., NYC, house-carpenter (28 July - 2 Aug. 1812); 5ft.
7in., age 34, dark complex., dark hair, blue eyes, carpenter
(Navy)
Smith, James, age 28, 6 years in U.S., wife & child, Mamakating,
Sullivan Co., tallow chandler (19-24 Oct. 1812)
Smith, James, age 27, 18 years in U.S., wife & 2 children, 95
Church St., NYC, printer (13-18 July 1812); 5ft. 7in., age 28,
light complex., fair hair, blue eyes, Church St., printer
(Navy)
Smith, James, age 26, 2 years in U.S., Fishkill, Dutchess Co.,
gentleman (12-17 Oct. 1812)
Smith, James, 5ft. 2in., age 25, dark complex., dark hair,
black eyes, coachman (Navy)
Smith, James T., 5ft. 5in., age 45, dark complex., dark hair,
blue eyes, Pearl St., umbrella (Navy)

Smith, John, age 53, 3 years in U.S., wife & child, 29 Division
St., NYC (20-25 July 1812); 5ft. 11in., age 53, light complex.,
brown hair, hazel eyes, Division St., tailor (Navy)

Smith, John, age 47, 9 years in U.S., wife & 7 children, Johnstown, Montgomery Co., farmer (18-24 Aug. & 31 Aug. - 5 Sept.
1812)

Smith, John, age 34, 17 years in U.S., wife & 3 children, City
of Albany, tailor, applied Apr. 1809 (17-22 Aug. 1812)

Smith, John, age 32, 11 years in U.S., wife & 4 children, 6 Rose
St., NYC, shoemaker (20-25 July 1812)

Smith, John, age 33, light complex., dark hair, blue
eyes, Anthony St., boot (Navy) - probably the same as the John
Smith, shoemaker, just above.

Smith, John, age 27, 5 years in U.S., wife & 2 children, 295
Broadway, NYC, umbrella maker (13-18 July 1812); 5ft. 5in.,
age 28, light complex., dark hair, dark eyes, Broadway, umbrella (Navy)

Smith, John, age 26, 1 year & 1 mo. in U.S., Schenectady, weaver
(17-22 Aug. 1812)

Smith, John, 5ft. 8in., age 25, pale complex., dark hair, grey
eyes, Oliver St., grocer (Navy)

Smith, John, age 24, 6 mos. in U.S., 107 Liberty St., NYC, bookkeeper (20-25 July 1812); 5ft. 10in., age 24, fair complex.,
dark hair, blue eyes, clerk, removed from NYC to Fishkill,
Dutchess Co. (Navy)

Smith, John, 5ft. 6½in., age 21, fair complex., fair hair, blue
eyes, Bancker St., baker (Navy)

Smith, Joseph, 5ft. 5in., age 38, brown complex., fair hair,
grey eyes, Front St., labourer (Navy)

Smith, Joseph, age 37, 6 years in U.S., Newburgh, Orange Co.,
laborer (19-24 Oct. 1812)

Smith, Joseph, age 25, 3 years in U.S., 88 Harman St., NYC,
butcher (28 July - 2 Aug. 1812); 5ft. 9½in., age 27, dark complex., light hair, black eyes, butcher (Navy)

Smith, Mark, 5ft. 7 3/4in., age 37, light complex., light hair,
grey eyes, Harlaem, sawyer (Navy)

Smith, Martin, age 41, 12 years in U.S., Seneca, Ontario Co.,
farmer (6-13 & 21-26 Sept. 1812)

Smith, Peter, age 39, 1 year & 2 mos. in U.S., wife & 4 children, 79 Gold St., NYC, professor of music (26-31 Oct. 1812)

Smith, Peter, 5ft. 7in., age 39, fair complex., brown hair, blue
eyes, engraver (Navy)

Smith, Ralph, age 25, 8 years in U.S., City of Albany, merchant,
applied 3 Apr. 1810 (17-22 Aug. 1812)

Smith, Robert S., age 38, 5 years & 6 mos. in U.S., wife & 4
children, corner Divine & Washington Sts., NYC, blacksmith
(20-25 July 1812)

Smith, Robert, age 35, 8 years in U.S., wife, Schoharie, clothier
(24-29 Aug. 1812)

Smith, Terrence, age 35, 1 year in U.S., Newburgh, Orange Co.,
laborer (19-24 Oct. 1812)

Smith, Terrence, 5ft. 6in., age 36, light complex., brown hair,
blue eyes, Elizabeth St., grocer (Navy)

Smith, Terrence, age 31, 10 years in U.S., wife & 3 children,
City of Albany, tobacconist (17-22 Aug. 1812)

Smith, Terence, age 25, 5 years & 11 mos. in U.S., wife & 2
children, 21 Barclay St., NYC, grocer (20-25 July 1812)

Smith, Thomas, age 31, 1 year & 10 mos. in U.S., wife & child,
Kingston, Ulster Co., weaver (7 Sept. & 19-24 Oct. 1812)

Smith, Thomas, age 30, 3 years & 5 mos. in U.S., wife & 4 children, 6 Desbrosses St., NYC, sawyer (26-31 Oct. 1812)

Smith, Thomas, age 29, 9 years in U.S., wife & child, 91 James
St., NYC, mariner (20-25 July 1812)

Smith, Thomas, age 28, 11 years & 1 mo. in U.S., New Windsor,
Orange Co., shoemaker (19-24 Oct. 1812)

Smith, Thomas, 5ft. 8in., age 26, fair complex., dark hair, grey
  eyes, Broome St., labourer (Navy)
Smith, Thomas, 5ft. 10in., age 22, light complex., black hair,
  blue eyes, labourer (Navy)
Smith, Thomas H., age 47, 17 years in U.S., Warwick, Orange Co.,
  farmer (28 July - 2 Aug. 1812)
Smith, William, age 46, 17 years in U.S., wife & 4 children,
  Ulysses, Tompkins Co., farmer (7-12 & 21-26 Sept. 1812)
Smith, William, age 39, 11 years in U.S., 5 in family, Seneca,
  Ontario Co., farmer (6-13 & 21-26 Sept. 1812)
Smith, William, age 38, 7 years in U.S., wife & 4 children, 22
  Chatham St., NYC, teacher (13-18 July 1812); 5ft. 7in., age
  38, light complex., dark hair, dark eyes, Chatham St.,teacher
  (Navy)
Smith, William, 4ft. 11½in., age 26, light complex., light hair,
  blue eyes, Harman St., cordwainer (Navy)
Smith, William, 5ft. 7in., age 25, fair complex., fair hair,
  grey eyes, watchmaker (Navy)
Smith, William, 5ft. 6in., age 23, fair complex., light hair,
  grey eyes, sash maker (Navy)
Smolner, James, age 25, 1 year & 4 mos. in U.S., wife & child,
  17 Liberty St., NYC, shoemaker (26-31 Oct. 1812)
Smollen, James, 5ft. 7in., age 26, light complex., light hair,
  blue eyes, Lombardy St., cordwainer (Navy)
Smyth, Frederick, age 26, 6 years in U.S., wife & child, 5 Cliff
  St., NYC, coffee mill maker (28 July - 2 Aug. 1812)
Smyth, William, age 20, 2 years in U.S., Brunswick, Rensselaer
  Co., merchant (10-15 Aug. 1812)
Snow, William, age 33, 5 years & 10 mos. in U.S., wife & 2 child-
  ren, Kingston, Ulster Co., tailor (19-24 Oct. 1812)
Soeman, Abraham E., age 24, 5 years in U.S., 237 Greenwich St.,
  NYC, merchant (20-25 July 1812)
Solis, Daniel, age 28, 8 years in U.S., 39 Norfolk St., NYC,
  quill manufacturer (20-25 July 1812); 5ft. 4in., age 29, light
  complex., dark hair, brown eyes, Broome St., quill (Navy)
Solis, Jacob J., 5ft. 3in., age 32, light complex., dark hair,
  dark eyes, Mount Pleasant, Westchester Co., quill (Navy)
Solis, Jacob O., age 32, 8 years & 8 mos. in U.S., wife, 49 First
  St., NYC, quill manufacturer (20-25 July 1812)
Solomon, John, 5ft. 6in., age 23, fair complex., brown hair,
  grey eyes, Water St., quill (Navy)
Solomons, Levy, age 41, 12 years & 9 mos. in U.S., wife & 4
  children, Albany City, chocolate manufacturer (28 July - 2 Aug.
  1812); it is stated he had been 12 years in U.S. and that he
  was a tobacconist (17-22 Aug. 1812)
Sommers, Charles George, age 21, 5 years in U.S., 13 Mott St.,
  NYC, accountant (3-8 Aug. 1812)
Somerville/Samerville, Archibald, age 35 on 14 Nov. last, 16
  years in U.S. on 14 July last, wife & child, Johnsburgh,
  Washington Co., farmer (24 Nov. 1812 & 21 Dec. 1812 - 23 Jan.
  1813)
Somerville, James, 5ft. 6in., age 26, light complex., light hair,
  Christopher St., printer (Navy)
Somerville/Samerville, John, 45 on 9 Mar. last, 16 years in U.S.
  on 14 July last, Johnsburgh, Washington Co., farmer (24 Nov.
  1812 & 21 Dec. 1812 - 23 Jan. 1813)
Somerville/Samerville, Samuel, age 40 on 18 Apr. last, 14 years
  in U.S. on 14 Jan. last, wife & 5 children, Johnsburgh, Washington Co., farmer (24 Nov. 1812 & 21 Dec. 1812 - 23 Jan. 1813)
Somerville/Samerville, Thomas, age 28 on 14 Dec. last, 14 years
  in U.S. on 10 Aug. last, wife & 3 children, Johnsburgh, Washington Co. (24 Nov. 1812 & 21 Dec. 1812 - 23 Jan. 1813)
Sammervill, Walter, 5ft. 9in., age 24, fair complex., brown hair,
  blue eyes, calico (Navy)

Soulden (or Soulder), Malachi, age 52 on 1 Nov. next, 7 years
    in U.S. on 17 Aug. last, Newport, Herkimer Co., superintendant
    of cotton factory (31 Oct. & 30 Nov. - 5 Dec. 1812)
Soulden (or Soulder), William, age 25 on 26 Apr. next, 5 years
    in U.S. on 19 Sept. inst., Vernon, Oneida Co., agent to a glass
    company (29 Sept. & 28 Sept. - 3 Oct. 1812)
Souray, Francis A., 5ft. 8in., age 30, light complex., brown
    hair, dark eyes, Division St., bookseller (Navy) -name is
    given in N.Y.C. Directory as Sowrey.
Southall, Solomon, 5ft. 8in., age 45, fair complex., dark hair,
    grey eyes, Cherry St., bellows (Navy)
Spear, Robert, age 34, 7 years in U.S., wife, 3 children, aunt
    & sister, 175 Greenwich St., NYC, storekeeper (3-8 Aug. 1812)
Spear, Robert, 5ft. 7½in., age 33, fair complex., brown hair,
    light eyes, Greenwich St., clerk (Navy)- probably the same as
    the above.
Spence, George, 5ft. 9in., age 29, fair complex., sandy hair,
    blue eyes, Warren St., servant (Navy)
Spence, George, age 28, 1 year & 8 mos. in U.S., wife, 41 Barclay
    St., NYC, grocer (20-25 July 1812)
Spencer, Benjamin A., age 39, 2 days in U.S., has a black slave,
    Brooklyn, Long Island, mariner (13-18 July 1812)
Spencer, Henry, 5ft. 8in., age 26, dark complex., dark hair,
    blue eyes, Cherry St., labourer (Navy)
Spinerly (?), William, 5ft. 5in., age 39, dark complex., brown
    hair, dark eyes, Greenwich St., button (Navy)
Spotswood, William, 5ft. 9in., age 37, fair complex., brown hair,
    grey eyes, Bowery, cabinetmaker (Navy)
Spratt, James, age 20, 2 mos. in U.S., 4 Bancker St., NYC, ac-
    countant (13-18 July 1812)
Spratt, Thomas, age 35, 3 years & 8 mos. in U.S., wife, 88 Bowery,
    NYC, grocer (20-25 July 1812)
Spratt, William, age 26, 1 year & 2 mos. in U.S., wife & child,
    New Windsor, Orange Co., blacksmith (19-24 Oct. 1812)
Spring, Alexander, 5ft. 11in., age 22, dark complex., black hair,
    brown eyes, removed from NYC to Utica, Oneida Co. (Navy)
Spring, John, age 36, 13 years in U.S., wife & child, Duanes-
    burgh, Schenectady Co., laborer (24-29 Aug. 1812)
Sproull, Nathaniel, age 24, 1 year & 1 mo. in U.S., Montgomery,
    Orange Co., schoolmaster (19-24 Oct. 1812)
Squire, William, 6ft., age 45, fair complex., brown hair, brown
    eyes, blacksmith (Navy)
Stacora, Thomas, age 25, 1 year & 4 mos. in U.S., Duanesburgh,
    Schenectady Co., tanner & currier (24-29 Aug. 1812)
Stafford, Aaron, age 31, 2 years & 2 mos. in U.S., wife, Clinton,
    Dutchess Co., spinner (12-17 Oct. 1812)
Stafford, Henry, age 35, 1 year & 1 mo. in U.S., wife, 80 Chapel
    St., NYC, segar maker (28 July - 2 Aug. 1812)
Stafford, Henry, 5ft. 3½in., age 30, light complex., brown hair,
    dark eyes, Walnut St., victualer (Navy)
Stafford, Robert, age 54, 9 years in U.S., wife & 4 children,
    Clinton, Dutchess Co., spinner (12-17 Oct. 1812)
Stainton (or Stanton?), John, age 37, 8 years in U.S., 5 in the
    family, Geneva, Ontario Co., farmer, applied June 1811 (15-22
    Aug. & 31 Aug. - 5 Sept. 1812)
Stainton, Robert, age 42, 8 years in U.S., Geneva, Ontario Co.,
    butcher, applied Feb. 1812 (15-22 Aug. & 31 Aug. - 5 Sept.
    1812)
Standring, James, age 28, 11 mos. in U.S., wife & child, Johns-
    town, Montgomery Co., whitesmith (6 Oct. - 4 Nov. & 9-14 Nov.
    1812)
Stanley, Adam, age 45, 16 years in U.S., wife & 6 children, 10
    Henry St., NYC, screw & rivet maker (13-18 July 1812); 5ft.
    6in., age 46, dark complex., dark hair, dark eyes, Henry St.,
    blacksmith (Navy)

Staple, George, 5ft. 10in., age 36, fair complex., brown hair,
blue eyes, labourer (Navy)
Starrat (or Starret?), Alexander, age 24, 6 years & 2 mos. in
U.S., wife & 2 children, Bethel, Sullivan Co., farmer, applied
10 Jan. 1810 (31 Aug. & 19-24 Oct. 1812)
Starrat, James, age 21, 6 years & 2 mos. in U.S., Bethel, Sullivan Co., farmer (31 Aug. & 19-24 Oct. 1812)
Starrat(or Starret?), John, age 48, 6 years & 2 mos. in U.S.,
wife & 4 children, Bethel, Sullivan Co., farmer (31 Aug. &
19-24 Oct. 1812)
Steadman, James, age 55, 15 years in U.S., wife & 2 children,
corner Pitt & Rivington Sts., NYC, gardener (13-18 July 1812)
Steadman, James, 5ft. 6½ir., age 45, dark complex., dark hair,
grey eyes, Rivington St., nursery (Navy)
Steele, Arthur, age 40, 3 mos. in U.S., Newburgh, Orange Co.,
laborer (19-24 Oct. 1812)
Steen, John, age 22, 8 years & 6 mos. in U.S., wife, 206 Church
St., NYC, carver (30 Nov. - 5 Dec. 1812)
Steeple, George, age 47, 7 years in U.S., 5 children, 110 Broad
St., NYC, laborer (20-25 July 1812)
Stephen, Robert, 5ft. 6in., age 39, brown complex., brown hair,
dark eyes, Bancker St., dyer (Navy)
Stephens, Edward, age 29, 2½ years in U.S., NYC, merchant (28
July - 2 Aug. 1812)
Stephens, John J., age 23, 3½ years in U.S., wife & 2 children,
NYC, tobacconist (28 July - 2 Aug. 1812)
Stephens, Thomas, age 39, 1 year in U.S., wife & 2 children, 43
Hudson St., NYC, salesman. (3-8 Aug. 1812)
Stephens, Thomas, 5ft. 8in., age 39, sandy complex., brown hair,
light eyes, Greenwich St., accountant (Navy)
Stephens, Thomas, age 32, 14 years in U.S., wife & 2 children,
45 Elm St., NYC, laborer (20-25 July 1812)
Stephenson, James, age 19, 6 years in U.S., Bethel, Sullivan Co.,
shoemaker (19-24 Oct. 1812)
Stephenson, John, age 30, 3 years in U.S., Kinderhook, Columbia
Co., farmer, applied June 1809 (7-12 Sept. 1812)
Stephenson, John, age 27, 5 years in U.S., wife & 2 children,
359 Greenwich St., NYC, clerk (20-25 July 1812); 5ft. 8in.,
age 27, light complex., brown hair, hazel eyes, removed from
NYC to Goshen, Orange Co. (Navy)
Stephenson, Samuel, age 21, 16 years in U.S., wife & 3 children,
Montgomery, Orange Co., weaver (19-24 Oct. 1812)
Stephenson, Thomas, age 28, 9 years in U.S., Kinderhook, Colum-
bia Co., farmer, applied June 1809 (7-12 Sept. 1812)
Stephenson, William, age 59, 9 years in U.S., wife & 9 children,
Kinderhook, Columbia Co., farmer, applied June 1809 (5 Sept.
& 7-12 Sept. 1812)
Sterlin, Thomas L., age 48, 16 years in U.S., wife & 4 children,
Rhinebeck, Dutchess Co., teacher (12-17 Oct. 1812)
Sterling, David, age 39, 9 years in U.S., Hudson, Columbia Co.,
tailor, applied 1810 (3-8 Aug. 1812)
Steven, William, age 32, 2 years in U.S., 5 in family, 34 Char-
lotte St., NYC, weaver (24-29 Aug. 1812); 5ft. 5in., age 32,
fair complex., dark hair, grey eyes, Catherine St., weaver
(Navy)
Stevens, John, age 32, 9 years in U.S., 2 children, 46 East
George St., NYC, boarding house keeper (10-15 Aug. 1812)
Stevens, John J., 5ft. 5in., age 23, light complex., light hair,
blue eyes, Middle Road, tobacco (Navy)
Stevens, Thomas, 5ft. 5in., age 35, light complex., fair hair,
brown eyes, Anthony St., labourer (Navy)
Stevenson, Isaac, 5ft. 8in., age 32, dark complex., black hair,
grey eyes, Greenwich St. grocer (Navy)
Stevenson, James, 5ft. 5½in., age 28, fair complex., brown hair,
grey eyes, Corlaers Hook, cartman (Navy)

Stevenson, James, 5ft. ¼in., age 19, fair complex., dark hair,
  blue eyes, stone cutter (Navy)
Stevenson, John, 5ft. 5in., age 34, light complex., brown hair,
  black eyes, Bloomingdale, labourer (Navy)
Stevenson, John, 5ft. 10in., age 33, light complex., brown hair,
  blue eyes, Gold St., shoemaker (Navy)
Stevenson, John, 5ft. 8in., age 27, light complex., brown hair,
  hazel eyes, Beach St., clerk (Navy)
Stevenson, William, age 28, 9 years in U.S., 4 in family, 83
  Murray St., NYC, cartman (20-25 July 1812); 5ft. 9in., age 28,
  dark complex., brown hair, grey eyes, Orange St., cartman
  (Navy)
Steward, Samuel, age 23, 20 years in U.S., Gorham, Ontario Co.,
  farmer (15-22 Aug. & 31 Aug. - 5 Sept. 1812)
Stewart, Alexander, age 63, 25 years in U.S., wife & 2 children,
  Saratoga Co., farmer (14-19 Sept. 1812)
Stewart, Alexander, age 55, in U.S. since Sept. 1809, wife, Broad-
  albin, Montgomery Co., farmer (18-24 Aug. & 31 Aug. - 5 Sept.
  1812)
Stewart, Alexander, age 24, 6 years in U.S., wife & child, 104
  Liberty St., NYC, carpenter (28 July - 2 Aug. 1812); 5ft. 4½in.,
  age 24, fair complex., brown hair, blue eyes, Mott St., car-
  penter (Navy)
Stewart, Alexander, 5ft. 10in., age 21, dark complex., brown
  hair, brown eyes, Mulberry St., labourer (Navy)
Stewart, Charles, age 27, 8 years in U.S., wife & 3 children,
  50 Cedar St., NYC, shipmaster (30 Nov. - 5 Dec. 1812)
Stewart, Charles, 5ft. 9in., age 24, dark complex., dark hair,
  dark eyes, Garden St., labourer (Navy)
Stewart, Cornelius, age 25, 11 years in U.S., Smithfield, Madi-
  son Co., farmer (3 Aug. 1812)
Stewart/Steward, Daniel, age 28 in Oct. last, 3 years in U.S.,
  wife & 2 children, Thurman, Washington Co., farmer (24 Nov. &
  21 Dec. 1812 - 23 Jan. 1813)
Stewart, Daniel, age 30, 12 years in U.S., wife & 2 children,
  Broadalbin, Montgomery Co., tailor (18-24 Aug. & 31 Aug. - 5
  Sept. 1812)
Stewart, Daniel, age 25, 3 years in U.S., wife & 2 children,
  Broadalbin, Montgomery Co., farmer (18-24 Aug. & 31 Aug. - 5
  Sept. 1812)
Stewart, David, age 35, 8 years in U.S., wife & 6 children,
  Bethel, Sullivan Co., farmer (31 Aug. & 19-24 Oct. 1812)
Stewart, David, age 26, 25 years in U.S., Saratoga Co., farmer
  (14-19 Sept. 1812)
Stewart, George, 5ft. 5in., age 36, brown complex.,brown hair,
  brown eyes, Pump St., cartman (Navy)
Stewart, George, age 32, 2 mos. in U.S., 121 Chamber St., NYC,
  mason (3-8 Aug. 1812)
Stewart, George, age 26, 4 years in U.S., Sugar Loaf St., NYC,
  merchant (28 Sept. - 3 Oct. 1812)
Stewart, Henry, age 36, 10 years in U.S., wife & 3 children,
  Minisink, Orange Co., laborer (19-24 Oct. 1812)
Stewart, Henry, age 24, 9 mos. in U.S., Montgomery, Orange Co.,
  shoemaker (19-24 Oct. 1812)
Stewart, James, age 44, 11 years in U.S., wife & 3 children,
  Johnstown, Montgomery Co., tailor (11-17 & 17-22 Aug. 1812)
Stewart, James, age 33, 11 years in U.S., Smithfield, Madison
  Co., farmer (1 Aug. & 10-15 Aug. 1812)
Stewart, James, 5ft. 10in., age 29, light complex., light hair,
  grey eyes, Water St., stone cutter (Navy)
Stewart, James, Sr., age 47, 11 years in U.S., wife & 9 children,
  Smithfield, Madison Co., farmer (1 Aug. & 10-15 Aug. 1812)
Stewart, James T., 5ft. 8½in., age 38, fair complex., grey hair,
  brown eyes, Water St., hatter (Navy)

Stewart, John, age 67, 11 years in U.S., wife, Mayfield, Mont-
gomery Co., farmer (15 Sept. - 5 Oct. & 5-10 Oct. 1812)
Stewart, John, age 52, 10 years in U.S., wife & 5 children,
Johnstown, Montgomery Co., stone mason (25 Aug. - 2 Sept. &
7-12 Sept. 1812)
Stewart, John, 5ft. 9in., age 50, dark complex., dark hair,
grey eyes, Cross St., grocer (Navy)
Stewart, John, age 35, 12 years in U.S., wife & 4 children,
Goshen, Orange Co., farmer (19-24 Oct. 1812)
Stewart, John, age 31, 3 years in U.S., wife, 131 Greenwich St.,
NYC, grocer (2-7 Nov. 1812); 5ft. 6½in., age 31, brown com-
plex., dark hair, black eyes, Greenwich St., grocer (Navy)
Stewart, John, age 31, 25 years in U.S., wife & 3 children,
Saratoga Co., farmer (14-19 Sept. 1812)
Stewart, John, 5ft. 9in., age 24, fair complex., red hair, grey
eyes, George St., clerk (Navy)
Stewart, John, age 23, 1 year in U.S., wife & 2 children, 78
Bancker St., NYC, laborer (28 July - 2 Aug. 1812)
Stewart, John, age 20, 1 year & 1 mo. in U.S., Cornwall, Orange
Co., weaver (19-24 Oct. 1812)
Stewart, Malcom, age 25, 12 years in U.S., Broadalbin, Montgo-
mery Co., tailor (18-24 Aug. & 31 Aug. - 5 Sept. 1812)
Stewart, Neal, age 28, 25 years in U.S., wife & 3 children, Sa-
ratoga Co., farmer (14-19 Sept. 1812)
Stewart, Peter, age 31, 8 years in U.S., wife, Hudson, Columbia
Co., physician (8 Sept. & 3-8 Sept. 1812)
Stewart, Robert, age 45, 11 years in U.S., wife & 4 children,
Smithfield, Madison Co., farmer (1 Aug. & 10-15 Aug. 1812)
Stewart, Robert, 5ft. 5in., age 25, light complex., dark hair,
blue eyes, Anthony St., shoemaker (Navy)
Stewart, Robert, age 22, 6 years in U.S., 56 Beaver St., NYC,
dyer (10-15 Aug. 1812)
Stewart, Robert, 5ft. 7in., age 22, fair complex., fair hair,
blue eyes, mariner (Navy)
Stewart, Thomas, age 42, 10 years in U.S., wife & 4 children,
Smithfield, Madison Co., farmer (1 Aug. & 10-15 Aug. 1812)
Stewart, Thomas, 5ft. 9in., age 32, light complex., fair hair,
brown eyes, Henry St., weaver (Navy)
Stewart, William, age 30, 1 mo. in U.S., NYC, gentleman (28
July - 2 Aug. 1812); 5ft. 10½in., age 30, light complex., red
hair, blue eyes, Broad St., gentleman (Navy); 5ft. 10 in., age
30, light complex., light hair, brown eyes, removed from NYC
to Salisbury (Mills), Orange Co. (Navy)
Stewart, William, 5ft. 9in., age 46, light complex., brown hair,
black eyes, gardener (Navy)
Stewart, William, 5ft. 11in., age 30, fair complex., black hair,
grey eyes, labourer (Navy)
Stewart, William, 5ft. 7in., age 27, dark complex., brown hair,
blue eyes, Laight St., cordwainer (Navy)
Stewart, William, age 25, 8 years in U.S., Bethel, Sullivan Co.,
farmer (31 Aug. & 19-24 Oct. 1812)
Stewart, William, age 23, in U.S. since Sept. 1802, Broadalbin,
Montgomery Co., carpenter (18-24 Aug. & 31 Aug. - 5 Sept. 1812)
Stewart, William, age 23, 3 years in U.S., Long Island, teacher
(28 July - 2 Aug. 1812)
Stiemple, George, age 26, 8 years in U.S., wife, Spring St.
NYC, cartman (20-25 July 1812)
Still, Luke, age 46, 9 years in U.S., wife & 2 children, Wall-
kill, Orange Co., farmer (19-24 Oct. 1812)
Still, William, age 28, 7 years in U.S., 150 William St., NYC,
clerk (28 July - 2 Aug. 1812); 5ft. 8in., age 28, fair complex.,
fair hair, blue eyes, John St., clerk (Navy)
Stinthy (or Struthy?), Robert, 5ft. 11in., age 36, dark complex.,
dark hair, grey eyes, Jay St., blacksmith (Navy)

Stirling, David, age 39, 9 years in U.S., Hudson, Columbia Co.,
    tailor, applied Feb. 1810 in Mayor's Court in Hudson (n.d.)
Stobo (?), James, age 34, 9 years in U.S., Schenectady, weaver
    (14-19 Sept. 1812)
Stoddart, John, age 24, 10 years in U.S., Chenango Co., brewer
    (10-15 Aug. 1812)
Stokes, Thomas B., age 17½, 14 years in U.S., NYC, clerk (26-31
    Oct. 1812)
Storey, Andrew, age 33, 9 mos. in U.S., Kingston, Ulster Co.,
    merchant, applied in June (...) (7 Sept. & 19-24 Oct. 1812)
Storey, Benjamin, 5ft. 4in., age 33, light complex., brown hair,
    blue eyes, Scammel, optic (Navy)
Storey, John, age 35, 2 years in U.S., wife & 2 children, 47
    Cherry St., NYC, plasterer (28 July - 2 Aug. 1812)
Storey, John, 5ft. 6½in., age 30, dark complex., dark hair, dark
    eyes, Roosevelt St., plasterer (Navy)
Storey, Thomas, 6ft., age 30, dark complex., brown hair, blue
    eyes, baker (Navy)
Story, Andrew, age 33, 13 years & 9 mos. in U.S., Ulster Co.,
    merchant (3-8 Aug. 1812); see Andrew Storey, above.
Strachan, Alexander, 5ft. 8in., dark complex., dark hair, dark
    eyes, Barclay St., blacksmith (Navy)
Straughan, Wm., age 29, 11 years in U.S., 4 in family, Naples,
    Ontario Co., farmer (15 Nov. 1812 - 3 Jan. 1813)
Stream, John, age 25, 1 year in U.S., Cornwall, Orange Co., car-
    penter (19-24 Oct. 1812)
Streeter, James, age 35, 21 years in U.S., wife & 6 children,
    Bethlehem, Orange Co., tailor (31 Aug. - 5 Sept. 1812)
Stringer, William, age 47 last Feb., 1 year in U.S. on 5 Aug.
    last, wife & 4 children, Eaton, Madison Co., farmer (31 Oct.
    & 30 Nov. - 5 Dec. 1812)
Strong, Duncan, 5ft. 5½in., age 34, dark complex., dark hair,
    black eyes, Front St., baker (Navy)
Strong, Thomas, 5ft. 11½in., age 24, dark complex., dark hair,
    dark eyes, brewer (Navy)
Strong, William, age 24, 1 year & 11 mos. in U.S., New Windsor,
    Orange Co., shoemaker (19-24 Oct. 1812)
Stuart, John, , age 24, 5 years in U.S., wife, 56 Leonard St.,
    NYC, clerk (13-18 July 1812); 5ft. 9½in., age 24, fair com-
    plex., red hair, grey eyes, removed from NYC to Goshen, Orange
    Co. (Navy)
Stuart, John, age 19, 2 years in U.S., 384 Pearl St., NYC, cooper
    (20-25 July 1812)
Stuart, Kenloch, age 47, 6 years & 9 mos. in U.S., wife & 2
    children, 271 Greenwich St., NYC, confectioner, applied 28
    Apr. 1810 (20-25 July 1812)
Stuart, William, age 28, 7 years in U.S., 37 Mulberry St., NYC,
    pedlar (28 July - 2 Aug. 1812)
Stuart, William, age 23, 1 year in U.S., Kips Bay, NYC, gardener
    (20-25 July 1812)
Stubbs, Edward, age 27, 4 years & 7 mos. in U.S., Wayne, Steuben
    Co., farmer, applied Sup. Court New York 31 Dec. 1807 (24 Aug.
    & 31 Aug. - 5 Sept. 1812)
Stubbs, John, age 24, 7 mos. in U.S., wife & 2 children, Arundel
    St., NYC, weaver (20-25 July 1812)
Stubbs, William, age 55, 4 years & 7 mos. in U.S., wife & 4
    children, Wayne, Steuben Co., farmer, applied Sup. Court N.Y.
    31 Dec. 1807 (31 Aug. - 5 Sept. 1812); wife apparently Marga-
    ret, age 40, and children: Cathrine, age 18, Michael, age 19,
    William, Jr., age 16,& Richard, age 13; Anna Ross, age 50, was
    with the family (24 Aug. 1812)
Sturges, William, age 43, 6 years & 3 mos. in U.S., wife & 8
    children, Kinderhook, Columbia Co., paper maker (3-8 Aug. 1812)
Styles, John Clinton, age 30, 6 mos. in U.S., Montgomery, Orange
    Co., bootmaker (19-24 Oct. 1812)

Styles, Robert, age 50, 7 years in U.S., 26 Front St., NYC, half-
   pay British officer (3-8 Aug. 1812)
Suffern, Thomas, age 24, 4 years in U.S., 6 Depeyster St., NYC,
   merchant, applied 20 July 1809 (13-18 July 1812); 5ft. 7in.,
   age 25, light complex., dark hair, blue eyes, Depeyster St.,
   tobacco (Navy)
Sullin (?), Michael, 5ft. 9in., age 25, dark complex., dark hair,
   blue eyes, Spring St., maltster (Navy)
Sullivan, John, 5ft. 7½in., age 25, light complex., fair hair,
   blue eyes, hatter (Navy)
Sullivan, Patrick, age 33, 6 years & 11 mos. in U.S., wife, corner Elizabeth & Dutch Sts., NYC, grocer (20-25 July 1812);
   5ft. 8½in., age 34, fair complex., light hair, blue eyes, Grand
   St., grocer (Navy)
Sullivan, Silvester, 5ft. 8in., age 22, fair complex., brown
   hair, grey eyes, Broad St., hairdresser (Navy)
Sullivan, Timothy, age 24, 9 years in U.S., 211 Water St., NYC,
   accountant (20-25 July 1812); 5ft. 9½in., age 26, dark complex., brown hair, blue eyes, Front St., accountant (Navy)
Summers, Peter, age 26, 1¼ years in U.S., NYC, laborer (28 July -
   2 Aug. 1812)
Summerville, John, 5ft. 11in., age 27, dark complex., black hair,
   grey eyes, Ferry St., leather (Navy)
Sutton, Michael, age 25, 1 year in U.S., 303 Water St., NYC,
   maltster, applied 14 Apr. 1811 (20-25 July 1812)
Sutton, Richard, age 34, 6 years in U.S., 169 Church St., NYC,
   boot- and shoemaker (2-7 Nov. 1812)
Sutton, Richard, 5ft. 11in., age 30, dark complex., brown hair,
   dark eyes, Church St., cordwainer (Navy) - perhaps the same
   as the Richard Sutton above.
Sutton, William, age 52, 28 years in U.S., wife, Schenectady,
   carpenter (10-15 Aug. 1812)
Swain/Swaine, John, age 33, 11 years & 6 mos. in U.S., wife & 6
   children, 20 William St., NYC, printer (17-22 Aug. 1812); 5ft.
   8in., age 35, sandy complex., brown hair, blue eyes, William
   St., printer (Navy)
Swan, William, age 27, 7½ years in U.S., wife & 2 children, 96
   William St., NYC, merchant, applied 10 July 1807 (20-25 July
   1812); 5ft. 9in., age 28, fair complex., dark hair, brown eyes,
   removed from NYC to Fishkill (Navy)
Swanny, Thomas, age 24, 8 years in U.S., corner Duane & Cross
   Sts., NYC, millwright (20-25 July 1812)
Swany, Ralph, 5ft. 7in., age 32, dark complex., brown hair, grey
   eyes, Bowery, gardener (Navy)
Sweeny, Dennis, 5ft. 11in., age 27, fair complex., fair hair,
   grey eyes, Pine St., milkman (Navy)
Sweeny, Hugh, 5ft. 5in., age 46, fair complex., dark hair, black
   eyes, mason (Navy)
Sweeny, Hugh, age 20, 6 years & 8 mos. in U.S., 64 Vesey St.,
   NYC, student of medicine (20-25 July 1812); 5ft. 6in., age 21,
   light complex., light hair, blue eyes, Vesey St., student of
   medicine (Navy)
Sweeny, John, 5ft. 8in., age 19, fair complex., fair hair, grey
   eyes, Greenwich St., wire worker (Navy)
Sweeny, Myles/Miles, age 30, 8 years in U.S., 14 Augustus St.,
   carpenter (20-25 July 1812); 5ft. 6in., age 30, light complex.,
   dark hair, black eyes, James Slip, carpenter (Navy)
Sweeny, Myles, age 27, 5 years in U.S., 250 Broadway, NYC, gardener (28 July - 2 Aug. 1812)
Sweeny, Richard, 5ft. 7in., age 38, dark complex., black hair,
   blue eyes, Bloomingdale, gardener (Navy)
Sweeny, Thomas, 5ft. 5in., age 25, light complex., light hair,
   grey eyes, Elm St., millwright (Navy)
Sweetman, John, 5ft. 6in., age 51, light complex., grey hair,
   grey eyes, Burling Slip, rope (Navy)

Swinnerton, John, age 40, 2 years in U.S., wife & 2 children,
  Manhattanville, manufacturer (5-10 Oct. 1812); 5ft. 10in.,
  age 40, fair complex., brown hair, blue eyes, Manhattan, wea-
  ver (Navy)
Swim(?), John, age 31, 10 mos. in U.S., wife, Newburgh, Orange
  Co., weaver (19-24 Oct. 1812)
Tackeberry, James, age 38 on 21 Sept. last, 5 years in U.S. on
  27 Aug. last, wife, uncle & aunt, Eaton, Madison Co., farmer,
  applied about 3 years ago (31 Oct. & 30 Nov. - 5 Dec. 1812)
Tackeberry, Nathaniel, age 42 last Feb., 5 years in U.S. on 28
  June last, wife & 7 children, Eaton, Madison Co., farmer (31
  Oct. & 30 Nov. - 5 Dec. 1812)
Taff, James, 5ft. 8in., age 25, dark complex., brown hair, blue
  eyes, Water St., labourer (Navy)
Taffery, John R., 6ft. 2in., age 27, light complex., sandy hair,
  grey eyes, clerk (Navy)
Talbot, Samuel W., 5ft. 2½in., age 15, fair complex., light hair,
  blue eyes, student (Navy)
Tannery, John, age 17, 5 years & 6 mos. in U.S., Newburgh, Orange
  Co., laborer (19-24 Oct. 1812)
Tarryhews, Robert, age 40, 7 years & 3 mos. in U.S., wife & 5
  children, Newburgh, Orange Co., laborer (19-24 Oct. 1812)
Tate, John, age 58, 12 years in U.S., wife, Montgomery, Orange
  Co., weaver (19-24 Oct. 1812)
Tate, Thomas, age 34, 12 years in U.S., wife & 2 children, Mont-
  gomery, Orange Co., weaver (19-24 Oct. 1812)
Taylor, Alexander, 5ft. 8in., age 34, dark complex., dark hair,
  light eyes, ship captain (Navy)
Taylor, Archibald, age 30, 5 years in U.S., wife & 3 children,
  Angelica, Allegany Co., farmer (14 Sept. & 21-26 Sept. 1812)
Taylor, David, 5ft. 8in., age 30, fair complex., light hair,
  blue eyes, Elm St., labourer (Navy)
Taylor, Edward, age 60, 13 years in U.S., wife & 3 children,
  Locke, Cayuga Co., miller, applied 1802 (21-26 Sept. & 5-10
  Oct. 1812)
Taylor, Edward C., age 25, 10 years in U.S., 98 William St., NYC,
  merchant (20-25 July 1812)
Taylor, George, 5ft. 4½in, age 34, light complex., light hair,
  black eyes, Murray St., cabinet (Navy)
Taylor, James, age 25, 3 years in U.S., 46 John St., NYC, ac-
  countant, applied 21 Dec. 1809 (20-25 July 1812)
Taylor, James, 5ft. 8in., age 24, dark complex., dark hair, grey
  eyes, accountant (Navy) - perhaps the same as the James Taylor
  above.
Taylor, James, age 25, 1 year & 4 mos. in U.S., wife, 93 Church
  St., NYC, carpenter (20-25 July 1812)
Taylor, John, age 45, 8 years & 10 mos. in U.S., Bethel, Sullivan
  Co., weaver (19-24 Oct. 1812 & 31 Aug. 1812)
Taylor, John, age 35, 7 years & 3 mos. in U.S., wife & 2 child-
  ren, 57 Orchard St., NYC, teacher (13-18 July 1812)
Taylor, John, 5ft. 9in., age 31, dark complex., black hair,
  brown eyes, Suffolk St., coachman (Navy)
Taylor, John, age 28, 5 years in U.S., 29 Augustus St., NYC,
  laborer (28 July - 2 Aug. 1812)
Taylor, John, age 26, 1 year & 9 mos. in U.S., wife, Bowery,
  NYC, manufacturer of calico (28 July - 2 Aug. 1812)
Taylor, John, 5ft. 8in., age 25, light complex., sandy hair,
  blue eyes, removed from NYC to Goshen, Orange Co. (Navy)
Taylor, Patrick H., age 27, 2½ years in U.S., NYC, gentleman
  (20-25 July 1812); 5ft. 11in., age 27, fair complex., brown
  hair, brown eyes, musician (Navy)
Taylor, Robert, age 28, 1 year in U.S., wife & 4 children, 117
  Bancker St., NYC, baker (26-31 Oct. 1812); 5ft. 4in., age 29,
  light complex., brown hair, blue eyes, James St., baker (Navy)

Taylor, Samuel P., 5ft. 3in., age 33, dark complex., dark hair,
brown eyes, Brooklyn, professor of music (Navy)
Taylor, Stephen, age 29, 10 years in U.S., wife & child, 20
Bancker St., NYC, pilot (24-29 Aug. 1812); 5ft. 5½in. age 29,
dark complex., dark hair, grey eyes, Harman St., pilot (Navy)
Taylor, Stephenson, 5ft. 5in., age 35, light complex., brown
hair, blue eyes, Leonard St., carpenter (Navy)
Taylor, Thomas, 5ft. 8in., age 37, light complex., light hair,
blue eyes, Elm St., painter (Navy)
Taylor, Thomas, age 28, 5 years in U.S., 122 Chamber St., NYC,
mason (28 July - 2 Aug. 1812); 5ft. 11in., age 29, fair com-
plex., light hair, blue eyes, Chapple St., mason (Navy)
Taylor, William, age 45, 9 years in U.S., Maiden Lane, NYC,
clothing store keeper (13-18 July 1812)
Taylor, William, age 21, 5 years in U.S., 146 Water St., accoun-
tant (20-25 July 1812)
Teas, Alexander, age 26, 2 years in U.S., wife & 2 children,
Greenwich St., weaver (10-15 Aug. 1812); 5ft. 6in., age 26,
dark complex., dark hair, hazel eyes, East Bank St., weaver
(Navy)
Teat, Thomas, age 55, 9 years in U.S., wife & 5 children, City
of Albany, merchant (17-22 Aug. 1812)
Teed, John, 5ft. 7in., age 45, fair complex., brown hair, grey
eyes, cartman (Navy)
Tedder, John, age 26, 5 weeks in U.S., wife & child, 164 Cherry
St., master mariner (20-25 July 1812)
Tedeligh, John, 5ft. 8in., age 35, dark complex., brown hair,
grey eyes, gardener (Navy)
Telford, George, age 42, 8 years in U.S., wife & 4 children,
Newburgh, Orange Co., laborer (19-24 Oct. 1812)
Teller, William, age 29, 2 years in U.S., wife & child, City of
Albany, carpenter (17-22 Aug. 1812)
Tenhous, Peter D., age 32, 11 years in U.S., Saratoga, boarding
house keeper (17-22 Aug. 1812)
Tennant, William, age 27, 3 years in U.S., NYC, merchant, applied
16 Jan. 1810 (20-25 July 1812)
Terquea, Joseph, age 25, 1 year & 6 mos. in U.S., wife, Schenec-
tady, shoemaker (31 Aug. - 5 Sept. 1812)
Terrence, James, 5ft. 11in., age 33, brown complex., black hair,
grey eyes, cotton manufacturer (Navy)
Thale (?), Robert, 5ft. 6in., age 50, light complex., brown hair,
grey eyes, Nassau St., servant (Navy)
Thanele, Thomas, 5ft., age 43, light complex., brown hair, dark
eyes, Maiden Lane, tailor (Navy)
Thiesher, G., age 32, 6 years in U.S., wife & 3 children, 201
Broadway, NYC, teacher (13-18 July 1812)
Thirkle, Thomas, age 27, 12 years in U.S., wife & child, City of
Albany, blacksmith (17-22 Aug. 1812)
Thomas, Angus, age 45, 16 years in U.S., wife & child, 117 Front
St., NYC, merchant (20-25 July 1812)
Thomas, Henry, 5ft. 4in., age 23, dark complex., brown hair,
hazel eyes, Ann St., carver (Navy)
Thomas, John, 5ft. 11in., age 64, brown complex., grey hair,
blue eyes, Harman St., brass founder (Navy)
Thomas, John, age 29, 1½ years in U.S., wife, 35 Roosevelt St.,
NYC, tailor (28 July - 2 Aug. 1812); 5ft. 7in., age 30, dark
complex., brown hair, hazel eyes, Warren St., tailor (Navy)
Thomas, John, 5ft. 2in., age 21, fair complex., black hair, blue
eyes, painter (Navy)
Thomas, Timothy, 5ft. 8in., age 50, dark complex., black hair,
fair eyes, Ann St., carpenter (Navy)
Thomas, William, age 52, 16 years in U.S., wife & child, Johnstown, Montgomery Co., weaver (15 Sept. - 5 Oct. & 5-10 Oct. 1812)
Thomlene, James, age 36, 11 years in U.S., Milton, Saratoga Co.,
clothier (31 Aug. - 5 Sept. 1812)

Thompson, Barnard, 5ft. 1in., age 22, light complex., light hair,
  brown eyes, Division St., chair painter (Navy)
Thompson, David, age 29, 8 years in U.S., 61 Cherry St., NYC,
  clerk (13-18 July 1812); 5ft. 3in., age 29, fair complex.,
  brown hair, blue eyes, clerk (Navy)
Thompson, Duncan, 5ft. 6in., age 42, light complex., brown hair,
  blue eyes, Lombardy St., tailor (Navy)
Thompson, Elliot, age 21, 13 years in U.S., Cornwall, Orange
  Co., carpenter (19-24 Oct. 1812)
Thompson, George, age 39, 1 year in U.S., wife & 7 children,
  Bergen Co., N.J., teacher (10-15 Aug. 1812)
Thompson, Henry, age 65, 11 years in U.S., wife & 9 children,
  Montgomery, Orange Co., farmer (19-24 Oct. 1812)
Thompson, Henry, age 27, 9 years in U.S., wife & 2 children,
  Kips Bay, mason (3-8 Aug. 1812); 5ft. 6in., age 27, dark com-
  plex., brown hair, grey eyes, Kips Bay, mason (Navy)
Thompson, Hugh, 5ft. 5in., age 43, fair complex., dark hair,
  grey eyes, weaver (Navy)
Thompson, James, age 61, 10 years in U.S., wife, Duanesburgh,
  Schenectady Co., farmer (10-15 Aug. 1812)
Thompson, James, age 50, 5 mos. in U.S., wife & 4 children,
  Wallkill, Orange Co., farmer (19-24 Oct. 1812)
Thompson, James, 5ft. 8in., age 46, dark complex., dark hair,
  hazel eyes, Greenwich St., weaver (Navy)
Thompson, James, age 38, 12 years in U.S., wife & 2 children, 5
  Batavia Lane, NYC, distiller (13-18 July 1812); 5ft. 4in.,
  age 39, light complex., brown hair, grey eyes, distiller (Navy)
Thompson, James, 5ft. 10in., age 31, fair complex., fair hair,
  blue eyes, Spring St., button (Navy)
Thompson, James, age 30, 1 year in U.S., wife & child, Montgo-
  mery, Orange Co., weaver (19-24 Oct. 1812)
Thompson, John, age 45, 1 year & 1 mo. in U.S., wife & 3 child-
  ren, Cornwall, Orange Co., weaver (21 Dec. 1812 - 23 Jan. 1813
  & 2 Jan. 1813)
Thompson, John, 5ft. 8in., age 44, light complex., light hair,
  blue eyes, Fair St., p... (illegible) (Navy)
Thompson, John, age 34, 17 years in U.S., wife & 4 children,
  Bloominggrove, Orange Co., carpenter (19-24 Oct. 1812)
Thompson, John, 5ft. 6in., age 33, fair complex., dark hair,
  blue eyes, Pump St., wheelwright (Navy)
Thompson, John, 5ft. 11½in., age 25, fair complex., brown hair,
  grey eyes, labourer (Navy)
Thompson, Joseph, 5ft. 11in., age 25, fair complex., black hair,
  blue eyes, Chapple St., slater (Navy)
Thompson, Nicholas, age 31, 2½ years in U.S., wife, Water St.,
  NYC, innkeeper (20-25 July 1812); 5ft. 10in., age 33, light
  complex., light hair, blue eyes, Water St., innkeeper (Navy);
  removed from NYC to Fishkill, Dutchess Co. (Navy)
Thompson, Ralph, age 25, 4 years & 6 mos. in U.S., Poughkeepsie,
  Dutchess Co., laborer (12-17 Oct. 1812)
Thompson, Robert, age 54, wife & 3 children, 29 Henry St., NYC,
  teacher (20-25 July 1812); 5ft. 9½in., age 55, fair complex.,
  grey hair, grey eyes, Mulberry St., teacher (Navy)
Thompson, Robert, age 43, 8 years in U.S., NYC, cabinetmaker
  (28 July - 2 Aug. 1812)
Thompson, Robert, 5ft. 7in., age 35, dark complex., dark hair,
  grey eyes, Moore St., cabinet (Navy)
Thompson, Thomas, age 46, 21 years in U.S., wife & 5 children,
  Wallkill, Orange Co., farmer (19-24 Oct. 1812)
Thompson, Thomas, age 28, 5 mos. in U.S., Poughkeepsie, Dutchess
  Co., laborer (12-17 Oct. 1812)
Thompson, Thomas, age 25, 10 years in U.S., wife & 2 children,
  420 Greenwich St., NYC, sawyer (20-25 July 1812); 5ft. 9in.,
  age 25, ruddy complex., sandy hair, blue eyes, Greenwich St.,
  pit sawyer (Navy)

Thompson, Timothy, age 26 on 24 June last, in U.S. since 25
Dec. 1810, Whitesborough, Oneida Co., weaver, from Northamp-
tonshire, England (10 Aug. & 17-22 Aug. 1812)
Thompson, William, age 34, 6 years in U.S., Penfield, Monroe
Co., farmer (5-15 & 24-29 Aug. 1812)
Thompson, William, age 32 in Apr. next, 1 year in U.S. on 12
July last, wife, Deerfield, Oneida Co., crown glass blower,
from Durham, England (29 Sept. & 28 Sept. - 3 Oct. 1812)

Thomson, Patrick, age 32, 2 years in U.S., Poughkeepsie, Dutchess
Co., storekeeper, applied 16 Oct. 1811 (3-8 Aug. 1812)
Thornbury, John, 5ft. 7½in., age 30, dark complex., red hair,
blue eyes, pedlar (Navy)
Thornell, Joseph, age 50, 9 years in U.S., 5 in family, Boyle,
Monroe Co., farmer, applied 13 Nov. 1811 (13-27 Sept. & 28
Sept. - 3 Oct. 1812)
Thornell, Thomas, age 43, 9 years in U.S., wife, Maiden Lane,
NYC, tailor (20-25 July 1812)
Thornton, Patrick, 5ft. 6in., age 28, black complex., black
hair, blue eyes, labourer (Navy)
Thornton, Thomas, age 66 last June, 11 years in U.S. on 28 June
last, wife & daughter, New Hartford, Oneida Co., farmer (26
Aug. & 28 Sept. - 3 Oct. 1812)
Thresher, George, 5ft. 7½in., age 35, dark complex., brown hair,
black eyes, teacher (Navy)
Tibbot, William, 5ft. 2in., fair complex., fair hair, blue eyes,
Pearl St., shoe (Navy)
Tibbut/Tibbuts, Jonathan, age 52, 9 years in U.S., wife & child,
Hudson, Columbia Co., laborer (3-8 Aug. 1812)
Tienan, Lawrence, age 34, 4 years in U.S., wife & 6 children,
City of Albany, laborer (17-22 Aug. 1812)
Tienor, James, age 28, 7 years in U.S., Utica, Oneida Co., clerk
(17-22 Aug. 1812)
Tobey, James, 5ft. 5in., age 35, dark complex., black hair,
black eyes, Augustus St., labourer (Navy)
Tobin, Thomas, 5ft. 7in., age 50, fair complex., grey hair,
brown eyes, labourer (Navy)
Todd, Isaac, age 66, 1 day in U.S., Broadway, NYC, servant (17-
22 Aug. 1812)
Todd, James, age 46, 18 years in U.S., 2 in family, 108 Church
St., NYC, carpenter (10-15 Aug. 1812); 5ft. 8in., age 46,
dark complex., brown hair, blue eyes, Green St., carpenter(Navy)
Todd, Michael, 11 years in U.S., wife & 3 children, Pearl St.,
NYC (20-25 July 1812)
Todd, Samuel, 5ft. 10in., age 26, fair complex., brown hair,
grey eyes, Bloomingdale, labourer (Navy)
Toher, John, age 24, 1 year in U.S., Monroe Works, Orange Co.,
cut nailor (17-22 Aug. 1812)
Tolay, Patrick, age 29, 5 years & 4 mos. in U.S., Poughkeepsie,
Dutchess Co., laborer (12-17 Oct. 1812)
Tolkeen, Charles, age 22, 4 mos. in U.S., 74 Courtlandt St., NYC,
"dry good agent" (28 July - 2 Aug. 1812)
Tomlinson, John, 5ft. 6in., age 39, fair complex., light hair,
blue eyes, Elizabeth St., machine (Navy)
Toner, Bryant, 5ft. 6in., age 22, dark complex., dark hair,
hazel eyes, servant (Navy)
Tonge, Christopher, 5ft. 11in., age 40, dark complex., dark
hair, Harlaem, starch (Navy)
Tonland, Edward, age 55, 28 years in U.S., wife & 7 children,
Montgomery, Orange Co., tailor (19-24 Oct. 1812)
Toole, Francis, age 23 on 10 Oct. next, 23 years in U.S.on 5 Nov.
next, wife & 3 children, Augusta, Oneida Co., farmer (31 Oct.
& 30 Nov. - 5 Dec. 1812)
Toole, Mark, 5ft. 5in., age 39, fair complex., dark hair, brown
eyes, servant (Navy)

Toole, William, 5ft. 10½in., age 40, sandy complex., sandy hair,
hazel eyes, Broad St., mason (Navy)

Topper, John, 5ft. 10in., age 37, fair complex., sandy hair,
grey eyes, Orchard St., teacher (Navy)

Topping, Henry, age 38, 1 year & 1 mo. in U.S., wife & 5 children, Schenectady, tallow chandler (28 July - 2 Aug. 1812)

Topping, John, age 30, 1 year in U.S., 417 Pearl St., NYC,
teacher (13-18 July 1812)

Topson, Bryon, age 26, 1½ years in U.S., Bloomingdale, gardener
(28 July - 2 Aug. 1812)

Toumain, Lucas, age 20, 4 years in U.S., 15 William St., NYC,
shoemaker (26-31 Oct. 1812)

Tower, John, age 24, 19 years in U.S., Phelps, Ontario Co.,
farmer (5-15 & 24-29 Aug. 1812)

Townsend, Thomas, 5ft. 8in., age 47, light complex., dark hair,
brown eyes, Elizabeth St., labourer (Navy)

Townsend, William, 5ft. 8in., age 27, dark complex., dark hair,
blue eyes, cooper (Navy)

Tracey, James, age 45, 9 years & 1 mo. in U.S., wife & 4 children, Shawangunk, Ulster Co., farmer (19-24 Oct. 1812)

Tracey, Thomas, age 30, 11 years in U.S., wife & 3 children,
New Paltz, Ulster Co., farmer (19-24 Oct. 1812)

Trainor, Peter, 5ft. 8in., age 48, dark complex., dark hair,
black eyes, Garden St., servant (Navy)

Tranor, Pat, 5ft. 8in., age 28, fair complex., sandy hair, light
eyes, weaver (Navy)

Traynor, Michael, age 23, 4 years in U.S., wife, Newburgh, Orange
Co., laborer (19-24 Oct. 1812)

Treaty, William, 5ft. 5in., age 40, dark complex., black hair,
black eyes, Elm St., labourer (Navy)

Trenor, James, age 29 on 28 Dec. last, 7 years in U.S. on 23
Aug. inst., Utica, Oneida Co., clerk to a merchant, from Dublin, Ireland (10 Aug. 1812)

Trenter, James, 5ft. 10in., age 25, fair complex., brown hair,
blue eyes, gardener (Navy)

Trenton, William, 5ft. 11in., age 38, light complex., brown hair,
blue eyes, carpenter (Navy)

Trespass, Caleb, 5ft. 9in., age 25, dark complex., dark hair,
dark eyes, Jacob St., leather dresser (Navy)

Trice, James, age 30, 6 years in U.S., City of Albany, merchant
(5-10 Oct. 1812)

Trimble, Edward, 5ft. 6in., dark complex., black hair, grey eyes,
porter (Navy)

Trimble, John, age 34, 12 years in U.S., wife & 3 children,
Bloominggrove, Orange Co., weaver (19-24 Oct. 1812)

Tronton (?), Richard, 5ft. 10in., age 40, fair complex., brown
hair, blue eyes, iron (Navy)

Trotter, Thomas, age 41, 11 years in U.S., wife & 4 children,
191 Bowery Lane, NYC, tallow chandler (20-25 July 1812); 5ft.
9in., age 42, light complex., "b"hair, "b" eyes, 191 Bowery,
soap (Navy)

Troy, Michael, 5ft. 11in., age 40, light complex., brown hair,
grey eyes, 304 Water St., farmer (Navy)

Trueman, Lucas, 5ft. 5in., age 21, dark complex., black hair,
blue eyes, William St., shoemaker (Navy)

Truman, George, age 36, 5 years & 10 mos. in U.S., wife & 3 children, 202 Broadway, NYC, hatter (20-25 July 1812); Trueman,
George, 5ft. 6in., age 33, light complex., dark hair, brown
eyes, Broadway, hatter (Navy)

Tuke, Michael, age 48 last Mar., 2 years in U.S. on 4 Oct. inst.,
wife & 7 children, Eaton, Madison Co., farmer (31 Oct. & 30
Nov. - 5 Dec. 1812)

Tule, Christian, 5ft. 10in., age 37, fair complex., dark hair,
blue eyes, Catherine Lane, cartman (Navy)

Tully, Francis, age 23, 5 years in U.S., wife & child, 130 Chamber St., NYC, coppersmith (17-22 Aug. 1812); 5ft. 6in., age 23, light complex., brown hair, blue eyes, Ann St., copper (Navy)

Tully, Patrick, 5ft. 5in., age 50, pale complex., brown hair, grey eyes, cooper (Navy)

Tully, Patrick, 5ft. 5in., age 49, fair complex., brown hair, blue eyes, Anthony St., coppersmith (Navy)

Tully, Patrick, 5ft. 10in., age 21, fair complex., dark hair, brown eyes, labourer (Navy)

Tumey, James, 5ft. 5in., age 25, light complex., fair hair, light eyes, Henry St., printer (Navy)

Turgle, Martin, age 51, 15 years in U.S., wife & 6 children, farmer (24-29 Aug. 1812)

Turnbull, Adam, age 33, 11 mos. in U.S., Duanesburgh, Schenectady Co., teacher (24-29 Aug. 1812)

Turnbull, George, age 51, 25 years in U.S., wife & 6 children, Duanesburgh, Schenectady Co., farmer (10-15 Aug. 1812)

Turnbull, George, age 30, 5 years in U.S., 4 in family, Seneca, Ontario Co., weaver (5-15 & 24-29 Aug. 1812)

Turner, Bartholomew, 5ft. 8in., age 27, fair complex., light hair, grey eyes, Manhattan, labourer (Navy)

Turner, James, age 30, 10 years & 1 mo. in U.S., wife & 2 children, Bloominggrove, Orange Co., laborer (19-24 Oct. 1812)

Turner, John, 6ft. 2in., age 42, dark complex., brown hair, dark eyes, Vesey St., grocer (Navy)

Turner, Levin, age 26, 24 years in U.S., wife & child, 146 Washington St., NYC, bookbinder (20-25 July 1812); 5ft. 7in., age 27, brown complex., brown hair, blue eyes, Washington St., bookbinder (Navy)

Turner, Thomas, age 25, 6 years in U.S., wife & child, Washington, Dutchess Co., farmer (12-17 Oct. 1812)

Turney, James, age 24, 10 years in U.S., wife & 3 children, 105 Henry St., NYC, printer (20-25 July 1812)

Turquand, Paul Leonard, age 35, 9 years & 11 mos. in U.S., Broome St., NYC, teacher (20-25 July 1812)

Twededale, William A., age 35, 2 years in U.S., City of Albany, teacher (17-22 Aug. 1812)

Tweedie/ Twedie, James, age 31, 10 years in U.S., wife & 4 children, Florida, Montgomery Co., tailor (25 Aug. - 2 Sept. & 7-12 Sept. 1812)

Tweedy, David, age 42, 18 years in U.S., wife & 4 children, Montgomery, Orange Co., weaver (19-24 Oct. 1812)

Twisley, William, age 52, 1 year in U.S., wife & 4 children, 83 Lumber St., NYC, grocer & laborer (20-25 July 1812)

Tyson, Henry, 5ft. 8in., age 37, light complex., brown hair, blue eyes, Jews Alley, shipwright (Navy)

Uffington, Thomas Spooner, age 34, 4 years & 10 mos. in U.S., wife & 3 children, 434 Greenwich St., NYC, gold beater (20-25 July 1812); 5ft. 9in., age 35, dark complex., dark hair, dark eyes, Greenwich St., gold beater (Navy)

Uncian, Isaac, 5ft. 8in., age 29, light complex., brown hair, blue eyes, servant (Navy)

Upfold, John, age 44 years & 4 mos., 11 years & 10 mos. in U.S., wife & 4 children, Fabius, Onondaga Co., preacher of the Gospel (3 Feb. - 10 May 1813)

Ure, Fleming, age 31, 12 years in U.S., Oswego, Onondaga Co., mason (18-25 Sept. 1812); listed as farmer (28 Sept. - 3 Oct. 1812)

Urquhart, Robert, 5ft. 8½in., age 22, fair complex., brown hair, blue eyes, Jones St., dyer (Navy)

Usher, Bloomfield, age 28, 5 years in U.S., wife & 3 children, 117 Elm St., NYC, hatter (13-18 July 1812)

228 NEW YORK

Usher, Luke, age 28, 2 years in U.S., wife & 2 children, Broadway, NYC, manufacturer of mineral waters (28 July - 2 Aug.
1812); 5ft. 4in., age 30, light complex., dark hair, brown
eyes, Broadway (Navy)
Ushouse, Jonathan, age 19, 16 years & 5 mos. in U.S., Poughkeepsie, Dutchess Cq., carpenter (12-17 Oct. 1812)
Valey, Elisha, 5ft. 4in., age 21, light complex., light hair,
light eyes, 122 Bowery, teacher (Navy)
Van Beuren, Valentine, 5ft. 5½in., age 25, light complex.,
sandy hair, dark eyes, Greenwich St., ship (Navy)
Van Cleck, Simon, age 37, 6 mos. in U.S., wife & 6 children,
Northumberland, Saratoga Co., farmer (31 Aug. - 5 Sept. 1812)
Vandenbrugh, Richard, age 60, 9 years in U.S., wife & 2 child-
ren, Newtown, Long Island, farmer, half-pay British captain
(28 July - 2 Aug. 1812)
Vane, David, age 65, 21 years in U.S., 7 children, New Windsor,
Orange Co., farmer (19-24 Oct. 1812)
Vane, James, age 29, 20 years in U.S., New Windsor, Orange Co.,
carpenter (19-24 Oct. 1812)
Vane, Moses, age 35, 21 years in U.S,, wife & 7 children, New
Windsor, Orange Co., farmer (19-24 Oct. 1812)
Van Embrugen, Gilbert, age 27, 21 years in U.S., wife, Bethle-
hem, Albany Co., shoemaker (31 Aug. - 5 Sept. 1812)
Van Wells, William, age 26, 8 years in U.S., Robinson St., NYC,
flax dresser (20-25 July 1812)
Van Wincle, David, Jr., age 25, 19 years in U.S., Newtown, Long
Island, cordwainer (20-25 July 1812); 5ft. 11in., age 26,
light complex., brown hair, blue eyes, Newtown, L.I., shoe-
maker (Navy)
Varty, Joseph, age 55, 1 year in U.S., wife, Scipio, Cayuga Co.,
farmer (7-12 & 21-26 Sept. 1812)
Veitch, Andrew D., 5ft. 11½in., age 24, light complex., dark
hair, blue eyes, removed from NYC to Fishkill, Dutchess Co.
(Navy)
Vey/Voy, William, age 23, 9 mos. in U.S., wife & child, 92 Mott
St., NYC, butcher (20-25 July 1812); 5ft. 6in., age 25, light
complex., black hair, grey eyes, Elizabeth St., butcher (Navy)
Vick, Samuel, 5ft. 5in., age 19, fair complex., light hair,
light eyes, William St., pin maker (Navy)
Vigham, John, age 33, 2 years & 8 mos. in U.S., Kingston, Ulster
Co., weaver (19-24 Oct. 1812); age given as 23 (7 Sept. 1812)
Vigham, Nathan, age 44, 2 years & 9 mos. in U.S., wife & 4 child-
ren, Kingston, Ulster Co., weaver (7 Sept. & 19-24 Oct. 1812)
Vincent, John, 10 mos. in U.S., wife & 2 children, Fourth St.,
NYC, ropemaker (20-25 July 1812)
Wade, Patrick, 5ft. 6in., age 20, dark complex., black hair,
grey eyes, Warren St., chair maker (Navy)
Wadsworth, Henry, 5ft. 10½in., age 25, fair complex., fair hair,
blue eyes, Roosevelt St., labourer (Navy)
Wagner, Richard, age 34, 9 years in U.S., 50 Pearl St., NYC,
distiller (31 Aug. - 5 Sept. 1812)
Waite, Henry, 5ft. 6in., age 38, light complex., light hair,
blue eyes, baker (Navy); age 41, 14 years in U.S., 7 in family,
Elm St., NYC, baker (28 July - 2 Aug. 1812)
Waite, William, age 32, 9 years in U.S., wife & child, Broadway,
NYC, carpenter (20-25 July 1812); 6ft., age 35, light complex.,
dark hair, dark eyes, Kips Bay, carpenter (Navy)
Wake, Thomas, age 31, 6 years in U.S., City of Albany, laborer
(17-22 Aug. 1812)
Wake, William, 5ft. 7in., age 35, light complex., light hair,
grey eyes, brewer (Navy)
Walford, Joseph R., 5ft. 6½in., age 21, light complex., brown
hair, brown eyes, gentleman, removed from NYC to Goshen, Orange
Co. (Navy)

Walker, David, age 46, 28 years in U.S., wife & 6 children,
Duanesburgh, Schenectady Co., mason (24-29 Aug. 1812)

Walker, George, age 40, 17 years in U.S., wife & 6 children,
Schenectady, farmer (24-29 Aug. 1812)

Walker, James, age 39, 14 years in U.S., wife & 4 children,
Smithfield, Madison Co,, farmer (4 Aug. & 10-15 Aug. 1812)

Walker, James, age 35, 7 years in U.S., wife & 2 children, 479
Greenwich St., NYC (20-25 July 1812); 5ft. 6in., age 35, fair
complex., grey hair, brown eyes, shuttle maker (Navy)

Walker, James, age 30 on 13 Dec. next, 2 years in U.S. on 3 Apr.
next, wife, Sullivan, Madison Co., miller, applied two different times some 3 or 4 years ago (31 Oct. & 30 Nov. - 5 Dec.
1812)

Walker, James, age 18, 1 year & 5 mos. in U.S., 247 Broadway,
merchant (20-25 July 1812)

Walker, John, age 64, 11 years in U.S., wife & child, Wawarsing,
Ulster Co., farmer (19-24 Oct. 1812)

Walker, John, age 43 on 3 Dec. next, 6 years in U.S. on 17 July
last, wife & 5 children, Whitestown, Oneida Co., blacksmith
(26 Aug. & 28 Sept. - 3 Oct. 1812)

Walker, John, age 20, 1 day in U.S., 6 Cherry St., NYC, merchant
(24-29 Aug. 1812)

Walker, Joseph, 5ft. 8in., age 47, dark complex., dark hair,
black eyes, blacksmith (Navy)

Walker, Peter, age 42, 7 years in U.S., Lyons, Ontario Co., farmer, applied June 1811 (15-22 Aug. & 31 Aug. - 5 Sept. 1812)

Walker, Richard, 5ft. 7in., age 28, fair complex., sandy hair,
grey eyes, cook (Navy)

Walker, Robert, 5ft. 6in., age 24, light complex., fair hair,
blue eyes, Mamaroneck, Westchester Co., weaver (Navy)

Walker, William, age 36, 8 years in U.S., wife & child, 39 Charlotte St., teacher (20-25 July 1812); 5ft. 7in., age 38, dark
complex., dark hair, dark eyes, Charlotte St., teacher (Navy)

Wall, John, 5ft. 2in., age 36, fair complex., sandy hair, dark
eyes, Catherine St., brewer (Navy)

Wall, Stephen, age 32, 3 years in U.S., wife & 5 children, 37
Augustus St., NYC, grocer, applied 15 July 1810 (20-25 July
1812); 5ft. 10in., age 33, fair complex., light hair, blue
eyes, grocer (Navy)

Wallace, James, age 35, 3 mos. in U.S., wife & 4 children, 27
Henry St., NYC, blacksmith (13-18 July 1812); 5ft. 10in., age
35, fair complex., fair hair, grey eyes, Bancker St., blacksmith (Navy)

Wallace, James, age 31, 10 years in U.S., 4 Mile Stone, professor
of mathematics, applied 24 July 1809 (20-25 July 1812)

Wallace, James, age 30, 13 years & 10 mos. in U.S., Newburgh,
Orange Co., laborer (19-24 Oct. 1812)

Wallace, James, 5ft. 8in., age 30, fair complex., brown hair,
blue eyes, Middle Road, tobacco (Navy)

Wallace, James, 5ft. 9in., age 27, dark complex., black hair,
brown eyes, Harlaem, h... (illegible) (Navy)

Wallace, James, age 26, 6 years in U.S., Fishkill, Dutchess Co.,
gardener (12-17 Oct. 1812)

Wallace, James, 5ft. 9in., age 25, sandy complex., dark hair,
grey eyes, Mott St., shoemaker (Navy)

Wallace, John, 5ft. 7in., age 33, dark complex., dark hair, brown
eyes, Greenwich St., weaver (Navy)

Wallace, Lawrence, 5ft. 8in., age 28, dark complex., dark hair,
dark eyes, Harlaem, farmer (Navy)

Wallace, Robert, age 50, 23 years in U.S., 4 children, Scipio,
Cayuga Co., farmer (7-12 & 21-26 Sept. 1812)

Wallace, Robert, age 46, 19 years in U.S., wife & 3 children,
Montgomery, Orange Co. farmer (19-24 Oct. 1812)

Wallace, Robert, age 23, 5 years in U.S., wife, 14 Charlotte St.,
NYC, cartman (20-25 July 1812)

Wallace, Thomas, age 20, 4 years in U.S., NYC, stone cutter (28
    July - 2 Aug. 1812); 5ft. 6in., age 20, brown complex., brown
    hair, brown eyes, Pell St., stone cutter (Navy)
Wallace, William, age 21, 2 years in U.S., Newburgh, Orange Co.,
    cabinetmaker (19-24 Oct. 1812)
Wallace, William, Jr., age 44, 17 years in U.S., wife & 4 child-
    ren, Wallkill, Orange Co., farmer (19-24 Oct. 1812)
Wallis, Alfred, 5ft. 7in., age 21, light complex., light hair,
    blue eyes, cordwainer (Navy)
Wallis, James, age 40, 1 year in U.S., wife & 2 children, 11
    Mulberry St., NYC, brewer (13-18 July 1812)
Walsh, Alexander, age 29, 17 years in U.S., 115 Front St., NYC,
    accountant (13-18 July 1812)
Walsh, Bartholomew, age 61, 8 years in U.S., wife & 5 sons, NYC,
    tobacconist, applied 27 Apr. 1810 (13-18 July 1812); 5ft. 5½in.,
    age 62, dark complex., dark hair, dark eyes, Henry St., segar
    (Navy)
Walsh, Bartholomew, Jr., 5ft. 6in., age 22, dark complex., dark
    hair, brass founder (Navy)
Walsh, Christopher T., age 32, 5 years in U.S., Montgomery,
    Orange Co., schoolmaster (19-24 Oct. 1812)
Walsh, Henry, 5ft. 7in., age 33, light complex., black hair,
    blue eyes, Cedar St., schoolmaster (Navy)
Walsh, James, age 34, 11 years in U.S., wife & 6 children, Sara-
    toga Co., farmer (14-19 Sept. 1812)
Walsh, John W., 5ft. 3in., age 32, fair complex., brown hair,
    grey eyes, painter (Navy)
Walsh, Patrick, age 29, 8 years in U.S., wife & child, NYC,
    schoolmaster, applied 26 Apr. 1810 (13-18 July 1812); 5ft.
    6½in., age 30, dark complex., dark hair, blue eyes, Doyer (?)
    St., schoolmaster (Navy)
Walsh, Patrick, age 21, 1½ years in U.S., 17 Bancker St., NYC,
    morocco dresser (20-25 July 1812)
Walsh, Richard, 5ft. 11in., age 50, dark complex., dark hair,
    grey eyes, Greenwich St., gardener (Navy)
Walsh, Thomas, age 30, 8 mos. in U.S., wife & 3 children, Mont-
    gomery, Orange Co., laborer (19-24 Oct. 1812)
Walsh, Thomas S., age 40, 7 years in U.S., wife & 6 children,
    42 Greenwich St., NYC, grocer (20-25 July 1812), 6ft., age 40,
    brown complex., dark hair, light eyes, removed from NYC to
    Rensselaer (Navy)
Waltby, William, age 49, 6 years & 11 mos. in U.S., wife & child,
    Otsego Co., farmer (31 Aug. - 5 Sept. 1812)
Walton, Charles, 5ft. 10in., age 28, light complex., brown hair,
    brown eyes, Water St., brushmaker (Navy)
Wanderhoun, John, 5ft. 7in., age 34, light complex., brown hair,
    brown eyes, Mamaroneck, Westchester Co., weaver (Navy)
Ward, Edmund/Edmond, age 20, 16 years in U.S., 201 Broadway,
    NYC, clerk (20-25 July 1812); 5ft. 7in., age 21, dark complex.,
    brown hair, dark eyes, Broadway, clerk (Navy)
Ward, Godfrey, 5ft. 5in., age 42, light complex., black hair,
    blue eyes (Navy)
Ward, John, 5ft. 6in., age 21, fair complex., light hair, blue
    eyes, William St., tanner (Navy)
Ward, Thomas, 5ft. 7in., age 24, brown complex., dark hair, blue
    eyes, Broad St., tobacco (Navy)
Wardale, William, age 62, 10 years in U.S., wife & child, 25
    Thomas St., NYC, carpenter (3-8 Aug. 1812)
Warden, Alexander, age 31, 12 years in U.S., Middlesex, Ontario
    Co., clerk in a store, applied Feb. 1812 (15-22 Aug. & 31 Aug. -
    5 Sept. 1812)
Wardle, James, age 34, 1 year & 4 mos. in U.S., Clinton, Dutchess
    Co., cotton carder (12-17 Oct. 1812)
Wardle, John, age 21, 1 year & 4 mos. in U.S., Clinton, Dutchess
    Co., spinner (12-17 Oct. 1812)

Wardrop, James, age 34, 2 years in U.S., 27 Hudson St., NYC,
merchant (20-25 July 1812)

Waring, Benjamin, age 39, 7 years in U.S., wife & 2 children,
21 Gold St., NYC, crodwainer (20-25 July 1812)

Wark, Benjamin, age 30, 3 years in U.S., 18 Stone St., NYC, feed
store keeper (17-22 Aug. 1812); 5ft. 9in., age 31, ruddy complex., grey hair, blue eyes, Front St., granary (Navy)

Wark, James, 5ft. 6in., age 25, fair complex., brown hair, grey
eyes, shoemaker (Navy)

Warne, James, 5ft. 4in., age 32, dark complex., brown hair, dark
eyes, Mulberry St., rigger (Navy)

Warren, Benjamin, age 53 last May, 1 year in U.S., wife & 2
children, Sangerfield, Oneida Co., farmer (26 Aug. & 28 Sept. -
3 Oct. 1812)

Warren, Weston, 5ft. 11in., age 26, fair complex., light hair,
blue eyes, Pearl St., coachman (Navy)

Wasson, William, age 31, 7 years in U.S., 3 in family, Seneca,
Ontario Co., farmer (5-15 & 24-29 Aug. 1812)

Waters, Andrew, 5ft. 10in., age 28, dark complex., dark hair,
dark eyes, labourer (Navy)

Waters, Charles, 5ft. 8in., age 23, fair complex., brown hair,
grey eyes, Cross St., bricklayer (Navy)

Waters, John, 5ft. 9in., age 36, dark complex., brown hair,
brown eyes, William St., labourer (Navy)

Waters, Patrick, 6ft., age 25, dark complex., brown hair, hazel
eyes, Augustus St., morocco (Navy)

Waters, Terrence, 5ft.6in., age 22, fair complex., brown hair,
blue eyes, gardener (Navy)

Waters, Thomas, 5ft. 6in., age 25, fair complex., brown hair,
grey eyes, labourer (Navy)

Waters, William, age 34, 8 years in U.S., 4 in family, Williamson, Ontario Co., farmer (5-15 & 24-29 Aug. 1812)

Watkins, William, age 41, 10 years in U.S., wife & child, 213
William St., NYC, shoemaker (19-24 Oct. 1812); 5ft. 10in., age
51, fair complex., grey hair, brown eyes, William St., shoemaker (Navy)

Watkinson, John, age 47, 6 years in U.S., wife & 3 children,
Duanesburgh, Schenectady Co., farmer (24-29 Aug. 1812)

Watkinson, William, age 39, 8 years in U.S., 4 in family, Benton,
Ontario Co., farmer (5-15 & 24-29 Aug. 1812)

Watland, William, 5ft. 9in., age 25, fair complex., dark hair,
brown eyes, Manhattanville, labourer (Navy)

Watmaster, William, 5ft. 8in., age 22, fair complex., fair hair,
brown eyes, manufacturer (Navy)

Watson, James, age 31, 7 years in U.S., wife & child, Wallkill,
Orange Co., weaver (19-24 Oct. 1812)

Watson, John, 5ft. 10in., age 45, dark complex., brown hair,
brown eyes, labourer (Navy)

Watson, John, 5ft. 8in., age 32, fair complex., brown hair, grey
eyes, Rose St., morocco (Navy)

Watson, John W., age 36, 1 year & 4 mos. in U.S., Brooklyn, agent
for a house in Liverpool (3-8 Aug. 1812)

Watson, Jonathan, age 48, 10 years in U.S., wife, NYC, shoemaker
(20-25 July 1812)

Watson, Joseph, age 30, 6 years in U.S., farmer (30 Aug. - 5 Sept.
1812)

Watson, Joseph, 5ft. 8in., age 30, light complex., brown hair,
blue eyes, cooper (Navy)

Watson, Michael, 6 years in U.S., wife, 44 Cross St., NYC, saddler (20-25 July 1812); 5ft. 8in., age 25, dark complex., dark
hair, dark eyes, Duane St., saddler (Navy)

Watson, Stephen, age 30, 6 years in U.S., Geneva, Ontario Co.,
farmer (7-12 Sept. 1812)

Watson, Wertley, 5ft. 11in., age 30, dark complex., brown hair,
dark eyes, Manhattanville, gardener (Navy)

Watt, Alexander, 5ft. 6in., age 39, brown complex., brown hair,
    blue eyes, Bloomingdale, gardener (Navy)
Watters, Thomas, age 24, 2 years in U.S., wife & child, 245
    William St., NYC, carpenter (20-25 July 1812)
Watts, John, age 42, 8 years in U.S., wife & 3 children, NYC,
    printer & bookseller (28 July - 2 Aug. 1812)
Watts, John, 5ft. 7in., age 45, fair complex., brown hair, brown
    eyes, Bowery Lane, stenotype (Navy) - perhaps the same as the
    John Watts above.
Watts, Joseph, age 28, 16 years in U.S., 1 child, Newburgh,
    Orange Co., painter (14 & 17-22 Aug. 1812)
Watts, Thomas, age 28, 5 years & 8 mos. in U.S., New Windsor,
    Orange Co., laborer (19-24 Oct. 1812)
Waugh, Peter, age 54, 18 years in U.S., 7 in family, Seneca,
    Ontario Co., farmer, states he applied & was naturalized in
    Pa. in 1801 but neglected to take his certificate (5-15 & 24-
    29 Aug. 1812)
Way, Francis, age 23, 6 mos. in U.S., Fishkill, Dutchess Co.,
    laborer (12-17 Oct. 1812)
Wayland, Charles, 4ft. 11in., age 22, fair complex., brown hair,
    dark eyes, Corlaers Hook, cordwainer (Navy)
Webb, Henry, 5ft. 7in., age 36, fair complex., light hair, grey
    eyes, Reed St., grocer (Navy)
Webb, James, age 21, 6 years in U.S., wife, 176 Bancker St.,
    NYC, ship carpenter, applied 16 Dec. 1809 (13-18 July 1812)
Webb, John, age 58, 8 years in U.S., 4 in family, White St.,
    NYC, carpenter (20-25 July 1812); 5ft. 10in., age 60, dark
    complex., brown hair, grey eyes, Duane St., carpenter (Navy)
Webb, John, age 47, 6 years & 5 mos., wife & 7 children, Water
    St., NYC, ship carpenter (20-25 July 1812)
Webb, Joseph, age 35, 2 years & 9 mos. in U.S., 5 in family, 37
    Augustus St., carpenter (20-25 July 1812)
Weble, Joseph, 5ft. 7in., age 34, fair complex., brown hair,
    light eyes, Cross St., carpenter (Navy)
Webster, Robert, age 27 on 10 Sept. 1812, 1 year in U.S. on 15
    Aug. last, wife & 3 children, Eaton, Madison Co., farmer (31
    Oct. & 30 Nov. - 5 Dec. 1812)
Weddel, Robert, age 64, 21 years in U.S., wife & 8 children,
    Johnsburgh, Washington Co., farmer (8 Dec. 1812); age given
    as 25 (7-19 Dec. 1812)
Weir, Robert, 5ft. 8in., age 30, dark complex., brown hair, blue
    eyes, Bowery, thread manufacturer (Navy)
Weller, Humphry, 5ft. 6in., age 31, light complex., brown hair,
    black eyes, Leonard St., miller (Navy)
Weller, W., age 62, 11 years in U.S., 2 children, 180 Front St.,
    NYC, bookkeeper (3-8 Aug. 1812)
Weller, William, 5ft. 6in., age 63, fair complex., brown hair,
    grey eyes, Leonard St., clerk (Navy)
Wells, John, age 29, 10 mos. in U.S., Clinton, Dutchess Co.,
    weaver (12-17 Oct. 1812)
Wells, Richard, 5ft. 8in., age 48, fair complex., brown hair,
    blue eyes, Maiden Lane, clerk (Navy)
Wells, William, 5ft. 8in., age 36, fair complex., light hair,
    grey eyes, (name of street illegible), instrument (Navy)
Wells, William, 5ft. 7½in., age 26, light complex., brown hair,
    blue eyes, Washington St., servant (Navy)
Welsh, Henry, age 33, 3 years in U.S., wife & 2 sisters, 367
    Greenwich St., merchant (20-25 July 1812)
Welsh, John, 5ft. 10in., age 44, fair complex., fair hair, blue
    eyes, Elm St., grocer (Navy)
Welsh, John, 5ft. 9in., age 42, dark complex., dark hair, blue
    eyes, gardener (Navy)
Welsh, Joseph, age 42, 8 mos. in U.S., 2 children, 40 Broadway,
    NYC, gentleman (20-25 July 1812)

Welsh, Martin, 5ft. 8in., age 36, fair complex., brown hair,
hazel eyes, Long Island, milkman (Navy)
Welsh, Patrick, 5ft. 8in., age 21, fair complex., brown hair,
brown eyes, Cherry St., morocco (Navy)
Welsh, Richard, 5ft. 10½in., age 23, fair complex., fair hair,
blue eyes, stocco (Navy)
Welshan, John W., 5ft. 4in., age 35, dark complex., black hair,
black eyes, Cliff St., tailor (Navy)
Welshman, Edward, 5ft. 7in., age 34, ruddy complex., brown hair,
black eyes, Leonard St., carpenter (Navy)
Wesh, William, age 26, 1 year in U.S., 104 Liberty St., NYC,
merchant (20-25 July 1812)
West, Bartholomew, 5ft. 5in., age 25, brown complex., brown
hair, black eyes, Gransburgh (?), labourer (Navy)
West, Beale, age 47, 8 years in U.S., Westchester, gardener (20-
25 July 1812)
West, David, 5ft. 9in., age 26, fair complex., fair hair, blue
eyes, Grand St., cartman (Navy)
West, John, 5ft. 5in., age 31, light complex., brown hair, blue
eyes, painter (Navy)
West, Nicholas, 5ft. 7in., age 38, brown complex., brown hair,
dark eyes, Leonard St., painter (Navy)
West, Vere, 4 in family, NYC (21-26 Sept. 1812); 5 ft. 7in.,
age 58, dark complex., dark hair, dark eyes, Lower Robinson
St., slater (Navy)
West, Thomas, 5ft. 5½in., age 27, light complex., brown hair,
brown eyes, Ann St., brush maker (Navy)
Wetherly, John, age 57, 8 years in U.S., wife, 25 James St. NYC,
cordwainer (20-25 July 1812)
Wetts, Richard, age 48, 7 years in U.S., wife, 59 Maiden Lane,
NYC, clerk, applied 29 June 1812 (13-18 July 1812)
Whale, Thomas, age 44, 3 years in U.S., wife & 5 children, Phila-
delphia, dancing master, applied Sept. 1809 (20-25 July 1812)
Whale, Thomas, 5ft. 7in., age 39, dark complex., dark hair, dark
eyes, teacher (Navy)
Whatson, Richard, 5ft. 6in., age 31, dark complex., brown hair,
dark eyes, Bowery, carpenter (Navy)
Wheatcroft, William, age 30, 8 years in U.S., wife & 2 children,
34 Vesey St., sailor (3-8 Aug. 1812)
Wheatley, John H., age 30, in U.S. 1 year & 3 mos., has man-ser-
vant, Bloomingdale, gentleman (13-18 & 20-25 July 1812)
Wheaton, William, age 26, 6 years in U.S., wife & child, 96
Catharine St., NYC, merchant tailor (13-18 July 1812); 5ft.
7½in., age 27, light complex., brown hair, grey eyes, Chatham
St., tailor (Navy)
Wheeler, James, 5ft. 5in., age 29, light complex., brown hair,
brown eyes, labourer (Navy)
Wheelock, Charles, 6ft., age 25, fair complex., brown hair,
black eyes, Elizabeth St., tallow chandler (Navy); 5 years in
U.S., age 25, Elizabeth St., NYC, tallow chandler (28 July -
2 Aug. 1812)
Whelan, Joseph, age 25, 7 years in U.S., Johnstown, Montgomery
Co., farmer (5-10 Oct. 1812)
Whiggam, George, age 28, 4 years in U.S., Montgomery, Orange Co.,
weaver (19-24 Oct. 1812)
Whiley, Alexander, 5ft. 5in., age 22, light complex., brown hair,
brown eyes, stone (Navy)
Whitager, John, 5ft. 8in., age 35, fair complex., brown hair,
grey eyes, Cliff St., coachman (Navy)
Whitaker, John, age 27 years & 2 mos., 3 years in U.S., wife &
2 children, Hudson, Columbia Co., cotton manufacturer (12 Aug.
& 17-22 Aug. 1812)
White, Andrew, age 23, 11 years in U.S., wife, Schenectady,
cooper (17-22 Aug. 1812)

White, Charles B., age 34, 11 years in U.S., wife & child, 35
  Catherine St., NYC, pocketbook maker (20-25 July 1812); 5ft.
  5½in., age 35, fair complex., dark hair, dark eyes, James St.,
  pocketbook (Navy)
White, Edward, 5ft. 7in., age 19, fair complex., dark hair, blue
  eyes, servant (Navy)
White, James, Jr., 5ft. 8½in., age 19, fair complex., brown hair,
  brown eyes, clerk (Navy)
White, John, age 32, 15 years in U.S., wife & 5 children, Front
  St., NYC, grocer (20-25 July 1812)
White, John, 6ft., age 30, light complex., brown hair, blue eyes,
  Manhattan, sawyer (Navy)
White, John, age 30, 8 years in U.S., wife & son, NYC, shoemaker
  (20-25 July 1812); 5ft. 7in., age 30, pale complex., brown
  hair, brown eyes, Middle Road, cordwainer (Navy)
White, John, 5ft. 8 3/4in., age 26, dark complex., brown hair,
  light eyes, Front St., rigger (Navy)
White, John, 5ft. 5in., age 23, fair complex., brown hair, brown
  eyes, Elm St., labourer (Navy)
White, Joseph, age 74, 11 years in U.S., wife & child, Duanesburgh, Schenectady Co., weaver (24-28 Aug. 1812)
White, Joseph, Jr., age 17, 11 years in U.S., Duanesburgh, Schenectady Co., apprentice (24-29 Aug. 1812)
White, Michael, 5ft. 3in., age 27, fair complex., brown hair,
  blue eyes, Broadway, drayman (Navy)
White, Philip, 5ft. 6in., age 22, ruddy complex., dark hair, blue
  eyes, weaver (Navy)
White, Richard, age 30, 7 mos. in U.S., 33 Lombardy St., NYC
  (20-25 July 1812)
White, Rowlin, 5ft. 7in., age 24, light complex., brown hair,
  blue eyes, Pachogue, Long Island, farmer (Navy)
White, Thomas, age 19, 11 years in U.S., Duanesburgh, Schenectady
  Co., cooper (24-29 Aug. 1812)
White, William, age 46, 3 years in U.S., 52 Pearl St., NYC, shoemaker (28 July - 2 Aug. 1812); 5ft. 6in., age 47, fair complex.,
  fair hair, grey eyes, Pearl St., cordwainer (Navy)
White, William, 5ft., age 26, light complex., light hair, light
  eyes, Charlotte St., shipwright (Navy)
Whitehead, John, age 40, 17 years in U.S., wife & child, 11 Jef-
  ferson St., NYC, shoemaker (3-8 Aug. 1812); 5ft. 8in., age 40,
  light complex., dark hair, Harman St., shoemaker (Navy)
Whitehead, John, 5ft. 9in., age 29, fair complex., sandy hair,
  black eyes, Mott St., brewer (Navy); age 30, 3 years in U.S.,
  Mott St., brewer (20-25 July 1812)
Whitehead, Sol, 5ft. 6in., age 27, dark complex., brown hair,
  black eyes, apprentice pilot (Navy)
Whitehouse, James, age 40, 10 years in U.S., wife & 5 children,
  Robinson St., NYC, merchant (13-18 July 1812); 5ft. 7in., age
  40, light complex., dark hair, blue eyes, removed from NYC to
  Columbia (Navy)
Whitesides, John, age 48, 10 years in U.S., wife & 5 children,
  Montgomery, Orange Co., farmer (19-24 Oct. 1812)
Whiticker, John, 5ft. 6in., age 51, dark complex., dark hair,
  grey eyes, skinner (Navy)
Whitley, Thomas, age 46, 8 years in U.S., wife & 2 children,
  City of Albany, shoemaker (17-22 Aug. 1812)
Whitnell, Isaac, age 27, 2 years in U.S., Waterford, Saratoga
  Co., teacher (31 Aug. - 5 Sept. 1812)
Whitnell, William, 5ft. 7in., age 30, light complex., brown hair,
  brown eyes, New Rochelle, Westchester Co., machine (Navy)
Whitson, Ephraim, 5ft. 2½in., age 26, fair complex., black hair,
  dark eyes, Maiden Lane, gunsmith (Navy)
Whittel, James, 5ft. 4 3/4in., age 27, fair complex., brown
  hair, blue eyes, shoemaker (Navy)

Whittingham, Charles, age 28, 21 years in U.S., 82 Harman St.,
  NYC, brass founder (13-18 July 1812); 5ft. 6½in., age 30, fair
  complex., dark hair, dark eyes, Harman St., brass founder (Navy)
Whittingham, Joseph, age 21, 21 years in U.S., 82 Harman St.,
  NYC, brass founder (20-25 July 1812); 5ft. 5½in., age 22, fair
  complex., dark hair, dark eyes, brass founder (Navy)
Whittingham, Richard, age 36, 21 years in U.S., wife & 3 child-
  ren, 124 Harman St., NYC, brass founder (13-18 July 1812);
  5ft. 6½in., age 36, fair complex., dark hair, dark eyes, Har-
  man St., brass founder (Navy)
Whylie, James, Jr., age 19, 2 years in U.S., 84 Pearl St., NYC,
  clerk (20-25 July 1812)
Wier, Archibald, age 35 on 1 Nov. next, 5 years in U.S. on 13
  Sept. next, wife, Russia, Herkimer Co., farmer, from Argyle,
  Scotland (29 Sept. & 28 Sept. - 3 Oct. 1812)
Wiggins, Thomas, age 46, 21 years in U.S., wife & 3 children,
  NYC, coachman (14-19 Sept. 1812)
Wigham, Isaac, age 34, 6 years in U.S., 38 Beekman St., NYC,
  merchant (20-25 July 1812); 5ft. 7in., age 34, dark complex.,
  dark hair, blue eyes, manufacturer (Navy); removed from NYC
  to Dutchess Co. (Navy)
Wight, Walter, 5ft. 6in., age 49, dark complex., sandy hair,
  blue eyes, Greenwich St., mason (Navy)
Wilcox, John, age 44, 7 years in U.S., wife & child, 6 Rynder
  St., NYC, comb maker (13-18 July 1812)
Wild, James, age 26 years & 5 mos., 6 years & 15 days in U.S.,
  wife & 2 children, Columbiaville, Columbia Co., cotton machine
  maker, applied at Mayor's Court in Hudson on 2 Jan. 1810 (12
  Aug. & 17-22 Aug. 1812)
Wild, John, age 14, 9 years in U.S., Boyle, Ontario Co., farmer
  (23-30 Aug. & 7-12 Sept. 1812)
Wild, Nathan, age 21 years & 9 mos., 1 year & 10 mos. in U.S.,
  Columbiaville, Columbia Co., fustian cutter (12 Aug. & 17-22
  Aug. 1812)
Wild, Thomas, Jr., age 17, 9 years in U.S., Boyle, Ontario Co.,
  joiner (23-30 Aug. & 7-12 Sept. 1812)
Wild, Thomas, Sr., age 41, 9 years in U.S., 7 in family, Seneca,
  Ontario Co., joiner, applied Feb. 1810 (23-30 Aug. & 7-12 Sept.
  1812)
Wildman, Richard, 5ft. 4in., age 27, brown complex., brown hair,
  blue eyes, Vandewater St., tailor (Navy)
Wilds, Storey, age 27, 8 years in U.S., Seneca, Ontario Co.,
  farmer (5-15 & 24-29 Aug. 1812)
Wilham, Joseph, 5ft. 4½in., age 19, light complex., light hair,
  hazel eyes, hatter (Navy)
Wilkins, David, age 31, 11 years in U.S., wife & 2 children, 64
  Warren St., NYC, grocer (20-25 July 1812); 5ft. 7in., age 32,
  dark complex., black hair, black eyes, Warren St., grocer (Navy)
Wilkin (or Wilkins), George, 5ft. 6in., age 27, fair complex.,
  fair hair, grey eyes, gun (Navy)
Wilkinson, John, 5ft. 11in., age 24, black complex., dark hair,
  dark eyes, Stagg Town, labourer (Navy)
Wilkinson, Samuel, 5ft. 8in., age 33, brown complex., light hair,
  blue eyes, Water St., clerk (Navy)
Wilkinson, Samuel, age 29, 1½ years in U.S., 30 Gold St., NYC,
  merchant (20-25 July 1812)
Wilks, George, age 27, 6 years in U.S., Jefferson Co., laborer
  (24-29 Aug. 1812)
Willen, John, age 28, 14 days in U.S., Grand St., NYC, whitesmith (21-26 Sept. 1812)
Willet, Gilbert C., said to be an officer under British pay,
  Montgomery, has not reported (2 Jan. 1813)
Willetts, Thomas, Jr., age 25, 9 years in U.S., brother aged 15,
  36 Dey St., merchant (20-25 July 1812); 5ft. 7in., light com-
  plex., black hair, hazel eyes, removed to Goshen (Navy)

William, James, 5ft. 7in., age 22, fair complex., light hair,
brown eyes, mariner (Navy)
Williams, Charles, 5ft. 10in., age 30, ruddy complex., brown
hair, brown eyes, printer (Navy)
Williams, David, age 17, 15 years in U.S., 62 N. Moore St., NYC,
stone cutter (26-31 Oct. 1812)
Williams, Evan, age 31, 12 years in U.S., wife & 5 children,
Clinton, Dutchess Co., laborer (12-17 Oct. 1812)
Williams, Evan, 5ft. 7½in., age 23, fair complex., dark hair,
blue eyes, Division St., carpenter (Navy)
Williams, George, 5ft. 10in., age 46, dark complex., black hair,
brown eyes, Harlaem, farmer (Navy)
Williams, George, age 25, 11 mos. in U.S., Bath, Steuben Co.,
laborer (25-31 Aug. & 7-12 Sept. 1812)
Williams, Henry, age 30 on 6 Dec. last, 11 years in U.S. on 1
July 1812, wife & 4 children, Steuben, Oneida Co., farmer,
from North Wales (26 Aug. & 28 Sept. - 3 Oct. 1812)
Williams, Henry, 5ft. 9in, age 32, fair complex., brown hair,
brown eyes, jeweler (Navy)
Williams, Isaac, 5ft. 11in., age 23, fair complex., brown hair,
blue eyes, Bancker St., baker (Navy)
Williams, James, age 44 on 14 Mar. next, 2 years in U.S. on 11
Sept. last, wife & 9 children, Madison, Madison Co., blacksmith (31 Oct. 1812); status given as farmer (30 Nov. - 5 Dec.
1812)
Williams, John, age 31, 9 mos. in U.S., 2 in family, 202 Broadway, NYC, tailor (20-25 July 1812)
Williams, John, 5ft. 7in., age 26, light complex., light hair,
grey eyes, Charlotte St., grocer (Navy)
Williams, John, 5ft. 7½in., age 23, dark complex., dark hair,
grey eyes, Broadway, tailor (Navy)
Williams, John, age 22 last June, 13 years in U.S., Utica, Onei-
da Co., clerk in a store, from South Wales (26 Aug. & 28 Sept. -
3 Oct. 1812)
Williams, John, 2d., age 32 on 2 Oct. next, 12 years in U.S. on
20 July last, wife & 2 children, Steuben, Oneida Co., farmer
(29 Sept. & 28 Sept. - 3 Oct. 1812)
Williams, Oulton, age 29, 5 years & 8 mos. in U.S., 34 Liberty
St., NYC, printer (20-25 July 1812)
Williams, Perry, age 31, 3 days in U.S., State St., NYC, merchant
(5-10 Oct. 1812)
Williams, Robert, age 54, 2 years in U.S., wife, 64 John St.,
NYC, shoemaker (20-25 July 1812); 5ft. 2in., age 54, dark com-
plex., dark hair, brown eyes, John St., shoemaker (Navy)
Williams, Robert, Jr., age 31, 2 years in U.S., wife & 2 child-
ren, 58 William St., NYC, shoemaker (20-25 July 1812); 5ft.
--in., age 32, dark complex., dark hair, dark eyes, William
St., shoemaker (Navy)
Williams, Thomas, 6ft., age 23, light complex., brown hair, blue
eyes, iron (Navy)
Williams, Thomas, age 21, 11 years in U.S., 12 Spring St., NYC,
laborer (28 July - 2 Aug. 1812)
Williams, William, 5ft. 8in., age 68, ruddy complex., grey hair,
dark eyes, boarding house (Navy)
Williams, William, age 33, 11 years in U.S., wife & 3 children,
Clinton, Dutchess Co., laborer (12-17 Oct. 1812)
Williams, William, age 29, 5 years in U.S. wife & child, Laight
St., NYC, servant (20-25 July 1812)
Williams, William, age 23, 16 years in U.S., wife, 62 N. Moore
St., NYC, stone cutter (26-31 Oct. 1812)
Williamson, Adam, 5ft. 5in., age 22, fair complex., brown hair,
blue eyes, Maiden Lane, suspenders (Navy)
Williamson, Peter, age 63, 5 weeks in U.S., Bushwick, L.I., mer-
chant (20-25 July 1812); 5ft. 5in., age 64, dark complex., dark
hair, grey eyes, gentleman, removed to Goshen (Navy)

Williamson, Stephen, age 21, 3 years in U.S., Liberty St., NYC,
dyer (20-25 July 1812)
Williamson, Thomas, age 26, 2 mos. in U.S., wife, 173 Bowery
Lane, NYC, weaver (20-25 July 1812)
Willis, Richard, 5ft. 7in., age 45, fair complex., fair hair,
brown eyes, labourer (Navy)
Williss, Robert, age 21, 8 years in U.S., Seneca, Ontario Co.,
farmer (5-15 Aug. 1812)
Williss, William, age 49, 8 years in U.S., 6 in family, Seneca,
Ontario Co., farmer (24-29 Aug. 1812)
Willis, William, 5ft. 7in., age 30, fair complex., brown hair,
blue eyes, Hammond St., weaver (Navy)
Willson, Abraham R., age 29, 16 years in U.S., 7 in family, 113
Hester St., NYC, btter (sic!) (20-25 July 1812)
Willson, Alexander, of Junius in Seneca Co., has refused to re-
port; his residence is "not admissable" (2-7 Oct. 1812)
Willson, Edward, age 19, 9 years in U.S., Boyle, Ontario Co.,
weaver (5-15 & 24-29 Aug. 1812)
Willson, George, age 21, 9 years in U.S., Boyle, Ontario Co.,
weaver (5-15 & 24-29 Aug. 1812)
Willson, James, age 32, 6 years in U.S., wife & 9 children, Au-
relius, Cayuga Co., distiller (5-10 Oct. 1812)
Willson, Thomas, age 21, 7 years in U.S., Seneca, Ontario Co.,
carpenter (5-15 Aug. 1812)
Willson, Zachariah, age 64, 9 years in U.S., 3 in family, Boyle,
Ontario Co., weaver (5-15 & 24-29 Aug. 1812)
Wilmot, James, 5ft. 9in., age 24, light complex., light hair,
grey eyes, shoemaker (Navy)
Wilson, Adam, age 35, 10 years in U.S., wife & 3 children, Green-
wich St., NYC, blacksmith, applied 17 Nov. 1809 (13-18 July
1812)
Wilson, Alexander, 5ft. 7in., age 39, ruddy complex., brown hair,
blue eyes, John St., baker (Navy)
Wilson, Alexander, age 28, 12 years in U.S., Wallkill, Orange Co.,
laborer (19-24 Oct. 1812)
Wilson, Charles, 5ft. 8½in., age 34, dark complex., brown hair,
blue eyes, Westchester, farmer (Navy)
Wilson, David, age 32, 10 years in U.S., wife & 3 children,
corner Crosby & Grand Sts., NYC, carpenter (20-25 July 1812)
Wilson, David, age 30, 1 year & 7 mos. in U.S., wife & 3 child-
ren, Montgomery, Orange Co., weaver (19-24 Oct. 1812)
Wilson, Edward, 5ft. 8in., age 24, light complex., brown hair,
blue eyes, morocco (Navy)
Wilson, James, 5ft. 8in., age 48, fair complex., brown hair,
dark eyes, Greenwich St., stone cutter (Navy)
Wilson, James, age 35, 11 years in U.S., wife & 4 children, Rome,
Oneida Co., weaver, naturalized 5 years ago, employed by James
Lynch (29 July & 3-8 Aug. 1812)
Wilson, James, 5ft. 7in., age 31, dark complex., dark hair, dark
eyes, labourer (Navy)
Wilson, James, age 21, 11 years in U.S., City of Albany, stone
cutter (17-22 Aug. 1812)
Wilson, James G., age 30, 29 years in U.S., Harlaem, shoemaker &
farmer (10-15 Aug. 1812)
Wilson, John, age 47, 14 years in U.S., wife & children, Sullivan
St., NYC, cartman, applied 1804 (20-25 July 1812)
Wilson, John, age 46, 11 years & 1 mo. in U.S., wife & 2 child-
ren, Montgomery, Orange Co., shoemaker (19-24 Oct. 1812)
Wilson, John, 5ft. 8in., age 45, fair complex., grey hair, grey
eyes, Rynder St., corset maker (Navy)
Wilson, John, age 40, 18 years in U.S., wife & 6 children, 98
Greenwich St., NYC, grocer (20-25 July 1812)
Wilson, John, age 31, 7 years in U.S., 3 in family, Geneva, On-
tario Co., farmer (11-25 & 26-31 Oct. 1812)

Wilson, John, 5ft. 5in., age 30, fair complex., fair hair, grey
    eyes, Bowery Lane, weaver (Navy)
Wilson, John, 5ft. 5in., age 29, dark complex., dark hair, dark
    eyes, Hester St., tailor (Navy)
Wilson, John, age 28, 7 years in U.S., Hamilton Square, NYC,
    gardener (20-25 July 1812)
Wilson, John, age 20, 5 years in U.S., City of Albany, laborer
    (5-10 Oct. 1812)
Wilson, John, age 19, 7 years in U.S., NYC, shoemaker (2-7 Nov.
    1812); 5ft. 7in., age 20, fair complex., light hair, blue
    eyes, shoe (Navy)
Wilson, John M., age 36, 9 years in U.S., wife & 5 children, 16
    Front St., NYC, physician (10-15 Aug. 1812)
Wilson, Joseph, 5ft. 3in., age 53, fair complex., brown hair,
    grey eyes, removed from NYC to Amenia, Dutchess Co. (Navy)
Wilson, Joseph, age 41, 12 years in U.S., wife & 4 children, 62
    Broadway, NYC, teacher of music (28 July - 2 Aug. 1812); 5ft.
    8in., age 42, dark complex., dark hair, blue eyes, teacher
    (Navy)
Wilson, Joseph, 5ft. 3in., age 23, fair complex., brown hair,
    grey eyes, Pearl St., accountant (Navy)
Wilson, Robert, 5ft. 9in., age 36, dark complex., brown hair,
    brown eyes, labourer (Navy)
Wilson, Robert, 5ft. 8in., age 22, light complex., brown hair,
    grey eyes, Hague St., morocco fin. (Navy)
Wilson, Robert A., 5ft. 6½in., age 30, ruddy complex., brown
    hair, dark eyes, Hester St., potter (Navy)
Wilson, Samuel, age 26, 8 years in U.S., Bath, Steuben Co., joi-
    ner (24 Aug. & 31 Aug. - 5 Sept. 1812)
Wilson, Stephen, 5ft. 7in., age 45, light complex., dark hair,
    brown eyes, Vesey St., carpenter (Navy)
Wilson, Thomas, age 50, 8 mos. in U.S., wife & 4 children, far-
    mer (10-15 Aug. 1812)
Wilson, Thomas, 5ft. 9in., age 40, dark complex., light hair,
    blue eyes, Cherry St., sawyer (Navy)
Wilson, Thomas, age 32, 6 years in U.S., wife & 3 children, Au-
    relius, Cayuga Co., distiller (19-24 Oct. 1812)
Wilson, Thomas, Jr., 5ft. 8in., age 31, red complex., red hair,
    brown eyes, Orange St. weaver (Navy)
Wilson, Thomas, age 28, 2 years in U.S., wife & 2 children, Mama-
    kating, Sullivan Co., shoemaker (19-24 Oct. 1812)
Wilson, Thomas, age 26, 1 year & 6 mos. in U.S., wife & child,
    Colonie, Albany Co., tobacconist (17-22 Aug. 1812)
Wilson, Thomas, age 21, 7 years in U.S., Seneca, Ontario Co.,
    carpenter (24-29 Aug. 1812)
Wilson, William, age 52, 6 years in U.S., wife & 4 children,
    Onondaga Co., farmer (3-8 Aug. 1812)
Wilson, William, 5ft. 5in., age 47, dark complex., dark hair,
    hazel eyes, Thompson St., stone cutter (Navy)
Wilson, William, age 46, 9 years in U.S., wife & 7 children,
    Thompson St., NYC, feed merchant (20-25 July 1812)
Wilson, William, age 44, 24 years in U.S., wife & 4 children,
    Johnstown, Montgomery Co., farmer (11-17 & 17-22 Aug. 1812)
Wilson, William, age 31, 11 years in U.S., wife & child, Kips
    Bay, NYC, gardener (20-25 July 1812); 5ft. 10in., age 32, fair
    complex., dark hair, brown eyes, Kips Bay, gardener (Navy)
Wilson, William, age 30, 1 year & 4 mos. in U.S., wife, Clinton,
    Dutchess Co., weaver (12-17 Oct. 1812)
Wilson, William, 5ft. 10in., age 29, brown complex., dark hair,
    blue eyes, ship (carpenter) (Navy)
Wilson, William, age 27, 10 years & 9 mos. in U.S., wife & child,
    20 Orange St., NYC, morocco dresser (20-25 July 1812); 5ft.
    9½in., age 27, fair complex., brown hair, brown eyes, Division
    St., morocco (Navy)

Wilson, William, age 23, 1 year & 2 mos. in U.S., wife & 2
children, Newburgh, Orange Co., mason (19-24 Oct. 1812)
Wilson, William, 5ft. 9in., age 22, light complex., brown hair,
blue eyes, Hudson St., stone (Navy)
Wilson, William, age 22, 11 years & 9 mos. in U.S., wife & 3
children, Newburgh, Orange Co., farmer (19-24 Oct. 1812)
Wilson, William D., age 26, 6 years in U.S., 13 Dey St., merchant
(20-25 July 1812); 5ft. 9in., age 26, light complex., light
hair, grey eyes, grocer (Navy)
Winde, William, age 23, 9 years in U.S., wife, 105 Mott St.,
NYC, shipwright (20-25 July 1812)
Winder, William, 5ft. 6in., age 30, dark complex., brown hair,
black eyes, Pump St., shipwright (Navy)
Windsor, Lloyd D., age 41, 12 years in U.S., wife & 2 children,
Broadway, NYC, teacher (20-25 July 1812); 5ft. 5½in., age 40,
fair complex., dark hair, blue eyes, Broadway, teacher (Navy)
Windsor, Solomon, age 56, 10 years in U.S., 2 in family, 76 Bar-
clay St., NYC, jeweler (20-25 July 1812); 5ft. 7in., age 58,
light complex., brown hair, grey eyes, Barclay St., jeweler
(Navy)
Winn, Mathew, 5ft. 4in., age 32, dark complex., black hair,
hazel eyes, apothecary (Navy)
Winterkaln, Thomas, age 49, 12 years in U.S., wife & 2 children,
116 Anthony St., NYC, pedlar (10-15 Aug. 1812)
Winterscale, Thomas, 5ft. 8in., age 50, fair complex., dark
hair, grey eyes, pedler (Navy)
Wintringham, Thomas, 5ft. 4in., age 38, light complex., dark
hair, light eyes, William St., mechanic (Navy)
Wishart, James, age 31, 5 years in U.S., wife & child, City of
Albany, laborer (17-22 Aug. 1812)
Witherspoon, John, 5ft. 11in., age 28, dark complex., brown hair,
dark eyes, Bowery Lane, weaver (Navy)
Witham, Joseph, age 23, 11 years in U.S., Maiden Lane, accoun-
tant (20-25 July 1812); 5ft. 9½in., age 35, dark complex.,
dark hair, brown eyes, Maiden Lane, accountant (Navy)
Witham, Joseph, Jr., age 19, 11 years in U.S., Ann St., NYC,
hatter (20-25 July 1812)
Witherly, John, 5ft. 4½in., age 57, fair complex., light hair,
light eyes, shoemaker (Navy)
Withnall, William, age 29, 11 mos. in U.S., Mamaroneck, Westchester Co., cotton machine maker (21-26 Sept. 1812); same as
William Witnell, above.
Womersley, Joshua, age 29, 2 years in U.S., Westchester Co.,
woolen manufacturer (17-22 Aug. 1812)
Wood, Anthony, 5ft. 7in., age 21, fair complex., brown hair,
grey eyes, Catherine St., tailor (Navy)
Wood, Charles, a tailor residing in New Windsor, Orange Co., has
not reported (2 Jan. 1813)
Wood, David, age 38, 11 years in U.S., 3 in family, Harlaem, yeo-
man (10-15 Aug. 1812); 5ft. 7in., age 37, fair complex., dark
hair, grey eyes, farmer (Navy)
Wood, Francis, 5ft. 9in.,age 39, fair complex., brown hair, grey
eyes, 173 Hester St., cartman (Navy)
Wood, George, 5ft. 9in., age 29, fair complex., dark hair, grey
eyes, servant (Navy)
Wood, James, age 33, 4 years in U.S., NYC, weaver (30 Nov. - 5
Dec. 1812); 5ft. 7in., age 33, dark complex., dark hair, blue
eyes, Chatham St., weaver (Navy)
Wood, John, 5ft. 6in., age 28, fair complex., fair hair, blue
eyes, Anthony St., labourer (Navy)
Wood, John West, age 44, 7 years in U.S., wife & child, Wawarsing,
Ulster Co., farmer (19-24 Oct. 1812)
Wood, Thomas, age 30, 6 years in U.S., 3 in family, Geneva, On-
tario Co., blacksmith (13-17 Sept. & 28 Sept. - 3 Oct. 1812)

Wood, William, age 45, 4½ years in U.S., wife, corner Oliver &
Water Sts., blockmaker (13-18 July 1812); 5ft. 6in., age 45,
light complex., dark hair, brown eyes, Oliver St., blockmaker
(Navy)

Wood, William, 5ft. 9in., age 35, fair complex., brown hair,
blue eyes, Wall St., coachman (Navy)

Wood, William, 5ft. 6½in., age 30, brown complex., brown hair,
blue eyes, Hudson St., weaver (Navy)

Woodbyene, Thomas, age 41, 5 years in U.S., wife, 63 East George
St., NYC, sawyer (28 July - 2 Aug. 1812)

Woodhead, John, age 20, 5 years in U.S., 39 Maiden Lane, NYC,
accountant (20-25 July 1812)

Woodhouse, John, age 32, 11 years in U.S., wife & 3 children,
Hudson, Columbia Co., currier (10-15 Aug. 1812)

Woods, Francis, age 41, 9 years in U.S., wife & 4 children, Hester St., NYC, cartman (20-25 July 1812)

Woods, George, age 28, 1 year & 4 mos. in U.S., Claremont, Westchester Co., servant (20-25 July 1812)

Woods, William, 5ft. 8in., age 39, dark complex., black hair,
dark eyes, manufacturer (Navy)

Woodward, John, 5ft. 7in., age 21, light complex., brown hair,
blue eyes, Maiden Lane, accountant (Navy)

Woofendale, Robert, age 68, 18 years in U.S., 7 children, 35
Little George St., NYC (20-25 July 1812)

Woolcock, Samuel T., age 21, 9 years in U.S., 175 William St.,
NYC, engraver (13-18 July 1812); 5ft. 5in., age 22, fair complex., light hair, blue eyes, William St., engraver (Navy)

Woolcock, Thomas, 5ft. 2in., age 24, brown complex., sandy hair,
light eyes, Gold St., coach lamp (Navy)

Wooldridge, John, 5ft. 5½in., age 56, fair complex., brown hair,
blue eyes, removed from NYC to Goshen (Navy)

Wooton, E., age 56, 1 year in U.S., wife, 303 Greenwich St.,
NYC, mechanic (20-25 July 1812)

Wormley, Joshua, 5ft. 9in., age 29, dark complex., black hair,
hazel eyes, woolen manufacturer (Navy)

Wright, Edmund, age 52, 23 years in U.S., wife & 5 children,
Scipio, Cayuga Co., distiller (21-26 Sept. 1812)

Wotherspoon, M., age 29, 4 years in U.S., 40 Broadway, NYC,
merchant (20-25 July 1812)

Wren, Isaac, 5ft. 10in., age 54, light complex., brown hair,
grey eyes, Division St., drayman (Navy)

Wright, Edmond, age 52, 23 years in U.S., wife & 5 children,
Scipio, Cayuga Co., distiller of whiskey (7-12 Sept. 1812)

Wright, John, age 43, 7 years & 10 mos. in U.S., 6 in family,
Troy, Rensselaer Co., cooper (28 July - 2 Aug. 1812)

Wright, John, age 25, 1 year in U.S., wife & child, Brooklyn,
Long Island, teacher (13-18 July 1812); 5ft. 9in., age 25,
fair complex., dark hair, blue eyes, teacher (Navy)

Wright, Thomas, age 37, 9 years in U.S., wife & 4 children, 111
Lombardy St., painter (28 July - 2 Aug. 1812)

Wybrants/Wybrand, Patrick, age 21, 9 mos. in U.S., 49 Pearl St.,
NYC, tailor (20-25 July 1812); 5ft. 6½in., age 22, dark complex., black hair, blue eyes (Navy)

Wylde, Nathaniel, age 24, 1 year & 3 mos. in U.S., has an apprentice, Cross St., NYC, machine maker (28 July - 2 Aug. 1812)

Wylder, Nathaniel, 5ft. 10in., age 25, light complex., brown
hair, grey eyes, collar (Navy)

Wylie, David, age 27, 8 years in U.S., wife, 95 Pump St., NYC,
grocer (20-25 July 1812)

Wylie, John, age 31, 7 years in U.S., 16 Broadway, NYC, merchant,
applied 23 May 1810 (13-18 July 1812)

Wymbs, John, 5ft. 10in., age 35, fair complex., fair hair, blue
eyes, pedler (Navy)

Yarwood, Henry, age 26 on 4 May last, 16 years in U.S. last July
nearly, Lee, Oneida Co., farmer, from Cheshire, England (29
Sept. & 28 Sept. - 3 Oct. 1812)

Yarwood, James, age 73, 15 years in U.S., wife, son, grandson
and daughter, Lee, Oneida Co., farmer (28 Sept. - 3 Oct. 1812)

Yarwood, Samuel, age 43 on 21 last May, 18 years in U.S. on 16
Jan. last, wife & 5 children, Lee, Oneida Co., farmer, from
Cheshire, England (29 Sept. & 28 Sept. - 3 Oct. 1812)

Yarwood, Samuel, age 20 on 11 of this Sept., 16 years in U.S. on
25 July last, Lee, Oneida Co., farmer (29 Sept. & 28 Sept. -
3 Oct. 1812)

Yates, Edward, age 35, 15 years in U.S., wife & 5 children,
Clinton, Dutchess Co., shoemaker (12-17 Oct. 1812)

Yates, Richard, age 48, 10 mos. in U.S., Hudson, Columbia Co.,
dyer (12 Aug. & 17-22 Aug. 1812)

Yeates, William, age 20, 8 years in U.S., 76 John St., NYC, cordwainer (20-25 July 1812)

Yeo, Richard, age 34, 1 year & 7 mos. in U.S., wife, 157 Water
St., NYC, glover & leather dresser (20-25 July 1812); 5ft.
7in., age 35, dark complex., dark hair, hazel eyes, Water St.,
glove (Navy)

Yeule, George, 5ft. 7in., age 30, fair complex., fair hair, blue
eyes, James St., suspended (Navy)

Young, Alexander, age 26, 8 years & 6 mos. in U.S., wife & child,
corner Grand & Orchard Sts., NYC, grocer (28 July - 2 Aug.
1812); 5ft. 10in., age 25, fair complex., dark hair, brown
eyes, Grand St., cartman - are they the same or two different
persons?

Young, David, age 38, Wallkill, Orange Co., weaver (19-24 Oct.
1812)

Young, George, age 30, 3 mos. in U.S., Cornwall, Orange Co.,
weaver (19-24 Oct. 1812)

Young, George, 5ft. 6½in., age 30, brown complex., brown hair,
grey eyes, Clinton Town, Dutchess Co., weaver (Navy) - perhaps
the same as the George Young above?

Young, Isaac, age 34, 7 years in U.S., wife & child, Montgomery,
Orange Co., cooper (19-24 Oct. 1812)

Young, James, age 20, 3 mos. in U.S., Cornwall, Orange Co., weaver (19-24 Oct. 1812)

Young, Johnson, age 20, 1 year & 1 mo. in U.S., Montgomery, Orange
Co., farmer (19-24 Oct. 1812)

Young, Joseph, age 22, 11 years & 3 mos. in U.S., Newburgh, Orange
Co., cabinetmaker (19-24 Oct. 1812)

Young, Moses, age 35, 11 years in U.S., mother, New Windsor,
Orange Co., weaver (19-24 Oct. 1812)

Young, Philip, age 25, 4 years & 9 mos. in U.S., corner Front &
Depeyster Sts., NYC, tobacconist (28 July - 2 Aug. 1812); 5ft.
7in., age 26, light complex., light hair, blue eyes, tobacco
(Navy)

Young, Thomas, age 45, 8 years in U.S., 6 in family, Seneca, Ontario Co., farmer (5-15 & 24-29 Aug. 1812)

Young, William, 5ft. 7in., age 37, light complex., light hair,
grey eyes, Pine St., baker (Navy)

Young, William, 5ft. 7in., age 34, fair complex., brown hair,
grey eyes, West Farms, Westchester Co., potter (Navy)

NEW JERSEY

Adams, George, age 30, in U.S. since 15 Sept. 1804, Newark, la-
bourer; family is in Europe (10 Oct.-26 Dec. 1812)
Adams, Robert, age 22, in U.S. since Dec. 1811, Paterson, turner
(5-12 Sept. 1812)
Adams, Samuel, age 34, in U.S. since 1803, wife & 3 children,
Trenton, shoemaker (1 Dec. 1812-1 May 1813)
Adock, Isaac, age 44, 18 years in U.S., wife & 2 children, Cum-
berland, miller (10 Oct.-26 Dec. 1812)
Ammerson, Daniel, age 15, in U.S. since 4 May 1800, Bloomfield,
cotton spinner (15-29 Aug. 1812)
Ammerson, Robert, age 48, in U.S. since 4 May 1800, wife & 5
children, Bloomfield, labourer (15-29 Aug. 1812)
Ammerson, Thomas, age 17, in U.S. since 4 May 1800, Springfield,
cotton spinner (15-29 Aug. 1812)
Anderson, James W,, age 26, in U.S. since 19 Jan. 1810, Newark,
merchant (1 Dec. 1812-1 May 1813)
Angus, William, age 32, in U.S. since 27 Apr. 1806, wife & 2
children, Bellville, carpenter (12-26 Sept. 1812)
Archibald, Robert, age 26, in U.S. since 20 May 1812, Paterson,
weaver (5-12 Sept. 1812)
Armitage, James, age 44, in U.S. since 25 June 1804, Newark, tai-
lor (26 Sept.-10 Oct. 1812)
Bantam, John, age 45, in U.S. since 2 July 1802, wife & 8 children,
Newark, blacksmith (15-29 Aug. 1812)
Barrows, James, age 39, in U.S. since 25 Aug. 1808, wife & 2
children, Paterson, weaver (5-12 Sept. 1812)
Baxter, George, age 36, in U.S. since 24 Dec. 1811, wife & 3
children, Bloomfield, cotton spinner (5-12 Sept. 1812)
Beachimp, Thomas, age 22, in U.S. since 25 May 1812, Paterson,
labourer (5-12 Sept. 1812)
Beatty, William, age 17, in U.S. since Feb. 1810, Newark, tanner
& currier (15-29 Aug. 1812)
Bell, James, age 24, in U.S. since 2 Sept. 1811, wife & 1 child,
Paterson, weaver (5-12 Sept. 1812)
Bigg, Archibald, age 34, in U.S. since 3 Sept. 1806, Elizabeth
Town, weaver (12-26 Sept. 1812)
Birney, William, age 24, in U.S. since 3 May 1812, wife, Bell-
ville, powder maker (12-26 Sept. 1812)
Bishop, Henry, age 21, in U.S. since Apr. 1811, Newark, shoe-
maker (8-15 Aug. 1812)
Black, John, age 22, in U,S. since 10 Mar. 1813, Newark (1 Dec.
1812-1 May 1813)
Blarnay, James, age 23, in U.S. since 2 Mar. 1812, Newark, potter
(26 Sept.-10 Oct. 1812)
Blaything, Joseph, age 27, in U.S. since 22 June 1807, wife & 3
children, Acquacknonk, paper maker (10 Oct.-26 Dec. 1812)
Bradford, Joseph, age 40, in U.S. since July 1804, wife, Essex
Co., agriculturist (15-29 Aug. 1812)
Bradley, John, age 27, in U.S. since 19 Dec. 1811, Newark, lock-
smith (26 Sept.-10 Oct. 1812)
Brady, Owen, age 26, in U.S. since 3 July 1812, Paterson, weaver
(12-26 Sept. 1812)
Bridge, Samuel, age 30, in U.S. since 25 July 1809, wife & child,
Bergen Co., cotton manufacturer; applied 21 Apr. 1810 in Essex
Pleas (26 Sept.-10 Oct. 1812)
Brooks, James, age 40, in U.S. since 12 July 1806, wife, Pater-
son, merchant (5-12 Sept. 1812)
Brown, Alexander, age 20, in U.S. since 16 May 1812, Paterson,
weaver (5-12 Sept. 1812)
Brown, John, age 24, 18 mos. in U.S., Dover, nailor (10 Oct.-26
Dec. 1812)
Buckley, John, age 35, in U.S. since 4 May 1810, wife & 5 child-
ren, Paterson, cotton carder (5-12 Sept. 1812)

Bury, John, age 29, in U.S since 7 Jan. 1811, wife & 2 children, Bloomfield, weaver (26 Sept.-10 Oct. 1812)

Bury, William, age 52, in U.S. since Aug. 1806, wife, Paterson, weaver (5-12 Sept. 1812)

Butterworth, Henry, age 49, in U.S. since June 1795, wife, Springfield, agriculturist (1 Dec. 1812-1 May 1813)

Byerley, John, age 25, in U.S. since May 1812, Byram, Sussex Co., agriculturist (1 Dec. 1812-1 May 1813)

Cai(e?)n, Menassa, in U.S. since 18 July 1806, wife & child, Flemington (10 Oct.-26 Dec. 1812)

Cairns, Hugh, age 24, in U.S. since 23 May 1812, Paterson, labourer (5-12 Sept. 1812)

Caldwell, John, age 27, in U.S. since 15 July 1806, wife, Newark, joiner (15-29 Aug. 1812)

Cammack, Hugh, age 22, in ¯.S. since 3 Sept. 1810, Newark, currier (1 Dec. 1812-1 May 1813)

Canavan, Michael, age 40, in U.S. since 10 Aug. 1800, Newark, painter (12-26 Sept. 1812)

Carmichael, Alexander, age 24, in U.S. since 7 Oct. 1805, Paterson, turner (5-12 Sept. 1812)

Carmichael, Owen, age 26, in U.S. since 18 June 1812, wife & 3 children, Paterson, weaver (5-12 Sept. 1812)

Carr, Alexander, age 20, in U.S. since 19 Sept. 1811, Bellville, powder maker (12-26 Sept. 1812)

Carroll, Owen, age 22, in U.S. since 8 Feb. 1812, Cape May, English teacher; applied 19 Feb. 1812 Cape May Pleas (12- 26 Sept. (1812)

Claridge, John, age 58, in J.S. since 15 Sept. 1801, 2 daughters, Springfield, turner (15-29 Aug. 1812)

Clark, James, age 23, in U.S. since 11 Dec. 1808, Newark, coach lace weaver (26 Sept.-10 Oct. 1812)

Clency, Dennis, age 24, in J.S. since 25 May 1812, Paterson, labourer (5-12 Sept. 1812)

Clou, James, age 21, in U.S. since 1 May 1812, Paterson, weaver (5-12 Sept. 1812)

Coe, Joshua, age 21, in U.S. since 26 Sept. 1811, Bellville, powder maker (12-26 Sept. 1812)

Coleman, John, age 27, in U.S. since Oct. 1804, wife & 4 children, Newark, laborer (15-29 Aug. 1812)

Conner, Michael, age 21, in U.S. since 1 Nov. 1811, Bellville, powder maker (12-26 Sept. 1812)

Corbett, George, age 18, in U.S. since May 1812, Paterson, weaver (5-12 Sept. 1812)

Courtney, Henry, age 25, in U.S. since 1 Nov. 1809, Crane Town, machine maker (26Sept.-10 Oct. 1812)

Coyel, Michael, age 30, 8 years in U.S., Dover, farmer (10 Oct.-26 Dec. 1812)

Craig, Richard, age 29, in U.S. since 29 July 1803, wife & 3 children, Bloomfield, labourer (15-29 Aug. 1812)

Crane, Samson J., age 27, in U.S. since 2 June 1811, Paterson, weaver (5-12 Sept. 1812)

Crawford, Robert, age 24, in U.S. since 17 May 1806, wife, Orange, shoemaker (12-26 Sept. 1812)

Cresty, William, age 28, 10 years in U.S., Dover, nailor (10 Oct.-26 Dec. 1812)

Daglerfield, Wooldridge, age 35, in U.S. since 5 Dec. 1802, wife & 3 children, Springfield, paper maker; applied Sept. term 1809 Essex Pleas (15-29 Aug. 1812)

Dale, James, age 26, in U.S. since 26 Sept. 1812, wife & child, Newark, manufacturer of wool (1 Dec. 1812-1 May 1813)

Daugherty, Mathew, age 27, in U.S. since 6 July 1803, wife & 2 children, Newark, nailor; applied Jan. term 1811 Essex Pleas (15-29 Aug. 1812)

Davidson, John, age 19, in U.S. since 14 May 1812, Paterson, weaver (5-12 Sept. 1812)

244 NEW JERSEY

Davis, David, age 24, in U.S. since Nov. 1811, Paterson, hatter
(5-12 Sept. 1812)
Davis, John, age 30, in U.S. since 4 Sept. 1810, wife & child,
Bellville, powder maker (12-26 Sept. 1812)
Delancy, William, age 32, in U.S. since 4 Sept. 1804, wife & 2
children, Paterson, labourer (5-12 Sept. 1812)
Dennis, Charles, age 25, in U.S. since 17 Mar. 1811, Hunterdon
Co., weaver (to 8 Aug. 1812)
Dickson, Patrick, age 23, in U.S. since 22 Sept. 1810, Paterson,
weaver (5-12 Sept. 1812)
Doak, Samuel, age 39, in U.S. since 10 Aug. 1804, wife & 6 child-
ren, Bloomfield, stone quarrier (15-29 Aug. 1812)
Donaldson, Thomas, age 26, in U.S. since 16 May 1812, Paterson,
weaver (5-12 Sept. 1812)
Dory, John, in U.S. since Oct. 1801, wife & 4 children, Trenton,
brewer (5-12 Sept. 1812)
Dougherty, Anthony, age 44, in U.S. since Dec. 1797, wife & 5
children, Newark, labourer (15-29 Aug. 1812)
Dougherty, George, age 21, in U.S. since 2 May 1812, Newark, labourer (15-29 Aug. 1812)
Dougherty, James, age 27, in U.S. since July 1812, Newark, labourer (15-29 Aug. 1812)
Doughty, Anthony, age 29, in U.S. since 17 Sept. 1801, Paterson,
weaver (5-12 Sept. 1812)
Dowlin, Miles, age 31, in U.S. since 11 Sept. 1801, Orange, cooper (10 Oct.-26 Dec. 1812)
Drummond, William, age 21, in U.S. since Dec. 1811, Newark, shoemaker (15-29 Aug. 1812)
Druny, John, age 34, in U.S. since 28 Oct. 1809, Newark, tailor
(12-26 Sept. 1812)
Dunn, Michael, age 23, in U.S. since 4 July 1804, wife, Newark,
labourer (15-29 Aug. 1812)
Dunson, Thomas, age 38, in U.S. since 13 Aug. 1812, wife & 2
children, Paterson, fustian cutter (5-12 Sept. 1812)
Dyson, James, age 26, 3½ years in U.S., wife & child, Trenton,
woolen clothier (1 Dec. 1812 - 1 May 1813)
Fagin, Peter, age 23, 7 years in U.S., Morris Town, labourer
(1 Dec. 1812 - 1 May 1813)
Faherty, William, age 29, in U.S. since 27 Sept. 1797, Newark,
cordwainer (15-29 Aug. 1812)
Farrell, John J.O., age 25, in U.S. since 20 Jan. 1811, wife &
child, Newark, merchant (15-29 Aug. 1812)
Ferguson, William, age 32, in U.S. since 13 Aug. 1811, wife & 2
children, Paterson, bleacher (5-12 Sept. 1812)
Field, Peter, age 33, in U.S. since Oct. 1809, wife & child,
Springfield, miller & millstone maker (12-26 Sept. 1812)
Finester, Daniel, age 18, in U.S. since 1 June 1811, Newark, shoe-
maker (15-29 Aug. 1812)
Fitzgerald, William, age 29, 8 years in U.S., wife & 3 children,
Morris Co., English teacher (10 Oct.-26 Dec. 1812)
Fleck, George, age 24, in U.S. since 20 Aug. 1806, Somerset Co.,
weaver & reedmaker (26 Sept. - 10 Oct. 1812)
Flinn, Michael, age 25, in U.S. since Sept. 1809, wife, Newark,
labourer (15-29 Aug. 1812)
Forman, Ezekiel, age 66, native of Monmouth Co., N.J., wife & 8
children, half pay British officer, receiving 35 pounds per
annum (to 8 Aug. 1812)
Forsyth, James, age 23, in U.S. since 3 Aug. 1812, Paterson, weaver (5-12 Sept. 1812)
Foster, Thomas, age 35, 7 years in U.S., wife, Randolph, agriculturist (1 Dec. 1812 - 1 May 1813)
Fox, Lawrence, age 24, in U.S. since Sept. 1810, Bellville, powder maker (12-26 Sept. 1812)
Frame, John, age 30, in U.S. since 13 Oct. 1803, Bloomfield, labourer (15-29 Aug. 1812)

Freeman, Thomas D., age 38, in U.S. since Feb. 1809, wife & 1
  child, South Amboy, labourer (1 Dec. 1812 - 1 May 1813)
Gaffery, James, age 18, in U.S. since 2 Dec. 1811, Bellville,
  powder maker (12-26 Sept. 1812)
Garttend, Owen, age 35, in U.S. since June 1804, wife & child,
  Trenton, potter 1 Dec. 1812 - 1 May 1813)
Gettey, James, age 24, in U.S. since 27 Nov. 1811, Paterson, mill-
  wright (5-12 Sept. 1812)
Gibb, James, age 64, in U.S. since 1801, widower, Hardwick, Sus-
  sex Co., English teacher (5-12 Sept. 1812)
Gillespie, Michael, age 34, in U.S. since 18 July 1812, wife &
  2 children, Newark, labourer (15-29 Aug. 1812)
Gillespie, Michael, age 26, in U.S. since June 1811, wife & child,
  Newark, labourer (15-29 Aug. 1812)
Goff, James, age 40, in U.S. since 27 July 1811, wife & 3 children,
  Springfield, paper maker (10 Oct. - 26 Dec. 1812)
Gordon, James, age 19, in U.S. since 18 June 1811, Paterson,
  weaver (5-12 Sept. 1812)
Gordon, Thomas, age 32, in U.S. since 1 July 1804, wife & child,
  Newark, muslin weaver; applied 2 July 1810 (15-29 Aug. 1812)
Graham, Guy, age 31, in U.S. since Apr. 1807, wife & 4 children,
  shoemaker (10 Oct.-26 Dec. 1812)
Grant, William, age 46, in U.S. since 20 May 1803, wife & 2
  children, Newark, labourer (12-26 Sept. 1812)
Gray, Gilbert, age 46, in U S. since 8 May 1801, Union Twp.,
  weaver (12-26 Sept. 1812)
Gray, James, age 32, in U.S. since Feb. 1811, wife & 2 children,
  Paterson, machine maker (5-12 Sept. 1812)
Griffith, Edward, age 31, in U.S. since 15 June 1804, wife & child,
  Elizabeth Town, manufacturer of earthen ware; applied 8 Mar.
  1809 (to 8 Aug. 1812)
Griffith, John, in U.S. since 22 Sept. 1808, Elizabeth Town, manu-
  facturer of earthen ware; applied 6 Sept. 1809 (to 8 Aug. 1812)
Griffith, Robert, age 25, in U.S. since 21 Apr. 1810, wife, Eliza-
  beth Town, manufacturer of earthen ware; on 15 July applied to
  clerk of Borough of Elizabeth and received certificate (to 8
  Aug. 1812)
Grogran, George, age 35, in U.S. since 17 Aug. 1803; wife & 2
  children, Newark, laborer (15-29 Aug. 1812)
Gruet, Frederick, age 24, in U.S. since June 1795, wife, Orange,
  fringe weaver (10 Oct.-26 Dec. 1812)
Gruett, Peter, age 31, in U.S. since 4 June 1795, Crane Town,
  physician (1 Dec. 1812 - 1 May 1813)
Haigh, Abraham, age 28, in U.S. since July 1812, Paterson, wool
  spinner (5-12 Sept. 1812)
Hamlon, Robert, age 30, in U.S. since 14 Apr. 1811, Hunterdon
  Co., spinner (to 8 Aug. 1812)
Hancock, William, age 36, in U.S. since June 1807, wife & 2
  children, Trenton, whitesmith (1 Dec. 1812 - 1 May 1813)
Harding, Richard B., age 31, in U.S. since 15 Sept. 1801, wife,
  Chatham, paper maker (12-26 Sept. 1812)
Hassall, James, age 40, in U.S. since 22 Sept. 1808, wife & child,
  Elizabeth Town, manufacturer of earthen ware; applied 7 Mar.
  1810 (to 8 Aug. 1812)
Hawthorn, Francis, age 40, in U.S. since 9 June 1811, wife & 8
  children, Newark, agriculturist (15-29 Aug. 1812)
Hedrick, David, age 27, in U.S. since 26 Mar. 1811, Paterson,
  cotton spinner (5-12 Sept. 1812)
Henderson, Jacob, age 40, in U.S. since Aug. 1800, wife & child,
  Elizabeth Town, twine maker (10 Oct.-26 Dec. 1812)
Henderson, John, age 50, in U.S. since Aug. 1795, Elizabeth Town,
  twine maker (10 Oct.-26 Dec. 1812)
Henderson, William, age 32, in U.S. since Aug. 1795, Elizabeth
  Town, twine maker (10 Oct.-26 Dec. 1812)

Hibbant, Thomas, age 44, in U.S. since 22 May 1807, wife & child, Bellville, farmer (10 Oct.-26 Dec. 1812)

Holliday, Thomas, age 30, in U.S. since 4 Sept. 1811, wife, Paterson, weaver (5-12 Sept. 1812)

Howard, John, age 56, in U.S. since 30 Sept. 1800, wife & 3 children, Paterson, cotton spinner (5-12 Sept. 1812)

Howard, Thomas, age 21, in U.S. since 11 May 1811, Paterson, cotton spinner (5-12 Sept. 1812)

Hugh, Simeon, age 26, in U.S. since July 1812, Paterson, wool carder (5-12 Sept. 1812)

Hughs, Jonathan, age 57, in U.S. since 22 June 1807, wife & 6 children, Aquacknonk, paper maker (10 Oct.- 26 Dec. 1812)

Humphries, Alexander, age 28, in U.S. since 1 May 1812, wife & 2 children, Newark, labourer (15-29 Aug. 1812)

Huston, Hugh, age 28, 1½ years in U.S., wife & 3 children, Morris Town, weaver (1 Dec. 1812 - 1 May 1813)

Hutchison, James McCullin, age 21, in U.S. since 18 Dec. 1811, Paterson, weaver (5-12 Sept. 1812)

Jackson, John, 5 years in U.S., New Brunswick, sailor (1 Dec. 1812 - 1 May 1813)

Jackson, Wm., age 26, in U.S. since June 1800, wife & 2 children, Bloomsbury, innkeeper (1 Dec. 1812 - 1 May 1813)

Johnston, Thomas, age 20, in U.S. since 29 Aug. 1811, Paterson, weaver (5-12 Sept. 1812)

Johnston, William, age 20, in U.S. since 2 May 1812, Paterson, weaver (5-12 Sept. 1812)

Kelley, Patrick, age 30, in U.S. since 17 July 1801, wife & 1 child, Springfield, tailor (26 Sept. - 10 Oct. 1812)

Kelley, William, age 27, in U.S. since July 1810, Orange, cooper (1 Dec. 1812 - 1 May 1813)

Kelly, Cornelius, age 36, in U.S. since 1 July 1811, wife & 3 children, Burlington Co. (26 Sept. - 10 Oct. 1812)

Kemble, Stephen, age 72, native of N.J., niece & 4 black servants, New Brunswick; he entered the British service in 1757 and continued in it until 1793, when he sold his Lt.-Col.'s commission and returned to New Brunswick; he receives a small annuity (8-16 Aug. 1812)

Knee, Daniel, age 21, in U.S. since Aug. 1809, Flemington (10 Oct.-26 Dec. 1812)

Laughard, Andrew, age 22, in U.S. since 26 Sept. 1810, Bellville, powder maker (12-26 Sept. 1812)

Linn, David, age 36, in U.S. since 1 July 1811, wife & 3 children, Paterson, millwright (5-12 Sept. 1812)

Lockhart, Thomas, age 27, in U.S. since 4 Apr. 1812, Bellville, millwright (5-12 Sept. 1812)

Lockland, William, age 21, in U.S. since 20 May 1812, Paterson, weaver (5-12 Sept. 1812)

Lynch, William, age 27, 8 years in U.S., Burlington Co. (10 Oct.- 26 Dec. 1812)

McCallister, Felix, age 25, in U.S. since 20 May 1811, wife, Newark, labourer (15-29 Aug. 1812)

McCannel, Maurice, in U.S. since 18 July 1806, Flemington (10 Oct.-26 Sept. 1812)

McClarky, Patrick, age 34, in U.S. since 7 Sept. 1797, wife & 4 children, Newark, labourer (12-26 Sept. 1812)

McCleery, James, age 44, in U.S. since 28 May 1812, wife & 1 child, Paterson, weaver (5-12 Sept. 1812)

McClennan, James, age 35, in U.S. since 2 Aug. 1804, wife, Bellville, powder maker (12-26 Sept. 1812)

McConnel, James, age 22, in U.S. since 10 May 1811, wife & child, Bellville, saltpeter refiner (12-26 Sept. 1812)

McConnell, John, age 22, in U.S. since 18 Oct. 1811, Bellville, powder maker (12-26 Sept. 1812)

Mc Connely, Patrick, age 50, in U.S. since 28 June 1811, wife & 4 children, Paterson, weaver (5-12 Sept. 1812)

McDonald, Archibald, age 30, in U.S. since 4 Oct. 1809, wife & 3
children, Rahway, wool spinner (26 Sept. - 10 Oct. 1812)
McDowal, William, age 48, in U.S. since Aug. 1797, Newark, rope-
maker (15-29 Aug. 1812)
McDowall, Alexander, age 22, in U.S, since 18 May 1811, Paterson,
carpenter (5-12 Sept. 1812)
McElvain, Daniel, age 23, in U.S. since 22 May 1808, Paterson,
weaver (5-12 Sept. 1812)
McEowen, Anthony, age 27, in U.S. since 28 Sept. 1806, Newark,
labourer (12-26 Sept. 1812)
McGall, Robert, age 24, in U.S. since 20 July 1811, Bellville,
powder maker (12-26 Sept. 1812)
Magee, Patrick, age 26, in U.S. since 20 May 1802, wife & child,
Paterson, labourer (5-12 Sept. 1812)
McGinley, Michael, age 22, in U.S. since June 1812, Paterson,
weaver (5-12 Sept. 1812)
McGlauchlan, Edward, age 33, in U.S. since 28 June 1811, widower,
Paterson, labourer (5-12 Sept. 1812)
McGlauchlen, Samuel, age 21, in U.S. since 16 June 1812, Newark,
currier (12-26 Sept. 1812)
McGregor, James, age 21, in U.S. since 9 June 1810, Paterson,
cotton spinner (5-12 Sept. 1812)
McGuire, Hugh, age 25, in U.S. since June 1812, Paterson, weaver
(5-12 Sept. 1812)
McIlray, David, age 38, in U.S. since 14 Nov. 1810, wife & 6
children, Paterson, weaver (12-26 Sept. 1812)
McKee, James, age 23, in U.S. since 28 June 1811, Paterson wea-
ver (5-12 Sept. 1812)
McLenahan, William, age 47, in U.S. since Sept. 1785, Trenton,
Methodist preacher (15-29 Aug. 1812)
McNeil, William, age 25, in U.S. since 9 June 1805, Paterson,
weaver (5-12 Sept. 1812)
Magafin, James, age 48, in U.S. since 28 June 1812, wife & 7
children, Paterson, weaver (5-12 Sept. 1812)
Malliff, Patrick, age 32, in U.S. since 13 Aug. 1811, Bellville,
powder maker (12-26 Sept. 1812)
Mann, James, age 46, in U.S. since 4 Apr. 1812, wife & 3 children,
Bellville, agriculturist (5-12 Sept. 1812)
Mason, John, age 42, in U.S. since 20 Oct. 1810, wife & 11 child-
ren, Bloomfield, cotton spinner; applied 19 Apr. 1811 Essex
Pleas (15-29 Aug. 1812)
Medowell, Cairnoan, age 60, in U.S. since 17 Sept. 1797, Cape
May, English teacher; applied Dec. 1798 Chillicothe Ohio Pleas
(10 Oct. - 26 Dec. 1812)
Miller, John, age 22, in U.S. since Sept. 1810, Crane Town, cot-
ton spinner (12-26 Sept. 1812)
Mitchel, Edward, age 48, in U.S. since Sept. 1803, wife, Pater-
son, weaver; applied April 1809 Essex Pleas (5-12 Sept. 1812)
Mitchel, John, age 34, in U.S. since 1 Nov. 1804, Bellville,
cooper (10 Oct.-26 Dec. 1812)
Montgomery, James, age 21, in U.S. since 3 Sept. 1810, Newark,
turner (12-26 Sept. 1812)
Montgomery, John, age 25, in U.S. since Aug. 1811, Paterson,
carpenter (5-12 Sept. 1812)
Montgomery, Robert, age 26, in U.S. since 1 Nov. 1810, wife & 2
children, Newark, tanner & currier (15-29 Aug. 1812)
Moore, Ephraim, age 30, in U.S. since 8 Dec. 1809, wife & 2 children, Bellville, labourer (10 Oct.-26 Dec. 1812)
Morgan, Morgan, age 44, in U.S. since 4 Oct. 1793, wife & 6
children, Bergen Co., Schuyler's mine, red & white lead manufacturer (12-26 Sept. 1812)
Morgan, William, age 32, in U.S. since 30 July 1801, Perth Amboy (10 Oct. - 26 Dec. 1812)
Morris, Solomon, age 22, in U.S. since 2 Oct. 1811, Bellville,
powder maker (12-26 Sept. 1812)

Mullegan, John, age 32, in U.S. since 20 June 1801, wife & 2 children, Newark, shoemaker (12-26 Sept. 1812)

Mullen, John, age 40, in U.S. since July 1801, wife & 3 children, Trenton, labourer (1 Dec. 1812 - 1 May 1813)

Munns (?), Charles, age 45, in U.S. since Nov. 1796, wife & child, Bellville, superintendent of powder manufactory (12-26 Sept. 1812)

Murphey, Patrick, age 27, in U.S. since June 1808, Paterson, labourer (5-12 Sept. 1812)

Murry, Francis, age 36, in U.S. since 1 Aug. 1806, wife & four children, Crane Town, machine maker (26 Sept. - 10 Oct. 1812)

Murry, James, age 46, in U.S. since 18 July 1810, wife & nine children, Bloomfield, cotton spinner (5-12 Sept. 1812)

Murry, William, age 28, in U.S. since Dec. 1798, Newark, merchant (15-29 Aug. 1812)

Neilson, James, age 21, in U.S. since 14 May 1812, wife, Paterson, weaver (5-12 Sept. 1812)

Norris, Richard, age 67, 16 years in U.S., wife, Mendham, wool comber (1 Dec. 1812 - 1 May 1813)

Oliver, William, age 40, in U.S. since 15 Nov. 1801, wife & five children, Newark, weaver (26 Sept. - 10 Oct. 1812)

O'Neil, Thomas, age 46, in U.S. since 6 May 1802, Bergen Co., teacher (10 Oct. -26 Dec. 1812)

Orr, William, age 22, 1 year in U.S., Mendham, teacher (1 Dec. 1812 - 1 May 1813)

Palmer, William, age 28, 2 years in U.S., wife & 3 children, Essex Co., farmer (to 8 Aug. 1812)

Patterson, Robert, age 29, in U.S. since 18 Apr. 1808, wife & 3 children, Paterson, superintendent weaver; applied this 12 Oct. at Essex Pleas (5-12 Sept. 1812)

Peacock, Thomas, age 54, in U.S. since 6 Aug. 1810, family now in Europe, Aquackanock, teacher (10 Oct. - 26 Dec. 1812)

Phelan, Thomas, age 23, in U.S. since 12 Dec. 1809, Newark, currier (12-26 Sept. 1812)

Pile, Thomas, age 29, in U.S. since 30 Nov. 1807, wife & child, Elizabeth Town, chemist (1 Dec. 1812 - 1 May 1813)

Pine, Robert, age 50, in U.S. since 25 June 1796, wife & four children, Acquacknock, miller (10 Oct. - 26 Dec. 1812)

Platt, Robert, age 27, in U.S. since Sept. 1803, wife, Newark, labourer (15-29 Aug. 1812)

Price, Ellis, age 25, in U.S. since 25 May 1801, wife & 2 children, Newark, shoemaker (26 Sept. - 10 Oct. 1812)

Price, John, age 33, in U.S. since 4 Aug. 1807, wife & 2 children, Elizabeth Town, chemist (1 Dec. 1812 - 1 May 1813)

Purford, William, age 24, in U.S. since 24 Sept. 1806, Newark, soap boiler (1 Dec. 1812 - 1 May 1813)

Purvis, John, age 33, since 3 July 1802, wife & 2 children, Bloomfield, paper maker; applied 19 Jan. 1808 Essex Pleas (15-29 Aug. 1812)

Racey, William, age 20, in U.S. since 11 May 1804, Newark, harness maker (12-26 Sept. 1812)

Ray, James, age 22, in U.S. since 15 June 1812, Bellville, powder maker (12-26 Sept. 1812)

Reder, Joseph, age 22, in U.S. since 19 May 1812, Bloomfield, weaver (12-26 Sept. 1812)

Reid, Daniel, age 34, in U.S. since 1 July 1811, wife & child, Paterson, carpenter (5-12 Sept. 1812)

Reid, William, age 33, in U.S. since 8 Aug. 1807, wife & two children, Union Twp., farmer (10 Oct. - 26 Dec. 1812)

Reppey, Matthew, age 37, in U.S. since 21 Nov. 1811, wife & 5 children, Paterson, sawyer (5-12 Sept. 1812)

Riley, James, age 16, in U.S. since 8 Apr. 1812, Paterson, weaver (5-12 Sept. 1812)

Roberts, St. George Espie, age 21, in U.S. since 26 Nov. 1811, Newark, teacher of languages (12-26 Sept. 1812)

Robertson, James, age 37, in U.S. since June 1811, Paterson, cotton manufacturer (5-12 Sept. 1812)

Rogers, David, age 34, in U.S. since 18 July 1800, widower, Paterson, weaver (5-12 Sept. 1812)

Rogers, John, Jr., age 22, in U.S. since 28 June 1801, Paterson, weaver (5-12 Sept. 1812)

Ross, Joseph, age 22, in U.S. since 27 June 1807, Aquacknack, clerk (10 Oct. - 26 Dec. 1812)

Ross, William, age 32, in U.S. since 15 Mar. 1811, wife & five children, Hunterdon Co., spinner (to 8 Aug. 1812)

Rourke, Hugh, age 30, in U.S. since 9 May 1801, wife & child, Bellville, powder maker (12-26 Sept. 1812)

Rusling, James, age 50, in U.S. since 1795, wife & 6 children, Morris Co,, agriculturist (15-29 Aug. 1812)

Sager, John, age 24, in U.S. since 10 June 1810, Paterson, painter & glazier (5-12 Sept. 1812)

Sanderson, Arthur, age 43, in U.S. since Aug. 1804, wife & 6 children, Bloomfield, labourer (15-29 Aug. 1812)

Sanderson, Robert, age 69, in U.S. since 10 Aug. 1804, widower, Bloomfield, stone quarrier (15-29 Aug. 1812)

Sanderson, William, age 46, in U.S. since Aug. 1804, wife & 7 children, Bloomfield, labourer (15-29 Aug. 1812)

Savage, John, age 58, in U.S. since June 1777, wife & child, Newark, labourer (12-26 Sept. 1812)

Scott, James, age 37, 15 years in U.S., Morris Town, miner (1 Dec. 1812 - 1 May 1813)

Scott, James, age 28, in U.S. since May 1808, wife & child, Newark, merchant (15-29 Aug. 1812)

Scott, William, age 26, in U.S. since 16 Nov. 1805, Newark, a brewer (10 Oct. - 26 Dec. 1812)

Scott, William, age 23, 3 nos. in U.S., Newton, Sussex Co., weaver (15-29 Aug. 1812)

Semon, William, in U.S. since 3 Oct. 1809, wife & 2 children, Flemington, merchant (10 Oct. - 26 Dec. 1812)

Sharp, Richard, age 35, in U.S. since 8 Aug. 1801, wife & three children, Pequnnac, turner (12-26 Sept. 1812)

Shaw, Michael Andrew, age 47, in U.S. since 11 Apr. 1811, Newark (1 Dec. 1812 - 1 May 1813)

Shawcross, James, age 33, in U.S. since 6 Jan. 1811, wife, Newark, agriculturist (5-12 Sept. 1812)

Sheldon, William, age 27, in U.S. since 2 Feb. 1806, wife & five children, Bloomfield, labourer (15-29 Aug. 1812)

Shepherd, James, age 28, in U.S. since 27 Nov. 1811, Paterson, reed maker (5-12 Sept. 1812)

Sheridan, Bernard Nugent, age 38, in U.S. since Aug. 1801, wife & 6 children, Aquacknonk, teacher (12-26 Sept. 1812)

Simon, Wm., age 34, in U.S. since 1809, wife & 3 children, Trenton, shopkeeper (1 Dec. 1812 - 1 May 1813)

Simpson, Samuel, age 22, in U.S. since 18 May 1812, Paterson, weaver (5-12 Sept. 1812)

Slammon, James, age 24, in U.S. since 9 Dec. 1810, wife & child, Paterson, weaver (5-12 Sept. 1812)

Slater, Robert, age 50, in U.S. since 13 Oct. 1804, widower, Paterson, machine maker (5-12 Sept. 1812)

Smith, John, age 28, in U.S. since 14 May 1806, wife & child, Bloomfield, fuller & dyer (12-26 Sept. 1812)

Snowden, Thomas, age 32, in U.S. since 16 July 1806, wife & child, Elizabeth Town, weaver (26 Sept. - 11 Oct. 1812)

Spratt, Thomas, age 20, in U.S. since 25 May 1812, Paterson, labourer (5-12 Sept. 1812)

Stark, Henry, age 24, in U.S. since 20 May 1812, Paterson, weaver (5-12 Sept. 1812)

Stevens, James, Jr., age 24, 15 years in U.S., wife & 2 children, Mendham, clothier (1 Dec. 1812 - 1 May 1813)

Stevens, William, age 23, in U.S. since 10 Nov. 1798, Newark, wool spinner (28 Sept. - 10 Oct. 1812)

Stevenson, James, age 24, in U.S. since 20 Sept. 1810, Bellville, powder maker (12-26 Sept. 1812)

Stevenson, John, age 34, in U.S. since 1 Aug. 1802, Paterson, weaver (5-12 Sept. 1812)

Stevenson, John, age 25, in U.S. since 8 June 1811, Bellville, powder maker (12-26 Sept. 1812)

Stevenson, William, age 44, in U.S. since 24 May 1812, widower, Paterson, weaver (5-12 Sept. 1812)

Stewart, George, age 22, in U.S. since 28 Jan. 1806, Newark, silver plater (12-26 Sept. 1812)

Sugar, George, age 26, in U.S. since 11 July 1810, wife, Paterson, carpenter (5-12 Sept. 1812)

Taylor, William, age 51, in U.S. since 6 July 1811, wife & six children, Newark, weaver (15-19 Aug. 1812)

Thompson, Joseph, age 25, in U,S. since 19 Aug. 1801, wife & 2 children, Paterson, dyer (5-12 Sept. 1812)

Thompson, Lewis, age 58, native of Monmouth Co., N.J., wife, 2 sons & 4 daughters, Monmouth Co., farmer, British half pay officer (to 8 Aug. 1812)

Thomson, John, age 33, in U.S. since 8 May 1801, wife, Bergen Co., teacher (5-12 Sept. 1812)

Thomson, William, age 36, in U.S. since 28 Sept. 1805, wife & 2 children, Paterson, weaver (5-12 Sept. 1812)

Tierney, Michael, age 29, in U.S. since 28 May 1811, wife & 2 children, Bellville, powder maker (12-26 Sept. 1812)

Tobein(?), Edmund, age 28, in U.S. since June 1801, Newark, labourer (12-26 Sept. 1812)

Tomlinson, Abel Arthur, age 26, in U.S. since 24 June 1811, wife & 2 children, Bloomfield, weaver (12-26 Sept. 1812)

Toole, James, age 19, in U.S. since 1 Nov. 1810, Newark, tanner & currier (15-29 Aug. 1812)

Torrance, James, age 33, in U.S. since 6 Apr. 1801, wife & three children, Newark, merchant (12-26 Sept. 1812)

Transon, Peter, age 20, in U.S. since 7 June 1811, wife & child, Newark, cooper (12-26 Sept. 1812)

Turner, Thomas Welsh, age 22, in U.S. since 18 June 1811, Bloomfield, weaver (12-26 Sept. 1812)

Upjohn, James, age 60, in U.S. since 1797, wife, 2 sons & seven daughters, Morris Co., agriculturist (15-29 Aug. 1812)

Valentine, Peter, age 25, 2 years in U.S., Dover, nailor (10 Oct. - 26 Dec. 1812)

Walker, John, age 29, in U.S. since 13 July 1801, Newark, agriculturist (15-29 Aug. 1812)

Waugh, David, age 18, in U.S. since 18 May 1812, Paterson, weaver (5-12 Sept. 1812)

Wedderburn, John, age 32, in U.S. since Sept. 1804, wife, Newark, weaver (1 Dec. 1812 - 1 May 1813)

Welsh, George, age 31, in U.S. since 30 Apr. 1811, family in Scotland, Newark, baker (15-29 Aug. 1812)

Westerman, Thomas, age 32, in U.S. since 18 Aug. 1811, wife & child, Paterson, cotton carder (5-12 Sept.1812)

Wharton, George, in U.S. since 29 Mar. 1812, wife & 6 children, Spring Garden, cotton spinner (12-26 Sept. 1812)

White, George, age 30, in U.S. since May 1801, wife & 2 children, New Brunswick, merchant (8-15 Aug. 1812)

White, William A., age 32, 14 years in U.S., wife & 3 children, Dover, nailor (10 Oct.-26 Dec. 1812)

Willitts, Thomas, age 49, in U.S. since May 1800, wife, New Brunswick, umbrella maker; applied 25 Feb. 1803 (8-16 Aug. 1812)

Wilson, Alexander, age 33, in U.S. since 3 July 1802, wife & 2 children, Bloomfield, paper maker; applied 19 Jan. 1808 Essex Pleas (15-29 Aug. 1812)

Wilson, Charles, age 27, 9 years in U.S., wife & 3 children,
  Morris Co., agriculturist (10 Oct. - 26 Dec. 1812)
Wilson, George, age 46, in U.S. since 4 Nov. 1804, 1 son, Newark,
  labourer (15-29 Aug. 1812)
Wilson, Michael, age 23, in U.S. since 28 June 1812, Newark,
  cooper (12-26 Sept. 1812)
Wilson, Samuel, age 21, in U.S. since 7 Sept. 1811, Bellville,
  powder maker (12-26 Sept. 1812)
Wilson, Thomas, age 37, in U.S. since 2 Apr. 1811, wife & child,
  Bloomfield, weaver (12-26 Sept. 1812)
Wilson, William, age 19, in U.S. since 20 July 1811, Bellville,
  powder maker (12-26 Sept. 1812)
Wood, William R., age 31, in U.S. since 3 Dec. 1806, wife & 1
  child, Newark, weaver (1 Dec. 1812 - 1 May 1813)
Woods, John, age 41, in U.S. since 23 Mar. 1810, wife & 1 child,
  Kingston, woolen clothier (1 Dec. 1812 - 1 May 1813)

DELAWARE

Aikin, Joseph, age 29, 3 years in U.S., Millcreek, weaver (to 8
Jan. 1814)
Akeroyd, Jeremiah, age 48, 5 years in U.S., wife & 3 children,
village of Stannton, woolen manufacturer (1-17 Aug. 1812)
Anderson, James, age 27, 7 years in U.S., wife & child, Newcastle,
weaver (4 Mar.-4 Apr. 1813)
Arbuckle, James, age 28, 9 years in U.S., wife & 2 children, Wil-
mington, printer (23 July - 1 Aug. 1812)
Bannister, Isaac, age 35, 20 mos. in U.S., wife & 5 children,
Brandywine, woolen manufacturer (17 May - 1 July 1813)
Barr, John, age 21, 15 mos. in U.S., Wilmington, weaver (1-17 Aug.
1812)
Barr, Paul, age 34, 6 years in U.S., wife & 4 children, Newcastle,
baker (4 Apr. - 17 May 1813)
Barrett, Hugh, age 48, 6 years in U.S., wife & 8 children, Brandy-
wine, weaver (to 1 Sept. 1813)
Barrett, John, age 22, 5 years in U.S., Christiana, spinner and
weaver (23 July - 1 Aug. 1812)
Beaty, John, age 45, 21 years in U.S., wife & 6 children, Mill-
creek, farmer (to 1 Sept. 1813)
Beaver, Thomas, age 20, 2 years in U.S., Brandywine, weaver (23
July - 1 Aug. 1812)
Beecross, Isaac, age 14, 3 mos. in U.S., village of Stannton,
woolen manufacturer (1-17 Aug. 1812)
Bell, Thomas H., age 25, 3 years in U.S., wife, Duckcreek, pain-
ter (13-31 Aug. 1812)
Bell, William, age 31, 28 years in U.S., wife & child, Sussex Co.,
mariner (23-30 July 1812)
Bennett, John, age 36, 4 years in U.S., Brandywine, weaver; ap-
plied, date unknown (23 July - 1 Aug. 1812)
Best, Adam, age 25, 1 mo. in U.S., Brandywine, woolen manufacturer
(23 July - 1 Aug. 1812)
Bingham, Moses, age 32, 7 years in U.S., Wilmington, weaver (23
July - 1 Aug. 1812)
Black, Andrew, age 35, 12 years in U.S., wife & 2 children, Bran-
dywine, weaver (23 July - 1 Aug. 1812)
Blayney, William, age 49, 6 years in U.S., wife & 4 children,
Christiana, machinist (to 5 Oct. 1814)
Bleek, Matthew, age 29, 2 years in U.S., Millcreek, weaver (to 4
Mar. 1813)
Bowden, William, age 28, 3 years in U.S., wife & 2 children,
Christiana, mariner; applied 26 Mar. 1813 (to 5 Oct. 1814)
Boyd, William, age 27, 6 mos. in U.S., Brandywine, scourer (23
July - 1 Aug. 1812)
Braden, Charles, age 37, 16 years in U.S., Brandywine, weaver (15
Sept. - 10 Oct. 1812)
Bradley, John, age 25, 2 years in U.S., Christiana, gunpowder
maker (23 July - 1 Aug. 1812)
Bradshaw, Samuel, age 46, 4 years & 3 mos. in U.S., wife & child,
Brandywine, weaver (16-23 July 1812)
Bradshaw, William, age 46, 1 year in U.S., Brandywine, weaver (23
July - 1 Aug. 1812)
Brady, Patrick, age 26, 6 years in U.S., Christiana, labourer (23
July - 1 Aug. 1812)
Breen, Francis, age 21, 8 mos. in U.S., Wilmington, tailor (to 4
Mar. 1813)
Brian, John, age 51, 20 mos. in U.S., Millcreek, weaver (1-15 Sept.
1812)
Brierly, John, age 37, 6 years in U.S., Wilmington, iron founder;
applied Philadelphia 20 Mar. 1813 (to 8 Jan. 1814)
Broadley, James, age 34, 6 years in U.S., wife & child, Christiana,
gunpowder maker (23 July - 1 Aug. 1812)

Brown, James, age 24, 15 mos. in U.S., Wilmington, weaver (1-17
Aug. 1812)

Buchanan, William, age 42, 18 years in U.S., wife & 6 children,
Millcreek, weaver (4 Mar. - 4 Apr. 1813)

Buck, James, age 22, 4 years in U.S., Christiana, gunpowder
maker (23 July - 1 Aug. 1812)

Buckley, Joshua, age 33, arrived 2 Mar. 1813 in Wilmington, a
machine maker (to 4 Mar. 1813); later in Lewes (to 1 Sept.
1813)

Bunting, Matthew, age 28, 12 years in U.S., wife & child, Millcreek, weaver (4 Apr. - 17 May 1813)

Burgess, William, age 34, 5 years in U.S., wife & 5 children,
Christiana, machinist (to 5 Oct. 1814)

Burnett, Robert, age 41, 1 year & 11 mos. in U.S., Wilmington,
farmer (23 July - 1 Aug. 1812); a Robert Burnet, age 43, on
10 May 1813 was ordered to Reading (28 Dec. 1813)

Burns, James, age 27, a mariner and deserter from the British
brig of war Mohawk in Chesapeake Bay, on 24 May 1813 was ordered to Reading (28 Dec. 1813)

Butler, George, age 36, wife & 7 children, Millcreek, weaver (to
1 Nov. 1813)

Callaghan, Jeremiah, age 28, 3 years in U.S., Wilmington, plaisterer (to 1 Nov. 1813)

Campbell, Colin, age 42, 14 years in U.S., wife & 5 children,
Brandywine, tailor (15 Sept. - 10 Oct. 1812)

Campbell, David, age 23, 13 years in U.S., Brandywine, tailor
(15 Sept. - 10 Oct. 1812)

Campbell, Joseph, age 64, 13 years in U.S., wife & 4 children &
grandchildren, Wilmington, weaver & gardener (15 Sept.-10 Oct.
1812)

Carlisle, James, age 27, 6 years in U.S., Brandywine, cooper(to
4 Mar. 1813)

Carr, Owen, age 35, 3 years in U.S., Christiana, gunpowder maker
(23 July - 1 Aug. 1812)

Caswell, Robert, age 39, 11 years in U.S., wife & 4 children,
Newcastle, farmer (15 Sept. - 10 Dec. 1812)

Cathcart, Gabriel, age 22, 2 years in U.S., Wilmington, engineer
(to 5 Oct. 1814)

Christy, William, age 21, 3 mos. in U.S., Brandywine, cordwainer
(4 Mar. - 4 Apr. 1813)

Clark, John, age 24, 1 year in U.S., Brandywine, shearman (23
July - 1 Aug. 1812)

Cleland, George, age 30, 8 years in U.S., wife & 2 children,
Newcastle, farmer (23 July - 1 Aug. 1812)

Colvin, John, age 22, 9 mos. in U.S., Brandywine, cloth weaver
(23 July - 1 Aug. 1812)

Conway, John, age 57, 19 years in U.S., wife & 9 children, Millcreek, farmer (1-15 Sept. 1812)

Cowen, George, age 30, 3 years in U.S., Christiana, weaver (to
1 Nov. 1813)

Cox, James, age 46, 9 years in U.S., wife & 7 children, Wilmington, trader and pedlar (16-23 July 1812)

Daugherty, Dennis, age 33, 10 years in U.S., wife & child, Millcreek, cotton manufacturer (4 Apr. - 17 May 1813)

Dickey, Isaac, age 30, 8 years in U.S., Millcreek, cloth manufacturer (23 July - 1 Aug. 1812)

Dickey, John, age 27, 3 years in U.S., wife & 2 children, Christiana, weaver and farmer (23 July - 1 Aug. 1812)

Doherty, Edward, age 32, 5 years in U.S., Concord, Sussex Co.,
merchant; applied last Apr. term Sussex Co. Court (23-30 July
1812)

Doras, Bernard, age 25, 1 year & 1 mo. in U.S., Wilmington, weaver (16-23 July 1812)

Dougherty, Daniel, age ..., 27 mos. in U.S., Christiana, machinist (to 5 Oct. 1814)

Dougherty, Patrick, age 30, 5 years in U.S., Christiana, gunpowder maker (23 July - 1 Aug. 1812)

Dougherty, Richard, age 35, 9 years in U.S., wife & 4 children,
Christiana, gunpowder maker (23 July - 1 Aug. 1812)

Dowdes, John, age 29, 15 years in U.S., wife & 6 children, Millcreek, labourer (1-15 Sept. 1812)

Downy, Michael, age 30, 4 years & 11 mos. in U.S., wife and 2
children, Wilmington, labourer (16-23 July 1812)

Elder, Matthew, age 20, 2 mos. in U.S., Christiana, weaver (17
Aug. - 1 Sept. 1812)

Fawcett, John, age 57, 1 year in U.S., Wilmington, farmer (to
1 Nov. 1813)

Ferguson, Charles, age 20, 7 mos. in U.S., Millcreek, weaver
(4 Apr. - 17 May 1813)

Ferguson, Thomas, age 34, 3 years in U.S., wife & 5 children,
Millcreek, weaver (4 Apr. - 17 May 1813)

Fitzpatrick, George, age 33, 8 years in U.S., wife, Christiana,
gardener (to 8 Jan. 1814)

Flanagan, Hugh, age 39, 11 years in U.S., Christiana, gunpowder
maker (23 July - 1 Aug. 1812)

Ford, James, age 23, 14 mos. in U.S., Christiana, blacksmith
(17 Aug. - 1 Sept. 1812)

Ford, John, age 46, 14 mos. in U.S., Christiana, blacksmith
(17 Aug. - 1 Sept. 1812)

Foster, Thomas, age 25, 20 mos. in U.S., Millcreek, weaver (4
Apr. - 17 May 1813)

Gallagher, Hugh, age 26, 6 years in U.S., wife, Wilmington, labourer (to 8 Jan. 1814)

Gallagher, John, age 21, 2 years in U.S., wife, Brandywine,
turnpike maker (17 May - 1 July 1813)

Gallaher, John, age 28, 10 years in U.S., Millcreek, labourer
(1-15 Sept. 1812)

Galloway, John, age 30, 22 mos. in U.S., Whiteclay Creek, machinist (to 5 Oct. 1814)

Garret, Michael, age 30, 8 years in U.S., wife & child, Millcreek, weaver (to 1 Sept. 1813)

Graham, James C., age 37, 11 years in U.S., wife & 4 children,
Millcreek, woolen manufacturer (16-23 July 1812)

Graham, Robert, age 38, 7 years in U.S., wife & 4 children, Millcreek, weaver (4 Apr. - 17 May 1813)

Greatrake, George (son of Lawrence), age 18, 12 years in U.S.,
Christiana, paper maker (4 Mar. - 4 Apr. 1813)

Greatrake, Henry, age 15, 12 years in U.S., Christiana (4 Mar. -
4 Apr. 1813)

Greatrake, Lawrence, age 55, 12 years & 2 mos. in U.S., wife &
8 children, Brandywine Paper Mills, paper maker; applied 2
July 1812 (16-23 July 1812); Lawrence (father) and George
(son) were ordered to Reading but in June were allowed to return; Lawrence by then had become naturalized (28 Dec. 1813)

Greatrake, Lawrence, Jr., age 20, 12 years in U.S., Christiana,
paper maker (4 Apr. - 17 May 1813)

Greer, James, age 37, 11 years in U.S., wife & 2 children,
Christiana, saltpeter refiner (23 July - 1 Aug. 1812)

Guy, Samuel, age 30, 1 year in U.S., wife, Wilmington, plaisterer (23 July - 1 Aug. 1812)

Hall, Thomas, age 52, 28 years in U.S., 3 children, Duckcreek,
cordwainer (13-31 Aug. 1812)

Hanlan, Robert, age 30, 2 years in U.S., Christiana, manufacturer (to 4 Mar. 1813)

Harper, Joseph, age 30, 19 years in U.S., wife & 3 children,
Brandywine, machinist (23 July - 1 Aug. 1812)

Harper, Thomas, age 35, 3 years in U.S., Whiteclay Creek, millwright (to 8 Jan. 1814)

Harper, Thomas, age 26, 19 years in U.S., Brandywine, calico
printer (23 July - 1 Aug. 1812)

Harrison, Thomas, age 24, 1 year in U.S., wife & child, Brandywine, weaver (23 July - 1 Aug. 1812)

Hemphill, Matthew, age 24, 6 mos. in U.S., Brandywine, weaver
(4 Mar. - 4 Apr. 1813)

Henderson, Samuel, age 31, 2 years & 10 mos. in U.S., wife & 2
children, Christiana, clergyman; applied 6 May 1812 (16-23 July
1812)

Henry, Daniel, age 56, 21 years in U.S., 3 children, Christiana,
farmer (4 Mar. - 4 Apr. 1813)

Henry, Patrick, age 27, 21 years in U.S., wife & 9 children,
Christiana, farmer (4 Mar. - 4 Apr. 1813)

Hill, Thomas, age 45, 12 years in U.S., Christiana, farmer (4
Mar. - 4 Apr. 1813)

Hodgson, George, age 30, 8 mos. in U.S., Christiana, machine
maker (23 July - 1 Aug. 1812)

Hodgson, Henry, age 21, 3 mos. in U.S., Christiana, machine maker (4 Mar. - 4 Apr. 1813)

Hodgson, Isaac, age 23, 14 mos. in U.S., Christiana, machine
maker (23 July - 1 Aug. 1812)

Hodgson, Richard, age 18, 8 mos. in U.S., Christiana, machine
maker (4 Mar. - 4 Apr. 1813)

Hodgson, Thomas, age 25, 14 mos. in U.S., Christiana, machine
maker (23 July - 1 Aug. 1812)

Hollers, James, age 40, 8 years in U.S., wife & 4 children, Millcreek, weaver (to 1 Nov. 1813)

Hughes, Francis, age 28, 5 weeks in U.S., Christiana, gunpowder
maker (23 July - 1 Aug. 1812)

Humphreys, Park, age 30, 22 days in U.S., wife, Christiana, labourer (23 July - 1 Aug. 1812)

Jack, James, age 47, 20 years in U.S., wife & 4 children, Wilmington, labourer (16-23 July 1812)

Jackson, George, age 24, 7 years in U.S., Millcreek, farmer (4
Apr. - 17 May 1813)

Jemison, George, age 34, 11 years in U.S., wife, Wilmington, labourer (23 July - 1 Aug. 1812)

Johnson, William, age 24, 13 years in U.S., wife & child, Wilmington, blacksmith (17 May - 1 July 1813)

Johnston, John, age 33, 9 years in U.S., wife & 2 children,
Christiana, farmer (17 May - 1 July 1813)

Jones, Richard, age 28, 12 years in U.S., wife & 2 children,
Christiana, farmer (4 Mar. - 4 Apr. 1813)

Joyce, Penny Wright, age 52, 8 years in U.S., wife & 4 children,
Newcastle, schoolmaster (1-17 Aug. 1812)

Kenning, James, age 36, 15 years in U.S., Christiana, weaver (1-
17 Aug. 1812)

Kerland, James, age 29, 18 mos. in U.S., Brandywine, manufacturer
(to 8 Jan. 1814)

Kerr, David, age 40, 1 year in U.S., Christiana, weaver (17 Aug. -
1 Sept. 1812)

Kirk, James, age 36, 11 years in U.S., wife & 4 children, Brandywine, weaver (23 July - 1 Aug. 1812)

Larkin, John, age 23, 4 years in U.S., iron rotter (to 5 Oct.
1814)

Lees, David, age 20, 5 years in U.S., Brandywine, spinner (23
July - 1 Aug. 1812)

Leonard, Francis, age 25, 3 years in U.S., Christiana, labourer
(17 May - 1 July 1813)

Linch, Hugh, age 27, 10 years in U.S., wife & 3 children, Wilmington, labourer (23 July - 1 Aug. 1812)

Little, William, age 32, 12 mos. in U.S., Brandywine, weaver (17
May - 1 July 1813)

Loughey, Daniel, age 27, 11 years in U.S., Christiana, labourer
(1-17 Aug. 1812)

Loughery, John, age 23, 3 mos. in U.S., Christiana, labourer (1-
17 Aug. 1812)

Lyons, Morty, age 47, 15 years in U.S., 1 child, Millcreek, labourer (1-15 Sept. 1812)

McAgeal, Robert, age 22, 2 years in U.S., Brandywine, spinner (23 July - 1 Aug. 1812)

McAllister, Charles, age 23, 7 mos. in U.S., Wilmington, carpenter (4 Mar. - 4 Apr. 1813)

McBride, Hugh, age 44, 11 years in U.S., wife & 4 children, Newcastle, farmer (15 Sept. - 10 Oct. 1812)

McBride, Patrick, age 28, 12 years in U.S., Millcreek, labourer (1-15 Sept. 1812)

McCabe, James, age 50, 20 years in U.S., 1 daughter, Christiana, labourer (to 5 Oct. 1814)

McCavoy, John, age 27, 1 year in U.S., Brandywine, weaver (23 July - 1 Aug. 1812)

McCredy, Francis, age 27, 5 years in U.S., Appoquimack, storekeeper (4 Apr. - 17 May 1813)

McCurdy, William, age 25, 30 mos. in U.S., Millcreek, blacksmith (to 5 Oct. 1814)

McDermot, Patrick, age 33, 11 mos. in U.S., wife, Christiana, gunpowder maker (23 July - 1 Aug. 1812)

McElmer, George, age 25, 23 years in U.S., Christiana, iron founder (to 5 Oct. 1814)

Macfarlan/McFarlane, Robert, age 30, in U.S. since 2 Mar. 1813, Wilmington, manufacturer (to 4 Mar. 1813); 8 May 1813 ordered to Reading, Pa., but in Oct. permitted to return to Wilmington (28 Dec. 1813)

McFarland, Samuel, age 22, 8 years in U.S., Christiana, machine maker (23 July - 1 Aug. 1812)

McFee, Hugh, age 28, 8 mos. in U.S., wife & child, Christiana, carpenter (17 Aug. - 1 Sept. 1812)

McGar, Patrick, age 25, 4 years in U.S., Christiana, labourer (23 July - 1 Aug. 1812)

McGilligan, Patrick, age 20, 15 mos. in U.S., Millcreek, labourer (1-15 Sept. 1812)

Macguire, Hugh, age 34, 3 years in U.S., Christiana, machinist (to 5 Oct. 1814)

McGulley, John, age 29, 5 years in U.S., Christiana, labourer (23 July - 1 Aug. 1812)

McIntire, Daniel, age 26, 8 mos. in U.S., Brandywine, weaver (23 July - 1 Aug. 1812)

McKeever, Daniel, age 21, 2 years in U.S., Millcreek, labourer (1-15 Sept. 1812)

McKenzie, William, age 28, 6 years & 10 mos. in U.S., Wilmington, millwright (4 Apr. - 17 May 1813)

McMullen, Joseph, age 21, 11 years in U.S., Wilmington, shoemaker (23 July - 1 Aug. 1812)

Macpherson, James, age 21, 9 mos. in U.S., Christiana, weaver (4 Mar - 4 Apr. 1813)

McQuaid, Michael, age 29, 6 years in U.S., Brandywine, weaver (15 Sept. - 10 Oct. 1812)

Magaw, Robert, age 30, 10 years in U.S., wife & 3 children, Christiana, weaver (4 Apr. - 17 May 1813)

Mahaffy, James, age 48, 1 year in U.S., wife, Christiana, machine maker (16-23 July 1812)

Mahaffy, Thomas, age 23, 1 year in U.S., Christiana, machine maker (16-23 July 1812)

Mallen, Thomas, age 25, 1 mo. in U.S., wife, Brandywine, weaver (23 July - 1 Aug. 1812)

Marshall, John, age 35, 10 years in U.S., Christiana, woolen manufacturer (5 Sept. - 10 Oct. 1812)

Matthews, Gilley, age 21, 4 years in U.S., wife & child, Christiana, gunpowder maker (23 July - 1 Aug. 1812)

Mayall, William, age 20, 2 years in U.S., Brandywine, weaver (23 July - 1 Aug. 1812)

Metcalf, Thomas, age 33, 2 years & 10 mos. in U.S., Christiana, cotton spinner (16-23 July 1812)

Miller, Andrew, age 24, 1 year in U.S., wife, Christiana, gunpowder maker (23 July - 1 Aug. 1812)

Miller, Joseph, age 35, 3 weeks in U.S., Lewes, brewer (to 1 Sept. 1813)

Mills, Allen, age 31, 10 years & 6 mos. in U.S., wife & 4 children, Brandywine paper mills, paper maker (16-23 July 1812)

Mitchel, John, age 25, 5 years & 3 mos. in U.S., wife & 1 child, Brandywine, farmer (23-30 July 1812)

Moon, Thomas, age 33, 16 mos. in U.S., Whiteclay Creek, tanner (1-17 Aug. 1812)

Moor, James, age 23, 28 mos. in U.S., Brandywine, weaver (to 5 Oct. 1814)

Morris, John, age 28, 14 or 15 years in U.S., wife, Broadcreek, mariner (to 1 Sept. 1813)

Morrison, Moses, age 22, 8 mos. in U.S., wife, Millcreek, manufacturer (23 July - 1 Aug. 1812)

Morrison, Robert, age 35, 5 years in U.S., wife & child, Wilmington, nail maker (23 July - 1 Aug. 1812)

Morrison, Thomas, age 27, 7 years in U.S., wife & 2 children, Wilmington, drayman (23 July - 1 Aug. 1812)

Mount, John, age 32, 12 years in U.S., wife & 4 children, Christiana, bricklayer (to 5 Oct. 1814)

Murphy, John, age 30, 6 years in U.S., Brandywine, labourer (23 July - 1 Aug. 1812)

Murphy, John, age 25, 7 mos. in U.S., Wilmington, butcher (4 Ma. - 4 Apr. 1813)

Murphy, Patrick, age 26, 6 years in U.S., Christiana, cotton spinner; applied Philadelphia 22 Mar. 1813 (to 8 Jan. 1814)

Murray, John, age 48, 21 years in U.S., wife & child, Millcreek, mason (1-15 Sept. 1812)

Nelson, Dawson, age 18, 6 weeks in U.S., Newcastle, farmer (23 July - 1 Aug. 1812)

Newsom, Robert, age 27, 4 years in U.S., Christiana, turnpike maker (16-23 July 1812)

North, John, age 30, 1 year in U.S., wife & 2 children, Christiana, labourer (23 July - 1 Aug. 1812)

O'Brien, Daniel, age 30, 1 year in U.S., Brandywine, labourer (23 July - 1 Aug. 1812)

Our, David, age 35, 17 years in U.S., Brandywine, cotton manufacturer (1-15 Sept. 1812)

Paget, George, age 34, 2 years in U.S., wife & 4 children, Christiana, gunpowder maker (23 July - 1 Aug. 1812)

Partington, John, age 29, 2 years & 9 mos. in U.S., Brandywine, spinner; applied 19 Oct. 1811 (23 July - 1 Aug. 1812)

Partington, Thomas, age 21, 2 years & 6 mos. in U.S., Christiana, spinner (4 Mar. - 4 Apr. 1813)

Partridge, William, age 35, 4 years & 1 mo. in U.S., wife & 2 children, Brandywine, cloth dyer; applied 3 years & 6 mos. since (16-23 July 1812)

Patterson, James, age 18, 6 years in U.S., Brandywine, weaver (4 Apr. - 17 May 1813)

Patterson, John, age 56, 6 years in U.S., Christiana, weaver (23 July - 1 Aug. 1812)

Patterson, Robert, age 20, 5 years in U.S., Brandywine, weaver (4 Apr. - 17 May 1813)

Patterson, William, age 30, 5 years & 11 mos. in U.S., wife, Christiana, weaver (16-23 July 1812)

Patton, Samuel, age 28, 1 year in U.S., Brandywine, weaver (23 July - 1 Aug. 1812)

Perkins, Nathaniel H. Clifford, age 27, 1 year & 3 mos. in U.S., Brandywine, cloth manufacturer (16 -23 July 1812)

Polk, Alexander, age 33, 17 mos. in U.S., wife & 6 children, Christiana, farmer (17 May - 1 July 1813)

Powell, Evan, age 21, 11 years in U.S., Wilmington, cabinetmaker
   (23 July - 1 Aug. 1812)
Powell, George W., age 22, 11 years in U.S., Brandywine, shear-
   man (23 July - 1 Aug. 1812)
Poyne, William, age 21, 5 years in U.S., Wilmington, shoemaker
   (23 July - 1 Aug. 1812)
Read, Joseph, age 35, 4 years & 1 mo. in U.S., wife & 2 children,
   Wilmington, conveyancer and accountant; applied 2 July 1812
   (16-23 July 1812)
Reed, Henry, age 27, in U.S. since Feb. 1812, wife, Christiana,
   machinist; applied to Judge Scott in Mar. ... (to 5 Oct. 1814)
Reed, William, age 24, 3 years in U.S., Christiana, woolen manu-
   facturer (17 May - 1 July 1813)
Reynolds, Andrew, age 22, 27 mos. in U.S., Millcreek, weaver (to
   5 Oct. 1814)
Reynolds, Roger, age 36, 12 years in U.S., wife & 2 children,
   Newport, labourer; applied 22 July 1801 (17 May - 1 July 1813)
Rogers, Barney, age 45, 13 years in U.S., wife & 2 children in
   Baltimore, Millcreek, labourer (1-15 Sept. 1812)
Rogers, Jonathan, age 27, 12 years in U.S., wife & 2 children,
   Millcreek, woolen manufacturer (4 Apr. - 17 May 1813)
Rogers, Samuel, age 29, 11 years in U.S., wife & child, Millcreek,
   woolen manufacturer (23 July - 1 Aug. 1812)
Ross, George, age 23, 2 years in U.S., Baltimore, mariner (to 1
   Sept. 1813)
Roundtree, Charles, age 33, 6 years in U.S., wife & 3 children,
   Wilmington, trunk maker (16-23 July 1812)
Russel, Hugh, age 40, 6 years in U.S., wife & child, Millcreek,
   weaver (4 Mar. - 4 Apr. 1813)
Savage, William, age 27, 19 mos. in U.S., wife, Whiteclay Creek,
   machinist (to 8 Jan. 1814)
Scott, Alexander, age 30, 9 mos. in U.S., Brandywine, spinner
   (4 Mar. - 4 Apr. 1813)
Scott, John, age 22, 3 years in U.S., Brandywine, shearman (23
   July - 1 Aug. 1812)
Semple, Samuel, age 30, in U.S. since 10 Aug. 1812, wife & child,
   Brandywine, weaver (to 5 Oct. 1814)
Sharkey, James, age 43, 11 years in U.S., wife & child, Chris-
   tiana, turnpike maker (17 Aug. - 1 Sept. 1812)
Sheedy, John, age 55, 12 years in U.S., Wilmington, labourer (23
   July - 1 Aug. 1812)
Shepherd, George, age 25, 11 mos. in U.S., wife & child, Brandy-
   wine, weaver (23 July - 1 Aug. 1812)
Shepherd, Peter, age 24, 1 year in U.S., Christiana, gunpowder
   maker (23 July - 1 Aug. 1812)
Sherwood, John, age 26, 7 years & 11 mos. in U.S., Wilmington,
   hatter (16-23 July 1812 & to 8 Jan. 1814)
Shivilen, Edward, age 24, 2 years in U.S., Christiana, gunpowder
   maker (23 July - 1 Aug. 1812)
Shivilen, John, age 27, 5 years in U.S., Christiana, gunpowder
   maker (23 July - 1 Aug. 1812)
Simpson, James, age 28, 4 years in U.S., wife, Brandywine, cloth
   weaver (23 July - 1 Aug. 1812)
Smith, Charles, age 47, 11 years in U.S., wife & 3 children,
   Stannton, soap boiler (1-17 Aug. 1812)
Smith, David, age 26, 11 years in U.S., Christiana, snuff maker
   (17 Aug. - 1 Sept. 1812)
Smith, John, age 39, 1 year in U.S., Brandywine, weaver (16 -23
   July 1812)
Smyth, John, age 23, 7 mos. in U.S., Brandywine, weaver (23 July -
   1 Aug. 1812)
Steen, George, age 21, 6 years in U.S., Christiana, house- car-
   penter (to 5 Oct. 1814)
Stewart, Charles, age 24, 10 years in U.S., wife & 4 children,
   Millcreek, weaver (to 1 Nov. 1813)

Stirling, John, age 21, 6 mos. in U.S., Christiana, weaver (23
    July - 1 Aug. 1812)
Stirling, Thomas, age 28, 7 years in U.S., wife, Brandywine, wea-
    ver (4 Mar.- 4 Apr. 1813)
Sturgeon, Edward, age 27, 10 years in U.S., wife & 4 children,
    Newcastle, tailor (to 4 Mar. 1813)
Taggert, Robert, age 21, 8 mos. in U.S., Brandywine, weaver (23
    July - 1 Aug. 1812)
Taylor, John, age 50, 12 years in U.S., wife & 6 children, Mill-
    creek, linen weaver (17 Aug. - 1 Sept. 1812)
Taylor, William, age 22, 18 years in U.S., Wilmington, plaisterer
    (23 July - 1 Aug. 1812)
Towit, Michael, age 29, 9 years in U.S., wife & child, Christiana,
    gunpowder maker (23 July - 1 Aug. 1812)
Trimbles, Daniel, age 32, 18 years in U.S., wife & child, Middle-
    ford, Sussex Co., collier (23-30 July 1812)
Turnbull, Adam, age 38, 11 mos. in U.S., wife & 2 children, New-
    castle, farmer (23 July - 1 Aug. 1812)
Vallely, Patrick, age 20, 6 weeks in U.S., wife, Christiana, wea-
    ver (23 July - 1 Aug. 1812)
Wagstaff, Hugh, age 25, 6 mos. in U.S., Christiana, machine maker
    (23 July - 1 Aug. 1812)
Wagstaff, James, age 32, 3 mos. in U.S., wife & 3 children, Wil-
    mington, spindle maker (to 8 Jan. 1814)
Walker, Arthur, age 32, 18 mos. in U.S., wife & child, Christiana,
    blacksmith (4 Mar. - 4 Apr. 1813)
Walker, John, age 53, 9 years in U.S., wife & 4 children, Mill-
    creek, weaver and dyer (to 5 Oct. 1814)
Wallace, George, age 39, 3 years in U.S., Brandywine, weaver (23
    July - 1 Aug. 1812)
Wallace, George, age 32, 11 years in U.S., wife & 2 children,
    Christiana, farmer; applied 22 July 1801 (23 July - 1 Aug. 1812)
Wallace, Moses, age 19, 2 years in U.S., Christiana, farmer (23
    July - 1 Aug. 1812)
Wallace, William, age 29, 2 years & 10 mos. in U.S., Christiana,
    wool spinner (23 July - 1 Aug. 1812)
Wardlow, John, age 23, 4 years in U.S., Christiana, turnpike
    maker (16-23 July 1812)
Weir, Arthur, age 24, 3 mos. in U.S., Brandywine, weaver (23 July -
    1 Aug. 1812)
Weir, Joseph, age 26, 30 mos. in U.S., Christiana, farmer (to 5
    Oct. 1814)
Welsh, Hugh, age 20, 2 years in U.S., Christiana, gunpowder maker
    (23 July - 1 Aug. 1812)
Welsh, John, age 24, 4 years in U.S., Brandywine, dyer (23 July -
    1 Aug. 1812)
Wheeler, John, age 66, 9 years in U.S., Wilmington, iron master;
    applied 18 July 1809 at Philadelphia (to 4 Mar. 1813)
Whiley, William, age 26, 5 years in U.S., Millcreek, weaver (17
    Aug. - 1 Sept. 1812)
White, Alexander, age 34, 12 years in U.S., wife & 3 children,
    Concord, Sussex Co., merchant; applied Apr. term 1800 in Court
    of Common Pleas, Sussex Co. (23-30 July 1812)
Williams, Richard, age 26, 11 years in U.S., wife, Brandywine,
    miller (16-23 July 1812)
Wilson, John, age 30, 1 year in U.S., Stannton, woolen manufac-
    turer (1-17 Aug. 1812)
Wiseman, Timothy, age 38, 13 years in U.S., Wilmington, butcher
    (to 4 Mar. 1813)
Young, George, age 21, 6 weeks in U.S., Christiana, weaver (23
    July - 1 Aug. 1812)
Young, John, age 24, 6 weeks in U.S., Wilmington, weaver (23 July -
    1 Aug. 1812)

PENNSYLVANIA

Adams, John, age 21, in U.S. since 27 Aug. 1811, labourer (25 Mar. 1813)

Adams, Thomas P., age 16, in U.S. since 3 Nov. 1811, 34 North 2nd St., clerk (17 May 1813)

Adams, William, age 30, in U.S. since 18 Sept. 1806, 50 Market St., hatter (2-7 Nov. 1812)

Ahern, Patrick, age 26, in U.S. since 1 July 1810, wife, s.w. corner 10th & Locust Sts., labourer (1-9 Sept. 1814)

Ainsworth, John, age 25, in U.S. since 22 May 1811, Malborough St. at Geo. Jones's, cotton weaver (1-31 Aug. 1814)

Alcorn, James, age 23, in U.S. since 15 June 1812, Vine, near Schuylkill 2nd St., weaver (22 Mar. 1813)

Alcorn, Robert, age 22, in U.S. since 3 May 1812, Pennsylvania Hospital, cell keeper (1-31 Aug. 1814)

Aldred, John, age 31, in U.S. since 15 June 1811, Germantown, weaver (20 Mar. 1813)

Alexander, James, age 34, in U.S. since Aug. 1792, wife & 2 children, Ridge Road near 1st turnpike gate, ladies' shoemaker (1-9 Sept. 1814)

Alexander, William, age 28, 6 years in U.S., Haverford, Delaware Co., gunpowder manufacturer (28 Apr. 1813)

Allen, William, age 30, in U.S. since May 1799, wife, 356 South 2nd St., mariner (23 Mar. 1813)

Allicant, Antonia (black man), age 25, in U.S. since 19 June 1814, mariner, deserter from _Albion_ 74 (30 June 1814)

Allison, Robert, age 26, in U.S. since 15 Nov. 1810, Bussleton, Phila. Co., wool-spinner (20 Mar. 1813)

Anderson, Alexander, age 22, in U.S. since Aug. 1808, 250 South 2nd St., storekeeper (23 July 1812)

Anderson, Clark, age 29, in U.S. since 29 Aug. 1808, wife and 3 children, 148 South St., M.D. (22 Mar. 1813)

Anderson, John, age 26, 2 years in U.S., Germantown, carpenter (25 July 1812)

Anderson, Thomas, age 18, in U.S. since 12 Nov. 1810, Lemond St., silver-plater (22 Mar. 1813)

Anderson, William, age 46, in U.S. since 4 Aug. 1801, wife and 4 children, Northern Liberties, Phila. Co., labourer (23 Mar. 1813)

Anderson, William, age 17, in U.S. since 10 Nov. 1810, corner Lemon & 8th Sts., silver-plater (26 Mar. 1813)

Andrews, John P., age 20, in U.S. since 22 Aug. 1812, 98 Market St., accountant (7-12 Dec. 1812)

Andrews, Joseph, age 47, in U.S. since 22 Oct. 1808, wife & one child, Sansom St., teacher (16 Mar. 1813)

Andrews, William Lyons, age 23, 10 mos. in U.S., 98 Market St., accountant; applied 17 June 1812 (25 July 1812)

Armstrong, William, age 28, in U.S. since 20 Aug. 1814, Phila., sailor (1-9 Sept. 1814)

Arthur, James, age 34, in U.S. since 1807, 2 North 10th St., storekeeper (22 Mar. 1813)

Arthur, Samuel, age 34, in U.S. since 1 Sept. 1803, Wm. Adgate's, 2 North 10th St., labourer (1-31 Aug. 1814)

Ashurst, Richard, age 29, in U.S. since 3 Aug. 1805, wife and 3 children, 76 Market St., trader; applied 8 July 1808 (31 May 1813)

Attewell, Francis, age 23, in U.S. since 6 July 1811, 1 Swanson St., tailor; wishes to leave U.S. as soon as convenient (20 July 1812)

Aubert, Peter, age 29, in U.S. since 19 Aug. 1810, Holmesburg, Phila. Co., wool-comber (10-14 Nov. 1812)

Bailey, Francis, age 26, in U.S. since 14 May 1807, 217 South St., distiller; applied 20 Sept. 1811 (22 Mar. 1813)

Bailey, James, age 31, in U.S. since Jan. 1784, Christian, below
10th St., coachman (3C Jan. 1814)

Baker, James, age 22, in U.S. since 19 June 1814, mariner, deserter from Albion 74 (30 June 1814)

Bald, Robert, age 28, in U.S. since 15 Feb. 1809, 25 North 9th
St., accomptant (20 July 1812)

Balderston, James, age 35, in U.S. since 20 Oct. 1810, at Bus-
kins's, Germantown, clothier (1-9 Sept. 1814)

Balf, Luke, age 22, in U.S. since Aug. 1810, 67 Dock St., shoemaker (22 Mar. 1813)

Balfe, Thomas, age 26, in U.S. since 4 Sept. 1810, wife & child,
55 South 5th St., bootmaker (26 Mar. 1813)

Ball, William, age 28, in U.S. since 1 Aug. 1798, wife, Eagles-
ville, Blockley Twp., coachman (21 July 1812)

Bamford, Joseph, age 39, in U.S. since 1 June 1805, wife and 5
children, 5 Filbert St., machine maker; applied 1 Apr. 1810
(25 July 1812)

Barber, Thomas, age 19, in U.S. since 12 May 1812, Market, 4th
from Schuylkill, weaver (20 Mar. 1813)

Barnard, William, age 23, 9 years in U.S., Phila., servant (1-31
Aug. 1814)

Barnes, Robert, age 29, in U.S. since 5 Nov. 1797, wife, 30 Chatham, Phila. Co., mariner (7-12 Dec. 1812)

Barnet, Edward, age 56, in U.S. since 22 Feb. 1806, 152 South
4th St., attorney-at-law; applied 11 June 1811 (22 Mar. 1813)

Barnett, Joseph, age 26, in U.S. since 14 May 1807, 244 South
3rd St., carter (17 Mar. 1813)

Barnett, Thomas, age 24, in U.S. since 28 Sept. 1805, North Christian St,, weaver (7-12 Dec. 1812)

Barnhurst, Joseph, age 30, in U.S. since Aug. 1811, wife & two
children, Currant Alley, Locust St., dye sinker (25 July 1812)

Barnhurst, Thomas, age 39, in U.S. since Aug. 1811, wife and two
children, Currant Alley, Locust St., copper plate maker (25
July 1812)

Barrett, George N., age 18, in U.S. since 20 Oct. 1796, 23 South
10th St., comedian (20 Mar. 1813)

Bartley, James, age 29, 2½ years in U.S., wife & 4 children, 5th
St. from Schuylkill, labourer (20-25 July 1812)

Bates, John, age 23, in U.S. since 1 June 1802, North Water St.,
baker; applied 29 June 1812 (11 Apr. 1814)

Baxter, William, age 22, in U.S. since Feb. 1811, Bustletown,
weaver (6 June 1814)

Beaumount, Thomas, age 39, in U.S. 2 years & 4 mos., wife and 2
children, Phila., comedian; applied 27 Sept. 1811 (27 Mar. 1813)

Beddell, John, age 41, in U.S. since May 1805, wife, Arch, near
3rd St,, skin-dresser (22 Mar. 1813)

Beerman, John Henry, age 30, in U.S. since 16 Apr. 1811, wife &
child, corner 4th Chesnut from Schuylkill, haircloth weaver
(20 July 1812)

Bell, James, age 25, in U.S. since Oct. 1810, 230 South 6th St.,
distiller (22 Mar. 1813)

Bell, John, age 33, in U.S. since Dec. 1809, 126 South 5th St.,
weaver; applied 11 Nov. 1812 (10 Jan. 1814)

Bell, Thomas, age 23, in U.S. since 13 May 1812, Holmesburgh,
Phila. Co., cotton-spinner (22 Mar. 1813)

Benner, John, age 30, in U.S. since 14 Oct. 1809, wife and child,
Spruce St. near Schuylkill, chemist (2-7 Nov. 1812)

Bennett, Uzziel, age 21, in U.S. since 17 June 1811, Filbert,
between 10th & 11th Sts., labourer (26 Mar. 1813)

Berry, John, age 23, in U.S. since 23 Mar. 1811, 62 Dock St.,
shoemaker (1-31 Aug. 1814)

Best, John, age 25, in U.S. since 9 July 1810, wife & 2 children,
Traquair's Court between 10th & Filbert Sts., labourer (19 Mar.
1813)

Biddle, Daniel, age 32, in U.S. since fall of 1803, wife & child, Front, between Race & Vine Sts., No. 185, mariner; applied 22 Sept. 1809 (25 July 1812)

Bigford, Samuel, age 25, in U.S. since 14 Aug. 1806, 21 Walnut St., shoemaker (22 Mar. 1813)

Bignell, John, age 20, in U.S. since 18 Apr. 1807, Race above 2nd St., hatter (28 Mar. 1814)

Black, James, age 28, 16 years in U.S., 94 Spruce St., plasterer (20 July 1812)

Blair, William, age 23, in U.S. since 29 July 1806, East Bradford Twp., Chester Co., labourer (22 Dec. 1812)

Blayney, William, age 47, 4 years in U.S., wife & 3 children, Germantown, Phila. Co., manufacturer (22 July 1812)

Bleakley, Matthew, age 23, 4 years in U.S., Locust, between 8th & 9th Sts., house-carpenter (21 July 1812)

Blinn, John, age 24, in U.S. since 31 May 1806, wife & 2 children, Penn St. near South, biscuit maker (1-31 Aug. 1814)

Bodkin, George, age 23, in U.S. since 3 May 1812, 13th St., between Pine & South Sts. (25 Mar. 1813)

Bogan, John, age 29, in U.S. since 15 Apr. 1806, Wilson & Taylor's factory, Falls of Schuylkill, manufacturer (1-9 Sept. 1814)

Boon, John, age 34, in U.S. since 31 Oct. 1800, wife & 2 children, 338 South Front St., dealer in rope, etc. (22 Mar. 1813)

Bordman, John, age 23, in U.S. since 15 June 1806, wife & child, Frankford, hatter; applied 24 Mar. 1813 (24 Mar. 1813)

Borland, John, age 21, in U.S. since 9 June 1812, corner 5th & Prune Sts., coachman (19 Mar. 1813)

Bottomley, Isaac, age 35, in U.S. since 19 Oct. 1799, Concord Twp., Delaware Co., woolen manufacturer (27 Apr. 1813)

Bottomley, Thomas, age 43, in U.S. since 26 Oct. 1810, Aston Twp., Delaware Co., woolen manufacturer (27 Apr. 1813)

Bowden, William, age 28, in U.S. since 25 Mar. 1810, wife & two children, 28 Little Water St., mariner (26 Mar. 1813)

Boyd, Hugh, age 46, in U.S. since 15 Dec. 1809, wife & 2 children, Germantown Road, N.L., grocer (25 Mar. 1813)

Boyle, Bernard, age 35, in U.S. since Oct. 1810, corner 6th & 8th Sts., grocer (20 July 1812)

Boyle, Patrick, age 24, 3½ years in U.S., wife, Catharine St., between 4th & 5th Sts., labourer (20 July 1812)

Boyle, Peter, age 30, in U.S. since 1 Nov. 1811, Blockley Twp., Phila. Co., labourer (2-7 Nov. 1812)

Bradford, William, age 36, in U.S. since 7 July 1803, wife and 5 children, Germantown, stocking-weaver (22 Mar. 1813)

Bradley, James, age 25, in U.S. since 18 May 1812, Callowhill, between 8th & 9th Sts., labourer (23 Mar. 1813)

Bradley, James, age 23, in U.S. since 1811, Nitre-Hall Mills, powder maker (6 Dec. 1813)

Bradley, John, age 30, in U.S. since 27 July 1801, wife, 295 South 3rd St., tailor (17 May 1813)

Bradshaw, Thomas, age 31, in U.S. since 10 Jan. 1801, wife and 2 children, 72 Christian St., mariner (25 Mar. 1813)

Bray, John, age 30, in U.S. since 5 Oct. 1805, wife & 3 children, 4 Elizabeth St., comedian (22 Mar. 1813)

Bridge, James, age 25, in U.S. since 19 Oct. 1811, 205 South 5th St., teacher (20 Mar. 1813)

Brien, James, age 21, in U.S. since 13 Sept. 1811, wife, Blockley Twp., Phila. Co., labourer (17 Nov. 1812)

Britton, Hugh, age 22, in U.S. since Nov. 1810, Falls of Schuylkill Wire Factory, wire drawer (1-9 Sept. 1814)

Brodill, Edward, age 25, in U.S. since 28 Oct. 1809, wife, Cox's Alley & Southwark, carpenter (22 Mar. 1813)

Brogan, Thomas, age 33, in U.S. since 12 Aug. 1811, Arch St. near 7th St., labourer (23 Mar. 1813)

Brooks, Francis, age 40, in U.S. since 14 May 1812, Northern Liberties, weaver (10-14 Nov. 1812)

Brown, Andrew, age 22, in U.S. since 25 Aug. 1798, 134 South 2nd St., cabinetmaker (1-31 Aug. 1814)
Brown, James, age 25, in U.S. since 17 Oct. 1811, Broad St. near New Market, cotton weaver (1-9 Sept. 1814)
Brown, John, age 28, in U.S. since July 1801, 77 Dock St., shoemaker (22 Mar. 1813)
Brown, John, age 26, in U.S. since 17 Nov. 1811, wife, Arch St., gentleman; applied 21 Jan. 1812 (24 Mar. 1813)
Brown, John, age 25, in U.S. since Aug. 1813, Falls of Schuylkill, labourer (1-9 Sept. 1814)
Brown, John, age 24, in U,S. since 10 Dec. 1810, Falls of Schuylkill, Phila. Co., farmer (10-14 Nov. 1812)
Brown, John, age 19, 2 years in U.S., Germantown, weaver (25 July 1812)
Brown, Robert, age 28, in U.S. since 29 Sept. 1810, 6 Prospect Alley, between Arch & Filbert Sts., stone cutter (1-31 Aug. 1814)
Brown, Stephen, age 26, 3 years in U.S., 70 South 2nd St., straw hat manufacturer (25 July 1812)
Brown, William, age 27, in U.S. since 25 Sept. 1808; wife & child, Noble St., tanner (1-31 Aug. 1814)
Brown, William, age 19, 2 years in U.S., Germantown, weaver (25 July 1812)
Brown, Wilson, age 21, 2 years in U.S., Germantown, weaver (25 July 1812)
Brownlee, William Craig, age 28, in U.S. since 21 Sept. 1808, wife & 2 children, 215 Lombard St., clergyman (15 Mar. 1813)
Buchanan, William, age 35, in U.S. since 4 July 1801, wife & 1 child, Upper Chichester Twp., Delaware Co., labourer (5 June 1813)
Bucknall, Benjamin, age 51, in U.S. since 10 Oct. 1811, wife & 3 children, 125 Chesnut St., japanner (21 July 1812)
Bucknall, James, age 24, in U.S. since 1 June 1811, 127 Chesnut St., japanner (23 July 1812)
Budin, Robert, age 22, in U.S. since 28 June 1811, 63 North 10th St., stone cutter (1-9 Sept. 1814)
Burnett, John, age 26, in U.S. since 3 July 1807, 132 North Water St., mariner (1 June 1813)
Burrows, John, age 35, in U.S. since 20 Apr. 1810, wife, Walnut St. between 2nd and Front Sts., clerk (22 Mar. 1813)
Burt, John, age 18, in U.S. since 31 Oct. 1810, Phila., clerk (1-31 Aug. 1814)
Burton, John, age 47, in U.S. since 1 July 1811, Blockley Twp., Phila. Co., woolen manufacturer (27 Nov. 1812)
Byrne, Patrick, age 22, in U.S. since 22 June 1807, 330 Market St., painter & glazier, served apprenticeship in Phila. (22 July 1812)
Caddow, Hugh, age 22, in U.S. since 4 Sept. 1810, wife, 5 Green-Leaf Alley, saddler (19 Mar. 1813)
Cain, Andrew, age 20, in U.S. since 12 Dec. 1803, Whitin Twp., Chester Co., with Wm. Couch, blacksmith (1-9 Sept. 1814)
Calahan, John, age 25, in U.S. since 23 Apr. 1814, shoemaker (23 May 1814)
Calver, James, age 35, in U.S. since 20 Mar. 1799, wife and two children, Phila., carpenter (1-31 Aug. 1814)
Campbell, Angus, age 21, in U.S. since 12 Oct. 1811, Springfield, Delaware Co., labourer (2-7 Nov. 1812)
Campbell, Eneas, age 40, in U.S. since 7 Aug. 1812, Phila., sawyer (1-31 Aug. 1814)
Campbell, James, age 35, in U.S. since 20 May 1806, wife and two children, 42 Plumb St., morocco-dresser (23 Mar. 1813)
Campbell, James, age 25, in U.S. since 1 Nov. 1807, wife, 202 South 3rd St., coachman (23 Nov. 1812)
Campbell, James, age 19, in U.S. since 1 June 1812, Lower Blockley, Phila. Co., farmer (18 Mar. 1813)

Campbell, John, age 28, in U.S. since 27 Sept. 1805, 10th St.,
stone cutter (7-12 Dec. 1812)
Campbell, Patrick, age 30, in U.S. since 17 Dec. 1811, wife & 3
children, 111 Plumb St., tailor (22 Mar. 1813)
Campbell, Walter, age 18, in U.S. since Dec. 1803, South near
3rd St., cordwainer (28 Nov. 1812)
Cane, James, age 28, in U.S. since 1 Nov. 1811, wife, corner
Shippen & 7th Sts., labourer (24 May 1813)
Cannon, William, age 24, in U.S. since 2 Aug. 1810, wife & child,
4th St. between Union & Spruce Sts., coachman (19 Mar. 1813)
Cantwell, William, age 19, in U.S. since 17 July 1812, 34 Callow-
hill St., clerk; he reported to marshal of District of Mass.
on 30 July 1812 (10-14 Nov. 1812)
Capper, John, age 28, in U.S. since 15 Apr. 1811, 113 North 8th
St., baker (7-12 Dec. 1812)
Carlile, Hudson, age 28, 4½ years in U.S., wife & 2 children,
corner Spruce & 8th Sts., labourer (20 July 1812)
Carmichael, John, age 20, in U.S. since 28 Oct. 1811, Hopkins's
Court, N.L., cotton-spinner (25 Mar. 1813)
Carr, Charles, age 39, in U.S. since 3 July 1801, wife, South St.
between 2nd & George Sts., hostler (23 Mar. 1813)
Carson, George, age 52, in U.S. since 6 Sept. 1794, wife, 101
South St., shoemaker (25 Mar. 1813)
Carson, John, age 23, in U.S. since 22 June 1807, Germantown,
weaver (25 Mar. 1813)
Carson, William, age 26, in U.S. since 15 Aug. 1807, wife & child,
South St., weaver (17 Mar. 1813)
Carter, John, age 52, in U.S. since 6 May 1809, wife & 4 children,
3 Carlisle Court, coachman; applied 15 June 1812 (21 July 1812)
Carusi, Gaetano, age 52, in U.S. since 26 Sept. 1809, wife and 3
children, Phila., musician (1-31 Aug. 1814)
Carvin, James, age 24, in U.S. since 25 June 1810, 144 Lombard
St., weaver (15 Mar. 1813)
Caskey, James, age 19, in U.S. since 17 Sept. 1811, 214 Arch St.,
printer (1-9 Sept. 1812)
Cassady, Hugh, age 26, in U.S. since 14 Aug. 1808, 5 North 5th
St., bottler (19 Mar. 1813)
Cassady, James, age 32, in U.S. since 11 Aug. 1812, wife & three
children, corner Walnut & 11th Sts., labourer (19 Mar. 1813)
Cassady, Patrick, age 23, in U.S. since 16 Aug. 1806, Arch St.
between 9th & 10th Sts., labourer (22 Mar. 1813)
Cassady, Patrick, age 23, in U.S. since 4 Aug. 1811, Front St.
above South St., porter (20 Mar. 1813)
Cassedy, Andrew, age 15, in U.S. since 1811, Nitre-Hall Mills,
powder maker (6 Dec. 1813)
Cassedy, Robert, age 30, 6 years in U.S., Haverford Twp., Dela-
ware Co., gunpowder manufacturer (28 Apr. 1813)
Cassedy, William, age 18, in U.S. since 1811, Nitre-Hall Mills,
powder maker (6 Dec. 1813)
Cathcart, Gabriel, age 21, in U.S. since 17 June 1812, North
Front St., engineer (2-7 Nov. 1812)
Catherwood, Hugh, age 23, in U.S. since 8 Nov. 1811, 217 South
St., labourer (1-9 Sept. 1814)
Catherwood, Robert, age 24, in U.S. since 24 Aug. 1810, 118 North
7th St., grocer (2-7 Nov. 1812)
Chesnut, William, age 29, 4 years & 8 mos. in U.S., 280 Market
St., grocer (24 July 1812)
Childs, Charles, age 35, in U.S. since 1 Oct. 1810, wife and 5
children, Fayette St. between 9th & 10th Sts., labourer (19
Mar. 1813)
Christie, William, age 31, in U.S. since 6 Sept. 1801, Mansion
House Hotel, clerk (24 July 1812)
Christy, Archibald, age 30, in U.S. since 31 Aug. 1811, wife &
child, East Bradford Twp., Chester Co., labourer (12 Dec. 1812)

Clare, Bartholomew, age 26, 2 years & 8 mos. in U.S., 15 Race
St., storekeeper (20 July 1812)
Clark, John, age 27, in U.S. since 1800, wife, Queen St. between
2nd & 3rd Sts., rigger (23 Mar. 1813)
Clark, Patrick, age 28, in U.S. since 1811, Nitre-Hall Mills,
powder maker (6 Dec. 1813)
Clark, William, age 22, in U.S. since 3 May 1811 (1-9 Sept. 1814)
Clarke, Edward, age 34, 11 years in U.S., wife, child & 2 servants,
92 North 7th St., teacher (24 July 1812)
Closey, Webb, age 25, in U.S. since June 1812, 61 South 2nd St.,
shoemaker (2-7 Nov. 1812)
Coal, Thomas, age 38, in U.S. since 20 June 1807, wife and four
children, Market St. near Schuylkill, shoemaker (20 Mar. 1813)
Coburn, Robert, age 26, in U.S. since 24 Aug. 1811, upper end of
Catharine St. and Passyunk Road, distiller (16 Nov. 1812)
Coleman, James, age 24, 1 year & 9 mos. in U.S., 7 South Wharves,
storekeeper (20 July 1812)
Collins, John, age 32, in U.S. since 15 Mar. 1809, Kensington,
Hanover St. at Mrs. Anderson's near Frankford Road, plasterer
(1-31 Aug. 1814)
Colvin, James, age 26, in U.S. since 1806, 2 North 10th St.,
paver (20 Mar. 1813)
Connell, Darby, age 23, in U.S. since 31 Aug. 1811, 236 South
St., carter (22 Mar. 1813)
Connelly, Henry, age 27, in U.S. since 7 Sept. 1810, corner 10th
& South Sts., type founder (25 July 1812)
Conner, James, age 30, in U.S. since 25 Aug. 1807, wife & child,
Lower Blockley Twp., Phila. Co., labourer (17 Mar. 1813)
Connery, John, age 37, in U.S. since 6 June 1803, wife and two
children, 4th near Spruce St., cabinetmaker (22 Mar. 1813)
Connor, James, age 25, 1 year in U.S., 5 Quarry St., soap boiler
(20-25 July 1812)
Conry, Michael, age 30, in U.S. since 13 July 1810, wife & child,
Loxley Court between Front & 2nd Sts., labourer (25 Mar. 1813)
Conway, Patrick, age 25, 6 years in U.S., corner Gaskill & Geo.
Sts., dry good merchant (20-25 July 1812)
Cooper, Charles, age 29, in U.S. since 4 July 1805, wife & child,
corner Catharine & Front Sts., copperplate maker (20 Mar. 1813)
Cornelius, Isaiah, age 22, in U.S. since Aug. 1795, Lombard near
6th St., shoemaker (22 Mar. 1813)
Couden, Joseph, age 21, in U.S. since 24 Aug. 1808, Juniper St.
between Market & Chesnut Sts., stone cutter (25 Mar. 1813)
Courtney, Thomas, age 25, in U.S. since 27 Aug. 1808, Water near
Race St., dealer (22 Mar. 1813)
Cowden, John, age 23, in U.S. since 14 Aug. 1808, wife, Locust
between 10th & 11th Sts., weaver (26 Mar. 1813)
Cowden, Robert, age 25, in U.S. since 26 Aug. 1806, wife and two
children, Blockley, Phila. Co., weaver; applied 13 Apr. 1813
(1-9 Sept. 1814)
Cox, John, age 33, in U.S. since 16 Sept. 1812, mother and four
sisters, corner of 6th and South Sts., labourer (1-9 Sept. 1814)
Cox, William, age 30, in U.S. since 25 May 1804, wife & 3 children,
corner Brown & St. John Sts., Northern Liberties, chair-maker
(22 July 1812)
Coyle, John, age 21, 9 mos. in U.S., 306 South 3rd St., teacher
of languages (21 July 1812)
Craig, John, age 30, in U.S. since 14 May 1807, wife & child,
283 North 3rd St., nail-cutter (25 Mar. 1813)
Crawford, John, age 51, in U.S. since 14 July 1812, Lower Blockley Twp., Phila. Co., labourer (19 Mar. 1813)
Creighton, Fletcher, age 19, in U.S. since 2 June 1812, 308 High
St., saddler (20 Mar. 1813)
Crockett, George, age 23, in U.S. since 2 Sept. 1811, 34 North
2nd St., accomptant (17 May 1813)

Cronin, Stephen, age 30, in U.S. since 10 May 1811, South 4th
between Spruce & Pine Sts., coachman (19 Mar. 1813)
Crossin, James, age 30, in U.S. since Sept. 1809, 3rd near Plumb
St., bricklayer (22 Mar. 1813)
Crumbley, William, age 25, in U.S. since 28 Aug. 1808, wife and
child, Locust & Spruce between 11th & 12th Sts., Prosperous
Alley, copperplate printer (1-9 Sept. 1814)
Curran, Thomas, age 20, 2 years & 1 mo. in U.S., 37 South Water
St., accomptant (20-25 July 1812)
Currey, Lawrence, age 32, in U.S. since 9 Sept. 1810, Holmsburgh,
Phila. Co., farmer (15 Mar. 1813)
Currin, Michael, age 24, in U.S. since 29 Aug. 1811, Walnut above
13th St., labourer (23 Mar. 1813)
Darragh, William, age 23, in U.S. since 17 Sept. 1807, corner
10th & Locust Sts., farmer (12 Dec. 1812)
Davenport, John, age 34, in U.S. since 1 Oct. 1803, wife and 5
children, 155 North 6th St., news-carrier (2-7 Nov. 1812)
Davidson, John, age 21, 8 Carters Alley, weaver (1-9 Sept. 1814)
Davis, William, age 35, in U.S. since 15 July 1807, wife and 3
children, 227 South St., carpenter (22 Mar. 1813)
Davis, William, age 31, in U.S. since 12 June 1810, wife, Scha-
kespear, Chesnut St., bookbinder (1-9 Sept. 1814)
Dean, Joseph, age 26, in U.S. since 15 June 1811, Blockley Twp.,
woolen manufacturer (22 Mar. 1813)
De Luce, Nathaniel, age 20, 10 mos. in U.S., corner Minor & 6th
Sts., professor of music (21 July 1812)
Denny, Dennis, age 32, in U.S. since 16 July 1809, 2 children,
Pine Alley, 2 doors from 4th St., labourer (1-9 Sept. 1814)
Dent, John, age 42, in U.S. since Oct. 1806, wife, between Mar-
ket & Chesnut Sts. near Schuylkill, hair manufacturer (16 Nov.
1812)
Denton, Gideon, age 25, in U.S. since 22 July 1805, 213 Race St.,
shoemaker (21 Mar. 1814)
Devitt, Thomas, age 23, in U.S. since 25 Oct. 1811, corner Penn
& Pine Sts., dealer (22 Mar. 1813)
Dickson, Thomas, age 27, in U.S. since 10 June 1811, wife & child,
Lombard St., between 11th & 12th Sts., ink manufacturer (17
Mar. 1813)
Dillan, James, age 26, 12 years in U.S., wife & 4 children, Hurst
St., copperplate printer (20-25 July 1812)
Dodamede, Thomas, age 24, in U.S. since 19 Nov. 1810, Water St.
between Walnut & Spruce Sts., mariner (25 July 1812)
Donaughey, John, age 21, in U.S. since 9 Nov. 1811, Northern Li-
berties, weaver (10-14 Nov. 1812)
Donaughy, Raler, age 23, in U.S. since 29 May 1807, corner 9th
and Vine Sts., iron founder (20 Mar. 1813)
Donley, James, age 33, 8 years in U.S., wife & 5 children, 77
North 5th St., stone paver; applied 10 Oct. 1811 (21 July 1812)
Donnelly, Hugh, age 24, in U.S. since Dec. 1811, corner South &
6th Sts., weaver (23 Mar. 1813)
Donnelly, Terrence, age 30, in U.S. since 20 Nov. 1810, 25 South
2nd St., trader (20 July 1812)
Dool, William, age 21, in U.S. since 2 May 1812, Falls of Schuyl-
kill, wire drawer (1-9 Sept. 1814)
Dougherty, Daniel, age 34, in U.S. since 16 July 1801, wife and
3 children, Falls of Schuylkill, wire drawer (1-9 Sept. 1814)
Dougherty, Hugh, age 24, in U.S. since 4 July 1810, Hartford Twp.,
Delaware Co., cotton spinner (15 Mar. 1813)
Dougherty, John, age 40, in U.S. since 8 July 1812, wife and two
children, Penn Twp., Phila. Co., farmer (1-9 Sept. 1814)
Dougherty, John, age 31, in U.S. since Nov. 1801, wife & 2 child-
ren, Kensington, Hanover St., labourer (1-9 Sept. 1814)
Dougherty, John, age 30, in U.S. since 20 June 1811, wife, Lower
Blockley Twp., Phila. Co., labourer (18 Mar. 1813)

Dougherty, Michael, age 40, in U.S. since July 1799, wife and 4
children, Kensington, fisherman (1-9 Sept. 1814)
Dougherty, William, age 32, in U.S. since 5 Aug. 1811, wife and
2 children, Falls of Schuylkill, wire drawer (1-9 Sept. 1814)
Dougherty, William, age 29, in U.S. since 13 June 1807, wife &
2 children, Washington St., labourer; applied 15 Oct. 1811
(15 Mar. 1813)
Dougherty, William, age 29, in U.S. since 5 Aug. 1812, wife & 2
children, Blockley Twp., Phila. Co., wire drawer (24 Mar. 1813)
Douglas, James, age 24, in U.S. since 18 Sept. 1809, Gaskill be-
tween 3rd & 4th Sts., accomptant; applied 20 Oct. 1810 (20 July
1812)
Dove, William, age 29, in U.S. since 27 Mar. 1806, corner Catha-
rine & Front Sts., labourer (27 Mar. 1813)
Downs, Thomas, age 28, in U.S. since 2 Sept. 1807, back of 12
Spruce St., sand-man (7-12 Dec. 1812)
Doyle, James, age 28, in U.S. since 1812, at Mr. Graham's in 13th
St. near Smith St., baker (1-9 Sept. 1814)
Doyle, James, age 22, in U.S. since 5 July 1811, wife, Spruce
St. above 10th St., shoemaker (20 Mar. 1813)
Doyle, Walter, age 32, in U.S. since 1 Aug. 1801, housekeeper,
357 Arch St., soap boiler (22 July 1812)
Drake, William, age 44, in U.S. since 7 Oct. 1809, wife & seven
children, Germantown, woolen manufacturer (20 Mar. 1813)
Drayton, James Thomas, age 35, in U.S. since 23 June 1811, 16
North 6th St., umbrella maker; applied 13 Apr. 1812 (20 July
1812)
Drips, Mathew, age 33, in U.S. since 21 Aug. 1807, wife & child,
Cherry Alley, between 13th & Juniper Sts., weaver (1-9 Sept.
1814)
Dugan, Michael, age 46, in U.S. since 20 Nov. 1802, corner 13th
and Walnut Sts., dealer (27 Nov. 1812)
Dugan, Patrick, age 32, in U.S. since 27 July, wife & child, 8th
St. from Schuylkill, between Race & Vine Sts., stone mason (1-
9 Sept. 1814)
Dunbar, Mathew, age 26, in U.S. since 14 May 1807, wife & child,
18 Filbert St., stone cutter (22 Mar. 1813)
Duncan, John, age 30, in U.S. since 1 May 1812, wife & 2 children,
George St. between 12th & 13th Sts., labourer (1-9 Sept. 1814)
Duncan, William, age 31, in U.S. since 1 Aug. 1808, wife & two
children, Sugar Alley, two doors above 6th St., drayman (1-9
Sept. 1814)
Dunlap, William, age 43, in U.S. since Sept. 1798, wife, Fitz-
water St., between 6th & 7th Sts., labourer (26 Mar. 1813)
Dunn, Robert, age 27, in U.S. since 23 Jan. 1811, wife, Prune St.,
principal of a military academy; applied 23 Jan. 1811; is now
married to an American lady (20 July 1812)
Dutton, John, age 35, in U.S. since 20 Sept. 1808, 164 South 6th
St., shoemaker; applied 22 June 1812 (5 Dec. 1812)
Dyster, Joseph Joshua, age 44, in U.S. since 5 May 1809, wife,
229 Arch St., bridge architect; applied 2 June 1809 (22 July
1812)
Eaden, William, age 25, in U.S. since 8 Sept. 1810, wife & child,
208 Market St., grocer (18 Mar. 1813)
Eakins, James, age 25, in U.S. since 2 Aug. 1803, wife & 2 child-
ren, between Market & Arch Sts. from Schuylkill, labourer (20
Mar. 1813)
Earp, George, age 25, in U.S. since Oct. 1794, 252 South 2nd St.,
storekeeper (23 July 1812)
Earp, Robert, age 23, in U.S. since Oct. 1794, 170 Market St.,
clerk (23 July 1812)
Egar, Thomas, age 23, in U.S. since 12 June 1812, Vine near
Schuylkill, 2nd St., weaver (22 Mar. 1813)
Elliot, Samuel, age 24, in U.S. since 17 Oct. 1809, wife & two
children, Broad St. labourer (2-7 Nov. 1812)

Ellis, Hugh, age 34, in U.S. since 17 Aug. 1804, wife and two children, 239 Market St., silver plater; applied 30 Apr. 1811 (24 July 1812)

Ellis, Richard, age 29, in U.S. since 28 July 1810, 383 Race St., manufacturer; applied 20 Oct. 1810 (23 Mar. 1813)

England, William, age 22, in U.S. since 8 May 1812, 170 3rd St., groom (22 Mar. 1813)

English, Edward, age 32, 3 years in U.S., wife & 3 children, 8 South St., grocer (21 July 1812)

Ennis, Michael Lewis, age 32, 11 years in U.S., 44 Spruce St., carpenter (20 July 1812)

Esler, James, age 32, in U.S. since 22 July 1807, wife & child, 236 South St., grocer (22 Mar. 1813)

Ester, Robert, age 22, in U.S. since 8 Nov. 1810, 8 Elizabeth's Alley, tailor (2-7 Nov. 1812)

Evans, Thomas, age 40, in U.S. since 18 July 1801, wife and six children, Kensington, carpenter; applied 25 Mar. 1813 (26 Mar. 1813)

Evenden, Thomas Loud, age 50, in U.S. since 9 Oct. 1811, wife, 88 North 5th St., pianoforte maker; part of his family is in Europe (24 July 1812)

Evers, Thomas, age 27, in U.S. since 19 June 1814, mariner, a deserter from Albion 74 (30 June 1814)

Ewing, Robert, age 22, in U.S. since 1 Aug. 1809, corner 6th & Chesnut Sts., labourer (26 Mar. 1813)

Ewing, William, age 28, in U.S. since Sept. 1809, Chestnut near Schuylkill, 6th St., blacksmith (22 Mar. 1813)

Farley, John, age 24, in U.S. since 26 June 1811, 250 Arch St., waiter (18 Mar. 1813)

Farquer, Francis, age 27, in U.S. since 15 Aug. 1803, wife and 2 children, 26 Spruce St., bricklayer (23 Mar. 1813)

Farquer, William, age 30, in U.S. since 15 Aug. 1803, wife and 3 children, 26 Spruce St., labourer (23 Mar. 1813)

Farrell, Francis, age 43, in U.S. since 16 June 1810, wife and daughter, Love Lane, schoolmaster; applied 22 June 1812 (21 Jan. 1814)

Farren, James, age 27, in U.S. since 2 June 1811, Germantown Road, labourer (22 Mar. 1813)

Farron, John, age 19, in U.S. since 4 Aug. 1811, Falls of Schuylkill, wire drawer (1-9 Sept. 1814)

Faulkner, Cornelius, age 26, 2 mos. in U.S., 97 South Front St., gentleman (20 July 1812)

Fearon, Robert, age 38, in U.S. since Jan. 1796, Market between 6th & 7th Sts., hackney-keeper (22 Mar. 1813)

Ferguson, Matthew, age 19, in U.S. since 1811, Nitre-Hall Mills, powder maker (6 Dec. 1813)

Ferguson, Robt., age 29, in U.S. since 4 June 1811, 208 Market St., farmer (15 Mar. 1814)

Feris, Robert, age 21, in U.S. since Sept. 1811, 98 Vine St., weaver (25 July 1812)

Finley, Napthali, age 26, in U.S. since 17 Mar. 1812, 240 North 3rd St., channeller(?); applied 7 Dec. 1813 (1 Feb. 1814)

Flanager, Daniel, age 20, in U.S. since 20 June 1811, 247 South 4th St., tailor (10-14 Nov. 1812)

Floyd, Henry, age 22, in U.S. since 26 May 1812, 16 Almond St., bottler (22 Mar. 1813)

Follard, Samuel, age 32, in U.S. since 16 Aug. 1807, near Upper Ferry, labourer (15 Mar. 1813)

Ford, George, age 25, 1 year in U.S., Fromberger's Court, accomptant (21 July 1812)

Forquer, Michael, age 38, in U.S. since 19 June 1807, 26 Spruce St., labourer (No. 1311)

Foster, William, age 32, in U.S. since 16 July 1802, 257 Catharine St., labourer; applied 27 Mar. 1813 (27 Mar. 1813)

Foster, William, age 23, in U.S. since 2 July 1811, wife, Shippen
St., labourer (15 Mar. 1813)
Fotten, William, age 22, in U.S. since 10 Oct. 1808, near the
centre square in South 13th St., weaver (22 Mar. 1813)
Fouder, Menasses, age 26, in U.S. since 24 Oct. 1811, wife and
child, corner 5th & Plumb Sts., tailor (15 Mar. 1813)
Fowke, Job, age 18, in U.S. since 20 Sept., 38 South Front St.,
merchant; says his stay in U.S. is uncertain, as he is under
direction of persons in England and Canada; applied 22 June
1812 (21 July 1812)
Fox, Joseph, age 24, in U.S. since July 1811, Germantown, spin-
ner (16 Dec. 1813)
Foxhill, Thomas, age 31, in U.S. since 17 June 1807, wife and
child, Fitzwater St., Southwark, Phila. Co., victualer (22
July 1812)
Foy, Henry, age 18, in U.S. since 8 July 1812, 31 Race St., labourer (19 Mar. 1813)
Francis, Frank Hewson, age 27, in U.S. since 30 Sept. 1812, 10th
between Filbert & Arch Sts., stone cutter (19 Mar. 1813)
Frazier, John, age 27, in U.S. since 24 Mar. 1807, wife & child,
South 5th St. near Queen St., thread manufacturer (24 Mar. 1813)
Frazier, William, age 33, in U.S. since 26 May 1810, wife and 4
children, South 5th St. near Queen St., thread manufacturer
(24 Mar. 1813)
Fretz, Moses, age 50, in U.S. since 8 June 1812, wife, Roxbo-
rough Twp., Phila. Co., farmer; his permanent residence is in
Lousi Twp., Lincoln Co., Upper Canada (2-7 Nov. 1812)
Fromenteau, Louis, age 61, in U.S. since Nov. 1809, 21 Prune St.,
merchant (22 July 1812)
Fry, George, age 52, in U.S. since 16 June 1793, Germantown, gar-
dener; applied 22 Mar. 1813 (22 Mar. 1813)
Fullerton, John, age 47, in U.S. since 15 Apr. 1814, wife and 5
children, corner of Old York Road & Coats St., Northern Liber-
ties, labourer (1-31 Aug. 1814)
Furey, James, age 30, in U.S. since 23 May 1807, wife and three
children, North 5th St. above Noble, labourer (24 Mar. 1813)
Furey, James, age 25, in U.S. since Aug. 1795, wife and child,
Middletown Twp., Delaware Co., weaver (22 Mar. 1813)
Galbraith, Hugh, age 31, in U.S. since 6 May 1812, wife and two
children, 46 Arch St., saddler (23 Mar. 1813)
Gallagher, John, age 20, in U.S. since 20 Aug. 1812, 85 South
Water St., dealer (22 Mar. 1813)
Gallagher, William, age 32, in U.S. since 21 May 1812, wife, 50
Christian St., paper-hanger; applied 4 June 1812 (26 Mar. 1813)
Gallaher, Philip, age 22, in U.S. since 1 Nov. 1810, Pine St.
near 12th St., labourer (22 Mar. 1813)
Gamble, John, age 36, 11 years in U.S., wife & 7 children, Phila.,
labourer (1-31 Aug. 1814)
Gardiner, Henry, age 47, in U.S. since 7 Dec. 1809, wife, 351
Market St., merchant; applied 3 July 1812 (22 July 1812)
Gates, Victor, age 49, in U.S. since 20 Sept. 1811, wife and 8
children, Blockley Twp., millwright (23 Mar. 1813)
Gaw, John, age 38, in U.S. since 30 Sept. 1799, wife & 2 children,
223 Callicohill (sp.?) St., drayman (22 Mar. 1813)
George, John, age 22, in U.S. since 1 Sept. 1811, 49 Chestnut St.,
clerk (23 July 1812)
George, John, age 21, in U.S. since Nov. 1806, wife, 4th & Ches-
nut Sts. from Schuylkill, haircloth manufacturer (25 July 1812)
Gibson, Valentine, age 28, in U.S. since 10 Oct. 1810, Holmes-
ville, Phila. Co., manufacturer (16-30 Sept. 1814)
Gibson, William, age 31, in U.S. since 10 Oct. 1810, wife & three
children, Holmesville, Phila. Co., manufacturer (1-9 Sept. 1814)
Gibson, William, age 25, in U.S. since 8 July 1811, wife & child,
Fitzwater St., tobacconist (15 Mar. 1813)

Gilbert, Christopher, age 29, in U.S. since Feb. 1802, 46 Spruce
   St., shoemaker (22 Mar. 1813)
Giles, George, age 32, in U.S. since Oct. 1805, wife & 2 children,
   67 Catharine St., rigger (2-7 Nov. 1812)
Gillespie, Francis, age 27, in U.S. since 28 Aug. 1806, wife & 3
   children, 101 Mary St., shoemaker (25 Mar. 1813)
Gillespie, Joseph, age 36, in U.S. since 7 July 1811, Passyunk
   Twp., at S. Girard's, farmer (1-31 Aug. 1814)
Gillespy, Andrew, age 40, in U.S. since 16 Sept. 1810, wife & 3
   children, Camden, gardener (20 July 1812)
Gillespy, George, age 28, in U.S. since 26 Oct. 1807, corner 9th
   & Lombard Sts., clerk (20 July 1812)
Gillespy, John, age 21, in U.S. since 29 Aug. 1808, wife, corner
   9th & Lombard Sts., grocer; applied 30 May 1812 U.S. District
   Court (20 July 1812)
Gilligan, Michael, age 24, in U.S. since 22 Oct. 1810, wife and
   child, 102 Plumb St., bricklayer (20 Mar. 1813)
Gillmor, William, age 26, in U.S. since 7 Dec. 1809, 1 Emly's
   Alley, shoemaker (23 July 1812)
Gilmer, John, age 25, in U.S. since 4 Sept. 1810, 2 North 10th
   St., carpenter (22 Mar. 1813)
Givin, Andrew, age 29, in U.S. since 10 Aug. 1809, wife & child,
   George St., Southwark 84, labourer (1-9 Sept. 1814)
Glacken, James, age 35, in U.S. since 24 June 1810, Locust St.
   between 10th & 11th Sts., labourer (16 Mar. 1813)
Glasgow, Edward, age 17, 6 mos. in U.S., 6 Pine St., grocer (20
   July 1812)
Glasgow, John, age 21, 1 year in U.S., 6 Pine St., grocer (20
   July 1812)
Glass, John, age 24, 14 mos. in U.S., 67 Dock St., last maker
   (21 July 1812)
Glenn, William, age 21, in U.S. since 17 Oct. 1809, 96 North 2nd
   St., clerk (22 Mar. 1813)
Gome, Christopher Wm., age 51, 7 years in U.S., 99 Cherry Alley,
   umbrella maker (21 July 1812)
Goodwin, John, age 26, in U.S. since 8 Aug. 1811, 104 Filbert St.,
   carter (7-12 Dec. 1812)
Goodwin, Roger, age 22, in U.S. since 8 Aug. 1811, corner South
   & 5th Sts., clerk (7-12 Dec. 1812)
Gorman, James, age 24, 1½ years in U.S., 52 South Water St.,
   storekeeper (20 July 1812)
Gowen, James, age 23, in U.S. since 23 July 1811, 83 North Water
   St., accomptant (24 July 1812)
Graham, David, age 54, in U.S. since Aug. 1800, Bett's Nail Fac-
   tory, 7th St. near High St., nail-header (1-9 Sept. 1814)
Graves, Thomas, age 30, in U.S. since 15 June 1812, Harford,
   Phila. Co., woolen-spinner (26 Mar. 1813)
Gray, Patrick, age 20, in U.S. since 1801, 236 Market St., tin-
   plate worker (26 Mar. 1813)
Greenfield, Edward B., age 23, in U.S. since 29 Oct. 1810, 74
   Locust St., millwright (3 Dec. 1812)
Greening, Richard, age 22, in U.S. since Dec. 1808, 9 Elfrith's
   Alley in Jno. Congers, shoemaker, a baker (1-31 Aug, 1814)
Greor, Joseph, age 26, in U.S. since 15 June 1812, wife, Cypress
   Alley, weaver; applied 29 Apr. 1814 (29 Apr. 1814)
Griffith, William, age 80, in U.S. since 3 Aug. 1804, Falls of
   Schuylkill, gentleman (23 Mar. 1813)
Griffith, William, age 33, in U.S. since 10 June 1792, wife and
   5 children, Penn Twp., Phila. Co., carpenter (24 Mar. 1813)
Grimes, Henry, age 32, in U.S. since 20 Aug. 1806, wife and two
   children, Moravian Alley, labourer (23 Mar. 1813)
Guthrie, George, age 26, in U.S. since 18 July 1811, corner
   South & 13th Sts., weaver (22 Mar. 1813)
Hagen, Andrew, age 25, 5½ years in U.S., wife & child, 3 George
   St., printer (20 July 1812)

Haig, Thomas, age 39, in U.S. since 16 Mar. 1808, wife and five
  children, Beach St., potter (2-7 Nov. 1812)
Hall, Richard, age 27, 4 years in U.S., wife, Smithfield Road
  above Frankford, weaver (1-31 Aug. 1814)
Hallowell, John, age 50, in U.S. since 1800, wife, Race St.,
  groom (26 Mar. 1813)
Hamill, Archibald, age 22, in U.S. since 10 Feb. 1810, 27 Straw-
  berry Alley, grocer; applied 22 Mar. 1813 (23 Mar. 1813)
Hamilton, Robert, age 27, in U.S. since 4 Aug. 1806, 94 Filbert
  St., stone cutter (19 Mar. 1813)
Hannah, Solomon, age 36, in U.S. since Nov. 1810, 98 ... St.,
  Phila., weaver (25 July 1812)
Hardigan, Mark, age 35, in U.S. since 25 June 1806, Northern
  Liberties, Phila. Co., currier (25 July 1812)
Hardinge, Samuel A., age 41, in U.S. since 25 Oct. 1797, wife,
  18 South 6th St., comedian (26 Mar. 1813)
Hardy, David, age 45, in U.S. since 31 Mar. 1811, wife, 231 South
  4th St., grocer (24 July 1812)
Hardy, Hugh, age 35, in U.S. since Sept. 1801, wife & 3 children,
  South 3rd St., teacher (25 July 1812)
Hardy, Thomas, age 31, in U.S. since 3 Aug. 1804, wife and three
  children, corner Spruce & Water Sts., carter (Mar. 1813)
Hargrave, David, age 23, in U.S. since 23 Apr. 1814, Front St.
  near Lombard, mariner, deserter from Albion 74 (23 June 1814)
Harkins, James, age 31, in U.S. since 17 July 1801, Sugar Alley,
  nail-cutter (25 Nov. 1812)
Harold, James, age 63, in U.S. since Feb. 1811, St. Mary's Church,
  South 4th St., Roman Catholic priest (1-31 Aug. 1814)
Harper, John P., age 30, 4 years & 10 mos. in U.S., wife and three
  children, 205 South St., grocer; applied 24 Sept. 1808 (25 July
  1812)
Harper, Robert, age 24, in U.S. since 20 May 1805, wife & child,
  12 Mary St., mariner; applied 28 Sept. 1810 (22 Mar. 1813)
Harpham, Jonathan, age 30, in U.S. since 30 June 1804, 217 South
  2nd St., storekeeper (20 July 1812)
Harpham, Simeon, age 24, in U.S. since 30 June 1804, 156 North
  2nd St., storekeeper (20 July 1812)
Harris, George, age 28, in U.S. since 4 June 1810, Haverford Twp.,
  Delaware Co., clothier (22 Mar. 1813)
Hartley, William, age 28, in U.S. since 28 June 1811, back of
  208 High St., reed-maker (20 Mar. 1813)
Harvey, David, age 21, in U.S. since 17 June 1811, Market St.
  near Schuylkill, weaver (26 Apr. 1813)
Harvey, James, age 37, in U.S. since 29 June 1801, wife and three
  children, 288 South 3rd St., carter (22 Mar. 1813)
Harvey, Robert, age 22, 5 years in U.S., wife & child, 12 Car-
  ter's Alley, tailor (22 July 1812)
Hastings, John, age 32, in U.S. since 7 July 1803, wife and three
  children, 45 South 4th St., turner (19 Mar. 1813)
Hastings, Robert, age 28, in U.S. since 2 June 1812, Germantown,
  weaver; applied 22 Mar. 1313 (22 Mar. 1813)
Hathwell, George H., age 34, in U.S. since 15 Oct. 1811, wife &
  3 children, 75 South Front St., carver & gilder & comedian (19
  Mar. 1813)
Haythorn, James, age 34, in U.S. since Aug. 1812, South 6th St.,
  morocco- leather dresser (26 Mar. 1813)
Hayward, William, age 31, in U.S. since 3 May 1804, 150 Chestnut
  St., waiter (18 Mar. 1813)
Hazard, Patrick, age 33, in U.S. since 16 Nov. 1801, Penn Twp.,
  Phila. Co., farmer & gardener (10-14 Nov. 1812)
Haze, Michael, age 29, in U.S. since 29 Nov. 1808, 10 Pear St.,
  hostler (19 Mar. 1813)
Henry, Felix, age 28, in U.S. since 2 May 1812, wife & 2 children,
  George St. near 11th St., carpenter (1-9 Sept. 1814)

Henry, James, age 22, in U.S. since 7 July 1812, P. Hagner's,
  Falls of Schuylkill, labourer (1-9 Sept. 1814)
Higgins, Nicholas, age 45, in U.S. since 24 Dec. 1811, wife,
  456 South Front St., wheelwright (22 Mar. 1813)
Highlands, Samuel, age 47, in U.S. since 8 Aug. 1795, wife & 4
  children, Juniper Alley, porter (20 Mar. 1813)
Hinchillwood, John, age 20, in U.S. since 1 Dec. 1810, Phila.,
  weaver (1-31 Aug. 1814)
Hindle, James, age 23, in U.S. since 29 July 1812, Globe Mill,
  Northern Liberties, manufacturer (1-9 Sept. 1814)
Hinsillwood, Thomas, age 18, in U.S. since 1 Nov. 1810, corner
  of 4th & Chestnut Sts., weaver (1-31 Aug. 1814)
Holland, Lawrence, age 35, in U.S. since 1798, wife & 2 children,
  Vine St. near Schuylkill, stone cutter (7-12 Dec. 1812)
Holmes, John, age 25, in U.S. since 27 Oct. 1804, wife & child,
  20 Sansom St., merchant; applied 27 Sept. 1808 (21 July 1812)
Holmes, John, age 24, in U.S. since 28 Sept. 1810, wife and two
  children, 178 South 6th St., grocer (10-14 Nov. 1812)
Hood, William, age 23, 1 year & 8 mos. in U.S., 298 Race St.,
  nailor (25 July 1812)
Houghy, Patrick, age 30, in U.S. since 16 July 1808, wife, corner
  Race & 6th Sts., labourer (8 Jan. 1814)
Howard, John, age 26, in U.S. since Oct. 1812, wife & child,
  North 2nd St. between Arch & Race Sts., coachman (26 Mar. 1813)
Howill, Henry, age 30, in U.S. since 20 Nov. 1810, Willings Alley,
  saddler (22 Mar. 1813)
Howlett, Samuel, age 47, in U.S. since 13 May 1798, Locust St.,
  factor (7-12 Dec. 1812)
Hughes, Lawrence James, age 25, in U.S. since 16 Mar. 1809, 117
  North 10th St., teacher (25 July 1812)
Humphrey, John, age 20, in U.S. since 2 May 1812, Nitre-Hall
  Mills, saltpeter refiner (6 Dec. 1813)
Hunt, Thomas, age 27, in U.S. since 16 May 1805, wife and two
  children, 10 Banner's Court, weaver (25 July 1812)
Hunter, David, age 28, in U.S. since 19 Sept. 1801, wife and 3
  children, Frankford, tanner (24 Mar. 1813)
Hunter, James, age 27, in U.S. since 14 Aug. 1811, Lancaster Co.,
  weaver (1-9 Sept. 1814)
Hussey, John, age 34, in U.S. since 10 Sept. 1811, wife, 2 Coa-
  tes's St., tallow chandler (2-7 Nov. 1812)
Hutchinson, John, age 26, in U.S. since 30 Sept. 1807, 10th be-
  tween Arch & Cherry Sts., stone cutter; he does not intend to
  become citizen of U.S. (1-9 Sept. 1814)
Hutchinson, John, age 25, in U.S. since 17 Oct. 1809, 255 South
  5th St., grocer (22 Mar. 1813)
Hutchinson, John, age 22, in U.S. since 3 May 1812, 13th between
  Pine & South Sts., weaver (25 Mar. 1813)
Inches, Thomas, age 45, in U.S. since 24 May 1801, wife, Kensington, Phila. Co., merchant (21 Nov. 1812)
Ingham, Jonas, age 58, 30 years in U.S., North 2nd near Vine St.,
  broker; he wishes to return to England (20-25 July 1812)
Iope, John William, age 37, in U.S. since Oct. 1803, wife and 5
  children, corner of 7th and Chestnut Sts. from Schuylkill, iron
  plate worker; applied 15 Sept. 1809 (23 Nov. 1812)
Irvins, John, age 30, in U.S. since 5 Nov. 1810, 98 Vine St.,
  weaver (25 July 1812)
Irwin, Anthony, age 25, in U.S. since 9 Sept. 1810, wife & three
  children, Holmesburgh, wool-comber (7-12 Dec. 1812)
Jackson, Luke, age 37, in U.S. since 28 Nov. 1811, 200 High St,,
  barkeeper (18 Mar. 1813)
Jackson, Thomas, age 50, in U.S. since Oct. 1810, 8 children,
  corner of Market & 13th Sts., gentleman (10-14 Nov. 1812)
Jackson, William, age 48, in U.S. since 21 Nov. 1809, Broad St.
  near the Water House, shoemaker; applied 19 Oct. 1811 (20 Mar.
  1813)

Jamieson, Andrew, age 29, in U.S. since 7 Dec. 1809, 61 North 4th St., accomptant; applied 26 May 1812 (21 July 1812)

Jamison, Thomas, age 26, in U.S. since 17 Nov. 1810, 4 Market St., clerk (23 July 1812)

Jeffers, John, age 24, in U.S. since 28 Sept. 1801, 5th from Schuylkill near Spruce St., blacksmith (20 Mar. 1813)

Jenkins, Launcelot, age 29, in U.S. since June 1802, wife and 3 children, Blockley Twp., Phila. Co., innkeeper (18 Mar. 1813)

Johnson, Robert, age 24, in U.S. since Dec. 1811, 13th near South St,, weaver (23 Mar. 1813)

Johnston, Daniel, age 23, in U.S. since 1 Aug. 1805, wife, 11 Wood St., carter (26 Mar. 1813)

Johnston, John, age 28, in U.S. since 13 Sept. 1810, Walnut St. between 12th & 13th Sts., carpenter (24 Mar. 1813)

Johnston, John, age 25, in U.S. since 26 Sept. 1805, Blockley Twp., Phila. Co., blacksmith (2-7 Nov. 1812)

Johnston, John, age 24, in U.S. since 5 June 1811, at Thomas Dobson's, North 2nd St., bookbinder (1-31 Aug. 1814)

Jones, David, age 28, 11 years in U.S., wife and two children, Southampton Twp., Bucks Co., farmer (25 July 1812)

Jones, Hugh, age 35, in U.S. since 20 July 1801, wife, Broad St. between Walnut & Locust Sts., milkman (25 July 1812)

Jones, John, age 23, in U.S. since 1794, 306 North St., cordwainer (2-7 Nov. 1812)

Jones, John, age 19, in U.S. since 14 Nov. 1810, 22 Harmony Court, comedian (19 Mar. 1813)

Jones, Thomas, age 20, in U,S. since 3 Sept. 1805, 131 Market St., merchant (23 Nov. 1812)

Jordan, Patrick, age 30, in U.S. since 10 Aug. 1806, wife & child, corner 10th & Filbert Sts., schoolmaster (20-25 July 1812)

Kane, Dennis, age 24, in U.S. since 1 Aug. 1806, wife & child, Callowhill St. between 5th & 6th Sts., shoemaker (1 Dec. 1813)

Kean, Roderick, age 37, in U.S. since 16 Aug. 1804, Ridge Road near the first turnpike gate, labourer; applied 3 Mar. 1812 (21 Feb. 1814)

Keany, Francis, age 27, in U.S. since 8 July 1804, Cheltenham Twp., Montgomery Co., gardener (2-7 Nov. 1812)

Keaton, John, age 41, in U.S. since 7 May 1814, near the Gap, Lancaster Road, farmer (1-9 Sept. 1814)

Keelar, Thomas William, age 30, 9 years & 1 mo. in U.S., wife & 4 children, 74 Arch St., copperplate printer; applied 21 June 1803 (20-25 July 1812)

Kelly, Bartholomew, age 23, in U.S. since 20 Dec. 1811, 23 Strawberry St., carver & gilder; applied 27 Dec. 1811 (23 July 1812)

Kelly, John, age 29, in U.S. since 23 May 1808, wife, 5 Prune St., hatter (10-14 Nov. 1812)

Kelly, Patrick, age 25, in U.S. since 21 May 1814, Front St. near Lombard, mariner, deserter from __Albion__ 74 (21 June 1814)

Kelly, Patrick, age 24, 2 years & 9 mos. in U.S., 351 South 2nd St., shoemaker (20 July 1812)

Kelly, William, age 28, in U.S. since 18 Oct. 1811, North 5th St., Northern Liberties, Phila., labourer (20 July 1812)

Kennedy, William, age 40, 2 years in U.S., 85 South 5th St., grocer; applied Mayor's Court, New York City, 1810 (21 July 1812)

Kennedy, William, age 31, in U.S. since 12 Dec. 1801, wife & five children, 46 Spruce St., boot- and shoemaker (22 Mar. 1813)

Kenney, James, age 37, in U.S. since 15 July 1801, 9 South 6th St., grocer (17 Mar. 1813)

Kent, James, age 26, in U.S. since Oct. 1809, 64 North 5th St., house-carpenter (20 July 1812)

Keogh, Patrick, age 38, 2 years & 7 mos. in U.S., 42 North 7th St., grocer (22 July 1812)

Kerr, James, age 24, in U.S. since 27 Aug. 1811, 222 South 6th St., distiller (22 Mar. 1813)

Kerr, William, age 21, in U.S. since Aug. 1802, at Js. Kerr's,
122 Market St., saddler (1-31 Aug. 1814)
Kershaw, John, age 28, in U.S. since 18 May 1806, wife, Blockley
Twp., Phila. Co., manufacturer (22 Mar. 1813)
Kilbourne, William, age 24, in U.S. since 2 May 1805, Strawberry
Alley 16 at Mrs. Lawrenson's, shoemaker (1-31 Aug. 1814)
Kilpatrick, William, age 30, in U.S. since 10 May 1812, 167 South
3rd St., carpenter (Mar. 1813)
Kincaid, John, age 22, in U.S. since Apr. 1814, at James Steward's
13th St. between Lombard & South Sts., labourer (1-31 Aug. 1814)
Kingsley, Thomas, age 27, in U.S. since 3 Dec. 1811, Holmesville,
Phila. Co., manufacturer (16-30 Sept. 1814)
Kinley, Philip, age 28, in U.S. since 15 June 1804, 67 Dock St.,
last-maker (21 Jan. 1814)
Kirk, John, age 43, in U.S. since 28 Feb. 1812, wife & 5 children,
Milton, Bucks Co., weaver (1-9 Sept. 1814)
Knapp, Thomas, age 25, in U.S. since Apr. 1800, 128 North Water
St., mariner (27 May 1813)
Knighton, Joseph, age 55, in U.S. since May 1804, wife & child,
26 Apple Tree Alley, stocking weaver (25 July 1812)
Kracht, Martin, age 46, in U.S. since Dec. 1806, wife & child,
New 2nd St., near Seth Craig's factory, labourer (1-9 Sept. 1814)
Lafferty, Bernard, age 24, in U.S. since 14 Sept. 1810, wife and
2 children, 38 Small St., grocer (22 Mar. 1813)
Laird, William, age 26, in U.S. since Aug. 1793, 99 Race St.,
tobacconist (23 July 1812)
Lamb, James, age 22, in U.S. since 8 July 1811, Falls of Schuyl-
kill, wire drawer (19 Sept. 1814)
Lamb, John, age 21, in U.S. since 10 May 1811, 135 South 4th St.,
accomptant (21 July 1812)
Lambert, Robert, age 52, in U.S. since 2 Sept. 1802, wife & seven
children, Blockley Twp., Phila. Co., millwright; applied 24
Sept. 1808 (No. 806)
Lamon, Andrew, age 52, in U.S. since 27 Nov. 1799, wife, corner
Race & 8th Sts., weaver (22 Mar. 1813)
Lancaster, William, Jr., age 22, in U.S. since 3 Sept. 1805, 2
in family, 46 George St., Southwark (20 July 1812)
Landers, Frederick, age 31, in U.S. since Aug. 1793, wife and 5
children, Ashton Twp., Delaware Co., tailor (25 Mar. 1813)
Larcomb, Richard, age 30, in U.S. since 28 Dec. 1814, wife and 2
children, 156 Spruce St., turner (1-9 Sept. 1814)
Large, Daniel, age 31, in U.S. since Jan. 1807, wife & 3 children,
448 North Front St., steam engine maker; applied 28 Apr. 1809
(25 July 1812)
Latta, William, age 30, in U.S. since 31 Oct. 1807, wife & child,
Broad St. between Locust & Spruce Sts., labourer (23 Mar. 1813)
Laughlin, Thomas, age 30, in U.S. since Oct. 1811, wife, at Ste-
phen Gerard's place, farmer (1-31 Aug. 1814)
Laughton, John, age 29, in U.S. since 20 May 1807, 87 South 4th
St., coachman; applied 20 Nov. 1809 (18 Mar. 1813)
Lawrence, John, age 67, in U.S. since July 1808, Currant Alley,
Locust St., fringe weaver (25 July 1812)
Leddy, Mick, age 24, in U.S. since 6 Apr. 1812, corner 5th and
Prune Sts., bottler (19 Mar. 1813)
Lee, David, age 19, in U.S. since 9 Oct. 1811, 69 Cherry Alley,
bookbinder (21 July 1812)
Lee, Dawson, age 26, in U.S. since 2 May 1805, wife & child, Queen
St. between 2nd & 3rd Sts., stone cutter (19 Mar. 1813)
Lee, James, age 23, in U.S. since 22 May 1808, wife, Juniper St.
near Race St., stone cutter (19 Mar. 1813)
Lepper, Arthur, age 33, in U.S. since 6 Sept. 1810, 78 North Wa-
ter St., weaver (25 Mar. 1813)
Leslie, William, age 22, in U.S. since 11 Sept. 1812, wife, cor-
ner 9th & Vine Sts., physician (19 Mar. 1813)

Lewis, Robert, age 23, 5 years in U.S., 132 South 3rd St., cordwainer; applied 25 Dec. 1809 (20-25 July 1812)

Liggett, George, age 32, in U.S. since 14 Oct. 1796, wife & child,
Little Pine St., carpenter (15 Feb. 1814)

Lloyd, Thomas, age 34, in U.S. since 10 Jan. 1805, 93 North 2nd
St., porter; he wishes to return to England to see his family
and for his health (21 May 1813)

Loague, William, age 25, in U.S. since 28 Sept. 1801, 1 child,
Spruce near 5th St. from Schuylkill, blacksmith (20 Mar. 1813)

Lockhart, Samuel, age 21, in U.S. since 21 May 1812, Malborough
St. at Geo. Jones's, cotton-spinner (1-31 Aug. 1814)

Logan, Patrick, age 28, in U.S. since 1 Aug. 1801, Guynned, Montgomery Co., cooper (1-9 Sept. 1814)

Logan, Thomas, age 24, in U.S. since 1 Aug. 1801, Guynned, Montgomery Co., tanner & currier (1-9 Sept. 1814)

Logue, James, age 27, in U.S. since 10 Dec. 1810, wife & child,
2nd St. between Market & Arch Sts., soap-boiler (20 Mar. 1813)

Long, Joseph, age 37, in U.S. since 25 Sept. 1807, Phila., ropemaker (14 Dec. 1813)

Long, Joseph, age 31, in U.S. since 5 Nov. 1804, wife & child,
corner German & 3rd Sts., grocer; applied 13 Oct. 1810 (19 Mar.
1813)

Lorange, Bolona, age 23, in U.S. since 2 Apr. 1810, corner of
Cherry & 8th Sts., carpenter (1-31 Aug. 1814)

Lorimore, Patrick, age 26, in U.S. since 29 Oct. 1811, Hopkins's
Court, N.L., turner (15 Mar. 1813)

Lougharry, Neill, age 28, in U.S. since 18 May 1812, corner 3rd
& Plumb Sts., grocer (22 Mar. 1813)

Loughead, Edward, age 24, in U.S. since 24 Oct. 1811, Shippen St.,
labourer (15 Mar. 1813)

Loughery, John, age 23, in U.S. since 3 May 1812, Cobs Creek,
Delaware Co., powder maker (22 Mar. 1813)

Loughran, Francis, age 25, in U.S. since 1 Feb. 1812, wife & 2
children, 112 Plumb St., weaver (22 Mar. 1813)

Love, Hugh, age 24, in U.S. since Sept. 1796, 552 North 3rd St.,
house-carpenter & joiner (2-7 Nov. 1812)

Lowry, Andrew, age 29, in U.S. since 17 July 1807, wife and two
children, South St. between 10th & 11th Sts., weaver (1-9 Sept.
1814)

Lucy, William, age 41, in U.S. since 24 May 1793, Hamilton Village near Phila., printer; applied Oct. 1802 in New York (20-
25 July 1812)

Lyddon, George, age 35, in U.S. since 8 July 1807, wife & child,
209 South St., soap-boiler (22 Mar. 1813)

Lynd, James, age 38, in U.S. since Aug. 1792, wife & 7 children,
24 North 2nd St., merchant; applied 17 June 1812 (24 July 1812)

Lyon, John, age 47, in U.S. since 20 Dec. 1812, Passyunk Twp.,
Phila. Co., botanist; first arrived in U.S. in 1795 and re-
mained until 29 Dec. 1811, when he returned to Europe (22 Dec.
1812)

Lyons, Coroner, age 25, in U.S. since 10 May 1810, 2nd St. between
Arch & Race Sts., hostler (20 Mar. 1813)

Lyons, John, age 31, in U.S. since 15 June 1803, Chestnut above
10th St., coachman (20 Mar. 1813)

Lyons, Peter, age 26, in U.S. since 18 May 1811, 13th St. between
Chestnut & High Sts., labourer; applied 23 Sept. 1814 (1-9 Sept.
1814)

McAffee, Joseph, age 20, in U.S. since 29 Aug. 1811, 61 North 4th
St., accomptant (21 July 1812)

McAfee, Robert, age 27, in U.S. since 20 May 1812, near Globe
Mill, shuttle maker; applied 11 Apr. 1814 (11 Apr. 1814)

McAlenon, Hugh, age 22, in U.S. since 9 Aug. 1810, 312 Market St.,
clerk (19 Mar. 1813)

Macauley, Isaac, age 27, in U.S. since 30 Aug. 1806, wife, No. 1
No. 12th St., floorcloth manufacturer (19 Mar. 1813)

McAvoy, John, age 28, in U.S. since 28 Oct. 1811, Globe Mill between 2nd & 3rd Sts., weaver (21 May 1813)

McBride, William, age 25, in U.S. since 2 July, 119 South 5th St.,
painter & glazier (20 Mar. 1813)

McBrine, Charles, age 30, in U.S. since 15 Aug. 1807, corner of
Washington St., labourer; applied 15 Oct. 1811 (15 Mar. 1813)

McCabe, Berney, age 28, in U.S. since 26 Aug. 1818, wife, Market St. near Schuylkill, grocer (22 Mar. 1813)

McCall, John, age 26, in U.S. since 23 Sept. 1809, near Globe
Mill, Northern Liberties, cotton spinner (22 July 1812)

McCamman, Samuel, age 46, in U.S. since 11 June 1811, Hartford,
Delaware Co., weaver (1-9 Sept. 1814)

McCanlees, James, age 29, in U.S. since 24 May 1806, Falls of
Schuylkill, labourer (1-9 Sept. 1814)

McCann, Charles, age 22, in U.S. since 15 Nov. 1807, wife, corner of Spruce & 8th Sts., grocer (20 Mar. 1813)

McCarry, James, age 22, in U.S. since 1 Sept. 1805, 14 Lombard
St., shoemaker (24 Mar. 1813)

McCarter, John, age 30, in U.S. since 30 May 1810, wife and two
children, Towns Mill, Phila. Co., weaver (1-9 Sept. 1814)

McCartey, David, age 31, in U.S. since Nov. 1810, corner Catharine & 5th Sts., Southwark, Phila. Co., dealer (23 July 1812)

Macartney, John, age 19, in U.S. since 29 Sept. 1811, 31 South
2nd St., clerk (2-7 Nov. 1812)

McCartney, Patrick, age 25, in U.S. since 8 Nov. 1811, wife and
child, Lower Merion Twp., Montgomery Co., weaver (2-7 Nov. 1812)

McCartney, Robert, age 26, in U.S. since 29 Sept. 1811, corner
7th & Race Sts., carpenter (17 Nov. 1812)

McCaulley, William, age 24, in U.S. since 7 May 1812, High & 5th
from Schuylkill, weaver (20 Mar. 1813)

McClaskey, Richard, age 26, 11 years in U.S., inmate in Black-
berry Alley, printer (20-25 July 1812)

McClean, John, age 21, in U.S. since 17 Dec. 1811, Doyle's Town,
Bucks Co., gentleman (10-14 Nov. 1812)

McClelland, Hugh, age 29, in U.S. since 16 July 1801, 61 North
4th St., clerk (23 July 1812)

McClennen, James, age 39, in U.S. since 14 July 1802, wife and 4
children, Abington, Montgomery Co., labourer (1-9 Sept. 1814)

McCloskey, Charles, age 21, in U.S. since 17 May 1812, South St.
between 9th & 10th Sts., drayman (22 Mar. 1813)

McCloskey, Michael, age 32, in U.S. since 30 Aug. 1806, wife and
3 children, 207 South 5th St., drayman (21 July 1812)

McClure, Thomas, age 23, in U.S. since 10 Oct. 1807, 134 South
2nd St., cabinetmaker (1-31 Aug. 1814)

McComb, John, age 26, in U.S. since 26 July 1812, corner 4th and
Christian Sts., pit sawyer (24 Feb. 1814)

McConnel, William, age 23, in U.S. since 10 Jan. 1806, South 4th
St. between Spruce & Pine Sts., printer (19 Mar. 1813)

McCormack, John, age 37, in U.S. since 6 Aug. 1796, 3rd St. near
German St., dealer (22 Mar. 1813)

McCormick, Henry, age 30, in U.S. since 18 July 1806, wife and 3
children, 10th St. near Locust St., labourer (20 Mar. 1813)

McCowen, William, age 28, in U.S. since Feb. 1810, 1 child, 60
Queen St., weaver (1-31 Aug. 1814)

McCoy, John, age 55, in U.S. since 20 Oct. 1812, 7 children, North
8th St., farmer (25 Mar. 1813)

McCoy, William, age 21, in U.S. since 13 Sept. 1810, Nicholson's
Court No. 4, at Widow Breamers, house-carpenter (1-31 Aug. 1814)

McCrackin, George, age 44, in U.S. since 26 July 1803, wife and
4 children, Aston Twp., District of Old Chester, weaver (1-31
Aug. 1814)

McCue, Edward, age 22, in U.S. since 4 July, Kensington, farmer
(1-9 Sept. 1814)

McCue, Michael, age 23, in U.S. since Oct. 1811, at Stephen Girard's place, farmer (1-31 Aug. 1814)

McCullogh, Michael, age 27, in U.S. since 27 July 1812, wife and
2 children, Small St. near 7th St., dealer (22 Mar. 1813)
McDavid, Thomas, age 33, in U.S. since 13 May 1812, wife and two
children, 4th St. near Schuylkill, labourer (18 Mar. 1813)
McDermott, John, age 38, in U.S. since 4 Nov. 1806, wife, 210
Arch St., skin dresser (23 Mar. 1813)
McDonough, John, age 23, in U.S. since 23 June 1812, Blockley
Twp., Phila. Co., labourer (18 Nov. 1812)
McDonough, Michael, age 21, in U.S. since 20 June 1812, Chestnut
& 5th from Schuylkill, labourer (20 Mar. 1813)
McElevan, Daniel, age 25, in U.S. since 22 May 1808, corner Vine
& Front Sts., Schuylkill, weaver (1-31 Aug. 1814)
McFadgen, Duncan, age 26, in U.S. since 16 Aug. 1808, 55 North
6th St., soap-boiler (20 Mar. 1813)
McFarlan, Samuel, age 51, in U.S. since 14 Sept. 1810, 21 South
3rd. St., grocer (1-9 Sept. 1814)
McGann, Andrew, age 48, in U.S. since 16 July 1810, Attleborough,
Bucks Co., stocking-weaver; applied 7 Sept. 1810 (2-7 Nov. 1812)
McGarrahill, John, age 38, in U.S. since 13 June 1806, Hart Tavern
on Frankford Road, gardener (25 Mar. 1813)
McGary, James, age 26, in U.S. since 7 July 1811, wife and two
children, Globe Mill, weaver (15 Feb. 1814)
McGary, John, age 32, in U.S. since 3 Aug. 1800, wife & child,
257 Catharine St., carter (23 Mar. 1813)
McGaw, John, age 36, in U.S. since 3 Dec. 1811, wife and five
children, 62 Coates's St., chandler (22 Mar. 1813)
McGee, Bernard, age 27, in U.S. since 1 Oct. 1809, near Lazaretto,
labourer (1-9 Sept. 1814)
McGee, Henry, age 26, in U.S. since 4 Mar. 1808, wife & 2 Children,
Vine near 10th St., labourer (19 Mar. 1813)
McGill, Anthony, age 28, in U.S. since July 1811, 202 North 2nd
St. at corner of 3rd & Noble Sts., labourer (1-9 Sept. 1814)
McGill, William, age 25, in U.S. since 9 July 1811, Holmesburgh,
Phila. Co., spinner (12 Dec. 1812)
McGirk, Patrick, age 33, in U.S. since 1 Nov. 1804, corner 13th
and Walnut Sts., labourer (27 Nov. 1812)
McGloane, Bernard, age 22, in U.S. since 6 July 1810, 99 North
9th St., weaver (25 Mar. 1813)
McGrath, James, age 28, in U.S. since 25 Aug. 1811, Norristown,
Montgomery Co., White Marsh Twp., farmer (1-9 Sept. 1814)
McGrath, Owen, age 27, in U.S. since 1 May 1812, corner Washing-
ton St., labourer (15 Mar. 1813)
Megraw, Thomas, age 27, in U.S. since 20 Jan. 1810, Northern Li-
berties, Phila. Co., farmer; applied 5 June 1812 (23 July 1812)
McGuigan, Felix, age 35, in U.S. since 14 Dec. 1807, wife, South
St. between 9th & 10th Sts., type founder; applied 16 Mar. 1810
(19 Mar. 1813)
Maguire, Charles, age 34, in U.S. since 9 Oct. 1809, 46 Spruce
St., shoemaker; applied 26 Mar. 1813 (27 Mar. 1813)
McGuire, Charles, age 26, in U.S. since 14 June 1803, wife and 1
child, Blockley Twp., Phila. Co., stone cutter (2 Dec. 1812)
Maguire, John, age 24, in U.S. since 13 June 1811, South 5th St.,
drayman (18 Mar. 1813)
McGuvan, Patrick, age 27, in U.S. since 16 Mar. 1810, wife,
Blockley Twp., Phila. Co., gardener (2-7 Nov. 1812)
McIlhenney, Robert, age 26, in U.S. since 1810, wife & 2 children,
5th St. Passyunk Road, carter (1-9 Sept. 1814)
McIlree, Mathew, age 28, in U.S. since Nov. 1809, Radnor Twp.,
Delaware Co., weaver (1-31 Aug. 1814)
McInaull, Hugh, age 24, in U.S. since 17 Oct. 1809, Cheltenham,
Montgomery Co., labourer (1-9 Sept. 1814)
McIntire, George, age 21, in U.S. since 1811, wife & child, Nitre-
Hall Mills, powder maker (6 Dec. 1813)
McIntire, James, age 27, in U.S. since 16 June 1806, Swanson St.
88, at Archibald Humes's, labourer (1-31 Aug. 1814)

McIntire, William, age 26, in U.S. since 28 Nov. 1811, German-
town, weaver (1-9 Sept. 1814)
McIntosh, Angus, age 32, in U.S. since 8 June 1812, Providence,
Montgomery Co., labourer (1-9 Sept. 1814)
McIntosh, John, age 35, in U.S. since 8 June 1812, Providence,
Montgomery Co., labourer (1-9 Sept. 1814)
McIntosh, John, age 25, in U.S. since Aug. 1812, corner Washing-
ton St., labourer (15 Mar. 1813)
McIntosh, William, age 31, in U.S. since 14 Aug. 1811, 201 North
4th St., carpenter (1-9 Sept. 1814)
McIntyre, John, age 21, in U.S. since 9 Oct. 1809, 10th St. near
Arch St., stone cutter (19 Mar. 1813)
McIver, Michael, age 20, in U.S. since 4 June 1809, 13th St. be-
tween Filbert & Arch Sts., labourer (25 Mar. 1813)
McKane, Alexander, age 26, in U.S. since 9 Oct. 1809, wife and
child, Race St. between 9th & 10th Sts., labourer (19 Mar. 1813)
McKay, Bernard, age 26, in U.S. since 3 Feb. 1811, wife and two
children, 16 Stampford's Alley, cork-cutter (23 Mar. 1813)
McKee, Bernard, age 28, in U.S. since 21 Apr. 1807, at brewer
George Pepper's, drayman (1-9 Sept. 1814)
McKee, Gabriel, age 23, in U.S. since 8 Sept. 1811, 240 Market
St., baker (22 Mar. 1813)
McKellar, Neil, age 42, in U.S. since 1 Oct. 1804, wife, George
St between 12th & 13th Sts., blacksmith; applied 25 Sept. 1814
(1-9 Sept. 1814)
McKelvey, William, age 30, in U.S. since 4 July 1802, Kingsessing
Twp., Phila. Co., labourer (24 Dec. 1812)
McKenna, Edward, age 20, in U.S. since Sept. 1810, 355 Arch St.,
labourer (23 Mar. 1813)
McKensie, Richard, age 26, in U.S. since 20 Nov. 1811, 42 South
3rd St., saddler (20 Mar. 1813)
McKenzie, John, age 24, in U.S. since 12 Oct. 1811, Springfield,
Delaware Co., labourer (2-7 Nov. 1812)
McKern, John, age 21, in U.S. since 26 Nov. 1811, Phila., labourer
(1-31 Aug. 1814)
McKernan, Peter, age 31, in U.S. since 15 June 1811, wife and 2
children, Upton Court, Northern Liberties, labourer (24 Mar.
1813)
Mackey, Dennis, age 33, in U.S. since 15 Sept. 1810, High St.
between Broad and 12th Sts., labourer (1-9 Sept. 1814)
Mackey, Patrick, age 33, in U.S. since 1812, Nitre-Hall Mills,
splitter of wood (1-31 Aug. 1814)
Mackey, Richard, age 46, 9 mos. & 2 days in U.S., wife and four
children, New 4th St., Northern Liberties, currier (20-25 July
1812)
Mackie, William, age 30, in U.S. since 27 Sept. 1807, wife and 3
children, White Marsh Twp., Montgomery Co., near Plymouth, labourer (1-9 Sept. 1814)
McKinley, Hugh, age 50, in U.S. since Aug. 1790, wife and four
children, Northern Liberties, Phila. Co., farmer (23 July 1812)
McLane, Laughlin, age 32, in U.S. since 19 Oct. 1811, wife and 7
children, corner of Race & 8th Sts., shoemaker (20 Mar. 1813)
McLaughlin, John, age 31, in U.S. since 18 Sept. 1805, Broad St.
near South St., labourer (26 Mar. 1813)
McLaughlin, Wm., age 26, in U.S. since 4 Oct. 1804, at Mr. Joseph
Sims's, Chestnut St., farmer (23 Mar. 1813)
McLean, James, age 24, in U.S. since 1 June 1811, 234 South 3rd
St., cabinetmaker (23 July 1812)
McLear, Francis, age 22, in U.S. since 11 May 1812, Moyamensing
Twp., Phila. Co., weaver (25 May 1813)
McMangle, Edward, age 30, in U.S. since May 1811, Falls of Schuyl-
kill, wire-drawer (1-9 Sept. 1814)
McMannamy, James, age 49, in U.S. since 9 Sept. 1792, wife and
child, 29 Pine Alley, labourer (26 Mar. 1813)

McManus, Bernard, age 32, in U.S. since 9 July 1804, wife and 3
children, 16 South 10th St., bookseller (7-12 Dec. 1812)
McManus, Owen, age 28, in U S. since 16 July 1806, wife and 3
children, 104 Filbert St., maltster (7-12 Dec. 1812)
McMichael, John, age 21, in U.S. since 13 Oct. 1808, 55 South
10th St., distiller (24 Mar. 1813)
McMillin, James, age 45, in U.S. since Apr. 1811, wife & five
children, Rose Alley, weaver; applied 3 May 1814 (3 May 1814)
McMullan, Hugh, age 20, in U.S. since 4 July 1801, Kennett Twp.,
Chester Co., farmer (7-12 Dec. 1812)
McMullan, James, age 25, in U.S. since 4 July 1801, Kennett Twp.,
Chester Co., weaver (7-12 Dec. 1812)
McMullen, Samuel, age 40, in U.S. since 28 Oct. 1800, Clymer's
Court, coachman (26 Mar. 1813)
McMullin, John, age 33, in U.S. since 8 July 1797, wife & four
children, Northern Liberties, Phila. Co., house-carpenter (23
July 1812)
McMullin, Samuel, age 22, in U.S. since Nov. 1800, 40 Chestnut
St., boot- and shoemaker (23 July 1812)
McMurdy, Jonathan, age 21, in U.S. since 8 Sept. 1796, Maria St.
No. 8, Northern Liberties, confectioner (1-31 Aug. 1814)
McMurdy, Robert, age 70, in U.S. since 8 Sept. 1796, wife & son,
8 Maria St., Northern Liberties, labourer (1-31 Aug. 1814)
McNeil, Thomas, age 37, in U.S. since 22 Sept. 1803, wife & four
children, 7 Spaford St., weaver; applied 20 Oct, 1813 (26 Jan.
1814)
McNeilly, John, age 23, in U.S. since 1 Nov. 1810, corner 4th &
Chestnut Sts., saddler (22 Mar. 1813)
McQuaid, Edward, age 28, in U.S. since 28 Nov. 1811, 113 South
5th St., weaver (16-30 Sept. 1814)
McShane, Charles, age 24, in U.S. since Sept. 1798, 15 South 7th
St., surgical instrument maker (25 July 1812)
McSorley, John, age 40, in U.S. since 11 Oct. 1811, wife and two
children, Strasburg, Lancaster Co., spinning wheel maker (1-9
Sept. 1814)
McVicker, Henry, age 34, in U.S. since 16 Oct. 1809, Falls of
Schuylkill, wire-drawer; applied 24 Mar. 1813 (24 Mar. 1813)
Mc Vicker, John, age 47, in U.S. since 21 Nov. 1811, Falls of
Schuylkill, wire-drawer; applied 24 Mar. 1813 (Mar. 1813)
McWilliams, John, age 30, in U.S. since Mar. 1811, wife & child,
Nitre-Hall Mills, powder maker (6 Dec. 1813)
Mackle, Joseph, age 22, in U.S. since 1810, Nitre-Hall Mills,
powder maker (6 Dec. 1813)
Magalian, Patrick, age 24, in U.S. since 15 Nov. 1810, boarder
with Robert McMullin, Gaskill St. between 4th & 5th Sts., wea-
ver (1-9 Sept. 1814)
Malcomson, Joseph, age 24, in U.S. since 25 Nov. 1809, Bucks Co.,
weaver (27 Apr. 1813)
Malholand, Henry, age 28, in U.S. since 28 Aug. 1808, South St.
between 5th & 6th Sts., labourer (19 Mar. 1813)
Mallin, Thomas, age 27, in U.S. since 27 July 1803, 99 South 2nd
St., calico printer; applied 3 July 1812 (23 July 1812)
Mallon, John, age 22, in U.S. since 14 Aug. 1810, Juniper Alley
between 10th & 11th Sts., waiter (19 Mar. 1813)
Malony, James, age 26, in U.S. since 23 Sept. 1811, Marshall's
Alley, 4th St. near Spruce St., coachman (19 Mar. 1813)
Manderson, James, age 23, in U.S. since 10 Aug. 1805, wife and 2
children, Kensington, Northern Liberties, grocer; applied 13
Apr. 1811 (21 May 1813)
Mangy, James, age 35, in U.S. since Sept. 1805, wife & child,
back of 120 Arch St., coachman (25 Mar. 1813)
Manion, Dennis, age 46, in U.S. since 30 June 1811, 1 daughter,
Globe Mill in North 4th St., spinner (1-9 Sept. 1814)
Marsden, Thos., age 30, in U.S. since 21 Apr. 1814, wife and 3
children, Frankford Rd., cotton manufacturer (21 June 1814)

Marren, Thomas, age 30, in U.S. since 5 Sept. 1811, Locust St.,
    groom (7-12 Dec. 1812)
Marshal, George, age 27, in U.S. since 25 Sept. 1804, wife and
    child, Catharine St. near 3rd St., morocco finisher (22 Mar.
    1813)
Martin, Andrew, age 23, in U.S. since 19 July 1807, wife, Abing-
    ton, Montgomery Co. (1-9 Sept. 1814)
Martin, James, age 36, 6 years in U.S., wife & 5 children, 369
    Market St., bookseller; applied 14 Aug. 1909 (23 July 1812)
Martin, James, age 24, in U.S. since 29 Aug. 1811, iron founder
    (15 Mar. 1813)
Martin, John, age 22, in U.S. since 19 June 1814, mariner, de-
    serten from Albion 74 (30 June 1814)
Martin, Peter, age 23, in U.S. since 18 May 1812, Callowhill St.
    between 8th & 9th Sts., baker (18 Mar. 1813)
Martin, William, age 34, in U.S. since 10 Sept. 1810, Cheltenham,
    Montgomery Co., farmer (16-30 Sept. 1814)
Maxwell, James, age 25, in U.S. since 12 Sept. 1811, wife & child,
    13th St. near South St., weaver (22 Mar. 1813)
May, Theodore, age 36, in U.S. since 4 Nov. 1812, Market St. at
    Wm. Hillerman's boarding house, physician; he came from Upper
    Canada to attend the medical meeting (10-14 Nov. 1812)
Maylin, Joseph, age 44, in U.S. since 20 May 1806, wife and one
    stepdaughter, 139 South 6th St., gentleman; applied 13 Oct.
    1810 (2-7 Nov. 1812)
Meade, Patrick, age 24, in U.S. since 25 June 1810, wife and 2
    children, 1 South 7th St., coachman (19 Mar. 1813)
Meliss, Andrew, age 26, in U.S. since Oct. 1808, 8 North Front
    St., accomptant; applied 28 Dec. 1811 (23 July 1812)
Metham, Prene, age 28, in U.S. since 10 Feb. 1810, wife, 181
    Chestnut St., butler (27 Nov. 1812)
Milanafe, Constantine, age 21, in U.S. since 28 Aug. 1810, Block-
    ley Twp., Phila. Co., labourer (2-7 Nov. 1812)
Miller, John, age 29, 1 year in U.S., 7th & Market Sts., grocer
    (25 July 1812)
Miller, John, in U.S. since 1 Oct. last, wife, 29 Callowhill St.,
    mariner (16 Nov. 1812)
Miller, William, age 30, in U.S. since 27 May 1806, Old Chester,
    Delaware Co., labourer (1-9 Sept. 1814)
Mills, Allen, age 31, in U.S. since 14 Jan. 1800, wife and four
    children, 86 South 11th St., paper maker (31 May 1813)
Mills, Edward, age 26, in U.S. since 1 Oct. 1810, wife & child,
    Shippen St. near 6th St., labourer (1-9 Sept. 1814)
Milner, George, age 40, in U.S. since Oct. 1805, wife and four
    children, 383 Race St., weaver (2-7 Nov. 1812)
Mingdey, James, age 35, in U.S. since Sept. 1805, wife and child,
    120 Arch St., coachman (27 Mar. 1813)
Mitchell, John, age 50, in U.S. since 10 June 1810, wife & three
    children, Germantown, millwright (22 Mar. 1813)
Mitchell, Robert, age 25, in U.S. since 29 Aug. 1808, 50 North
    3rd St., labourer (1-9 Sept. 1814)
Moffat, Spencer, age 31, in U.S. since 14 July 1802, wife and 2
    children, corner Brown & 2nd Sts., grocer (24 Mar. 1813)
Moffet', William, age 28, in U.S. since 18 Oct. 1809, Oxford Twp.,
    Phila. Co., farmer (1 June 1813)
Mogridge, Augustus, age 24, in U.S. since 20 Dec. 1812, wife,
    Mansion House Hotel, farmer (21 Dec. 1812)
Monaghan, Henry, age 23, in U.S. since 27 July 1811, 40 Cherry
    Alley, blacksmith (23 Mar. 1813)
Moneypenny, James, age 31, in U.S. since 1 Sept. 1803, wife & 3
    children, corner South & 13th Sts., copperplate printer (22
    Mar. 1813)
Montgomery, Hugh, age 53, in U.S. since 4 Aug. 1806, wife & 8
    children, Vine St., grocer (23 Mar. 1813)

Moody, John, age 24, in U.S. since 5 Oct. 1808, wife, Oxford, Phila. Co., labourer (1-9 Sept. 1814)

Moody, John, age 23, in U.S. since 22 Sept. 1810, 92 Spruce St., printer (22 Mar. 1813)

Mooney, John, age 20, in U.S. since May 1812, 32 Vine St., distiller, deserter from Albion 74 (25 May 1814)

Mooney, Thomas, age 26, in U.S. since 26 Dec. 1810, wife & one child, 5 Green Leaf Alley, coachman (20 Mar. 1813)

Moore, Edward, age 24, in U.S. since 27 Sept. 1808, wife & child, George St. between 10th & 11th Sts., labourer (20 Mar. 1813)

Moore, Henry, age 28, in U.S. since June 1811, wife, 3rd St. near German St., Southwark, porter (16 Mar. 1813)

Moore, James, age 30, in U.S. since June 1808, wife & 2 children, North 6th St. between Coates & Green Sts., soap-boiler; applied 10 Oct. 1811 (1-31 Aug. 1812)

Moore, Samuel, age 40, in U.S. since 13 July 1807, wife, 21 North 6th St., labourer (1-9 Sept. 1814)

Morgan, James, age 24, in U.S. since 17 June 1801, corner Locust & 8th Sts., hostler (20 Mar. 1813)

Morgan, John, age 19, in U.S. since 29 Sept. 1809, 74 Locust St., brass founder (25 July 1812)

Morgan, Thomas, age 28, in U.S. since Nov. 1794, at Wm. H. Morgan's, 111 Chestnut St., carver & gilder (1-31 Aug. 1814)

Morris, Evan, age 23, in U.S. since July 1801, 9 Fayette St., shoemaker (2-7 Nov. 1812)

Morrison, Thomas, age 20, in U.S. since 8 July 1801, at Mr. Thompson's, 200 North 2nd St., weaver (1-31 Aug. 1814)

Morrow, Samuel, age 48, in U.S. since 27 Aug. 1809, 3 children, Frankford, teacher (24 Mar. 1813)

Mortimer, John, age 40, in U.S. since 9 Mar. 1809, wife & child, 104 Mulberry St., teacher; applied 2 Feb. 1810 (24 July 1812)

Moxam, William, age 55, in U.S. since 8 June 1793, wife and 3 children, Southwark, carpenter; applied 16 July 1812 (23 Mar. 1813)

Moxly, John, age 27, in U.S. since 29 Sept. 1812, North 8th St., oil-maker (22 Mar. 1813)

Moyne, John, age 35, in U.S. since 22 July 1811, wife and two children, 34 Mary St., shoemaker (26 Mar. 1813)

Muirhead, Alexander, age 34, in U.S. since 11 Sept. 1810, No. 26 Chestnut St., merchant; applied 23 Mar. 1811 (24 July 1812)

Mulcahy, John, age 25, in U.S. since 15 Nov. 1805, 4 Crab St., house-carpenter (24 Mar. 1813)

Mulheran, John, age 30, in U.S. since 1 Aug. 1803, wife, 6th St., labourer (20 Mar. 1813)

Mullaniff, Jas., age 26, in U.S. since 24 Sept. 1811, Penn Twp., in Turner's Lane, labourer (26 Mar. 1813)

Mullowney, Jeremiah, age 22, in U.S. since 10 May 1811, Spruce St. between 4th & 5th Sts., blacksmith (27 Mar. 1813)

Murphy, Bernard, age 24, in U.S. since 22 July 1812, 118 Market St., oyster-seller (2-7 Nov. 1812)

Murphy, Patrick, age 25, in U.S. since 16 Aug. 1807, Roxborough Twp., Phila. Co., carder & spinner (22 Mar. 1813)

Murphy, Patrick, age 21, 1 year in U.S., 14 Carter's Alley, weaver (21 July 1812)

Murray, Daniel, age 24, in U.S. since 28 Aug. 1811, corner 13th & Market Sts., assistant in a store (22 Mar. 1813)

Murray, James, age 47, in U.S. since 2 Oct. 1811, wife & child, 389 Race St., stocking-weaver (1-9 Sept. 1814)

Murray, James, age 28, in U.S. since 20 Aug. 1795, 128 North Water St., mariner (27 May 1813)

Murray, John, age 45, in U.S. since 13 Sept. 1809, wife and six children, Taylor's Alley between 2nd & Front Sts., labourer (26 Mar. 1813)

Murray, Michael, age 28, in U.S. since 26 Feb. 1809, South St. near Front St., labourer (22 Mar. 1813)

Murta, William, age 41, in U.S. since 27 Oct. 1810, wife & child, 146 South 8th St., bottler (20-25 July 1812)

Naily, Archibald, age 22, in U.S. since 22 Aug. 1812, wife, Race St. between 7th & 8th Sts. from Schuylkill, drayman (1-9 Sept. 1814)

Naily, Robert, age 23, in U.S. since 22 Aug. 1812, Race St. between 7th & 8th Sts. from Schuylkill, weaver (1-9 Sept. 1814)

Nave, Benjamin, age 25, in U.S. since 1794, wife, 30 Catherine St., mariner (24 Dec. 1812)

Nelson, Thomas, age 22, in U.S. since 1 June 1812, Broad St. near Walnut St., weaver (23 Mar. 1813)

Newman, John, age 40, in U.S. since 4 May 1802, wife & 2 children, 6 South Water St., grocer (21 July 1812)

Nichols, James A., age 36, in U.S. since Aug. 1804, wife & child, between 11th & 12th & Locust & Walnut Sts., baker (1-9 Sept. 1814)

Nicholson, Patrick, age 24, in U.S. since 22 May 1808, South St. between 5th & 6th Sts., labourer (19 Mar. 1813)

Nickland, George, age 25, in U.S. since 14 Dec. 1806, 62 Market St., attending grocery store (24 July 1812)

Norris, John, age 31, in U.S. since 1 Oct. 1807, wife and six children, Columbia, Lancaster Co., tinsmith (26 Mar. 1813)

Nottingham, William, age 28, in U.S. since 17 June 1807, wife, 2 children & 1 servant, 57 Union St., merchant; applied 6 Feb. 1809; he is married to a lady, native of New Jersey, daughter of a Revolutionary officer (22 July 1812)

Nowlen, Peter, age 38, 2 years in U.S., wife & child, 257 South St., labourer (20 July 1812)

Nulty, Owen, age 23, in U.S. since Aug. 1809, Holmesburgh, Phila. Co., carpenter (12 Dec. 1812)

O'Bryan, Simon, age 23, in U.S. since 9 June 1812, 39 North 2nd St., labourer (1-9 Sept. 1814)

O'Bryan, Thomas, age 58, in U.S. since 20 Dec. 1810, 194 Lombard St., weaver; applied 22 Mar. 1813 (27 Mar. 1813)

O'Conner, John, age 25, in U.S. since Sept. 1810, wife and four children, Phila., labourer (1-31 Aug. 1814)

O'Conner, John, age 22, in U.S. since 20 Sept. 1811, wife, St. Mary's St., between 7th & 8th Sts., bricklayer (1-9 Sept. 1814)

O'Hara, Arthur, age 30, 2½ years in U.S., 17 Walnut St., labourer (20 July 1812)

O'Neil, John, age 26, in U.S. since 23 June 1807, wife, 101 Vine St., assistant brewer (21 July 1812)

O'Neill, Hugh, age 27, in U.S. since 10 May 1812, Schuylkill between Vine & Callowhill Sts., labourer (1-9 Sept. 1814)

O'Neill, John, age 22, in U.S. since 1 June 1812, 200 South St., labourer (1-9 Sept. 1814)

Ore, Thomas, age 50, in U.S. since 1794, wife and 3 children, Filbert St. between 8th and 9th Sts., cotton machine maker (25 July 1812)

Orington, John, age 21, in U.S. since 10 Aug. 1805, corner 9th and South Sts., house-carpenter (22 Mar. 1813)

Orr, James, age 33, 2 weeks in U.S., Phila., weaver (1-31 Aug. 1814)

Orr, Joseph, age 33, in U.S. since 15 May 1812, wife, Bristol Twp., Phila. Co., weaver (16 Dec. 1813)

Osborne, George C., age 28, in U.S. since 24 Mar. 1807, wife & 3 children, Washington St., manufacturer (22 Dec. 1813)

Osborne, Samuel, age 21, in U.S. since 18 May 1812, back of 46 Arch St., saddler (22 Mar. 1813)

Osman, William, age 39, in U.S. since 5 May 1804, wife & child, Arch St. above 9th St., coachman (25 Mar. 1813)

O'Sullivan, John, age 22, in U.S. since 20 Feb. 1810, 64 South 8th St., gentleman; is awaiting letter from his parents to determine whether to be allowed to remain in U.S. (2-7 Nov. 1812)

Owens, David, age 26, in U.S. since 28 Aug. 1802, wife, corner
of Locust & 8th Sts., coachman (20 Mar. 1813)

Owens, Owen, age 26, in U.S. since May 1801, wife & 2 children,
Lower Dublin, Phila. Co., farmer (10-14 Nov. 1812)

Owens, William, age 43, in U.S. since 1 July 1798, wife and six
children, Harrogate, Phila. Co., farmer (20 Mar. 1813)

Palmer, Richard, age 51, in U.S. since 15 July 1794, wife & hired
girl, 145 North 2nd St., cotton manufacturer (25 July 1812)

Palmer, Thomas, age 51, in U.S. since 5 Nov. 1798, Lower Dublin
Twp., Phila. Co., storekeeper (25 Mar. 1813)

Palmer, Thomas, age 36, in U.S. since Sept. 1801, wife, Catharine
St. near Front St., labourer (22 Mar. 1813)

Parker, Benjamin, age 26, in U.S. since Nov. 1807, wife, two
children, mother-in-law & 1 apprentice, 258 South St., cabinet-
and chairmaker; applied 5 Sept. 1811 (25 July 1812)

Parker, James, age 30, in U.S. since 26 June 1812, wife & female
servant, Germantown, cotton spinner (22 July 1812)

Parker, Thomas, age 29, 3 years in U.S., Germantown, manufacturer
of blankets for U.S. (20 July 1812)

Parry, Robert, age 44, in U.S. since 30 June 1801, wife and two
children, 58 South Front St., gardener (19 Mar. 1813)

Parsons, Thomas, age 23, in U.S. since 3 Sept. 1814, 35 Plumb
St., Southwark, sailmaker (1-9 Sept. 1814)

Passmore, Samuel, age 35, in U.S. since 20 July 1805, wife and 4
children, South 8th St., cabinetmaker (1-31 Aug. 1814)

Patterson, John, age 25, in U.S. since 29 Sept. 1807, Lane St.
between 7th & 8th Sts., stone cutter; does not intend to become citizen of U.S. (1-9 Sept. 1814)

Patterson, Joseph, age 25, in U.S. since 8 June 1811, Broad St.
near Walnut St. (22 Mar. 1813)

Patterson, Nicholas, age 25, in U.S. since 26 Aug. 1814, sailor
(1-9 Sept. 1814)

Patton, James, age 32, in U.S. since 1 Oct. 1810, 104 Filbert St.,
labourer (26 Mar. 1813)

Patton, William, age 56, in U.S. since Oct. 1811, wife & child,
corner of Locust & 13th Sts., labourer; wishes to return to
Europe in a cartel (20 Nov. 1812)

Patton, William, age 23, in U.S. since 31 Aug. 1806, corner of
13th & Locust Sts., potter (2-7 Nov. 1812)

Pearce, Thomas P., age 38, in U.S. since 18 July 1800, wife & 5
children, 100 Lombard St., dealer (27 Mar. 1813)

Pearot, Abraham, age 34, in U.S. since Oct. 1804, wife, Rasberry
Alley,coach spring maker (7 Apr. 1814)

Penn, William, age 36, in U.S. since Apr. 1807, wife, Easton (20
Mar. 1813)

Penrose, William, age 29, in U.S. since Apr. 1810, 13th St. between Filbert & Arch Sts., labourer (15 May 1813)

Perrin, William, age 46, in U.S. since 20 May 1806, 28 South St.,
dealer (7-12 Dec. 1812)

Perry, James, age 21, in U.S. since 21 Aug. 1812, Frankford, at
Stacy Gillingham's, labourer (1-31 Aug. 1814)

Phillips, Peter, age 50, in U.S. since 8 Aug. 1806, 4 children,
71 North 7th St., chemist (23 Mar. 1813)

Pigott, Edward, age 66, 12 years in U.S., maid, servant & child,
Lower Providence Twp., Montgomery Co., farmer; applied 27 Jan.
1801 (23 July 1812)

Pigott, Robert, age 38, in U.S. since 1 May 1809, corner of Vine
& 7th Sts., labourer (23 Mar. 1813)

Pinkerton, John, age 49, in U.S. since 29 Sept. 1809, Blockley,
Phila. Co., stone-mason (2 Dec. 1812)

Pinkerton, John, age 47, in U.S. since 1811, Nitre-Hall Mills,
powder-maker (6 Dec. 1813)

Plews, William, age 22, in U.S. since 5 Aug. 1805, corner South
& 9th Sts., wire worker (20 July 1812)

Pollin, Peter, age 34, in U.S. since 13 May 1803, wife & child,
46 South 3rd St., shoemaker (29 May 1813)
Porter, James, age 27, in U.S. since 3 Sept. 1810, Lombard St.
between 5th & 6th Sts. from Schuylkill, weaver (7 Mar. 1814)
Porter, James, age 26, in U.S. since 16 Aug. 1807, wife and 3
children, corner of 13th & Vine Sts., storekeeper (1-9 Sept.
1814)
Porter, William, age 22, in U.S. since 3 May 1812, wife, between
Race & Vine Sts., above Centre Square, saddler (30 Apr. 1813)
Pounder, Jonathan, age 28, 5 years in U.S., wife & child, 352
North 3rd St., bookbinder (20 July 1812)
Powell, John, age 28, 5 years & 2 mos. in U.S., 86 South 11th
St., painter & glazier (23 July 1812)
Power, William, age 31, in U.S. since 24 Sept. 1804, Wilson &
Taylor's Factory, Falls of Schuylkill, manufacturer (1-9 Sept.
1814)
Punshon, Robert, age 35, in U.S. since 3 Sept. 1802, wife and 5
children, West Whiteland Twp., Chester Co., minister of the
Gospel (17 May 1813)
Pybus, John, age 42, in U.S. since 20 Oct. 1805, wife, one child,
five apprentices & a hired girl, corner Vine & 5th Sts., grocer
and shoe-seller (24 July 1812)
Queen, Charles, age 22, in U.S. since 29 Aug. 1811, iron founder
(15 Mar. 1813)
Queen, James, age 21, in U.S. since 5 July 1810, Kensington, far-
mer (24 Mar. 1813)
Queen, Manuel, age 24, in U.S. since 14 Oct. 1805, wife & child,
94 Filbert St., stone-cutter (19 Mar. 1813)
Queen, Patrick, age 22, in U.S. since 9 June 1811, corner Washington St., labourer (15 Mar. 1813)
Quig, William, age 26, in U.S. since 20 Sept. 1810, near Mr. Ha-
milton's in Blockley, labourer (1-9 Sept. 1814)
Quin, James, age 30, in U.S. since 24 May 1801, 6th St. below
Shippen St., stone-cutter (22 Mar. 1813)
Quinn, John, age 45, in U.S. since 10 Aug. 1812, Holmesville,
manufacturer (16-30 Sept. 1814)
Quinton, Alexander, age 30, in U.S. since 2 Sept. 1810, wife &
3 servants, Pennsbury Manor, Bucks Co., farmer; applied 3 June
1812 (1-9 Sept. 1814)
Ramsey, Thomas, age 22, in U.S. since 29 Aug. 1811, wife, German
St. near 3rd St., shoemaker (30 Nov. 1812)
Rankin, Arthur, age 22, in U.S. since 17 Apr. 1811, Kentucky,
woolen spinner (23 Mar. 1813)
Rankin, Hugh, age 20, in U.S. since 1 Oct. 1810, 118 North 7th
St., grocer (2-7 Nov. 1812)
Rayfield, William J., age 31, in U.S. since 20 May 1803, wife,
221 South Front St., accomptant (22 July 1812)
Rebum, John, age 29, in U.S. since 7 Aug. 1806, wife & 2 children,
192 Queen St., tailor; applied 7 Dec. 1812 (7-12 Dec. 1812)
Reed, Alexander, age 24, in U.S. since 19 Sept. 1802, wife and
child, 152 Arch St., printer (7-12 Dec. 1812)
Reed, James, age 24, in U.S. since 22 June 1807, Frankford, wea-
ver (25 Mar. 1813)
Reed, John, age 39, in U.S. since 18 Oct. 1811, wife, Race St.
between 7th & 8th Sts. from Schuylkill, weaver (1-9 Sept. 1812)
Reed, Thomas, age 24, in U.S. since 1811, Nitre-Hall Mills, powder maker (6 Dec. 1813)
Regan, John, age 35, in U.S. since 22 Aug. 1806, wife and five
children, 13th St. between Filbert & Arch Sts., carter (25 Mar.
1813)
Reiley, Patrick, age 45, in U.S. since 18 Oct. 1798, wife and 4
children, Frankford, Phila. Co., labourer (22 Mar. 1813)
Reilly, Bernard, age 25, in U.S. since 4 Aug. 1812, 4th St. above
Callowhill St. at Noah Underwood's, weaver (1-31 Aug. 1814)

Reilly, Michael, age 21, in U.S. since 10 May 1812, 24 Cherry
Alley, blacksmith (24 Mar. 1813)
Reilly, Paul, age 27, 5 years in U.S., 32 North 7th St., grocer
(20-25 July 1812)
Reilly, Patrick, age 29, in U.S. since 1 June 1807, corner Crown
& Vine Sts., sugar refiner; applied 13 Oct. 1809 (22 July 1812)
Rice, Michael, age 40, in U.S. since 16 Aug. 1806, Arch St. near
7th St., labourer (23 Mar. 1813)
Richardson, John, age 37, in U.S. since 12 June 1807, 216 South
2nd St., shoemaker (2-7 Nov. 1812)
Richmond, Robert, age 23, in U.S. since 2 Feb. 1810, Hamilton's
Village, printer (22 Mar. 1813)
Riley, Edward, age 33, in U.S. since 1 Aug. 1812, 28 South 3rd
St., gunsmith (17 May 1813)
Riley, James, age 29, in U.S. since 2 June 1812, 21 Lombard St.,
tailor; applied 1 Apr. 1813 (17 Feb. 1814)
Roberts, John, age 38, 8 years in U.S., Bristol Twp., Phila. Co.,
clothier (16 Dec. 1813)
Robinson, David, age 30, in U.S. since 19 June 1814, mariner, a
deserter from Albion 74 (30 June 1814)
Robinson, John, age 21, in U.S. since 30 Oct. 1811, 121 North
5th St., soap-boiler (2 Dec. 1812)
Robinson, John, age 20, in U.S. since 20 Dec. 1810, between Mar-
ket & Chestnut Sts., labourer (26 Mar. 1813)
Robinson, Thomas, age 22, in U.S. since 1 Sept. 1810, Chester Co.,
farmer (22 Mar. 1813)
Robinson, William, age 24, in U.S. since 19 June 1814, mariner,
deserter from Albion 74 (30 June 1814)
Robotham, William, age 46, in U.S. since 19 July 1801, wife, near
the New Prison, Phila., tailor (25 Nov. 1812)
Robson, John, age 40, 9 years in U.S., wife & child, Garden St.,
Spring Garden, Phila. Co., dealer in cattle; applied 10 July
in Superior Court of Pa. (20 July 1812)
Rodden, Hugh, age 21, in U.S. since 1 May 1812, Upton Court,
Northern Liberties, labourer (24 Mar. 1813)
Rodgers, Thomas, age 47, in U.S. since 20 Dec. 1811, wife and 8
children, 11th St. near Race St., assistant at a grocery store
(23 Mar. 1813)
Rodgers, Thomas, age 27, in U.S. since 1810, Nitre-Hall Mills,
powder maker (6 Dec. 1813)
Roebuck, John Wood, age 30, in U.S. since 14 June 1806, wife and
child, Germantown, stocking-weaver (22 Mar. 1813)
Rogers, John, age 22, in U.S. since 3 June 1812, Walnut St.,
teacher (23 Mar. 1813)
Rogers, John, age 22, in U.S. since 17 May 1805, 72 South 4th
St., cabinetmaker (2-7 Nov. 1812)
Ronaldson, Richard, age 40, in U.S. since 28 Aug. 1811, South St.,
letter founder; applied 1 Oct. 1811; was in U.S. from 15 Aug.
1801 to 3 Jan. 1807 (20 July 1812)
Roston, James, age 26, in U.S. since 27 Dec. 1807, Holmesburgh,
Phila. Co., spinner (12 Dec. 1812)
Rowand, John, age 22, in U.S. since 24 Aug. 1811, corner of 12th
and Pine Sts., weaver (24 July 1812)
Rushton, Edward, age 25, in U.S. since 5 Oct. 1805, wife & child
10th St. between Arch St. and Cherry Alley, accomptant (22 July
1812)
Russel, Charles, age 30, in U.S. since 14 July 1803, wife & 2
children, Upper Merion, Montgomery Co., labourer (1-9 Sept.
1814)
Russell, Eli, age 34, in U.S. since 25 July 1801, wife, Haver-
ford Twp., Delaware Co., farmer (28 Nov. 1812)
Ryan, Dennis, age 21, in U.S. since 2 Jan. 1800, between Walnut
& Spruce Sts., coachman (25 Mar. 1813)
Ryan, Thomas, age 22, in U.S. since 10 Aug. 1810, 190 Chestnut
St. (25 Mar. 1813)

Sargent, Thomas, age 38, in U.S. since 25 May 1805, wife and 3
  children, 3 Cherry St., tavern-keeper; applied 9 June 1812
  (24 July 1812)
Scanal, John, age 22, in U.S. since 22 July 1809, Haverford,
  Delaware Co., weaver (2-7 Nov. 1812)
Scanlon, Peter, age 23, in U.S. since 1 May 1810, at George Ser-
  vice's in Willings Alley, skin-dresser (1-9 Sept. 1814)
Scotney, Thomas, age 39, in U.S. since 24 July 1804, wife, 85
  South 5th St., labourer (7-12 Dec. 1812)
Scott, Andrew, age 28, in U.S. since 11 May 1812, Locust St.
  between 12th & 13th Sts., weaver (27 Mar. 1813)
Scott, Henry, age 23, in U.S. since 1810, Nitre-Hall Mills, pow-
  der maker (6 Dec. 1813)
Scott, James, age 24, 1 year in U.S., wife & child, Germantown,
  weaver (25 July 1812)
Scott, John, age 26, in U.S. since 15 Sept. 1797, 2 sisters, 9
  South 6th St., umbrella maker (20 July 1812)
Scott, Joseph, age 24, in U.S. since 11 May 1812, Locust St.,
  between 12th & 13th Sts., carter (27 Mar. 1813)
Scott, Robert, age 22, in U.S. since Dec. 1795, wife, South Front
  St. near Prime St., Southwark, ropemaker (2-7 Nov. 1812)
Scott, William, age 25, in U.S. since 17 May 1812, 243 South 6th
  St., dyer (1-9 Sept. 1814)
Selby, Richard Stephen, age 46, in U.S. since 15 Jan. 1809, 76
  South St., storekeeper (25 July 1812)
Shackleton, Thomas G., age 33, in U.S. since 9 Nov. 1810, wife &
  3 children, 74 Locust St., firsting (firstling?) cutter (7-12
  Dec. 1812)
Shannon, John, age 24, in U.S. since 17 May 1811, 205 South 4th
  St., weaver (1-9 Sept. 1814)
Sharing, John, age 28, in U.S. since 22 Mar. 1811, 246 South 3rd
  St., baker (23 July 1812)
Sharwin, Thomas, age 20, in U.S. since 23 May 1810, South St.
  between 10th & 11th Sts., weaver (20 Mar. 1813)
Shaughnassy, Andrew, age 27, in U.S. since 15 June 1812, 27 Mar-
  ket St. at Mr. Clyne's, clerk (4 Dec. 1812)
Shaw, Joseph, age 33, in U.S. since 30 Oct. 1805, 65 Locust St.,
  minister (22 Mar. 1813)
Shaw, Michael Andrew, age 47, 18 mos. in U.S., 13 South 2nd St.,
  gentleman (20 July 1812)
Shaw, Robert, age 32, in U.S. since 29 Aug. 1801, wife & 4 child-
  ren, Frankford, labourer (24 Mar. 1813)
Shaw, Thomas, age 35, 2 years in U.S., at the Bull's Head, North
  2nd St., Northern Liberties, cotton spinner (20-25 July 1812)
Shea, John, age 26, in U.S. since 5 Oct. 1810, wife & 2 children,
  between 10th & Filbert Sts., stone-cutter (19 Mar. 1813)
Sherrins, William, age 30, in U.S. since 1793, wife & 3 children,
  St. John St. between 3rd and 4th Sts., labourer (24 Nov. 1812)
Shields, Peter, age 28, in U.S. since 29 Aug. 1808, wife and 3
  children, South St., drayman (15 Mar. 1813)
Shortt, John H., age 36, in U.S. since 25 Nov. 1807, 118 North
  5th St., gentleman; applied 28 July 1812 (22 Dec. 1812)
Shuborne, William, age 41, 7 years in U.S., wife & 4 children,
  52 Swanson St., baker (20 July 1812)
Siddall, Joseph, age 19, in U.S. since 5 Oct. 1810, Phila., sur-
  veyor (1-31 Aug. 1814)
Simpson, John, age 23, in U.S. since 24 Sept. 1809, corner Prune
  & 5th Sts., turner (22 Mar. 1813)
Simpson, William, age 20, in U.S. since 8 Jan. 1811, wife & 2
  children, 5th St. from Schuylkill, between Market and Chestnut
  Sts., weaver (1-31 Aug. 1814)
Small, Rhodery, age 30, in U.S. since 15 Nov. 1803, wife and 2
  children, Arch St. near 8th St., bottler (19 Mar. 1813)
Smiley, John, age 45, in U.S. since 18 May 1810, Race St. between
  7th & 8th Sts. (2-7 Nov. 1812)

Smiley, William, age 36, in U.S. since 26 Oct. 1812, 14 Cherry
St., merchant; he came tc U.S. to settle accounts of Andrew
Smiley, lately dec'd, and intends to return to Europe as soon
as said accounts are settled (10-14 Nov. 1812)
Smith, Alexander, age 22, in U.S. since 20 Aug. 1812, 49 Chestnut
St., labourer (23 Mar. 1813)
Smith, Charles, age 25, in U.S. since 29 May 1806, inmate at Mrs.
Patterson's in South 5th St., Southwark, weaver (22 Mar. 1813)
Smith, Colin, age 43, in U.S. since 24 Nov. 1807, 37 Market St.,
accomptant; applied 29 Dec. 1810 (24 July 1812)
Smith, Edward, age 31, in U.S. since 29 May 1806, Pennsylvania
Hospital, cell-keeper (1-31 Aug. 1814)
Smith, Edward, age 23, in U.S. since Apr. 1812, corner of 4th &
Plumb Sts., labourer (19 Mar. 1813)
Smith, Patrick, age 20, in U.S. since 8 July 1812, inmate at
South 7th St. near Pine St., labourer (2-7 Nov. 1812)
Smith, Richard, age 43, 18 years & 8 mos. in U.S., 31 North 2nd
St., accomptant (24 July 1812)
Smith, Terence, age 21, in U.S. since July 1811, 169 North 3rd
St., grocer (2-7 Nov. 1812)
Smith, William, age 60, in U.S. since 26 Oct. 1802, wife, Rox-
borough Twp., Phila. Co., weaver (2-7 Nov. 1812)
Smyth, Frederick, age 80, 50 years in U.S., Phila. & Roxborough,
gentleman (18 Mar. 1813)
Smyth, James, age 45, 8 mos. in U.S., wife & 5 children, German-
town, Phila. Co., weaver (22 July 1812)
Smyth, Robert, age 26, in U.S. since 26 Sept. 1810, at a cotton
factory in Vine St. near Schuylkill, weaver (1-31 Aug. 1814)
Soffe, John, age 40, in U.S. since July 1804, wife & 2 children,
Moyamensing Twp., Phila. Co., shoemaker (22 July 1812)
Somerville, Thomas, age 22, in U.S. since 1 May 1811, Eagle Fur-
nace near Schuylkill, iron founder (15 Mar. 1813)
Spavin, Robert, age 42, in U.S. since 21 Feb. 1802, wife and 5
children, in Askins Alley between Spruce & Locust Sts., black-
smith (22 Mar. 1813)
Spencer, James, age 28, in U.S. since 15 Apr. 1807, wife & child,
Moyamensing Twp., Phila. Co., victualer (22 July 1812)
Spraggs, Richard, Sr., age 66, in U.S. since 18 Oct. 1798, 17
Dock St., trader (21 Feb. 1814)
Stayley, George, age 19, in U.S. since 20 Dec. 1812, Mansion House
Hotel, merchant (21 Dec. 1812)
Steel, James, age 20, in U.S. since 18 Aug. 1811, 11th St. near
Race St., stone cutter (1-9 Sept. 1814)
Steel, Thomas, age 28, in U.S. since 18 May 1812, wife & 2 child-
ren, 4th St. from Schuylkill near Market St., weaver (22 Mar.
1813)
Steele, Phillip Millington, age 30, in U.S. since 17 May 1806,
Upper Makefield Twp., Bucks Co., teacher; applied 4 Dec. 1806
(20 Nov. 1812)
Sterling, Hugh, age 26, in U.S. since 14 July 1807, wife & child,
2 Race St., nail-cutter (25 July 1812)
Stevenson, John, age 23, in U.S. since 19 June 1814, mariner,
deserter from <u>Albion</u> 74 (30 July 1814)
Stevenson, Thomas, age 23, in U.S. since 29 Aug. 1811, South 3rd
St., No. 66, tanner (1-31 Aug. 1814)
Stevenson, William, age 32, in U.S. since 29 May 1804, wife and
4 children, Weaver's Alley near 13th St., labourer (15 Mar. 1814)
Stevenson, William, age 24, in U.S. since 4 Aug. 1810, wife & 1
child, Wood St. between 5th & 6th Sts., carter (28 Apr. 1813)
Steward, David, age 27, in U.S. since 14 May 1807, Rowland Mills,
Montgomery Co., labourer in ironworks (1-9 Sept. 1814)
Stewart, James, age 21, in U.S. since 8 Aug. 1802, wife and three
children, Middletown Twp., Delaware Co., weaver ; applied 22
Mar. 1813 (22 Mar. 1813)

Stewart, John, age 29, in U.S. since 26 Sept. 1810, Parker's
Factory, Prune St., weaver (1-9 Sept. 1814)
Stewart, Samuel, age 23, in U.S. since 17 June 1812, corner 6th
& Coates's St., turner (2-7 Nov. 1812)
Stewart, Thomas, age 54, in U.S. since 27 May 1805, wife and 4
children, back of 58 Zane St., gentleman (25 Mar. 1813)
Stewart, Thomas, age 20, in U.S. since 2 June 1812, Upper Block-
ley Twp., Phila. Co., coachman (19 Mar. 1813)
Stewart, Thomas, age 14, in U.S. since 26 May 1812, 208 South
3rd St., gentleman (18 May 1813)
Sturt, Mathew, age 25, in U.S. since 4 July 1806, wife, Juniper
St. near Race St., labourer (19 Mar. 1813)
Such, William, age 21, in U.S. since 28 Nov. 1810, corner of
Walnut St. & Columbia Ave., groom (20 Mar. 1813)
Sullivan, Owen, age 21, in U.S. since 18 June 1812, Cheltenham,
Phila, Cc., fuller (1-9 Sept. 1814)
Summerfield, James, age 38, 19 years in U.S., wife & 6 children,
Christian St., Southwark, mariner (19 Mar. 1813)
Summerville, Patrick, age 23, in U.S. since 27 Aug. 1811, High
St. between 3rd & 4th Sts, from Schuylkill, weaver (20 Mar. 1813)
Sweeny, John, age 45, in U.S. since 2 Apr. 1812, near the Centre
Square, carpenter (23 Mar. 1813)
Taggert, John, age 24, in U.S. since 14 Nov. 1810, wife & child,
Locust St. above 9th St., stone cutter (1-9 1814)
Tappan, Joseph, age 30, in U.S. since Sept. 1813, Phila., farmer
& labourer; he says he travelled from Montreal to Phila; his
name is possibly Tappau? (3 Dec. 1813)
Tate, John, age 28, in U.S. since Oct. 1810, corner of 10th &
Race Sts., labourer (2-7 Nov. 1812)
Tate, John, age 24, in U.S. since 1 Oct. 1810, 42 South 3rd St.,
saddler (20 Mar. 1813)
Taylor, James, age 55, in U.S. since 18 Nov. 1809, Northern Li-
berties, Phila. Co., cotton spinner (23 Nov. 1812)
Taylor, James, age 23, 2½ years in U.S., Germantown, Phila. Co.,
machine maker (20-25 July 1812)
Taylor, Richard, age 19, in U.S. since 23 Nov. 1813, 3 North 4th
St., accomptant (15 Dec. 1813)
Taylor, Robert, age 53, 2½ years in U.S., wife & 5 children, Mar-
ket St, corner of Schuylkill & 7th Sts., carpenter (20-25 July
1812)
Taylor, Thomas, age 38, in U.S. since 29 Aug. 1811, Falls of
Schuylkill, wire drawer (1-9 Sept. 1814)
Tee, James, age 22, in U.S. since 15 June 1811, at Mr. McMahon's
on Township Road leading to Germantown, labourer (1-9 Sept.
1814)
Templeman, John, age 39, in U.S. since 15 June 1807, wife, Oxford
Twp., Phila. Co., grocer (10-14 Nov. 1812)
Thompson, Alexander, age 34, in U.S. since 14 Oct. 1811, wife &
child, Broad & 13th Sts. near Arch & Race Sts., weaver (1-9
Sept. 1814)
Thompson, David, age 28, in U.S. since 8 May 1812, George St.
between 12th & 13th Sts., labourer (1-9 Sept. 1814)
Thompson, James C., 3 years & 11 mos. in U.S., 137 Market St.,
dry good merchant; applied 15 Sept. 1809 (24 July 1812)
Thompson, John, age 50, in U.S. since 27 July 1803, 194 Lombard
St., grocer; applied 12 Oct. 1807 (22 Mar. 1813)
Thompson, Robert, age 18, in U.S. since 19 Oct. 1811, 15 Market
St., clerk (22 Mar. 1813)
Thompson, William R., age 37, in U.S. since 11 Sept. 1796, wife
& 4 children, Salisbury Twp., Lancaster Co., trader (27 Mar.
1813)
Thompson, William R., age 23, 4 years & 8 mos. in U.S., 15 High
St., grocer; applied 15 Sept. 1809 (24 July 1812)
Thorp, Issachar, age 37, in U.S. since 7 Oct. 1809, wife and 3
children, Bristol Twp., calico printer (24 Mar. 1813)

Thorp, James, age 35, in U.S. since 7 Oct. 1809, wife & child,
Bristol Twp., Phila. Co., calico printer (16 Dec. 1813)
Tizzard, Samuel, age 24, in U.S. since Aug. 1803, wife, 321
North 2nd St., printer; applied 2 Oct. 1809 (23 July 1812)
Todd, William, age 26, in U.S. since Aug. 1803, wife, Race St.
near 8th St., drayman (25 July 1812)
Tracey, Hugh, age 23, in U.S. since 30 June 1811, 115 High St.,
confectioner (26 Mar. 1813)
Travers, Smith, age 29, in U.S. since 27 Oct. 1810, 16 Pine St.,
teacher (2-7 Nov. 1812)
Tremayne, John, age 49, in U.S. since 1 Jan. 1810, 323 High St.,
physician; applied 13 Sept. 1811 (22 July 1812)
Trendell, Thomas, age 45, in U.S. since 17 May 1804, wife, 299
Arch St., teacher; applied 9 Mar. 1810 (20 July 1812)
Tribell, Francis, age 27, in U.S. since 3 Jan. 1808, 6 South
Water St., mariner (25 Mar. 1813)
Tucker, William, age 72, in U.S. since 18 Sept. 1807, 2 From-
berger's Court, teacher of shorthand writing; applied 20 Nov.
1807 (24 July 1812)
Tunney, Philip, age 35, in U.S. since 1796, wife, Pine St. be-
tween 10th & 11th Sts., mariner (18 Mar. 1814)
Turner, John, age 21, in U.S. since 19 June 1814, mariner, de-
serter from Albion 74 (30 June 1814)
Tutton, Gardine, age 27, in U.S. since 7 Aug. 1807, wife & child,
Frankford, powder manufacturer (26 Mar. 1813)
Tweed, William, age 23, in U.S. since 3 Sept. 1810, 23 South 3rd
St., barkeeper (22 Mar. 1813)
Underwood, William, age 21, in U.S. since 1 July 1810, St. John
St. between 2nd & 3rd Sts., drayman (25 Mar. 1813)
Wade, John, age 23, 4 years in U.S., 14 Carter's Alley, paper-
stainer; applied 12 Oct. 1811 (21 July 1812)
Walker, John, age 28, in U.S. since 15 June 1812, wife & three
children, 11th St. near Race St., weaver (22 Mar. 1813)
Walker, Thomas, age 24, 10 mos. in U.S., wife, 94 Spruce St.,
saddler (21 July 1812)
Wallace, Samuel, age 21, in U.S. since 1811, Nitre-Hall Mills,
powder maker (6 Dec. 1813)
Wallace, Thomas, age 27, in U.S. since 26 Oct. 1811, wife & four
children, North 7th & Shippen Sts., weaver (1-9 Sept. 1814)
Wallace, William, age 29, in U.S. since 27 Sept. 1809, Plumb St.,
weaver (20 Mar. 1813)
Walls, James, age 20, in U.S. since May 1811, 125 South 6th St.,
blacksmith (22 Mar. 1813)
Walsh, James, age 23, in U.S. since 10 Aug. 1812, wife, 5 Fil-
bert St., labourer (1-9 Sept. 1814)
Walsh, Richard, age 23, in U.S. since 2 Dec. 1811, at John Carr's
in Walnut St. between 10th & 11th Sts., plasterer (1-9 Sept.
1814)
Ward, John, age 22, in U.S. since 30 Aug. 1811, 85 South Water
St., assistant clerk (22 Mar. 1813)
Warner, William, age 20, in U.S. since 29 Nov. 1810, corner of
Walnut St. & Columbia Ave., coachman (20 Mar. 1813)
Warren, John, age 24, 2 weeks in U.S., Phila., calico printer
(1-31 Aug. 1814)
Warren, William, age 45, 5 years in U.S., wife & 2 sons, 385
South 2nd St., trader; applied 21 Oct. 1810 (20 July 1812)
Wason, Archibald, age 24, in U.S. since 17 June 1811, wife, 219
Filbert St., drayman (19 Mar. 1813)
Waters, John, age 30, in U.S. since 12 Sept. 1801, wife & one
male child, Holmesburgh, Phila. Co., teamster (12 Dec. 1812)
Watson, George, age 20, in U.S. since 1811, Nitre-Hall Mills,
powder maker (6 Dec. 1813)
Watson, James, age 19, in U.S. since 1810, Nitre- Hall Mills,
powder maker (6 Dec. 1813)
Watt, James, age 21, in U.S. since 8 July 1811, 80 North 9th St.,
weaver (23 Mar. 1813)

Watt, John, age 52, in U.S. since 4 Aug. 1812, Weavers Alley between 12th & 13th Sts. & Walnut & Locust Sts., labourer; applied 28 Oct. 1812 (1-9 Sept. 1814)

Watt, John, age 51, in U.S. since 4 Aug. 1812, at Daniel Croson's in Locust St., between 12th & 13th Sts., weaver; he intends to return to Ireland as soon as possible (18 Mar. 1813)

Watt, John, age 50, in U.S. since 8 July 1811, wife & 7 children, North 9th St., gentleman (23 Mar. 1813)

Watt, John, age 18, in U.S. since 8 July 1811, 123 South 11th St., stone cutter (1-9 Sept. 1814)

Watt, William, age 24, in U.S. since 15 Sept. 1810, 50 North 4th St., clerk; applied 4 Oct. 1810 (28 Apr. 1813)

Watts, James, age 23, in U.S. since 1 Sept. 1811, Pine St. near 12th St., carpenter (25 Mar. 1813)

Weatherhead, John, age 22, 9 mos. in U.S., Germantown, carpenter (20 July 1812)

Webb, Thomas, age 32, in U.S. since 31 Mar. 1809, corner of Lombard St., shoemaker (1 Apr. 1814)

Webster, George, age 33, in U.S. since Feb. 1811, wife, 405 Market St., brush-maker; is married to a citizen's daughter (24 July 1812)

Weir, John, age 27, in U.S. since 14 Sept. 1810, wife & child, Falls of Schuylkill, marble-sawyer (23 Mar. 1813)

Weir, John B., age 30, in U.S. since 1 Sept. 1803, wife and five children, 125 North 11th St., saddler (22 Mar. 1813)

Welsh, Richard Ellis, age 21, in U.S. since 7 Apr. 1809, 127 South 3rd St., clerk; wishes to return to Europe (22 Mar. 1813)

Wetherill, Richard, age 23, in U.S. since 14 June 1812, Providence Twp., Delaware Co., at Thomas Bowen's factory, weaver (1-31 Aug. 1814)

Whelan, William, age 29, in U.S. since 8 May 1803, wife and six children, 131 Chestnut St., grocer; applied 20 Feb. 1809 (10-14 Nov. 1812)

White, George, in U.S. since 16 July 1807, 2 Pear St., bottler (2-7 Nov. 1812)

White, James, age 34, in U.S. since 19 May 1801, wife & child, 11 Gaskill St., mahogany-sawyer (23 Mar. 1813)

White, James, age 30, in U.S. since 20 Oct. 1810, wife & child, 98 Vine St., weaver (25 July 1812)

White, James, age 30, in U.S. since 19 Nov. 1810, northwest corner of Lombard & 5th Sts., grocer; applied 20 Mar. 1812 at New York (21 July 1812)

White, James, age 23, in U.S. since 17 June 1811, Market St. near Schuylkill, weaver (27 Mar. 1813)

White, John, age 40, in U.S. since Feb. 1802, wife & child, 6 South Water St., mariner (25 Mar. 1813)

Whitten, John, age 31, in U.S. since 29 Nov. 1810, Marple Twp., Delaware Co., weaver (1-31 Aug. 1814)

Wiley, John, age 21, in U.S. since 5 Nov. 1811, northwest corner of Arch & 2nd Sts., grocer (17 Nov. 1812)

Williams, Albert, age 24, in U.S. since 26 Aug. 1814, sailor (1-9 Sept. 1814)

Williams, Griffith, age 40, in U.S. since 1 Aug. 1801, wife, Harrogate, Phila. Co., farmer (20 Mar. 1813)

Williams, James, age 29, in U.S. since 15 July 1809, 14 Moravian Alley, coachman (1-31 Aug. 1814)

Williams, Richard, age 46, in U.S. since Aug. 1800, Broad St. between Walnut & Chestnut Sts., shoemaker (25 Nov. 1812)

Williams, Robert, age 40, in U.S. since Mar. 1811, wife & three children, Blockley Twp., machine maker (22 Mar. 1813)

Williamson, Stephen, age 22, in U.S. since 9 Aug. 1809, Cherry St., a few doors above 11th St. in home of Robt. Boggs, silk dyer (1-9 Sept. 1814)

Wilson, Alexander, age 45, in U.S. since 4 Sept. 1809, Elmesley's Alley, turner (23 Mar. 1813)

Wilson, Francis, age 36, in U.S. since July 1801, wife and six
  children, Abington, Montgomery Co., labourer (1-9 Sept. 1814)
Wilson, George, age 23, in U.S. since 1811, Nitre-Hall Mills,
  saltpeter refiner (6 Dec. 1813)
Wilson, John, age 21, in U.S. since 23 Oct. 1811, Catharine St.
  near Front St., shoemaker (22 Mar. 1813)
Wilson, Thomas, age 48, in U.S. since 1 May 1801, wife and three
  children, 24 North 10th St., stone cutter (2-7 Nov. 1812)
Wilson, Thomas, age 38, in U.S. since 1 May 1811, at Dr. Blair's
  in Germantown, manufacturer (1-9 Sept. 1814)
Wilson, Thomas, age 22, in U.S. since 1811, Nitre-Hall Mills,
  powder maker (6 Dec. 1813)
Wilson, William, age 30, in U.S. since 1807, Nitre-Hall Mills,
  saltpeter refiner (6 Dec. 1813)
Wilson, William, age 30, in U.S. since 26 Sept. 1809, Bucking-
  ham Twp., Bucks Co., stone mason (2-7 Nov. 1812)
Wilson, William, age 26, in U.S. since 20 Dec. 1812, 265 South
  5th St., merchant (21 Dec. 1812)
Winn, Thomas, age 30, in U.S. since Aug. 1795, wife, 122 Swan-
  son St., mariner (3 Dec. 1812)
Winpenny, Samuel, age 38, in U.S. since 17 Dec. 1806, wife and 5
  children, Germantown, manufacturer of broadcloths; applied 2
  Jan. 1813 (15 Mar. 1813)
Winter, William R., age 21, in U.S. since 17 Mar. 1810, Chester,
  N.J., farmer (1-9 Sept. 1814)
Withington, Thos. Scholes, age 22, in U.S. since 30 Apr. 1810,
  193 Walnut St., merchant; applied 20 Apr. 1811 (21 Dec. 1812)
Wonch(or Winch?), James, age 30, in U.S. since 12 Jan. 1804,
  corner of South & Penn Sts., mariner (No. 1427)
Woods, Patrick, age 26, 1 mo. in U.S., corner 10th & Locust Sts.,
  wheelwright (20-25 July 1812)
Woods, William, age 29, in U.S. since 16 June 1806, wife, 10
  North 8th St., grocer (24 July 1812)
Wooley, Milling, age 32, in U.S. since 14 Oct. 1813, at Henry
  Hawkins's factory in Ridge Road, weaver; applied 15 Dec. 1813
  (16 Dec. 1813)
Worthington, Thomas B., age 25, in U.S. since 20 May 1805, North
  2nd St., weaver; applied 24 July 1812 (24 May 1813)
Wotherspoon, Robert, age 23, in U.S. since 11 June 1811, 2nd St.
  near the Globe Mill, Northern Liberties, manufacturer (23 July
  1812)
Wright, Benjamin, age 27, in U.S. since 2 May 1806, wife, three
  children & 7 apprentices, 115 North 2nd St., brushmaker; ap-
  plied 27 June 1812 (22 July 1812)
Wright, Henry, age 24, in U.S. since 21 July 1809, 112 North
  Front St., mariner (16 Mar. 1813)
Wright, John, age 32, in U.S. since 6 Apr. 1803, wife and two
  children, Trotter's Alley, accomptant (22 July 1812)
Wright, William, age 26, in U.S. since 20 Aug. 1805, Passyunk
  Twp., Phila. Co., accomptant (26 May 1813)
Wyatt, Thomas, age 28, in U.S. since 21 Oct. 1811, wife & three
  children, Blockley Twp., cloth manufacturer (7 Dec. 1813)
Wylie, Samuel B., age 36, in U.S. since 21 Oct. 1797, wife and 2
  children, Walnut above 11th St., minister of Gospel (19 Mar. 1813)
Yeates, Edman, Jr., age 29, 7 years & 8 mos. in U.S., wife and 2
  children, South 5th St., tin manufacturer & coppersmith (23
  July 1812)
Young, Andrew, age 23, in U.S. since 7 Sept. 1809, wife, Roxbo-
  rough Twp., Phila. Co., machine maker (2-7 Nov. 1812)
Young, Edward, age 20, in U.S. since 18 May 1811, Germantown, car-
  penter (23 Mar. 1813)
Young, John, age 24, in U.S. since 25 June 1808, 2 North 10th St.,
  bottler (22 Mar. 1813)
Young, William, age 26, in U.S. since Apr. 1794, Sterling Alley,
  carver & gilder, 9 years apprentice in NYC (24 July 1812)

MARYLAND

Abatt(?), Benjamin, age 23, 2 years in U.S., Baltimore, cooper
(11 Oct. 1813)
Adams, John, age 41, 5 years in U.S., Baltimore, wife, shoemaker
(11 Oct. 1813)
Adams, John, age 34, 10 years in U.S., wife, Washington Co., innkeeper (8-22 Aug. 1812)
Adger, Samuel, age 18, 6 mos. in U.S., Baltimore, clerk (25 July -
1 Aug. 1812); see Samuel Edgar below.
Ainsley/Ainslie, Peter, age 24, 1 year in U.S., Baltimore, minister of the Gospel (8-22 Aug. 1812
Alexander, Thomas, age 24, 2 years in U.S., Baltimore, grocer
(22 Aug. - 2 Sept. 1812)
Alford, James, age 22, 3 years in U.S., Baltimore, weaver (11 Oct.
1813)
Allen, John, age 26, 5 years in U.S., wife, Fell's Point, Baltimore, mathematical instrument maker (10-18 July 1812); the next
year he has a child (11 Oct. 1813)
Allen, Michael, age 48, 16 years in U.S., Montgomery Co., stone
mason (22 Aug. - 2 Sept. 1812)
Anderson, James, age 34, 11 years in U.S., wife & 2 children,
Westminster, plasterer (8-22 Aug. 1812)
Anderson, Robert, age 25, 6 years in U.S., wife & child, Balti-
more, weaver (18-25 July 1812); the next year he has another
child (11 Oct. 1813)
Andrews, Andrew L., age 25, 3 years in U.S., Baltimore, stone
quarrier (11 Oct. 1813)
Andrews, James, age 33, 9 years in U.S., wife, Baltimore, bleacher
(8-22 Aug. 1831)
Arbuckle, Thomas, age 28, 9 years in U.S., Baltimore, accountant
(10-18 July 1812); in 1813 he is described as clerk and has
been removed to Carlisle (10 Oct. 1813)
Armat, Christopher, age 27, 9 years in U.S., wife & 3 children,
Baltimore, merchant (10-18 July 1812)
Armat, William, age 20, 16 years in U.S., Baltimore, clerk (10-
18 July 1812)
Armstrong, Francis, age 40, 18 mos. in U.S., Baltimore, 4 child-
ren, labourer (11 Oct. 1813)
Armstrong, Walter, age 35, 6 years in U.S., wife & 4 children,
Baltimore, iron founder (11 Oct. 1813)
Arnold, David, age 34, 7 years in U.S., Hagerstown, weaver (8-22
Aug. 1812)
Arthur, Francis, age 20, 7 years in U.S., Baltimore, clerk (18-
25 July 1812)
Ashton, John, age 36, 1 year in U.S., wife & child, Washington
Co., weaver (8-22 Aug. 1812)
Ashton, Joseph, age 34, 10 years in U.S., Washington Co., weaver
(8-22 Aug. 1812)
Auchincloss, Arthur, age 34, 12 years in U.S., wife & child, New
York, merchant (18-25 July 1812)
Auchincloss, John, age 23, 9 years in U.S., wife, Baltimore, dry
good merchant; applied 12 Jan. 1812 (10-18 July 1812)
Audain, John, age 64, 3 years in U.S., Fell's Point, Baltimore,
Church of England clergyman (10-18 July 1812)
Baker, John, age 39, 9 years in U.S., wife & 4 children, Balti-
more, stone mason (10-18 July 1812)
Baker, Robert, age 23, 1 year in U.S., Baltimore, cotton card
manufacturer (10-18 July 1812)
Banks, George, age 30, 11 years in U.S., wife, Baltimore, pain-
ter & glazier (18-25 July 1812)
Banks, William, age 31, 10 days in U.S., wife, Baltimore, merchant
(10-18 July 1812)

Barker, John, age 25, 15 mos. in U.S., wife & 3 children, Baltimore, iron founder (18-25 July 1812)
Barker, John, age 24, 3 years in U.S., Baltimore, wife & 3 children, weaver (11 Oct. 1813)
Barker, William, age 50, 15 mos. in U.S., wife & 4 children, Baltimore, iron founder (18-25 July 1812)
Barnet, William, age 23, 19 mos. in U.S., Baltimore, weaver (11 Oct. 1813)
Barnet, William, age 22, 2 years in U.S., Baltimore, painter (11 Oct. 1813)
Barney, Patrick, age 27, 6 years in U.S., Baltimore, wife, storekeeper (11 Oct. 1813)
Barnfield, Barzillar, age 48, 2 years & 6 mos. in U.S., 6 children, Baltimore, cloth weaver (10-18 July 1812)
Barr, William, age 20, 2 years in U.S., Baltimore, clerk (10-18 July 1812)
Bartlett, John, age 45, 12 years in U.S., 5 children, Washington Co., house-carpenter (8-22 Aug. 1812)
Bartlett, Richard, age 33, 11 years in U.S., wife, Washington Co., house-carpenter (8-22 Aug. 1812)
Barton, Robert, age 35, 20 years in U.S., wife & 5 children. Baltimore Co., farmer (11 Oct. 1813)
Baxter, C., age 26, 6 years in U.S., wife & child, Baltimore, rigger (11 Oct. 1813)
Beard, Hugh, age 36, 7 years in U.S., wife & 2 children, Baltimore, paver; applied Mar. 1810 (11 Oct. 1813)
Bedford, William T., age 46, 10 years in U.S., wife & 4 children, Baltimore Co., merchant (1-8 Aug. 1812)
Bell, John, age 46, 5 years in U.S., wife & 4 children, Baltimore, painter (18-25 July 1812)
Bell, Thomas C., age 21, 7 years in U.S., Baltimore, painter (11 Oct. 1813)
Benckert/Benckhart, John D., age 24, 10 years in U.S., wife, Baltimore, morocco manufacturer (10-18 July 1812); in 1813 age is given as 26, with 12 years in U.S. (11 Oct. 1813)
Beresford, William, age 26, 5 years in U.S., Baltimore Co., moulder (11 Oct. 1813)
Bevard, James, age 47, 21 years in U.S., wife & 3 children, Baltimore, carter (8-22 Aug. 1812)
Birch, William, age 34, 11 mos. in U.S., Baltimore, paper hanger (18-25 July 1812)
Birnie, Clotworthy, age 47, 2 years in U.S., wife & 9 children, Frederick Co., farmer (8-22 Aug. 1812)
Black, William, age 37, 11 years in U.S., Cecil Co., linen weaver (8-22 Aug. 1812)
Blair, Hugh, age 21, 6 years in U.S., Baltimore, cabinetmaker; applied Apr. 1812 (11 Oct. 1813)
Bland, Samuel, age 28, 7 years in U.S., wife & child, Baltimore Co., millwright (25 July - 1 Aug. 1812)
Bolston, John, age 25, 4 years in U.S., wife & child, Baltimore, nailor (11 Oct. 1813)
Bolton, B.B., age 38, 2 years in U.S., wife & 3 children, Baltimore, pianoforte maker (11 Oct. 1813)
Bond, Henry, age 19, 4 years in U.S., Baltimore (2-12 Sept. 1812)
Bond, Thomas, age 20, 2 years in U.S., Baltimore, clerk 2-12 Sept. & 11 Oct. 1813)
Bond, Timothy, age 40, 10 years in U.S., wife, Baltimore, millwright (11 Oct. 1813)
Bourne, Thomas, age 23, 7 days in U.S., Baltimore, seaman (18 Sept. - 31 Oct. 1812)
Bowghton (or Boughton?), Thomas, age 61, 19 years in U.S., wife & child, Baltimore, cooper (18-25 July 1812)
Boyd, James, age 45, 3 years in U.S., wife & 2 children, Baltimore, millwright (11 Oct. 1813)

Boyd, Peter, age 29, 5 years in U.S., 3 children, Baltimore, soap
and candle manufacturer (10-18 July 1812); applied Mar. 1811
(11 Oct. 1813)
Boyd, Samuel, age 26, 2 years in U.S., wife, Baltimore, carpenter (11 Oct. 1813)
Boyle, Edward, age 30, 3 years in U.S., wife & 2 children, Baltimore, weaver (11 Oct. 1813)
Boyle, John, age 35, 2 years in U.S., Baltimore, minister of the
Gospel (22 Aug. - 2 Sept. 1812)
Boyle, Patrick, age 20, 16 years in U.S., Baltimore, paper hanger (11 Oct. 1813)
Bradlee, Newton, age 45, 17 years in U.S., Prince George's Co.,
schoolmaster; applied 22 Apr. 1806 but clerk did not have copy
of the oath of allegiance (25 July - 1 Aug. 1812)
Brady, Francis, age 25, 5 years in U.S., wife & child, Baltimore,
trader (18-25 July 1812)
Brahney, James, age 23, 3 years in U.S., Baltimore, clerk (11 Oct.
1813)
Branham, Peter, age 30, 16 years in U.S., wife & 2 children, Bal-
timore, cooper (11 Oct. 1813)
Brevett/Brevitt, Joseph, age 43, 15 years in U.S., 5 children,
Baltimore, physician (18-25 July 1812); in 1813 wife mentioned
(11 Oct. 1813)
Brinkett, William, age 40, 3 years in U.S., Baltimore Co., wea-
ver; applied Mar. 1812 (11 Oct. 1813)
Broefreau, David W., age 40, 6 years in U.S., Baltimore, teacher
(25 July - 1 Aug. 1812)
Brook, Thomas, age 34, 5 years in U.S., Baltimore, teacher; ap-
plied 18 July 1811 (25 July - 1 Aug. 1812)
Brouillett, Charles, age 23, 18 mos. in U.S., Baltimore, confec-
tioner (18-25 July 1812)
Brown, Archibald, age 20, 12 years in U.S., Montgomery Co., far-
mer (22 Aug. - 2 Sept. 1812)
Brown, Edward, age 26, 9 years in U.S., wife & 3 children, Bal-
timore, labourer (18-25 July 1812)
Brown, John, age 38, 5 years in U.S., Baltimore, bricklayer (16
Sept. - 31 Oct. 1812)
Brown, John, age 37, 16 mos. in U.S., wife, Baltimore, weaver of
coach lace; applied June 1811 (10-18 July 1812)
Brown, John, age 37, 2 years in U.S., wife, Baltimore Co., far-
mer; applied June 1811 (11 Oct. 1813)
Brown, John, age 28, 6 years in U.S., Baltimore, seaman; applied
June 1812 (11 Oct. 1813)
Brown, Samuel, age 43, 7 years in U.S., wife, Baltimore Co., ba-
ker (18-25 July 1812); by fall of 1813 a child had been born
(11 Oct. 1813)
Brown, Thomas, age 54, 12 years in U.S., wife & child, Montgomery
Co., farmer (22 Aug. - 2 Sept. 1812)
Bunce, Robert Spencer, age 31, 10 years in U.S., Worcester Co.,
schoolmaster; applied 16 May 1812 (8-22 Aug. 1812)
Bungie, Robert, age 27, 18 years in U.S., Baltimore, musical in-
strument maker (11 Oct. 1813)
Burke, John, age 48, 5 years in U.S., Baltimore, labourer (11 Oct.
1813)
Burke, Thomas, age 34, 6 years in U.S., Baltimore, teacher; ap-
plied Mar. 1810 (11 Oct. 1813)
Burn, William, age 41, 28 years in U.S., Baltimore, bookkeeper
(11 Oct. 1813)
Burn, William, age 40, 7 years in U.S., Fell's Point, Baltimore,
clerk (10-18 July 1812)
Burnet, Thomas, age 36, 22 years in U.S., wife & 5 children,
Montgomery Co., farmer (22 Aug. - 2 Sept. 1812)
Burnitt, Richard, age 33, 9 years in U.S., wife & child, Balti-
more, cordwainer (10-18 July 1812)

Burnup, John, age 32, 5 years in U.S., wife & 3 children, Baltimore, pump maker (11 Oct. 1813)

Burroughs, Isaac, age 28, 3 years in U.S., Baltimore, wharfinger;
applied Jan. 1812 (18-25 July 1812)

Burrows, Richard, age 22, 8 days in U.S., Baltimore (1-8 Aug.
1812)

Burrows, Thomas, age 28, 7 years in U.S., Baltimore, saddler (11
Oct. 1813)

Byrne, Timothy, age 42, 9 years in U.S., wife, Baltimore, millstone maker (18-25 July 1812)

Calahan, James, age 35, 12 years in U.S., Baltimore, grocer (11
Oct. 1813)

Caldwell, George, age 48, 7 years in U.S., Emmitsburg, weaver
(8-22 Aug. 1812)

Caldwell, Henry, age 20, 9 mos. in U.S., Hagerstown, clerk (8-22
Aug. 1812)

Callaghan/Calleghin, Peter, age 26, 5 years in U.S., Baltimore,
shoemaker (18-25 July 1812)

Callighan, James, age 25, 3 years in U.S., Baltimore, trader (2-
12 Sept. 1812)

Campbell, Archibald, age 36, 5 years in U.S., wife & 4 children,
Baltimore Co., miner (1-8 Aug. 1812)

Campbell, Arthur, age 46, 24 years in U.S., Montgomery Co., farmer (22 Aug. - 2 Sept. 1812)

Campbell, Daniel, age 23, 2 years in U.S., Baltimore, clerk (11
Oct. 1813)

Campbell, James, age 28, 11 years in U.S., Baltimore, storekeeper
(11 Oct. 1813)

Campbell, James, age 14, 1 year in U.S., Baltimore Co., miner (1-
8 Aug. 1812)

Campbell, Wm., age 23, 20 mos. in U.S., Baltimore, labourer (11
Oct. 1813)

Cannon (?), John, age 38, 3 years in U.S., Baltimore, clerk (18-
25 July 1812)

Cannon, Martin, age 61, 21 years in U.S., wife & 7 children,
Montgomery Co., farmer (22 Aug. - 2 Sept. 1812)

Cannon, Patrick, age 20, 2 years in U.S., Baltimore, labourer; removed to Philadelphia (11 Oct. 1813)

Cardwell, Abraham C., age 23, 10 days in U.S., Baltimore, merchant
(18 Sept. - 31 Oct. 1812)

Carmichael, Edward, age 29, 6 years in U.S., wife & 2 children,
Baltimore, sawyer of mahogany (16 Sept. - 31 Oct. 1812)

Carmichael, John, age 48, 6 years in U.S., wife & 6 children,
Baltimore, weaver & dyer (18 -25 July 1812)

Carmichael, John, age 20, 2 years in U.S., Baltimore Co., cotton
spinner (11 Oct. 1813)

Carney, Michael, age 25, 6 years in U.S., Baltimore, pedlar (11
Oct. 1813)

Carney, Patrick, age 30, 8 years in U.S., wife & 2 children,
Washington Co., labourer (8-22 Aug. 1812)

Carrington, Edward Douglass, age 23, 6 mos. in U.S., Baltimore
Co., mariner (10-18 July 1812)

Carrington, James, age 37, 1 year in U.S., wife & 4 children,
Baltimore Co., gentleman (10-18 July 1812)

Carroll, Daniel, age 27, 9 years in U.S., wife, Baltimore, drayman (18-25 July 1812); by Oct. 1813 he had a child (11 Oct. 1813)

Carroll, Dennis, age 48, 2 years in U.S., Baltimore, tobacconist;
applied June 1813 (11 Oct. 1813)

Carroll, John, age 40, 4 years in U.S., wife & 3 children, Baltimore Co., clerk (11 Oct. 1813)

Carroll, Patrick, age 35, 8 years in U.S., wife & 3 children,
Baltimore, storekeeper (11 Oct. 1813)

Carroll, Patrick, age 34, 11 years in U.S., 3 children, Baltimore,
carter (18-25 July 1812)

Carroll, Thomas, age 29, 18 years in U.S., wife & child, Balti-
more, whitesmith (25 July - 1 Aug. 1812)
Carroll, William, age 43, 10 years in U.S., wife & 3 children,
Washington Co., tailor (8-22 Aug. 1812)
Casey, John, age 32, 10 years in U.S., wife & child, Baltimore,
cooper (31 Oct. 1812 - 6 Jan. 1813)
Cassady/Cassiday, Christopher, age 27, 18 mos. in U.S., Balti-
more, tailor (10-18 July 1812)
Cassady, John, age 28, 6 years in U.S., Frederick Town, farmer
(8-22 Aug. 1812)
Catherall, William, age 29, 7 years in U.S., wife & child, Bal-
timore, cooper (1-8 Aug. 1812)
Caugham, Alex., age 20, 2 years in U.S., Baltimore, plumber (11
Oct. 1813)
Cavanaugh, Peter, age 35, 18 mos. in U.S., wife, Baltimore, inn-
keeper; applied Mar. 1812 (10-18 July 1812)
Cavanaugh, Peter, age 34, 7 years in U.S., wife, Baltimore, ta-
vern-keeper; applied Mar. 1812, naturalized (11 Oct. 1813)
Cayhoo, Michael, age 40, 20 years in U.S., 7 children, Washing-
ton Co., weaver (8-22 Aug. 1812)
Chaill, Michael, age 68, 8 years in U.S., wife & child, Balti-
more, drayman (25 July - 1 Aug. 1812)
Chambers, Joseph, age 28, 12 years in U.S., wife & 2 children,
Baltimore, ropemaker (18 Sept. - 31 Oct. 1812)
Chambers, Robert, age 54, 14 years in U.S., Baltimore, weaver
(11 Oct. 1813)
Chapman, George, age 24, 7 years in U.S., wife & child, Balti-
more, clerk (18-25 July 1812)
Chapman, Jonathan, age 23, 3 years in U.S., wife & child, Balti-
more Co., farmer (11 Oct. 1813)
Chapman, Jonathan, age 22, 2 years in U.S., wife & child, Balti-
more, dry good merchant (18-25 July 1812)
Charsty, Edward, age 29, 3 years in U.S., Baltimore Co., iron-
monger/ blacksmith (11 Oct. 1813)
Chester, Edward, age 28, 2 years in U.S,, wife & child, Balti-
more Co., miner (8-22 Aug. 1812)
Chrisholm, Alexander, age 33, 9 years in U.S., wife, Baltimore,
stone cutter (11 Oct. 1813)
Christie, William, age 22, 6 weeks in U.S., Cecil Co., stone
mason (8-22 Aug. 1812)
Clacton (?), Thomas, age 43, 18 mos. in U.S., wife & 6 children,
Baltimore, tailor (11 Oct. 1813)
Clark, Barnard, age 40, 15 years in U.S., Baltimore, slop shop
keeper (18-25 July 1812)
Clark, Hugh, age 23, 11 years in U.S., Frederick Town, distiller
(8-22 Aug. 1812)
Clark, Patrick, age 49, 22 years in U.S., 4 children, Baltimore,
labourer (1-8 Aug. 1812)
Clunside(?), William, age 36, 10 years in U.S., Washington Co.,
gardener; applied 1811 (8-22 Aug. 1812)
Coleman, Alexander, age 33, 6 years in U.S., Baltimore, weaver
(18-25 July 1812)
Coleman, Benjamin, age 26, 7 years in U.S., wife, Baltimore,
printer (11 Oct. 1813)
Coleman, Patrick, age 31, 4 years in U.S., Baltimore, storekeeper
(18-25 July 1812)
Coleman, Thomas, age 31, 14 years in U.S., wife & child, Balti-
more, tobacconist (11 Oct. 1813)
Colfer, John, age 30, 8 years in U.S., Baltimore, mariner (25
July - 1 Aug. 1812)
Colvin, John, age 30, 10 years in U.S., Baltimore, mason (11 Oct.
1813)
Conme(?), James, age 26, 2 years in U.S., Baltimore, soap boiler;
removed to Washington (11 Oct. 1813)

Connall, Thomas. age 32, 2 years in U.S., wife & 2 children, Baltimore, labourer (11 Oct. 1813)

Connell, Philip, age 48, 27 years in U.S., wife & 8 children, Montgomery Co., butcher (22 Aug. - 2 Sept. 1812)

Connelly, James, age 21, 2 years in U.S., Baltimore, paper printer (11 Oct. 1813)

Connelly, Patrick, age 32, 17 years in U.S., Ann Arundel Co., ditcher (31 Oct. 1812 - 6 Jan. 1813)

Connolly, Thomas, age 38, 14 years in U.S., wife & 4 children, button mould maker; naturalized (11 Oct. 1813)

Connor, Peter, age 23, 2 years in U.S., Baltimore, clerk (10-18 July 1812)

Conway, James, age 23, 19 years in U,S., Baltimore, machine maker (11 Oct. 1813)

Conway, John, age 30, 2 years in U.S., Baltimore, weaver (11 Oct. 1813)

Conway, William D., age 27, 10 years in U.S., Baltimore, bookseller; applied Mar. 1810 (10-18 July 1812)

Cook, John, age 28, 9 years in U.S., wife & child, Liberty Town, farmer (8-22 Aug. 1812)

Cooper, James, age 25, 9 years in U.S., Baltimore, cooper; applied 6 July 1812)

Corr, Owen, age 31, 1 year in U.S., wife & 2 children, Taney Town, house-carpenter (8-22 Aug. 1812)

Corrie, James, age 44, 8 years in U.S., wife & 2 children, Baltimore, house-carpenter (10-18 July 1812); by next fall he has another child (11 Oct. 1813)

Corrill, Hugh, age 40, 1 year in U.S., wife, Baltimore, weaver (18-25 July 1812)

Costello, Edmond, age 35, 2 years in U.S., wife & 2 children, Baltimore, labourer (11 Oct. 1813)

Costello, James, age 25, 13 years in U.S., Baltimore, tailor; naturalized (11 Oct. 1813)

Costello, James J., age 23, 15 years in U.S., Baltimore, tailor (18-25 July 1812)

Costigan, William, age 29, 16 mos. in U.S., Cecil Co., machine maker (8-22 Aug. 1812)

Coudan, Robert, age 46, 11 years in U.S., wife, Baltimore, weaver (18 -25 July 1812)

Coulson, Patrick, age 31, 9 years in U.S., wife & 2 children, Baltimore, house-carpenter (18-25 July 1812)

Coulson, Thomas, age 47, 4 years in U.S., wife & 5 children, Baltimore, manufacturer of law papers (10-18 July 1812)

Courtney, Henry, age 25, 4 years in U.S., Baltimore Co., machine maker (11 Oct. 1813)

Cousins, John, age 31, 27 years in U.S., Baltimore, chair maker (11 Oct. 1813)

Cowen, Thomas, age 36, 5 years in U.S., wife & 2 children, Baltimore, carpenter (11 Oct. 1813)

Cowen, Thomas, age 25, 11 years in U.S., Baltimore, shoemaker (18 Sept. - 31 Oct. 1812)

Craig, George, age 26, 22 mos. in U.S., Baltimore, cordwainer (25 July - 1 Aug. 1812)

Craig, John, age 25, 6 years in U.S., Baltimore, teacher; applied 17 Nov. 1809 (18-25 July 1812)

Craig, Robert H., age 32, 5 years in U.S., Baltimore, teacher of military tactics; applied Dec. 1811 (10-18 July 1812)

Crawford, John, age 25, 2 years in U.S., Prince George's Co., farmer (11 Oct. 1813)

Creach/Crea, Hugh, age 30, 11 years in U.S., wife & 2 children, Baltimore, soap & tallow chandler (10-18 July 1812)

Creighton, Robert, age 30, 1 year in U.S., Baltimore Co., machine maker (25 July - 1 Aug. 1812)

Creswell, John, age 38, 5 years in U.S., wife & 4 children, Baltimore Co., teacher; applied Sept. 1811 (10-18 July 1812)

Crocket, David, age 30, 7 years in U.S., Baltimore, saddler; applied 23 Sept. 1809 (11 Oct. 1813)

Crook, Daniel, age 24, 2 years in U.S., Baltimore, butcher (18-25 July 1812); by Oct. 1813 he had married (11 Oct. 1813)

Crook, Henry, age 42, 7 years in U.S., wife & child, Baltimore, weaver (18-25 July 1812)

Crossan/Crossin, John, age 21, 14 mos. in U.S., Baltimore, labourer (16 Sept. - 31 Oct. 1812)

Culbertson, John, age 22, 13 mos. in U.S., Cecil Co., machine maker (8-22 Aug. 1812)

Cunningham, Hugh, age 30, 16 years in U.S., Baltimore, clerk (11 Oct. 1813)

Cunningham, Stephen, age 38, 19 mos. in U.S., wife & 3 children, Baltimore, tanner (11 Oct. 1813)

Cunningham, William, age 26, 5 years in U.S., Hagerstown, weaver (8-22 Aug. 1812)

Curghy, Barnard, age 24, 2 years in U.S., wife & 2 children, Baltimore, ship-carpenter (11 Oct. 1813)

Curran, Martin, age 32, 2 years in U.S., wife & child, Baltimore, labourer (11 Oct. 1813)

Curran, Thomas, age 26, 2 years in U.S., wife & child, Baltimore, labourer (11 Oct. 1813)

Curron (for Curran?), Matthew, age 30, 2 years in U.S., Baltimore, labourer (11 Oct. 1813)

Curtain, Lawrence, age 22, 5 days in U.S., Baltimore, clerk (1-8 Aug. 1812)

Daley, John, age 32, 2 years in U.S., Baltimore, pedlar (18-25 July 1812); by Oct. 1813 he was married (11 Oct. 1813)

Dalton, Patrick, age 26, 18 mos. in U.S., Baltimore, mahogany sawyer (11 Oct. 1813)

Davidson, John, age 43, 5 mos. in U.S., Baltimore Co., machine maker (25 July - 1 Aug. 1812)

Davis, George, age 42, 5 years in U.S., Baltimore, harness maker (11 Oct. 1813)

Davis, James, age 42, 7 years in U.S., wife, Baltimore, stationer (11 Oct. 1813)

Davis, William, age 29, 8 years in U.S., Baltimore, shoemaker (11 Oct. 1813)

Deary, John, age 36, 2 years in U.S., Baltimore, weaver (11 Oct. 1813)

Dickey, William, age 22, 5 years in U.S., Hagerstown, clerk (8-22 Aug. 1812)

Dickin (?), Alexander, age 20, 2 years in U.S., Baltimore Co., cotton spinner (11 Oct. 1813)

Dicks, John, age 22, 2 years in U.S., Baltimore, tailor (11 Oct. 1813)

Dobson, George, age 29, 3 years in U.S., Baltimore, printer (11 Oct. 1813)

Dodds, Robert, age 26, 9 years in U.S., New Windsor, physician; applied Aug. 1810 (8-22 Aug. 1812)

Dolen, Daniel, age 26, 2 years in U.S., Baltimore, labourer (11 Oct. 1813)

Dolen, John, age 28, 21 years in U.S., wife & 4 children, Baltimore, labourer (11 Oct. 1813)

Donely, James, age 24, 18 mos. in U.S., Baltimore, weaver (11 Oct. 1813)

Done(ly?), John, age 40, 18 years in U.S., wife & 6 children, Montgomery Co., farmer (22 Aug. - 2 Sept. 1812)

Donnaugh, Patrick, age 23, 2 years in U.S., Baltimore, labourer (11 Oct. 1813)

Donnelly, Daniel, age 42, 5 years in U.S., wife & child, Baltimore, pedlar (25 July - 1 Aug. 1812); by fall of 1813 has had another child (11 Oct. 1813)

Donohoo, Barney, age 38, 12 years in U.S., wife & 4 children, Baltimore, pedlar (11 Oct. 1813)

Donohoo, John, age 29, 1½ years in U.S., Baltimore, pedlar (11 Oct. 1813)

Donohoo, Michael, age 19, 16 years in U.S., Baltimore, labourer (11 Oct. 1813)

Donohoo, Patrick, age 50, 16 years in U.S., wife & 8 children, Ann Arundel Co., farmer (31 Oct. - 6 Jan. 1813)

Donohoo, Patrick, age 27, 16 years in U.S., wife & 3 children, Baltimore, shoemaker (11 Oct. 1813)

Donohoo, Thomas, age 21, 17 years in U.S., Ann Arundel Co., farmer (11 Oct. 1813)

Donovan, Jeremiah, age 39, 13 years in U.S., wife, Baltimore, grocer (1-8 Aug. 1812)

Dougherty, C., age 28, 2 years in U.S., wife & child, Baltimore, sugar boiler (11 Oct. 1812)

Dougherty, Daniel, age 30, 7 years in U.S., wife, Baltimore, type founder (11 Oct. 1813)

Dougherty, John, age 42, 15 years in U.S., wife & child, Baltimore, labourer (11 Oct. 1813)

Dougherty, John, age 34, 9 years in U.S., wife, Baltimore, livery stable keeper (11 Oct. 1813)

Dougherty, John, age 30, 12 years in U.S., wife, Frederick Co., farmer (8-22 Aug. 1812)

Dougherty, Owen, age 50, 2 years in U.S., wife & 6 children, Baltimore, labourer (11 Oct. 1813)

Dougherty, Patrick, age 18, 2 years in U.S., Baltimore, labourer (11 Oct. 1813)

Dougherty, Patrick, wife & 4 children, Baltimore, turner (11 Oct. 1813)

Dougherty, Rody, age 34, 9 years in U.S., Baltimore, labourer (18-25 July 1812)

Dougherty, Roger, age 22, 2 years in U.S., Baltimore, pedlar (11 Oct. 1813)

Dougherty, Samuel, age 18, 2 years in U.S., Baltimore, saddler (11 Oct. 1813)

Douglass, A., age 22, 2 years in U.S., Baltimore, bookbinder (11 Oct. 1813)

Doyle, John, age 27, 19 mos. in U.S., Baltimore, cabinetmaker (11 Oct. 1813)

Drips, William, age 29, 9 years in U.S., wife & child, Washington Co., manager at forge (8-22 Aug. 1812)

Drum, Oliver, age 25, 8 years in U.S., Baltimore, labourer (11 Oct. 1813)

Duddy, Henry, age 22, 2 years in U.S., Baltimore, weaver (11 Oct. 1813)

Duff, John, age 26, 2½ years in U.S., Baltimore, comedian (11 Oct. 1813)

Duffy, John, age 30, 2 years in U.S., Baltimore, labourer (11 Oct. 1813)

Dulany, William, age 33, 8 years in U.S., wife, Baltimore, carpenter (11 Oct. 1813)

Dumply, James, age 30, 9 years in U.S., wife, Baltimore, gardener (11 Oct. 1813)

Dunlap, George, age 19, 18 mos. in U.S., Baltimore, porter seller (2-12 Sept. 1812)

Dunlop, E., age 31, 2 years in U.S., Baltimore, weaver (11 Oct. 1813)

Edgar, David, age 28, 7 years in U.S., wife, Baltimore, grocer & flour merchant; applied 11 Nov. 1809 (8-22 Aug. 1812)

Edgar, Samuel, age 18, 18 mos. in U.S., Baltimore, clerk (11 Oct. 1813)

Edmondson/Edmonson, Thomas G., age 22, 2 years in U.S., Baltimore, clerk (10-18 July 1812)

Edmons/Edmund, John, age 35, 12 years in U.S., wife, Baltimore, labourer (18-25 July 1812)

Edwards, John, age 38, 6 years in U.S., wife & 2 children, Baltimore Co., gardener (8-22 Aug. 1812)

Elliott, Joseph, age 43, 19 years in U.S., Montgomery Co., teacher (22 Aug. - 2 Sept. 1812)

Elton, Miles, age 22, 2 years in U.S., Baltimore, weaver (11 Oct.
1813)

Elvige, Robert, age 34, 5 years in U.S., Baltimore, cabinetmaker (11 Oct. 1813)

Evans, Hugh W., age 23, 3 years in U.S., Baltimore, merchant's
clerk; applied 7 Mar. 1811 (18-25 July 1812)

Evans, Thomas, age 26, 8 years in U.S., wife & child, Baltimore,
house-carpenter (1-8 Aug. 1812); by Oct. 1813 he has another
child (11 Oct. 1813)

Everett, James, age 41, 9 years in U.S., wife & 4 children, Baltimore, tanner (11 Oct. 1813)

Faherty, B., age 45, 16 years in U.S., wife & 6 children, Ann
Arundel Co., farmer (2-12 Sept. 1812)

Faherty, Charles, age 36, 18 years in U.S., Ann Arundel Co.,
farmer (2-12 Sept. 1812)

Faherty, Manus, age 24, 2 years in U.S., Baltimore, labourer
(31 Oct. 1812 - 6 Jan. 1813)

Faherty, Michael, age 46, 3 years in U.S., Baltimore, labourer
(11 Oct. 1813)

Faherty, Patrick, age 48, 20 years in U.S., wife & 4 children,
Ann Arundel Co., farmer (2-12 Sept. 1812)

Faherty, Patrick, age 28, 19 mos. in U.S., Baltimore, labourer
(11 Oct. 1813)

Faherty, Peter, age 48, 18 years in U.S., Ann Arundel Co., ditcher (2-12 Sept. 1812)

Fanning, Dennis, age 30, 9 years in U.S., wife & child, Baltimore, grocer (11 Oct. 1813)

Farquharson, Charles, age 32, 11 years in U.S., Baltimore, house-
carpenter (25 July - 1 Aug. 1812); by Oct. 1813 he is married
(11 Oct. 1813)

Farquarson, John, age 56, 11 years in U.S., wife & 4 children,
Dorchester Co., merchant; applied 17 July 1811 (22 Aug. - 2
Sept. 1812)

Farrell, Francis, age 27, 1 year in U.S., Baltimore, student of
divinity (18-25 July 1812)

Farrell, James W., age 28, 5 years in U.S., Baltimore, lumber
merchant; applied 9 Mar. 1810 (10-18 July 1812)

Faultler, John, age 41, 18 years in U.S., wife, Washington Co.,
tailor (8-22 Aug. 1812)

Fenby, Peter, age 25, 19 years in U.S., Baltimore, cooper (18-25
July 1812); wife & 2 children, naturalized (11 Oct. 1813)

Fenwick, James, age 27, 18 mos. in U.S., Baltimore Co., miller
(11 Oct. 1813)

Ferguson, Charles, age 27, 6 years in U.S., Baltimore, stone cutter (25 July - 1 Aug. 1812)

Fitsimmons, Wm., age 26, 9 years in U.S., Baltimore Co., carpenter (11 Oct. 1813)

Flint, Thomas, age 21, 10 days in U.S., Baltimore, merchant (18
Sept. - 31 Oct. 1812)

Forrest, James, age 33, 3 years in U.S., Baltimore, baker (11 Oct.
1813)

Forman, Christian, age 31, 12 years in U.S., wife & 3 children,
Baltimore, butcher (18-25 July 1812)

Forsight, Robert, age 22, 6 mos. in U.S., Baltimore, weaver (18-
25 July 1812)

Forster, Francis, age 33, 8 years in U.S., wife & 3 children,
Baltimore, hatter; applied Dec. 1807; naturalized (11 Oct.
1813)

Foxlow, Joseph F., age 28, 5 years in U.S., wife, Cecil Co.,
wheelwright (8-22 Aug. 1812)

Frailey, John, age 23, 2 years in U.S., Baltimore, labourer (11 Oct. 1813)

Frazier, James, age 30, 1 mo. in U.S., Baltimore, carver & guilder (2-12 Sept. 1812)

Fryer, Thomas, age 26, 2 years in U.S., Baltimore, tailor (8-22 Aug. 1812)

Fulton, John, age 25, 2 years in U.S., Baltimore Co., shoemaker (11 Oct. 1813)

Fulton, Thomas, age 22, 2 years in U.S., Baltimore, weaver (11 Oct. 1813)

Funston, Andrew, age 25, 6 years in U.S., Baltimore, storekeeper (18-25 July 1812)

Funston, Robert, age 28, 13 mos. in U.S., wife & 2 children, Baltimore, storekeeper (11 Oct. 1813)

Gallagher, Hugh, age 37, 10 years in U.S., wife & 2 children, Baltimore, miller (11 Oct. 1813)

Gallagher, Leslie, age 27, 5 years in U.S., Baltimore, grocer; applied Oct. 1811 (10-18 July 1812)

Galt, Richard/Richardson, age 25, 10 years in U.S., Baltimore, clerk; applied Sept. 1809, naturalized (10-18 July 1812 & 11 Oct. 1813)

Gamble, Alexander, age 35, 8 years in U.S., Baltimore, drayman (11 Oct. 1813)

Gamble, Thomas, age 51, 18 years in U.S., wife & 3 children, Baltimore Co., tanner & currier (16 Sept. - 31 Oct. 1812)

Garrity, Patrick, age 57, 28 years in U.S., wife & 6 children, Washington Co., tailor (8-22 Aug. 1812)

George, Archibald, age 22, 27 mos. in U.S., Baltimore, clerk (18-25 July 1812)

George, John, age 21, 7 years in U.S., Baltimore, haircloth manufacturer (11 Oct. 1813)

George, Robert, age 42, 3 mos. in U.S., Baltimore, tobacconist (18-25 July 1812)

Gibson, Andrew, age 23, 13 mos. in U.S., Cecil Co., tanner (8-22 Aug. 1812)

Gilbert, David, age 30, 6 years in U.S., wife & child, Baltimore Co., shoemaker (25 July - 1 Aug. 1812)

Gilbert, Joseph, age 30, 2 years in U.S., wife & 2 children, Baltimore, labourer (11 Oct. 1813)

Gilbert, Peter R., age 43, 20 years in U.S., wife & 5 children, Frederick Town, weaver (8-22 Aug. 1812)

Gilday, P., age 30, 11 years in U.S., wife & child, Baltimore, bricklayer (11 Oct. 1813)

Giles, James, age 25, 2 years in U.S., Baltimore Co., weaver (25 July - 1 Aug. 1812)

Gilleran, Lackey, age 40, 11 years in U.S., wife & 2 children, Baltimore, labourer (11 Oct. 1813)

Gilmor, Henry, age 47, 13 years in U.S., wife, Washington Co., schoolmaster (8-22 Aug. 1812)

Ginn, James, age 40, 6 years in U.S., wife & 4 children, Cecil Co., linen weaver (8-22 Aug. 1812)

Glass, James, age 21, 5 years in U.S., Cecil Co., tanner (8-22 Aug. 1812)

Gorden, Alen, age 29, 15 mos. in U.S., Washington Co., clerk (8-22 Aug. 1812)

Gott, James, age 28, 2 years in U.S., wife & 3 children, mahogany sawyer (11 Oct. 1813)

Gowan, George, age 30, 14 years in U.S., Baltimore, hatter (11 Oct. 1813)

Gowan, John, age 40, 17 years in U.S., wife & child, Baltimore, soap boiler (8-22 Aug. 1812)

Grady, Anthony, age 29, 20 mos. in U.S., wife & 3 children, Baltimore, drayman (11 Oct. 1813)

Graham, Thomas, age 34, 15 years in U.S., wife, Baltimore, calico printer (11 Oct. 1813)

Graham, William, age 40, 8 days in U.S., Baltimore (1-8 Aug. 1812)
Graham, William, age 32, 7 years in U.S., wife & 4 children,
  Baltimore (8-22 Aug. 1812)
Graham, Wm., age 26, 7 years in U.S., wife & 3 children, Balti-
  more, scowman (11 Oct. 1813)
Graham, Wm., age 26, 6 years in U.S., wife & 4 children, Balti-
  more, storekeeper (11 Oct. 1813)
Grayham, John, age 46, 19 years in U.S., 2 children, Frederick
  Town, porter seller (8-22 Aug. 1812)
Grayham, Samuel, age 29, 19 years in U.S., Baltimore, painter &
  glazier (18-25 July 1812)
Green, William, age 48, 15 years in U.S., wife & 3 children, Bal-
  timore, shoemaker (11 Oct. 1813)
Gregg, Alexander, age 26, 10 years in U.S., Baltimore, grocer
  (22 Aug. - 2 Sept. 1812); applied Sept. 1808 (11 Oct. 1813)
Gregg, Andrew, age 20, 7 years in U.S., Baltimore, clerk; ap-
  plied Sept. 1809 (10-18 July 1812)
Griffin, Anthony, age 26, 19 mos. in U.S., Baltimore, tailor (11
  Oct. 1813)
Griffin, Hugh, age 26, 2 years in U.S., Baltimore, pedlar (11
  Oct. 1813)
Griffin, William, age 21, 19 mos. in U.S., Baltimore, cordwainer
  (11 Oct. 1813)
Griffith, Edward, age 30, 2 years in U.S., 2 children, Baltimore,
  tailor (11 Oct. 1813)
Griffith, Thomas, age 28, 2 years in U.S., wife & child, Balti-
  more, slater (11 Oct. 1813)
Grimes, O, age 21, 19 mos. in U.S., Baltimore, dyer (11 Oct.
  1813)
Guilday, Michael, age 30, 6 years in U.S., wife & child, Union
  Town, tailor (8-22 Aug. 1812); Baltimore (11 Oct. 1813)
Guinan, John, age 23, 15 mos. in U.S., Emmitsburg, hawker & ped-
  lar (8-22 Aug. 1812)
Haddington, William, age 37, 10 years in U.S., wife & 2 children,
  Baltimore Co., farmer & gardener (1-8 Aug. 1812)
Hagan, Peter, age 40, 13 years in U.S., wife & child, Frederick
  Town, farmer; applied Feb. 1810 (8-22 Aug. 1812)
Haigh, Samuel, age 40, 8 years in U.S., family now in Md., Balti-
  more, merchant (10-18 July 1812)
Haines, Martin, age 50, 28 years in U.S., wife & child, Taney
  Town, turner (8-22 Aug. 1812)
Hall, James, age 23, 2 years in U.S., wife & child, Baltimore,
  weaver (11 Oct. 1813)
Hall, John, age 23, 18 years in U.S., wife & child, Washington
  Co., shoemaker (8-22 Aug. 1812)
Hamilton, Hugh, age 50, 19 years in U.S., wife & 4 children, Bal-
  timore, carter (11 Oct. 1813)
Hamilton, James, Jr., age 24, 6 years in U.S., Baltimore, dry
  good merchant & grocer; applied Oct. 1811 (10-18 July 1812)
Hamilton, Nathaniel, age 27, 7 years in U.S., Baltimore, gardener
  (10-18 July 1812)
Hamilton, Robert, age 23, 2 years in U.S., wife & child, Balti-
  more, labourer (11 Oct. 1813)
Hammil, Patrick, age 31, 13 years in U.S., wife & 3 children,
  Washington Co., farmer (22 Aug. - 2 Sept. 1812)
Harbison, Robert, age 29, 11 years in U.S., wife & child, Balti-
  more, grocer (11 Oct. 1813)
Harrison, Wm. E.H., age 25, 4 years in U.S., Ann Arundel Co.,
  schoolmaster (2-12 Sept. 1812)
Harden, Wm., age 31, 1 year in U.S., wife, Baltimore, clerk (18-
  25 July 1812)
Hardesty, John, age 33, 7 years in U.S., wife, Baltimore, merchant
  (18 Sept. - 31 Oct. 1812)
Hardisty, John, age 40, 8 years in U.S., wife, Kent Co., labourer
  (11 Oct. 1813)

Hargell, James, age 45, 8 years in U.S., wife & 4 children, Baltimore, gardener (11 Oct. 1813)

Harper, Joseph, age 24, 5 mos. in U.S., Worcester Co., teacher (22 Aug. - 2 Sept. 1812)

Harris, John W., age 29, 5 years in U.S., wife & 3 children, Baltimore, tailor (11 Oct. 1813)

Harris, Joseph, age 24, 4 years in U.S., Baltimore, servant (11 Oct. 1813)

Harrison, Edward, age 27, 2 years in U.S., Frederick Co., weaver of muslin (8-22 Aug. 1812)

Harrison, James, age 46, 18 mos. in U.S., wife & child, Baltimore, shoemaker (11 Oct. 1813)

Harrison, Richardson, age 28, 9 mos. in U.S., Baltimore Co., weaver (18-25 July 1812)

Harrison, Wm., age 31, 8 years in U.S., wife & 4 children, Baltimore, stone mason (11 Oct. 1813)

Harrison, W.E.H., age 26, 4 years in U.S., Ann Arundel Co., teacher (11 Oct. 1813)

Harwood, James, age 25, 8 years in U.S., Baltimore, storekeeper (11 Oct. 1813)

Harwood, James, age 27, 7 years in U.S., Baltimore, porter (11 Oct. 1813)

Harwood, Thomas, age 38, 11 years in U.S., Baltimore, merchant (10-18 July 1812)

Harwood, Thomas, age 31, 11 years in U.S., Baltimore, grocer; naturalized (11 Oct. 1813)

Haslam, John, age 34, 11 years in U.S., wife & 4 children, Baltimore, veterinary surgeon (10-18 July 1812); by Oct. 1813 he has another child and he has been naturalized (11 Oct. 1813)

Hay, John, age 28, 6 years in U.S., Cecil Co., schoolmaster (16 Sept. - 31 Oct. 1812)

Hays, Maurice, age 27, 10 years in U.S., Frederick Co., labourer (8-22 Aug. 1812)

Hazlett, Robert, age 31, 11 years in U.S., Frederick Town, miller (8-22 Aug. 1812)

Heincken, C. W., age 18, 2 years in U.S., Baltimore Co. (8-22 Aug. 1812)

Hemphill, Joseph, age 20, 4 years in U.S., Hagerstown, clerk (8-22 Aug. 1812)

Henry, Francis, age 31, 13 years in U.S., Baltimore, nailor; naturalized (11 Oct. 1813)

Henry, William, age 32, 11 years in U.S., wife & 3 children, Montgomery Co., shoemaker (22 Aug. - 2 Sept. 1812)

Heron, Alexander, age 30, 11 years in U.S., Baltimore, dry good merchant (10-18 July 1812)

Heron, Alexander, age 33, 11 years in U.S., Baltimore, grocer (11 Oct. 1813)

Hestom, William, age 23, 2 years in U.S., wife & child, Baltimore, labourer (11 Oct. 1813)

Heyland, Marcus, age 28, 8 years in U.S., Baltimore, merchant; applied 11 Mar. 1810 (18-25 July 1812)

Highen, Samuel, age 48, 9 mos. in U.S., wife & 3 children, Baltimore, weaver (18-25 July 1812)

Holmes, James, age 31, 7 years in U.S., wife & 2 children, Baltimore, bottler of ale/porter seller; applied 9 Nov. 1809 (25 July - 1 Aug. 1812 & 11 Oct. 1813)

Horne, Thomas, age 38, 11 years in U.S., wife, Baltimore, bricklayer (25 July - 1 Aug. 1812)

Howard, George W,, age 29, 3 years in U.S., wife & 4 children, Baltimore, teacher (25 July - 1 Aug. 1812)

Hugham, Samuel, age 48, 2 years in U.S., wife & 3 children, Baltimore, weaver (11 Oct. 1813)

Hughes, Robert, age 43, 5 years in U.S., wife & 4 children, Cecil Co., linen weaver (8-22 Aug. 1812)

Humes, Thomas, age 30, 12 years in U.S., Baltimore, distiller
   (18-25 July 1812)
Hunter, James, age 38, 6 mos. in U.S., Baltimore, weaver (18-25
   July 1812)
Hutchison, James, age 45, 5 years in U.S., Baltimore, weaver (18-
   25 July 1812)
Inglesby, Wm., age 30, 12 years in U.S., wife & 3 children, Bal-
   timore, tallow chandler; naturalized (11 Oct. 1813)
Irvine, Daniel, age 30, 3 years in U.S., wife & 2 children, Bal-
   timore, shoemaker (11 Oct. 1813)
Irwen, Wm., age 24, 3 years in U.S., wife & child, Baltimore,
   cabinetmaker (11 Oct. 1813)
Jackson, George, age 34, 2 years in U.S., Montgomery Co., farmer
   (22 Aug. - 2 Sept. 1812)
Jackson, John, age 42, 14 years in U.S., wife & 2 children, Baltimore, weaver (11 Oct. 1813)
Jackson, John, age 37, 11 years in U.S., child, Baltimore, cordwainer (8-25 July 1812)
Jackson, John, age 35, 11 years in U.S., wife & child, Baltimore,
   cordwainer (11 Oct. 1813)
James, James W,, age 23, 2 years in U.S., wife, Baltimore, baker
   (18-25 July 1812); by Oct. 1813 he has another child (11 Oct.
   1813)
Jamieson, Samuel, age 25, 2 years in U.S., wife & child, Balti-
   more, manufacturer (11 Oct. 1813)
Jephson, John, age 42, 26 years in U.S., wife, Baltimore, cord-
   wainer (10-18 July 1812)
Johnson, Archibald, age 21, 3 years in U.S., Baltimore, labourer
   (11 Oct. 1813)
Johnson, Frederick, age 30, 4 years in U.S., wife & 3 children,
   Baltimore Co., stone mason (11 Oct. 1813)
Johnson, George, age 24, 2 years in U.S., Baltimore, clerk (11
   Oct. 1813)
Johnson, James, age 48, 18 years in U.S., Washington Co., mason
   (8-22 Aug. 1812)
Johnson, James, age 27, 3 years in U.S., wife & 2 children, Bal-
   timore, waterman (11 Oct. 1813)
Johnson, James, age 22, 2 years in U.S., Baltimore, teacher of
   the English language (10-18 July 1812)
Johnson, James M., age 30, 5 years in U.S., wife & 5 children,
   Montgomery Co., cotton manufacturer (22 Aug. - 2 Sept. 1812)
Johnson, John, age 32, 9 years in U.S., wife & child, Baltimore
   Co., weaver (11 Oct. 1813)
Johnson, John, age 25, 4 years in U.S., wife & 2 children, Bal-
   timore, ship-carpenter (11 Oct. 1813)
Johnson, William, age 22, 3 years in U.S., Baltimore, clerk (18-
   25 July 1812)
Jones, David, age 48, 5 years in U.S., wife & 3 children, Balti-
   more Co., farmer (18-25 July 1812)
Jordan, Robert, age 24, 4 years in U.S., Washington Co., distil-
   ler (8-22 Aug. 1812)
Jourdan, Alic, age 37, 2 years in U.S., wife & 3 children, Bal-
   timore Co., weaver (25 July - 1 Aug. 1812)
Kagin; Thomas, age 39, 17 mos. in U.S., Baltimore, cotton weaver
   (1-8 Aug. 1812)
Kain, Daniel, age 49, 18 years in U.S., wife, Baltimore, carpen-
   ter (11 Oct. 1813)
Kane, Anthony, age 26, 6 years in U.S., Baltimore, storekeeper
   (11 Oct. 1813)
Kee, Andrew, age 47, 12 years in U.S., wife & 3 children, Washing-
   ton Co., labourer (8-22 Aug. 1812)
Keenan, Charles, age 26, 2 years in U.S., Baltimore, weaver (25
   July - 1 Aug. 1812)
Keith, Robert, age 20, 2 years in U.S., Baltimore, bricklayer
   (11 Oct. 1813)

Kelly, James, age 20, 8 mos. in U.S., Baltimore, maltster (31
   Oct. 1812 - 6 Jan. 1813)
Kelly, Michael, age 47, 5 years in U.S., wife & child, Baltimore
   Co., weaver (8-22 Aug. 1812)
Kelly, Terrance, age 33, 14 years in U.S., wife, Baltimore, stone
   mason (11 Oct. 1813)
Kennedy, Wm., age 26, 11 years in U.S., wife & child, Baltimore
   Co., teacher (18-25 July 1812)
Keny, Joseph, age 27, 7 years in U.S., wife & 2 children, Balti-
   more, tavern-keeper (11 Oct. 1813)
Kerby, Cornelius, age 34, 10 years in U.S., wife & 2 children,
   Baltimore, clerk (11 Oct. 1813)
Kerby, Cornelius, age 31, 1 year in U.S., wife & 3 children,
   Baltimore, merchant (18-25 July 1812)
Kerr, William, age 24, 3 years in U.S., Baltimore, pedlar (11
   Oct. 1813)
Kerrigh (?), John, age 21, 8 mos. in U.S., Baltimore, stone cut-
   ter (18-25 July 1812)
Kershaw, Samuel, age 37, 12 years in U.S., Baltimore, shoemaker
   (18-25 July 1812)
Keys, Hugh, age 28, 9 years in U.S., wife & 4 children, Frederick
   Town, merchant; applied Aug. 1811 (8-22 Aug. 1812)
Kiernan, James, age 25, 7 years in U.S., Baltimore, dyer (11 Oct.
   1813)
Kiernan, John, age 32, 8 years in U.S., Baltimore, trader; ap-
   plied 1 Nov. 1809 (10-18 July 1812); clerk (11 Oct. 1813)
Kiernan, Michael, age 46, 12 years in U.S., wife & 5 children,
   Baltimore, labourer (11 Oct. 1813)
Kiernan, Patrick, age 32, 3 years in U.S., Baltimore, drayman
   (11 Oct. 1813)
Kilpatrick, James, age 29, 2 years in U.S., wife & child, Balti-
   more, labourer (11 Oct. 1813)
King, Richard, age 49, 15 years in U.S., wife & 5 children, Bal-
   timore, shoemaker (18-25 July 1812)
King, William, age 38, 6 years in U.S., 2 children, Baltimore,
   stone mason (11 Oct. 1813)
Kirkland, Alexander, age 25, 3 years in U.S., Baltimore, clerk;
   applied Jan. 1812 (18-25 July 1812)
Kirvin, Robert, age 47, 13 years in U.S., wife, Baltimore, weaver (11 Oct. 1813)
Knoe, Dean, age 25, 18 mos. in U.S., Baltimore, clerk (11 Oct.
   1813)
Knox, William, age 25, 5 mos. in U.S., Baltimore, storekeeper
   (25 July - 1 Aug. 1812)
Lane, John, age 45, 6 years in U.S., Frederick Co., shepherd
   (8-22 Aug. 1812)
Laughlin, Allen, age 29, 10 years in U.S., Funks Town, labourer
   (8-22 Aug. 1812)
Lawless, Mathew, age 30, 7 years in U.S., Baltimore, grocer (18-
   25 July 1812)
Lawson, John, age 33, 9 years in U.S., wife & 6 children, Baltimore Co., cotton manufacturer (10-18 July 1812)
Leasr(?), George, age 52, 2 years in U.S., Baltimore, calico
   printer (11 Oct. 1813)
Leche, David, age 22, 4 years in U.S., Baltimore, storekeeper,
   (10-18 July 1812)
Legbury, John, age 37, 11 years in U.S., wife & 3 children, Bal-
   timore, millwright (11 Oct. 1813)
Le Guerrier, Pierre, age 22, 19 mos. in U.S., Baltimore, confec-
   tioner (18-25 July 1812)
Leonard, Hugh, age 30, 11 years in U.S., Newcastle, labourer (18-
   25 July 1812); age given as 35 (11 Oct. 1813)
Leslie, John, age 19, 1 year in U.S., Baltimore, clerk (10-18
   July 1812)

Lewis, Lewis D., age 28, 11 years in U.S., wife, Baltimore, wheelwright (11 Oct. 1813)

Lewis, Thomas, age 31, 6 years in U.S., wife & child, Baltimore Co., farmer (8-22 Aug. 1812)

Lewis, Thomas, age 30, 7 years in U.S., wife & 2 children, Baltimore Co., labourer (11 Oct. 1813)

Lewliss, Robert, age 32, 7 years in U.S., Washington Co., cooper (8-22 Aug. 1812)

Lidenna, John, age 26, 2 years in U.S., Baltimore, labourer (11 Oct. 1813)

Linden, Daniel, age 32, 4 years/ in U.S., wife & 4 children, Baltimore, labourer (11 Oct. 1813)

Lindsey, James, age 39, 12 years in U.S., wife & 3 children, Baltimore Co., carder (25 July - 1 Aug. 1812)

Lindsey, Thomas, age 16, 11 mos. in U.S., Hagerstown, clerk (8-22 Aug. 1812)

Littleboy, George, age 38, 6 mos. in U.S., mother, Baltimore, military plume maker & cornbaker (10-18 July 1812)

Lockert, Patrick, age 34, 12 years in U.S., Washington Co., labourer (8-22 Aug. 1812)

Lorman, Wm., age 25, 6 years in U.S., Baltimore, drayman (11 Oct. 1813)

Lormor(?), Samuel, age 36, 15 years in U.S., wife & 3 children, Baltimore, drayman (11 Oct. 1813)

Lowe, John, age 24, 1 year in U.S., Baltimore Co., cotton spinner (10-18 July 1812)

Lowry, Edward B., age 36, 6 years in U.S., wife & 3 children, Baltimore, teacher; applied 7 Mar. 1811 (25 July - 1 Aug. 1812)

Lowry, Robert, age 29, 2 years in U.S., Baltimore, tailor (11 Oct. 1813)

Lumb, Abraham, age 30, 3 years in U.S., wife & 3 children, Baltimore, weaver (11 Oct. 1813)

Lumb, Abraham, age 29, 3 years in U.S., Baltimore Co., wire drawer (10-18 July 1812)

Lydann, Patrick, age 78, 24 years in U.S., wife & 2 children, Montgomery Co., farmer (22 Aug. - 2 Sept. 1812)

Lydann, Peter, age 32, 24 years in U.S., Montgomery Co., farmer (22 Aug. - 2 Sept. 1812)

Lydann, Timothy, age 47, 24 years in U.S., wife & 5 children, Montgomery Co., farmer (22 Aug. - 2 Sept. 1812)

Lynch, James, age 26, 3 years in U.S., Baltimore, weaver (11 Oct. 1813)

McBean, Angus, age 34, 9 years in U.S., Baltimore, grocer (11 Oct. 1813)

McBride, Edward, age 38, 18 years in U.S., wife & 3 children, Baltimore, stone cutter; naturalized (11 Oct. 1813)

McBrierty, Anthony, age 30, 11 years in U.S., wife & child, Baltimore, cooper (11 Oct. 1813)

McCabe, Hugh, age 29, 2 years in U.S., wife & child, Baltimore, cotton weaver (11 Oct. 1813)

McCann, Charles, age 20, 2 years in U.S., Baltimore, waterman (11 Oct. 1813)

McCann, Peter, age 36, 9 years in U.S., wife & child, Baltimore, tobacconist (11 Oct. 1813)

McCannon, Wm., age 48, 22 years in U.S., wife & child, Baltimore, cooper (11 Oct. 1813)

McCarter, James, age 20, 5 years in U.S., Baltimore, paper hanger (11 Oct. 1813)

McCartney, James, age 20, 20 mos. in U.S., Baltimore, storekeeper (11 Oct. 1813)

Mc Cartney, Peter, age 28, 6 years in U.S., Baltimore, cooper (18-25 July 1812)

McCauley, James, age 29, 3 years in U.S., Baltimore, bricklayer (11 Oct. 1813)

McCaw, Robert, age 39, 14 years in U.S., wife, Frederick Co.,
   weaver (8-22 Aug. 1812)
McClean, Charles, age 36, 3 years in U.S., wife & 3 children,
   Baltimore, innkeeper; applied Mar. 1812 (10-18 July 1812)
McClean, Charles, age 37, 3 years in U.S., wife & 4 children,
   Baltimore, storekeeper; applied Jan. 1812; naturalized (11
   Oct. 1813)
McCleary, John, age 48, 15 years in U.S., wife & 4 children,
   Hagerstown, schoolmaster; applied 1801 (8-22 Aug. 1812)
McClellan, John, age 27, 5 years in U.S., Baltimore, baker (11
   Oct. 1813)
McClelland, John, age 21, 2 years in U.S., Hagerstown, clerk
   (8-22 Aug. 1812)
McColley, Robert, age 25, 6 years in U.S., Baltimore, labourer
   (11 Oct. 1813)
McConnell, Thomas, age 28, 1½ years in U.S., Baltimore, teacher
   (11 Oct. 1813)
McCormick, John, age 29, 13 years in U.S., wife & child, Balti-
   more Co., drayman (11 Oct. 1813)
McCormick, William, age 23, 2 years in U.S., wife & child, Bal-
   timore, weaver (11 Oct. 1813)
McCracker, John, age 24, 5 years in U.S., Washington Co., stone
   cutter (8-22 Aug. 1812)
McCready, Charles, age 25, 7 years in U.S., Baltimore, teacher
   (18-25 July 1812)
MacCristal, James, age 22, 4 years in U.S., Ann Arundel Co.,
   collier (31 Oct. 1812 - 6 Jan. 1813)
Maccuene, James, age 22, 2 years in U.S., Baltimore, weaver (11
   Oct. 1813)
MacCulley, James, age 41, 20 years in U.S., Baltimore, tailor
   (18-25 July 1812)
Mc Dermot, Henry, age 30, 7 years in U.S., Baltimore, labourer
   (11 Oct. 1813)
McDermot, Stephen, age 26, 3 years in U.S., Baltimore, weaver
   (11 Oct. 1813)
McDevinness, James, age 38, 15 years in U.S., wife & 4 children,
   Baltimore Co., tanner (18-25 July 1812)
McDonald, Alexander, age 47, 11 years in U.S., wife & 4 children,
   Baltimore, labourer (10-18 July 1812)
McDonald, Alexander, age 27, 12 years in U.S., wife & child,
   Baltimore, carter (11 Oct. 1813)
McDonald, Charles, age 25, 3 years in U.S., Baltimore, carpenter
   (11 Oct. 1813)
MacDonald, Henry, age 28, 9 years in U.S., Baltimore, grocer
   (11 Oct. 1813)
McDonald, James, age 32, 6 years in U.S., wife & 4 children,
   Baltimore, blacksmith (11 Oct. 1813)
McDonald, John, age 27, 19 mos. in U.S., wife, Baltimore Co.,
   machine maker (25 July - 1 Aug. 1812)
McDonald, Lawrence, age 19, 19 mos. in U.S., Baltimore Co.,
   machine maker (25 July - 1 Aug. 1812)
McDonald, Patrick, age 23, 2 years in U.S., Baltimore, drayman
   (11 Oct. 1813)
McDonald, Thomas, age 34, 9 years in U.S., wife & 4 children,
   Baltimore, labourer (11 Oct. 1813)
McDuel, George, age 25, 4 years & 3 mos. in U.S., St. Mary's,
   painter (8-22 Aug. 1812)
McDuell, John, age 23, 5 years in U.S., wife, Baltimore, painter
   (8-22 Aug. 1812)
MacEnally, Peter, age 26, 8 mos. in U.S., brother, Baltimore Co.,
   weaver (18-25 July 1812)
McFadon, Charles, age 47, 18 years in U.S., wife & 3 children,
   Baltimore, tailor (25 July - 1 Aug. 1812)
McFarlan, Michael, age 28, 8 years in U.S., wife & 3 children,
   Baltimore, labourer (11 Oct. 1813)

McFarland, John, age 38, 24 years in U.S., Baltimore, tailor (18-
25 July 1812)

MacFarland, Patrick, age 33, 12 years in U.S., wife & child, Baltimore, stone mason (11 Oct. 1813)

McFarlane, John, age 38, 25 years in U.S., Baltimore, tailor (11
Oct. 1813)

McFarling, Peter, age 25, 7 years in U.S., Funks Town, mason (8-
22 Aug. 1812)

Magauran, James C., age 25, 7 years in U.S., wife, Baltimore,
lumber merchant (18-25 July 1812)

McGee, Edward, age 35, 20 years in U.S., Frederick Town, labourer
(8-22 Aug. 1812)

McGee, Eugene, age 20, 1 year in U.S., Baltimore, student of divinity (18-25 July 1812)

McGee, John, age 28, 7 years in U.S., Baltimore, teacher (18-25
July 1812)

Magee, Patrick, age 22, 21 mos. in U.S., wife, Baltimore, pedlar
(11 Oct. 1813)

McGinn, James, age 32, 10 years in U.S., wife & 3 children, Baltimore, tailor (25 July -1 Aug. 1812)

McGinnis, Thomas, age 24, 5 years in U.S., wife & child, Frederick
Town, labourer (8-22 Aug. 1812)

McGuch, Andrew, age 35, 10 years in U.S., wife & 2 children, Baltimore Co., carpenter (11 Oct. 1813)

McGuigen, Alexander, age 26, 3 years in U.S., Baltimore, weaver
(11 Oct. 1813)

McGuigen, Roger, age 44, 6 years in U.S., Baltimore, distiller
(11 Oct. 1813)

McGuire, Francis, age 28, 2 years in U.S., wife & child, Baltimore, storekeeper (11 Oct. 1813)

McGurk, John, age 30, 17 years in U.S., Baltimore, bricklayer
(11 Oct. 1813)

McHeinekey, Christian, age 18, 2 years in U.S., Baltimore Co.,
farmer (11 Oct. 1813)

McIlhany, Alexander, age 24, 2 years in U.S., Baltimore, chandler (11 Oct. 1813)

McIlhany, Henry, age 22, 2 years in U.S., Baltimore, baker (11
Oct. 1813)

McIlherin, Dennis, age 30, 5 years in U.S., wife & child, Baltimore, drayman (25 July - 1 Aug. 1812)

Macilroy, John, age 43, 2½ years in U.S., wife & 4 children, Baltimore, storekeeper (11 Oct. 1813)

MacIntire, Alexander, age 48, 19 mos. in U.S., Baltimore, baker
(11 Oct. 1813)

McIntire, William H., age 19, 2 years in U.S., Baltimore, clerk
(10-18 July 1812)

McIntosh, Andrew, age 34, 9 years in U.S., Baltimore Co., miner
(8-22 Aug. 1812); stone cutter (11 Oct. 1813)

McIntosh, Samuel, age 32, 3 years in U.S., Baltimore, merchant
(18-25 July 1812); clerk (11 Oct. 1813)

McKauna, Anthony, age 53, 9 years in U.S., wife & 7 children,
Baltimore, storekeeper (11 Oct. 1813)

MacKee, William, age 32, 8 years in U.S., Cecil Co., house- carpenter (8-22 Aug. 1812)

McKee, William, age 27, 4 years in U.S., Baltimore, clerk; applied 10 Sept. 1810 (10-18 July 1812)

MacKelden, Joseph, age 31, 18 mos. in U.S., wife & 2 children,
Baltimore, storekeeper (18-25 July 1812)

McKenney, Anthony, age 51, 9 years in U.S., wife & 3 children,
Baltimore, storekeeper

McKenney, Wm., age 37, 6 years in U.S., wife, Baltimore, butcher;
applied Mar. 1810 (11 Oct. 1813)

MacKey, George, age 33, 25 years in U.S., wife & 2 children, Baltimore, grocer (11 Oct. 1813)

McKey, Thomas, age 26, 2 years in U.S., Baltimore, blacksmith
(11 Oct. 1813)
McKiernan, Michael, age 52, 17 years in U.S., Trap Town, school-
master (8-22 Aug. 1812)
McKim, John, age 46, 16 years in U.S., wife & 3 children, Balti-
more, carpenter; naturalized (11 Oct. 1813)
MacKisic, John, age 29, 11 years in U.S., Baltimore, tobacconist
(18-25 July 1812)
Mackowin, Daniel, age 25, 6 years in U.S., Baltimore, clerk (11
Oct. 1813)
McLaughlin, Alexander, age 24, 5 years in U.S., Baltimore, la-
bourer (11 Oct. 1813)
McLaughlin, John, age 24, 2 years in U.S., wife, Taney Town,
tailor (8-22 Aug. 1812)
MacMillan, William, age 25, 6 years in U.S., Baltimore, weaver
(10-18 July 1812)
McMullen, Timothy, age 27, 6 years in U.S., Baltimore, cooper
(11 Oct. 1813)
MacMurrey, Patrick, age 30, 10 years in U.S., Baltimore, paver
(11 Oct. 1813)
McNall, John, age 26, 9 years in U.S., wife, Frederick Town,
house-carpenter; applied Aug. 1811 (8-22 Aug. 1812)
McNeal, James, age 25, 6 years in U.S., Baltimore, accountant;
applied 6 May 1812 (10-13 July 1812)
McNulty, Hugh, age 26, 2 years in U.S., Baltimore, pedlar (11
Oct. 1813)
McNulty, Patrick, age 34, 3 years in U.S., wife & 2 children,
Baltimore, labourer; applied Mar. 1810; naturalized (11 Oct.
1813)
MacPherson, William, age 36, 4 years in U.S., 1 child, Baltimore,
minister of the Gospel (1-8 Aug. 1812)
MacQueen, Alexander, age 30, 6 years in U.S., wife & child, Bal-
timore, dyer (11 Oct. 1813)
McRelly(?), Peter, age 30, 9 years in U.S., wife & 4 children,
Baltimore, bootmaker (11 Oct. 1813)
McRoberts, Andrew, age 21, 7 years in U.S., Washington Co., dis-
tiller (8-22 Aug. 1812)
Maddigan, Paul, age 26, 11 years in U.S., wife & 2 children, Bal-
timore, carter; naturalized (11 Oct. 1813)
Maher, Timothy, age 35, 18 mos. in U.S., Baltimore, carpenter (11
Oct. 1813)
Major, John Rudolph, age 30, 9 years in U.S., Baltimore, cooper
(18-25 July 1812)
Maloy, Patrick, age 28, 9 years in U.S., Baltimore, livery stable
keeper (11 Oct. 1813)
Manion, Dennis, age 46, 13 mos. in U.S., daughter, Baltimore Co.,
cotton spinner (18-25 July 1812)
Martin, George, age 30, 12 years in U.S., Baltimore Co., stone
quarrier (11 Oct. 1813)
Martin, John, age 45, 17 years in U.S., wife & child, Baltimore,
ornamental sash maker (18-25 July 1812)
Martin, John, age 46, 2 years in U.S., wife & 8 children, Balti-
more, labourer (11 Oct. 1813)
Martin, John, age 18, 3 years in U.S., Baltimore, stone cutter
(11 Oct. 1813)
Matthews, Edward, age 48, 11 years in U.S., wife & child, Montgomery Co., minister of the Gospel (22 Aug. - 2 Sept. 1812);
wife (only), Ann Arundel Co., naturalized (11 Oct. 1813)
Matthews, John, age 48, 12 years in U.S., Baltimore Co., farmer
(11 Oct. 1813)
Mayfield, Thomas, age 33, 9 years in U.S., wife & 3 children,
Baltimore, wire drawer (11 Oct. 1813)
Meany, George F., age 32, 6 years in U.S., wife & child, Baltimore, baker (8-22 Aug. 1812)

Melcher, Jacob, age 20, 5 years in U.S., Baltimore, cooper (1-8 Aug. 1812)

Mels, Charles, age 32, 12 years in U.S., wife & 4 children, Frederick Co., weaver of cloth (8-22 Aug. 1812)

Merritt, Samuel, age 21, 2 years in U.S., Baltimore, clerk (11 Oct. 1813)

Michall, David, age 34, 6 years in U.S., Hagerstown, weaver (8-22 Aug. 1812)

Mickle, Andrew, age 30, 4 years in U.S., wife & child, Baltimore, tailor (11 Oct. 1813)

Miller, Ann, age 55, 11 years in U.S., 1 son, Hagerstown, weaver (8-22 Aug. 1812)

Miller, Frederick, age 26, 10 days in U.S., Baltimore (25 July - 1 Aug. 1812)

Miller, James, age 21, 3 years in U.S., State of Ohio, clerk (8-22 Aug. 1812)

Miller, John, age 28, 10 years in U.S., wife, Baltimore, foreman of Union manufactory (10-18 July 1812)

Miller, John, age 28, 9 years in U.S., wife & child, Baltimore, coach lace manufacturer (11 Oct. 1813)

Miller, Samuel, age 33, 3 weeks in U.S., Baltimore, physician (10-18 July 1812)

Miller, William, age 21, 11 years in U.S., Hagerstown, weaver (8-22 Aug. 1812)

Milne, Robert, age 26, 2 years in U.S., Baltimore, calico printer (11 Oct. 1813)

Mitchell, Spencer, age 35, 16 years in U.S., Prince George's Co., physician; applied but objected to the word "forever" (25 July - 1 Aug. 1812)

Moffet, John, age 28, 2 years in U.S., Baltimore, weaver (11 Oct. 1813)

Moffitt, William, age 23, 7 years in U.S., Hagerstown, merchant; applied Mar. 1809 (8-22 Aug. 1812)

Mollony, O., age 27, 8 years in U.S., Baltimore, bricklayer (11 Oct. 1813)

Monteith, Robert, age 30, 11 years in U.S., Baltimore, jeweller; applied Sept. 1809 (11 Oct. 1813)

Moon, Allen, age 23, 1½ years in U.S., Baltimore, ship-carpenter (11 Oct. 1813)

Moonay, Thomas, age 28, 3 years in U.S., Baltimore, painter (18-25 July 1812)

Mooney, Cornelius, age 43, 11 years in U.S., wife & 6 children, Baltimore Co., bleacher (18-25 July 1812)

Mooney, John, age 60, 1 year & 2 mos. in U.S., 3 children, Baltimore, weaver (10-18 July 1812)

Mooney, John, age 29, 1 year in U.S., Baltimore, weaver (18-25 July 1812)

Moore, James, age 42, 1 year in U.S., Baltimore, weaver (18-25 July 1812)

Moore, Robert S., age 27, 11 years in U.S., Baltimore, clerk & tanner (10-18 July 1812); applied Sept. 1810 (11 Oct. 1813)

Morgan, Dennis, age 40, 20 years in U.S., wife & 2 children, Washington Co., schoolmaster (8-22 Aug. 1812)

Morress, Gideon, age 39, 16 years in U.S., St. Mary's Co., cabinetmaker; applied 5 Aug. 1812 (8-22 Aug. 1812)

Morrison, Neal, age 32, 10 years in U.S., wife & 11 children, Baltimore, carpenter; applied Sept. 1810 (11 Oct. 1813)

Morse, Barney, age 30, 7 years in U.S., wife & 2 children, Baltimore, labourer (11 Oct. 1813)

Mortimer, John, age 30, 12 years in U.S., wife & 4 children, Baltimore, watchman (11 Oct. 1813)

Morton, Samuel, age 34, 6 years in U.S., wife & 3 children, Baltimore, manufacturer (11 Oct. 1813)

Mudyman, Wm., age 44, 1 year in U.S., wife & 2 children, Baltimore, weaver (18-25 July 1812)

Mulkirn, Peter, age 23, 5 years in U.S., Cecil Co., weaver (25
  July - 1 Aug. 1812)
Murphy, Philip, age 22, 28 mos. in U.S., Baltimore Co., dyer &
  bleacher (18-25 July 1812)
Murray, James, age 45, 3 years in U.S., wife & 8 children, Bal-
  timore Co., spinner (11 Oct. 1813)
Murrill, John, Jr., age 28, 7 years in U.S., Washington Co.,
  merchant; applied Apr. 1809 (22 Aug. - 2 Sept. 1812)
Muskett, John, age 37, 11 years in U.S., wife & 3 children, Bal-
  timore, tavern-keeper (18-25 July 1812)
Muskett, John, age 34, 11 years in U.S., wife & 2 children, Bal-
  timore, storekeeper (11 Oct. 1813)
Nattalli, Joseph, age 35, 8 years in U.S., wife & 3 children,
  Baltimore, bookkeeper (11 Oct. 1813)
Naughton, John, age 21, 18 mos. in U.S., Baltimore, tailor (11
  Oct. 1813)
Nazum, Edward, age 40, 20 mos. in U.S., Creager Town, schoolmas-
  ter; applied Aug. 1812 (11 Oct. 1813)
Neilson, John, age 34, 1 year in U.S., wife & child, Baltimore,
  weaver (11 Oct. 1813)
Nelson, Joseph, age 24, 7 years in U.S., Hagerstown, bricklayer
  (8-22 Aug. 1812)
Nevill, Thomas, age 24, 2 years in U.S., Baltimore, carpenter
  (11 Oct. 1813)
Newland, John, age 38, 4 years in U.S., wife & child, Baltimore,
  brewer (11 Oct. 1813)
Newton, Isaac, age 40, 8 years in U.S., wife & 6 children, Baltimore Co., innkeeper; applied Mar. 1812 (11 Oct. 1813)
Nicholson, Christopher, age 31, 10 years in U.S., wife & 6 children, Baltimore, cordwainer (8-22 Aug. 1812)
Noble, Alexander, age 33, 3 years in U.S., wife & child, Balti-
  more, dyer (18-25 July 1812); by the next Oct. his age is 34
  and he has another child (11 Oct. 1813)
Norman, John, age 26, 18 mos. in U.S., wife & child, Baltimore,
  brass founder (11 Oct. 1813)
Nowland, John, age 38, 3 years in U.S., wife & child, Baltimore,
  clerk (18-25 July 1812)
Nugent, Neal, age 36, 6 years in U.S., wife & 4 children, Balti-
  more, tavern-keeper (10-13 July 1812)
Oakley, Thomas, age 43, 5 years in U.S., Baltimore, gardener (25
  July - 1 Aug. 1812)
Oakley, Thomas, age 30, 6 years in U.S., Baltimore, gardener (11
  Oct. 1813)
Oakley, William, age 43, 7 years in U.S., wife & 2 children, Bal-
  timore, carter (18-25 July 1812)
O'Brien, Matthew, age 25, 14 years in U.S., Baltimore, merchant
  (10-18 July 1812)
O'Connor, Eugene, age 49, 17 years in U.S., wife & 2 children,
  Baltimore, teacher (11 Oct. 1813)
O'Connor, John, age 23, 16 years in U.S., Baltimore, physician
  (10-18 July 1812)
O'Donnell, Barny, age 30, 9 years in U.S., wife, Baltimore, store-
  keeper (18-25 July 1812)
O'Donnell, James, age 27, 7 years in U.S., Baltimore, drayman
  (10-18 July 1812)
O'Donnell, Patrick, age 21, 2 years in U.S., Baltimore, cord-
  wainer (11 Oct. 1813)
O'Flaherty, Patrick, age 36, 17 years in U.S., Frederick Town,
  ditcher (8-22 Aug. 1812)
O'Heare, John, age 47, 10 years in U.S., Baltimore, clerk (8-22
  Aug. 1812)
O'Kely, Wm., age 44, 7 years in U.S., wife & 2 children, Balti-
  more, carter (11 Oct. 1813)
Oldfield, John J.C., age 24, 6 years in U.S., Baltimore, clerk
  (10-18 July 1812)

O'Neale, Arthur, age 45, 17 years in U.S., Baltimore, storekeeper (11 Oct. 1813)

O'Neale, Robert, age 24, 2 years in U.S., wife, Baltimore, tailor (11 Oct. 1813)

O'Neil, Barnard, age 45, 9 years in U.S., wife & 2 children, Cecil Co., weaver; applied Sept. 1809 (25 July - 1 Aug. 1812)

Orchard, John, age 42, 11 years in U.S., wife, Baltimore, teacher (18-25 July 1812)

O'Rourke/O'Rorke, Peter, age 33, 2 years in U.S., wife & child, Baltimore, brick mason (8-22 Aug. 1812); next year his age is given as 37 (11 Oct. 1813)

Orr, Alexander, age 23, 1 year in U.S., Baltimore, turner; applied 16 July 1812 (10-18 July 1812)

Osborne, Andrew, age 24, 5 years in U.S., Baltimore, storekeeper; applied 7 May 1812 (18-25 July 1812)

Owen, Thomas, age 34, 8 years in U.S., wife & 2 children, Baltimore, merchant (10-18 July 1812); next year he is called manufacturer (11 Oct. 1813)

Paley/Payley, William, age 27, 7 years in U.S., Baltimore, clerk; applied Mar. 1811 (10-18 July 1812 & 11 Oct. 1813)

Park, John, age 37, 8 years in U.S., wife & 4 children, Baltimore, shoemaker (10-18 July 1812)

Park, Thomas, age 37, 17 years in U.S., wife & 5 children, Hagerstown, labourer (8-22 Aug. 1812)

Parker, Ezra, age 24, 5 years in U.S, Baltimore, commission merchant; applied Mar. 1811 (10-18 July 1812); later called grocer (11 Oct. 1813)

Parker, Henry, age 51, 2 years in U.S., Baltimore, weaver (11 Oct. 1813)

Parnell, John, age 22, 4 years in U.S., Baltimore, seaman (11 Oct. 1813)

Partington, Richard, age 41, 18 mos. in U.S., wife & 4 children, Baltimore Co., cotton spinner (18-25 July 1812)

Patterson, George, age 21, 2 years in U.S., Baltimore, weaver (11 Oct. 1813)

Patterson, John, age 28, 2 years in U.S., Baltimore, painter (11 Oct. 1813)

Patterson, Joseph M., age 43, 10 years in U.S., Baltimore, pedlar (10-18 July 1812)

Patterson, Joseph, age 26, 2 years in U.S., Baltimore, weaver (11 Oct. 1813)

Pawlick, John, age 46, 6 years in U.S., wife, Baltimore Co., weaver (11 Oct. 1813)

Pennman, John, age 23, 4 mos. in U.S., Baltimore, paper hanger (18-25 July 1812)

Perry, John, age 24, 6 years in U.S., Baltimore, gun maker (11 Oct. 1813)

Perry, John T., age 22, 3 years in U.S., Baltimore, shoemaker (11 Oct. 1813)

Perry, Richard, age 26, 16 years in U.S., wife & child, Baltimore, bridle bit maker (1-8 Aug. 1812)

Phelan, Edward, age 40, 6 years in U.S., wife, Baltimore, clerk (18-25 July 1812); next year age is given as 44 (11 Oct. 1813)

Pherson, M., age 48, 4 years in U.S., Baltimore, labourer (11 Oct. 1813)

Phillips, Peter, age 43, 3 weeks in U.S., 1 servant, Baltimore, gentleman; came to Baltimore to recover health (10-18 July 1812)

Phillips, Peter Pile, age 17, 3 weeks in U.S., Baltimore, gentleman; came to recover health (10-18 July 1812)

Phillips, Robert, age 35, 8 years in U.S., wife & 2 children, Baltimore, calico printer (11 Oct. 1813)

Phillips, Thomas, age 23, 7 years in U.S., Baltimore, bottler (11 Oct. 1813)

Pickering, Wm., age 35, 7 years in U.S., wife, Baltimore, mariner (11 Oct. 1813)

Pierson, Thomas, age 38, 11 years in U.S., wife & 5 children,
Baltimore, skin dresser (1-8 Aug. 1812); naturalized (11 Oct.
1813)
Pilgrim, Nathaniel, age 35, 15 years in U.S., wife, Baltimore,
plane maker (11 Oct. 1813)
Pine, Rare, age 47, 11 years in U.S., Washington Co., house-car-
penter (8-22 Aug. 1812)
Platt, John, age 38, 2 years in U.S., wife & 2 children, Balti-
more Co., cotton machine maker (1-8 Aug. 1812)
Poor, Thomas, age 47, 12 years in U.S., wife & 2 children, Bal-
timore, cabinetmaker (11 Oct. 1813)
Poppleton, Thomas, age 47, 2 years in U.S., wife, Baltimore, land
surveyor & draughtsman (10-18 July 1812)
Porter, John, age 36, 2 years in U.S., wife & 3 children, Balti-
more, weaver (11 Oct. 1813)
Porter, Robert, age 34, 4 years in U.S., Baltimore, weaver (11
Oct. 1813)
Powell, Patrick Bourk, age 47, 3 years in U.S., wife & child,
Baltimore Co., storekeeper (8-22 Aug. 1812)
Powers, James, age 26, 7 years in U.S., Baltimore, storekeeper
(10-18 July 1812)
Powers, Michael, age 27, 5 years in U.S., wife, Baltimore, wea-
ver (11 Oct. 1813)
Pryor, Edward, age 45, 7 years in U.S., wife & 3 children, Bal-
timore, dyer (25 July - 1 Aug. 1812)
Quie, Samuel, age 27, 2 years in U.S., Baltimore Co., weaver (11
Oct. 1813)
Quinn, Patrick, age 24, 7 mos. in U.S., Baltimore, student of di-
vinity (18-25 July 1812)
Raney, David, age 31, 9 years in U.S., wife & 4 children, Balti-
more, shoemaker (11 Oct. 1813)
Ready, David, age 43, 5 years in U.S., Baltimore, weaver (11 Oct.
1813)
Reardon, Morrice, age 49, 23 years in U.S., wife & 7 children,
Baltimore Co., shoemaker (25 July - 1 Aug. 1812)
Reder, Arthur, age 50, 12 years in U.S., wife, Baltimore, malt-
ster (16 Sept. - 31 Oct. 1812)
Reed, George, age 27, 5 years in U.S., wife, Baltimore, brush
maker (11 Oct. 1813)
Reed, Henry, age 25, 2 years in U.S., wife, Baltimore, whitesmith;
applied Mar. 1812 (11 Oct. 1813)
Reed, John, age 30, 3 years in U.S., Baltimore, gardener (11 Oct.
1813)
Reed, Patrick, age 26, 9 years in U.S., Baltimore, drayman (11
Oct. 1813)
Reeve, John, age 35, 28 years in U.S., Frederick Town, blacksmith
& farmer (8-22 Aug. 1812)
Reeve, John, age 37, 10 years in U.S., Baltimore, blacksmith (11
Oct. 1813)
Reeve, Thomas, age 36, 3 years in U.S., Baltimore, storekeeper
(2-12 Sept. 1812)
Reeves, Thomas, age 43, 8 years in U.S., Baltimore, grocer (11
Oct. 1813)
Reily, Patrick, age 30, 9 years in U.S., wife & 2 children, Bal-
timore, drayman (11 Oct. 1813)
Reyburn, Thomas G., age 22, 2 years in U.S., wife, Baltimore,
clerk (18-25 July 1812)
Ricard, James, age 46, 8 mos. in U.S., wife & 3 children, Balti-
more, tailor (18-25 July 1812)
Rice, Charles, age 36, 8 years in U.S., wife & 4 children, Funks
Town, mason (8-22 Aug. 1812)
Rich, Thomas, age 63, 24 years in U.S., Montgomery Co., farmer
(22 Aug. - 2 Sept. 1812)
Ringrose, John W., age 22, 14 years in U.S., wife, Baltimore,
tailor (11 Oct. 1813)

Risk, John, age 30, 2 years in U.S., Baltimore, weaver (11 Oct. 1813)

Ritchie, James, age 19, 4 years in U.S., Baltimore, clerk (10-18 July 1812)

Roach, James, age 50, 15 years in U.S., Washington Co., labourer (8-22 Aug. 1812)

Robertson, George, age 25, 2 years in U.S., Baltimore, storekeeper (11 Oct. 1813)

Robertson, John B., age 35, 11 years in U.S., Ann Arundel Co., clerk (31 Oct. 1812 - 6 Jan. 1813)

Robinson, Edward, age 46, 11 years in U.S., wife & child, Baltimore, shoemaker (25 July - 1 Aug. 1812)

Robinson, Henry, age 25, 6 years in U.S., Baltimore, stationer (11 Oct. 1813)

Robinson, John, age 28, 6 years in U.S., wife, Hagerstown, merchant; applied Mar. 1809 (8-22 Aug. 1812)

Robinson, Peter, age 26, 2 years in U.S., Baltimore, storekeeper (11 Oct. 1813)

Robinson, Thomas, age 29, 2 years in U.S., wife & child, Baltimore, sugar baker (11 Oct. 1813)

Robinson, Thomas, age 22, 5 years in U.S., Baltimore, grocer; applied Jan. 1812 (18-25 July 1822)

Robinson, William, age 22, 1 year in U.S., Hagerstown, clerk (8-22 Aug. 1812)

Rocher, Michael, age 42, 12 years in U.S., Baltimore, weaver (11 Oct. 1813)

Rodley, Robert, age 31, 11 years in U.S., wife & child, Baltimore, shoemaker (10-18 July 1812)

Roe(?), John, age 36, 8 years in U.S., wife & 2 children, Baltimore Co., cotton manufacturer (10-18 July 1812)

Rogers, Alexander, age 23, 8 years in U.S., Baltimore Co., machine maker (11 Oct. 1813)

Rogers, David, age 36, 5 years in U.S., Baltimore, cabinetmaker (11 Oct. 1813)

Rogers, John, age 24, 7 weeks in U.S., Baltimore, student of divinity (18-25 July 1812)

Rogers, John, age 25, 2 years in U.S., Baltimore, carpenter (10-18 July 1812); removed to Alexandria (11 Oct. 1813)

Rogers, Patrick, age 32, 5 years in U.S., wife & 2 children, Baltimore, cooper (11 Oct. 1813)

Rogers, William, age 60, 28 years in U.S., Frederick Town, gunsmith (8-22 Nov. 1812)

Role, James, age 28, 8 years in U.S., Baltimore, sawyer of mahogany (16 Sept. - 31 Oct. 1812)

Roney, Patrick, age 27, 8 years in U.S., Baltimore, hack driver (11 Oct. 1813)

Royla (?), George, age 35, 2 years in U.S., Baltimore cotton carder (11 Oct. 1813)

Rupell, John, age 35, 10 years in U.S., Baltimore, carpenter (11 Oct. 1813)

Rusher, William, age 31, 5 years in U.S., Kent Co. (31 Oct. 1812 - 6 Jan. 1813)

Ryan, James, age 34, 15 years in U.S., wife & 2 children, Baltimore, labourer (11 Oct. 1813)

Ryan, James, age 31, 15 years in U.S., wife & 2 children, Baltimore, farmer (18-25 July 1812)

Ryan, John, age 50, 28 years in U.S., wife & 5 children, Ann Arundel Co., farmer (2-12 Sept. 1812)

Ryan, Thomas, age 31, 5 years in U.S., Baltimore, tavern-keeper (2-12 Sept. 1812)

Ryr, George, age 35, 5 mos. in U.S., Baltimore Co., cotton spinner (25 July - 1 Aug. 1812)

Samoin(?), Joseph, age 40, 7 years in U.S., wife & 3 children, Baltimore, rigger; naturalized (11 Oct. 1813)

Sandell, Edward, age 36, 17 years in U.S., Baltimore, silversmith & watchmaker (10-18 July 1812)

Saunders, Walter, age 33, 10 years in U.S., wife & child, Liberty Town, schoolmaster; applied 17 Aug. 1811 (8-22 Aug. 1812)

Savage, Patrick D., age 25, 5 years in U.S., Frederick Co., a
weaver of cloth (8-22 Aug. 1812)

Scott, David, age 30, 2 years in U.S., wife & 2 children, Baltimore, millwright (11 Oct. 1813)

Scott, Henry, age 26, 6 years in U.S., wife, Baltimore, merchant;
applied Mar. 1811 (10-18 July 1812); by Oct. 1813 he has had
a child (11 Oct. 1813)

Scott, John, age 40, 9 years in U.S., wife & 3 children, Frederick Co., farmer (8-22 Aug. 1812)

Scott, John, age 34, 2 years in U.S., Baltimore, porter (11 Oct.
1813)

Scott, John, age 30, 2 years in U.S., Baltimore, storekeeper
(10-18 July 1812)

Scott, Thomas, age 31, 9 years in U.S., Baltimore, distiller (11
Oct. 1813)

Scott, Timothy, age 21, 2 years in U.S., Baltimore, type founder
(11 Oct. 1813)

Share, Joseph, age 33, 15 years in U.S., wife & 5 children, Baltimore, brass founder (11 Oct. 1813)

Shaw, Alexander, age 46, 17 years in U.S., 3 children, Baltimore,
carpenter (25 July - 1 Aug. 1812)

Shaw, James B., age 25, 8 years in U.S., Baltimore, carpenter
(11 Oct. 1813)

Shaw, Joseph, age 29, 3 years in U.S., wife & child, Baltimore
Co., cotton spinner (18-25 July 1812)

Sheay, Michael, age 20, 14 years in U.S., Baltimore, carpenter
(11 Oct. 1813)

Sheely, Edmund, age 44, 12 years in U.S., wife & 2 children,
Baltimore, shoemaker (11 Oct. 1813)

Sheridan, Thomas, age 26, 2 years in U.S., Baltimore, weaver
(11 Oct. 1813)

Sheridan, William, age 23, 2 years in U.S., Washington Co., distiller (8-22 Aug. 1812)

Sherry, James, age 20, 2 years in U.S., Baltimore, porter seller
(25 July - 1 Aug. 1812)

Short, John, age 34, 5 years in U.S., wife & 3 children, Baltimore, manufacturer of artificial mineral waters (10-18 July
1812); the next year 5 children are mentioned (11 Oct. 1813)

Shuffling, T., age 28, 5 years in U.S., Baltimore Co., shoemaker
(11 Oct. 1813)

Simpson, John, age 50, 25 years in U.S., wife, Hagerstown, farmer (8-22 Aug. 1812)

Simpson, Martin, age 24, 6 years in U.S., Baltimore, manufacturer
of thread; removed to New York (11 Oct. 1813)

Simpson, Samuel, age 29, 2 years in U.S., Baltimore Co., weaver
(11 Oct. 1813)

Sinnott, John D., age 27, 11 years in U.S., wife & 2 children,
Baltimore, physician & professor; applied 30 Mar. 1812 (10-18
July 1812)

Sloan, Hugh, age 23, 12 years in U.S., Baltimore, shoemaker (11
Oct. 1813)

Smith, Alexander, age 22, 6 years in U.S., Baltimore, baker (16
Sept. - 31 Oct. 1812)

Smith, Andrew, age 40, 1 year in U.S., New York, merchant (18-25
July 1812)

Smith, Archibald, age 27, 5 years in U.S., Baltimore, waterman
(11 Oct. 1813)

Smith, James, age 29, 19 years in U.S., wife & child, Baltimore
Co., shoemaker (25 July - 1 Aug. 1812)

Smith, James, age 24, 2 years in U.S., Prince George's Co., powder maker (22 Aug. - 2 Sept. 1812)

Smith, John, age 50, 6 years in U.S., Baltimore, machine maker
(11 Oct. 1813)
Smith, John, age 44, 5 years in U.S., wife, Baltimore, cordwainer
(1-8 Aug. 1812)
Smith, John, age 30, 9 years in U.S., wife & 2 children, Balti-
more, stone cutter (18-25 July 1812)
Smith, John, age 30, 6 years in U.S., Baltimore, baker (18-25
July 1812)
Smith, John, age 30, 4 years in U.S., Baltimore, bricklayer (11
Oct. 1813)
Smith, Joseph, age 22, 18 mos. in U.S., Baltimore, pedlar (11
Oct. 1813)
Smith, William, age 37, 7 years in U.S., wife, St. Mary's Co.,
cordwainer; applied 4 Aug. 1812 (8-22 Aug. 1812)
Somerville, John, age 39, 3 years in U.S., Baltimore, merchant
(10-18 July 1812)
Sproeton, John, age 58, 5 years in U.S., Cecil Co., farmer (8-
22 Aug. 1812)
Steele, Thomas, age 24, 6 years in U.S., wife & child, Balti-
more, shoemaker (11 Oct. 1812)
Stewart, Adam, age 28, 3 years in U.S., wife & 6 children, piano-
forte maker (11 Oct. 1813)
Stewart, Andrew, age 31, 3 years in U.S,, wife & child, Balti-
more, slater (25 July - 1 Aug. 1812)
Stewart, James, age 28, 18 mos. in U.S., wife & 3 children,
pianoforte maker (11 Oct. 1813)
Stewart, James, age 23, 7 years in U.S., Baltimore, clerk (10-
18 July 1812)
Stewart, Samuel, age 43, 2 years in U.S., wife & child, Baltimore,
storekeeper (11 Oct. 1813)
Stocks, James, age 46, 2 years in U.S., Baltimore Co., wire-
drawer (10-18 July 1812)
Stocks, James, age 46, 2 years in U.S., Baltimore, weaver (11
Oct. 1813)
Stone, James, age 31, 9 years in U.S., Washington Co., labourer
(8-22 Aug. 1812)
Stuart, Robert, age 30, 9 years in U.S., wife & 4 children, Mont-
gomery Co., teacher (22 Aug. - 2 Sept. 1812)
Swaine, Henry, age 41, 14 years in U.S., wife & 3 children, Bal-
timore, bricklayer (11 Oct. 1813)
Sweeny, Patrick, age 45, 2 years in U.S., Baltimore, tobacconist
(11 Oct. 1813)
Sweeny, William, age 46, 2 years in U.S., Baltimore, tobacconist
(11 Oct. 1813)
Sweetman, James, age 21, 4 years in U.S., Baltimore, plane maker
(11 Oct. 1813)
Tate, Alexander, age 22, 5 years in U.S., Baltimore, merchant
(16 Sept. - 31 Oct. 1812)
Tatum, Joseph J., age 38, 6 years in U.S., wife & 2 children,
Baltimore, brush maker (22 Aug. - 2 Sept. 1812)
Taylor, James, age 23, 3 years in U.S., Baltimore Co., cotton
spinner(18-25 July 1812)
Taylor, James, age 23, 2 years in U.S., Baltimore Co., weaver
(8-22 Aug. 1812)
Tellrany, Gregory, age 31, 6 years in U.S., wife & child, Bal-
timore, baker (11 Oct. 1813)
Terry, Michael, age 28, 14 years in U.S., wife, Frederick Town,
labourer (8-22 Aug. 1812)
Thomas, John, age 32, 1 year in U.S., wife & 3 children, Balti-
more, house-carpenter (18-25 July 1812)
Thomas, John, age 33, 13 years in U.S., wife & 2 children, Bal-
timore, carpenter (11 Oct. 1813)
Thomas, William, age 48, 27 years in U.S., wife & 2 children,
Hagerstown, carpenter (8-22 Aug. 1812)

Thompson, John, age 22, 5 years in U.S., wife, Baltimore, pedlar
(11 Oct. 1813)
Thompson, Robert, age 24, 2 years in U.S., Baltimore, weaver (11
Oct. 1813)
Thompson, Thomas, age 33, 1 year in U.S., Baltimore, day labou-
rer (10-18 July 1812)
Thomson, Charles, age 55, 30 years in U.S., 2 children, Dorches-
ter Co., cordwainer (8-22 Aug. 1812)
Thomson, James, age 38, 26 years in U.S., wife, Washington Co.,
labourer (8-22 Aug. 1812)
Thomson, William, age 23, 8 days in U.S., Baltimore (1-8 Aug.
1812)
Thornton, Seagood, age 30, 12 years in U.S., wife & 2 children,
Baltimore, seaman (18-25 July 1812)
Tiernan, Patrick, age 26, 7 years in U.S., Baltimore, merchant
(18-25 July 1812)
Tinckler, Thomas, age 53, 1 year in U.S., Baltimore, cedar cooper
(10-18 July 1812)
Tolle, Martin, age 21, 2 years in U.S., Baltimore, labourer (11
Oct. 1813)
Torrance, James, age 28, 5 years in U.S., Frederick Town, weaver
(8-22 Aug. 1812)
Tracy, Patrick, age 33, 10 years in U.S., wife & 2 children,
Prince George's Co., labourer (22 Aug. - 2 Sept. 1812)
Turner, George, Jr., age 27, 9 years in U.S., Cecil Co., weaver
(8-22 Aug. 1812)
Turner, John, age 19, 1 year in U.S., Baltimore Co., loom maker
(25 July - 1 Aug. 1812)
Tweedle, James, age 25, 2 years in U.S., Baltimore Co., reed
maker (1-8 Aug. 1812)
Urquback, John, age 24, 2 years in U.S., Baltimore, millwright
(11 Oct. 1813)
Usher, R.W., age 21, 5 years in U.S., Baltimore, labourer (16
Sept. - 31 Oct. 1812); name given as Richard (11 Oct. 1813)
Vance, John, age 26, 10 years in U.S., Baltimore, bookseller &
stationer ; applied Mar. 1811 (10-18 July 1812)
Vance, Thomas, age 22, 7 years in U.S., Baltimore, bookseller
(10-18 July 1812)
Varner, Robert, age 55, 20 mos. in U.S., wife & 4 children, Bal-
timore, weaver (11 Oct. 1813)
Virtue, Allen, age 25, 7 years in U.S., wife & 2 children, Bal-
timore, labourer (11 Oct. 1813)
Virtue, David, age 25, 2 years in U.S., wife & child, Baltimore
Co., farmer (11 Oct. 1813)
Waddell, Francis, age 45, 19 years in U.S., Baltimore, distiller
(11 Oct. 1813)
Waddell, Mathew, age 43, 5 years in U.S., wife & 4 children, Bal-
timore Co., superintendent of U. manufacturing company (18-25
July 1812)
Waefer, James, age 32, 9 years in U.S., Baltimore, grocer (10-18
July 1812)
Wafer, George, age 27, 9 years in U.S., Baltimore, storekeeper
(25 July - 1 Aug. 1812)
Walker, Thomas B., age 35, 10 years in U.S., wife, Baltimore,
pianoforte manufacturer (10-18 July 1812
Walker, William, age 32, 11 years in U.S., wife & 2 children,
Hagerstown, barber (8-22 Aug. 1812)
Walsh, Matthew, age 30, 14 years in U.S., Prince George's Co.,
millwright (22 Aug. - 2 Sept. 1812)
Ward, Hugh, age 21, 1 year in U.S., Baltimore Co., turner & filer
(18-25 July 1812)
Ward, James (coloured man), age 36, 2 years in U.S., wife & child,
Baltimore, teacher of the English language (10-18 July 1812)
Warren, Henry, age 18, 7 years in U.S., Baltimore, painter (11 Oct.
1813)

Watson, John, age 55, 7 years in U.S., Baltimore, tobacconist;
    applied Feb. 1812 (25 July - 1 Aug. 1812)
Watson, John, age 24, 2 years in U,S., Prince George's Co.,
    powder maker (22 Aug. - 2 Sept. 1812)
Webb, Charles, age 27, 2 years in U.S., wife & child, Baltimore,
    soap boiler (31 Oct. 1812 - 6 Jan. 1813)
Webb, James, age 40, 12 years in U.S., wife & 2 children, Prince
    George's Co., cabinetmaker; applied 1810 (22 Aug. - 2 Sept.
    1812)
Webster, John, age 32, 9 mos. in U.S., wife & 2 children, Balti-
    more, weaver (18-25 July 1812); wife is not listed in Oct. of
    1813 (11 Oct. 1813)
Weslie, John, age 36, 2 years in U.S., wife & 4 children, Balti-
    more Co., weaver (11 Oct. 1813)
West, Richard, age 57, 2 years in U.S., wife & 4 children, Bal-
    timore, copper refiner (11 Oct. 1813)
West, William, age 28, 8 years in U.S., wife & 3 children, Bal-
    timore, storekeeper; naturalized (11 Oct. 1813)
West, William, age 26, 12 years in U.S., wife & child, Baltimore,
    block & pump maker (18-25 July 1812)
Westerman, William, age 36, 15 mos. in U.S., wife & 5 children,
    Baltimore Co., cotton spinner (25 July - 1 Aug. 1812)
Whelan, James, age 29, 16 years in U.S., wife, Baltimore, dray-
    man (11 Oct. 1813)
Whelan, Peter, age 23, 2 years in U.S., Baltimore, labourer (11
    Oct. 1813)
White, James, age 20, 2 years in U.S., Baltimore Co., weaver (11
    Oct. 1813)
White, Joseph, age 21, 6 years in U.S., wife & child, Baltimore,
    cotton spinner (11 Oct. 1813)
Williams, Abraham R., age 35, 15 years in U.S., wife & 5 children,
    Baltimore, cotton spinner (11 Oct. 1813)
Williams, James, age 30, 9 years in U.S., Baltimore, clerk (25
    July - 1 Aug. 1812); by Oct. of next year he has a wife (11
    Oct. 1813)
Williams, John, age 33, 9 years in U.S., wife & 4 children, Bal-
    timore, tailor (10-18 July 1812)
Williams, John, age 30, 7 years in U.S., wife & 2 children, Bal-
    timore, stone cutter (10-18 July 1812)
Williams, Robert, age 25, 9 years in U.S., Baltimore, seaman (8-
    22 Aug. 1812)
Wilson, Hall, age 23, 16 mos. in U.S., Baltimore Co., machine
    maker; applied 25 May 1812 (8-22 Aug. 1812)
Wilson, John, age 25, 13 mos. in U.S., Baltimore Co., tinsmith
    (8-22 Aug. 1812)
Wilson, Philip, age 47, 16 mos. in U.S., wife & 3 children, Bal-
    timore Co., machine maker; applied 25 May 1812 (8-22 Aug. 1812)
Wilson, Robert, age 34, 18 mos. in U.S., wife & 4 children, Bal-
    timore, millwright (11 Oct. 1813)
Winwood, Thomas, Jr., age 28, 3 years in U.S., wife, Baltimore,
    grocer; applied Mar.; naturalized (11 Oct. 1813)
Wood, Henry, age 27, 6 years in U.S., Frederick Town, labourer
    (8-22 Aug. 1812)
Woodville, Wm., age 20, 1 year in U.S., Baltimore, merchant (18-
    25 July 1812)
Woodward, Thos., age 37, 2 years in U.S., wife & 2 children, Bal-
    timore, calico printer (11 Oct. 1813)
Wright, Malcom, age 27, 12 years in U.S., Baltimore, tin plate
    worker (11 Oct. 1813)
Wrightson, Robert, age 30, 3 years in U.S., wife & child, Balti-
    more, tavern-keeper; applied Mar. 1811 (10-18 July 1812)
Wrightson, Robert, age 30, 4 years in U.S., wife & child, Balti-
    more, shoemaker (11 Oct. 1813)
Young, George, age 34, 11 years, 11 mos. & 11 days in U.S., wife
    & child, Kent Co., cordwainer; applied Sept. 1811(8-22 Aug. 1812)

Young, John, age 36, 6 years in U.S., wife & 2 children, Baltimore, seaman (16 Sept. - 31 Oct. 1812)

VIRGINIA

Adams, Samuel, age 50, 16 years in U.S., wife & 3 children, Cul-
peper, merchant (14-21 Nov. 1812)
Adams, William, age 39, 13 years in U.S., wife & 1 child, Eliza-
beth City Co., mariner; a land holder and a seaman on board
the revenue cutter (1 Sept. 1812)
Aldridge, William Jos., age 61, in U.S. since 1795, 1 daughter,
Fauquier Court House, merchant (1-8 & 16 Aug. 1812)
Alexander, David, age 22, 4 years & 5 mos. in U.S., Petersburg,
Dinwiddie Co., pedlar (1 Sept. 1812)
Allison, William, age 17, 2 years in U.S., Petersburg, clerk;
applied in Philadelphia 1 Jan. 1810 (16-21 & 21-27 Mar. 1813);
5ft. 7in., fair complex., fair hair, grey eyes (No. 2)
Alton, Geo., age 21, 10 years & 4 mos. in U.S., Wythe Co., miner;
applied May 1811 (14-21 Nov. 1812)
Anderson, James, age 20, 3 years in U.S., Petersburg, clerk (21-
27 Mar. 1813); 5 ft. 7 in., fair complex., red hair, grey eyes,
ordered to Brunswick Court House (Nos. 2 & 5)
Anderson, John, age 34, 2 years in U.S., wife & 1 child, Henrico
Co., farmer & gardener (16-21 Mar. 1813 & No. 5)
Angus, William, age 25, in U.S. since Oct. 1810, Richmond City,
clerk; applied 29 May 1812 (14 July-1 Aug. 1812)
Armstrong, James, age 41, in U.S. since 1804, Petersburg, clerk;
applied 6 Nov. 1811 (1-8 Aug. 1812)
Atkinson, Geo., age 19, in U.S. since Oct. 1805, Richmond, clerk
& miller (to 16 Mar. 1813 & No. 4)
Atkinson, Richard, age 28, 5 years in U.S., Petersburg, merchant
(25 Dec. 1812-21 Feb. 1813); 5 ft. 9½ in., brown complex., dark
hair, blue eyes, sent 18 Mar. 1813 to Pearson Co., N.C. (No. 1)
Atkinson, Richard, age 23, in U.S. since Oct. 1805, Cartersville,
Cumberland Co., merchant (22-29 Aug. 1812)
Atkinson, Robert, age 26, in U.S. since Sept. 1800, Richmond,
clerk; applied 22 June 1812 (1-8 Aug. 1812 & No. 4)
Auslow, Thomas, age 36, in U.S. since 1 Nov. Richmond City. grocer
(14 July-1 Aug. 1812)
Babes, Geo., age 24, 9½ years in U.S., Accomack, schoolmaster
(14-21 Nov. 1812)
Bailie, Samuel, age 30, 5 years in U.S., mother & 3 sisters,
Abingdon, schoolmaster; applied May 1812 Sup. Ct. Washington
Co. (21 Nov.-25 Dec. 1812)
Bains, David, age . . . (No. 4)
Barber, James, age 34, 1 year & 2 mos. in U.S., wife & 3 children,
Norfolk Boro, saddler (1 Sept.1812)
Barclay, David, age 31, in U.S. since Sept. 1805, 3 in family,
Richmond City, merchant; applied 10 Dec. 1811; 6 ft. 2 in,
fair complex., dark hair, blue eyes, ordered (18 Mar. 1813) to
Lynchburg (14 July-1 Aug. 1812 & No. 1)
Bennett, Thomas, age 45, in U.S. since 1789, wife & 5 children,
Petersburg, merchant (13-17 Oct. 1812 & 21-27 Mar. 1813; 6 ft.,
florid complex., grey hair, blue eyes, ordered (21 Mar. 1813)
to·Charlottsville (No.2)
Biddle, James, age 38, 17 years in U.S., Petersburg, merchant
(21-27 Mar. 1813)
Biggard, Robert, age 39, 14 years in U.S., Chestervield, ditcher
(16-21 Mar. 1813); brown complex. dark hair, grey eyes (No. 1)
Bigham, James, 5 ft. 9 in., age 25, dark complex., dark hair;
hazel eyes (No.2)
Bigham, John, age 25, 5 years in U.S., Richmond, gardener (21-
27 Mar. 1813)
Black, William, age 24, in U.S. since 1807, Lynchburg, merchant;
applied 27 Jan. 1812 (22-29 Aug. 1812)
Bogues, Robert, age 28, 1½ years in U.S., Richmond, gunsmith
(13 May 1813)

Brady, Patrick, age 47, in U.S. since 1795, wife & 4 children,
Fauquier Co., merchant (17-22 Aug. 1812)
Braidwood, John, age 28, 1 year in U.S. Goochland Co., teacher
of the deaf and dumb (4-11 Apr. 1813)
Braine, James, age 47, in U.S. since Oct. 1804, 7 in family,
Richmond City, merchant; applied 23 Mar. 1809 (14 July-1 Aug.
1812)
Bramsly, Wm., age 22, 12 years in U.S., cabinetmaker (21 Nov.-
25 Dec. 1812)
Brander, Hector, age 22½, 3 years in U.S, wife, Petersburg,
miller (21-27 Mar. 1813); 5 ft. 10 in., pale complex., dark
hair, grey eyes (No. 2)
Branegin, Nicholas, age 53, in U.S. since 1784, 4 in family,
Lunenburg Co., blacksmith (17-22 Aug. 1812)
Bream, James, 5 ft. 9 in., age 47, dark complex., dark hair, grey
eyes, sent (18 Mar. 1813) to Goochland Co. (No. 1)
Brough, Kepple, age 42, 11 years in U.S.; Rockbridge; wishes to
be naturalized (14-21 Nov. 1812)
Brown, Alexander, age 31, in U.S. since Nov. 1799, wife, Pittsylvania Co., farmer; applied 23 Apr. 1811 (reported 10 Sept.
1812)
Brown, John, age 70, 16 years in U.S., Grayson Co., farmer; applied Grayson Co. Oct. 1812 (25 Dec. 1812-21 Feb. 1813)
Brown, John, age 41, 25 years in U.S., Petersburg, schoolmaster
(16-21 Mar. 1813)
Brown, John 5 ft. 9 in., age 39, dark complex., black hair, black
eyes (No. 1)
Bryan, Daniel, age 21, 2 years in U.S., Petersburg, manufacturer
of mineral maters (16-21 Mar. 1813); 5 ft. 10 in., dark complex., black hair, grey eyes (No. 1)
Bryan, Jos., age 41, 2 years in U.S., tailor (21 Nov.-25 Dec.
1812)
Bryce, James, age 32, 10 years in U.S., Norfolk Boro, merchant
(1 Sept. 1812)
Brydie, Charles, age 34, in U.S. since Oct. 1792, 4 in family,
Lunenburg Co., merchant, postmaster at Lunenburg Court House
(14 July-1 Aug. 1812)
Buchanan, Alexander, age 19, in U.S. since Oct. 1810, Richmond,
tanner; applied Dec. 1810 (1-8 Aug. 1812 & No. 4)
Callow, John R., age 38, in U.S. since Apr. 1807, Richmond,
stocker of muskets (1-8 Aug. 1812 & No. 4)
Campbell, David, age 28, 8 years in U.S., Lynchburg, tailor; applied 1808 (14 July 1812)
Campbell, James, age 16, in U.S. since July 1810, Lunenburg Co.,
apprentice to merchant (9-16 Aug. 1812)
Cantelo, William J., age 24, 2 years in U.S., wife, Norfolk Boro,
farmer (1 Sept. 1812)
Carilson, Samuel, (21 Mar. 1813) 5 ft. 8 in., age 29, dark complex., black hair, black eyes (No. 2)
Carlisle, Allen, age 25, 11 mos. in U.S., Norfolk Boro, house-
carpenter (1 Sept. 1812)
Carson, George, age 46, in U.S. since Sept. 1789, wife & 5
children, Cumberland Co., merchant; applied Bottetout Co. March
1794; passport to North Carolina (17-22 Aug. 1812 & 12 Apr.-
9 May 1813)
Casey, William, age 64, 30 years in U.S., wife & 2 children, Fauquier Co., weaver (12 Apr.-9 May 1813)
Caskie, James, age 22, in U.S. since July 1807, Manchester, merchant; applied 13 Jan. 1812 (14 July-1 Aug. 1812); on 30 Mar.
1813 5 ft. 10 in., fair complex., auburn hair (No. 3)
Caskie, John, age 22, in U.S. since 1807 when he came to U.S. at
solicitation of his uncle, Alexander Kerr, who had come to U.S. in
1794, Manchester, merchant; Caskie, from Scotland, served in
the U.S. militia; applied 9 Mar. 1812; was allowed to return
to Manchester (14 July-1 Aug. 1812 & 4 Sept. 1813 & 16 Mar. 1813)

Christie, Jos., age 18, in U.S. since 1810, Fredericksburg, clerk, nephew to a gentleman who has been a citizen upwards of 30 years; applied Aug. 1812 (16 Aug. 1812)

Clarke, George, age 30, in U.S. since Oct. 1805, Richmond City, tailor (5-12 Sept. 1812 & No.4)

Clarke, John, age 60, in U.S. since Sept. 1801, 7 in family, Richmond, grocer (1-8 Aug. 1812); 5 ft. 6 in., brown complex., brown hair, grey eyes (No. 3)

Cleland, Robert S., age 23, 1 year & 7 mos. in U.S., Norfolk Boro, teacher (1 Sept. 1812)

Cochran, Marcus, age 23, in U.S. since 9 Oct. 1809, Richmond, clerk (n.d.); 6 ft., florid complex., dark hair, dark eyes (No. 2)

Coggin, William, age 57, 20 years in U.S., Norfolk Boro, labourer (1 Sept. 1812)

Collingworth, Jonathan, age 31, in U.S. since July 1806, Richmond, brewer(1-8 Aug. 1812); 5 ft. 8 in., brown complex., black hair, hazel eyes (No. 3)

Conner, Edward, age 27, 7 years in U.S., wife, Hanover Co., painter (16-21 Mar. 1813); 5 ft. 4 in., fair complex., dark hair, grey eyes (No. 1)

Cooke, Peter, age 42, in U.S. since Oct. 1795, Prince Geo. Co., teacher (14 July-1 Aug. 1812); 5 ft. 9 in., fair complex., sandy hair, blue eyes (No. 2)

Cooney, John, age 50, in U.S. since 31 July 1784, 6 in family, Bedford, schoolmaster (14 July 1812)

Craig, John, age 45, 5 years in U.S., Westmorland, weaver; applied Circuit Court of Washington Nov. 1808 (31 Aug. 1812)

Crawford, Thomas, age 21, 5 ft, 11 in., fair complex., dark hair, blue eyes (No. 1)

Currie, James, Jr., age 22, in U.S. since Mar. 1811, Richmond, farmer; applied May 1812 (14 July-1 Aug. 1812 & No. 4)

Cuthbert, William, age 25, in U.S. since 1806, Petersburg, clerk (1-8 Aug. 1812 & No.5)

Davidson, Samuel, age 29, Petersburg, cabinetmaker (21-27 March 1813)

Davis, George, age 25, 2 years in U.S., Norfolk Boro, speculator; "a man of bad character" (1 Sept. 1812)

Dakings/Deakings, Joseph, age 50, in U.S. since Oct. 1793, 5 in family, Richmond City, merchant (14 July-1 Aug. 1812)

Delaney, Michael, age 21, 2 years in U.S., Norfolk Boro, tanner (1 Sept. 1812)

Dixon, James Johnston, age 37, 10 years in U.S., wife & 7 children, Richmond, bookbinder; applied 1803 in New York (to 16 Mar. 1813 & No. 4)

Dixson, William S., age 18, in U.S. since Feb. 1811, Richmond, clerk (to 16 Mar. 1813); 5 ft. 11 in., fair complex., auburn hair, grey eyes (No. 2)

Dobie, Thomas, age 29, in U.S. since Sept. 1808, Richmond, currier (1-8 Aug. 1812 & No. 4)

Dolan, Martin, 17 years in U.S., wife & 4 children, Richmond, gun-maker (16-21 Mar. 1813 & No. 5)

Donaldson, Adam, age 47, 21 years in U.S., res. of Fredericksburg about 9 years and of Virginia since 1791, wife & 1 child, Fredericksburg, shopkeeper; he came to America as an indented servant; in 1801 he married a woman born in Madison Co., Va., by whom he has 1 son (10 Aug. 1812 and letter of 27 Mar. 1813)

Douthart/Douthat, R., age 55, 28 years in U.S., 3 children, Rockbridge Co., tanner, magistrate & postmaster; has served in the militia (14-21 Nov. 1812)

Dunbar, James, age 23, in U.S. since 1809, Richmond, manufacturer (25 Aug. 1812)

Dunlop, N., age 19, in U.S. since Mar. 1805, Richmond, clerk (1-8 Aug. 1812)

Dunn, Andrew, age 23, in U.S. since Apr. 1812, wife & 5 children, Richmond, clerk (5-12 Sept. 1812 & 21-27 Mar. 1813); 5 ft. 6 in., fair complex., dark hair, grey eyes (No. 2)

Dunn, Thomas, age 24, in U.S. since Nov. 1810, Petersburg, merchant; (18 Mar. 1813) 5 ft. 11 in., florid complex., dark hair, grey eyes (No.1)

Dyball, Geo., age 18, in U.S. since Apr. 1812, Richmond, apprentice (to 16 Mar. 1813 & No. 4)

Elliott, Hugh, age 35, 15 years in U.S., wife & 3 children, Rockbridge Co., farmer (14-21 Nov. 1812)

Elliott, William, age 44, in U.S. since 1798, Rockbridge Co. (12-26 Sept. 1812)

Evans, Hugh Wm., age 24, 4 years in U.S., Baltimore, clerk; applied March 1811 (reported 23 May 1813)

Evans, Thos. E., age about 24, paroled at Lexington by the Marshal of Virginia (n.d.)

Ewing, John, age 29, in U.S. since Nov. 1803, 6 children, Richmond, tanner; applied Dec. 1309 (1-8 Aug. 1812 & No.4)

Ewing, William, age 25, in U.S. since Nov. 1811, Richmond, teacher; applied May 1812 (1-8 Aug. 1812)

Ewing, Wm., age 25, 2 years in U.S., Richmond, clerk; applied 8 Jan. 1812 (No. 4)

Facton, Jeremiah, age 25, in U.S. since Jan. 1808, Charles City Co., gardener (22-29 Aug. 1812)

Farley, James, age 32, 4 years & 4 mos. in U.S., wife, Rockbridge, farmer (14-21 Nov. 1812)

Farr, Thomas, age 38, in U.S. since 1810, wife & 2 children, Petersburg, paper maker (12-26 Sept. 1812); his age is 39 in report of 16-21 Mar. 1813; No. 1, in Mar. 1813 lists a Thomas Farr, age 41, 5 ft. 9 in., dark complex., dark hair, blue eyes

Farrar, J.H., age 14, in U.S. since Jan. 1801, Petersburg, apothecary & druggist (1-8 Aug. 1812)

Farrar, Thomas, age 85, 23 years in U.S., Norfolk Boro (1 Sept. 1812)

Fedeman, Symerville, age 35, in U.S. since Aug. 1806, 1 in family, Richmond, powder maker (reported 4 Aug. 1812)

Ferguson, Joseph, age 48, 10 years in U.S., wife & 2 children, Petersburg, shoemaker (21-27 Mar. 1813); 5 ft. 8 in., dark complex., dark hair, hazel eyes (No. 2)

Fife, Robert B., age 20, 2 years in U.S., Fredericksburg, farmer; applied Spotsylvania July 1810; belongs to the volunteers (23 Aug. 1812)

Finn, George, age 43, 1 year & 9 mos. in U.S., wife, Norfolk Boro, currier (1 Sept. 1812)

Fraser/Frazer, Francis, age 23, 5 years in U.S., Petersburg, dyer (21-27 Mar. 1813); 5 ft. 5 in., brown complex. black hair, grey eyes (No.2)

Frowell (or Frovell?), Isaac, age 29, 5 mos. in U.S., Petersburg, tallow chandler (21-27 Mar. 1813); 5 ft. 5 in., dark complex., black hair, black eyes, ordered to Fluvanna Court House (No. 2)

Gibson, John, age 28, in U.S. since 1810, Fauquier Court House, weaver (9-16 Aug. 1812)

Gill, Christopher, age 24, 9 years in U.S., Richmond, plasterer (16-21 Mar. 1813 & No.5)

Gill, John, age 29, 20 years in U.S., Richmond, stucco-worker (16-21 Mar. 1813); 5 ft. 8 in., fair complex., brown hair, blue eyes (No.1)

Gilliat, Martha C., age 27, in U.S. since Apr. 1806, 1 in family, Richmond (1-8 Aug. 1812)

Gordon, Alexander, age 18, 3 mos. in U.S., Falmouth, clerk (27-Mar.-4 Apr. 1813)

Gordon, James, age 65, 8 years in U.S., Henrico Co., carpenter (16-21 Mar. 1813); 5 ft. 10 in., fair complex., grey hair, grey eyes (No.1)

Gordon, John, age 37, 11 years in U.S., Richmond, clerk (21-27
    Mar. 1813); 5 ft. 6 in., dark complex., dark hair, dark eyes,
    ordered to Cartersville (No.2)
Gordon, Wm., Jr., age 19, in U.S. since 1807, Falmouth, clerk to
    a merchant; applied 12 July 1811 to court of Fredricksburg
    (16 Aug. 1812)
Graham, Gilbert, age 25, in U.S. since May 1804, Manchester,
    clerk, several years member of voluntary company of Manchester
    (14 July-1 Aug. 1812); removed to Lynchburgh (No.5); allowed
    to return to Manchester (4 Sept. 1813)
Graham, James, age 51, in U.S. since 31 Aug. 1787, Lynchburg,
    doctor; applied Oct. 1808 (10-14 Nov. 1812)
Grimshaw, Samuel, age 30, in U.S. since Sept. 1805, Henrico Co.,
    farmer (5-12 Sept. 1812)
Haffey, Michael, age 18, 1 year in U.S., Petersburg, nail maker
    (21-27 Mar. 1813); 5 ft. 7 in., fair complex., reddish hair,
    grey eyes (No.2)
Haffey, Roderick, age 25, 1 year in U.S., wife & 4 children,
    Petersburg, nail maker; applied Phila. 1805 (21-27 Mar. 1813);
    5 ft. 7 in., fair complex., reddish hair, blue eyes (No. 2)
Hardy, David, age 36, in U.S. since 2 Oct. 1811, Richmond, grocer
    (to 16 Mar. 1813); 5 ft. 7 in., florid complex. grey hair, grey
    eyes (No.2)
Hardy, William, age 30, 1 year & 9 mos. in U.S., wife & 1 child,
    Norfolk Boro, cabinetmaker (1 Sept. 1812)
Hayes, Matthias, age 32, 17 years in U.S., Henrico Co., gardener
    (16-21 Mar. 1813); 5 ft. 10 in., dark complex., dark hair, blue
    eyes (No. 1)
Heaton, John, age 38, in U.S. since Aug. 1809, 1 in family, Wood.
    Co., farmer (9-16 Aug. 1812)
Henderson, Alexander, age 47, 20 years in U.S., Petersburg, gar-
    dener (21-27 Mar. 1813); 5 ft. 10 in., brown complex., dark
    hair, dark eyes (No.2)
Henderson, John, age 30, in U.S. since 30 Aug. 1806, Richmond,
    grocer; applied 13 Aug. 1810 (14 July-1 Aug. 1812)
Henderson, Robert, age 24, in U.S. since Jan. 1806, Petersburg,
    clerk (1-8 Aug. 1812 & 27 Mar.-4 Apr. 1813); 6 ft., light com-
    plex., dark hair, hazel eyes (No.3)
Hendron, Samuel, age 55, 16 years in U.S., wife & 3 children,
    Rockledge Co., weaver (14-21 Nov. 1812)
Henry, James, age 40, in U.S. since Feb. 1808, native of Ireland,
    Richmond, merchant (1-8 Aug. 1812; he came to settle affairs
    of his brother John, who died in Va. 22 Aug. 1807 (letter of
    13 Mar. 1813); 5 ft. 6 in., dark complex., dark hair, grey eyes,
    removed to Charlottesville (No.3); was paroled by marshal at
    Charlottesville
Herron, James, age 40, 2 years & 4 mos. in U.S., Norfolk Co.,
    farmer (1 Sept. 1812)
Herron, Nathaniel, age 51, 20 years in U.S., Norfolk Boro, mer-
    chant (1 Sept. 1812)
Herron, Patrick, age 27, 2 years & 6 mos. in U.S., Norfolk Boro,
    merchant (1 Sept. 1812)
Hetherton, Andrew, age 35, in U.S. since Jan. 1804, 4 in family,
    Richmond City, tailor (14 July-1 Aug. 1812)
Hetherton, William, age 36, 12 years in U.S., Powhatan Co., far-
    mer/ditcher; applied Sept. or Oct. 1809 (21 Nov.-25 Dec. 1812 &
    4-11 Apr. 1813)
Heywood, Joseph, age 29, 4 years in U.S., Petersburg, cotton
    spinner (21-27 Mar. 1813); 5 ft. 6 in., fair complex., light
    hair, grey eyes (No.2)
Hilles, John, age 32, in U.S. since 1808, wife & 4 children,
    Fredericksburg, weaver (10 Aug. 1812)
Hogan, John, age 28, in U.S. since Aug. 1803, Rockbridge Co.,
    storekeeper (to 16 Mar. 1813)

Hundell, John, age 58, 32 years in U.S., wife & 10 children,
Fauquier Co., farmer (12 Apr.-9 May 1813)

Hume, Wm., age 33, 17½ years in U.S., Culpeper, teacher (23 Aug.
1812)

Hutchison, Andrew, age 35, 9 years in U.S., 4 children, Richmond,
tailor (No.4)

Hutchison, William, age 31, in U.S. since May 1802, Richmond,
grocer; applied June 1812 (14 July-1 Aug. 1812); 5 ft. 5 in.,
fair complex., fair hair, dark eyes; sent to Rockingham Co.
(No.1)

Hutchison, William, 5 ft. 11 in., age 36 (Apr. 1813), dark complex., black hair, hazel eyes (No.3)

Hyde, Daniel, age 47, 20 years in U.S., wife & 4 children, Spotsylvania Co., farmer (25 Dec. 1812-21 Feb. 1813)

Irvin, John, age 35, in U.S. since 1802, Rockbridge Co., merchant
(12-26 Sept. 1812)

Irvine, George, age 21, in U.S. since 1810, Petersburg, clerk; 6
ft., fair complex., auburn hair, grey eyes (5-12 Sept. 1812 & No.2)

Isaac, Anthony, age 34, in U.S. since May 1806, wife, Richmond,
slater (22-29 Aug. 1812); age is given as 35 and he has wife
and 1 child (16-21 Mar. 1813); 5 ft. 7 in., fair complex.,
brown hair, hazel eyes, ordered to Fluvanna Court House (No.2)

Isaacs, Gabriel, age 21, in U.S. since May 1811, Powhatan Co.,
storekeeper (to 16 Mar. 1813)

Jackson, Jno., Sr., age 45, 10 years in U.S., 4 children, Wythe
Co., farmer; applied May 1811 (14-21 Nov. 1812)

Jackson, Jno., Jr., age 40, 10 years in U.S., 5 children, Wythe
Co., miner; applied May 1811 (14-21 Nov. 1812)

Jackson, Joseph, age 46, 10 years in U.S., 4 children, Wythe Co.,
miner; applied May 1811 (14-21 Nov. 1812)

Jackson, Thos., Sr., age 65, 10 years in U.S., 5 children, Wythe
Co., miner; applied May 1811 (14-21 Nov. 1812)

Jameson, Andrew, age 24, 4 years & 9 mos. in U.S., Lynchburg,
merchant; applied Nov. 1810 (10-14 Nov. 1812)

Johnson/Johnston, Arthur, age 20, 5 years in U.S., Petersburg,
packer (21-27 Mar. 1813); 5 ft. 5 in., fair complex., reddish
hair, dark eyes (No.2)

Johnston, Hugh, age 22, in U.S. since 1810, Richmond, tailor (5
Sept. 1812)

Jones, Noah, age 28, 12 years in U.S., wife & 2 children, Richmond, dyer (to 16 Mar. 1813 & No.4)

Jones, Robert C.M., age 46, 20 years in U.S., Petersburg, painter;
applied Phila. 1806 (21-27 Mar. 1813); 5 ft. 7 in., florid complex., dark hair, grey eyes (No.2)

Kincaid, James, age 23, 6 years in U.S., Richmond, tallow chandler
(16-21 Mar. 1813); 5 ft. 7 in., sallow complex., black hair,
black eyes (No.1)

Kingston, James P., age 27, 6 years in U.S., Philadelphia, merchant; gone to Philadelphia (21-27 Mar. 1813); 6 ft., fair complex., light hair, hazel eyes (No.1)

Kippen, George, age 23, in U.S. since 3 Jan. 1804, Richmond,
clerk; applied 30 May 1812 (1-8 Aug. 1812); allowed to return
to Richmond (4 Sept. 1813)

Knipe, Lauet (or Lanet?), age 33, 9 years in U.S., 5 children,
Wythe Co., miner; applied May 1811 (14-21 Nov. 1812)

Kyle, David, age 14, 1 month in U.S., Bottetout, merchant (14-21
Nov. 1812)

Kyle, Hazlet, age 19, 2 years in U.S., Bottetout, merchant (14-
21 Nov. 1812)

Kyle, James, age 18, 2 years in U.S., Lynchburg, clerk (10-14 Nov.
1812)

Kyle, Robert, age 22, 5 years in U.S., Bottetout, merchant (14-
21 Nov. 1812)

Lambert, Patrick, age 40, 13 years in U.S., Carterville, merchant
(17 May 1813)

Lambert, Thomas, age 31, 10 years in U.S., wife & 3 children,
  Norfolk Boro, shoemaker (27 Mar.-4 Apr. 1813); 5 ft. 4 in.,
  fair complex., red hair, blue eyes, ordered to Fluvanna Court
  House (No.3)
Lamon, John, age 32, in U.S. since 1801, 5 in family, Charles
  Town, Jefferson Co., weaver; applied July 1812 (13-17 Oct. 1812)
Lang, Ob., age 35, 3 years & 11 mos. in U.S. (selling an estate
  of a deceased brother), Rockbridge, accountant; applied in New
  Hampshire but not granted (14-21 Nov. 1812)
Laughlin, Hugh, age 39, 7 years & 2 mos. in U.S., wife & 3 chil-
  dren, Rockbridge, weaver (14-21 Nov. 1812)
Laurie/Lawrie, William, age 22, in U.S. since 30 Sept. 1807,
  Richmond City, clerk; applied 20 June 1812 (5-12 Sept. 1812);
  removed to Lynchburg (No.5); allowed to return to Richmond (4
  Sept. 1813)
Lawson, Oswald, age 33, 3½ years in U.S., Norfolk, clerk (21-27
  Mar. 1813); 5 ft. 7½ in., florid complex., dark hair, blue eyes,
  ordered to Charlottsville (No.2)
Leigh, Sir Egerton, age about 53, paroled by Marshal of Va. at
  Lexington (n.d.)
Leslie, Alexander, age 46, 14 years in U.S., Richmond, baker
  (16-21 Mar. 1813 & No.5)
Leslie, Alexander, Jr., age 22, in U.S. since Aug. 1809, Rich-
  mond, clerk; applied 13 Jan. 1812 (14 July-1 Aug. 1812); re-
  moved to Lynchburgh (No.5); allowed to return to Richmond (4
  Sept. 1813)
Liggat, Alexander, native of Ireland, brother of John Liggat,
  age 28, arrived Baltimore 1806 and applied there Mar. 1811,
  Falmouth, merchant (23 Aug. 1812 & a petition)
Lighton, James, age 23, 15 years in U.S., wife, Norfolk Boro,
  mariner (1 Sept. 1812)
Lockridge, John, age 37, 11 years in U.S., wife & 2 children,
  Petersburg, tailor; applied Dec. 1807 (21-27 Mar. 1813); 5 ft.
  7 in., fair complex., fair hair, grey eyes (No. 2)
Lowndes, Elizabeth, age 53, in U.S. since 1805, 6 in family,
  Petersburg, potter (12-26 Sept. 1812)
Lownds/Lownes, John, age 16, 8 years in U.S., Petersburg, potter
  (21-27 Mar. 1813); 5 ft. 3 in., fair complex., brown hair, black
  eyes (No.2)
Lownds/Lownes, Thomas, age 20, 8 years in U.S., Petersburg, pot-
  ter (21-27 Mar. 1813); 5 ft. 8 in., fair complex., brown hair,
  grey eyes (No.2)
Lynch, Peyton, age 32, 5 years in U.S., wife & 3 children, Peters-
  burg, blacksmith; applied 2 July 1810 (16-21 Mar. 1813); 5 ft.
  6 in., fair complex., fair hair, grey eyes (No.1)
McArter, John, age 31, 1½ years in U.S., Richmond, gardener (to
  16 Mar. 1813)
McArter/McCart, John, age 33, in U.S. since Sept. 1810, 3 children,
  Richmond, bacon merchant (14 July-1 Aug. 1812 & No. 4)
McCaskey/McClatchy, Richard, age 35, in U.S. since 19 May 1812,
  Richmond, miller (to 16 Mar. 1813 & No.40)
McClure, James, age 51, 17 years in U.S., wife & 2 sons, Richmond,
  merchant (21-27 Mar. 1813); 5 ft. 6 in., brown complex., light
  hair, blue eyes (No.2)
McCundy/McCunday, Andrew, age 31, 11 years in U.S., wife & 2
  children, Rockbridge Co., farmer (14-21 Nov. 1812)
McDermott, Patrick, age 30, in U.S. since Aug. 1811, wife & 1
  child, Richmond, labourer (report 22 Sept. 1812)
McDonald, John, age 35, in U.S. since April 1805, 6 in family,
  Richmond City, grocer (14 July-1 Aug. 1812); 5 ft. 6 in, ruddy
  complex., dark hair, blue eyes (No.1)
McEuen/McEwen, John, age 27, 8 years in U.S., Richmond, stone
  cutter (16-21 Mar. 1816); 5 ft. 4 in., fair complex., fair
  hair, grey eyes (No.1)

Magee, Andrew, age 27, 9 years in U.S., Petersburg, clerk; ap-
plied 1 Jan. 1810 (16-21 Mar. 1813); 5 ft. 9 in., dark complex., dark hair, blue eyes (No.1)
McGillivie(?), John, age 21, in U.S. since Dec. 1809, Richmond,
clerk; applied 6 June 1812 (14 July-1 Aug. 1812); removed to
Lynchburg No.5)
McIntyre/McIntire, George, age 30, in U.S. since 1804, wife,
sister & 2 children, Hampton, physician (14 July-1 Aug. and
1 Sept. 1812)
McKee/McKie, Robert, age 45, 28 years in U.S., wife, Rockbridge
Co., farmer; applied May 1811 (14-21 Nov. 1812)
McKenna, Hugh L., 5 ft. 10 in., age 24 (18 Mar. 1813), fair complex., sandy hair, hazel eyes (No.1)
McKenzie, H.F., age 21, in U.S. since June 1808, Petersburg,
clerk; applied 18 Aug. 1809 (12-26 Sept. 1812)
Mackey, John, age 23, in U.S. since 13 June 1807, Richmond, cotton manufacturer; applied Providence, R.I. (reported 14 June
1812)
McKim, William, age 28, 3 years in U.S., Chesterfield Co., far-
mer (to 16 Mar. 1813 & No.4)
*McLaughlin/McGlaughlin, age 25, 15 mos. in U.S., Greenbrier Co.,
carpenter; applied 24 Sept. 1812(14-21 Nov. 1812 & 12 Oct. 1812)
McMillan/McMullin, Hector, age 24, in U.S. since Nov. 1810, Petersburg, clerk (14 July-1 Aug. 1812); 5 ft. 11 in., dark complex.,
black hair, grey eyes (No.1)
Mack...?, Edward, age 47, 23 years in U.S,, cabinetmaker (report
7 Sept. 1812)
Man, Andrew, age 43, 23 years in U.S., Richmond, gardener (No.5)
Marno, James, age 50, 27 years in U.S,, wife & 5 children, Prin-
cess Anne Co., farmer (1 Sept. 1812)
Mearns, James, age 28, 10 years & 6 mos. in U.S., Southampton
Co., merchant (1 Sept. 1812); on 30 Mar. 1813, now aged 29,
5 ft. 8 in., brown complex., black hair, blue eyes, ordered
to Greensvill Co. (No.3)
Meran, John, age 41, 1 year & 2 mos. in U.S., Norfolk Boro, far-
mer (summary)
Michael, Stanford, age 34, 28 years in U.S., wife & 2 children,
Norfolk Boro, bricklayer & stone mason (14 Nov. 1812)
Mickle, William, age 28, 11 years in U.S., Petersburg, collector;
applied 1 Jan. 1810 (16-21 Mar. 1813); 5 ft. 10 in., florid
complex., dark hair, hazel eyes (No.1)
Milbourn, Geo., age 47, 20 years in U.S., Culpeper, farmer (31
Aug. 1812)
Milbourn, Stephen, age 59, 16 years in U.S., Culpeper, 5 child-
ren, farmer (31 Aug. 1812)
Milbourn, Thos., age 58, 16 years in U.S., wife & 2 children,
Culpeper, farmer (31 Aug. 1812)
Milbourn, Wm., age 56, 16 years in U.S., Culpeper, farmer (31
Aug. 1812)
Miller, George, age 35, 11 years in U.S., wife & 4 children,
Henrico Co., paper maker (27 Mar.-4 Apr. 1813); 5 ft. 10 in.,
fair complex., dark hair, dark eyes (No.3)
Miller, Hugh, age 41, 16 years in U.S., wife & 4 children, Rich-
mond, blacksmith (to 16 Mar. 1813)
Miller, Joseph, age 45, 7 weeks in U.S., Norfolk Boro (27 Mar.-
4 Apr. 1813); 5 ft. 7 in., fair complex., brown hair, blue
eyes, ordered to Fluvanna Court House (No.3)
Miller, Robert, age 60, 9 years in U.S., Richmond, weaver (16-21
Mar. 1813); 5 ft. 7 in., brown complex., dark hair, grey eyes
(No.1)
Milling, John, age 39, 10 years in U.S., 1 child, Wythe Co.,
miner; applied May 1811 (14-21 Nov. 1812)
Mitchell, Andrew, age 22, 2 years in U,S., Abingdon, merchant
(21 Nov.-25 Dec. 1812)
* Given name is Wm.

Mitchell, Thomas, age 39, 8 mos. in U.S., 4 children, Portsmouth, Norfolk Co., teacher (1 Sept. 1812)

Montgomery, William, age 46, 10 years in U.S., 3 children, Hampton, Elizabeth City Co., shoemaker (1 Sept. 1812)

Moore, Richard Adams, age 30, in U.S. since 1797, 1 child, Petersburg, apothecary & druggist (1-8 Aug. 1812 & 16-21 Mar. 1813); 5 ft. 7½ in., fair complex., dark hair, blue eyes (No.1)

Moore, William, age 56, 33 years in U.S., 1 child, Richmond, grocer (21-27 Mar. 1813); 5 ft. 5 in., brown complex., black hair, grey eyes, ordered to Louiza Co. (No.2)

Moran, John, age 41, 1 year & 2 mos. in U.S., Norfolk Boro, farmer (1 Sept. 1812)

Morris, James, age 26, in U.S. since Sept. 1803, Richmond, merchant (grocer); applied 18 Feb. 1809 (1-8 Aug. 1812 & No.4)

Muir, William, age 22, in U.S. since Oct. 1807, native of North Britain, Falmouth, clerk; applied 8 Jan. 1812; has served in the militia (14 July-1 Aug. & 16 Aug. 1812); 5 ft. 10 in., fair complex, fair hair, hazel eyes (No.1)

Mullin, Hugh, age 41, 16 years in U.S., wife & 4 children, Richmond, dyer (No.4)

Murphy, John, age 22, 6 mos. in U.S., Norfolk Boro, tanner & currier (1 Sept. 1812)

Murray, Michael K., age 35, 12 years in U.S., wife, Chesterfield, physician (4-11 Apr. 1813); 5 ft. 8 in., fair complex., dark hair, grey eyes (No.3)

Naughtrop, James, age 30, 13 years in U.S., Fincastle, merchant (14-21 Nov. 1812)

Neale/Neal, William, age 39, 6 years in U.S., wife & 4 children, Richmond, upholsterer; applied Baltimore 1812 (16-21 Mar. 1812 & No.5)

Neilson, Hall, age 25, 8 years in U.S., native of Ireland, Richmond, merchant; applied Richmond 31 May 1809 (to 16 Mar. 1813 & statement of 6 May 1813); 5 ft. 10 in., fair complex., sandy hair, grey eyes, removed to Mecklenburg Co. & in Mar. 1813 received permission to travel to Washington, D.C. (to 16 Mar. 1813 & No.3); letter of Robert Neilson of 20 June 1813 from Washington states that family consists of 7 brothers & 2 sisters; John Neilson for about 14 or 15 years has been resident of Augusta, Ga.; Samuel has been resident there about 9 years; Thomas was a resident of Hagerstown, Md., but in fall of 1806 removed to Petersburg, Va.; Hall arrived in U.S. in autumn of 1807; William and James arrived in U.S. in fall of 1811 and settled in Norfolk, Va.

Neilson, James, age 25, 2 years & 10 mos. in U.S., Norfolk Boro, merchant; applied May 1812 (1 Sept. 1812); 5 ft. 6 in., fair complex., auburn hair, ordered to Mecklenburg Co. (No.3)

Neilson, William H., age 28, 1 year & 8 mos. in U.S., Norfolk Boro, merchant; applied May 1812 (1 Sept. 1812); 5 ft. 7 in., fair complex., red hair, blue eyes, ordered to Mecklenburg Co. (No.3)

Nelson, Alexander, age 33, 11 years in U.S., wife & 3 children, Rockbridge Co., farmer (14-21 Nov. 1812)

Nisbett, Archibald, age 28, in U.S. since May 1803, Richmond City, merchant; applied 1 June 1812 (17-22 Aug. 1812)

Nisbet, David, age 23, in U.S. since May 1803, Richmond, clerk; applied March 1812 (1-8 Aug. 1812)

Nixon, James, age 57, in U.S. since May 1807, 2 in family, Richmond City, soap boiler & tallow chandler (22-29 Aug. 1812); the 2 in family are children (No.4)

Nixon, Robert Spencer, age 32, in U.S. since July 1793, Richmond City, collector; made application in New York but does not recall when (9-16 Aug. 1812)

Noble, John, age 28, 16 years in U.S., wife, Fredericksburg, bookbinder (23 Aug. 1812)

Orr, James, age 19, 2 years & 4 mos. in U.S., Petersburg, clerk
(14-21 Nov. 1812); in Mar. 1813 age 20, fair complex., light
hair, blue eyes (No.1)
Osborne, Samuel, age 51, 17 years in U.S., Norfolk Boro, seeds-
man (1 Sept. 1812)
Pamphres (?), David, age 25, 8 years in U.S., Lynchburg, tailor;
applied 1808 (10-14 Nov. 1812)
Patterson, George, age 20, 1½ years in U.S., Petersburg, storekeeper (16-21 Mar. 1813); 5 ft. 6 in., fair complex., dark hair,
blue eyes (No.1)
Patterson, William, age 27, 10 years in U.S., emigrated from Ireland in 1803, Richmond, merchant; applied at Court in Bottetout Co. on 11 Feb. 1810 (21-27 Mar. 1813); 6 ft., fair complex., dark hair, grey eyes, ordered to Augusta Co. (No.2)
Pearce/Peirce, Samuel, age 38, 9 years in U.S., Petersburg, saddler (27 Mar.-4 Apr. 1813); 5 ft. 4 in., ruddy complex., dark
hair, hazel eyes (No.3)
Percival, George, age 72, 3 mos. in U.S., wife, Lynchburg, butcher (10-14 Nov. 1812)
Percival, George, age 20, 1 year & 3 mos. in U.S., Lynchburg,
carpenter (10-14 Nov. 1812)
Percival, John, age 27, 5 years in U.S., Lynchburg, carpenter
(10-14 Nov. 1812)
Pettit, Patrick, age 18, 2 years & 8 mos. in U.S., Norfolk Boro,
merchant's clerk (1 Sept. 1812)
Placide, Alexander, age 28, 5 years in U.S., Norfolk Boro, teacher
(1 Sept. 1812)
Polack, Abraham, age 15, in U.S. since 5 Aug. 1811, Richmond,
clerk (9-16 Aug. 1812)
Pollock, John, age 18, Norfolk Boro, merchant's clerk (1 Sept.
1812)
Potts, James, age 21, 1 year & 2 mos. in U.S., Norfolk Co., rope-
maker (1 Sept. 1812)
Potts, Thomas, age 30, in U.S. since June 1810, Richmond, merchant;
applied 28 Mar. 1812 (or May?)(1-8 Aug. 1812); removed to Win-
chester (No.5)
Power, Francis, age 40, in U.S. since April 1807, Richmond, prof.
of languages and mathematics (1 Apr. 1812)
Preston, Sam., age 38, 17 years in U.S., wife & 3 children,
Washington Co., farmer; applied 28 Oct. 1812 at Superior Court
Washington Co. (21 Nov.-25 Dec. 1812)
Pullin, Geo., age 29, 3 years in U.S., wife, Richmond, innkeeper
(to 16 Mar. 1813)
Purvis, James, age 38, 1 year & 10 mos. in U.S., wife & 1 child,
Norfolk Boro, agent to establish a manufactory; has left the
U.S. for England (1 Sept. 1812)
Rae, Frederick, age 27, in U.S. since Oct. 1810, Richmond, school-
master; applied 22 June 1812 (1-8 Aug. 1812)
Rae, Richard, age 27, 3 years in U.S., Richmond, schoolmaster
(No.4)
Ralston, Peter, age 30, in U.S. since Nov. 1803, 2 in family,
Richmond City, bacon curer; applied 3 Aug. 1809 (14 July-1 Aug.
1812)
Ralston, Robert, age 25, in U.S. since Jan. 1811, Richmond City,
physician; applied 1812 (14 July-1 Aug. 1812 & 27 Mar.-4 Apr.
1813); 6 ft., brown complex., black hair, blue eyes (No.3)
Rawson, Robert, age 26, 3 years in U.S., Richmond, tavern-keeper
(to 16 Mar. 1813 & No.4)
Rattray, David, age 40, 15 years in U.S., Powhatan, grocer, sent
to Amherst Co. (4-11 Apr. 1813)
Rattray, David, age 36, 21 years in U.S., Powhatan Co., farmer
(12 Apr.-9 May 1813) - all crossed out in document
Read, Wm. F., age 27, in U.S. since 1804, wife & 1 child, Fredericksburg, saddler; applied ½ year ago in N.Y., 4 years ago
in Baltimore, 3 Aug. in Spotsylvania (10 Aug. 1812)

Redman, Timothy, age 27, in U.S. since Aug. 1809, Richmond City, carpenter (17-22 Aug. 1812 & No.4)

Rice, John, age 25, 8 years in U.S., Richmond, physician (16-21 Mar. 1813 & No.5)

Riddle, James, age 38, 5 ft. 6 in., brown complex., black hair, hazel eyes, ordered to Charlottsville (21 Mar. 1813 - No.2)

Ripley, Thomas B., age 22, 2 years in U.S., Richmond, builder of powder mills; passport to St. Mary, Georgia (12 Apr.-9 May 1813)

Ritchie, James, age 33, in U.S. since Nov. 1806, 3 children, Petersburg, sword-maker (1-8 Aug. 1812 & No.4)

Ritchie, William B., age 18, 2 years in U.S., Petersburg, merchant/clerk; applied 1 Jan. 1810 (14-21 Nov. 1812 & 16-21 Mar. 1813); 5 ft. 7 in., fair complex., dark hair, blue eyes (No.1)

Roach, Patrick, age 40, 5 years in U.S., Henrico Co., bookbinder (16-21 Mar. 1813)

Roberts, Richard, age 22, 9 years in U.S., Middlesex Co., clerk (12 Apr.-9 May 1813)

Roberts, Thomas, age 19, in U.S. since 20 Oct. 1810, Richmond City, clerk (17-22 Aug. 1812)

Robinson, John, age 42, in U.S. since Apr. 1802, Lynchburg, comm. merchant; applied 24 Aug. 1812 (5-12 Sept. 1812)

Rocke, Patrick, age 40, 5 years in U.S., Richmond, bookbinder (No.5) = Patrick Roach above.

Rose, Alexander, age 59, 30 years in U.S., 2 children, Petersburg, carpenter (21-27 Mar. 1813); 5 ft. 6 in., brown complex., fair hair, blue eyes (No.2)

Rose, David, age 30, in U.S. since Mar. 1805, Petersburg, millwright(to 16 Mar. 1813) = (?) John Rose, age 30, 8 years in U.S., Petersburg, miller, 5 ft. 7 in., brown complex., black hair, hazel eyes (21-27 Mar. 1813 & No.2)

Rose, William, age 33, in U.S. since May 1803, 3 in family, Richmond City, trader (17-22 Aug. 1812)

Rowson, Robert, age 26, 3 years in U.S., Richmond, tavern-keeper (16 Mar. 1813) = Robert Rawson above

Rutter, John, age 32, 9 years in U.S., wife & 2 children, Madison Co., miller (12 Apr.-9 May 1813)

Ryan, Lawrence, age 23, in U.S. since Aug. 1811, Richmond, labourer (1-8 Aug. 1812)

Ryan, William, age 35, in U.S. since 4 June 1811, Richmond, shoemaker; applied July 1811 (1-8 Aug. 1812)

Sanderson/Saunderson, William, age 38, in U.S. since 29 Apr. 1800, 3 children, Richmond, boot- and shoemaker; applied 1809 (22-29 Aug. 1812 & No. 4)

Sapple, Thomas, age 30, 1 year & 2 mos. in U.S., wife & 2 children, Norfolk Boro, cooper (1 Sept. 1812)

Scallan, James, age 21, 2 years & 9 mos. in U.S., Alexandria, clerk; applied March 1813; has passport from Washington (4-11 Apr. 1813); 5 ft. 8 in., fair complex., light hair, grey eyes (No.3)

Scallan, William, age 20, 3 years in U.S., Norfolk Boro, tanner & currier (1 Sept. 1812)

Scott, George, age 25, in U.S. since Oct. 1809, Richmond, clerk (1-8 Aug. 1812); removed to Lynchburg (No.5); allowed to return to Richmond (4 Sept. 1813)

Scott, Hugh, age 38, son of a citizen of Glasgow, came to U.S. 1801, married in Norfolk and has 2 children, weaver by trade, Norfolk Boro, purchases & sells lumber (1 Sept. 1812); 5 ft. 7 in., brown complex., dark hair, blue eyes, ordered to Augusta Co. (No.3)

Scott, James, age 42, 6 years in U.S., wife, Leesburg, schoolmaster (14-21 Nov. 1812)

Sharp, Robert, age 18, in U.S. since Apr. 1811, Richmond, clerk, removed to Amherst Court House (1-8 Aug. 1812 & No.5)

Simpson, John, age 40, 17 years in U.S., wife & 1 child, manufacturer of mineral waters (16-21 Mar. 1813); 5 ft. 9 in., dark
complex., black hair, blue eyes (No.1)

Sinton, Thomas, age 23, 2½ years in U.S., Richmond, carpenter 16-
21 Mar. 1813); 5 ft. 9 in., sallow complex., black hair, blue
eyes (No.1)

Sinton, William, age 24, 3 years in U.S., Richmond, clerk (to 16
Mar. 1813)

Smith, D.R., age 23, 4 years in U.S., Powhatan Co., ditcher (21-
27 Mar. 1813)

Smith, William, native of Scotland, about 6 years in U.S., Newport, about 4 miles from Dumfries, a nephew of George Smith
(letter of 5 May 1813)

Snell, James, age 31, 12 years in U.S., Richmond, hatter (16-21
Mar. 1813); 5 ft. 11 in., fair complex., sandy hair, grey eyes
(No.1)

Sommerville, George, age 22, in U.S. since 14 Aug. 1807, Harrison
Co., farmer (n.d.)

Sommerville, Thomas, age 55, in U.S. since 14 Aug. 1807, 8 in
family, Harrison Co., farmer; applied Sept. 1810 (n.d.)

Southgate, Charles, age 52, in U.S. since Sept. 1803, 2 in family, Richmond, musician; applied 16 Sept. 1809 (14 July-1 Aug.
1812 & No.4)

Stacy/Stacey, Frederick, age 45, 1 year in U.S., Petersburg,
overseer; applied Philadelphia 1806 (21-27 Mar. 1813); 5 ft.
10 in., fair complex., auburn hair, blue eyes (no.3)

Stanford, Michael, age 34, 28 years in U.S., wife & 2 children,
Norfolk Boro, bricklayer & stone mason (1 Sept. 1812)

Stevenson, William, age 32, 5 years & 5 mos. in U.S., Petersburg,
merchant; applied 7 Nov. 1807 in Hus. Court in Petersburg (21
Nov.-25 Dec. 1812); 5 ft. 11 in., fair complex., fair hair,
hazel eyes (No.1)

Stewart, Norman, age 30, arrived in Va. in May 1802, then aged
19; applied U.S. Circuit Court, Va., on 16 Oct. 1807 (petition);
5 ft. 6 in., dark complex., dark hair, grey eyes, removed to
Fluvanna Court House (No.3)

Stewart/Stuart, Thomas, age 24, in U.S. since Dec. 1809, Richmond, clerk; applied 18 June 1812 (1-8 Aug. 1812 & No.4); removed to Prince Edward (No.5); allowed to return to Richmond
(4 Sept. 1813)

Stewart, Wm., age 24, 1 year in U.S., tailor (21 Nov.-25 Dec.
1812)

Sullin, Geo., 3 years in U.S., wife, Richmond, innkeeper (No.4)

Sullivan, Martin, in U.S. since July 1806, Richmond City, clerk;
applied 15 July 1812 (14 July-1 Aug. 1812 & No.4)

Swales, Henry, age 41, 16 years in U.S., wife & 3 children, Richmond, bricklayer (reported 20 May 1813)

Thompson, James, age 44, 5 ft. 5 in., brown complex, black hair,
hazel eyes (No.2)

Thompson, John, age 27, in U.S. since Aug. 1809, Richmond, clerk
(14 July-1 Aug. 1812); 5 ft. 9 in., ruddy complex., black hair,
grey eyes (No.2); Christian Thompson, widow, in letter of 20
Mar. 1813, writes that she came to U.S. in 1801 with her husband, Balfour Thompson; Balfour died in the summer of 1812 and
left his brother, John Thompson, as his clerk and storekeeper;
John Thompson, age about 28, was paroled by the Marshal of Va.
at Charlottesville (n.d.)

Thompson, John, age 25, 8 years in U.S., wife, Petersburg, nail
maker (21-27 Mar. 1813); 5 ft. 7 in., fair complex., light hair,
grey eyes, sent to Philadelphia (No.1)

Thompson, Thomas J., age 44, 18 years in U.S., wife & 1 child,
Petersburg, collector (21-27 Mar. 1813)

Thompson, William, age 24, 4 years in U.S., Petersburg, merchant;
applied at Philadelphia Oct. 1810 (25 Dec. 1812-21 Feb. 1813);
age in Mar. 25, 5 ft. 7 in. fair complex., fair hair, grey eyes (2)

Toel, Peter, age 37, in U.S. since 1803, 3 in family, Lynchburg, farmer; applied 13 July 1812 (10-14 Nov. 1812)
Topping, John B., age 22, 2½ years in U.S., wife, Rockbridge Co., merchant (14-21 Nov. 1812)
Tradar, Francis, age 25, 5 years in U.S., Petersburg, dyer (report of 23 Mar. 1813)
Tracey, John, age 29, 8 years in U.S., Petersburg, soap boiler (16-21 Mar. 1813); 5ft. 10in., fair complex., sandy hair, blue eyes (No. 1)
Tucker, Henry W., age 23, in U.S. since July 1810, Charlotte Court House, student of medicine (9-16 Aug. 1812)
Tychurst/Tychirst, William, age 30, 6 years in U.S., wife, Richmond, stage driver (27 Mar.-4 Apr. 1813 & No.5)
Vaughan, Thomas, age 22, 1 year in U.S., Norfolk Boro, merchant's clerk (1 Sept. 1812)
Vevers, John, age 32, in U.S. since 1806, 1 in family, Fauquier Court House, tailor (1-8 Aug. 1812)
Vickers, John, age 35, 11 years in U.S., 1 child, Norfolk Boro, barber, "of immoral habits" (1 Sept. 1812)
Walker, John, age 18, in U.S. since 1811, Manchester, clerk; applied 6 June 1812 (14 July-1 Aug. 1812); removed to Lynchburg (No.5); allowed to return to Manchester (4 Sept. 1813)
Walker, William, age 33, 16 years in U.S., wife, Norfolk Co., miller (1 Sept. 1812)
Wallace, Thomas, age 12, in U.S. since Nov. 1812, Richmond City (17-22 Aug. 1812); 5 ft., fair complex.,red hair, grey eyes (No.1)
Walsh, Michael H., age 24, 2 years in U.S., Richmond, hatter; reported in Vermont (report of 27 May 1813)
Warel, Edmund, age 30, 7 years in U.S., Richmond, flour inspector (to 16 Mar. 1813 and No.4)
Watson, John, age 26, in U.S. since 1 June 1811, Richmond City, millwright (13-17 Oct. 1812)
Watts, Archibald, age 25, 5 years in U.S., wife & 1 child, Norfolk Boro, gunsmith (1 Sept. 1812)
Wauhop, James, age 30, 13 years in U.S., Fincastle, merchant (report 3 Oct. 1812)
West, Thomas, age 42, in U.S. since Nov. 1806, wife, Richmond, painter (report 28 Oct. 1812)
White, Matthew, age 27, 10 years in U.S., Rockbridge Co., merchant (14-21 Nov. 1812)
White, Peter, age 20, 2 years in U.S., Louisa, teacher; applied Louisa Court 1812 (23 Aug. 1812)
White, Robert, in U.S. since 1794, 6 in family, Rockbridge Co., merchant; applied 1807 (12-26 Sept. 1812)
Whitehouse, Joseph T., age 45, 4 mos. in U.S., wife & 2 children, Norfolk Boro, whitesmith (1 Sept. 1812)
Williams, Thos., age 30, 4 years in U.S., wife, Richmond, stone cutter; applied in Hustings Court in Richmond (to 16 Mar. 1813 & No.4)
Wilson, David, age 50, in U.S. since Dec. 1807, 4 in family, Northumberland, farmer; applied 8 July 1812 (13-17 Oct. 1812)
Wilson, Edward, age 47, 18 years in U.S., wife & 3 children, Princess Anne Co., farmer & merchant (1 Sept. 1812)
Wilson, George, age 48, 18 years in U.S., wife & six children, Richmond, cabinetmaker; applied Philadelphia 1806 (21-27 Mar. 1813); 5 ft. 7 in., brown complex., dark hair, black eyes (No.2)
Wilson, Robert, age 42, 21 years in U.S., Richmond, teacher (report 3 July 1813)
Wilson, Robert, age 26, 7 years in U.S., Fredericksburg (report 23 May 1813)
Wilson, Thomas, age 22, 3 years in U.S., Petersburg, storekeeper (16-21 Mar. 1813); 5 ft. 8 in., fair complex., light hair, blue eyes (No.1)

Wright, William, age 43, in U.S. since Dec. 1802, 6 children,
    Richmond, brewer (1-8 Aug. 1812 & No.4)

334   NORTH CAROLINA

NORTH CAROLINA

Adams, Charles L., age 22, 9 years in U.S., wife, Wilmington,
    saddler (2-7 Sept. 1812)
Aiton, Thomas, age 34, 17 years in U.S., Ashville, cotton- bag-
    gin(g) tailor (7-14 Sept. 1812)
Anderson, Augur, age 43, 10 years in U.S., wife and 5 children,
    Richmond Co., farmer (14 Sept. - 12 Oct. 1812)
Anderson, John, age 48, 10 years in U.S., wife and 7 children,
    Richmond Co., farmer (14 Sept. - 12 Oct. 1812)
Balhour, Charles, age 42, 19 years in U.S., wife and 6 children,
    Richmond Co., farmer (14 Sept. - 12 Oct. 1812)
Barley, John, age 40, 8 years in U.S., Smithville, rigger (14
    Sept. - 12 Oct. 1812)
Barrie, James, age 25, 6 years in U.S., Newbern, merchant; ap-
    plied 13 May 1812 (10 Nov. 1812 - 12 Jan. 1813)
Baxter, John, age 46, 10 years in U.S., wife and 5 children,
    Fayetteville, tavern-keeper (7-14 Sept. 1812)
Black, John, age 60, 22 years in U.S., wife and 2 children, Rich-
    mond, farmer (12 Jan. - 20 Feb. 1813)
Blue, John, age 58, 9 years in U.S., wife and 5 children, Robe-
    son Co. farmer (14 Sept. - 12 Oct. 1812)
Broadfoot, William, age 26, 4 years in U.S., Fayetteville, mer-
    chant (24 Aug. - 2 Sept. 1812)
Buchanan, Duncan, age 46, 20 years in U.S., wife & child, Rich-
    mond Co., farmer (14 Sept. - 12 Oct. 1812)
Buchanan, Duncan, age 45, 20 years in U.S., wife, Richmond Co.,
    farmer (24 Aug. - 2 Sept. 1812)
Buchanan, John, age 49, 21 years in U.S., wife & 4 children,
    Richmond Co., farmer (14 Sept. - 12 Oct. 1812)
Buckley, Samuel P., age 30, 12 years in U.S., wife & 3 children,
    Edenton, tinsmith (2-7 Sept. 1812)
Caldwell, John, age 32, 11 years in U.S., Morganton Co., merchant;
    applied Sept. 1812 (12 Oct. - 10 Nov. 1812)
Calhoun, Duncan, age 52, 22 years in U.S., wife & 6 children,
    Richmond Co., farmer (14 Sept. - 12 Oct. 1812)
Calhoun, Duncan, age 48, 21 years in U.S., wife & 8 Children,
    Richmond Co., farmer (14 Sept. - 12 Oct. 1812)
Campbell, Alexander, age 35, 25 years in U.S., wife & 3 children,
    Richmond Co., farmer (14 Sept. - 12 Oct. 1812)
Campbell, Angus, age 34, 24 years in U.S., wife & child, Cumber-
    land, farmer (12 Jan. - 20 Feb. 1813)
Campbell, Colin, age 64, 21 years in U.S., 5 children, Richmond
    Co., farmer (14 Sept. - 12 Oct. 1812)
Campbell, Daniel, age 54, 22 years in U.S., wife & 5 children,
    Cumberland, farmer (12 Jan. - 20 Feb. 1813)
Campbell, Daniel, age 44, 10 years in U.S., wife & 4 children,
    Richmond, farmer (12 Jan. - 20 Feb. 1813)
Campbell, Daniel, age 39, 24 years in U.S., wife & 5 children,
    Richmond Co., farmer (14 Sept. - 12 Oct. 1812)
Campbell, Hugh, age 47, 8 years in U.S., wife & 4 children, Rich-
    mond, farmer (7-14 Sept. 1812)
Campbell, John, age 50, 24 years in U.S., wife & 5 children,
    Moore, farmer (12 Jan. - 20 Feb. 1813)
Campbell, John, age 37, 20 years in U.S., father, mother, wife &
    2 children, Robeson, farmer (7-14 Sept. 1812)
Campbell, Neil, age 60, 23 years in U.S., wife & 5 children, Cum-
    berland, farmer (12 Jan.-20 Feb. 1813)
Camron, Daniel, age 60, 1 year in U.S., wife & 2 children, Rich-
    mond Co., farmer (14 Sept. - 12 Oct. 1812)
Camron, John, age 43, 22 years in U.S., wife & 4 children, Rich-
    mond, farmer (7-14 Sept. 1812)
Carlile, John, age 28, 4 years & 11 mos. in U.S., Wilmington,
    clerk (16-24 Aug. 1812)

Carlile, John (not above), was removed from Washington for using
  improper expression about the war and is in Elizabeth Town -
  age 23, 5ft. 9in., light complex., light hair, blue eyes (1
  Dec. 1813)
Carmichael, Daniel, age 76, 22 years in U.S., 3 children, Rich-
  mond Co., farmer (14 Sept. - 12 Oct. 1812)
Carmichael, Duncan, age 66, 21 years in U.S., 1 child, Richmond
  Co., farmer (14 Sept. - 12 Oct. 1812)
Carmichael, Hugh, age 38, 8 years in U.S., wife & child, Robeson
  Co., farmer (14 Sept. - 12 Oct. 1812)
Carmichael, John, age 60, 32 years in U.S., wife & child, Rich-
  mond Co., farmer (14 Sept. - 12 Oct. 1812)
Carnock, David, age 35, 14 years in U.S., Wilmington, commission
  merchant (2-7 Sept. 1812)
Charlin, John, age 66, 1 year in U.S., wife & 3 children, Rich-
  mond Co., farmer (14 Sept. - 12 Oct. 1812)
Chatman, Valentine, age 29, 8 years in U.S., Warrenton, cabinet-
  maker (24 Aug. - 2 Sept. 1812)
Christholm, Alexander, age 26, 9 years in U.S. (14 Sept. - 12
  Oct. 1812)
Christholm, James, age 39, 9 years in U.S., wife & 5 children,
  Robeson Co., farmer (14 Sept. - 12 Oct. 1812)
Colhoun, Archibald, age 44, 10 years in U.S., wife & 2 children,
  Richmond, farmer (12 Jan. - 20 Feb. 1813)
Colhoun, Archibald, age 43, 21 years in U.S., wife & 3 children,
  Richmond Co., farmer (14 Sept. - 12 Oct. 1812)
Collins, Benjamin, age 24, 9 years in U.S., Halifax, merchant;
  applied Aug. 1812 (24 Aug. - 2 Sept. 1812)
Colquhoun, Duncan, age 52, 22 years in U.S., wife & 6 children,
  Richmond, cooper (24 Aug. - 2 Sept. 1812)
Colquhoun, Duncan, age 48, 22 years in U.S., wife & 8 children,
  Richmond (24 Aug. - 2 Sept. 1812)
Combs, Samuel, age 30, years in U.S., Raleigh, bookbinder;
  applied Feb. 1812 (7 July - 16 Aug. 1812)
Conway, Francis B., age 23, 5 years in U.S., Newbern, vendue
  master; applied 28 Oct. 1808 (10 Nov. 1812 - 12 Jan. 1813)
Cooper, James, age 25, 10 years in U.S., Granville, carpenter
  (10 Nov. 1812 - 12 Jan. 1813)
Corrie, John, age 51, 21 years in U.S., wife & 4 children, Robe-
  son Co., farmer (14 Sept. - 12 Oct. 1812)
Cox, George, age 58, 23 years in U.S., wife & 7 children, Moore,
  farmer; receives half pay as reduced lieutenant and will not
  become citizen lest he lose his pension (7 July - 16 Aug. 1812)
Crockat, John, age 19, 5 years in U.S., Warrenton, clerk (24 Aug. -
  2 Sept. 1812)
Crockat, William, age 33, 11 years in U.S., Warrenton, sailor;
  has applied (24 Aug. - 2 Sept. 1812)
Culbreth, Archibald, age 60, 20 years in U.S., 2 children, Robe-
  son Co., farmer (14 Sept. - 12 Oct. 1812)
Currie, Angus, age 50, 22 years in U.S., wife & 8 children, Moore,
  farmer (12 Jan. - 20 Feb. 1813)
Currie, Angus, age 42, 20 years in U.S., wife & 5 children, Robe-
  son Co., farmer (14 Sept. - 12 Oct. 1812)
Currie, Archibald, age 50, 21 years in U.S., wife & 7 children,
  Moore, farmer (12 Jan. - 20 Feb. 1813)
Currie, John, age 32, 7 years in U.S., wife & 3 children, Robe-
  son Co., farmer (14 Sept. - 12 Oct. 1812)
Currie, Lauchlen, age 41, 21 years in U.S., wife & 4 children,
  Moore, farmer (12 Jan. - 20 Feb. 1813)
Dallas, Peter, age 60, 21 years in U.S., wife & 9 children, Robe-
  son Co., farmer (14 Sept. - 12 Oct. 1812)
Davidson, William, age 27, 7 years in U.S., Granville, farmer
  (24 Aug. - 2 Sept. 1812)
Dickson, John, age 26, 4 years in U.S., Cumberland, merchant;
  applied spring 1812 (24 Aug. - 2 Sept. 1812)

Doyle, George, age 22, 4 mos. in U.S., Wilmington, cooper (16-
24 Aug. 1812)

Edgar, Patrick N., age 34, 12 years in U.S., no occupation; he
lives on proceeds of his estate in Ireland and is unwilling
to be naturalized lest he lose his estate thereby (24 Aug. -
2 Sept. 1812)

Ferguson, Murdo, age 56, 9 years in U.S., wife & 8 children,
Moore, farmer (12 Jan. - 20 Feb. 1813)

Fox, William, age 28, 5 years in U.S., Edenton, merchant (2-7
Sept. 1812)

Gillis, Alexander, age 43, 10 years in U.S., wife & 4 children,
Cumberland, farmer (12 Jan. - 20 Feb. 1813)

Gillis, Archibald, age 63, 24 years in U.S., wife, Moore, farmer
(12 Jan. - 20 Feb. 1813)

Gillis, Archibald, age 45, 24 years in U.S., wife & 5 children,
Richmond Co., farmer (14 Sept. - 12 Oct. 1812)

Gillis, Hector, age 46, 1 year in U.S., wife & 2 children, Richmond Co., farmer (14 Sept. - 12 Oct. 1812)

Gillis, John, age 60, 24 years in U.S., wife & 7 children, Cumberland, farmer (12 Jan. - 20 Feb. 1813)

Gillis, John, age 45, 24 years in U.S., wife & 2 children, Robeson Co., farmer (14 Sept. - 12 Oct. 1812)

Gillis, Malcom, age 67, 23 years in U.S., wife & 3 children,
Cumberland, farmer (12 Jan. - 20 Feb. 1813)

Gillis, Malcom, age 50, 10 years in U.S., wife & 6 children,
Richmond Co., farmer (14 Sept. - 12 Oct. 1812)

Gillis, Neil, age 50, 1 year in U.S., wife & 5 children, Richmond Co., farmer (14 Sept. - 12 Oct. 1812)

Gillis, Norman, age 45, 24 years in U.S., wife & 5 children,
Robeson Co., farmer (14 Sept. - 12 Oct. 1812)

Gillis, Roderick, age 38, 23 years in U.S., wife & 4 children,
Cumberland, farmer (12 Jan. - 20 Feb. 1813)

Gillis, Swain, age 28, 24 years in U.S., Cumberland Co., farmer
(14 Sept. - 12 Oct. 1812)

Gorrie, John, age 30, 5 years in U.S., Wilmington, merchant (16-
24 Aug. 1812)

Graham, Archibald, age 37, 8 years in U.S., wife & 4 children,
Richmond, farmer (7-14 Sept. 1812)

Graham, Daniel, age 25, 9 years in U.S., wife, Robeson Co., farmer (14 Sept. - 12 Oct. 1812)

Graham, Dugald, age 75, 9 years in U.S., 3 children, Robeson Co.,
farmer (14 Sept. - 12 Oct. 1812)

Graham, George, age 23, 8 years in U.S., Robeson, tailor (7-14
Sept. 1812)

Graham, James, age 40, 8 years in U.S., wife & 6 children, Richmond Co., farmer (14 Sept. - 12 Oct. 1812)

Graham, John, age 46, 9 years in U.S., wife & 8 children, Richmond Co., farmer (14 Sept. - 12 Oct. 1812)

Graham, John, age 31, 9 years in U.S., wife & 2 children, Robeson Co., farmer (14 Sept. - 12 Oct. 1812)

Graham, Neill, age 67, 8 years in U.S., Robeson Co., farmer (14-
Sept. - 12 Oct. 1812)

Grant, John, age 70, 10 years in U.S., wife & 3 children, Richmond Co., farmer (14 Sept. - 12 Oct. 1812)

Grant, John, age 70, 10 years in U.S., wife & 3 children, Richmond, blacksmith (24 Aug. - 2 Sept. 1812)

Grayham, Daniel, age 76, 24 years in U.S., wife & 4 children,
Richmond, farmer (12 Jan. - 20 Feb. 1813)

Hall, George, age 35, 10 years in U.S., Raleigh, merchant (7
July - 16 Aug. 1812)

Hamilton, Alexander, age 25, 5 years in U.S., Granville, merchant;
applied Mar. 1810 (24 Aug. - 2 Sept. 1812)

Hamilton, Patrick, age 22, 5 years in U.S., Granville, merchant;
applied Mar. 1810 (24 Aug. - 2 Sept. 1812)

Hanrahan, John, age 25, 1 year in U.S., Washington, merchant (10 Nov. 1812 - 12 Jan. 1813)

Hatridge, Alexander, age 30, 8 years in U.S., Wilmington, merchant (16 -24 Aug. 1812)

Henderson, James, age 32, 9 years in U.S., Fayetteville, merchant; applied 1809 (12 Oct. - 10 Nov. 1812)

Herrwell, John, age 41, 2 years in U.S., wife, Wilmington, ship-carpenter (16-24 Aug. 1812)

Higham, Thomas, age 40, 5ft. 3 in., dark complex., black hair, black eyes, removed to Fayetteville (1.Dec. 1813)

Hogg, James, age 47, 14 years in U.S., wife & 8 children, Orange Co., lawyer (12 Oct. - 10 Nov. 1812)

Hoyle, Jackson P., age 36, 17 years in U.S., Edenton, merchant (2-7 Sept. 1812); 6ft., light complex., light hair, blue eyes, removed to and now confined in Edenton; of "poor character" - had gone & obtained certificate from neutral power (1 Dec. 1813)

Hulan, John, age 23, 10 years in U.S., Fayetteville, shoemaker (24 Aug. - 2 Sept. 1812)

Hutchison, George, age 40, 9 years in U.S., Wilmington, merchant; applied 1809 (14 Sept. - 12 Oct. 1812)

Jeffey, James, 4 years in U.S., Warrenton, merchant; applied Apr. 1812 (16-24 Aug. 1812)

Johnson, Alexander, 8 years in U.S., wife & 5 children, Robeson Co., farmer (12 Jan. - 20 Feb. 1813)

Johnston, Duncan, age 42, 10 years in U.S., wife & child, Robeson Co., farmer (14 Sept. - 12 Oct. 1812)

Johnston, James, age 25, 14 years in U.S., Halifax, merchant; applied Oct. 1809 (7 July - 16 Aug. 1812)

Johnston, John, age 22, 5 years in U.S., Hanover Co., farmer (14 Sept. - 12 Oct. 1812)

Johnston, Niel, age 46, 10 years in U.S., wife & 5 children, Richmond, farmer (7-14 Sept. 1812)

Kelley, Daniel, age 52, 26 years in U.S., wife & 4 children, Robeson Co., farmer (12 Jan. - 20 Feb. 1813)

Kirkpatrick, Watson, age 22 years & 10 mos., 3 years in U.S., Wilmington, merchant (16-24 Aug. 1812)

Lawson, James, age 33, 1 year & 11 mos. in U.S., wife and two children, Fayetteville, cabinetmaker (24 Aug. - 2 Sept. 1812)

Leach, Archibald, age 27, 3 years in U.S., Richmond, farmer (7-14 Sept. 1812)

Leach, Dugald, age 46, 9 years in U.S., wife & 6 children, Robeson Co., farmer (12 Jan. - 20 Feb. 1813)

Leach, Dugald, age 30, 9 years in U.S., wife & 2 children, Richmond, farmer (7-14 Sept. 1812)

Leach, John, age 59, 8 years in U.S., wife & 3 children, Robeson, farmer (7-14 Sept. 1812)

Leach, John, age 50, 8 years in U.S., wife & 6 children, Richmond, farmer (12 Jan. - 20 Feb. 1813)

Leach, John, age 27, 8 years in U.S., mother & sister, Richmond Co., farmer (7-14 Sept. 1812)

Livington, Peter, age 58, 8 years in U.S., wife & 3 children, Robeson Co., farmer (14 Sept. - 12 Oct. 1812)

Love, Robert, age 26, 1 year in U.S., Rutherford Co., farmer; applied Oct. 1812 (12 Oct. - 10 Nov. 1812)

Lovington, Duncan, age 54, 21 years in U.S., wife & 3 children, Richmond Co., farmer (14 Sept. - 12 Oct. 1812)

Lucas, Archibald, age 72, 20 years in U.S., Richmond Co., farmer (14 Sept. - 12 Oct. 1812)

Lutherland, Alexander, age 40, 8 years in U.S., wife & 9 children, Richmond Co., farmer (7-14 Sept. 1812)

Lyon, William, age 33, 12 years in U.S., wife & child, Lenoir (10 Nov. 1812 - 12 Jan. 1813)

McBride, Alexander, age 27, 8 years in U.S., wife & child, Robeson Co., farmer (14 Sept. - 12 Oct. 1812)

McBryan, John, age 33, 8 years in U.S., wife & 4 children, Robeson Co., farmer (12 Jan. - 20 Feb. 1813)

McCall, Daniel, age 27, 19 years in U.S., wife & child, Fayetteville, tailor (24 Aug. - 2 Sept. 1812)

McCaskill, K., age 50, 10 mos. in U.S., 1 child, Moore Co., farmer (14 Sept. - 12 Oct. 1812)

McCay, Alexander, age 30, 20 years in U.S., wife & 3 children,
Robeson Co., farmer (14 Sept. - 12 Oct. 1812)

McColl, D., age 50, 20 years in U.S., wife & 7 children, Cumberland Co., farmer (12 Oct. - 10 Nov. 1812)

McColl, Daniel, age 70, 25 years in U.S., wife & 2 children,
Richmond Co., farmer (14 Sept. - 12 Oct. 1812)

McColl, Duncan, age 58, 21 years in U.S., wife & 5 children,
Richmond Co., farmer (14 Sept. - 12 Oct. 1812)

McColl, H., age 32, 9 years in U.S., Fayetteville, merchant (12
Oct.- 10 Nov. 1812)

McColl, Hugh, age 67, 21 years in U.S., wife & child, Richmond
Co., farmer (14 Sept. - 12 Oct. 1812)

McColl, John, age 70, 20 years in U.S., 1 child, Richmond, farmer (7-14 Sept. 1812)

McColl, John, age 67, 20 years in U.S., wife & 5 children, Cumberland Co., farmer (12 Oct. - 10 Nov. 1812)

McColl, John, age 55, 9 years in U.S., wife & 7 children, Cumberland, farmer (12 Jan. - 20 Feb. 1813)

McColl, John, age 38, 20 years in U.S., wife & 4 children, Richmond, farmer (7-14 Sept. 1812)

McComay (or McCornay?), Duncan, age 40, 20 years in U.S., wife &
10 children, Richmond Co., farmer (14 Sept. - 12 Oct. 1812)

McCormage, John, age 54, 21 years in U.S., wife & 7 children,
Richmond Co., farmer (14 Sept. - 12 Oct. 1812)

McCrainey, Kinneth, age 40, 24 years in U.S., wife & 4 children,
Richmond Co., farmer (14 Sept. -12 Oct. 1812)

McCrainey, Malcom, age 64, 10 years in U.S., wife, Robeson Co.,
farmer (14 Sept. -12 Oct. 1812)

McCrainey, Neill, age 32, 24 years in U.S., wife & 4 children,
Cumberland, farmer (12 Jan. - 20 Feb. 1813)

McCranmon, Malcom, age 70, 25 years in U.S., wife & 7 children,
Moore, farmer (12 Jan. - 20 Feb. 1813)

McCullam, Archibald, age 26, 8 years in U.S., wife, Robeson Co.,
farmer (12 Jan. - 20 Feb. 1813)

McCullam, Duncan, age 50, 20 years in U.S., wife & 3 children,
Cumberland, farmer (12 Jan. - 20 Feb. 1813)

McDenomin, John, age 54, 10 years in U.S., wife & 5 children,
Robeson Co., farmer (14 Sept. - 12 Oct. 1812)

McDonald, Alexander, age 56, 10 years in U.S., wife & 4 children,
Moore, farmer (12 Jan. - 20 Feb. 1813)

McDonald, Angus, age 45, 21 years in U.S., wife & 7 children,
Richmond Co., farmer (14 Sept. - 12 Oct. 1812)

McDonald, Angus, age 45, 10 years in U.S., wife & 7 children,
Moore, farmer (12 Jan. - 20 Feb. 1813)

McDonald, Archibald, age 35, 9 years in U.S., wife & child, Robeson Co., farmer (14 Sept. - 12 Oct. 1812)

McDonald, Daniel, age 53, 20 years in U.S., wife & 9 children,
Richmond Co., farmer (14 Sept. - 12 Oct. 1812)

McDonald, Daniel, age 52, 10 years in U.S., wife & 3 children,
Moore, farmer (12 Jan. - 20 Feb. 1813)

McDonald, Daniel, age 50, 25 years in U.S., wife & 7 children,
Robeson Co., farmer (14 Sept. - 12 Oct. 1812)

McDonald, Daniel, age 46, 20 years in U.S., wife & 4 children,
Robeson Co., farmer (14 Sept. - 12 Oct. 1812)

McDonald, Daniel, age 26, 7 years in U.S., wife, Richmond Co.,
farmer (14 Sept. - 12 Oct. 1812)

McDonald, Hugh, age 55, 12 years in U.S., wife & 2 children,
Richmond, farmer (12 Jan. - 20 Feb. 1813)

McDonald, John, age 60, 8 years in U.S., wife & 4 children, Cumberland, farmer (12 Jan. - 20 Feb. 1813)

McDonald, John, age 40, 9 years in U.S., wife & 5 children, Richmond Co., farmer (14 Sept. - 12 Oct. 1812)

McDonald, John, age 35, 9 years in U.S., Richmond Co., farmer (14 Sept. - 12 Oct. 1812)

McDonald, John, age 25, 1 year in U.S., Richmond Co., farmer (14 Sept. - 12 Oct. 1812)

McDonald, Kennith, age 19, 1 year in U.S., Richmond Co., farmer (14 Sept. - 12 Oct. 1812)

McDonald, Lauchlin, age 47, 7 years in U.S., wife & 4 children, Richmond Co., farmer (14 Sept. - 12 Oct. 1812)

McDonald, Lauchlin, age 27, 22 years in U.S., Richmond Co., farmer (14 Sept. -12 Oct. 1812)

McDonald, Norman, age 17, 1 year in U.S., Richmond Co., farmer (14 Sept. -12 Oct. 1812)

McDonald, Roderick, age 56, 22 years in U.S., wife & 2 children, Cumberland, farmer (12 Jan. - 20 Feb. 1813)

McDuffee, Angus, age 30, 9 years in U.S., wife & 2 children, Richmond Co., farmer (14 Sept. -12 Oct. 1812)

McDuffie, Murdo, age 24, 10 years in U.S., Robeson Co., farmer (12 Jan. - 20 Feb. 1813)

McDuffie, Neil, age 33, 10 years in U.S., wife & 2 children, Robeson Co., farmer (14 Sept. -12 Oct. 1812)

McDugal, Alexander, age 51, 20 years in U.S., wife & 9 children, Robeson Co., farmer (14 Sept. - 12 Oct. 1812)

McDugald, Duncan, age 57, 17 years in U.S., wife & 4 children, Richmond Co., farmer (7-14 Sept. 1812)

McDugald, Samuel, age 56, 21 years in U.S., wife & 3 children, Robeson Co., farmer (14 Sept. - 12 Oct. 1812)

McEachen, Daniel, age 45, 8 years in U.S., wife & 8 children, Cumberland, farmer (12 Jan. - 20 Feb. 1813)

McFadgen, Archibald, age 52, 27 years in U.S., wife & 7 children, Cumberland, fuller (7-14 Sept. 1812)

McFerson, M., age 22, 9 years in U.S., Fayetteville, clerk (12 Oct. - 10 Nov. 1812)

McGager, Duncan, age 72, 9 years in U.S., wife & 3 children, Robeson Co., farmer (14 Sept. - 12 Oct. 1812)

McGanan, John, age 65, 10 years in U.S., wife & 7 children, Robeson Co., farmer (14 Sept. -12 Oct. 1812)

McGevere, H., age 29, 11 years in U.S., Fayetteville, merchant; applied 1807 (12 Oct. - 10 Nov. 1812)

McGilberry, Chalchom, age 25, 9 years in U.S. (14 Sept. - 12 Oct. 1812)

McGilberry, Daniel, age 53, 7 years in U.S., wife & 5 children, Richmond Co., farmer (14 Sept. - 12 Oct. 1812)

McGilberry, Daniel, age 47, 9 years in U.S., wife & 3 children, Richmond Co., farmer (14 Sept. - 12 Oct. 1812)

McGill, Donnall, age 30, 8 years in U.S., 6 persons in family, Richmond, farmer (7-14 Sept. 1812)

McGilvery, A., age 24, 20 years in U.S., Fayetteville, clerk (7-14 Sept. 1812)

McGilverry, Alexander, age 27, 7 years in U.S., wife & 2 children, Richmond, farmer (7-14 Sept. 1812)

McGreggor, Archibald, age 33, 8 years in U.S., wife & 5 children, Cumberland, farmer (12 Jan. - 20 Feb. 1813)

McGugan, Daniel, age 30, 8 years in U.S., wife & 7 children, Robeson Co., farmer (14 Sept. - 12 Oct. 1812)

McGuir, John, age 29, 5 years in U.S., Bertie, schoolmaster (10 Nov. 1812 - 12 Jan. 1813)

McInnis, Angus, age 32, 10 years in U.S., wife, sister, 3 children, Richmond Co., farmer (7-14 Sept. 1812)

McInnis, Daniel, age 60, 20 years in U.S., wife & 4 children, Moore, farmer (12 Jan. -20 Feb. 1813)

McInnis, Duncan, age 49, 10 years in U.S., Cumberland, farmer (12 Jan. - 20 Feb. 1813)

McInnis, Duncan, age 27, 20 years in U.S., wife & 4 children,
Moore, farmer (12 Jan. - 20 Feb. 1813)
McInnis, James, age 46, 20 years in U.S., wife & 5 children,
Richmond Co., farmer (14 Sept. - 12 Oct. 1812)
McInnis, John, age 29, 20 years in U.S., wife & 4 children, Moore,
farmer (12 Jan. - 20 Feb. 1813)
McIntagart, Daniel, age 55, 20 years in U.S., 1 child, Robeson
Co., farmer (14 Sept. - 12 Oct. 1812)
McIntagart, Gilbert, age 56, 21 years in U.S., wife & 6 children,
Robeson Co., farmer (14 Sept. - 12 Oct. 1812)
McIntire, Alex., age 36, 10 years in U.S., Fayetteville, merchant
(12 Oct. - 10 Nov. 1812)
McIntire, John, age 50, 21 years in U.S., wife & 2 children,
Cumberland, clergyman (12 Jan. - 20 Feb. 1813)
McIntyre, Nicholas, age 55, 20 years in U.S., wife & child, Cum-
berland, farmer (12 Jan. -20 Feb. 1813)
McKaskal, Allen, age 45, 1 year in U.S., Robeson Co., tailor (12
Jan. - 20 Feb. 1813)
McKaskal, Daniel, age 50, 1 year in U.S., wife & 5 children, Ro-
beson Co., farmer (12 Jan. -20 Feb. 1813)
McKaskal, Daniel, age 33, 1 year in U.S., Robeson Co., farmer
(12 Jan. - 20 Feb. 1813)
McKaskee, Donald, age 39, 21 years in U.S., wife & 5 children,
Richmond Co., farmer (14 Sept. - 12 Oct. 1812)
McKaskee, John, age 57, 10 years in U.S., wife & 5 children,
Richmond Co., farmer (14 Sept. -12 Oct. 1812)
McKassel, Petel (or Petet?), age 25, 1 year in U.S., Robeson Co.,
farmer (14 Sept. -12 Oct. 1812)
McKay, Daniel, age 25, 20 years in U.S., Robeson Co., farmer (14
Sept. - 12 Oct. 1812)
McKay, Duncan, Sr., age 65, 10 years in U.S., 2 children, Rich-
mond Co., farmer (7-14 Sept. 1812)
McKay, Hugh, age 32, 20 years in U.S., Robeson Co., farmer (14
Sept. - 12 Oct. 1812)
McKay, Malcom, age 50, native American, Cumberland Co., farmer;
during the Revolution he joined the British army and at present
receives pay of a reduced ensign from the British govt. (12
Oct. - 10 Nov. 1812)
McKenzie, Duncan, age 57, 22 years in U.S., wife & 4 children,
Cumberland, farmer (12 Jan.- 20 Feb. 1813)
McKenzie, John, age 55, 21 years in U.S., wife & 7 children,
Richmond, farmer (12 Jan. - 20 Feb. 1813)
McKinnon, Alexander, age 47, 10 years in U.S., wife, Richmond
Co., farmer (14 Sept. -12 Oct. 1812)
McKinnon, Daniel, age 48, 25 years in U.S., wife, Moore, farmer
(12 Jan. -20 Feb. 1813)
McKinnon, John, age 44, 9 mos. (or 34 years?) in U.S., 2 children,
Robeson Co., farmer (14 Sept. - 12 Oct. 1812)
McKinnon, Mardo, age 46, 10 years in U.S., wife & 4 children,
Richmond Co., farmer (14 Sept. - 12 Oct. 1812)
McKinnon, Neil, age 65, 9 years in U.S., wife & 2 children, Rich-
mond Co., farmer (14 Sept. -12 Oct. 1812)
McKinnon, Neil, age 55, 21 years in U.S., wife & 7 children,
Richmond Co., farmer (14 Sept. - 12 Oct. 1812)
McKou, Hugh, age 45, 20 years in U.S., wife & 6 children, Robe-
son Co., farmer (14 Sept. - 12 Oct. 1812)
McKrain, Keneth, age 30, 25 years in U.S., wife & 4 children,
Richmond, farmer (24 Aug. - 2 Sept. 1812)
McLain, Daniel, age 35, 10 years in U.S., wife & 4 children,
Richmond, carpenter (24 Aug. - 2 Sept. 1812)
McLain, John, age 24, 10 years in U.S., wife & child, Richmond
Co., farmer (14 Sept. - 12 Oct. 1812)
McLauchlan, John, age 47, 1 year in U.S., wife & 5 children,
Richmond, tailor (24 Aug. - 2 Sept. 1812)

McLauchlen, Archibald, age 80, 8 years in U.S., wife & 4 children, Richmond, farmer (7-14 Sept. 1812)

McLauchlen, John, age 43, 9 years in U.S., wife & 5 children, Robeson, farmer (7-14 Sept. 1812)

McLauchlin, John, age 47, 21 years in U.S., Richmond Co., farmer (14 Sept. - 12 Oct. 1812)

McLauchlin, Lauchlen, age 28, 7 years in U.S., mother, brother & 2 sisters, Robeson Co., farmer (12 Jan. - 20 Feb. 1813)

McLauchlin, Neill, age 58, 8 years in U.S., wife & 6 children, Cumberland, farmer (12 Jan. - 20 Feb. 1813)

McLauchlin, Robert, age 48, 10 years in U.S., wife & 7 children, Moore, farmer (12 Jan. - 20 Feb. 1813)

McLauren, Angus, age 34, 20 years in U.S., wife & 4 children, Richmond Co., farmer (14 Sept. - 12 Oct. 1812)

McLauren, Donald, age 40, 20 years in U.S., wife & 6 children, Richmond Co. farmer (14 Sept. - 12 Oct. 1812)

McLaurin, Angus, age 33, 22 years in U.S., wife & 4 children, Richmond, blacksmith (24 Aug. - 2 Sept. 1812)

McLaurin, Daniel, age 40, 22 years in U.S., wife & 6 children, Richmond, wheelwright (24 Aug. - 2 Sept. 1812)

McLaurin, Maurice, age 60, 22 years in U.S., wife & 4 children, Richmond, farmer (24 Aug. - 2 Sept. 1812)

McLeach, Daniel, age 34, 9 years in U.S., wife, Robeson Co., farmer (12 Jan. - 20 Feb. 1813)

McLean, Angus, age 25, 8 years in U.S., Moore, farmer (12 Jan. - 20 Feb. 1813)

McLean, Archibald, age 43, 9 years in U.S., wife & 3 children, Robeson Co., farmer (14 Sept. - 12 Oct. 1812)

McLean, Donald, age 39, 9 years in U.S., wife, Richmond Co., farmer (14 Sept. - 12 Oct. 1812)

McLean, Duncan, age 70, 22 years in U.S., 2 children, Richmond Co., farmer (14 Sept. - 12 Oct. 1812)

McLean, Hector, age 35, 10 years in U.S., wife & 2 children, Robeson Co., farmer (14 Sept. - 12 Oct. 1812)

McLean, John, age 45, 21 years in U.S., wife & 3 children, Robeson Co., farmer (14 Sept. - 12 Oct. 1812)

McLean, John, age 40, 10 years in U.S., wife & 4 children, Richmond Co., farmer (14 Sept. - 12 Oct. 1812)

McLean, John, age 38, 20 years in U.S., wife & 8 children, Robeson Co., schoolmaster (12 Jan. - 20 Feb. 1813)

McLean, John, age 26, 9 years in U.S., Robeson Co., farmer (14 Sept. - 12 Oct. 1812)

McLean, Norman, age 60, 22 years in U.S., wife & 3 children, Richmond, farmer (12 Jan. - 20 Feb. 1813)

McLellon, Daniel, age 51, 19 years in U.S., wife & 6 children, Richmond Co., farmer (14 Sept. - 12 Oct. 1812)

McLeod, Daniel, age 30, 10 years in U.S., wife & 4 children, Richmond Co., farmer (14 Sept.- 12 Oct. 1812)

McLeod, Duncan, age 25, 22 years in U.S., Cumberland, farmer (12 Jan. - 20 Feb. 1813)

McLeod, John, age 23, 10 years in U.S., wife & 2 children, Richmond, farmer (24 Aug. - 2 Sept. 1812)

McLeod, John, age 23, 10 years in U.S., wife & 2 children, Richmond Co., farmer (14 Sept. - 12 Oct. 1812)

McLeod, Murdo, age 60, 9 years in U.S., wife & 3 children, Richmond Co., farmer (14 Sept. - 12 Oct. 1812)

McLeod, Murdoch, Sr., age 64, 10 years in U.S., wife & 3 children, Richmond (24 Aug. - 2 Sept. 1812)

McLeon (sic!), Daniel, age 45, 10 years in U.S., wife & 3 children, Richmond Co., farmer (14 Sept. - 12 Oct. 1812)

McLeore, John, age 52, 24 years in U.S., wife & 9 children, Cumberland, farmer (12 Jan. - 20 Feb. 1813)

McLeore, Norman, age 50, 21 years in U.S., wife & 8 children, Robeson Co., farmer (12 Jan. -20 Feb. 1813)

McLerain, Hugh, age 63, 21 years in U.S., three sons and several daughters, Richmond, farmer (24 Aug. - 2 Sept. 1812)

McLerran, Hugh, age 63, 21 years in U.S., 2 children, Richmond Co., farmer (14 Sept. - 12 Oct. 1812)

McLerron, Hugh, age 61, 21 years in U.S., wife & 7 children, Richmond, farmer (7-14 Sept. 1812)

McMahon, Samuel, age 23, 2 years in U.S., Raleigh, merchant; he will apply at next court in Halifax (7 July - 16 Aug. 1812)

McMillan, Alexander, age 34, 9 years in U.S., wife & 4 children, Richmond, farmer (7-14 Sept. 1812)

McMillan, Alin, age 34, 3 years in U.S., wife & 4 children, Richmond (24 Aug. - 2 Sept. 1812)

McMillan, Donald, age 50, 9 years in U.S., wife & 7 children, Robeson, farmer (7-14 Sept. 1812)

Mc Millan, Edward, age 29, 9 years in U.S., wife & 3 children, Richmond Co., farmer (14 Sept. - 12 Oct. 1812)

McMillan, John, 9 years in U.S., wife & 8 children, Robeson Co., farmer (12 Jan.- 20 Feb. 1813)

McMillan, Malcom, age 60, 10 years in U.S., wife & 5 children, Robeson, farmer (7-14 Sept. 1812)

McMillan, Malcom, age 50, 22 years in U.S., wife & 6 children, Moore, farmer (12 Jan. -20 Feb. 1813)

McMillan, Malcom, age 43, 9 years in U.S., wife & 6 children, Richmond, farmer (7-14 Sept. 1812)

McNair, Barnard, age 67, 26 years in U.S., wife, Robeson Co., farmer (12 Jan. -20 Feb. 1813)

McNeil, John, age 32, 20 years in U.S., wife & 4 children, Robeson Co., farmer (14 Sept. - 12 Oct. 1812)

MacNeil, Neil, age 44, 20 years in U.S., wife & 7 children, Richmond Co., farmer (14 Sept. - 12 Oct. 1812)

McNiel, Daniel, age 56, 8 years in U.S., Cumberland, claims at law; on half pay as captain; wishes to remain in U.S. until suit in which he is interested is settled (7 July - 16 Aug. 1812)

McNiell, John, age 56, 24 years in U.S., wife & 5 children, Moore, farmer (12 Jan. - 20 Feb. 1813)

McPhee, Angus, age 34, 10 years in U.S., wife & 2 children, Richmond, farmer (24 Aug. - 2 Sept. 1812)

McPherson, Duncan, age 54, 9 years in U.S., wife & 3 children, Richmond Co., farmer (14 Sept. - 12 Oct. 1812)

McPherson, Neil, age 53, 24 years in U.S., wife, Richmond Co., farmer (14 Sept. - 12 Oct. 1812)

McRae, Malcom, age 56, 21 years in U.S., wife & 8 children, Robeson Co., farmer (12 Jan. -20 Feb. 1813)

McRae, Peter, age 51, 24 years in U.S., wife & 4 children, Richmond Co., farmer (14 Sept. - 12 Oct. 1812)

McSwain, Angus, age 70, 10 years in U.S., wife & 2 children, Richmond Co., farmer (14 Sept. - 12 Oct. 1812)

McSwain, Daniel, age 55, 22 years in U.S., 2 children, Robeson Co., farmer (14 Sept. - 12 Oct. 1812)

McSwain, Daniel, age 52, 22 years in U.S., wife, Richmond Co., farmer (14 Sept. - 12 Oct. 1812)

McSwain, Daniel, age 32, 10 years in U.S., wife & child, Richmond Co., farmer (14 Sept. - 12 Oct. 1812)

McSwain, Finlay, age 64, 9 years in U.S., wife & 3 children, Richmond Co., farmer (14 Sept. - 12 Oct. 1812)

McSwain, Finlay, age 47, 22 years in U.S., wife & 6 children, Richmond Co., farmer (14 Sept. - 12 Oct. 1812)

Martin, Alexander, age 54, 24 years in U.S. wife & 4 children, Cumberland, farmer (12 Jan. -20 Feb. 1813)

Martin, Alexander, age 20, 1 year in U.S., Richmond Co., farmer (14 Sept. - 12 Oct. 1812)

Martin, Donua (for Donald?), age 45, 1 year in U.S., wife and 3 children, Cumberland, farmer (12 Jan. - 20 Feb. 1813)

Martin, Richard, age 48, 12 years in U.S., Wilmington, grocer (16-24 Aug. 1812)

Maurison, Norman, age 45, 24 years in U.S., wife & 9 children, Richmond (24 Aug. - 2 Sept. 1812)

Maxwell, Thomas, age 26, 2 years in U.S., wife & child, Fayetteville, saddler (7-14 Sept. 1812)

Mofat, James, age 53, 16 years in U.S., Edenton, merchant (2-7 Sept. 1812)

Moison, John, age 25, 24 years in U.S., mother, 2 sisters and 3 orphan children, Richmond, farmer (24 Aug. - 2 Sept. 1812)

Montgomery, William, 11 years in U.S., wife & 3 children, Warren (10 Nov. 1812 - 12 Jan. 1813)

Moore, Thomas, age 30, 3 years in U.S., wife & child, Fayetteville, brass founder (7-14 Sept. 1812)

Morison, Malcom, age 50, 10 years in U.S., 4 children, Richmond, farmer (24 Aug. - 2 Sept. 1812)

Morrison, John, age 67, 10 years in U.S., 5 children, Richmond Co., farmer (14 Sept. - 12 Oct. 1812)

Morrison, John, age 52, 24 years in U.S., wife, Richmond Co., farmer (14 Sept. -12 Oct. 1812)

Morrison, John, age 32, 10 years in U.S., wife & 2 children, Robeson Co., farmer (2 Jan. - 20 Feb. 1813)

Morrison, John, age 27, 24 years in U.S., mother, 2 sisters and 3 orphan children, Richmond Co., farmer (7-14 Sept. 1812) = John Moison, above?

Morrison, Mahom, age 55, 10 years in U.S., wife & 4 children, Richmond Co., farmer (14 Sept. - 12 Oct. 1812)

Morrison, Malcom, age 41, 10 years in U.S., wife & 2 children, Richmond Co., farmer (14 Sept. - 12 Oct. 1812)

Morrison, Murdo, age 56, 24 years in U.S., wife & 2 children, Richmond Co., farmer (14 Sept. -12 Oct. 1812)

Morrison, Norman, age 67, 3 years in U.S., wife & child, Richmond Co., farmer (14 Sept. - 12 Oct. 1812)

Morrison, Norman, age 60, 22 years in U.S., wife & 5 children, Robeson Co., farmer (14 Sept. - 12 Oct. 1812)

Morrison, Norman, age 47, 10 years in U.S., wife & 6 children, Richmond Co., farmer (14 Sept. - 12 Oct. 1812)

Morrison, William, age 41, 24 years in U.S., wife & 6 children, Richmond Co., farmer (14 Sept. - 12 Oct. 1812)

Mulone/ Mulan, Anthony, age 36, 8 years in U.S., Wilmington, engaged in settling two estates (7 July - 16 Aug. 1812); 5ft. 6in., dark complex., dark hair, black eyes, removed to Hillsborough (1 Dec. 1813)

Munroe, Alexander, age 44, 9 years in U.S., Robeson Co., farmer (14 Sept. - 12 Oct. 1812)

Munroe, Daniel, age 42, 22 years in U.S., wife, Richmond Co., farmer (14 Sept. - 12 Oct. 1812)

Munroe, Daniel, age 32, 10 years in U.S., wife & 4 children, Richmond, farmer (7-14 Sept. 1812)

Munroe, Donald, age 35, 10 years in U.S., wife & 6 children, fisherman (24 Aug. - 2 Sept. 1812)

Munroe, Peter, age 30, 10 years in U.S., wife & 4 children, Robeson, farmer (7-14 Sept. 1812)

Munroe, Robert, age 60, 9 years in U.S., wife & 5 children, Richmond, farmer (7-14 Sept. 1812)

Murphy, Muras, age 56, 8 years in U.S., wife & 8 children, Robeson Co., farmer (14 Sept. - 12 Oct. 1812)

Neale, James, age 30, 9 years in U.S., wife & child, Wilmington, tavern-keeper (2-7 Sept. 1812)

Nicholson, Peter, age 20, 10 years in U.S., Robeson Co., farmer (12 Jan. - 20 Feb. 1813)

Nicholson, S., age 26, 11 years in U.S., Fayetteville, merchant (12 Oct. - 10 Nov. 1812)

O'Connor, Dennis, 9 years in U.S., Northampton, merchant; applied 22 Mar. 1806 (24 Aug. - 2 Sept. 1812)

Patterson, Alexander, age 60, 26 years in U.S., wife & 8 Children, Richmond, farmer (7-14 Sept. 1812)

Patterson, Archibald, age 25, 10 years in U.S., wife, Richmond Co., farmer (14 Sept. - 12 Oct. 1812)

Patterson, Daniel, age 28, 9 years in U.S., mother, brother and 2 sisters, Richmond, farmer (12 Jan. - 20 Feb. 1813)

Patterson, John, age 36, 8 years in U.S., wife & 5 children, Robeson Co., farmer (12 Jan. - 20 Feb. 1813)

Patterson, Peter, age 28, 10 years in U.S., wife, Richmond Co., farmer (14 Sept. - 12 Oct. 1812)

Peeling, Luke, age 35, 5 years in U.S., Gates Co., schoolmaster (2-7 Sept. 1812)

Priest, Angus, age 46, 8 years in U.S., wife & 7 children, Richmond Co., farmer (7-14 Sept. 1812)

Rankin, Robert, age 27, 9 years in U.S., Wilmington, hatter (2-7 Sept. 1812)

Ray, A., age 70, 20 years in U.S., wife & 3 children, Cumberland Co., farmer (12 Oct. - 10 Nov. 1812)

Ray, Daniel, age 50, 20 years in U.S., wife & 6 children, Cumberland Co., farmer (12 Oct. - 10 Nov. 1812)

Ray, Duncan, age 47, 21 years in U.S., wife & 11 children, Moore, farmer (12 Jan. - 20 Feb. 1813)

Ray, John, age 50, 20 years in U.S., wife & 3 children, Cumberland, farmer (12 Jan. - 20 Feb. 1813)

Ray, John, age 32, 20 years in U.S., Cumberland Co., farmer (12 Oct. - 10 Nov. 1812)

Redmond, Maurice, age 18, 4 mos. in U.S., Tarborough, clerk (16-24 Aug. 1812)

Reston, Thomas C., age 22, 1 year & 7 mos. in U.S., Wilmington; applied Feb. 1811; he is engaged in settling affairs of his grandfather and uncle, who resided and died in N.C. (16- 24 Aug. 1812)

River, Alexander, age 48, 10 years in U.S., wife & 3 children, Robeson Co., farmer (14 Sept. - 12 Oct. 1812)

Roberson, John, 4 years in U.S., Orange, sawyer; applied 25 Sept. 1812 (10 Nov. 1812 - 12 Jan. 1813)

Robinson, William, 11 years in U.S., Orange, sawyer; applied 23 Sept. 1812 (10 Nov. 1812 - 12 Jan. 1813)

Shaw, Angus, age 56, 20 years in U.S., wife & 5 children, Robeson Co., farmer (14 Sept. - 12 Oct. 1812)

Shaw, Archibald, age 48, 10 years in U.S., wife & 2 children, Cumberland, farmer (12 Jan. - 20 Feb. 1813)

Shaw, Daniel, age 64, 22 years in U.S., wife & 2 children, Robeson Co., farmer (14 Sept. - 12 Oct. 1812)

Shaw, John, age 50, 21 years in U.S., wife & 7 children, Robeson Co., farmer (14 Sept. - 12 Oct. 1812)

Shaw, Matthew, age 50, 8 years in U.S., wife & 6 children, Raleigh, grocer & "sperit" maker; applied May 1811 (7 July - 16 Aug. 1812)

Shaw, Neil, age 69, 10 years in U.S., wife & 4 children, Robeson Co., farmer (14 Sept. - 12 Oct. 1812)

Shaw, William, age 34, 12 years in U.S., Washington, merchant (10 Nov. 1812 - 12 Jan. 1813)

Shay, John L., age 15, 3 years in U.S., Tarborough, clerk (16-24 Aug. 1812)

Simpson, Robert, age 35, 1 year & 6 mos. in U.S., wife & four children, Wilmington (16 - 24 Aug. 1812)

Smith, Archibald, age 44, 10 years in U.S., wife & 2 children, Richmond, farmer (12 Jan. -20 Feb. 1813)

Smith, Duncan, age 53, 26 years in U.S., wife & 10 children, Robeson Co., farmer (12 Jan. - 20 Feb. 1813)

Smith, John, age 60, 21 years in U.S., wife & 6 children, Robeson Co., farmer (14 Sept. - 12 Oct. 1812)

Smith, Neil, age 60, 10 years in U.S., wife & 2 children, Robeson Co., farmer (14 Sept. - 12 Oct. 1812)

Smith, Samuel, age 33, 4 years in U.S., wife & child, Fayette-
    ville, shoemaker (24 Aug. - 2 Sept. 1812)
Stewart, Daniel, age 55, 21 years in U.S., wife & 6 children,
    Cumberland, farmer (7-14 Sept. 1812)
Stewart, Malcom, age 51, 21 years in U.S., wife & 9 children,
    Robeson, farmer (7-14 Sept. 1812)
Stewart, Peter, age 63, 1 year in U.S., wife & 5 children, Rich-
    mond Co., farmer (14 Sept. - 12 Oct. 1812)
Stewart, Santiago, Fayetteville, age 26, 5ft. 8in., dark complex.,
    dark hair, blue eyes, removed to Fayetteville as having no
    visible employment (1 Dec. 1813)
Sullivan, James, age 28, 5 years in U.S., Fayetteville, shoemaker
    (7-14 Sept. 1812)
Sweetman, Michael, age 24, 2 years in U.S., Halifax, clerk; ap-
    plied 17 Nov. 1812 (10 Nov. 1812 - 12 Jan. 1813)
Telchrire (or Gelchrire?), John, age 36, 9 years in U.S., wife
    & 4 children, Robeson Co., farmer (12 Jan. - 20 Feb. 1813)
Tindan, Archibald, age 31, 22 years in U.S., wife & child, Robe-
    son Co., farmer (14 Sept. - 12 Oct. 1812)
Tinlaton, Malcom, age 57, 16 years in U.S., wife & 4 children,
    Cumberland, farmer (12 Jan. -20 Feb. 1813)
Torry, James, age 67, 23 years in U.S., wife & 3 children, Cum-
    berland, farmer; was a commissary in the Revolution and is a
    pensioner of the British government (12 Jan. - 20 Feb. 1813)
Tullock, Charles, age 30, 4 years in U.S., Robeson, millwright
    (24 Aug. - 2 Sept. 1812)
Walker, John, age 29, 9 years in U.S. (14 Sept. - 12 Oct. 1812)
Watson, Daniel, age 35, 9 years in U.S., wife & 2 children, Rich-
    mond Co., shoemaker (7-14 Sept. 1812)
White, Donald, age 35, 4 years in U.S., wife & 3 children, Rich-
    mond Co., preacher & farmer; applied Oct. 1811 (14 Sept. - 12
    Oct. 1812)

SOUTH CAROLINA

Abbott, Sam, age 50, 13 years in U.S., 2 in family, Charleston, schoolmaster (22-31 July 1812)

Adams, John, age 34, 22 years in U.S., Irishman, 8 in family, Chester District, farmer (10-19 Sept. 1812)

Adare, John, age 27, 24 years in U.S., Irishman, Chester District, farmer and shoemaker (31 Aug. - 8 Sept. 1812)

Aitchison, Robert, age 28, 13 years in U.S., Charleston, clerk (22-31 July 1812)

Anderson, Thomas, age 26, 20 years in U.S., Abbeville District, overseer (10 Sept. - 17 Oct. 1812)

Anderson, Wm., age 73, 20 years in U.S., 3 in family, Abbeville District, weaver (10 Sept. - 17 Oct. 1812)

Armour, John, age 48, 21 years in U.S., 10 in family, Chester District, farmer (31 Aug. - 8 Sept. 1812)

Arnet, James, age 55, 11 years in U.S., York District, farmer (10-29 Sept. 1812)

Bar, John, age 28, 21 years in U.S., York District, farmer (10 - 29 Sept. 1812)

Barr, David, age 52, 22 years in U.S., 4 in family, York District, farmer (10-29 Sept. 1812)

Beswick, John, age 69, 11 years in U.S., 2 in family, Charleston, vendue cryer (22-31 July 1812)

Birnie, George, age 22, 7 years in U.S., Charleston, accountant (22-31 July 1812)

Blair, Jos., age 35, 3 mos. in U.S., York District, farmer (10-29 Sept. 1812)

Blair, Saml., age 45, 3 mos. in U.S., 2 in family, York District, farmer (10-19 Sept. 1812)

Boisseau, Jas. E., age 21, 7 years in U.S., Abbeville District, clerk (10 Sept. - 17 Oct. 1812)

Bold, William, age 28, 16 years in U.S., Beaufort, planter (22-31 July 1812)

Bradley, Andrew, age 50, 21 years in U.S., 8 in family, Abbeville District, farmer (10 Sept.-17 Oct. 1812)

Bradshaw, Thomas, age 22, 20 years in U.S., Irishman, Chester District, blacksmith (31 Aug.-8 Sept. 1812)

Brander, James, age 20, 3 days in U.S., Charleston, silversmith (22-31 July 1812)

Brooke, John L., age 58, 18 years in U.S., 4 in family, Pendleton, farmer; one of Geo. III men (10 Sept.-17 Oct. 1812)

Brooks, Thomas, age 45, 8 years in U.S., 4 in family, Charleston, merchant (22-31 July 1812)

Brown, Robert, age 37, 16 years in U.S., 6 in family, Charleston, factor and planter; applied July 1800 (22-31 July 1812)

Bruce, Jno., age 57, 20 years in U.S., from Ireland, Orangeburgh, farmer (10 Sept.-17 Oct. 1812)

Bryce, John, age 23, 11 years in U.S., Richland District, currier (10-29 Sept. 1812)

Buchan, Rev. Dr. John, age 29, 2 years in U.S., Charleston, minister (22-31 July 1812)

Burns, Samuel, age 50, 7 years in U.S., Irishman, 11 in family, Chester District, stone and brick mason; applied 5 April 1809 (31 Aug.-8 Sept. 1812)

Calder, William, age 30, 6 years in U.S., Charleston, merchant (22-31 July 1812)

Caldwell, William, age 20, 19 years in U.S., Scotchman, York District, farmer (31 July-29 Aug. 1812)

Calhoun, Alexr., age 49. 17 years in U,S., 4 in family, Pendleton, farmer (to 10 Nov. 1812)

Campbell, James, age 30, 9 years in U.S., Charleston, merchant; applied 22 Aug. 1810 (22-31 July 1812)

Campbell, Josias, age 30, 11 years in U.S., 3 in family, Kershaw District, carpenter; made a denizen 21 Jan. 1808 (31 July-29 Aug. 1812)

Carey, Richard Y., age 24, 1 year & 3 mos. in U.S., Kershaw(?),
  overlooker (10-19 Sept. 1812)
Carmoohorn, Richard, age 29, 8 years in U.S., Charleston, mer-
  chant (22-31 July 1812)
Carson, William, age 20, 5 years in U.S., Charleston, clerk; he
  does not intend to become a citizen (22-31 July 1812)
Carvalho, D.M., age 25, 10 mos. in U.S., Charleston, lapidary;
  he does not intend to become a citizen (22-31 July 1812)
Cathcart, David, age 47, 12 years in U.S., 4 in family, Chester
  District, farmer (31 Aug.-8 Sept. 1812)
Catherwood, J.J., age 24, 5 years in U.S., Charleston, watchmaker
  (1-10 Aug. 1812)
Cavalho, E.N., age 44, 5 years in U.S., 1 in family, Charleston,
  minister (22-31 July 1812)
Clements, Finlater, age 34, 7 years in U.S., 3 in family, Charles-
  ton, merchant; applied May 1812 (22-31 July 1812)
Cooper, Mathew, age 38, 6 years in U.S., Charleston, merchant
  (22-31 July 1812)
Crawford, Wm., age 40, 2 years in U.S., 4 in family, Pendleton,
  farmer; one of Geo. III ten (10 Sept.-17 Oct, 1812)
Cromwell, Saml., age 39, 12 years in U.S., Charleston, bricklayer
  (to 8 Aug. 1812)
Cruckshanks, Robert, age 24, 1 year in U.S., Charleston, grocer
  (22-31 July 1812)
Dailey, Thos., age 45, 27 years in U.S., 10 in family, Barnwell
  District, minister (31 July-29 Aug. 1812)
Dalgliesh, A., age 29, 8 years in U.S., Charleston Neck, clerk;
  does not wish to become a citizen (to 8 Aug. 1812)
Davidson, Andrew, age 25, 20 years in U.S., 3 in family, York
  District, farmer (10-29 Sept. 1812)
Davidson, Hugh, age 29, 21 years in U.S., 4 in family, Kershaw
  District, farmer (10-19 Sept. 1812)
Davidson, Wm., age 30, 11 years in U.S., Abbeville District,
  farmer (10 Sept.-17 Oct. 1812)
Davis, William, age 35, 11 years in U.S., 2 in family, Charleston,
  grocer (22-31 July 1812)
Delavaur, Francis, age 24, 3 mos. in U.S., Irishman, 2 in family,
  Beaufort, merchant (to 10 Nov. 1812)
Delavour, Isabella, age 34, 8 mos. in U.S., Beaufort, merchant
  (to 10 Nov. 1812)
Demsey, Thos., age 26, 8 years in U.S., Charleston, grocer (to
  8 Aug. 1812)
Dench (or Deuch?), J.C., age 35, 4 years in U.S., Andersonville,
  schoolmaster (10-29 Sept. 1812)
Dench (or Deuch?), Maria Jane, age 8, 4 years in U.S., Anderson-
  ville (10-29 Sept. 1812)
Dench (or Deuch?), Mariah E., age 32, 4 years in U.S., Anderson-
  ville, schoolmistress (10-29 Sept. 1812)
Devine, Thomas, age 32, 14 years in U.S., Charleston, clerk (22-
  31 July 1812)
Dick, James, age 29, 4 years in U.S., Charleston, merchant (22-
  31 July 1812)
Dickey, James, age 30, 11 years in U.S., Irishman, 6 in family,
  Chester District, farmer (to 10 Nov. 1812)
Dickson, James, age 52, 19 years in U.S., 5 in family, York Dis-
  trict, minister (10-29 Sept. 1812)
Donough, David, age 47, 24 years in U.S., Irishman, 7 in family,
  Laurens, farmer; married in U.S. (10 Sept.-17 Oct. 1812)
Douglass, Campbell, age 31, 11 years in U.S., Charleston, grocer
  (22-31 July 1812)
Dunlap, Jas., age 45, 2 years in U.S., 6 in family, Kershaw Dis-
  trict, farmer (31 July-29 Aug. 1812)
Dunlop, John B., age 24, 10 mos. in U.S., Charleston, merchant
  (22-31 July 1812)

Dunn, Andrew, age 55, 20 years in U.S., Irishman, 4 in family,
    Chester District, farmer (10-19 Sept. 1812)
Dunn, David, age 30, 20 years in U.S., Irishman, 5 in family,
    Chester District, farmer (10-19 Sept. 1812)
Dyer, William, age 29, 7 years in U.S., Irishman, 2 in family,
    Newberry District, farmer (31 July-29 Aug. 1812)
Elcook (or Elcock?), John, age 40, 11 years in U.S., Charleston,
    gardner (1-10 Aug. 1812)
English, Jno., age 23, 20 years in U.S., York District, farmer
    (10-29 Sept. 1812)
Ervin, John, age 31, 2 years in U.S., 5 in family, York District,
    farmer (10-29 Sept. 1812)
Ewing, James, age 24, 3 years in U.S., Pinckneyville, farmer (10
    Sept.-17 Oct. 1812)
Ewing, John, age 36, 21 years in U.S., Irishman, 5 in family,
    York District, farmer (31 July-29 Aug. 1812)
Ewing, Wm., age 34, 22 years in U.S., Scotchman, 6 in family,
    York District, farmer (31 July-29 Aug. 1812)
Farus, Wm., age 28, 7 years in U.S., Irishman, 4 in family, Ches-
    ter District, farmer (to 10 Nov. 1812)
Faulkner, Arthur, age 70, 30 years in U.S., York District, school-
    master (10-29 Sept. 1812)
Finch, Hugh, age 40, 18 years in U.S., 8 in family, York District,
    farmer and tailor (10-29 Sept. 1812)
Flanklow, Philip, age 50, 16 years in U.S., Englishman, 4 in fa-
    mily, Orangeburgh, farmer (10 Sept.-17 Oct. 1812)
Fleming, John, age 24, 20 years in U.S., Irishman, Newberry Dis-
    trict, farmer (31 July-29 Aug. 1812)
Fleming, Joseph, age 49, 20 years in U.S., Irishman, 4 (born here)
    in family, Newberry District, farmer (31 July-29 Aug. 1812)
Fulton, Thomas, age 31, 10 years in U.S., 3 in family, Beaufort
    District, overseer (10-29 Sept. 1812)
Furse, James, age 38, 7 years in U.S., 5 in family, Barnwell Dis-
    trict, planter (31 July-29 Aug. 1812)
Gallenek, Patrick, age 26, 7 years in U.S., Irishman, wife,
    Orangeburgh, clerk (10 Sept.-17 Oct. 1812)
Gibson, Alexander, age 27, 7 years in U.S., Charleston, merchant
    (22-31 July 1812)
Gillespie, Jas., age 41, 27 years in U.S., Irishman, Chester Dis-
    trict, farmer and hatter (31 Aug.-8 Sept. 1812)
Gilmer, Jno., age 41, 22 years in U.S., 8 in family, Abbeville
    District, shoemaker (10 Sept.-17 Oct. 1812)
Gleghorn, John, age 46, 23 years in U.S., Irishman, 12 in family,
    Chester District, farmer (10-19 Sept. 1812)
Goldsmith, Abm., age 56, 13 years in U.S., 2 in family, Charles-
    ton, merchant (31 July-29 Aug. 1812)
Goldsmith, Morris, age 28, 16 years in U.S., 6 in family, Charles-
    ton, merchant; a denizen since 1806 (31 July-29 Aug. 1812)
Gordon, Aaron, age 52, 15 years in U.S., 8 in family, Chester
    District, farmer (31 Aug.-8 Sept. 1812)
Gordon, C.P., age 27, 8 years in U.S., Charleston, clerk; applied
    9 Nov. 1809 (to 8 Aug. 1812)
Gordon, James, age 57, 26 years in U.S., Irishman, 8 (born here)
    in family, Newberry District, bricklayer (31 July-29 Aug. 1812)
Gould, Thomas, age 38, 13 years in U.S., 4 in family, Charleston,
    painter and glazier (22-31 July 1812)
Grace, P.H., age 33, 3 years in U.S., Charleston, cabinetmaker
    (to 8 Aug. 1812)
Graham, Wm., age 26, 23 years in U.S., Irishman, 3 in family,
    Chester District, farmer (10-19 Sept. 1812)
Grahame, Archibald, age 25, 8 years in U.S., Charleston, merchant;
    applied June 1809 (22-31 July 1812)
Graw, Thos., age 25, 1 year & 8 mos. in U.S., wife & 1 child,
    Charleston, accomptant (1-10 Aug. 1812)

Green, John Gray, age 40, 10 years in U.S., wife & 1 child, St. Paul's Parish, innkeeper (22-31 July 1812)

Green, Richard, age 51, 29 years in U.S., Richland District, shoemaker (10-29 Sept. 1812)

Groves, H.L., age 54, 21 years in U.S., Abbeville District, joiner (10 Sept.-17 Oct. 1812)

Hacket, William, age 57, 23 years in U.S., Irishman, 1 in family, York District, farmer (31 July-29 Aug. 1812)

Hacket, Wm., age 20, 1 year in U.S., Irishman, York District, farmer (31 July-29 Aug. 1812)

Hall, James, age 35, 11 years in U.S., Charleston, stone cutter (22-31 July 1812)

Hancock, George, age 22, 12 years in U.S., Charleston, cabinetmaker (to 8 Aug. 1812)

Harmon, John, age 52, 24 years in U.S., Irishman, 6 in family, Chester District, farmer 31 Aug.-8 Sept. 1812)

Harper, Thomas, age 32, 4 years in U.S., 1 in family, Charleston, hatter (22-31 July 1812)

Harrison, John, age 43, 20 years in U.S., Irishman, 5 in family, Greenville, farmer; married in U.S. (10 Sept.-17 Oct. 1812)

Hatton, Eliza, age 45, 8 mos. in U.S., Beaufort (to 10 Nov. 1812)

Hatton, Marian, age 16, 8 mos. in U.S., Beaufort (to 10 Nov. 1812)

Hay, Charles, age 47, 4 years in U.S., Irishman, 2 in family, Chester District, farmer (31 Aug.-8 Sept. 1812)

Hedly, John, age 45, 11 years in U.S., 4 in family, Charleston, schoolmaster (22-31 July 1812)

Heffernand, John, age 47, 9 years in U.S., 10 in family, Charleston, cabinetmaker; applied May 1811 (1-10 Aug. 1812)

Henhouse, John, age 25, 21 years in U.S., from Ireland, Greenville, farmer (10 Sept.-17 Oct. 1812)

Herbert, L., age 37, 9 years in U.S., York District, schoolmaster (10-29 Sept. 1812)

Hermon, James, age 30, 20 years in U.S., Irishman, 6 (born here) in family, Newberry District, farmer (31 July-29 Aug. 1812)

Hetherington, Geo., age 24, 1 year in U.S., wife & 1 child, Abbeville District, weaver and planter (10 Sept.-17 Oct. 1812)

Hethrington, Edward, age 35, 16 years in U.S., Irishman, Orangeburgh District, farmer (31 Aug.-8 Sept. 1812)

Hewson, Thos., age 29, 13 years & 11 mos. in U.S., Charleston, clerk; says he applied (1-10 Aug. 1812)

Heynes, Jas., age 34, 14 years in U.S., 3 in family, Charleston, grocer (1-10 Aug. 1812)

Hill, Alexr., age 45, 21 years in U.S., Irishman, 6 in family, York District, farmer (31 July-29 Aug. 1812)

Hill, Alexr., age 23, 21 years in U.S., Irishman, York District, farmer (31 July-29 Aug. 1812)

Hopkins, John, age 47, 23 years in U.S., Irishman, 5 in family, York District, farmer (31 July-29 Aug. 1812)

Horden, John, age 45, 16 years in U.S., 1 in family, Charleston, tobacconist (22-31 July 1812)

Hornhill, Robert, age 53, 21 years in U.S., 7 in family, Chester District, farmer (31 Aug.-8 Sept. 1812)

Hua, B,, 18 years in U.S., 4 in family, York District, merchant (10-29 Sept. 1812)

Hudgeons, J.B., age 41, 24 years in U.S., 9 in family, Pendleton, farmer; "a good citizen" (10 Sept.-17 Oct. 1812)

Hunter, Nathan, Sr., age 68, 23 years in U.S., Irishman, 2 in family, Newberry District, farmer (31 July-29 Aug. 1812)

Hunter, Nathan, Jr., age 26, in U.S. 23 years, Irishman, Newberry District, farmer (31 July-29 Aug. 1812)

Hyams, Henry, age 21, 2 years in U.S., Charleston, store keeper (22-31 July 1812)

Hyams, Mordecai, age 21, 2 years in U.S., Charleston, store keeper (22-31 July 1812)

Ingraham, Richard, age 62, 12 years in U.S., 8 in family, York
    District, farmer and carpenter (10-29 Sept. 1812)
Ingraham, Thomas, age 24, 12 years in U.S., York District, far-
    mer (10-20 Sept. 1812)
Ingram, Jno., age 26, 12 years in U.S., 4 in family, York District,
    farmer (10-29 Sept. 1812)
Irvin, Archibald, age 25, 6 years in U.S., Irishman, Newberry
    District, hatter (31 July-29 Aug. 1812)
Jackson, Joseph, age 25, 12 years in U.S., Charleston, merchant
    (22-31 July 1812)
Jamieson, Alexr., age 55, 18 years in U.S., Irishman, 11 in fa-
    mily, Chester District, farmer (to 10 Nov. 1812)
Johnston, Arch. S., age 27, 6 years in U.S., 4 in family; St.
    Bartholomew's Parish, planter; applied 1806 (22-31 July 1812)
Junkin, David, age 18, 8 mos. in U.S., Irishman, Newberry District,
    farmer (31 July-29 Aug. 1812)
Junkin, John, age 24, 5 years in U.S., Irishman, 2 in family,
    Chester District, schoolmaster (10-19 Sept. 1812)
Junkin, Samuel, age 30, 7 years in U.S., Irishman, 1 in family,
    Newberry District, farmer (31 July-29 Aug. 1812)
Keating, Michael, age 23, 2 years in U.S., Charleston, clerk (22-
    31 July 1812)
Kelly, Daniel, age 25, 22 years in U.S., Kershaw District, over-
    looker (31 July-29 Aug. 1812)
Kelly, John, age 31, 25 years in U.S., 3 in family, Kershaw Dis-
    trict, blacksmith (31 July-29 Aug. 1812)
Kennedy, John, age 36, 12 years in U.S., Prince William, farmer
    (to 10 Nov. 1812)
Kennedy, Thos., age 68, 25 years in U.S., Irishman, 4 in family,
    Chester District, farmer; applied 1792 to County Court of S.C.
    (31 Aug.-8 Sept. 1812)
Kerr, Daniel, age 52, 13 years in U.S., 2 in family, York District,
    shoemaker (31 July-29 Aug. 1812)
Kile, John, age 35, 24 years in U.S., 2 in family, Kershaw District,
    farmer (31 July-29 Aug. 1812)
Kilkenny, Timothy, age 31, 11 years in U.S., Charleston, clerk;
    "one of the quota of this district" (1-10 Aug. 1812)
Kilpatrick, Jas., age 34, 24 years in U.S., Irishman, 4 in family,
    Chester District, farmer (31 Aug.-8 Sept. 1812)
King, John, age 23, 6 years in U.S., Charleston, clerk (22-31 July
    1812)
Kirk, David, age 60, 19 years in U.S., Irishman, 4 in family,
    Chester District, farmer and weaver (31 Aug.-8 Sept. 1812)
Laverty, Jas., age 40, 9 years in U.S., 6 in family, Spartanburgh
    District, farmer (31 Aug.-8 Sept. 1812)
Lee, Robert, age 56, 19 years in U.S., 2 in family, Chester Dis-
    trict, farmer (31 Aug.-8 Sept. 1812)
Leghorn, George, age 30, 1 year & 8 mos. in U.S., Charleston,
    clerk (1-10 Aug. 1812)
Leitch, Duncan, age 25, 9 years in U.S., 1 in family, Charleston,
    grocer (22-31 July 1812)
Lenmon, Moses, age 52, 21 years in U.S., Irishman, 7 in family,
    Chester District, farmer (to 10 Nov. 1812)
Lip(r?)man, Abraham, age 35, 4 years in U.S., 1 in family, Charles-
    ton, watchmaker (22-31 July 1812)
Livingston, Gordon, age 21, 1 year & 6 mos. in U.S., wife, Charles-
    ton, grocer (1-10 Aug. 1812)
Love, John, age 45, 21 years in U.S., Irishman, 10 in family, York
    District, farmer (31 July-29 Aug. 1812)
Love, Robert, age 36, 21 years in U.S., Irishman, 4 in family,
    York District, farmer and wheelwright (31 July-29 Aug. 1812)
Love, Wm., age 42, 21 years in U.S., Irishman, 2 in family, York
    District, farmer and distiller (31 July-29 Aug. 1812)
Lowdon, George, age 40, 21 years in U.S., 8 in family, Chester
    District, farmer (31 Aug.-8 Sept. 1812)

Lyle, Mathew, age 64, 16 years in U.S., 6 in family, Kershaw
    District, farmer; receives pension of 20 pounds per annum from
    the British government for his services in the Revolution (31
    July-29 Aug. 1812)
Lyle, Robertson, age 23, 16 years in U.S., 2 in family, Kershaw
    District, farmer (31 July-29 Aug. 1812)
McArthur, Andrew, age 47, 21 years in U.S., Irishman, 7 in family,
    York District, farmer (31 July-29 Aug. 1812)
McArthur, John, age 29, 21 years in U.S., 2 in family, Kershaw
    District, farmer (31 July-29 Aug. 1812)
McCaherin, John, age 25, 22 years in U.S., York District, wagon
    maker (10-29 Sept. 1812)
McCarte, Jas., age 31, 7 years in U.S., Barnwell District, la-
    bourer (31 July-29 Aug. 1812)
McCaskill, Alexander, age 53, 10 years in U.S., 6 in family, Ker-
    shaw District, farmer (10-19 Sept. 1812)
Mc Caskill, Donald, age 22, 9 years in U.S., Kershaw District,
    farmer (10-19 Sept. 1812)
McCaskill, Peter, age 19, 10 years in U.S., Kershaw District,
    farmer (10-19 Sept. 1812)
Mc Clintosh, Robert, age 26, 24 years in U.S., Irishman, Chester
    District, farmer (to 10 Nov. 1812)
McCoon, John, age 23, 21 years in U.S., from Ireland, Greenville,
    farmer (10 Sept.-17 Oct. 1812)
McCullock, Robert, age 45, 21 years in U.S., 7 in family, York
    District, farmer and weaver (10-29 Sept. 1812)
McCullough, Samuel, age 24, 23 years in U.S., 3 in family, York
    District, blacksmith (10-29 Sept. 1812)
Mc Cullough, Wm., age 25, 23 years in U.S., 4 in family, York
    District, wagon maker (10-29 Sept. 1812)
McDowell, Thos., age 40, 8 mos. in U.S., Irishman, 6 in family,
    Chester District, farmer (31 Aug.-8 Sept. 1812)
McFarlane, M., age 27, 8 years in U.S., Charleston, clerk (22-31
    July 1812)
McGregor, Neil, age 40, 14 years in U.S., 3 in family, Charleston,
    gardener and grain merchant (22-31 July 1812)
McGuffie, A., age 29, 11 years in U.S., Charleston; he thinks he
    will not become a citizen (1-10 Aug. 1812)
McGriffin, Wm., age 50, 29 years in U.S., 7 in family, Pendleton,
    farmer (10-19 Sept. 1812)
McIntosh, Angus, age 23, 10 years in U.S., Kershaw District, far-
    mer (10-19 Sept. 1812)
McIntosh, Daniel, age 23, 10 years in U.S., Kershaw District,
    farmer (10-19 Sept. 1812)
McKellar, Jas., age 31, 5 years in U.S., 1 in family, Malborough
    District, (min?)ister (31 Aug.-8 Sept. 1812)
McKelvey, Hugh, age 44, 22 years in U.S., 7 in family, Chester
    District, farmer (31 Aug.-8 Sept. 1812)
McKinnon, Charles, age 23, 20 years in U.S., Kershaw District,
    farmer (10-19 Sept. 1812)
McKinnon, Laughlan, age 50, 20 years in U.S., 2 in family, Ker-
    shaw District, farmer (10-19 Sept. 1812)
McKinsey, John, age 19, 1 year in U.S., Camden, clerk (to 8 Aug.
    1812)
McKinstry, James, age 38, 24 years in U.S., Irishman, 4 in family,
    Chester District, farmer (to 10 Nov. 1812)
McLean, Daniel, age 24, 11 years in U.S., Kershaw District, black-
    smith (10-19 Sept. 1812)
McLean, James, age 41, 19 years in U.S., Camden, schoolmaster (to
    8 Aug. 1812)
McLean, John, age 30, 20 years in U.S., 2 in family, Kershaw
    District, hatter (10-19 Sept. 1812)
McLean, Oliver, age 45, 21 years in U.S., 9 in family, York Dis-
    trict, schoolmaster (10-29 Sept. 1812)

McLeod, Archibald, age 66, 20 years in U.S., 4 in family, Kershaw District, farmer (10-19 Sept. 1812)

McLeod, Daniel, age 23, 10 years in U.S., wife, Kershaw District, farmer (10-19 Sept. 1812)

McLeod, Roderick, age 25, 10 years in U.S., 2 in family, Kershaw District, farmer (10-19 Sept. 1812)

McLeod, William, age 18, 10 years in U.S., Kershaw District, farmer (10-19 Sept. 1812)

McMillan, Daniel, age 35, 23 years in U.S, 5 in family, Chester District, merchant (31 Aug.-8 Sept. 1812)

McMillan, Hugh, age 64, 23 years in U.S., 5 in family, Chester District, farmer (31 Aug.-8 Sept. 1812)

McMillan, Jas., age 25, 22 years in U.S., 3 in family, Chester District, turner (31 Aug.-8 Sept. 1812)

McMillan, Wm., age 76, 20 years in U.S., Irishman, 4 in family, Chester District, farmer (to 10 Nov. 1812)

McMullan, Archibald, age 52, 29 years in U.S., 8 in family, Abbeville District, planter (10 Sept.-17 Oct. 1812)

McNary, Patrick, age 35, 14 years in U.S., Irishman, 5 (born here) in family, Newberry District, farmer (31 July-29 Aug. 1812)

McNaught, Archibald, age 26, 1 year in U.S., Kershaw District, weaver (10-19 Sept. 1812)

McNaughton, Donald, age 38, 9 years in U.S., 5 in family, Kershaw District, farmer (10-19 Sept. 1812)

NcNeill, Jas., Sr., age 46, 23 years in U.S., Irishman, 8 (born here) in family, Newberry District, farmer (31 July-29 Aug. 1812)

McNeill, James, Jr., age 24, 23 years in U.S., Irishman, Newberry District, blacksmith (31 July-29 Aug. 1812)

McNinch, John, age 47, 18 years in U.S., 1 in family, Chester Village, merchant; holds a very considerable estate in this country (22-31 July 1812)

McSwine, Malcom, age 33, 10 years in U.S., 4 in family, Kershaw District, farmer (10-19 Sept. 1812)

McVicar, A., age 20, 1 year in U.S., Charleston, butcher (22-31 July 1812)

McWhorter, A., age 29, 21 years in U.S., 5 in family, York District, farmer (10-19 Sept. 1812)

McWhorter, Jno., age 24, 20 years in U.S., York District, farmer (10-19 Sept. 1812)

McWhorter, Thos., age 22, 20 years in U.S., York District, farmer (10-19 Sept. 1812)

Magwood, Robert, age 50, 5 years in U.S., Charleston, M.D.; applied Jan. 1810; a denizen (22-31 July 1812)

Martin, David, age 44, 21 years in U.S., 8 in family, Chester District, farmer (31 Aug.-8 Sept. 1812)

Matheson, Rodk., age 25, 6 years in U.S., Camden, merchant; applied Nov. 1811 (to 8 Aug. 1812)

Melrose, Thos., age 40, 6 years in U.S., wife & 1 child, Christ Church Parish, overseer (1-10 Aug. 1812)

Miller, John, age 29, 20 years in U.S., 3 in family, York District, farmer (10-29 Sept. 1812)

Miller, Joseph, age 31, 20 years in U.S., Scotchman, 2 in family, York District, farmer (31 July-29 Aug. 1812)

Miller, Robert M., age 24, 23 years in U.S., Abbeville District, farmer (10 Sept.-17 Oct. 1812)

Moffet, Andrew, age 18, 6 mos. in U.S., Charleston, clerk; does not intend to become a citizen (22-31 July 1812)

Monies, Hugh, age 21, 5 years in U.S., Charleston, merchant (to 8 Aug. 1812)

Moore, David, age 30, 6 years in U.S., Kershaw District, cabinetmaker (31 July-29 Aug. 1812)

Moore, John, age 57, 24 years in U.S., 10 in family, Abbeville District, mason (10 Sept.-17 Oct. 1812)

Moore, Robert, age 47, 27 years in U.S., Irishman, 7 (born here)
  in family, Newberry District, farmer (31 July-29 Aug. 1812)
Moore, Thos., age 33, 23 years in U.S., 6 in family, Chester
  District, tailor (31 Aug.-8 Sept. 1812)
Moorehouse, John, age 49, 12 years in U.S., Spartanburgh District,
  tailor (31 Aug.-8 Sept. 1812)
Mordecai, Noah, age 33, 3 years in U.S., Charlyton District, mer-
  chant (31 Aug.-8 Sept. 1812)
Morris, Ainsley, age 17, 6 years in U.S., Charleston, merchant
  (22-31 July 1812)
Morris, Simpson, age 38, 6 years in U.S., 2 in family, Charleston,
  merchant (22-31 July 1812)
Morrison, Wm., age 34, 11 years in U.S., 4 in family, Abbeville
  District, planter (10 Sept.-17 Oct. 1812)
Muirhead, James, age 20, 16 years in U.S., Charleston, clerk
  (1-10 Aug. 1812)
Mullen, James, age 52, 9 years in U.S., 8 in family, York Dis-
  trict, farmer (10-29 Sept. 1812)
Mullens, Mathew, age 27, 11 years in U.S., Irishman, Prince Wil-
  liam, merchant (to 10 Nov. 1812)
Munfoard, Jas., age 45, 21 years in U.S., 7 in family, Chester
  District, farmer (31 Aug.-8 Sept. 1812)
Nebit, Frances (sic!), age 52, 22 years in U.S., Scotchman, 9 in
  family, York District, farmer (31 July-29 Aug. 1812)
Neeland, A., age 55, 20 years in U.S., 3 in family, York District,
  farmer (10-29 Sept. 1812)
Neeland, James, age 30, 20 years in U.S., 4 in family, York Dis-
  trict, farmer (10-29 Sept. 1812)
Neely, Samuel, age 58, 20 years in U.S., Irishman, 5 in family,
  York District, farmer and distiller (31 July- 29 Aug. 1812)
Nisbet, Jas., age 34, 9 years in U.S., Charleston Neck, gardener;
  applied June 1811 (to 8 Aug. 1812)
Nisbet, John, age 33, 23 years in U.S., 6 in family, Chester Dis-
  trict, farmer (31 Aug.-8 Sept. 1812)
O'Donovan, Ml., 9 years in U.S., 1 in family, Charleston (22-31
  July 1812)
Omelverry (or Omelveny?), Wm., age 48, 19 years in U.S., Irish-
  man, 8 in family, Chester District, farmer (31 Aug.-8 Sept. 1812)
O'Neal, Joseph, age 45, 21 years in U.S., Irishman, 2 in family,
  York District, farmer (31 July-29 Aug. 1812)
O'Rawe, John, age 29, 5 years in U.S., Charleston, clerk; applied
  May 1812 (22-31 July 1812)
Orr, John, age 61, 21 years in U.S., Irishman, 8 in family, Ches-
  ter District, schoolmaster (31 Aug.-8 Sept. 1812)
Otes, John, age 47, 11 years in U.S., Charleston, storekeeper
  (1-10 Aug. 1812)
Parker, Wm. D., age 36, 9 years in U.S., Kershaw District, cabi-
  netmaker; applied Nov. 1811 (31 July-29 Aug. 1812)
Patrick, Robert, age 32, 3 mos. in U.S., York District, farmer
  (10-29 Sept. 1812)
Patterson, Jas., age 19, 9 years in U.S., Irishman, Chester Dis-
  trict, hatter (31 Aug.-8 Sept. 1812)
Patterson, John, age 19, 3 days in U.S., Charleston, flax-dresser
  (22-31 July 1812)
Patterson, Peter, age 27, 5 years in U.S., Pendleton, tailor (10-
  19 Sept. 1812)
Paul, Dunbar, age 21, 1 year & 8 mos. in U.S., Charleston, clerk
  (22-31 July 1812)
Peacock, Richard, age 28, 4 years in U.S., Charleston, tanner and
  currier (22-31 July 1812)
Peake, John Lamp, age 25, 6 years in U.S., 1 in family, Charles-
  ton, merchant (22-31 July 1812)
Pearson, Joseph, age 40, 18 years in U.S., 3 in family, York
  District, farmer (10-29 Sept. 1812)

Peebles, Geo. L., age 38, 13 years in U.S., 4 in family, Spartanburgh District, schoolmaster (31 Aug.-8 Sept. 1812)

Percy, Barnd. Elliott, age 26, 4 years in U.S., Charleston; does not wish to become a citizen (22-31 July 1812)

Peters, George, age 47, 10 years in U.S., 5 in family, Charleston, schoolmaster; applied June 1812 (22-31 July 1812)

Pierce, Edward, age 66, 32 years in U.S., Charleston Neck, accomptant (to 8 Aug. 1812)

Ponny, Jno., age 25, 4 years in U.S., Charleston, millwright; does not widh to become a citizen (to 8 Aug. 1812)

Price, Thos., age 34, 2 years & 5 mos. in U.S., wife, Charleston, clerk (1-10 Aug. 1812)

Pyne, John, age 45, 5 years in U.S., planter; applied March 1810; is a denizen (22-31 July 1812)

Quirim, Wm., age 24, 23 years in U.S., 3 in family, York District, farmer (10-29 Sept. 1812)

Quise, James, age 50, 23 years in U.S., Irishman, 7 in family, York District, farmer (31 July-29 Aug. 1812)

Redmond, Wm., age 31, 6 years in U.S., Union District, farmer (10 Sept.-17 Oct. 1812)

Reid, Isaiah, age 52, 22 years in U.S., 8 in family, York District, turner (31 Aug.-8 Sept. 1812)

Rendell, G., age 36, 5 years in U.S., 1 in family, Charleston, broker; has taken oath of allegiance to England and does not wish to become citizen of U.S. (22-31 July 1812)

Reyers, James, age 24, 3 years in U.S., Irishman, York District, enlisted soldier (31 July-29 Aug. 1812)

Reynolds, Joshua, age 27, 5 years in U.S., Camden, clerk (to 8 Aug. 1812)

Richards, Adam, age 37, 5 years in U.S., 4 in family, Pendleton, weaver; applied Oct. term 1811 (10-19 Sept. 1812)

Richardson, F.R., age 21, 3 years in U.S., Charlyton District, student-at-law (31 Aug.-8 Sept. 1812)

Richardson, John, age 47, 10 years in U.S., wife, St. Helena, planter (to 10 Nov. 1812)

Richey, Andrew, age 36, 11 years in U.S., 5 in family, Abbeville District, farmer (10 Sept.-17 Oct. 1812)

Robertson, James, age 45, 20 years in U.S., Irishman, Newberry District, hatter (31 July-29 Aug. 1812)

Robertson, Jas., age 17, 2 years in U.S., Charleston, clerk (1-10 Aug. 1812)

Robinson, John, age 46, 20 years in U.S., 4 in family, Chester District, farmer (31 Aug.-8 Sept. 1812)

Rodmant, John, age 34, 22 years in U.S., Irishman, 7 in family, Chester District, farmer (10-19 Sept. 1812)

Ross, Daniel, age 40, 11 years in U.S., Charleston, lumber merchant (22-31 July 1812)

Ross, Robert, age 23, 22 years in U.S., Irishman, 3 in family, Chester District, farmer (31 Aug.-8 Sept. 1812)

Ryan, Lawrence, age 28, 4 years in U.S., Charleston, student-at-law (22-31 July 1812)

Savage, Anthony, age 43, 27 years in U.S., Irishman, 6 in family, Greenville, farmer; married in U.S. (10 Sept.-17 Oct. 1812)

Schollay, James, age 40, 6 years in U.S., Charleston (22-31 July 1812)

Scollay, John, age 21, 5 years in U.S., Charleston, clerk; does not wish to become a citizen (22-31 July 1812)

Scott, Thos., age 18, 3 years in U.S., Savannah, merchant; does not wish to become a citizen (to 8 Aug. 1812)

Scott, William, age 36, 14 years in U.S., 5 in family, Charleston, millwright (to 18 Aug. 1812)

Shaw, David, age 39, 3 years in U.S., Charleston, surgeon (22-31 July 1812)

Shaw, W.D., age 26, 13 years in U.S., 1 in family, Charleston, merchant (22-31 July 1812)

Shields, Henry, age 35, 9 years in U.S., Charleston Neck, grocer
(to 8 Aug. 1812)

Simpson, Charles R., age 25, 5 years in U.S., single, Charleston,
merchant; does not intend to become a citizen (22-31 July 1812)

Simpson, Hugh, age 42, 20 years in U.S., Scotchman, 11 in family,
York District, farmer (31 July-29 Aug. 1812)

Simpson, Joseph, age 44, 25 years in U.S., Irishman, 8 in family,
Chester District, farmer (to 10 Nov. 1812)

Simpson, Thomas, age 40, 20 years in U.S., 7 in family, York
District, farmer (10-29 Sept. 1812)

Sloan, Jno. J., age 34, 7 years in U.S., 4 in family, York District, mechanic (10-29 Sept. 1812)

Smith, Andrew, age 50, 27 years in U.S., Scotchman, wife, Greenville, farmer; "a good Republican" (10 Sept.-17 Oct. 1812)

Smith, John, age 33, 14 years in U.S., 1 in family, Charleston,
shipwright (22-31 July 1812)

Smith, John, age 27, 10 years in U.S., Charleston, accomptant
(22-31 July 1812)

Smith, Joseph, age 26, 20 years in U.S., 4 in family, York District, farmer (10-29 Sept. 1812)

Smith, Robert, age 29, 24 years in U.S., Irishman, York District,
schoolmaster (31 July-29 Aug. 1812)

Smith, Wm., age 46, 12 years in U.S., 7 in family, Abbeville
District, weaver (10 Sept.-17 Oct. 1812)

Standcombe, Richard, age 40, 1 year in U.S., 4 in family, Charleston, sawyer; does not wish to take up arms against his country
(22-31 July 1812)

Stewart, John, age 42, 24 years in U.S., 4 in family, Abbeville
District, planter (10 Sept.- 17 Oct. 1812)

Surr, John C., age 25, 9 years in U.S., St. Paul's Parish, tutor
(1-10 Aug. 1812)

Swawbey, Jos. A., age 34, 12 years in U.S., Barnwell District;
itinerant (31 July-29 Aug. 1812)

Sweeny, Patrick, age 38, 14 years in U.S., Charleston, millwright
(22-31 July 1812)

Sweeny, Thomas, age 24, 7 years in U.S., 2 in family, Charleston,
clerk (22-31 July 1812)

Tait, Jas., age 37, 14 years in U.S., George Town, merchant (to
18 Aug. 1812)

Tart, Wm. McDowall, age 24, 2 years in U.S., Charleston, merchant;
does not wish to become a citizen (22-31 July 1812)

Tatem, William, age 24, 11 years in U.S., Charleston, clerk (22-
31 July 1812)

Taylor, Archibald, Jr., age 30, 15 years in U.S., Georgetown
District, merchant (31 July-29 Aug. 1812)

Tennant, Robert, age 25, 5 years in U.S., Charleston, accomptant
(22-31 July 1812)

Teppens, George, age 50, 20 years in U.S., 4 in family, Chester
District, farmer (31 Aug.-8 Sept. 1812)

Terry, George, age 48, 4 years in U.S., from Great Britain, 11 in
family, Greenville, farmer (10 Sept.-17 Oct. 1812)

Terry, James, age 25, 4 years in U.S., from Great Britain, Greenville, farmer (10 Sept.-17 Oct. 1812)

Thomas, Jno., age 26, 6 years in U.S., Charleston Neck, clerk
(to 8 Aug. 1812)

Thomb, Samuel, age 25, 1 year in U.S., Irishman, 4 in family,
Lawrence District, farmer (to 10 Nov. 1812)

Thompson, Daniel, age 36, 16 years in U.S., Malborough District,
ditcher (31 Aug.-8 Sept. 1812)

Thompson, James, age 21, 8 years in U.S., 2 in family, Abbeville
District (10 Sept.-17 Oct. 1812)

Thompson, John, age 48, 11 years in U.S,, 2 in family, Abbeville
District, weaver (10 Sept.-17 Oct. 1812)

Trescot, Joseph, age 26, 5 years in U.S., single, Charleston,
merchant; applied May 1812 (22-31 July 1812)

Turnbull, Gavin, age 46, 15 years in U.S., 1 in family, Charleston, schoolmaster (22-31 July 1812)
Turner, William, age 32, 18 years in U.S., 3 in family, Charleston, assistant lamplighter (22-31 July 1812)
Veale, Jno., age 53, 29 years in U.S., York District, schoolmaster (10-29 Sept. 1812)
Walker, Hugh, age 45, 10 years in U.S., Irishman, 8 in family, York District, farmer (31 July-29 Aug. 1812)
Wallace, James, age 27, 25 years in U.S., 2 in family, York District, farmer (31 July-29 Aug. 1812)
Wallace, Jas., age 24, 21 years in U.S., Scotchman, 3 in family, York District, farmer (31 July-29 Aug. 1812)
Waller, Wm., age 28, 18 mos. in U.S., Charlyton District, sadler; applied May 1811 (31 Aug.-8 Sept. 1812)
Waugh, A.R., age 27, 6 years in U.S., 3 in family, Charleston, merchant; applied 1808 (22-31 July 1812)
Wham, Benjamin, age 68, 14 years in U.S., 1 in family, Chester District, farmer (31 Aug.-8 Sept. 1812)
Wham, Wm., age 35, 14 years in U.S., 8 in family, Chester District, wheelwright (31 Aug.-8 Sept. 1812)
Wham, Wm., age 35, 14 years in U.S., 8 in family, Chester District, wheelwright (31 Aug.-8 Sept. 1812)
Wheeler, Josiah, age 22, 2 years in U.S., Charleston, accomptant (22-31 July 1812)
White, Daniel, age 33, 6 years in U.S., 3 in family, Charleston, butcher (1-10 Aug. 1812)
White, James, age 30, 5 years in U.S., 7 in family, Charleston, grocer; applied 20 May 1811 (1-10 Aug. 1812)
Wilson, James, age 48, 21 years in U.S., 10 in family, York District, wheelwright (31 Aug.-8 Sept. 1812)
Wilson, Thomas, age 57, 22 years in U.S., Irishman, 8 (born here) in family, Newberry District, farmer (31 July- 29 Aug. 1812)
Wilson, William, age 22, 1 year in U.S., 1 in family, Charleston, butcher (22-31 July 1812)
Wincey, James, age 46, 4 years in U.S., 4 in family, Charleston, blacksmith (22-31 July 1812)
Woodside, James, age 47, 5 years in U.S., Irishman, 2 in family, Greenville, shoemaker; married in U.S. (10 Sept.-17 Oct. 1812)
Work (or Wark?), John, age 29, 11 years in U.S., tallow chandler; one of the quota from Charleston (1-10 Aug. 1812)
Workman, Robert, age 51, 21 years in U.S., Irishman, 10 in family, York District, farmer and distiller (31 July-29 Aug. 1812)
Wright, Robert, age 28, 8 years in U.S., 1 in family, Charleston, carpenter (22-31 July 1812)
Wright, Thomas, age 29, 4 years in U.S., Irishman, 2 in family, Greenville, cooper (10-Sept.-17 Oct. 1812)
Young, Robert, age 26, 3 mos. in U.S., Irishman, 2 in family, York District, farmer (31 July-29 Aug. 1812)
Young, Zach., age 26, 9 years in U.S., Charleston, gardener (to 8 Aug. 1812)

GEORGIA

Abbott, Edmund, age 16, 4 years & 11 mos. in U.S., Frederica, merchant's clerk (4-10 Aug. 1812)

Anderson, William, age 23, 6 years in U.S., Augusta, theatrical performer (4-10 Aug. 1812)

Askew, James, age 38½, 14 years in U.S., wife & 3 children, Augusta, teacher (25-31 Aug. 1812)

Barron, Alexander, age 23, 1 year & 9 mos. in U.S., Savannah, house-carpenter; applied Nov. 1810 in New York (4 Aug. 1812)

Bennoch, Alexander, age 21, 3 years in U.S., Augusta, merchant's clerk; applied 22 Apr. 1812 (4-10 Aug. 1812)

Bennoch, Peter, age 26, 6 years & 9 mos. in U.S., Augusta, merchant; applied 18 Oct. 1811 (4-10 Aug. 1812)

Blue, Daniel, age 55, 22 years in U.S., wife, 7 children & 5 slaves, Camden Co., half pay British subaltern & corn planter (4-10 Aug. 1812)

Bolan, Richard, age 33, 9 years & 6 mos. in U.S., Augusta, merchant; applied Apr. 1806 (11-17 Aug. 1812)

Bones, John, age 20, 1 year & 8 mos. in U.S., Augusta, merchant's clerk (4-10 Aug. 1812)

Bradly, James, age 42, 5 years in U,S., wife & 2 children, Augusta, tailor (11-17 Aug. 1812)

Brown, Mo(rse?), age 34, 14 years in U.S., wife & 3 children, Savannah, pilot (27 July - 5 Aug. 1812)

Brown, Robert, age 40, 1 year & 8 mos. in U.S., Augusta, Catholic priest; applied Apr. 1812 (4-10 Aug. 1812)

Burke, Francis R., age 36, 4 years in U.S., Savannah (27 July - 5 Aug. 1812)

Burke, Thomas, age 23, 12 years in U.S., Augusta, theatrical performer (4-10 Aug. 1812)

Byrns, Stevens, age 28, 2 years & 3 mos. in U.S., Savannah, gunsmith (4 Aug. 1812)

Campbell, James, age 18, 2 years in U.S., Augusta, clerk; reported 16 Nov. (2 Oct. - 31 Dec. 1812)

Carnochan, David, age 38, 1 year in U.S., McIntosh Co., distiller (1 Sept. - 1 Oct. 1812)

Carnochan, William, age 36, 1 year in U.S., McIntosh Co., sugar planter; applied Feb. 1812 (1 Sept. - 1 Oct. 1812)

Caulfield, Thomas, age 42, 6 years in U.S., Augusta, theatrical performer (4-10 Aug. 1812)

Chaplin, Joseph H., age 19, 5 years & 11 mos. in U.S., Savannah, merchant's clerk (27 July - 5 Aug. 1812); 6 ft., fair complex., brown hair, black eyes, Augusta, passport 29 Mar. 1813 (27 Apr. 1813); entitled to indulgence (1 July 1813)

Charlton, George, age 26, 10 years in U.S., Savannah, merchant (27 July - 5 Aug. 1812); 5 ft. 1 in., florid complex., dark hair, blue eyes, Augusta, passport, 27 Mar. 1813 (27 Mar. 1813)

Cooper, John, age 26, 3 years & 5 mos. in U.S., wife and 1 child, Savannah, tailor (25-31 Aug. 1812)

Corbett, William, age 43, 4 years & 8 mos. in U.S., Washington, merchant; applied June term 1812 (25-31 Aug. 1812)

Cowan, John, age 22 years & 10 mos., 8 years & 8 mos. in U.S., Savannah, merchant's clerk (4-10 Aug. 1812)

Dale, John, age 46, 1 year & 7 mos. in U.S., Greensboro, planter (18-24 Aug. 1812)

Dalrymple, Thomas, age 25, 10 mos. in U.S., Savannah, merchant's clerk (27 July - 5 Aug. 1812); 5 ft. 7½ in., dark complex., dark hair, blue eyes, Augusta, passport 29 Mar. 1813 (27 Apr. 1813); entitled to indulgence (1 July 1813)

Davidson, Adam, age 21, 1 year & 4 mos. in U.S., Savannah, merchant (27 July - 5 Aug. 1812)

Davies, John, age 58, 17 years in U.S., wife & 2 children, Savannah, grocer (4-10 Aug. 1812)

Daviss, John, age 60, 5 ft. 7 in., fair complex., grey hair, blue
eyes, Effingham Co., passport 29 Mar. 1813 (27 Apr. 1813)
Drummond, Walter, age 47, 11 years in U.S., Savannah, millwright
(27 July - 5 Aug. 1812)
Dunn, Charles Chapman, age 24, 8 years & 6 mos in U.S., Augusta,
druggist; applied Jan. 1812 (4-10 Aug. 1812)
Elliott, Henry, age 25, 5 ft. 3 3/4 in, dark complex., dark hair,
black eyes, thin person, oval visage, clerk, paroled 3 Feb.
1814 to Augusta (19 Feb. 1814)
Fitzgerald, John G., age 39, 8 years in U.S., wife & 2 children,
Camden Co., planter, half pay lieutenant in British service
(25-31 Aug. 1812)
Fleming, John, age 30, 4 years in U.S., Savannah (usual residence
New York), merchant (27 July - 5 Aug. 1812)
Frazer/Fraser, James, age 19, 4 years & 6 mos. in U.S., Augusta,
merchant(4 Aug. 1812); 5 ft. 8 in., age 20, fair complex.,
brown hair, blue eyes, Augusta, passport 26 Mar. 1813 (27 Apr.
1813)
Hall, Durham T., age 22 years & 6 mos., 4 years & 6 mos. in U.S.,
Savannah, merchant (27 July - 5 Aug. 1812)
Hall, Henry T., age 21, 2 years & 10 mos. in U.S., Savannah,
merchant's clerk (27 July - 5 Aug. 1812)
Harper, James, age 20, 4 mos. in U.S., Augusta, merchant's clerk
(18-24 Aug. 1812)
Harper, William, age 18½, 2 years in U.S., Augusta, merchant's
clerk (18-24 Aug. 1812)
Hastings, Bryan, age 25, 5 years in U.S., wife and child in
Philadelphia, Augusta (usual residence Philadelphia), merchant;
applied Nov. 1811 at Mayor's Court, Philadelphia (4 Aug. 1812)
Henderson, Henry, age 21 years & 5 mos., Savannah, pilot (27 July -
5 Aug. 1812)
Hill, James, age 25, 10 years in U.S., Savannah, merchant; applied
Jan. 1812 at Superior Court, Chatham Co., Ga.; associated with
the volunteers in the Florida expedition in June 1812; 5 ft.
9½ in., fair complex., red hair, hazel eyes, Augusta, passport
24 Mar. 1813 (4 Aug. 1812, 27 Apr. 1813, 1 July 1813)
Homan, Isaac, age 46, 2 years in U.S., wife & child, Augusta,
teacher (4-10 Aug. 1812)
Horrocks, Thomas, age 45, 7 years in U.S., wife, Savannah, merchant; applied since declaration of war (27 July - 5 Aug. 1812)
Horsfall, James W., age 22, 6 years & 9 mos. in U.S., Augusta,
merchant (4 Aug. 1812)
Ker, George, age 55, 17 years in U.S., wife, sister-in-law & 8
children, Savannah, half-pay captain in British service (27
July - 5 Aug. 1812)
Key, Robert, age 22, 9 years in U.S., Savannah, pilot (27 July -
5 Aug. 1812)
Logan, John, age 19, 1 year & 8 mos. in U.S., Savannah, merchant's
clerk (27 July - 5 Aug. 1812); 5 ft. 4½ in., fair/florid complex., dark brown hair, dark blue eyes, stout person, oval vi-
sage, passport to Augusta 20 Dec. 1813 (27 Apr. 1813 & 19 Feb.
1814
Loudon, Robert, age 26, 4 years in U.S., Louisville, weaver (11-
17 Aug. 1812)
Low, John, age 21 years & 4 mos., 3 years in U.S., Savannah, apprentice to pilot (27 July - 5 Aug. 1812)
McAdam, John, age 26, 3 years & 4 mos. in U.S., Lexington, merchant (4-10 Aug. 1812)
McCay, John, age 37, 1 year & 7 mos. in U.S., wife & 2 children,
Savannah, umbrella maker (4 Aug. 1812)
McDowell, Thomas, age 19, 7 mos. in U.S., Savannah,merchant's
clerk (4 Aug. 1812)
McFarlane, James, age 36, 9 years & 6 mos. in U.S., Savannah,
bookseller (27 July - 5 Aug. 1812)

McHenry, James, age 24, 6 years in U.S., Savannah, merchant; applied 5 Dec. 1811 (27 July - 5 Aug. 1812)

McIntyre, A.C., age 20, 5 years in U.S., Savannah, printer's apprentice (27 July - 5 Aug. 1812)

McKenzie, John, age 26, 6 years & 3 mos. in U.S., Augusta, merchant; applied 18 Oct. 1811 (11-17 Aug. 1812)

McKenzie, Kenneth, age 23, 1 year in U.S., Augusta, clerk (4-10 Aug. 1812)

Mackie, John, age 21 years & 6 mos., 1 year & 6 mos. in U.S., Augusta, merchant's clerk (4-10 Aug. 1812)

Mackie, William, age 24, 7 years in U.S., Augusta, merchant (-10 Aug. 1812)

Maclea, William, age 23, 1 year in U.S., Augusta, merchant's clerk (4-10 Aug. 1812)

McLeod, Roderick, age 24, 5 years in U.S., Savannah, merchant; applied 10 Feb. 1812 (11-17 Aug. 1812); age 25, 5 ft. 11½ in., fair complex., brown hair, blue eyes, passport to Augusta 29 Mar. 1813 (27 Apr. 1813)

McNish, John, age 30, 9 years in U.S., Savannah, merchant (27 July - 5 Aug. 1812)

McNish, John, age 32, 5 ft. 11½ in., dark complex., black hair, hazel eyes, passport 24 Mar. 1813 to Augusta (27 Apr. 1813)

McQuin, John, age 23, 8 years in U.S., Augusta, merchant; applied 6 Oct. 1809 (11-17 Aug. 1812)

Maddin, John, age 18, 11 mos. in U.S., Jackson Co., tailor; reported 10 Nov. (2 Oct.-31 Dec. 1812)

Manson, Andrew, age 26, 3 years in U.S., Brunswick, merchant (27 July - 5 Aug. 1812)

Martin, John, age 24, 7 years in U.S., Augusta, merchant (4-10 Aug. 1812)

Matheson, Duncan, age 27, 5 years & 6 mos. in U.S., Augusta, merchant; applied 18 Apr. 1811 (4-10 Aug. 1812)

Matheson, Murdoch, age 22, 2 years & 6 mos. in U.S., Augusta, merchant; applied Apr. 1812 in Superior Court, Chatham Co. (4 Aug. 1812); 5 ft. 9½ in., fair complex, brown hair, hazel eyes, thin person, oval visage, paroled to Augusta 21 Dec. 1813 (27 Apr. 1813 & 19 Feb. 1814)

Middleton, John, age 41, 17 years in U.S., wife & 2 children, Savannah, house-carpenter; applied since declaration of war (4 Aug. 1812)

Miller, Arthur G., age 27, 13 years in U.S., Savannah, merchant; reported 30 Oct. (2 Oct. - 31 Dec. 1812)

Moon, Benjamin, age 23, 1 year & 9 mos. in U.S., Augusta, shopkeeper (11-17 Aug. 1812)

Moses, Philip, age 20, 6 mos. in U.S., Augusta, watchmaker (4 Aug. 1812)

Morison, John, age 32, 10 years in U.S., planter, born in Pensacola, West Florida (1 Sept. - 1 Oct. 1812)

Murray, George, age 35, 9 years & 8 mos. in U.S., Richmond Co., planter; applied 26 Apr. 1809 (18-24 Aug. 1812)

Nisbet, Alexander, age 34, 2 years & 9 mos. in U.S., Augusta, saddler (4-10 Aug. 1812)

Norman, Joseph, age 27, 5 years in U.S., Augusta, saddler; applied Apr. 1812 (4-10 Aug. 1812)

O'Connor, Peter, age 27, 5 years & 2 mos. in U.S., Augusta, merchant; applied 1810 (4 Aug. 1812)

Patterson, James, age 21, 2 years & 8 mos. in U.S., St. Simons, clerk (11-17 Aug. 1812)

Quin, Edward, age 21, 3 years in U.S., Augusta, merchant's clerk (4-10 Aug. 1812)

Ralston, George, age 46, 18 years in U.S., Savannah, merchant (27 July - 5 Aug. 1812); age 47, 5 ft. 10 in., florid complex., dark hair, hazel eyes, passport to retire to Washington 24 Mar. 1813 (27 Apr. 1813)

Rawson, William, age 21, 1 year & 8 mos. in U.S., Savannah, merchant's clerk (27 July - 5 Aug. 1812)

Reid, George, age 30, 5 years in U.S., Savannah, merchant's clerk;
applied 10 Feb. 1812 (27 July - 5 Aug. 1812); 5 ft. 5 in., fair
complex., sandy hair, blue eyes, passport 26 Mar. 1813 to Augusta (27 Apr. 1813); entitled to indulgence (1 July 1813)

Relph, George, age 24, 2 years in U.S., Savannah, merchant's
clerk (27 July - 5 Aug. 1812); 5 ft. 9 in., fair complex.,
brown hair, blue eyes, passport 29 Mar. 1813 to Augusta (27
Apr. 1813); entitled to indulgence (1 July 1813)

Ritchie, Stewart, age 42, 7 years in U.S,, wife, Camden Co.,
planter (25-31 Aug. 1812)

Sinclair, Alexander, age 25, 2 years in U.S., Savannah, merchant's
clerk (27 July - 5 Aug. 1812); 5 ft. 5 in., dark complex., brown
hair, hazel eyes, passport 25 Mar. 1813 to Indian Bluff (27 Apr.
1813); entitled to indulgence (1 July 1813)

Smith, John, age 20, 1 year & 7 mos. in U.S., Augusta, merchant's
clerk (4 Aug. 1812); age 21, 5 ft. 10 in., fair complex., brown
hair, blue eyes, stout person, oval visage, ordered to retire
to interior (27 Apr. 1813); entitled to indulgence (1 July
1813); paroled 21 Dec. 1813 to Augusta (19 Feb. 1814)

Smith, Thomas, age 26 years & 6 mos., 9 years in U.S., Camden
Co., overseer (11-17 Aug. 1812)

Smith, Thomas, age 27, 9 years in U.S., Camden Co., planter (25-
31 Aug. 1812)

Smith, William, age 21, 7 years in U.S., Augusta, merchant's
clerk; applied 16 Apr. 1812 (4-10 Aug. 1812); 5 ft. 9 in., fair
complex., brown hair, dark eyes, thin person, oval visage, paroled 20 Dec. 1813 to Augusta (19 Feb. 1814)

Smith, William, age 19, 2 years in U.S., Savannah, merchant's
clerk (27 July - 5 Aug. 1812); age 20, 5 ft. 9½ in., fair complex., dark hair, hazel eyes, ordered 26 Mar. 1813 to interior
(27 Apr. 1813)

Stewart, Mathew W., age 21, 10 years & 10 mos. in U.S., Whitmarsh
Island, planter; applied since declaration of war (4 Aug. 1812)

Truval (?), Richard, age 22, 2 years in U.S., Camden Co., mariner
(25-31 Aug. 1812)

Tully, John, age 21, 4 years & 10 mos. in U.S., Augusta, merchant's
clerk (4 Aug. 1812)

Vaughan, Francis W., age 16, 4 mos. in U.S., Milledgeville, apprentice, reported 11 Nov. (2 Oct. - 31 Dec. 1812)

Wallace, Norman, age 28, 8 years & 6 mos. in U.S., Savannah, merchant; applied 10 Jan. 1812 (27 July - 5 Aug. 1812); 5 ft.
5½ in., fair complex., dark hair, hazel eyes; ordered to Augusta 24 Mar. 1813 (27 Apr. 1813)

Wallen, Elias, age 28, 6 years in U.S., wife, Augusta, merchant;
applied 17 Apr. 1812 (4-10 Aug. 1812)

Wallen, Joseph, age 22, 3 years in U.S., Augusta, clerk; applied
15 Apr. 1812 (11- 17 Aug. 1812)

Willson, John, age 25, 3 years & 8 mos. in U.S., wife, Washington
Co., house-carpenter; applied 15 Jan. 1811 (25-31 Aug. 1812)

Winlock, William, age 26, 2 years in U.S., Savannah, seaman (27
July - 5 Aug. 1812)

Wood, John, age 61, 9 years in U.S., wife & daughter, Camden Co.,
planter (11-17 Aug. 1812)

Young, John G., age 25, 3 years & 4 mos. in U.S., wife & child,
Savannah, house-carpenter (27 July - 5 Aug. 1812)

LOUISIANA

Armstrong, Conway, age 24, in U.S. since Aug. 1806, wife & child
(natives of New York), New York, bricklayer (11-17 Aug. 1812)
Atkinson, Joseph, age 25, 6 years in U.S., New Orleans, carpenter (12-26 Oct. 1812)
Bailey, Thomas, age 41, 17 years in U.S., wife & 3 children, Feliciana, planter (12-26 Cct. 1812)
Barton, Thomas, age 35, 10 years in U.S., New Orleans, carpenter
(1 Apr. - 1 May 1813)
Bassett, Thomas, age 30, 8 years in U.S., New Orleans, teller of
the branch bank; claims citizenship (17-24 Aug. 1812); 5 ft.
6 in., fair complex., light hair, blue eyes, ordered to Opelousas (3 May 1813); returned to New Orleans contrary to the
notice of 23 Feb. 1813 (n.d.)
Binner, Alexander, discharged 1 Jan. 1813 from U.S. naval service as a British subject, has not reported (8 Feb. 1813)
Boyce, Joseph, a storekeeper near St. Francisville, has not reported (6 Jan. 1813)
Burnside, Robert, age 29, in U.S. since 28 Sept. 1803, wife &
child (both born in U.S.), New Orleans, teacher; applied 14
Jan. 1812 (11-17 Aug. 1812)
Casey, Henry, age 26, 7 years in U.S., New Orleans, grocer (1
Apr. - 1 May 1813); 5 ft. 10 in., fair complex., chestnut hair,
blue eyes, in La. 7 years, ordered to Opelousas (3 May 1813)
Casey, Thomas, age 22, 7 years in U.S., New Orleans, bricklayer
(1 Apr. - 1 May 1813)
Chauveau, Charles, age 28, 4 years in U.S., no permanent residence, no occupation; wishes to return to his native Canada
(26 Oct. - 16 Nov. 1812); 5 ft. 11 in., fair complex., dark
hair, light eyes, 4 years in La., ordered to Opelousas (3 May
1813)
Clague, Richard, age 31, in U.S. since Sept. 1803, New Orleans,
merchant; applied 20 Mar. 1811 (11-17 Aug. 1812); 5 ft. 9½ in.,
fair complex., black hair, grey eyes, in La. about 7 years, ordered to Opelousas (3 May 1813); returned to New Orleans contrary to notice of 23 Feb. 1813 (n.d.)
Clermont, Joseph D., age 38, 15 years in U.S., 2 sons, Pointe
Coupee, planter (28 Sept. - 12 Oct. 1812)
Colwell, Patrick, age 24, 5 years in U.S., Attakapas, shoemaker
(26 Oct.- 16 Nov. 1812)
Connoll, James, seaman, discharged 31 Dec. 1812 from U.S. armed
vessel as alien (6 Jan. 1813)
Connollin, Michael, age 22, 5 years in U.S., New Orleans, merchant; thinks he applied June 1807 in New York (31 Aug. - 7
Sept. 1812)
Considin, Michael, age 22, 18 mos. in La., 5 ft. 5½ in., fair
complex., dark hair, hazel eyes, ordered to Opelousas (3 May
1813)
Crosbie, Henry, age 23, 3 mos. in U.S., New Orleans, merchant;
he came to U.S. on mercantile business and intends to return
to Great Britain as soon as possible (17-24 Aug. 1812)
Davis, John, discharged 11 Jan. 1813 from U.S. naval service as
a British subject, has not reported (8 Feb. 1813)
Davis, William, planter near St. Francisville, formerly captain
in British service, has resided about 8 years in U.S., is married to a native of this city and has several children; he was
a resident of West Florida before it was taken by the U.S. (6
Jan. 1813)
Doyle, John K. (?), planter near St. Francisville, has not reported (6 Jan. 1813)
Dwyer, Andrew, age 32, 3 years in U.S., New Orleans, storekeeper
(31 Aug. - 7 Sept. 1812)

Ferguson, James, age 23, 5 years in U.S., Attakapas, grazier;
    does not recollect when he applied (26 Oct. - 16 Nov. 1812)
Ferguson, Thomas L., age 29, 7 years in U.S., Attakapas, grazier;
    does not recall when he applied (26 Oct. - 16 Nov. 1812)
Fitzgerald, Robert, age 31, 16 mos. in U.S., native of Ireland,
    New Orleans, merchant (17-24 Aug. 1812); 5 ft. 9 in., dark
    complex., black hair, grey eyes, 18 mos. in La., ordered to
    Opelousas (3 May 1813)
Fitzpatrick, John, age 27, 6 years in U.S., New Orleans, grocer
    (31 Aug. - 7 Sept. 1812); 5 ft. 10 in., fair complex., chestnut
    hair, light eyes, ordered to Opelousas (3 May 1813)
Graig, George, age 27, 5 years in U.S., wife, Attakapas, planter
    (12-26 Oct. 1812)
Graig, John, age 16, 3 years in U.S., Attakapas, student at law
    (12-26 Oct. 1812)
Graig, William, age 30, 3 years in U.S., wife, Attakapas, gar-
    dener (12-26 Oct. 1812)
Greeves(?), John G., age 25, 5 ft. 8 in., fair complex, light
    hair, blue eyes, in La. since May 1810, ordered to Natchitoches
    (3 May 1813)
Griffith, James, discharged 11 Jan. 1813 from U.S. naval service
    as British subject, has not reported (8 Feb. 1813)
Hagan, John, age 25, in U.S. since Aug. 1808, New Orleans, gro-
    cer (11-17 Aug. 1812); 5 ft. 11 in., fair complex., light hair,
    blue eyes, ordered to Opelousas (3 May 1813)
Hall, Thomas, age 30, 3 mos. in U.S., New Orleans, mariner (7-14
    Sept. 1812)
Hewitt, Robert, age 24, 10 years in U.S., New Orleans, house-
    joiner (1 Apr. - 1 May 1813)
Hood, George, age 21, 3 years in U.S., New Orleans, merchant
    (1 Jan. - 1 Apr. 1813)
Hopkins, James, age 27, 5 years in U.S., wife, New Orleans, tai-
    lor (17-24 Aug. 1812)
Hudson, John H., age 35, 5 ft. 11 in., fair complex., light hair,
    blue eyes, in La. since 1804, ordered to Attakapas (3 May 1813);
    returned to New Orleans contrary to notice of 23 Feb. 1813 (n..d.)
Humphreys, John, age 40, 11 years in U.S., 1 child, New Orleans,
    mariner, discharged from U.S. Navy as an alien (16 Nov. 1812 -
    4 Jan. 1813)
Jackson, Humphrey, age 28, 6 years in U.S., Attakapas, planter;
    applied 8 Oct. 1812 Superior Court La. (16 Nov. 1812 - 4 Jan.
    1813)
Johnston, William, age 16, 3 years in U.S., New Orleans, ship
    carpenter, discharged from U.S. navy as an alien (16 Nov. 1812 -
    4 Jan. 1813)
Jones, William, age 31, in U.S. since 9 July 1803, New Orleans,
    baker; his father, residing in Baltimore, is a naturalized
    citizen (11-17 Aug. 1812)
Jones, William, seaman, discharged 31 Dec. 1812 from U.S. armed
    vessel as an alien (6 Jan. 1813)
Kary, William V., planter, residing near Pinkneyville, has not
    reported (6 Jan. 1813)
Kennedy, Kenneth, age 21, in U.S. since Jan. 1812, New Orleans,
    merchant's clerk (11-17 Aug. 1812); age 22, 5 ft. 6 in., fair
    complex., light hair, blue eyes, in La. since Jan. 1812, or-
    dered to Opelousas (3 May 1813)
Kerr, Christopher, age 22, in U.S. since Mar. 1805, New Orleans,
    merchant's clerk (11-17 Aug. 1812); 5 ft. 8 in., light complex.,
    light hair, grey eyes, ordered to Opelousas (3 May 1813)
Kingston, Edward, age 25, 2 years & 6 mos. in U.S., New Orleans,
    merchant; applied Sept. 1810 (31 Aug. - 7 Sept. 1812)
Law, John, age 22, 10 years in U.S., New Orleans, carpenter (1
    Apr. - 1 May 1813)
Lawson, William McFarland, age 28, 2 years in U.S., New Orleans,
    carpenter (1 Jan. - 1 Apr. 1813)

Layton, Robert, age 27, 6 years in U.S., wife & child, New Or-
    leans, ship chandler; his family are natives of U.S. (31 Aug. -
    7 Sept. 1812)
Lee, John, seaman, discharged 31 Dec. 1812 as an alien from a
    U.S. armed vessel (6 Jan. 1813)
Littlejohn, John, age 22, 5 ft. 4 in., fair complex., light hair,
    blue eyes, in La. since Jan. 1810, ordered to Opelousas (3
    May 1813); returned to New Orleans contrary to notice of 23
    Feb. 1813 (n.d.)
Lowman, Cornelius, age 33, 14 years in U.S., Baton Rouge (12-26
    Oct. 1812)
Lyran (?), Daniel, age 45, 12 years in U.S., New Orleans, hatter
    (1 Apr. - 1 May 1813)
McCann, Thomas, age 45, 18 years in U.S., wife & 5 children, New
    Orleans, carpenter (1 Apr. - 1 May 1813)
McCarty, Michael, age 30, 14 years in U.S., Feliciana, surveyor
    (28 Sept. - 12 Oct. 1812)
McCauley, James, age 46, 20 years in U.S., St. Francisville,
    tailor (28 Sept. - 12 Oct. 1812)
McConley, James, age 39, 3 years in U.S., New Orleans, carpenter
    (1 Apr. - 1 May 1813)
McConnoughy, Thomas, seaman, discharged 31 Dec. 1812 from U.S.
    armed vessel as enemy alien (6 Jan. 1813)
McCue, Owen, age 34, 9 years in U.S., New Orleans, seaman (14-
    28 Sept. 1812)
McCusker, Terry, age 22, 7 mos. in U.S., New Orleans, clerk (7-
    14 Sept. 1812); age 23, 5 ft. 9 in., fair complex., light hair,
    blue eyes, in La. since Feb. 1812, ordered to Natchitoches (3
    May 1813)
McDonough, Thomas, age 22, 6 years in U.S., New Orleans, marine
    in service of U.S. (7-14 Sept. 1812)
McDowell, Hugh, age 50, 30 years in U.S., wife & son, Feliciana,
    weaver (12-26 Oct. 1812)
McGowan, Robert, age 25, 5 years in U.S., New Orleans, black-
    smith (31 Aug. - 7 Sept. 1812)
McMaster, Samuel, age 26, in U.S. since Dec. 1807, wife (native
    of New Orleans), New Orleans, merchant (11-17 Aug. 1812); 5 ft.
    10 in., fair complex., dark hair, grey eyes, ordered to Ope-
    lousas (3 May 1813); returned to New Orleans contrary to the
    notice of 23 Feb. 1813 (n.d.)
McQuilley, Bryan, age 48, 21 years in U.S., wife & 4 children,
    Feliciana, planter (14-28 Sept. 1812)
M(?)ark, Samuel, age 34, 9 years in U.S., New Orleans, wire wor-
    ker (1 Apr. - 1 May 1813)
Marole (?), Hypolite, age 38, 9 years in U.S., St. Francisville,
    weaver (31 Aug. - 7 Sept. 1812)
Mather, James, age 65, in U.S. since Jan. 1808, New Orleans, a
    planter; applied 19 Oct. 1808 Supreme Court of Eastern District
    of Pa. (16 Nov. 1812 - 4 Jan. 1813)
Miller, William, discharged 11 Jan. 1813 from U.S. naval service
    as British subject, has not reported (8 Feb. 1813)
Milne, Andrew, age 23, in U.S. since May 1806, New Orleans, mer-
    chant (11-17 Aug. 1812); returned to New Orleans contrary to
    notice of 23 Feb. 1813 (n.d.)
Muggat (or Muggah?), John, age 30, 8 years in La., 5 ft. 9 in.,
    fair complex., light hair, grey eyes, ordered to Opelousas
    (3 May 1813); returned to New Orleans contrary to notice of 23
    Feb. 1813 (n.d.)
Murrills, Charles W., age 24, 12 years in U.S., Baton Rouge, a
    soldier in the garrison (26 Oct. - 16 Nov. 1812)
Nicholas, Daniel R., age 23, 11 years in U.S., St. Francisville,
    tailor (28 Sept. - 12 Oct. 1812)
Norris, Patrick, age 25, 5 years in La., 5 ft. 7 in., fair com-
    plex., light hair, blue eyes; ordered to Opelousas(3 May 1813);
    returned to New Orleans contrary to notice of 23 Feb. 1813 (n.d.)

Nugent, H.P., age 40, 19 years in U.S., wife, New Orleans, teacher (14-28 Sept. 1812)

O'Brien, Dennis, age 25, 15 years in U.S., New Orleans, carpenter (1 Apr. - 1 May 1813)

Parker, Henry R., discharged 11 Jan. 1813 from U.S. naval service as a British subject, has not reported (8 Feb. 1813)

Passaw, George D., age 39, 11 years in U.S., Pointe Coupee, planter; applied in Pennsylvania (31 Aug. - 7 Sept. 1812)

Patterson, Charles, age 33, 12 years in U.S., New Orleans, ship
chandler (31 Aug. - 7 Sept. 1812); 5 ft. 8 in., light complex.,
light hair, blue eyes, 5 years in La., ordered to Opelousas
(3 May 1813); returned to New Orleans contrary to notice of
23 Feb. 1813 (n.d.)

Pearse, Edward, age 45, 6 years in U.S., Parish of Plaquemines,
planter; applied 1808 District Court of Columbia (16 Nov. 1812 -
4 Jan. 1813)

Perry, Robert, for several years resident in U.S., living near
St. Francisville, formerly a lieutenant in the British navy,
on half pay until early part of 1810, was resident of West
Florida before it was taken by U.S. (6 Jan. 1813)

Phelan, William, age 29, 2 years in U.S., New Orleans, soap boiler (1 Apr. - 1 May 1813)

Porter, Alexander, Jr., age 25, in U.S. since July 1805, Co. of
Attakapas, attorney-at-law; applied 7 Dec. 1812 District Court,
District of La. (16 Nov. 1812 - 4 Jan. 1813)

Porter, James, age 20, 8 mos. in U.S., Attakapas, student at law
(12-26 Oct. 1812)

Power, James, age 24, 3 years in U.S., New Orleans, carpenter
(14-28 Sept. 1812)

Ramsay, James, age 33, in U.S. since 13 Feb. 1802, New Orleans,
merchant; he resided 6 years in Charleston and since then in
New Orleans (11-17 Aug. 1812)

Reader, Samuel Lee, age 23, 9 years in U.S., New Orleans, painter
(1 Apr. - 1 May 1813)

Reilly, James F, age 25, 5 years in U.S., New Orleans, soldier
(1 Jan. - 1 Apr. 1813)

Richardson, William, age 37, 8 years in U.S., Attakapas, planter
(26 Oct. - 16 Nov. 1812)

Roberts, John, discharged 11 Jan. 1813 from U.S. naval service
as a British subject, has not reported (8 Feb. 1813)

Robinson, John B., age 29, in U.S. since July 1809, New Orleans,
teacher (11-17 Aug. 1812)

Rogers, Samuel, age 33, 11 years in U.S., St. Francisville, currier (31 Aug. - 7 Sept. 1812)

Scanlan, James, age 31, in U.S. since Aug. 1810, New Orleans,
sugar baker (11-17 Aug. 1812)

Skimmin (or Shimmin?), John, age 26, 4 years in U.S., New Orleans,
carpenter (1 Apr. - 1 May 1813)

Smith, John, seaman, discharged 31 Dec. 1812 from U.S. armed
vessel as alien (6 Jan. 1813)

Sterling, Alexander, near St. Francisville, planter, has not reported (6 Jan. 1813)

Sterling, John, near St. Francisville, planter, has not reported
(6 Jan. 1813)

Stewart, Christopher L., age 32, 8 years in U.S., wife, New Orleans, planter (31 Aug. - 7 Sept. 1812)

Thompson, John, discharged 11 Jan. 1813 from U.S. naval service
as British subject, has not reported (8 Feb. 1813)

Toole, Patrick, age 26, 5 years in U.S., New Orleans, tinman (1
Apr. - 1 May 1813)

Wheelen, Conrad, discharged 11 Jan. 1813 from U.S. naval service
as British subject, has not reported (8 Feb. 1813)

Wheeler, Isaac, age 23, in U.S. since 2 June 1805, New Orleans,
merchant; applied 21 June 1805 in Pa. (11-17 Aug. 1812)

Wilkinson, John, age 21, 3 years in U.S., Baton Rouge in the
   garrison, a soldier (26 Oct. - 16 Nov. 1812)
Williams, David C., age 28, in U.S. since 6 Oct. 1804, wife and
   child (both born in U.S.), New Orleans, ship broker (11-17 Aug.
   1812)
Williams, William B., discharged 11 Jan. 1813 from U.S. naval
   service as British subject, has not reported (8 Feb. 1813)
Wilson, James, discharged 31 Dec. 1812 from U.S. armed vessel
   as enemy alien, has not reported (6 Jan. 1813)
Witly, Christopher, age 42, 16 years in U.S., Parish of St. Helena, planter (28 Sept. - 12 Oct. 1812)

OHIO

Abbercrombie, Hugh, 21 years in U.S., wife & 8 children, Butler
 Co., farmer, native of Ireland (18 Sept. - 16 Oct. 1812)
Adams, James, 18 mos. in U.S., wife & child, Jefferson Co.,
 farmer, native of Ireland (18 Sept. - 16 Oct. 1812)
Allan, William, age 41, 11 years in U.S., wife & 2 children,
 Guernsey Co., farmer, native of England (1-18 Sept. 1812)
Allen, Austin, age 29, 5 years in U.S., Stark Co., farmer, na-
 tive of Ireland (19 Feb. - 11 May 1813)
Ashburn, Thomas, age 43, 7 years in U.S., wife & 5 children,
 Hamilton Co., farmer, native of England; applied Apr. 1812
 Court of Common Pleas, Hamilton Co. (18 Sept. - 16 Oct. 1812)
Bailhache, John, age 25, 2 years in U.S., Chillicothe, printer,
 native of England (1-18 Sept. 1812)
Baxter, James, age 56, 22 years in U.S., wife & 8 children, Ha-
 milton Co., farmer, native of Ireland (18 Sept. - 16 Oct. 1812)
Bechard, James, age 35, 5 years in U.S., wife & 5 children,
 Guernsey Co., cordwinder (18 Dec. 1812 - 19 Feb. 1813)
Bell, George, age 23, 2 years in U.S., Chillicothe, nailor, a
 native of Ireland (30 July - 5 Aug. 1812)
Bibb, Edward, age 45, 17 years in U.S., wife & 3 children, But-
 ler Co., farmer, native of North Wales (18 Sept. - 16 Oct. 1812)
Biggart, John, age 44, 14 years in U.S., wife & 5 children,
 Franklin, farmer, native of Ireland (1-18 Sept. 1812)
Birch, Richard, age 65, 6 mos. in U.S., wife, Butler Co., far-
 mer, native of England (16 Oct. - 18 Dec. 1812)
Birch, Richard, Jr., age 39, 6 mos. in U.S., wife & 6 children,
 Butler Co., farmer, native of England (16 Oct. - 18 Dec. 1812)
Blacker, Edward, age 26, 7 years in U.S., Butler Co., weaver;
 applied Sept. 1810 in Court of Brunswick, N.J. (16 Oct. - 18
 Dec. 1812)
Booth, James M., 8 years in U.S., wife, Marietta, cabinetmaker,
 native of England; applied 13 Aug. 1811 (5-19 Aug. 1812)
Bowman, Isaac, age 37, 9 years in U.S., wife & 2 children, Stark
 Co., cabinetmaker; applied 10 Dec. 1811 in Jefferson Co. (18
 Dec. 1812 - 19 Feb. 1813)
Breadon, Robert, age 40, 20 years in U.S., wife & 8 children,
 Ross Co., farmer, native of Ireland (1-18 Sept. 1812)
Brown, Robert, 9 years in U.S., wife & 2 children, Hamilton Co.,
 weaver, native of Ireland (18 Sept. - 16 Oct. 1812)
Calder, Alexander, age 56, 11 years in U.S., wife & 5 children,
 Columbiana Co., farmer, native of Scotland (18 Dec. 1812 - 19
 Feb. 1813)
Campbell, John, age 38, 15 years in U.S., wife & 5 children,
 Hamilton Co., farmer, native of Ireland; applied 3 Aug. 1812
 Court of Common Pleas, Hamilton Co. (18 Sept. - 16 Oct. 1812)
Carsons, John, age 27, 3 years in U.S., wife & child, Cincinnati,
 bookseller, native of Scotland (18 Sept. - 16 Oct. 1812)
Childs, James, age 37, 12 years in U.S., wife & 5 children,
 Trumbull Co., house-joiner, native of England; applied Nov.
 1809 (16 Oct. - 18 Dec. 1812)
Clark, John, age 47, 20 years in U.S., wife & 7 children, Ha-
 milton Co., farmer, native of Ireland (18 Sept. - 16 Oct. 1812)
Clark, William, age 45, 3 years in U.S., wife & 7 children, Ma-
 rietta, shoemaker, native of England (1-18 Sept. 1812)
Clingan, John, 20 years in U.S., 5 children, Miami Co., farmer,
 native of Ireland (18 Sept. - 16 Oct. 1812)
Corbet, Peter, age 29, 6 years in U.S., Guernsey Co., farmer
 (18 Dec. 1812 - 19 Feb. 1813)
Craigmiles, Alexander, age 35, 7 years in U.S., wife & 3 children, Hamilton Co., distiller, native of Ireland (16 Oct. - 18
 Dec. 1812)

Danby, Thomas, 5 years in U.S., wife, Cincinnati, clerk, native
of Ireland; applied spring of 1810 in Court of Common Pleas of
Clermont Co. (18 Sept. - 16 Oct. 1812)

Davis, Daniel E., age 48, 11 years in U.S., 4 children, Chillicothe, shoemaker, native of England (30 July - 5 Aug. 1812)

Davis, David, age 25, 11 years in U.S., Delaware Co., farmer
(18 Dec. 1812-19 Feb. 1813)

Davis, John D., age 44, 12 years in U.S., wife & 2 children, Delaware Co., farmer (18 Dec. 1812 - 19 Feb. 1813)

Davis, Richard, age 53, 11 years in U.S., wife & 4 children, Delaware Co., weaver (18 Dec. 1812 - 19 Feb. 1813)

Dun, Robert, age 28, 3 mos. in U.S., Chillicothe, merchant, native of Scotland (16 Oct. - 18 Dec. 1812)

Dupuis, Francis, 14 years in U.S., Miami Co., labourer, native
of Lower Canada; does not wish to be naturalized (18 Sept. -
16 Oct. 1812)

Edwards, Edward Henry, age 23, 2 years in U.S., Chillicothe, a
clerk (30 July - 5 Aug. 1812)

Ewbanks, John, age 61, 6 years in U.S., wife & 10 children, Indiana Territory, native of England (18 Sept. - 16 Oct. 1812)

Ferguson, Arthur, age 51, 3 years in U.S., wife & 8 children,
Hamilton Co., brewer, native of Scotland; applied Apr. 1812
Court of Common Pleas, Hamilton Co. (18 Sept. - 16 Oct. 1812)

Francis, David, age 41, 16 years in U.S., wife & 3 children, Butler Co., farmer, native of North Wales (18 Sept. - 16 Oct. 1812)

Frazer, Duncan, age 51, 8 years in U.S., wife & 3 children, Columbiana Co., farmer, native of Scotland (18 Dec. 1812 - 19 Feb.
1813)

Fulton, John S., age 24, 1 year in U.S., Chillicothe, shoemaker,
native of Nova Scotia (30 July - 5 Aug. 1812)

Gilland, Robert, age 21, 2 mos. in U.S., Chillicothe, clerk, native of Ireland (1-18 Sept. 1812)

Goff, William Commins, age 29, 12 years in U.S., wife & 3 children, Clermont Co., stocking weaver, native of Ireland (18 Sept.-
16 Oct. 1812)

Gray, Alexander, 4 years in U.S., Chillicothe, clerk, native of
Ireland; applied Apr. 1811 in Court of Common Pleas, Ross Co.
(8 Sept. - 16 Oct. 1812)

Gray, Francis E., age 22, 9 years in U.S., Hamilton Co., paper
maker, native of Ireland (1-18 Sept. 1812)

Greenham, Joseph, age 24, 10 years in U.S., Hamilton Co., distiller, native of England (18 Sept. - 16 Oct. 1812)

Grigg, John, age 41, 9 years in U.S., 1 child, Clinton Co., shoemaker, native of Ireland (18 Sept. - 16 Oct. 1812)

Grimes, John, age 38, 9 years in U.S., wife & 3 children, Champaign Co., farmer, native of North Britain; applied Jan. 1811
(1-18 Sept. 1812)

Gwillym, Morgan, age 43, 17 years in U.S., wife & 2 children,
Butler Co., farmer, native of Wales (16 Oct. - 18 Dec, 1812)

Gwilym, William, 16 years in U.S., wife & 4 children, Butler Co.,
farmer, native of South Wales (18 Sept. - 16 Oct. 1812)

Hanagan, Hugh, age 35, 15 years in U.S., Pickaway Co., schoolmaster, native of Ireland (19 Feb. - 11 May 1813)

Hicks, William, 1 year in U.S., wife & 4 children, Champaign Co.,
farmer, native of Ireland (18 Sept. - 16 Oct. 1812)

Highway, Samuel, age 25, 8 years in U.S., wife & child, Green
Co., farmer, native of England (18 Sept. - 16 Oct. 1812)

Holmes, Robert, age 28, 10 years in U.S., Chillicothe, clerk, a
native of Ireland; applied 10 Jan. 1812 (1-18 Sept. 1812)

Horrocks, Edward, age 35, 18 mos. in U.S., 4 children, Cincinnati,
baker, native of Ireland (18 Sept. - 16 Oct. 1812)

Hoskins, Richard, age 50, 28 years in U.S., wife & 7 children,
Delaware Co., farmer (16 Oct. - 18 Dec. 1812)

Hurdus, Adam, age 53, 8 years in U.S., wife & 5 children, Cincinnati, cotton manufacturer, native of England (18 Sept. -16 Oct.1812

Hurdus, James, age 23, 7 years in U.S., Cincinnati, upholsterer, native of England (18 Sept. - 16 Oct. 1812)

Ireson, William, age 35, 11 years in U.S., wife & 2 children, Columbiana Co., farmer, native of Scotland (18 Dec. 1812- 19 Feb. 1813)

Irwin, James, age 30, 9 years in U.S., Cirileville, Pickaway Co., merchant, native of Ireland; applied 10 Jan. 1812 U.S. Circuit Court, Chillicothe (30 July - 5 Aug. 1812)

Irwin, William, age 34, 9 years in U.S., wife & 4 children, Ross Co., farmer, native of Ireland (5-19 Aug. 1812)

Jenkins, William, age 35, 5 years in U.S., Washington Co., mill-wright, native of Scotland (18 Dec. - 16 Oct. 1812)

Johnston, James, age 36, 5 years in U.S,, wife & 4 children, Co-lumbiana Co., farmer, native of Scotland (18 Dec. 1812 - 19 Feb. 1813)

Johnston, Michael, 10 years in U.S., Jefferson Co., clock- and watchmaker, native of Ireland (18 Sept. - 16 Oct. 1812)

Johnston, Robert H., age 30, 7 years in U.S., wife & 2 children, Ross Co., farmer, native of Nova Scotia (1-18 Sept. 1812)

Jones, Evan, age 49, 11 years in U.S., 2 children, Butler Co., blacksmith, native of South Wales (18 Sept. - 16 Oct. 1812)

Jones, John, age 62, 19 years in U.S., wife & 3 children, Hamil-ton Co., gardener, native of England (18 Sept. - 16 Oct. 1812)

Jones, Maurice, 11 years in U.S., wife & 4 children, Butler Co., farmer, native of Wales (16 Oct. - 18 Dec. 1812)

Landree, Simon, 16 years in U.S., wife & 7 children, Hamilton Co., cooper, native of England (18 Sept. - 16 Oct. 1812)

Liddill, George, age 38, 6 years in U.S., wife & 3 children, Trumbull Co., farmer, native of Ireland (18 Sept. - 16 Oct. 1812)

Lightfoot, Christopher, age 31, 9 years in U.S., wife & 4 child-ren, Green Co., farmer, native of England (16 Oct. - 18 Dec. 1812)

Linfester, John, age 21, 5 years in U.S., Guernsey Co., cooper (18 Dec. 1812 - 19 Feb. 1813)

Long, Robert, age 35, 12 years in U.S., Chillicothe, soap boiler, native of Ireland (30 July - 5 Aug. 1812)

Long, Wm., Sr., age 68, 14 years in U.S., wife & 10 children, Ross Co., farmer, native of America, has resided in Nova Sco-tia (1-18 Sept. 1812)

Lowry, James, age 55, 15 years in U.S., wife & 4 children, Ross Co., schoolmaster, native of Ireland (1-18 Sept. 1812)

Lowry, Robert, age 63, 8 years in U.S., 3 children, Trumbull Co., farmer, native of Ireland (16 Oct. - 18 Dec. 1812)

McCann, Samuel, 12 years in U.S., wife & 3 children, Muskingum Co. (19 Feb. - 11 May 1813)

McCullough, Hugh, 10 years in U.S., wife & 4 children, Warren Co., weaver, native of Ireland (16 Oct. - 18 Dec. 1812)

McDoned, John, age 56, 8 years in U.S., wife & 10 children, Co-lumbiana Co., farmer, native of Scotland (18 Dec. 1812 - 19 Feb. 1813)

McIntosh, Alexander, age 63, 7 years in U.S., 4 children, Colum-biana Co., farmer, native of Scotland (18 Dec. 1812 - 19 Feb. 1813)

McIntosh, William, age 37, 10 years in U.S., wife & 2 children, Columbiana Co., farmer, native of Scotland (18 Dec. 1812 - 19 Feb. 1813)

McLean, Allan, age 45, 6 years in U.S., wife & child, Columbiana Co., farmer, native of Scotland (18 Dec. 1812 - 19 Feb. 1813)

McMakin, James, age 36, 7 years in U.S., wife & 4 children, Cin-cinnati, weaver, native of Ireland; applied Aug. 1812 Court of Common Pleas, Hamilton Co. (18 Sept. - 16 Oct. 1812)

McPhail, John, age 45, 10 years in U.S., Columbiana Co., farmer, native of Scotland (18 Dec. 1812 - 19 Feb. 1813)

Marshal, Abraham, age 39, 11 years in U.S., Champaign Co., labourer, native of England; will not become citizen; wishes
time to arrange his business and then will go to Canada; his
property in U.S. is worth not more than $100 (1-18 Sept. 1812)

Marshall, George, 15 mos. in U.S., Jefferson Co., dyer, native
of Ireland (18 Sept. - 16 Oct. 1812)

Marshall, Joseph, 15 mos. in U.S., wife & child, Jefferson Co.,
weaver, native of Ireland (18 Sept. - 16 Oct. 1812)

Marshall, William, 15 mos. in U.S., wife & 3 children, Jefferson
Co., farmer, native of Ireland (18 Sept. - 16 Oct. 1812)

Martin, Henry, Sr., age 49, 3 years in U.S., wife & child, Hamilton Co., farmer, native of England (1-18 Sept. 1812)

Masson, Lewis, 14 years in U.S., Miami Co., labourer, native of
Lower Canada; does not wish to be naturalized (18 Sept. - 16
Oct. 1812)

Mayrand, Henry Guillaume, 12 years in U.S., Miami Co., merchant,
native of Canada (18 Sept. - 16 Oct. 1812)

Miller, James, age 21, 2 years in U.S., Chillicothe, clerk; applied Apr. 1810 in Co. of Baltimore (1-18 Sept. 1812)

Miller, Joseph, age 37, 11 years in U.S., wife & 2 children,
Chillicothe, nailor, native of Ireland (30 July - 5 Aug. 1812)

Miller, William, age 17, 4 mos. in U.S., Chillicothe, nailor,
native of Ireland (1-18 Sept. 1812)

Mitchell, William, age 29, 16 years in U.S., New Philadelphia,
Methodist preacher, native of Ireland (1-18 Sept. 1812)

Morrison, Moses, age 45, 21 years in U.S., wife, Hamilton Co.,
farmer, native of Ireland (18 Sept. - 16 Oct. 1812)

Napier, George, age 67, 5 years in U.S., wife & 4 children,
Washington Co., farmer, native of Scotland (18 Sept. - 16 Oct.
1812)

Nevens, William, age 40, 24 years in U.S., wife & 6 children,
Ross Co., wheelwright, native of Ireland (5-19 Aug. 1812)

Nicholas, James, 15 years in U.S., wife & 4 children, Butler Co,,
blacksmith, native of South Wales (18 Sept. - 16 Oct. 1812)

Nicks, James, age 28, 10 years in U.S., wife & 2 children, Cincinnati, carpenter, native of Ireland (16 Oct. - 18 Dec. 1812)

Nixon, Robert, age 27, 14 years in U.S., wife & 2 children, Butler Co., farmer, native of Ireland (18 Sept. - 16 Oct. 1812)

Noble, Alexander, age 51, 6 years in U.S., wife & 6 children,
Columbiana Co., farmer, native of Scotland (18 Dec. 1812 - 19
Feb. 1813)

O'Brien, Patrick, age 22, 3 years in U.S., Hamilton Co., weaver,
native of Ireland (18 Sept. - 16 Oct. 1812)

Ogier, Thomas, age 32, 2 years in U.S., wife, Guernsey Co., farmer, native of England (18 Dec. 1812 - 19 Feb. 1813)

Ogier, William, age 43, 5 years in U.S., wife & 4 children,
Guernsey Co., farmer (18 Dec. 1812 - 19 Feb. 1813)

Orr, Thomas, age 25, 6 years in U.S., wife, Chillicothe, copper
and tin plate worker, native of Ireland; applied 2 Jan. 1809
Hustings Court in Petersburg, Va. (30 July - 5 Aug. 1812)

Patterson, Edward, age 15, 18 mos. in U.S., Licking Co., farmer,
native of Ireland (19 Feb. - 11 May 1813)

Patterson, Robert, age 23, 18 mos. in U.S., Licking Co., farmer,
native of Ireland (19 Feb. - 11 May 1813)

Penny, David, age 25, 6 years in U.S., wife & 4 children, Delaware Co., farmer (18 Dec. 1812 - 19 Feb. 1813)

Perry, Robert, age 26, 10 years in U.S., wife & child, Delaware
Co., farmer (18 Dec. 1812 - 19 Feb. 1813)

Philips, John, age 26, 6 years in U.S., wife & 4 children, Delaware Co., farmer (18 Dec. 1812 - 19 Feb. 1813)

Pollock, William, age 35, 2 years in U.S., wife & 4 children,
Chillicothe, shoemaker, native of Nova Scotia (30 July - 5 Aug.
1812)

Port, James, 17 years in U.S., wife & 5 (sic!) children, Butler
Co., farmer, native of Ireland (16 Oct. - 18 Dec. 1812)

Port, John, 17 years in U.S., Butler Co., farmer, native of Ireland (16 Oct. - 18 Dec. 1812)

Price, James, age 39, 5 years in U.S., wife & 5 children, Cincinnati, baker, native of Wales (16 Oct. - 18 Dec. 1812)

Price, Rees, age 42, 4 years in U.S., wife & 4 children, Butler Co., tavern-keeper, native of England (18 Sept. - 16 Oct. 1812)

Ritchie, John, age 37, 18 years in U.S., 7 in family, Montgomery Co., farmer (16 Oct. - 18 Dec. 1812)

Robertson, John, 8 years in U.S., wife & 3 children, Ross Co., weaver, native of North Britain (19 Feb. - 11 May 1813)

Robins, William, age 46, 2 years in U.S., Chillicothe, malster and brewer, native of Ireland; applied Mar. 1811 Co. Court, Sunbury, Pa. (30 July - 5 Aug. 1812)

Rose, Charles, age 26, 5 years in U.S., Stark Co., shoemaker, native of Island of Guernsey (19 Feb. - 11 May 1813)

Ross, William, age 27, 9 years in U.S., Chillicothe, clerk, a native of Britain (5 Aug. - 19 Aug. 1812)

Sarchet, John, age 28, 5 years in U.S., wife & 4 children, Guernsey Co., blacksmith (18 Dec. 1812 - 19 Feb. 1813)

Sarchet, Peter, age 53, 2 years in U.S., wife & 4 children, Hamilton Co., native of England (18 Sept. - 16 Oct. 1812)

Skeed, Thomas, age 37, 1 year in U.S., wife & 6 children, Ross Co., farmer, native of Nova Scotia (30 July - 5 Aug. 1812)

Smith, Finlay, age 57, 7 years in U.S., wife & 4 children, Columbiana Co., farmer, native of Scotland (18 Dec. 1812 - 19 Feb. 1813)

Smith, Stewart, age 50, 16 years in U.S., wife & 5 children, Delaware Co., farmer (18 Dec. 1812 - 19 Feb. 1813)

Stephens, Blackall, age 28, 6 years in U.S., wife & 2 children, Cincinnati, saddler, native of Ireland (18 Sept. - 16 Oct. 1812)

Tagart, Samuel, age 24, 6 years in U.S., Chillicothe, merchant, native of Ireland; applied 10 Jan, 1812 in U.S. Circuit Court, Ohio District, at Chillicothe (30 July - 5 Aug. 1812)

Taner, Charles, age 52, 25 years in U.S., wife & 3 children, Cincinnati, cooper, native of Ireland (16 Oct. - 18 Dec. 1812)

Teas, Samuel, age 44, 4 years in U.S., wife & 4 children, Chillicothe, house-carpenter, native of Nova Scotia (30 July - 5 Oct. 1812)

Tobias, John, age 40, 16 years in U.S., 5 children, Hamilton Co., farmer, native of North Wales (18 Sept. - 16 Oct. 1812)

Vaughan, John, 11 years in U.S., wife & 3 children, Cincinnati, farmer, native of Wales (16 Oct. - 18 Dec. 1812)

Walker, David, age 45, 21 years in U.S., wife & 5 children, Hamilton Co., native of Ireland (18 Sept. - 16 Oct. 1812)

Ward, John, age 49, 12 years in U.S., wife & 9 children, Hamilton Co., farmer, native of England (18 Sept. - 16 Oct. 1812)

Warnock, William, age 47, 20 years in U.S., wife & 10 children, Ross Co., farmer, native of Ireland (5-19 Aug. 1812)

Wells, Robert, age 22, 11 years in U.S., Marietta, cabinetmaker, native of Ireland; applied 18 Aug. 1811 Court of Common Pleas, Washington Co. (5-19 Aug. 1812)

White, Charles, age 17, 6 mos. in U.S., Belmont Co., clerk, native of Scotland (19 Feb. - 11 May 1813)

Whittaker, James, age 30, 7 years in U.S., Cincinnati, lime burner, native of England (16 Oct. - 18 Dec. 1812)

Wilson, Brown, 15 years in U.S., wife & 3 children, Butler Co., farmer; applied 1807 Court of Common Pleas (18 Sept. - 16 Oct. 1812)

Wilson, John, 15 years in U.S., 5 children, Butler Co., farmer, native of England; applied 1807 Court of Common Pleas (18 Sept. - 16 Oct. 1812)

Witchell, John, age 21, 10 years in U.S., Belmont Co., farmer, native of Ireland (18 Sept. - 16 Oct. 1812)

Wooley, George, age 53, 5 years in U.S., 10 children, Hamilton Co., weaver, native of England (16 Oct. - 18 Dec. 1812)

Worthington, Philip, age 6C, 5 years in U.S., wife & 3 children, Marietta, tin plate maker, native of England; applied 3 Aug. 1812 (5-19 Aug. 1812)

Wrigley, John, 17 years in U.S., wife & 2 children, Cincinnati, weaver, native of England (18 Sept. - 16 Oct. 1812)

Youart, James, age 41, 17 years in U.S., wife & 7 children, Miami Co., carpenter, native of Ireland (16 Oct. - 18 Dec. 1812)

Youart, Samuel, age 33, 14 years in U.S., wife & child, Cincinnati, carpenter, native of Ireland (16 Oct. - 18 Dec. 1812)

KENTUCKY

Beaty, Robert, age 49, 20 years in U.S., 2 in family, Lexington, weaver (9 Sept. 1812)

Bell, William, age 22, 22 mos. in U.S., Shelbyville, storekeeper (9 Sept. 1812)

Betts, James, age 33, 8 years in U.S., Georgetown, farmer (9 Sept. 1812)

Bishop, Robert H., age 36, 10 years in U.S., 6 in family, Lexington, preacher; applied Apr. 1811 (9 Sept. 1812)

Booth, William, age 30, 3 years in U.S., Lexington, merchant; applied May 1810 (9 Sept. 1812)

Bridges, John, age 28, 11 years in U.S., 5 in family, Lexington, tallow chandler (9 Sept. 1812)

Dewhurst, George, age 32, 11 years in U.S., 6 in family, Lexington, cabinetmaker (9 Sept. 1812)

Essex, William, age 49, 16 years in U.S., 5 in family, Lexington, bookbinder (9 Sept. 1812)

Essex, William, age 20, 16 years in U.S., Lexington, apprentice to bookbindery (9 Sept. 1812)

Garner, Thomas, age 45, 18 mos. in U.S., 6 in family, Lexington, merchant (9 Sept. 1812)

Hanley, Thomas, age 29, 2 years in U.S., Lexington, tanner; applied Aug. 1811 (9 Sept. 1812)

Harris, John, age 27, 6 years in U.S., Fayette Co., speculator; applied 9 Sept. 1812)

Levett, Augustus P., age 5C, 4 years in U.S., Lexington, manufacturer of oil floor cloth (9 Sept. 1812)

Lochlin, James, age 33, 12 years in U.S., 7 in family, Lexington, tailor (9 Sept. 1812)

Long, William, age 28, 9 years in U.S., Lexington, manufacturer of hemp (9 Sept. 1812)

Manly, Jos. D., age 46, 28 mos. in U.S., 5 in family, Lexington, teacher in grammar school; applied 3 Dec. 1811 (9 Sept. 1812)

Millar, John M., age 32, 8 years & 8 mos. in U.S., Lexington, house-carpenter; applied 14 Mar. 1810 (9 Sept. 1812)

Milligan, William, age 59, 29 years in U.S., 6 in family, Lexington, wheelwright (9 Sept. 1812)

Monks, John, age 26, 10 years in U.S., Lexington, weaver (9 Sept. 1812)

Pollock, Gavin, age 26, 6 years in U.S., Lexington, weaver (9 Sept. 1812)

Price, John, age 33, 7 years in U.S., 2 in family, Lexington, cotton spinner (9 Sept. 1812)

Sheriff, Anthony, age 43, 13 mos. in U.S., 4 in family, Lexington, merchant (9 Sept. 1812)

Smith, William, age 40, 11 years in U.S., 7 in family, Lexington, manufacturer (9 Sept. 1812)

Sprake, Thomas, age 52, 10 years in U.S., 8 in family, Lexington, butcher (9 Sept. 1812)

Sproule, Charles, age 25, 7 years in U.S., 4 in family, Frankfort, merchant & manufacturer (9 Sept. 1812)

Stephenson, William, age 3C, 14 mos. in U.S., Fayette Co., weaver (9 Sept. 1812)

Wolly, John, age 23, 5 years in U.S., Lexington, weaver (9 Sept. 1812)

EAST TENNESSEE

Ackles, John, age 67, 22 years in U.S., from Ireland, 2 daugh-
ters & 1 grandchild, Greene Co., weaver but pursues farming
(8-15 Sept. 1812)
Anderson, George, age 45, 19 years in U.S., wife, Rhea Co, far-
mer (29 Sept. - 6 Oct. 1812)
Anderson, John, age 39, 12 years in U.S., wife & 5 children,
Greene Co., wheelwright (15-22 Sept. 1812)
Anderson, William, age 46, 21 years in U.S., 5 in family, Blount
Co., tanner (18-25 Aug. 1812)
Beatty, Hugh, age 37, 21 years in U.S., from Ireland, wife & 4
children, Knox Co., farmer (3-18 Aug. 1812)
Bell, Alexander, age 46, 20 years in U.S., wife & 6 children,
Sevier Co., farmer (6 Oct. - 3 Nov. 1812)
Black, Thomas, age 60, 36 years in U.S., from England, wife & 8
children, Carter Co., collier (1-8 Sept, 1812)
Blackbourn, James, age 50, 33 years in U.S., 7 children, Anderson
Co,, tailor (6 Oct. - 3 Nov. 1812)
Blain, Robert, age 29, 21 years in U.S., wife & 4 children,
Grainger Co., merchandizing (25 Aug. - 1 Sept. 1812)
Brice, William, age 52, 30 years in U.S., wife & 8 children,
Hawkins Co., carpenter (6 Oct. - 3 Nov. 1812)
Brown, Alexander, age 31 on 19 Nov, next; he and his wife arri-
ved at Petersburg, Va., on 25 Nov. 1799; time in U.S. to this
20 Aug. will be 12 years, 8 mos. and 26 days; residence on Fall
Creek, Pittsylvania Co., Va., 6 miles north from Danville; he
was formerly a merchant; at present he is settling old business
and making a crop; applied 23 Apr. 1811 at Pittsylvania Court
(6 Oct. 1812)
Brown, Alexander, age 24, 8 years in U.S., Greenville, weaver
(25 Aug. - 1 Sept. 1812)
Brown, John, age 22, 8 years in U.S., Grainger Co., clerk to a
merchant (6 Oct. - 3 Nov. 1812)
Cain, Hugh, age 52, 29 years in U.S., from Ireland, wife & seven
children, Hawkins Co., farmer (3-18 Aug. 1812)
Campbell, Samuel, age 51, 23 years in U.S., wife & 10 children,
Blount Co., farmer (6 Oct. - 3 Nov. 1812)
Canfield, John, age 50, 15 years in U.S., Sullivan Co., stone
mason (6 Oct. - 3 Nov. 1812)
Carry, Dennis, age 46, 16 years in U.S., from Ireland, wife & 7
children, Knox Co., farmer (3-18 Aug. 1812)
Casey, Alexander, age 45, 28 years in U.S., from Ireland, wife &
child, Roane Co., farmer; served as a soldier under Gen, Wayne
(8-15 Sept. 1812)
Catherwood, Hugh, age 38, 2 years in U.S., Sullivan Co., farmer
(6 Oct. - 3 Nov. 1812)
Conyers, Bartholomew, age 64, 26 years in U.S., from England,
wife & 2 children, Jefferson Co., farmer; applied 1788 at
court in Fredericksburg, Va., but obtained no certificate (1-8
Sept. 1812)
Cooney, John, schoolmaster; residence on Ivy Creek, Bedford Co.,
Va., 8 miles from Lynchburg; with wife & 5 children arrived at
Alexandria, Va., on 31 July 1784 and to this 5 Sept. 1812 it
will be 28 years, 1 month & 4 days; his age 50 on 9 Mar. last
(6 Oct. 1812)
Cooper, Thomas, age 79, 35 years in U.S., wife & 12 children,
Anderson Co., farmer (22-29 Sept. 1812)
Crozier, Arthur, age 49, 22 years in U.S., wife & 7 children,
Anderson Co., farmer (22-29 Sept. 1812)
Currin, John, age 35, 14 years in U.S., from Ireland, wife & 3
children & 3 slaves, Bledsoe Co., farmer (8-15 Sept. 1812)
Dewoody, Wm., age 58, 28 years in U.S., wife & 8 children, Greene
Co., publican (25 Aug. - 1 Sept. 1812)

Dinnel, Thomas, age 42, 18 years in U.S., wife & 6 children,Jefferson Co., farmer (29 Sept. - 6 Oct. 1812)

Dinnil, Thomas, age 42, 14 years in U.S., Jefferson Co., farmer (25 Aug. - 1 Sept. 1812)

Doherty, George, age 24, about 1 year in U.S., Claiborne Co., clerk to a merchant (29 Sept. - 6 Oct. 1812)

Dury, William, age 42, 23 years in U.S., Blountsville, merchant (6 Oct. - 3 Nov. 1812)

Eaken, Benjamin, age 18, 2 years in U.S., from Ireland, Knox Co., labourer (3-18 Aug. 1812)

Eaken, George, age 30, 2 years in U.S., from Ireland, Knox Co., Methodist preacher (3-18 Aug. 1812)

Elliott, Mons, age 31, 11 years in U.S., from Ireland, wife, Blount Co., farmer (1-8 Sept. 1812)

Farquharson, Robert, age 32, 13 years in U.S., from Scotland, Knoxville, merchant (3-13 Aug. 1812)

Farrell, James, age 37, 21 years in U.S., wife & 7 children, Jefferson Co., teacher (22-29 Sept. 1812)

Ferguson, Alex., age 44, 27 years in U.S., wife & 6 children, Knox Co., farmer, from Ireland (25 Aug. - 1 Sept. 1812)

Ferguson, Henry, age 47, 27 years in U.S., wife & 6 children, Washington Co., farmer (5 Oct. - 3 Nov. 1812)

Ferguson, Thomas, age 41, 21 years in U.S., wife & 5 children, Washington Co., tailor (5 Oct. - 3 Nov. 1812)

Ford, William, age 53, 35 years in U.S., wife & 8 children, Greene Co., weaver, "rather fond of whiskey" (8-15 Sept. 1812)

From, Archibald, age 40, 27 years in U.S., 10 in family, Blount Co., farmer (18-25 Aug. 1812)

Furguson, John, age 35, 22 years in U.S., wife & 4 children, Washington Co., tailor (15-22 Sept. 1812)

Furguson, Robert, age 45, 38 years in U.S., 7 in family, Blount Co., farmer (18-25 Aug. 1812)

Gamble, Thomas, age 52, 28 years in U.S., from Ireland, wife & 3 children, Blount Co., farmer (8-15 Sept. 1812)

Ganet, William, age 53, 29 years in U.S., 8 in family, Blount Co., farmer, justice of the peace (18-25 Aug. 1812)

Garvin, John, age 50, 27 years in U.S., wife & 3 children, Greene Co., farmer (15-22 Sept. 1812)

Gass, Samuel, age 48, 27 years in U.S., from Ireland, wife and 11 children, Jefferson Co., farmer (1-8 Sept. 1812)

Gault, John, age 52, 19 years in U.S., from Ireland, wife and 7 children, Blount Co., farmer (8-15 Sept. 1812)

Gill, Thomas, age 36, 16 years in U.S., wife & 4 children, Grainger Co., farmer; says he was naturalized at Edington, N.C., but has no certificate (6 Oct. - 3 Nov. 1812)

Gill, Wm. M., age 35, 20 years in U.S., wife & 3 children, Rhea Co., farmer (29 Sept. - 6 Oct. 1812)

Glass, John, age 40, 23 years in U.S., wife & 6 children, Blount Co,, farmer (3-24 Nov. 1812)

Gould, John, age 40, 27 years in U.S., from Ireland, wife & 5 children, Blount Co., farmer (8-15 Sept. 1812)

Gould, Samuel, age 46, 27 years in U.S., from Ireland, wife & 5 children, Blount Co., farmer (8-15 Sept. 1812)

Graham, Hugh, age 27, 6 years in U.S., from Ireland, Claiborne Co., merchant (1-8 Sept. 1812)

Graves, George, age 29, 24 years in U.S., wife, Sevier Co,, shoemaker (22-29 Sept. 1812)

Greer, James, age 47, 29 years in U.S., 4 children, Knox Co., farmer, from Ireland (25 Aug. - 1 Sept. 1812)

Gregory, Robert, age 27, 12 years in U.S., wife & 2 children, Greene Co., schoolmaster (25 Aug. - 1 Sept. 1812)

Gunning, David, age 60, 18 years in U.S., Sullivan Co., labourer (3 Nov. 1812 - 1 Feb. 1813)

Hope, Thomas, age 55, 27 years in U.S., wife & 8 children, Knox Co., house-joiner, from England (25 Aug. - 1 Sept. 1812)

Horton, Isaac, age 53, 33 years in U.S., wife & 7 children, An-
   derson Co., farmer (22-29 Sept. 1812)
Humes, Thomas, age 45, 27 years in U.S., from Ireland, wife & 3
   children, Knoxville, merchant (3-18 Aug. 1812)
Hunter, Francis, age 62, 36 years in U.S., from Ireland, wife &
   9 children, Grainger Co., weaver (1-8 Sept. 1812)
Huston, Hugh, age 19, 2 years in U.S., from Ireland, Claiborne
   Co., labourer (1-8 Sept. 1812)
Huston, William, age 21, 6 years in U.S., from Ireland, Claiborne
   Co., labourer (1-8 Sept. 1812)
Jack, William, age 37, 22 years in U.S., wife & 5 children, Haw-
   kins Co., farmer (3 Nov. 1812 - 1 Feb. 1813)
Jackson, James, age 52, 15 years in U.S., wife & 11 children,
   Carter Co., collier (22-29 Sept. 1812)
Jentson, Joseph, age 27, 3 years in U.S., Roane Co., farmer; he
   would prefer living under govt. of Great Britain (1-8 Sept. 1812)
Johnson, Theophilus, age 29, 17 years in U.S., wife, Rhea Co.,
   hatter (15-22 Sept. 1812)
Johnson, Wm., age 32, 23 years in U.S., wife & 3 children, Knox
   Co., farmer (25 Aug. - 1 Sept. 1812)
Johnston, James, age 23, 19 years in U.S., Hawkins Co., hosier
   (6 Oct. - 3 Nov. 1812)
Johnston, Joseph, age 49, 26 years in U.S., wife & child, Rhea
   Co., farmer (29 Sept. - 6 Oct. 1812)
Kennady, Hugh, age 26, 16 years in U.S., Knox Co., physician; he
   "has never had an education nor a course of reading suitable
   to his profession." (25 Aug. - 1 Sept. 1812)
Kennedy, James, age 43, 16 years in U.S., wife & 6 children, Knox
   Co., Presbyterian preacher, from Ireland (25 Aug. - 1 Sept.
   1812)
Ketcham, William, age 43, 29 years in U.S., wife & 5 children,
   Grainger Co., farmer (25 Aug. - 1 Sept. 1812)
Kyle, John, age 51, 29 years in U.S., wife & 3 children, Greene
   Co., tailor; in 1784 took oath of allegiance to U.S. (15-22 Sept.
   1812)
Lawson, Andrew, age 26, about 12 years in U.S., Sevier Co., far-
   mer (22-29 Sept. 1812)
Lawson, Anthony, Jr., age 29, 12 years in U.S., wife & 3 children,
   Sevier Co., stone mason (22-29 Sept. 1812)
Lawson, Robert, age 26, about 12 years in U.S., wife & 3 children,
   Sevier Co., saddler (22-29 Sept. 1812)
Lindsey, Mathew, age 59, 26 years in U.S., from Ireland, wife &
   2 children, Knox Co., farmer (3-18 Aug. 1812)
Lindsey, Moses, age 27, 26 years in U.S., from Ireland, Knoxville,
   saddler (3-18 Aug. 1812)
Lindsey, Robert, age 30, 26 years in U.S., from Ireland, wife &
   2 children, Knoxville, tanner (3-18 Aug. 1812)
Lohery, John, age 55, 25 years in U.S., wife & 9 children, An-
   derson Co., farmer (6 Oct. - 3 Nov. 1812)
Long, James, age 42, 21 years in U.S., 10 in family, Blount Co.,
   schoolmaster (18-25 Aug. 1812)
Long, William, age 37, 21 years in U.S., from Ireland, wife & 4
   children, Blount Co., farmer (1-8 Sept. 1812)
McAffry, Terence, age 38, 16 years in U.S., from Ireland, wife &
   3 children, Knox Co., carpenter (3-18 Aug. 1812)
McBath, Wm., age 60, 20 years in U.S., from Ireland, wife & 3
   children, Knox Co., schoolmaster (25 Aug. - 1 Sept. 1812)
McCanse, James, age 26, 11 years in U.S., Hawkins Co., distiller
   (6 Oct. - 3 Nov. 1812)
McCartney, John, age 52, 28 years in U.S., wife & 14 children,
   Blount Co., farmer (15-22 Sept. 1812)
McCloskey, John, age 48, 31 years in U.S., 8 children, Jefferson
   Co., tailor; "subject to intoxication" (25 Aug. - 1 Sept. 1812)
McClure, Robert, age 48, 24 years in U.S., wife & 4 children, Knox
   Co., farmer (25 Aug. - 1 Sept. 1812)

McClure, Robert, age 30, 30 years in U.S., wife & child, Washington Co., farmer (3 Nov. 1812 - 1 Feb. 1813)
McColly, Samuel, age 42, 14 years in U.S., from Ireland, wife & 6 children, Roane Co., farmer (8-15 Sept. 1812)
McCormick, Wm., age 32, 13 years in U.S., Rhea Co., tanner (15-22 Sept. 1812)
McCulley, James, age 50, 28 years in U.S., from Ireland, wife & 6 children, Blount Co., farmer (8-15 Sept. 1812)
McCulley, Robert, age 44, 22 years in U.S., 8 in family, Blount Co., farmer, justice of the peace (18-25 Aug. 1812)
McFarland, Mathew, age 38, 19 years in U.S., Jefferson Co., schoolmaster; has applied (25 Aug. - 1 Sept. 1812)
McHenry, Alex., age 50, 22 years in U.S., wife & 5 children, Knox Co., farmer (25 Aug. - 1 Sept. 1812)
McHenry, Robert, age 55, 28 years in U.S., wife & 4 children, Carter Co., shoemaker (22-29 Sept. 1812)
McIntyre, John, age 40, 24 years in U.S., from England, wife & 4 children, Cocke Co., labourer (8-15 Sept. 1812)
McKee, John, age 67, 28 years in U.S., wife & child, Blount Co., farmer (3-24 Nov. 1812)
McKee, John, Jr., age 37, 28 years in U.S., from Scotland, wife & 5 children, Blount Co., farmer (1-8 Sept. 1812)
McKennady, Adam, age 23, 16 years in U.S., Knox Co., physician (25 Aug. - 1 Sept. 1812)
MacKin, Edward, age 45, 21 year in U.S., wife & 8 children, Washington Co., tanner (15-22 Sept. 1812)
McMillan, Alex., Jr., age 37, 8 years in U.S., from Ireland, wife & 7 children, Knox Co., farmer (1-8 Sept. 1812)
McNutt, John, age 53, 20 years in U.S., wife & 5 children, Washington Co., weaver & farmer (15-22 Sept. 1812)
Marshall, John, age 49, 20 years in U.S., wife & 7 children, Sevier Co., farmer (22-29 Sept. 1812)
Martin, Robert, age 39, 17 years in U.S., wife & 8 children, Jefferson Co., farmer (25 Aug. - 1 Sept. 1812)
Martin, Samuel, age 31, 13 years in U.S., from Ireland, Roane Co., merchant; applied Sept. 1808 (1-8 Sept. 1812)
Matison, John, age 37, 17 years in U.S., 7 in family, Sevier Co., stone mason (25 Aug. - 1 Sept. 1812)
Miller, John, age 63, 15 years in U.S., from Ireland, Knox Co., farmer (25 Aug. - 1 Sept. 1812)
Miller, Samuel, age 52, 28 years in U.S., wife & 7 children, Roane Co., farmer (22-29 Sept. 1812)
Mills, Thomas, age 28, 7 years in U.S., wife & 3 children, Jefferson Co., farmer (3 Nov.1812 - 1 Feb. 1813)
Mitchell, James, age 63, 51 years in U.S., wife & 3 children, Sevier Co., shoe- and bootmaker; served in the Revolutionary War and took oath of allegiance to the U.S. (15-22 Sept. 1812)
Moffat, William, age 40, 18 years in U.S., wife & 2 children, Hawkins Co., house-joiner (25 Aug. - 1 Sept. 1812)
Moffet, Samuel, age 38, 8 years in U.S., from Ireland, wife & 5 children, Grainger Co., farmer (3-18 Aug. 1812)
Moffet, Thomas, age 28, 1 year in U.S., from Ireland, wife & 2 children, Grainger Co., farmer (18-25 Aug. 1812)
Moffet, ... (name torn away), age 42, 10 years in U.S., from Ireland, wife & 2 children, Grainger Co., farmer; applied Oct. 1809 (25 Aug. - 1 Sept. 1812)
Mooney, Joseph, age 48, 28 years in U.S., from Ireland, wife & 4 children, Jefferson Co., tanner and currier (1-8 Sept. 1812)
Moore, George, age 24, 16 years in U.S., wife & 2 children, Roane Co., farmer (22-29 Sept. 1812)
Moore, James, age 50, 16 years in U.S., wife & 8 children, Roane Co., farmer (22-29 Sept. 1812)
Moore, John, Sr., age 72, 15 years in U.S., wife, Knox Co., farmer (25 Aug. - 1 Sept. 1812)

Moore, John, Jr., age 24, 15 years in U.S., wife & 2 children,
Knox Co., shoemaker (25 Aug. - 1 Sept. 1812)
Morrow, John, age 31, 7 years in U.S., from Ireland, wife & child,
Knox Co., farmer (3-18 Aug. 1812)
Morrow, William, age 47, 21 years in U.S., from Ireland, wife &
6 children, Knoxville, tanner (3-18 Aug. 1812)
Murphey, Edward, age 55, 30 years in U.S., wife & 9 children,
Sevier, farmer (6 Oct. - 3 Nov. 1812)
Murray, Robert, age 46, 15 years in U.S., from Ireland, wife &
9 children, Knox Co., stone mason (3-18 Aug. 1812)
Nelson, Thomas, age 49, 23 years in U.S., wife & 6 children,
Washington Co., farmer (15-22 Sept. 1812)
Nenney, Patrick, age 49, 24 years in U.S., wife & 8 children,
Jefferson Co., merchant (22-29 Sept. 1812)
Nolan, Thomas, age 28, 7 years in U.S., Rhea Co., hatter (25
Aug. - 1 Sept. 1812)
Nugent, James, age 55, 27 years in U.S., wife & 6 children, Haw-
kins Co., millwright (6 Oct. - 3 Nov. 1812)
Nugent, James, age 45, 27 years in U.S., wife & 6 children, Haw-
kins Co., millwright (3-24 Nov. 1812)
Orr, James, age 48, 27 years in U.S., Blount Co., farmer (6 Oct.
3 Nov. 1812)
Park, Andrew, age 27, 8 years in U.S., from Ireland, wife & 2
children, Greene Co., house-carpenter (8-15 Sept. 1812)
Park, James, age 47, 8 years in U.S., wife & 6 children, Greene
Co., farmer (25 Aug. - 1 Sept. 1812)
Preston, Alexander, age 29, 10 years in U.S., Sevier Co., mer-
chant (15-22 Sept. 1812)
Robertson, Wm., age 63, 36 years in U.S., wife & 2 children,
Sevier Co., farmer (29 Sept. - 6 Oct. 1812)
Robinson, Valentine, age 57, 31 years in U.S., from England,
wife & 9 children, Cocke Co., schoolmaster (8-15 Sept. 1812)
Rogan, Daniel, age 41, 21 years in U.S., Sullivan Co., clerk to
a merchant (6 Oct. - 3 Nov. 1812)
Simpson, John, age 34, 6 years in U.S., Sullivan Co., clerk to
a merchant (6 Oct. - 3 Nov. 1812)
Simpson, Robert, age 51, 27 years in U.S., from Ireland, wife &
4 children, Greene Co., weaver (8-15 Sept. 1812)
Sloan, William, age 38, 20 years in U.S., from Ireland, wife &
8 children, Bledsoe Co., by trade a hatter but pursues farming
(8-15 Sept. 1812)
Small, William, age 56, 28 years in U.S., 8 in family, Roane Co.,
farmer (1-8 Sept. 1812)
Smith, John M., age 52, 28 years in U.S., wife & 8 children,
Washington Co., stone mason (15-22 Sept. 1812)
Sproull, John, age 39, 22 years in U.S., wife & child, Jefferson
Co., farmer; naturalized summer 1795 in Franklin Co., Pa., but
took no copy of record (3 Nov. 1812 - 1 Feb. 1813)
Stephenson, John, age 33, 16 years in U.S., 5 in family, Roane
Co., weaver (1-8 Sept. 1812)
Stone, Lawrence, age 32, 10 years in U.S., Grainger Co., labou-
rer (6 Oct. - 3 Nov. 1812)
Taylor, James, age 58, 30 years in U.S., wife & 7 children, An-
derson Co., farmer (6 Oct. - 3 Nov. 1812)
Thompson, John, age 49, 22 years in U.S., from Ireland, wife &
8 children, Knox Co., farmer (25 Aug. - 1 Sept. 1812)
Welch, Edmond, age 47, 23 years in U.S., from Ireland, wife & 5
children, Knox Co., ironmaster (25 Aug. - 1 Sept. 1812)
Woods, Wm., age 45, 18 years in U.S., from Ireland, wife & 4
children, Knox Co., farmer (25 Aug. - 1 Sept. 1812)
Work, Joseph, age 47, 20 years in U.S., from Ireland, wife & 7
sons, Roane Co., farmer (8-15 Sept. 1812)
Wright, George, age 55, 18 years in U.S., from Ireland, wife,
Knox Co., miller (25 Aug. - 1 Sept. 1812)

Wright, Hanse, age 40, 11 years in U.S., wife & 4 children, Hawkins Co., shoemaker (6 Oct. - 3 Nov. 1812)
Wright, John, age 32, 15 years in U.S., from Ireland, wife & 2
children, Knox Co., farmer (25 Aug. - 1 Sept. 1812)
Wright, Patrick, age 40, 17 years in U.S., Sullivan Co., labourer (3 Nov. 1812 - 1 Feb. 1813)
Wright, Robert, age 28, 18 years in U.S., from Ireland, wife &
4 children, Knox Co., labourer (25 Aug. - 1 Sept. 1812)

WEST TENNESSEE

Allen, William, age 22, 2 years in U.S., Nashville, merchant's
clerk (11-18 Aug 1812)
Anderson, John, age 50, 17 years in U.S,, wife & 2 children,
Nashville, cashier of the Nashville Bank; married in West Tennessee (1-8 Sept. 1812)
Badlum, James, age 27, 3 years in U.S., Davidson Co., bricklayer
(8-15 Sept. 1812)
Barry, James, age 32, 8 years in U.S., wife & child, Gallatin,
physician; married in West Tennessee (18-25 Aug. 1812)
Boyd, John, age 48, 11 years in U.S., Davidson Co., painter (4-
11 Aug. 1812)
Boyd, Robert, age 43, 11 years in U.S., wife & 3 children, David-
son Co., painter; married in West Tennessee (4-11 Aug. 1812)
Brown, Thomas, age 16, 2 years in U.S., Nashville, cordwainer
(1-8 Sept. 1812)
Buchanan, Robert, age 27, 3 years in U.S., Fayettesville, merchant
(18 - 25 Aug. 1812)
Burland, Thomas M., age 28, 3 years in U.S., wife & child, David-
son Co., farmer; applied 26 Nov. 1811; married in West Tennes-
see (8-15 Sept. 1812)
Cary, Michael, age 22, 2 years in U.S., Davidson Co., weaver &
spinner (4-11 Aug. 1812)
Champney, Thomas, age 53, 12 years in U.S., wife & 6 children in
Europe, Davidson Co., physician (11-18 Aug. 1812)
Craven, William P., age 26, 11 years in U.S., Smith Co., teacher
(25 Aug. - 1 Sept. 1812)
Crocket, Robert, age 27, 11 mos. in U.S., Gallatin, merchant's
clerk (25 Aug. - 1 Sept. 1812)
Culbert, George, age 23, 11 mos. in U.S., Sumner Co., tanner &
currier (25 Aug. - 1 Sept. 1812)
Culbert, Thomas, age 28, 5 years in U.S., Gallatin, merchant's
clerk (25 Aug. - 1 Sept. 1812)
Esdal, David, age 23, 6 years in U.S., Nashville, innkeeper (18-
25 Aug. 1812)
Evans, Hugh, age 24, 2½ years in U.S., wife (married in England)
& child, Nashville, painter (1-8 Sept. 1812)
Gordon, James, age 31, 11 years in U.S., wife (married in West
Tennessee) & 2 children, Williamson Co., haberdasher (11-18
Aug. 1812)
Hanna, James, age 43, 1 year in U.S., wife & 7 children, Nash-
ville, merchant 22 Sept. - 6 Oct. 1812)
Henderson, Hugh, age 24, 3 years in U.S., wife (married in North
Carolina), Williamson Co., merchant; applied 31 Oct. 1809 (1-
8 Sept. 1812)
Higgins, Bernard, age 21, 2 years in U.S., wife, Nashville, cot-
ton spinner (11-18 Aug. 1812)
Homes, William, age 49, 24 years in U.S., wife (married in West
Tennessee) & 2 children, Davidson Co., farmer (18-25 Aug. 1812)
Hume, William, age 40, 12 years in U.S., wife (married in West
Tennessee) & 3 children, Davidson Co., minister of the Gospel
and professor in Cumberland College (11-18 Aug. 1812)
Johnson, Andrew, age 46, 21 years in U.S., wife (married in West
Tennessee) & 2 children, Franklin, brick maker (1-8 Sept. 1812)
Kingston, Paul, age 33, 10 years in U.S., wife (married in West
Tennessee) & 2 children, Nashville, shoemaker (11-18 Aug. 1812)

Kingston, Richard, age 32, 6 years in U.S., wife (emigrated with him) & 4 children, Davidson Co., farmer (11-18 Aug. 1812)

Kirkman, Thomas, Sr., age 60, 16 mos. in U.S., wife & grand-daughter (both emigrated with him), Nashville, gentleman (4-11 Aug. 1812)

Kirkman, Thomas, Jr., age 35, 7 years in U.S., wife & 5 children (all emigrated with him), Nashville, merchant; applied 11 July 1811 (4-11 Aug. 1812)

Landers, William, age 40, 12 years in U.S., wife & 4 children, Sumner Co., tanner (1-8 Sept. 1812)

McAffry, John, age 28, 16 years in U.S., Davidson Co., cabinet-maker (15-22 Sept. 1812)

McBean, Daniel, age 40, 11 years in U.S., Nashville, cabinet-maker (11-18 Aug. 1812)

McCann, John, age 42, 20 years in U.S., wife (married in America) & 6 children, Sumner Co., farmer (18-25 Aug. 1812)

McCann, William, age 39, 20 years in U.S., Davidson Co., cooper (11-18 Aug. 1812)

McClure, William, age 24, 2 years in U.S., Clarksville, farmer (22 Sept. - 6 Oct. 1812)

McCormack, Lawrence, age 40, 23 years in U.S., Davidson Co., farmer (11-18 Aug. 1812)

McGillvary (?), William, age 28, 7 years in U.S., Franklin, tai-lor (8-15 Sept. 1812)

McKerahan, Charles, age 30, 11 years in U.S., wife, Nashville, Windsor chair maker (25 Aug. - 1 Sept. 1812)

McPhail, Angus, age 25, 11 years in U.S., Franklin, tailor (8-15 Sept. 1812)

O'Callaghan, Patrick, age 30, 14 years in U.S., Lincoln Co., stone & brick mason (18-25 Aug. 1812)

Osborn, Alfred M., age 23, 17 years in U.S., Davidson Co., tailor (1-8 Sept. 1812)

Park, Joseph, age 40, 22 years in U.S., Nashville, late a mer-chant (8-15 Sept. 1812)

Ramsey, Thomas, age 30, 8 years in U.S., Nashville, merchant (22 Sept. - 6 Oct, 1812)

Sanders, Francis, age 41, 19 years in U.S., wife (married in West Tennessee) & child, Davidson Co., tanner (18-25 Aug. 1812)

Stewart, William, age 40, 17 years in U.S., wife (married in America) & 4 children, Davidson Co., farmer (18-25 Aug. 1812)

Stothart, Robert, age 46, 19 years in U.S., wife (married in West Tennessee) & 3 children, Nashville, late merchant (4-11 Aug. 1812)

Stuart, James, age 26, 7 years in U.S., Williamson Co., house-carpenter (25 Aug. - 1 Sept. 1812)

Walker, Robert T., age 19, 11 mos. in U.S., Nashville, merchant's clerk (25 Aug. - 1 Sept. 1812)

Western, Thomas, age 27, 2 years in U.S., wife (married in Eng-land) & 2 children, Nashville, painter (1-8 Sept. 1812)

Williamson, John age 54, 21 years in U.S., wife & child, David-son Co., farmer (25 Aug. - 1 Sept. 1812)

Wright, John, age 46, 9 mos. in U.S., Nashville, storekeeper (18-25 Aug. 1812)

Wright, Joseph, age 43, 18 years in U.S., wife & 7 children, Wil-liamson Co., weaver (1-8 Sept. 1812)

Young, Peter A., age 17, 15 years in U.S., Nashville, merchant's clerk (15-22 Sept. 1812)

ILLINOIS

Amlin, Louis, age 45, in U.S. since 1789, Cahokia, engagee (12-19 Oct. 1812)

Archambeau, Joseph, age 50, in U.S. since 1794, wife, Kaskaskia, tavern-keeper (5-2 Oct. 1812)

Atcheson, William. age 59, in U.S. since 1790, wife & 4 children, Turkey Hill, farmer (5-12 Oct. 1812)

Bernerlie, Michel, age 22, in U.S. since 1808, Cahokia, engagee, now a volunteer doing duty (12-19 Oct. 1812)

Bernie, Charles, age 22, in U.S. since 1808, Cahokia, engagee (12-19 Oct. 1812)

Berthelmi, Jacques (alias Monplaisir), age 39, in U.S. since 1791, wife & child, Cahokia, farmer (5-12 Oct. 1812)

Bertrand, Simon, age 26, in U.S. since 1805, wife, Cahokia, blacksmith (5-12 Oct. 1812)

Beaunoyer, Paul, age 49, in U.S. since 1789, Cahokia, journeyman (5-12 Oct. 1812)

Bourdeau, Jacques (alias James), age 28, in U.S. since 1796, wife & 5 children, Cahokia, farmer (5-12 Oct. 1812)

Cayeu, Michel, age 30, in U.S. since 1797, Cahokia, engagee (12-19 Oct. 1812)

Charlier, Pierre, age 50, in U.S. since 1783, wife & child, Cahokia, wheelwright (5-12 Oct. 1812)

Chatillon, Louis (alias Gadin), age 26, in U.S. since 1794, Cahokia, engagee, now a volunteer doing duty (12-19 Oct. 1812)

Daout, Ettienne, age 23, in U.S. since 1806, Cahokia, engaged as a clerk, now a volunteer doing duty (12-19 Oct. 1812)

Demette, Francois, age 46, in U.S. since 1786, wife & 3 children, Cahokia, carpenter (5-12 Oct. 1812)

Despot, Charles, age 39, in U.S. since 1804, Cahokia, engagee boatman (5-12 Oct. 1812)

Dupré, Francois, age 37, in U.S. since 1790, wife & 2 children, Cahokia, farmer (12-19 Oct. 1812)

Farriere, Francois, age 32, in U.S. since 1800, wife & child, Cahokia, farmer and tavern-keeper (12-19 Oct. 1812)

Fauché, Antoine, age 32, in U.S. since 1800, Cahokia, engagee, a volunteer doing duty (12-19 Oct. 1812)

Gamlin, Michel, age 33, in U.S. since 1795, wife & 4 children, Cahokia, farmer (12-19 Oct. 1812)

Gamlin, Pierre, age 37, in U.S. since 1795, Cahokia, farmer (12-19 Oct. 1812)

Gendron, Baptiste, age 42, in U.S. since 1789, wife & 3 children, Cahokia, farmer (12-19 Oct. 1812)

Gendron, Louis, age 47, in U.S. since 1788, wife & 6 children, Cahokia, farmer (12-19 Oct. 1812)

Gendron, Tousaint, age 35, in U.S. since 1800, Cahokia, farmer (12-19 Oct. 1812)

Gravelle, Joseph, age 42, in U.S. since 1792, Cahokia, engagee (12-19 Oct. 1812)

Gregoire, Louis, age 28, in U.S. since 1804, Cahokia, engagee, a volunteer doing duty (12-19 Oct. 1812)

Guerin, Ange, age 36, in U.S. since 1795, wife & 2 children, Cahokia, farmer (5-12 Oct. 1812)

Guerin, Pierre, age 34, in U.S. since 1795, wife & 3 children, Cahokia, farmer (5-12 Oct. 1812)

Lalage, Fr.(?), age 24, in U.S. since 1804, Cahokia, engagee (5-12 Oct. 1812)

Lalonde, Baptiste, age 31, in U.S. since 1802, Cahokia, engagee (5-12 Oct. 1812)

Lamotte, Joachim, age 26, in U.S. since 1804, wife & child, Cahokia, engagee, a volunteer doing duty (12-19 Oct. 1812)

Langevain, Jean Louis, age 25, in U.S. since 1808, Cahokia, engagee, volunteer in militia service (12-19 Oct. 1812)

Lavaniere, Pierre, age 25, in U.S. since 1804, Cahokia, engagee,
  now volunteer in militia service (12-19 Oct. 1812)
Le Compte, Julien, age 49, in U.S. since 1791, wife & 5 children,
  Cahokia, farmer (5-12 Oct. 1812)
Letems, Panal, age 47, in U.S. since 1784, wife & 7 children,
  Cahokia, farmer (5-12 Oct. 1812)
Mallet, Joseph, age 23, in U.S. since 1804, Cahokia, engagee
  (5-12 Oct. 1812)
Manegle, Baptiste, age 37, in U.S. since 1797, engagee, Cahokia
  (12-19 Oct. 1812)
Manegle, Joseph, age 48, in U.S. since 1783, wife & 4 children,
  Cahokia, farmer and merchant (5-12 Oct. 1812)
Martelle, Amable, age 23, in U.S. since 1805, Cahokia, engagee,
  a volunteer doing duty (12-19 Oct. 1812)
Martin, Pierre, age 35, in U.S. since 1794, wife & 5 children,
  Cahokia, farmer, now a lieutenant in county militia (5-12 Oct.
  1812)
Mears, William, age 37, in U.S. since 1794, Cahokia, attorney
  (12-19 Oct. 1812)
Menard, Francois, age 37, in U.S. since 1792, 1 child, Kaskas-
  kia, trader (5-12 Oct. 1812)
Menard, John, age 29, in U.S. since 1797, wife & 5 children,
  Kaskaskia, farmer (5-12 Oct. 1812)
Menard, Peter, age 43, in U.S. since 1786, wife & 5 children,
  Kaskaskia, farmer; he has held civil and military commissions
  and has served in Council of the Indiana Territory (5-12 Oct.
  1812)
Paradis, Baptiste, age 28, in U.S. since 1801, wife & child, Ca-
  hokia, farmer (12-19 Oct. 1812)
Peltier, Louis, age 46, in U.S. since 1788, wife & 4 children,
  Cahokia, farmer (5-12 Oct. 1812)
Pinconneau, Augustus, age 32, in U.S. since 1796, wife & 2 child-
  ren, Cahokia, tavern-keeper (5-12 Oct. 1812)
Pinconneau, Ettienne, age 40, in U.S. since 1789, 2 children,
  Cahokia, farmer (5-12 Oct. 1812)
Pinconneau, Francois, age 26, in U.S. since 1802, Cahokia, enga-
  gee, a volunteer doing duty (12-19 Oct. 1812)
Pinconneau, Louis, age 42, in U.S. since 1793, wife & 4 children,
  Cahokia, ferryman (5-12 Oct. 1812)
Pinconneau, Louison, age 47, in U.S. since 1784, wife & 7 child-
  ren, Cahokia, merchant (5-12 Oct. 1812)
Proux, Joseph, age 26, in U.S. since 1806, Cahokia, engagee boat-
  man (5-12 Oct. 1812)
Prudhomme, Louis, age 26, in U.S. since 1804, Cahokia, engagee,
  generally winters in Indian country (5-12 Oct. 1812)
Rouillau, Louis, age 45, in U.S. since 1786, wife & 9 children,
  Cahokia, farmer (5-12 Oct. 1812)
St. Denis, Antoine, age 22, in U.S. since 1806, Cahokia, engagee
  (5-12 Oct. 1812)
St. Germain, Jean Louis, age 48, in U.S. since 1784, 1 child,
  Cahokia, farmer (5-12 Oct. 1812)
Touchette, Joseph, age 52, in U.S. since 1787, wife & 7 children,
  Cahokia, farmer & tavern-keeper (5-12 Oct. 1812)
Tremblé, Tousaint, age 22, in U.S. since 1806, Cahokia, engagee,
  volunteer doing duty (12-19 Oct. 1812)
Turcotte, Francois, age 43, in U.S. since 1790, wife & 2 children,
  Cahokia, tavern-keeper (5-12 Oct. 1812)
Vizina (?), Joseph, age 46, in U.S. since 1784, wife & child,
  Cahokia, blacksmith (5-12 Oct. 1812)

MISSOURI

Bristlin, Barnet, age 34, in U.S. since 1802, wife & 4 children,
St. Genevieve, plasterer, born in Ireland (4 Oct. 1812)
Byrne, Morgan, age 40, 13 years in U.S., wife & child, Cape Gi-
rardeau, farmer, born in Ireland (1 Sept. 1812)
Byrne, Moses, age 34, 13 years in U.S., wife & child, Cape Gi-
rardeau, farmer, born in Ireland (13 Sept. 1812)
Carey, Hugh, age 26, in U.S. since Dec. 1806, St. Genevieve,
boot- and shoemaker, born in Ireland (1 Sept. 1812)
Chenier, Ignace, age 42, in U.S. since 12 Sept. 1812, at A. Che-
nier's, St. Louis, no occupation stated (20 Sept. 1812)
Clark, John, age 54, in U.S. since 1790, St. Louis, minister of
the Gospel, born in Scotland (1 Sept. 1812)
Davis, Samuel, age 19, in U.S. since 1806, wife & child, St. Genevieve, baker, born in England (1 Sept. 1812)
Devinney, James, age 49, in U.S. since 1791, wife & child, Mis-
souri, merchant, born in Ireland (1 Sept. 1812)
Dolan, Michael, age 37, in U.S. since 1793, St. Genevieve, tailor,
born in Ireland (4 Oct. 1812)
Gamble, James, age 32, 10 years in U.S., St. Genevieve, farmer,
born in Scotland (1 Sept. 1812)
Gibson, Edward, age 33, in U.S. since 1804, Missouri, joiner &
cabinetmaker (1 Sept. 1812)
Hunter, Josiah, age 52, 29 years in U.S., wife & 7 children,
District of Cape Girardeau, farmer, born in Ireland (13 Sept.
1812)
Keeley, David, age 33, in U.S. since 1801, St. Ferdinand, District of St. Louis, builder-architect, born in Ireland (20 Sept.
1812)
Kerr, Charles, age 26, in U.S. since 1810, St. Genevieve, farmer,
born in England (4 Oct. 1812)
Kerr, Edward, age 23, in U.S. since 1810, St. Genevieve, farmer,
born in England (4 Oct. 1812)
Lagotrie, Narcisse, age 43, in U.S. since 12 Sept. 1812; his fa-
mily is in Canada; he is at A. Chenier's in St. Louis (20 Sept.
1812)
McManes, Patrick, age 42, in U.S. since 1782, St. Genevieve, la-
bourer, born in Ireland (4 Oct. 1812)
Moor, James, age 48, in U.S. since 12 July 1794, wife & 6 child-
ren, St. Louis, house-joiner, born in Ireland (1 Sept. 1812)
Morrison, John, age 47, 16 years in U.S., wife & 4 children,
District of Cape Girardeau, farmer, born in Ireland (13 Sept.
1812)
Roche, John, age 30, 10 years in U.S., St. Genevieve, farmer (1
Sept. 1812)
Spencer, George and Robert, farmers, residing in the District of
St. Charles, have not reported (20 Sept. 1812)

Early in August 1812 a number of persons sought passports to depart from New York for the West Indies in two cartels, the sloop <u>Sally</u>, of 92 tons, for Bermuda, and the brig <u>Isabella</u>, of 135 tons for Bermuda, Antigua and St. Croix. The following are passengers and crew on the <u>Sally</u>:

Bostock, Benjamin J., age 23, 6ft. 1in., fair complex., hazel eyes, light hair, born Barbados, attorney-at-law

Bostock, Louisa E., age 20, 5ft. 3in., fair complex., blue eyes, born Bermuda

Brown, James, age 34, 5ft. 9in., light complex., grey eyes, light hair, born Conn., mate of the <u>Sally</u>

Cunningham, Westley, age 32, 5ft. 8in., light complex., grey eyes, dark hair, born Baltimore, seaman on the <u>Sally</u>

Donwoody, Sue (black), age 50, born Bermuda, servant

Euers, Samuel, age 30, 5ft. 7½in., fair complex, grey eyes, light hair, born Ireland, farmer

Evins, Luther, age 42, 5ft. 5in., dark complex., dark eyes, dark hair, born R.I., capt. of the <u>Sally</u>

Forbes, Francis, age 70, 5ft. 8½in., fair complex., blue eyes, grey hair, born Bermuda, physician

Harkness, James, age 9, born Ireland

Lee, William A.B., age 16, 4ft. 10in., light complex., dark eyes, dark hair, from N.Y., seaman on the <u>Sally</u>

Lightbourn, Ann (wife of Wm.), age 54, 5ft. 5in., fair complex., blue eyes, grey hair, born Bermuda

Lightbourn, Frances, age 29, 5ft. 7in., fair complex., blue eyes, light hair, born Bermuda

Lightbourn, Louisa, infant

Lightbourn, Martha F., age 18 mos.

Lightbourn, Mary Ann, age 23, 5ft. 5in., fair complex., blue eyes, dark hair, born Macklesfield

Lightbourn, Nancy, age 6, 3ft. 5½in., fair complex., blue eyes, light hair, born Turk Islands

Lightbourn, Nathaniel, age 26, 5ft. 9½in., fair complex., blue eyes, light hair, born Bermuda, merchant

Lightbourn, William, age 59, 5ft. 10in., fair complex., blue eyes, grey hair, born Bermuda, gentleman

Lightbourn, William W., age 23, 6ft., fair complex., blue eyes, light hair, born Bermuda, gentleman

Newby, Francis (black), age 32, 5ft. 10in., black complex., black hair, born N.C.

Parker, Eliza J., age 14, 5ft. 1in., fair complex., blue eyes, light hair, born Bermuda

Perkins, Samuel, age 25, 5ft. 7in., light cimplex., grey eyes, dark hair, born Mass., seaman on the <u>Sally</u>

Popham, William, age 27, 5ft. 4in., dark complex., hazel eyes, auburn hair, born Bermuda, chairmaker

Sayers, Frederica, age 18, 5ft. 1in., dark complex., black eyes, brown hair, born Scotland

Spencer, Benjamin, age 39, 5ft. 8in., dark complex., grey eyes, light hair, born Bermuda, mariner

Spencer, Syke (black), age 14, born Bermuda, servant

Tatim, Jenny, age 15, dark complex., born Bermuda, servant

Taylor, Colin Falconar, age 25, 5ft. 7½in., fair complex., blue eyes, light hair, born Scotland, teacher

Tremingham, Hannah (mulatto), age 18, born Bermuda, servant

White, Richard, age 30, 5ft. 7in., brown complex., hazel eyes, black hair, born Barbados

Wood, Ann, age 18, born Ireland

Wood, William, age 44, 5ft. 7in., dark complex., dark eyes, black hair, born Isle ....(illegible)

The following are passengers and crew on the <u>Isabella</u>:

Dewint, Peter C., age 35, 5ft. 4in., sallow complex., black eyes, dark hair, born St. Croix

Dumford, Eliza S., age 45, fair complex., blue eyes, brown hair,
    born in England
Dumford, Henry (son of Eliza S.), age 19, fair complex., black
    eyes, black hair, born Bermuda
Dumford, John (son of Eliza S.), age 21, fair complex., black
    eyes, black hair, born Bermuda
Fisher, John, age 12, fair complex., black eyes, brown hair,
    born Bermuda
Forbes, Francis, age 71, 5ft. 8in., fair complex., blue eyes,
    grey hair, born Bermuda
Ketchum, Alfred (son of John & Susanna), age 14, 5ft., fair com-
    plex., grey eyes, light hair, born U.S.
Ketchum, Edgar, age 1 (infant child of John & Susanna), fair com-
    plex., dark eyes, brown hair, born U.S.
Ketchum, Emeline, age 3, 3ft. 1½in., fair complex., dark eyes,
    brown hair, born Barbados
Ketchum, Fanny (child of John & Susanna), age 11, 4ft. 5½in.,
    fair complex., grey eyes, brown hair, born U.S.
Ketchum, John Jauncey, age 42, 5ft. 10in., fair complex., grey
    eyes, brown hair, born Bermuda
Ketchum, Joseph (son of John & Susanna), age 9, 4ft. 2½in., fair
    complex., blue eyes, brown hair, born U.S.
Ketchum, Louisa (child of John & Susanna), age 15, 5ft. 2in.,
    fair complex., grey eyes, brown hair, born U.S.
Ketchum, Sally (child of John & Susanna), age 7, 3ft. 11in., fair
    complex., blue eyes, brown hair, born U.S.
Ketchum, Susanna (wife of John Jauncey), age 37, 5ft. 5in., fair
    complex., grey eyes, brown hair, born U.S.
Popham, Wm., age 26, 5ft. 4in., dark complex., dark eyes, sandy
    hair, born Bermuda
Spencer, Benjamin A., age 39, 5ft. 8in., brown complex., blue
    eyes, light hair, born Bermuda
Taylor, Colin F., age 25, 5ft. 8in., fair complex., grey eyes,
    auburn hair, born Scotland
Caty (black), servant, age 15, 5ft. 1in., born U.S.
Prince (black), servant, age 35, 5ft. 7in., born Bermuda
Syke (black), servant of Benjamin A. Spencer, age 12, 5ft., born
    Bermuda
Crew consisted of John O'Tuill (master), a mate, a cook, a ste-
ward, four men & a boy.

Disposition of requests for indulgence by suspected persons:

Allen, Mr., of Mass. - request rejected; removed to Worcester
on 28 June 1813; an "unruly" man.

Auchincloss, Hugh, of NYC - request rejected 10 July 1813; indulged for a time but then removed.

Bates, Mr., of NYC - temporary indulgence because of indisposi-
tion of his wife - 9 July removed to within 3 miles of NYC.

Bryan, William, of NYC - ordered removed to interior; was interceded for by John Ferrers.

Coljier, John, of NYC - removed 12 July 1813; wanted permission
to go to England.

Courtney, Lord, of NYC - removed 9 July 1813 to interior.

Davidson, Thomas, of Philadelphia - removed 17 July 1813 to 5 or
6 miles from Philadelphia - indulged because of his wife's
health.

Donaldson, Adam, of Fredericksburg - removed 25 June 1813 to
the interior but later allowed to return on account of his
marriage.

Dyff, Anthony D., of NYC - on 16 June 1813 removed to a few
miles from NYC but later allowed to return on account of his
marriage & declaration.

Farrow, Mr. - on 17 June 1813 applied for leave to depart from
the country.

Gray, Mr. E. - removed to interior but interceded for by Mr. M.
McKibbin.

Greatrake, Lawrence, of Washington, D.C. - on 26 May 1813 removed to interior & limited to a farm; he may return when the
British have removed their squadron.

Hadden, David, of NYC - on 14 July 1813 removed to Long Island
because New York is a military base.

Henry, James, of Richmond, Va. - on 23 May 1813 removed to
Charlottesville, Va., with leave to return to Richmond for a
limited time.

Higham, Thomas, of Charleston, S.C. - removed to interior but
because of health allowed to travel to the spring in Va. &
N.Y.

Highley, Mr. - his case found in letter of 21 June from John
Lefferts, member of Congress.

Hodges, Tyzack, of NYC - his case is explained to John Gaillard,
member of Congress.

Jackson, Dr., of Boston - removed to interior.

Jackson, Henry, of Lancaster, Pa. - ordered removed on 27 Sept.
1813 but indulgence granted.

Kenedy, Burns, of Philadelphia - indulgence granted and is allowed to travel into interior for his health (14 July 1813)

Lambert, Thomas, of Norfolk, Va. - ordered removed 31 July 1813;
he was imprisoned for misconduct in consequence of his being
a mechanic; after a long confinement he was released.

Lanson, Oswald, of Norfolk, Va. - removed to Charlottesville;
his case is being examined.

Lawrence, Nathaniel, of NYC - ordered removed 26 June 1813 but
allowed to return to be married and then to reside in Westchester Co.

Liggat, Alexander, of Falmouth, Va. - on 3 July ordered removed
to interior but because of his timely declaration, marriage,
etc., was allowed to return.

McLymont, Peter, of NYC - 22 June 1813 ordered to be removed;
he desired permission to leave the country.

Mitchell, William, of NYC - 22 June 1813 ordered removed; he desired permission to leave the country.

Murray, John, of NYC - on 6 July 1813 ordered removed to interior
but he came to U.S. as a minor and is of good character and so
was indulged.

Neilson, Hall, of Richmond, Va. - 24 June 1813 ordered removed
   to interior but because of timely declaration and because of
   his not being engaged in commerce he was granted indulgence.
Neilson, James & William H., of Petersburg, Va. - 24 June 1813
   ordered removed to interior but indulgence was granted them
   because of timely declaration and their not being engaged in
   commerce.
Newport, George, of NYC - 14 July 1813 ordered removed; case
   explained to Rufus King.
Phenix, F., of NYC - 2 July 1813 ordered removed; he sought permission to leave the country.
Potts, Mr., of NYC - 12 July 1813 ordered removed; case explained to Hon. W.B. Bullock.
Reeves, Wm. T.P., of NYC - 22 June 1813 ordered removed; he desired permission to leave the country.
Robertson, Gilbert, of Columbia, N.Y. - 16 July 1813 ordered
   removed but was allowed to visit the watering places in New
   York.
Russell, Henry, of NYC - 22 June 1813 ordered removed; he wanted
   leave to depart from the country.
Sewell, Geo. W., of NYC - ordered removed.
Stewart, James, of New London, Conn. - 18 June 1813 ordered
   removed to interior; he was formerly "an English sub agent."
Stewart, John, of NYC - 22 June 1813 ordered removed to interior;
   he wanted permission to leave the country.
Swann, William, of NYC - 16 June 1813 ordered removed but he
   was later allowed to return because of his services as a
   militia officer.
Tullock, Charles, of North Carolina - on 29 May 1812 was im-
   prisoned for misconduct.
Whitall, John, of Germantown - was indulged; see letter to the
   Marshal of Pa., folio 196.
Williamson, Peter, of NYC - see letter to Marshal of N.Y., folio
   192.
Wilson, John, of Charleston, S.C. - 29 June 1813 ordered re-
   moved but allowed to remain because of excellent character.
Wright, James - 16 June 1813 ordered to prison; case is found
   in letter from the Marshal of Md. to the Marshal of D.C.
Yeates, Edmund, of Philadelphia - ordered removed to interior;
   he lacked qualifications; case is explained in letter to Geo.
   Logan.

INDEX 387

Balger, James 1; John 1;
Lestshay 1
Balhour (for Balfour?),
Charles 334
Ball, Abraham 63; William
48, 63, 261; William W.
63
Ballantine/Ballentine,
James 63; Robert 63
Ballard, Henry 63
Bally, James 12
Balster, Oliver S. 63
Bamford, Joseph 261
Banaclough, John 63
Banager, Stephen 1
Bancraft, John 1
Banks, George 292; John
63; Robert 63; Rose 1;
William 292
Bannan/Banon/Banen,
Michael 63; Patrick 63;
Samuel 63
Bannigan, Thos. 12
Bannister, Isaac 252
Banos, Patrick 63
Bantam, John 242
Baptist, Isaac 63
Baraclaugh, Wm. 53
Barber, James 320; Samuel
63; Thomas 261
Barclay, David 320; Henry
63; James 63; John 63;
William 63
Bard, Joseph 63
Bark, Francis 64
Barker, John 64, 293;
William 48, 293
Barla, James 64
Barland, William G. 64
Barlas, William 64
Barley, John 334
Barlow, John 64
Barnard, John 64; William
261
Barnes/Barns, Andrew 64;
Francis 64; John 64;
Robert 64, 261; Sarah
12; William 12, 64;
William, Jr. 64
Barnet/Barnett, David 64;
Edward 261; Elias 64;
Joseph 261; Thomas 1,
261; William 293
Barney, James 12; John
64; Patrick 293
Barnfield, Barzillar 293
Barnhurst, Joseph 261
Barr/Bar, David 346; Enos
1; James 64; John 64,
252, 346; Mathew 64;
Paul 252; William 293
Barra, William 64
Barradale, William 64
Barrett, Ezekiel 64;
George N. 261; Hugh
252; John 64, 252;
Michael 64
Barrisford, - Gen. 120
Barron, Alexander 357;
Patrick 65
Barrows, James 242
Barry/Barrie, Betsey 12;
Edward 12; George Sol.
65; James 65, 334, 377;
John 65; Joshua 12,
Lawrence 65; Moses 65;
Peggy 12; Peter 64, 65;

Barry/Barrie (cont.),
Thomas 12; William 12,
53, 65
Bartis, James 65
Bartlett, Emeline 12;
John 12, 293; Mary 12;
Mary Ann 12; Richard
293; William 12
Bartley, James 261;
Michael 65; William 65
Bartor/Barten, Elizabeth
40; George 53; James 65;
Johannes 65; John 12,
40; Penelope 12;
Richard 65; Robert 293;
Thomas 361; William 65
Bartran, Andrew 65
Bascome, Cornelius 65
Bass, William 65
Bassett, Thomas 361
Bates, - Mr. 384; Abigail
12; Abigel A. 12;
Barrabas 12; Charles 12;
James T. 10; John 65,
261; Joseph 65; Mary B.
12; Thomas 65
Bathe, Elizabeth 12; John
12; Mary 12
Baxter, C. 293; George
242; James 366; John 53,
65, 334; William 65,
261
Beachinp, Thomas 242
Beador, Robert 66
Beakey/Beaky, George
Thomas 66
Bean, Joseph R. 12
Beard, Hugh 293
Beardman, Samuel 19
Beatty/Beaty/Baty, Hugh
372; James 66; John 66,
252; Mathew 66; Robert
65, 66, 371; Samuel 66;
William 66, 242
Beaumont/Beaumount, Joseph
66; Samuel 66; Thomas
261
Beaunoyer, Paul 379
Beaver, Thomas 252
Bechard, James 366
Beck, William 66
Beddell, John 261
Bedford, William T. 293
Beecross, Isaac 252
Beer, Joseph 12
Beerman, John Henry 261
Beers, Edward 66
Beggs, Jon 66
Begnal, John 66
Belder, Wilford 66
Bell, Alexander 372;
David 66; Francis 66;
George 66, 366; Hugh 66;
James 66, 242, 261;
Jane 12; John 66, 261,
293; Leonard 66; Mar-
garet 12; Richard 67;
Samuel 12; Thomas 67,
261; Thomas C. 293;
Thomas H. 252; William
67, 252, 371; Wm. H. 53
Bellich, William 67
Bellows, Jona. Bradley 39
Beltor, John 67
Benckert/Benckhart, John
D. 293
Benford, Edward 67

Bennan, John 48
Benner, John 67, 261
Bennet/Bennett, Alexander
67; Henry 67; James 53,
67; John 252; John M.
67; Morris 67; Obadiah
1; Reuben 67; Robert 67;
Thomas 320; Uzziel 261;
Bennie, John 67
Bennis, John 67
Bennoch, Alexander 357;
Peter 357
Bensaken/Bunsaken, Samuel
67, 77
Benson, James 12; Jane 12;
John 67; Mary Ann 12;
Paul 67; Robert 67;
Sarah 12; Thomas 12
Bentley, William 48
Benton, Samuel 67; Thomas
67; William 67; William
H. 67
Beresford, William 293
Berford, Peter O. 68
Bernerlie, Michel 379
Bernie, Charles 379
Berry, Godfrey 68; John
261
Berthelmi (alias Monplai-
sir), Jacques 379
Bertrand, Simon 379
Best, Adam 252; John 261
Beswick, John 346
Beton, Thomas 68
Bettely, Andrew 12; Eliza-
beth 12; Mary 12;
Thomas 12
Betts, James 371
Betty/Bety, Richard 68;
William 68
Bevan, George 68; Wm. 53
Bevard, James 293
Beverly, John 68
Beyman, John 68
Beynon, John 68
Beynow, John D. 68
Bibb, Edward 366
Bibby, T. 68
Biddle, Daniel 262; James
320
Bigford, Samuel 262
Bigg, Archibald 242
Biggard, Robert 320
Biggart, John 366
Bigger, William 68
Biggs, Alexander 68
Bigham, Hamilton 68;
James 320; John 320
Bignell, John 262
Bilbrough, Joseph 68
Bill, John 68
Billue, John 68
Bingham, Moses 252;
Robert 48
Bingle, Richard 68
Binner, Alexander 361
Bins, Joseph 68
Birch, Richard 366;
Richard, Jr. 366;
William 293
Bird, Joseph 68
Birney/Birnie, Clot-
worthy 293; George 346;
William 242
Birrel, Henry 68
Birtree, Jacob 68

www.ingramcontent.com/pod-product-compliance
Lightning Source LLC
Chambersburg PA
CBHW060131280326
41932CB00012B/1481